W9-CSX-482

APOLOGIA PRO VITA SUA

Apologia Pro Vita Sua

BEING A HISTORY OF
HIS RELIGIOUS OPINIONS

BY

JOHN HENRY ~~CARDINAL~~ NEWMAN

*Edited, with an Introduction
and Notes, by*

MARTIN J. SVAGLIC

'Commit thy way to the Lord and trust
in Him, and He will do it. And He will
bring forth thy justice as the light, and
thy judgment as the noon-day.'

OXFORD
AT THE CLARENDON PRESS
1967

Oxford University Press, Ely House, London W. 1

GLASGOW NEW YORK TORONTO MELBOURNE WELLINGTON
CAPE TOWN SALISBURY IBADAN NAIROBI LUSAKA ADDIS ABABA
BOMBAY CALCUTTA MADRAS KARACHI LAHORE DACCA
KUALA LUMPUR HONG KONG TOKYO

PRINTED IN GREAT BRITAIN

68-75872

8/3/19 Rludy. 6-14-28 (a)

CONTENTS

Contents

EDITOR'S INTRODUCTION

1. *Kingsley vs. Newman:*
A Score of Twenty Years or More

IN 1841 John Henry Newman had little thought of leaving the Anglican Church. He was still the leader of a movement which, radiating from Oxford since 1833 and called now by its name, had aroused multitudes of the educated laity and clergy to a moral fervour and a zeal for the welfare of the Church of England unknown among them since the seventeenth century. And in July of that year he published an essay intended in part as a warning to those of his followers who, dismayed by recent events, were wavering in their allegiance to Anglicanism.

The Oxford men, or Tractarians as they were called after the tracts in which they proclaimed their principles, had asserted for the Church of England a continuity with the Catholic Church which made of Protestantism only an incidental, often an unfortunate, reformation rather than an essentially different concept of the nature of the church and the function of the clergy. Their view was much like that of Henry VIII, of many of the great Caroline divines and the Non-jurors, of the Irish recluse Alexander Knox and his friend Bishop Jebb of Limerick; but it had never before been proclaimed with such intensity or elaborated so thoroughly as by the Tractarians.

Theirs was the Catholic Church of the early centuries, without the later Roman corruptions, as they considered them: a dogmatic church with rites and sacraments through which was conveyed the grace of God that all men needed to live a good life and attain salvation. On the basis of such a concept alone could their church survive the growth of liberal rationalism on the one hand, and on the other the concomitant encroachments of a reformed parliament swayed more now than ever by political expedience rather than zeal for the integrity of a revealed religion. And on this basis alone, more and more of the Tractarians had come to believe, did the Church of England have any real claim on their allegiance.

Protestant and liberal reaction to the new movement developed slowly at first, but by 1836 both the Evangelicals and the early Broad Churchmen, followers of Archbishop Whately of Dublin and Thomas Arnold of Rugby, had taken alarm at what they saw as a return to the errors and the obscurantism of Popery. As the Catholic character of the Oxford Movement became more and more evident, High Churchmen and even bishops, whose apostolical succession and authority had never been so firmly asserted as by the Tractarians, began to join the outcry against them. The Protestant reaction culminated in February 1841, on the publication of Newman's Tract 90, advancing the claim that the Thirty-nine Articles of the Church of England, to which all university students and clergymen had to subscribe and which had hitherto been almost invariably regarded as sealing the Establishment with an essentially Protestant character, were to be interpreted not in the sense of their Reformation framers or adopters but in conformity with ancient Catholic doctrine.

Protests rang throughout England. Typical of the Protestant reaction was that of a young Cambridge man, Charles Kingsley, in a letter to his mother:

> I have been reading the *Edinburgh Review* (April 1841) on No. 90 of the *Tracts for the Times.* . . . Whether wilful or self-deceived, these men are Jesuits, taking the oath to the Articles with moral reservations which allow them to explain them away in senses utterly different from those of their authors. All the worst doctrinal features of Popery Mr. Newman professes to believe in.[1]

Newman himself, more or less prepared for the outburst, consented to stop the Tracts, though only on the understanding that the principles of Tract 90 were not to be officially condemned. In high hopes of weathering the storm, therefore, and ironically on the eve of the three blows which he says in the *Apologia* finally broke his own faith in the catholicity of Anglicanism, he wrote an essay called 'Private Judgment', in which, in the spirit of St. Paul's injunction: 'Let every man abide in the same calling wherein he was called', he warned those disturbed by the reception of Tract 90 against the consequences of changing their religion:

[1] *The Life and Works of Charles Kingsley* (19 vols., London, 1902), i. 59.

. . . whatever be the intrinsic merits of Private Judgment, yet, if it at all exerts itself in the direction of proselytism and conversion, a certain *onus probandi* lies upon it, and it must show cause why it should be tolerated. . . . we are far indeed from saying that it is never to advance in the direction of change or revolution, else the Gospel itself could never have been introduced; but we consider that serious religious changes have a *prima facie* case against them; they have something to get over, and have to prove their admissibility, before it can reasonably be allowed; and their agents may be called upon to suffer, in order to prove their earnestness, and to pay the penalty of the trouble they are causing.[1]

After four years of reflection Newman himself made the act of private judgement he had warned his followers against. Convinced at last that the Church of England, by such events as the widespread episcopal repudiation of Tract 90, had shown it was not a part of the Catholic Church and that the Roman 'corruptions' were legitimate developments of the Apostolic deposit of faith, he entered the Roman Catholic Church on October 9, 1845. In the next few years hundreds of Anglicans, both clergy and laity, followed the example of a man who had been so quietly powerful a preacher, so stimulating a thinker, and so magnetic a personality that men of all shades of opinion had acclaimed him a unique figure at Oxford and the greatest single influence in the Anglican Church since John Wesley. The religious peace he had found remained, so far as we know, for the rest of his life: even in the saddest days of his future there was never to be for him anything like the ordeal of spiritual dryness reflected in the 'terrible' sonnets of his admirer and fellow convert Gerard Manley Hopkins. But he was indeed called upon to suffer in order to prove his earnestness and to pay the penalty of the trouble he was causing. That suffering came to him first through the behaviour of those he had left, and later through that of those he had joined.

Newman's conversion or secession or perversion, as it was variously called, was a heavy blow to the Church of England and brought the Oxford Movement, in its first phase at least, to a dismaying close. Conversions to Rome were then rare.

---

[1] *Essays Critical and Historical*, ii. 337. Unless otherwise indicated, all references to Newman's works are to the standard Longmans edition (39 vols., London, 1898–1903). References to the *Apologia* are to the present edition.

Although Catholic Emancipation had been granted in 1829, the Roman Church in England, after generations of repression, was small, poor, and unimportant; and even in Catholic countries, though something of a revival was under way, the Church had lost most of its influence among the intellectual classes. To Liberals it was a fossil. To Evangelicals it was Antichrist. To Anglo-Catholics it was an overbearing and partly corrupt rival which, though a sister church and in many ways to be respected, was on English soil a usurper. Newman himself had spoken harshly against Rome and kept his followers on guard against her. How, then, apart from pride or resentment against the bishops' treatment of him, if not from actual treachery to his church in the interest of Rome, could such an extraordinary act as his conversion be possibly explained?

Newman was prepared for the worst that could be said. He did not expect the forbearance of a Pusey or a Keble from lesser men than his fellow leaders, men who did not know him well enough to trust his motives and who genuinely felt that he had done a great wrong. Indeed, he wrote in 1864, censures of a convert by those who do not follow him 'are necessary for their own position'. In the face of daily conversions to Rome,

> . . . it became very necessary for those who had no doubts or diffi-
> culties to show to all who wavered or might waver, that there was
> something faulty in the mode in which the seceding parties had sever-
> ally detached themselves from their original communion,—some fault
> such as to invalidate the testimony of each, and to destroy its logical
> and rhetorical force.[1]

A few charges against his honesty he was drawn into answering, such as those of the Evangelical controversialist George Stanley Faber between 1847 and 1849.[2] But for the most part he ignored them, refusing to impute motives to his critics: 'He leaves his critics to that Judgment to which he himself appeals.'[3]

The criticism that Newman met in the early fifties, when he turned active polemicist, he fully expected, considering it 'in a certain sense a rule of the game'.[4] The author of the *Difficulties of Anglicans*, who contended that the logical issue of the Oxford Movement was submission to Rome and drew an ironical

---

[1] 'John Keble', in *Essays Critical and Historical*, ii. 425.
[2] See *Apologia*, pp. 169–70. [3] *Essays*, ii. 427.
[4] See his letter of Jan. 8, 1864, to X.Y., Esq., *Apologia*, Appendix A, p. 344.

picture of a state-controlled Establishment, was delivering a challenge. In 1851 he extended it to an even greater body of English Christians in his *Present Position of Catholics in England*, reducing to a rollicking absurdity the prejudices on which he held that the Protestant view of Catholicism was based. In the years of the Gorham Judgement and the restoration of the Catholic hierarchy to England, Newman was only one, if the most skilful, of many such writers on all sides. He sometimes answered his critics when larger interests than his person were involved,[1] and he made no attempt to shield himself by his clerical profession: 'I cannot reprobate, in a free country like this, the ridicule of individuals, whoever they are; and I think it would be a very evil day when it was forbidden. . . . And this permission must be suffered to the case of persons who bear a religious profession. . . .'[2] For the most part, however, though he realized that his activities must have been painful or bewildering to many, he continued to ignore personal attacks. Not a few of his countrymen, he knew, would class him with certain Catholics for whom 'a strong distrust' must be felt: 'proselytizing priests . . . who, like Dr. Newman, have turned round upon their mother-Church (I had almost said their mother-country) with contumely and slander'.[3]

The one criticism he could not reconcile himself to even with great effort, the one which for more than seventeen years caused him deep sorrow, was the one never uttered in words: it was the silence, with all it implied, of his oldest and closest friends, most of whom had remained Anglicans. Pusey, Marriott, Keble, Church, Rogers, Copeland, and others were men of too fine a conscience and too great a knowledge of Newman to permit of any indulgence in bitterness or recrimination. Yet Newman's move had plunged them into sorrow, and both their feelings and a sense of duty to their own church seemed to rule out a perpetuation of the old ties. It was they who made themselves dead to him, Newman always felt, and when a chance meeting with his former curate Copeland in 1862 offered the opportunity for a renewal of friendship, he was quick to take advantage of it. But while the

[1] See, for example, his correspondence with the Bishop of Norwich on Newman's view of miracles, which the bishop had attacked: *Present Position*, pp. 407–16.

[2] Ibid., pp. 203–4.

[3] Charles Kingsley, 'What, Then, Does Dr. Newman Mean?' reprinted in Appendix B, p. 365.

estrangement lasted, he felt it deeply. Looking back in 1863 on the long period of silence, he wrote to Isaac Williams: 'My friends, I confess, have *not* been kind. . . .'[1] Even his family had kept him at a distance, as we know from the moving letter he wrote to his sister Jemima when, after the success of the *Apologia*, she finally invited him to her home once again.[2]

For all his asceticism and detachment, Newman had been and remained one of the most affectionate of men. The years from 1833 to 1841 he remembered as 'in a human point of view, the happiest time of my life. I was truly at home.'[3] The poignancy of the loss of Oxford and the long separation from family and friends only became sharper as he began to lose favour with Catholics, too; and in 1863 he could write to Keble:

> You are always with me a thought of reverence and love, and there is nothing I love better than you, and Isaac, and Copeland, and many others I could name, except Him Whom I ought to love best of all and supremely. May He Himself, Who is the over-abundant compensation for all losses, give me His own Presence, and then I shall want nothing and desiderate nothing, but none *but* He, *can* make up for the loss of those old familiar faces which haunt me continually.[4]

If his treatment by Protestants was painful, however, that which Newman received for a time from Catholics, including some of his fellow converts, was even more so, until it culminated in his almost morbid streak of depression in the early 1860s.

The call to Dublin in 1852 in the service of the projected Catholic University, which he hoped to build into a centre for English-speaking Catholics of that Christian humanism he depicts so compellingly in the *Idea of a University*, meant for Newman a return to the kind of work he had long regarded as especially suited to his character and mission in life, both as a Fellow of Oriel and a priest of the Oratory of St. Philip Neri. As he said in 1859 of another educator, 'his calling was for a college life—for the quietness and peace, for the opportunities of devotion, for the gradual formation of young minds, for the literary leisure, which a place of education afforded him'.[5]

[1] Wilfrid Ward, *The Life of John Henry Cardinal Newman* (2 vols., London, 1912), i. 650.
[2] See Meriol Trevor, *Newman: Light in Winter* (London, 1963), pp. 505–6.
[3] *Apologia*, p. 76.
[4] Ward, *Life*, i. 591. See also *Present Position*, p. 245.
[5] *Sermons Preached on Various Occasions*, p. 256.

His mission was still, as it had long been, to combat the 'liberalism' which, reinterpreting or abandoning the traditional dogmas of orthodoxy, seemed well on the road to infidelity and ultimate moral anarchy. The Roman Catholic Church was alone strong enough to resist this gravest of dangers, he had come to believe, but this did not mean that Catholics themselves, any more than Christians in general, were equipped for the task. The aristocracy of talent was more than ever on the side of unbelief, as the new science and the 'higher criticism' had made clear. And Catholics could no longer afford to be, like Cardinal Wiseman, 'so outsided, so slow to throw [themselves] into other minds, so sanguine, so controversial & unphilosophic in . . . attitude of mind'. He would do all he could to encourage and develop the frame of mind that alone offered the hope of success. As he wrote in 1863,

> . . . the Church must be prepared for converts, as well as converts prepared for the Church . . . and Catholics in England, from their very blindness, cannot see that they are blind. To aim then at improving the conditions, the status, of the Catholic body, by a careful survey of their argumentative basis, of their position relatively to the philosophy and the character of the day, by giving them juster views, by enlarging and refining their minds, in one word, by education . . . has been my line. . . .[1]

And thus, in the natural rhythm of a temperament so deeply conditioned by the dialectic of that perennial Oxford textbook, the *Nicomachean Ethics*, the Newman who was a conservative at an increasingly liberal Oxford became a liberal when faced with the extreme conservatism of Rome. Over the years he became, in fact, the most persuasive of spokesmen for the *aggiornamento* in Catholicism to be espoused in part by Leo XIII and in its fullness by John XXIII.

Newman felt certain of the great extension, 'soon after my life', of 'those principles which are so near my heart';[2] and the Catholic revival in England and especially the second Vatican Council are his vindication. As one of the participating bishops has written, that Council could 'in a very exact sense . . . be

[1] *Autobiographical Writings*, ed. Henry Tristram (London and New York, 1957), pp. 258 and 259.
[2] Ward, *Life*, i. 593.

called *his* Council, the fulfillment of his vision and the justification of his theology. . .'.

It is not only that Cardinal Newman has been cited in debate by the
Council Fathers more frequently and more prominently than any other
authority, not excepting the Angelic Doctor, St. Thomas Aquinas,
himself. It is not only that in the welter of publications, articles and
books, which has proliferated since the first adumbration of the Council,
his name and his works have been quoted more extensively than those
of any other theologian or historian. His influence is pervasive. . . . It
is in fact, under the Holy Ghost, the guiding spirit of the Council as
a whole, and Newman's thought is basic in all its deliberations. Unless
the totally unforeseen should come to pass, the final decisions will
inevitably bear his stamp.[1]

But the Roman Church of the nineteenth century, on every side
facing its gravest problems since the Reformation, could not
yet see the wisdom of Newman's point of view.

His own plans for the Catholic University (he had already
established a good library and a scientific laboratory, and had
spent liberally of his own funds to erect a beautiful chapel) had
to be abandoned when Newman found that the most influential
members of the Irish hierarchy seemed disinclined to give him
as Rector the authority he needed to carry out a programme of
liberal education which scarcely fulfilled their own wish for a
kind of lay seminary. *The Idea of a University* has since become
a classic, and the National University of Ireland arose from the
apparent destruction of Newman's plans. But all Newman
could know when in 1858 he returned in disillusionment to
England was that years of hope and struggle had borne little
fruit and that as he approached old age, his mission was still to
be accomplished.

England was to mean not peace but more failure. In 1853 a
strain had developed between Newman's Oratory in Birmingham and its offshoot, the more prosperous London Oratory
under Frederick Faber. As the years passed, it grew worse, each
house seeing the activity of the other as a threat to its own
independence. It was Newman's view that the London group
had seriously damaged his reputation at Rome and in the
English Catholic body by charges to the effect that he wanted

[1] Bishop Robert J. Dwyer, 'Listening In', *The Register* (Denver, Colorado), xl
(Jan. 19, 1964), p. 1.

una specie di Generalato over the Oratory in England and was personally too sensitive and unyielding.[1]

In 1857 Newman had been formally notified by Cardinal Wiseman of the English bishops' request that he undertake a new translation of the Bible. He responded eagerly with his time and money in preparing the great work, hoping to consider in an Introduction some of the major problems of Scriptural interpretation in an age of revolutionary scholarship. His translators were already at work in the Birmingham Oratory when Wiseman, a gifted man of perhaps too many interests (whose carelessness about documents had already cost Newman dearly in the libel suit an ex-Dominican friar had brought against him in 1852), began to temporize about how expenses were to be met and in short to wash his hands of the whole affair. He was not well and faced a crisis in his own administration. Newman attributed his strange behaviour to disappointment that the London Oratory was not to play a major role in the new project.[2] In any event, Newman felt that he now had no real choice but to give it up. It meant a unique opportunity lost, this time through painful negligence, if not distrust on Wiseman's part since the quarrel between the Oratories.

In 1859, to save it from condemnation and at the express wish of his own bishop, Newman accepted the editorship of the *Rambler*, a learned Catholic periodical of liberal tendencies already in disfavour with the hierarchy for such remarks as the young Sir John Acton's that although St. Augustine was indeed the greatest Doctor of the West, 'he was also the father of Jansenism'.[3] In July of that year Newman published an article, 'On Consulting the Faithful in Matters of Doctrine', the underlying purpose of which was to advance the idea that on such current questions as educational policy laymen should indeed be consulted and in short to initiate the development of what is called today a theology of the laity. Because he spoke of a temporary suspense of the function of the *ecclesia docens* during

---

[1] The story of this quarrel was first told in any detail by Meriol Trevor, *Newman: Light in Winter*, pp. 73–165. It seems clear from her account that Newman was right in principle, but it is hard not to feel that with greater tact and flexibility he could have resolved the matter.

[2] See Ward, *Life*, i. 428; and Trevor, *Newman: Light in Winter*, pp. 169–73.

[3] See Newman, *On Consulting the Faithful in Matters of Doctrine*, ed. John Coulson (London and New York, 1961), p. 4.

the Arian controversy, when so many of the bishops wavered or espoused the Arian view, Newman found himself delated to Rome for heresy before the year was out. Rome took no official action, and the matter was later dropped after Newman's explanation,[1] though not before suspicions harmful to Newman had been aroused in the highest circles. Indeed, the editor of Newman's essay describes its publication as 'an act of political suicide from which his career within the Church was never fully to recover'.[2]

For some time Newman's books had been selling poorly. His health was impaired, and a sense of approaching death frequently overtook him, so that he could write in 1860 after reading 'Tithonus' in the *Cornhill*: 'I liken myself to Tithonus . . . fading out from the world, and having nothing to do with its interests or its affairs. I have fallen off in flesh and shrunk up during the past year, and am like a grey grasshopper or the evaporating mist of the morning. And, as I get older, so do trouble and anxieties seem to multiply.'[3] In fact, his greatest trouble was at hand. Within eighteen months he was to have lost favour with so many of his co-religionists that a well-known Catholic publisher could advise against his connexion with any periodical as dangerous to its success: 'The great objection to Newman is his . . . for one reason or another, unpopularity.'[4]

It was his suspected position on the temporal power of the papacy which darkened to blackness the cloud under which Newman had been living. As papal territory was being seized by Victor Emmanuel and Cavour, most Catholics rallied to the support of the embattled Pio Nono. A man of great charm, ability, and one-time liberal tendencies, the Pope had since 1848 felt betrayed by liberals; and he considered religion itself as in grave danger from the anticlerical Left. The days of strong ultramontanism had arrived. Those who, like Montalembert and Lacordaire in France, Döllinger in Germany, and his brilliant disciple, the future Lord Acton, in England, looked toward a christianizing and assimilation of the modern political and cultural temper were challenged by the larger group, led by men like Louis Veuillot in France and Manning and W. G.

---

[1] See his *Arians of the Fourth Century*, pp. 445–68.
[2] *On Consulting the Faithful*, ed. Coulson, p. 2.
[3] Ward, *Life*, i. 601–2.   [4] Ibid., p. 526.

Ward in England, for whom that temper was so obviously hostile to religion, especially Catholicism, that any *rapprochement* was out of the question. When in 1861 the *Rambler*, now edited by Acton and the impetuous convert Richard Simpson, took the *other* side on the question of the temporal power, Catholics were shocked by what looked almost like treason. And since Newman had once been connected with the *Rambler*, his name was linked with theirs. It was thought by many that Newman had something to do with a strong criticism of Manning's position which appeared in the December 1860 issue, and Manning himself apparently turned against Newman at this time.[1] The fact was that Newman, devoted to the Pope and always respectful of ecclesiastical authority, had repeatedly warned the editors of the *Rambler* against a sharpness of tone well calculated to arouse opposition. His own wish, as always, was for a *via media* between extremist positions. He feared the tendency of all too many Catholics like Manning to regard the temporal power, as then constituted, as a necessary part of Christian doctrine.

Refusing to surrender his powers of discrimination in what was clearly a matter of private judgement, Newman maintained an attitude of reserve on the question, which to many was little better than disloyalty. Yet during all the trouble and sorrow of these years, when he feared that his influence had been destroyed and that his mission was to remain unfulfilled, he suffered no diminution of religious faith, indulged in no recriminations, and could still maintain a balanced perspective. In July 1862 he finally scotched a persistent rumour that he was about to return to the Church of England—it had proved impervious to calmer denial—with a stinging and widely reprinted letter to one of the newspapers that had circulated it: '"The net is broken and we are delivered." I should be a consummate fool (to use a mild term), if in my old age I left "the land flowing with milk and honey" for the city of confusion and the house of bondage.'[2]

[1] See Edward Kelly, S.J., 'The *Apologia* and the Ultramontanes', *Newman's 'Apologia': A Classic Reconsidered*, ed. Vincent F. Blehl, S.J., and Francis X. Connolly (New York, 1964), pp. 27–28.

[2] Ward, *Life*, i. 581. This letter, containing phrases like 'the thought of the Anglican service makes me shiver', brought Newman to his 'lowest point' of popularity among Anglicans and was widely criticized in the press as unfeeling and ungrateful. Yet it was also a turning-point, since when an Anglican friend wrote to

But to a Catholic friend who contemplated starting an historical review, he could write:

> [N]othing would be better than a historical Review, but who would bear it ? Unless one doctored all one's facts one would be thought a bad Catholic. The truth is, there is a keen conflict going on just now between two parties, one in the Church and one out of it. And at such seasons extreme views alone are in favour and a man who is not extravagant is thought treacherous. I sometimes think of King Lear's daughters and consider that they after all may be found the truest who are in speech more measured.[1]

Ama nesciri and *spernere se sperni* were among the chief lessons of Newman's patron saint, Philip Neri, and Newman himself had strong inclinations to a life of devotion and obscurity. The anguish that suffuses the journal of the years between 1859 and 1864 comes far less from wounded pride than from the knowledge that his isolation was proving harmful to the interests nearest his heart: the Oratory itself, the preparatory school opened there in 1859 but now threatened by Newman's eclipse, and his own special work in life for religion: 'Let not the contempt which comes on *me*, injure the future of my Oratory', he pleaded in his journal. 'And again, O teach me . . . teach me how to employ myself most profitably, most to Thy glory, in such years as remain to me: for my apparent illsuccess discourages me much. O my God, I seem to have wasted these years that I have been a Catholic. What I wrote as a Protestant has had far greater power, force, meaning, success, than my Catholic works—& this troubles me a great deal.'[2] Three years later, in 1863, he writes:

> . . . I look back on my years at Oxford and Littlemore with tenderness . . . it was the time in which I had a remarkable mission—but how am I changed even in look! . . .
>
> . . . I am noticing all this opposition and distrust, not on their own account, for St. Philip had them abundantly, but because they have (to all appearance) succeeded in destroying my influence & my usefulness. Persons who would naturally look towards me, converts who

protest Newman's 'great want of charity', he replied that Protestants had treated him 'very unkindly' for seventeen years. 'This touched Keble.' The meeting with Copeland and the *Apologia* did the rest. See *Autobiographical Writings*, pp. 260–1.
  [1] Ward, *Life*, i. 571–2.
  [2] *Autobiographical Writings*, p. 253.

would naturally come to me, inquirers who would naturally consult me, are stopped by some light or unkind word said against me. I am *passé*, in decay; I am untrustworthy. . . .[1]

The idea of writing another book is never far from his mind. 'The notion of my publishing a book', he wrote to a friend in 1861, 'is one of those bright thoughts which I wish I could execute as easily as persons can report it of me . . . I wish it were [true].'[2] On the eve of the *Apologia* he admits that 'if I could believe it to be God's will, [I] would turn away my thoughts from ever writing anything, and should see, in the superintendence of these boys, the nearest return to my Oxford life. . . .'[3] He clearly cannot believe it to be God's will; yet he had always been an occasional writer, and there was no one now to provide him with an occasion. He could never write his life for its own sake. To a friend who asked him for an account, he described it as 'a short tale, without adventure, without interest except for myself'.[4] He had no intention of writing a defence of himself alone: 'Theologians and ascetic writers tell us', he had written in another connexion, 'that the perfection of a Christian lies in never pleading his own cause. . .'. But he had added, '*except when accused of error of faith*, for such error is dishonourable to God'. His example of such an error was 'treachery to the cause of truth'.[5]

On December 30, 1863, Newman received in the mail from a person unknown to him a copy of *Macmillan's Magazine* for January 1864, containing an enthusiastic review, signed 'C.K.', of volumes seven and eight of James Anthony Froude's ultra-Protestant *History of England*. Certain passages were marked.[6] In the course of a slashing attack by the reviewer on the demoralization he attributed to the doctrine of papal authority, Newman read:

It was not till more than one generation had grown up and died with the Bible in their hands, that Englishmen and Germans began to understand (what Frenchmen and Italians did not understand) that

---

[1] Ibid., pp. 254 and 257.   [2] Ward, *Life*, i. 605.
[3] Ibid., p. 613.   [4] Ibid., p. 608.   [5] Ibid., p. 541.
[6] In a letter of Feb. 24, 1864, the sender identified himself as William Pope, a former Anglican and now a Roman Catholic clergyman, adding: 'To your teaching, I say it with great thankfulness, my three sisters, my brother, and myself owe our conversion. . . .' (MS. *Apologia* Letters, Birmingham Oratory.)

they were to be judged by the everlasting laws of a God who was no respecter of persons.

So, again, of the virtue of truth. Truth for its own sake, had never been a virtue with the Roman clergy. Father Newman informs us that it need not, and on the whole ought not to be; that cunning is the weapon which Heaven has given to the Saints wherewith to withstand the brute male force of the wicked world which marries and is given in marriage. Whether his notion be doctrinally correct or not, it is at least historically so.

The writer, as Newman soon learned, was the Reverend Charles Kingsley, Professor of Modern History at Cambridge, chaplain to the Queen, recent tutor of the Prince of Wales, and one of the best-known authors of the day. Newman had received his occasion. As far back as 1851, when he was writing that there was not much wisdom in complaining against the insulting of individuals, he had added: 'But the case is very different when the religious rite is insulted, and the individual for the sake of the rite.'[1] And in 1862 he had advised Wetherell, Acton's assistant in editing the new *Home and Foreign Review*, how to meet the very charge of 'treachery to the cause of truth': 'I think it is the duty of one who has occasion to notice this charge made against him to *be indignant*.'[2]

What followed is so well known as to require only a brief summary here. The reader will find all the relevant documents in Appendix A and B of the present edition of the *Apologia*. Without asking any redress, Newman called the attention of Messrs. Macmillan to 'a grave and gratuitous slander' for which no justification from any words of his had been offered. This was the heart of the matter. From first to last, in all the correspondence which Newman published in February after Kingsley refused to offer more than a brief and fundamentally ambiguous apology in place of the offensively insinuating one he first proposed ('No man knows the use of words better than Dr. Newman'), Kingsley, normally the most open of men, could not be forced to behave in the manly fashion that Newman had called for in his letter to 'X. Y.'[3] Beyond referring to 'many passages' and to the sermon 'Wisdom and Innocence', preached

[1] *Present Position of Catholics*, p. 204.   [2] Ward, *Life*, i. 541.
[3] See Appendix A, p. 345, 'X. Y.' was Alexander Macmillan, one of the founders of the firm, who said he would prefer the anonymity that Newman had offered him in a letter of Jan. 28. (MS. *Apologia* Letters, Birmingham Oratory.)

at St. Mary's in 1843, he simply refused to cite any specific words of Newman to justify his categorical accusation; yet he continued to refer, even in his final apology, to Newman's 'words'. The fact is that Kingsley could find no words to prove his precise charge, for as one of his biographers says, 'what Newman had preached was quite the reverse' of Kingsley's report:

> In describing the weapons with which the Christian Church defends itself, prayer, holiness, and innocence, he had said that to the world of physical strength these weapons were so incomprehensible that it must believe that the Church conquered by craft and hypocrisy. 'The words "craft" and "hypocrisy" are but the version of "wisdom" and "harmlessness", in the language of the world.'[1]

And yet, as later events were to prove, Kingsley had no intention of giving up the charge, as against Newman or the Roman clergy. He was at the moment either too proud to avow on the one hand that he could not find a definite passage, or too timid to admit on the other that he had not changed his mind. In his own pamphlet answering Newman's, he was to offer as an explanation for his conduct that 'he had been informed (by a Protestant) that [Newman] was in weak health, that he wished for peace and quiet, and was averse to controversy'.[2]

To his correspondence with Kingsley, published on February 12 as a one shilling pamphlet entitled *Mr. Kingsley and Dr. Newman: A Correspondence on the Question Whether Dr. Newman Teaches That Truth Is No Virtue?* Newman, with the approval of Edward Badeley, a well-known lawyer and friend who had earlier advised him that Kingsley's proposed reparation was clearly insufficient, appended his devastating 'Reflections' in the form of a dialogue, turning Kingsley's charge back upon himself:

> Mr. Kingsley relaxes: 'Do you know, I like your *tone*. From your *tone* I rejoice, greatly rejoice, to be able to believe that you did not mean what you said.'
>
> I rejoin: '*Mean* it! I maintain I never *said* it, whether as a Protestant or as a Catholic.'
>
> Mr. Kingsley replies: 'I waive that point.'

[1] Robert B. Martin, *The Dust of Combat* (London, 1959), p. 238.
[2] Appendix B, p. 356.

I object: 'Is it possible ? What ? waive the main question! I either
said it or I didn't. You have made a monstrous charge against me;
direct, distinct, public. You are bound to prove it as directly, as distinctly, as publicly;—or to own you can't.'

'Well', says Mr. Kingsley, 'if you are quite sure you did not say it,
I'll take your word for it; I really will.'

My *word!* I am dumb. Somehow I thought that it was my *word* that
happened to be on trial. The *word* of a Professor of lying, that he does
not lie!

But Mr. Kingsley re-assures me: 'We are both gentlemen', he says.
'I have done as much as one English gentleman can expect from
another.'

I begin to see: he thought me a gentleman at the very time that he
said I taught lying on system. After all, it is not I, but it is Mr. Kingsley
who did not mean what he said. 'Habemus confitentem reum.'

Newman had warned from the start that he would consider
Kingsley's letters public property, and Kingsley acknowledged
that he had 'every right to do so'. Newman concluded his
pamphlet by observing that the correspondence constituted 'a
real satisfaction to those principles of historical and literary
justice to which he has given so rude a shock. Accordingly I
have put it into print, and make no further criticism on Mr.
Kingsley.'

If Kingsley had had the wisdom to accept this stinging but
merited rebuke, he might well have come off with a fair amount
of public sympathy as the almost pathetically helpless victim of
a probably hypersensitive and certainly none too popular man,
variously referred to during the progress of the controversy as a
lion, an ape, a bear, and a serpent. The *Saturday Review* of
February 27, 1864, which heralded the dispute as the liveliest
since the days of Bentley and Boyle, spoke of 'the old lion'
rousing himself in his den, and concluded with a description of
one remaining for the most part in serene solitude and peaceful
rest, 'but springing out now and then with the lithe and supple
crash of the serpent, erect, defiant, and pitiless, and hissing with
scorn, when the hour of vengeance arrived and a helpless victim
were within reach of his cruel fangs'.[1] And the week before,
the literary editor of the *Spectator*, R. H. Hutton, had spoken
of Kingsley as a perhaps 'too helpless victim' of Newman's
'undue scorn' and of a 'more than adequate literary retribution'.[2]

[1] xvii. 255.   [2] xxxvii. 206 and 207.

But the reviews said other things as well. They said that Newman was fundamentally in the right, and they said things quite as unflattering to Kingsley as anything in Newman's pamphlet. Hutton, whose opinion carried all the more weight as coming from a known admirer of Kingsley, more than anyone else prepared the way for Newman's critical and popular rehabilitation by the extensive publicity he gave to every stage of the controversy and by the progressively warmer admiration for Newman which he displayed. The other reviewers appear to have followed his lead.[1] *Loose Thoughts for Loose Thinkers* was the sub-title of one of Kingsley's works. According to Hutton, it represented only

too closely the character of his rough but manly intellect, so that a more opportune Protestant ram for Father Newman's sacrificial knife could scarcely have been found . . . the thicket in which he caught himself was, as it were, of his own choosing, he having rushed into it, quite without malice, but also quite without proper consideration of the force and significance of his own words. Mr. Kingsley is really without any case at all . . . and we think he drew down upon himself fairly the last keen blow of the sacrificial knife by what we must consider a very inadequate apology for his rash statement.[2]

The *Saturday Review* was more cutting:

Mr. Kingsley's habit of mind is a very unfortunate one for a serious investigator of truth. He is only deficient in the accomplishments of accuracy and gravity. To weigh his words is not so important as to calculate their force. Lively, impetuous, vigorous, hasty, too quick in forming judgments, and too vehement in expressing them, he is a brilliant partisan but a very unsafe teacher . . . he is apt to be careless in investigating the grounds of what ought to be his judgments, but which are his prejudices. He is the most sensational writer of history who ever disdained the labour of reading.[3]

Newman's pamphlet created a minor literary sensation. In the first impression only 500 copies had been run off, but in less than two months, 1,737 were sold.[4]

---

[1] This view of Hutton's importance was that of a contemporary critic, G. L. Craik. It has been generally accepted, and Newman's letters to Hutton in the Birmingham Oratory lend support to it. See Ward, *Life*, ii. 4.

[2] *The Spectator*, xxxvii (1864), 206–7.   [3] xvii (Feb. 27, 1864), 254.

[4] Letter of William Longman, Apr. 7, 1864, MS. *Apologia* Letters, Birmingham Oratory.

Even rasher than before, smarting under such an attack, and badly advised by friends, Kingsley began his extraordinary reply. 'I am answering Newman now,' he wrote to a correspondent, 'and though of course I give up the charge of conscious dishonesty, I trust to make him and his admirers sorry that they did not leave me alone. I have a score of more than twenty years to pay, and this is an instalment of it.'[1]

On March 20 he published his pamphlet *What, Then, Does Dr. Newman Mean?* Even today, after more than a century has passed, the reader who has never seen this work (reprinted in Appendix B) will be startled by the passionate intensity and bitterness of Kingsley's attack on Newman. 'I struck as hard as I could', he later admitted.[2] The bluntness of tone and confusion of purpose which have given the pamphlet its reputation even among Kingsley's admirers for 'bad logic and hot-headed obtuseness'[3] are evident from the start: 'I have declared Dr. Newman to have been an honest man up to the 1st of February, 1864. It was, as I shall show, only Dr. Newman's fault that I ever thought him to be anything else. It depends entirely on Dr. Newman whether he shall sustain the reputation which he has so recently acquired.' The crude innuendo was proof enough that Newman had rightly judged the sincerity of the apologies he had been offered.

For the rest, the pamphlet is, from the very title-page, a farrago of passages torn from the carefully qualified context of Newman's Anglican sermons 'Wisdom and Innocence' and 'The Apostolical Christian'; of actual misstatements, as in Kingsley's claim that he was so far just to Newman 'that No. 90, which made all the rest of England believe him a dishonest man, had not the same effect on me': a claim contradicted by early letters to Fanny Grenfell and his mother[4] and to be explained, perhaps, on the ground that the Kingsley of 1864 had come to realize that Newman's principles of interpretation were instructive for liberals, too;[5] of blatant appeals to popular sentiment and prejudice ('Englishmen know how to

[1] Letter of Mar. 9, 1864. MS. *Apologia* Letters, Birmingham Oratory.
[2] In a letter of June 8 to Macmillan. See Margaret Farrand Thorp, *Charles Kingsley* (Princeton, N.J., and London, 1937), p. 160.
[3] Ibid., p. 158.
[4] See *Life and Works of Charles Kingsley*, i, pp. 59 and 73.
[5] See Guy Kendall, *Charles Kingsley and His Ideas* (London, 1947), p. 149.

guard the women whom God has committed to their charge');
and in general of the protests of an outraged, simple, bluff
common sense against the knave or fool who could adopt the
system of unnatural asceticism, wild legends, and crafty ethics
which Newman had upheld even before joining the Church
responsible for it.

Even by Kingsley's admirers there was scarcely an attempt
to defend so unfortunate an outburst. The reaction of the influential journals of opinion was again substantially that of
Hutton: 'Mr. Kingsley . . . aggravates the original injustice a
hundredfold . . . has done himself pure harm by this rejoinder.'[1]
In private George Eliot described Kingsley's pamphlet as
'thoroughly vicious' writing which deserved to be 'thoroughly
castigated': a 'mixture of arrogance, coarse impertinence and
unscrupulousness with real intellectual incompetence'.[2]

Intellectually incompetent Kingsley may have been, but in
his person at least, he was anything but vicious. Matthew
Arnold, a great admirer of Newman, was to call Kingsley 'the
most generous man I have ever known'.[3] His parishioners loved
him. He was a zealous crusader for social justice. He had
hitherto invariably displayed a forthright, courageous spirit.
Why, then, did he go out of his way in the first place to attack a
man whom he had never met and who was now eclipsed and
retired ? And what did he mean by saying that his pamphlet
was only one instalment of a score of more than twenty years ?

It should be said at the outset, before discussing the motives
more or less peculiar to his own temperament, that perhaps a
better case can be made out for Kingsley's attack than has
been made thus far, and that on at least three counts. First, the
charge that truth for its own sake 'had never been a virtue with
the Roman clergy', while intolerably broad and unfair, was by
no means peculiar to Kingsley and certainly contained its grain
of truth in a church under fire from many sides since the Reformation. Newman's own already cited admission in 1864,
advising a friend against starting an historical review, that
'[u]nless one doctored all one's facts one would be thought a

---

[1] The review is cited at some length by Ward, *Life*, ii. 11–12, from the *Spectator* of Mar. 26, 1864.

[2] *The Letters of George Eliot*, ed. Gordon S. Haight (7 vols., New Haven and London, 1954–5), iv. 158–9.

[3] Quoted by Leslie Stephen, 'Charles Kingsley', *DNB* (1909), xi. 180.

bad Catholic', if it does not imply actual lying, at least points
to the prevalence of an *a priori* clerical mentality resistant to
the objective investigation and acceptance of historical evidence.
Years later it was to give a disedifying revelation of itself in the
protracted controversy between the Abbé Gasquet and Professor Coulton.[1] More recently, Professor Trevor-Roper has
asserted that it colours the work of several English Catholic
clerical historians.[2]

Acton had been gravely scandalized by this mentality, seeing
it as sometimes involving even the 'wilful lie', as in the case of
the Jesuit biographer who always wrote of Pope Paul III's
'nephews' instead of his son and grandchildren. And he advised
Newman that although eminent minds in the worlds of letters
and public affairs conceded his victory over Kingsley in the
first pamphlet 'and the failure of the attack upon you in Kingsley's reply', still they thought a 'general defence of the Catholic
clergy' would be 'very difficult'. Acton advised Newman to
undertake a frank discussion of 'the policy which is adopted in
order to avoid scandal', a 'practice of proscribing truth and
positively encouraging falsehood in the Church'.[3] Newman did
so indirectly and with great skill in his 'General Answer to
Mr. Kingsley', now the fifth chapter of the *Apologia*.

Second, it must be granted that Kingsley's view of the
Oxford Movement as 'wilful or self-deceived' Popery was fairly
typical, not only of the Evangelical but even of the cultivated
liberal mentality of Victorian England. To say that there were
Catholic elements in the Church of England was one thing;
but to attempt, before a nation that had long regarded Protestantism as synonymous with progress and patriotism, to advance a
theory that despite all obvious changes its church had remained
essentially Catholic, seemed so clearly to challenge history and
common sense as to render the motives or the sanity of its pro-
ponents questionable. It was a task, said *The Times*, of 'extraordinary wildness and visionariness'.[4] The Tractarians were well
aware of their danger and tried to proceed cautiously, with

---

[1] See M. D. Knowles, *Cardinal Gasquet as an Historian* (London, 1957).

[2] H. R. Trevor-Roper, *Historical Essays* (London, 1957), pp. 113–18 and *passim*.
Professor Trevor-Roper's outlook on English history bears some resemblance to
Kingsley's and Froude's.

[3] Letter of Apr. 10, 1864, MS. *Apologia* Letters, Birmingham Oratory.

[4] June 16, 1864, p. 12.

reserve or 'economy', that is, without a full disclosure at every point of the consequences of positions they were taking. Newman admits in the *Apologia* that

> . . . while I was working simply for the sake of the Anglican Church, I did not at all mind, though I found myself laying down principles in its defence, which went beyond that particular kind of defence which high-and-dry men thought perfection, and even though I ended in framing a kind of defence, which they might call a revolution, while I thought it a restoration. Thus, for illustration, I might discourse upon the 'Communion of Saints' in such a manner (though I do not recollect doing so,) as might lead the way towards devotion to the Blessed Virgin and the Saints on the one hand, and towards prayers for the dead on the other. In a memorandum of the year 1844 or 1845, I thus speak on the subject: 'If the Church be not defended on establishment grounds, it must be upon principles, which go far beyond their immediate object. Sometimes I saw these further results, sometimes not. Though I saw them, I sometimes did not say that I saw them:—so long as I thought they were inconsistent, *not* with our Church, but only with existing opinions, I was not unwilling to insinuate truths into our Church, which I thought had a right to be there. . . .[1]

To Newman, since he was not trying to benefit Rome but England, such a procedure was only a matter of good rhetoric in a difficult situation; to Kingsley and others, it was reprehensible craftiness. Newman himself hesitated to reprint the sermon 'Wisdom and Innocence' in his first pamphlet because he saw that people who did not know him might indeed misinterpret it. His friend Badeley agreed and advised him not to reprint it.[2] As for Tract 90, it too had been written for a special audience of troubled Anglo-Catholics, and unless its novel and fairly subtle premisses were carefully mastered—and perhaps even then—it would inevitably appear strained at times and sophistical. As Newman wrote to Pusey on March 1, 1863, the fact that Tract 90 had been one among other means 'of keeping up a high Church party among the English clergy . . . is no reason that you should be dragged through the mud by a composition of mine, which, viewed in the concrete, might have much in it, which had better not have been there'.[3]

---

[1] p. 154.   [2] See letters of Feb. 3 and 4, 1864, in MS. *Apologia* Letters.
[3] MS. Pusey Letters 1860–4, Birmingham Oratory. Newman later said that he could no longer accept his interpretation of Article XXXI but otherwise felt that the argument of Tract 90 was sound. See his *Via Media*, ii. 351–6.

The charge of sophistry against Newman, particularly by rationalists, was not uncommon. J. A. Froude, Leslie Stephen, and T. H. Huxley were among those who felt, in varying degree, that it was present in his thought. 'That Newman triumphantly vindicated his personal character', wrote Leslie Stephen, 'is . . . beyond doubt. The best that can be said for Kingsley is that he was aiming at a real blot on the philosophical system of his opponent; but, if so, it must be also allowed that he contrived to confuse the issue, and by other obvious misunderstandings to give a complete victory to a powerful antagonist.'[1] Elsewhere Stephen explained what he meant about Newman's system:

> Newman has a scepticism of his own . . . he sometimes sanctions that dangerous mode of apology which would destroy the validity of the reasoning process itself in order to evade reasonable conclusions. Such, for example, is the remarkable passage in which he meets the objection from the incompatible assertions of Scripture and science as to the motion of the sun, by saying that till we know what motion is we may suppose both the apparently contradictory assertions to be true.[2]

This was the passage which destroyed J. A. Froude's faith in Newman as a spiritual guide, after the subtleties of Tract 90 had shaken it.[3] It had a strong influence in convincing Kingsley that Newman 'was trying to undermine the grounds of all rational belief and human science' in order to get his 'victims . . . to believe anything, and rush blindfold into superstition'.[4]

Third, Newman's journals contain periodic recognitions that among his venial sins like 'self complacency' and 'rudeness' was 'inaccuracy in speech sometimes approaching to lying'.[5] One cannot make much of this, for it is the self-accusation of a scrupulous man writing about 'the absolute necessity of avoiding little sins, if we would be real Christians',[6] and men of such spirituality are commonly harder in judging themselves than the

---

[1] 'Charles Kingsley', *DNB* (1909), xi. 179.

[2] 'Newman's Theory of Belief', *An Agnostic's Apology* (London, 1903), pp. 179–80.

[3] See *The Nemesis of Faith* (2nd ed., London, 1849), pp. 157–8.

[4] Quoted by Guy Kendall, *Charles Kingsley and His Ideas*, p. 150, from an 1858 letter of Kingsley to the marine biologist Philip Henry Gosse. For the original passage in Newman and his own explanation, see *University Sermons*, pp. 347–9.

[5] *Autobiographical Writings*, p. 232. See also pp. 188, 210, 225.

[6] Ibid., p. 230.

general run of even good men. Still, there are signs in Newman, especially when he was pressed by opponents, of occasional disingenuousness of sorts, as in his slightly exaggerated account in the Preface to the *Apologia* of how unprepared he was to tell his story; or his technically correct but still misleading disclaimer of the monastic character of Littlemore in the letter to his bishop of April 14, 1842;[1] or in the remark in his letter to Kingsley of January 7 that when he received his letter acknowledging the authorship of the offending review in *Macmillan's*, he was amazed, as no person whom he had 'ever seen or heard of' had occurred to him as the author. This may well have been his initial reaction on seeing the marked passage, but since Kingsley's name appeared on the cover of *Macmillan's* as the author of the review article, it is difficult to believe that Newman had not learned the truth before receiving Kingsley's letter of acknowledgement.[2] It is perhaps true also that in his reply to Kingsley, Newman overstated the irregularity of his preaching from 1841 in order to break up the attendance of young men; for he did preach regularly enough in Michaelmas Term 1842 and Hilary Term till Easter, 1843, a period during which half of the *Sermons on the Subjects of the Day* were preached, including the one Kingsley objected to.[3]

Yet even if these three points in extenuation are granted and allowed to modify the indictment under which the reputation of Kingsley has suffered for his attack on Newman, they are not sufficient to explain or justify the intensity, the bitterness, and the persistence of that attack. Kingsley's feelings about Newman were shared neither by his spiritual mentor F. D. Maurice nor by his brother-in-law James Anthony Froude, whose book Kingsley was reviewing and who regarded Newman as one of the two most remarkable men he had ever met, the other being

---

[1] *Apologia*, p. 161.

[2] Cf. R. B. Martin, *The Dust of Combat*, p. 242. It was the *Athenaeum* (Mar. 26, 1864, p. 430) which first implied a doubt of Newman's statement here. In his letter to 'X. Y., Esq.' in the Correspondence, Newman had said that he saw the initials at the end of the review and the name of the Editor (David Masson) on the cover, but insisted that they 'conveyed to me absolutely no idea whatever. I am not defending myself, but merely stating what was the fact . . .'. The name of 'The Rev. Professor Kingsley' appears on the cover as the author of the review-article on Froude's book.

[3] See *Apologia*, p. 277, and the letter by Douglas E. Pett in *TLS* (Feb. 17, 1961), p. xvi. See also *Apologia*, n. 277. 35.

Carlyle.[1] Nor does such a feeling appear to have been shared by
any others (save perhaps the later Whately) who had ever known
Newman well, no matter how much they came to differ from
him intellectually and spiritually: e.g. Hawkins of Oriel, Palmer
of Worcester, or Mark Pattison of Lincoln. For Kingsley's
ultimate motivation, we must look further.

Under the influence of Carlyle and others, Kingsley had
gradually developed a theory of history, which he expounded at
Cambridge in the years preceding his attack on Newman, to the
effect that the Reformation revindicated the sanctity of marriage
and the family and restored the Teutonic freedoms and virtues.
These had been destroyed in the Middle Ages by the descendants of conquering Rome's lawyers, the clergy, who had
adopted 'those arms of quibbling and craft, which religious men
too often fancy are the proper arms of "the Saints" against "the
world"'.[2] Kingsley 'neither thought nor studied systematically,
and his beliefs were more matters of instinct than of reason'.[3]
He had come to look with increasing distaste on any but a
natural or 'scientific' theology, one which renewed much of the
spirit of his earlier deism, ignored the Atonement, denied eternal
punishment, and made sin hardly more than a matter of passing
regret.[4] Is it surprising that a man who in March 1864 could
write from Nimes, where he had gone for a rest:

> We saw today the most wonderful Roman remains. . . . the remark-
> able thing was the Roman ladies' baths in a fountain bursting up out
> of the rock. . . . All is standing, and could be used tomorrow, if the
> prudery of the priests allowed it. Honour to those Romans—with all
> their sins, they were the cleanest people the world has ever seen.[5]

—that such a man was genuinely outraged by the passage he
quotes in his pamphlet from Newman's *Difficulties of Anglicans*, affirming that the Catholic Church 'holds it better for the

[1] See Froude's 'The Oxford Counter-Reformation', *Short Studies on Great
Subjects* (4 vols., London, 1886), iv, esp. pp. 270–93.
[2] *The Roman and the Teuton* (Cambridge and London, 1864), p. 292.
[3] Leslie Stephen, 'Charles Kingsley', *DNB*.
[4] For an analysis of Kingsley's theology, see Walter E. Houghton, 'The Issue
Between Kingsley and Newman', *Theology Today*, iv (1947), 80–101: '. . . the clash
between Kingsley and Newman is the fundamental clash, both then and now, between Protestant Liberalism and Christian Orthodoxy, whether Roman Catholic
or Evangelical', a battle which for Newman 'is the central and unifying strand of
his life'.
[5] *Life and Works*, iii. 211.

sun and moon to drop from heaven, for the earth to fail, and for all the many millions on it to die of starvation in extremest agony, as far as temporal affliction goes, than that one soul, I will not say should be lost, but should commit one single venial sin, should tell one wilful untruth, or should steal one poor farthing without excuse' ?[1] That, not having the temperament to make an open-minded study of complex theological and ethical problems, he could only cry out again and again: 'What, then, does Dr. Newman mean ?'

The ultimate basis of Kingsley's hostility to Newman, the Tractarians, and Rome itself, however—more important than his distrust of casuistry or 'economy' or sacerdotalism—appears to have been psychological. As a young man Kingsley had been torn between the exclusive demands of an austere Evangelical religion and such worldly concerns as scientific pursuits and the attractions of physical love. The scepticism, indulgence, and vigorous physical activity of his early years at Cambridge were an attempt at a resolution which proved impossible for a man of Kingsley's temperament and inheritance. Some religious faith was necessary to him. At one point he confessed that he was wavering between 'deism or the highest and most monarchical system of Catholicism'.[2] And Catholicism, as Kingsley understood it, led even more than his childhood faith to a Manichean asceticism, not without a beauty of its own, which turned its back on the natural world. The same inability to make distinctions which made the work of Roman casuists like Alfonso Liguori so abhorrent to him made it possible for him to write: 'Were I a Romanist, I should look on a continuance in the state of wedlock as a bitter degradation to myself and my wife.'[3]

[1] Appendix B, p. 372. Kingsley also wishes to know how Newman can reconcile such a statement with the teachings of St. Alfonso Liguori on equivocation; but it is clear that he considers the statement absurd in itself. And there is little doubt that the majority of his countrymen would have agreed with him. As the *Saturday Review* put it: '[I]f this is a true character of the Creator . . . Dr. Newman's religious history forms an Apology for Atheism infinitely more mischievous than all that the Encyclopaedists, or Daimonists, or believers in the new philosophy of the divinity of the Sun, have ever speculated or suggested.' (xvii [1864], 787.) Cf. John Dewey, *The Quest for Certainty* (New York and London, 1929), pp. 51-52.

[2] *Life and Works*, i. 52.

[3] Quoted from a letter to an anonymous correspondent by Kendall, *Charles Kingsley and His Ideas*, p. 147. Kendall adds: 'Roman Catholics and Tractarians certainly did not and do not regard marriage as having the nature of sin . . . it is

In 1839 Kingsley met and fell in love with Fanny Grenfell, who had also known the attraction of Catholicism. It was the turning-point of his life. His marriage in 1844 is the root of the process by which he came to reconcile the world and the spirit and find peace of mind at last. 'Amavimus, Amamus, Amabimus' runs the inscription on the Kingsley tombstone. *Love* became the key-word of his life. Henceforth anything which theatened so intense and pure a bliss, the very fulfilment of man's nature and therefore indisputably good, was a thing of evil, an intolerable dissonance in the perfect harmony of the natural and supernatural borne in upon him by his own experience and strengthened by his reading of Carlyle. The celibacy which Rome demanded for her clergy was therefore a tool of craft rather than an aid to a higher virtue. Kingsley embarked on a lifelong crusade against monasticism, beginning in 1842 with a never completed prose life of St. Elizabeth of Hungary, which he intended as a wedding present for Fanny.[1] In 1848 it was published as a verse drama, *The Saint's Tragedy*, an object lesson on the inhumanity of asceticism, with the aim of making Protestants surer of the grounds on which they 'assert the purity and dignity of the offices of husband, wife, and parent' and deterring young men 'from the example of those miserable dilettanti, who in books and sermons are whimpering meagre second-hand praises of celibacy . . . '.

Many of Kingsley's most typical ideas were in varying degree shared by other prominent Victorians: e.g. his pan-German Protestant view of history ('the welfare of the Teutonic race is the welfare of the world'[2]) was substantially that of Carlyle, Tennyson, J. A. Froude, Shaftesbury and the Baron Bunsen, the historian E. A. Freeman, and indeed of the English

one thing to say that for those who have a vocation to the celibate life it is possible to attain to a higher spiritual state than can be attained by others who have not that vocation, and another to "forbid marriage", an attitude which the early Church condemned as heresy. . . .'

All the same, it must be said in Kingsley's defence that despite the Christian exaltation of marriage as a sacrament against various more or less Manichean heresies that condemned it, there did persist in patristic and medieval orthodox Christianity a tradition denigrating conjugal relations as at least venially sinful because of the element of concupiscence involved. See the articles on marriage in *Dictionnaire de théologie catholique*, ix, pt. ii (1927), esp. cols. 2090–6 and 2177–80.

[1] Martin, *The Dust of Combat*, pp. 71–75.
[2] *The Roman and the Teuton*, p. 338.

and Prussian courts; his rhapsodic exaltation of married love finds a near parallel in Browning and perhaps especially in Coventry Patmore, himself ironically a Catholic convert; and the anti-ascetic, anti-monastic note may be heard in many works such as Browning's 'Fra Lippo Lippi', Tennyson's 'St. Simeon Stylites' and more subtly in *The Idylls of the King*. But no other writer gave himself with such fervour and persistence to the propagation of all of them.

Hypatia (1853), which Kingsley considered his most important novel, is above all one long attack on Tractarianism by means of a portrait of fifth-century Alexandrian Catholicism. It makes of Bishop Synesius, the indulgent athlete and Platonic philosopher who refused to be consecrated unless he could keep his wife, a more attractive figure than the Patriarch Cyril, who is seen as little more than a crafty bigot, and even than Augustine himself, a greater and wiser man indeed but, it is delicately implied, disappointed in love. The hero, Raphael Aben-Ezra, on the point of becoming a Christian, changes his mind on learning that the father of a lovely Christian maiden he admires (her name is Victoria) is encouraging her to go into a convent:

I had actually deluded myself into the fancy that the Deity of the Galileans might be, after all, the God of our old Hebrew forefathers—of Adam and Eve, of Abraham and David, and of the rest who believed that children and the fruit of the womb were an heritage and gift which cometh of the Lord—and that Paul was right—actually right—in his theory that the Church was the development and fulfilment of our old national polity. . . . I must thank you for opening my eyes to a mistake which, had I not been besotted for the moment, every monk and nun would have contradicted by the mere fact of their existence, and reserve my nascent faith for some Deity who takes no delight in seeing his creatures stultify the primary laws of their being.[1]

Later, when old Miriam is about to reveal herself as the mother of Raphael, she tells first how she had originally become 'a Christian nun, and shut herself up to see visions, and dream dreams, and fattened her own mad self-conceit upon the impious fancy that she was the spouse of the Nazarene' but had left the convent when, God having refused to protect her from the barbarian invader by whom she was to have a child, she 'knew it all for a lie! a lie!'

[1] *Hypatia* (2 vols., London, 1853), ii. 41.

'"And you knew it for what it is," cried Raphael through his sobs, as he thought of Victoria, and felt every vein burning with righteous wrath!'[1]

Kingsley, who with the aid of F. D. Maurice had steered his course between the Scylla of pantheism and the Charybdis of the Tractarians, portrayed his ideal in Raphael, who found the former (Hypatia) inadequate and confused and the latter (Cyril and his followers) fanatical and unscrupulous. It was the same burning with righteous wrath that undoubtedly coursed through his own veins when he read in Newman's sermon 'The Apostolical Christian':

> But, if the truth must be spoken, what are the humble monk, and the holy nun, and other regulars, as they are called, but Christians after the very pattern given us in Scripture ? What have they done but this— continue in the world the Christianity of the Bible. . . . Did our Saviour come on earth suddenly, as He will one day visit, in whom would he see the features of the Christians he and his apostles left behind them, but in them ?[2]

Newman's assurance that such a model did not command literal imitation he ignored. 'Monks and nuns the only perfect Christians' is the way the impassioned Kingsley read it. 'What more ?' he cries.[3] He does indeed have other objections to make, but none that he might have felt as strongly as this—so strongly as to make it quite impossible for him to judge dispassionately either the words or the religion of the speaker. Newman's conversion (a 'moral suicide', Kingsley called it, a 'dive into the Roman avernus');[4] Kingsley's genuine abhorrence of post-Jesuit Catholicism, as he viewed it; the obloquy which fell on him for sheltering the disillusioned ex-Tractarian J. A. Froude, after the storm raised by the latter's sceptical *Nemesis of Faith*;[5] the conversion for a time to Catholicism of Mrs. Kingsley's sister Charlotte, the future Mrs. Froude; the controversial works of Newman the Catholic, with their caustic

---

[1] *Hypatia*, ii. 352.

[2] Appendix B, p. 358. For the original passage, see *Sermons on the Subjects of the Day*, pp. 290–1.

[3] Appendix B, p. 359.   [4] Epilogue to *Yeast, Life and Works*, xv. 273.

[5] In a letter to Maurice of Jan. 8, 1864, Alexander Macmillan expressed the opinion that '[o]ld passages about Froude and others have left a bitter flavour in his thoughts and feelings about the great pervert'. Quoted by Margaret Thorp, *Charles Kingsley*, p. 155.

irony against the Establishment and the prejudices of Protestants; the attacks on Kingsley by the Tractarians, who in 1863 under the leadership of Dr. Pusey had protested so strongly against his being granted a D.C.L. by Oxford that he felt it best to withdraw his name—all these factors had a share, no doubt, in strengthening his aversion to the leader he had once called 'that great genius, John Henry Newman',[1] and of whom Lancelot, the hero of *Yeast*, pondering his 'thin wan face, full of unfathomable thoughts', is led to reflect: 'What a man! . . . or rather the wreck of what a man! Oh, for such a heart, with the thews and sinews of a truly English brain!'[2] But they derived their force from working on a mind already convinced that Newman, the Tractarians, and the Roman Church, whose power for moral regeneration he could not wholly deny, were a living and constant challenge to his own and life's highest values. His real 'score of more than twenty years' is to be found in his confession that 'Love saved me!' from the Tracts. They 'struck at the root of our wedded bliss'.[3]

Newman, of course, could know little of all this. He knew at once, however, that Kingsley had at last given him the opportunity for the book he had 'for years wished to write . . . as a duty'.[4] Even before the publication of Kingsley's pamphlet, he had considered answering the original attack with a spiritual autobiography. What he regretted then was not Kingsley's charges so much as the fact that they had not gone far enough: 'If they would have gone on, speaking of "Roman duplicity", "St. Alfonso", or my own delinquence in *act*, such as No. 90, Whately's charge against me of remaining a crypto-papist in the Anglican Church, then I could have written what would have been *worth* writing, both as regards the doctrine of Truth, and my own history. But this apparently is not on the cards.'[5] It was to be 'on the cards' after all, however, for Newman's pamphlet had goaded Kingsley into spelling out his charges, and they now read almost as if they had been levelled according to Newman's own directions.

---

[1] Preface to the fourth edition of *Yeast*, *Life and Works* xv. x.
[2] Ibid., p. 209.
[3] Quoted by Kendall from the preface to Kingsley's unpublished prose Life of St. Elizabeth, *Charles Kingsley and His Ideas*, p. 25.
[4] Letter to Keble, Apr. 27, 1864. See Ward, *Life*, ii. 22.
[5] Letter to Edward Badeley of Jan. 15, 1864. MS. *Apologia* Letters.

When Kingsley's pamphlet was first announced, Newman wrote to Badeley that he looked forward to it as something 'for which of course I have prepared myself from the first'.

I mean, I never have had an opportunity to defend myself as to various passages in my life and writings, and I have always looked forward to the possibility of that opening being presented to me. I have for a long time been attempting to arrange my letters and papers with a view to it. Unluckily I have not yet got further than 1836—and what I shall chiefly want is 1841–1845. However, I must take things as they come.[1]

Keble suggested that he spare himself the labour of answering 'such trash as Mr. Kingsley's' and guard his health for the great task of the age: 'We (if I may say) want you, dear J. H. N.—all Christendom wants you—to take your stand against the infidelity wch seems to [be] so fast enveloping us all.'[2] But Newman realized full well that unless he first vindicated his own name before Protestant and Catholic alike, the ears of all too many of his countrymen would be deaf to anything he might in the future say. The favour of the literary critics had given him the chance to appeal now from Philip drunk to Philip sober. The publisher Longman urged immediate action. It was Newman's own score of twenty years or more. As he wrote to his old friend Church on April 23, 1864:

It has always been on my mind that perhaps some day I should be called on to defend my honesty while in the Church of England. . . . I have considered that if anyone with his name made an elaborate charge on me, I was bound to speak.

. . . I know well that Kingsley is a furious foolish fellow,—but he has a name,—nor is it anything at all to me that men think I got the victory in the Correspondence several months ago,—that was a contest of ability,—but now he comes out with a pamphlet bringing together a hodge podge of charges against me all about dishonesty. Now friends who know me say: 'Let him alone,—no one credits him', but it is not so. This very town of Birmingham, of course, knows nothing of me, and his pamphlet on its appearance produced an effect. The evangelical party has always spoken ill of me, and the pamphlet seems to justify them. The Roman Catholic party does not know me;—the fathers of our school boys, the priests, &c., &c., whom I cannot afford to let think

---

[1] Letter of Mar. 8, 1864, MS. *Apologia* Letters.
[2] Letter of Apr. 25, 1864, ibid.

badly of me. Therefore, thus publicly challenged, I must speak, and, unless I speak strongly, men won't believe me in earnest.[1]

He spoke strongly enough to be heard from England to the Antipodes.

2. *The Writing of the* Apologia

That Newman could write, in less than three months, the many-sided account of his spiritual history which is the *Apologia*, then the longest and still the most varied of his works, is an extraordinary testimony to his powers of concentration. It becomes more understandable, however, as we realize that the *Apologia*, like Kingsley's attack, was due to no sudden impulse but was rather the product of many years of reflection on various personal attacks and the desirability or possibility of answering them; on the nature of persuasion; on the essentials of good biography; and above all on the previous life of one who had felt since his Evangelical youth that, as life was primarily a series of transactions between God and the individual soul, the contemplation of things past afforded him the best opportunity of tracing God's hand at work, until the places and friends he so deeply loved had assumed the importance of actors in a divinely conceived drama. 'Let us humbly and reverently attempt to trace His guiding hand in the years which we have hitherto lived', he had long ago urged in a sermon called 'Remembrance of Past Mercies'. And as Jacob 'delighted lovingly to trace, and gratefully to acknowledge, what had been given, leaving the future to itself', so Newman, as we have seen, was in the years of his sorrow making the *Apologia* possible by 'living in memory rather than in hope, counting times, recording seasons, keeping days; having his history by heart, and his past life in his hand'.[2]

He directed the *Apologia* not to Kingsley, whom he considered beyond persuasion, but to the English public at large, which he knew shared many of Kingsley's views. Kingsley's pamphlet had 'poisoned the wells' against him by casting so much doubt on his character and by implication on his patriotism that no detailed answer to each of the charges would have any

[1] Ward, *Life*, ii. 19–20.
[2] *Parochial and Plain Sermons*, v. 84, 80, and 82.

real chance to penetrate minds already so hardened against him, even if such minds were capable of following the subtleties of complex theological and ethical problems. Yet Newman had no perplexity as to the method of answering Kingsley, not because he wished to write an autobiography for its own sake, but because he never doubted the truth of what Aristotle's *Rhetoric* and his own experience had taught him: that in persuasion, personal influence was of the first and utmost importance since, except in mathematical science, conviction depended not on the intellect alone but on the right state of mind and heart which made successful reasoning possible. And the heart is 'commonly reached, not through the reason, but through the imagination, by means of direct impressions, by the testimony of facts and events, by history, by description. Persons influence us, voices melt us, looks subdue us, deeds inflame us.'[1] In the writings of the Fathers of the Church, in Scripture itself, 'dogma and proof' were 'at the same time hagiography'.[2] Newman would subdue his readers and make them believe he was an honest Englishman, not so much by argument, at least at first, as by giving them his living mind in action: by giving them himself.

He would keep for the last chapter direct answers to Kingsley's charges against himself and the Roman clergy he had been made to represent; there, those who wished to examine them might do so in at least a more open, perhaps now a sympathetic, frame of mind.[3] In the story itself there would be no special pleading for Roman Catholicism, he assured the Anglican friends whose aid he rather hesitantly appealed for: 'I have no

---

[1] *Discussions and Arguments*, p. 293.

[2] *Historical Sketches*, ii. 223. The very title of Newman's story, *Apologia pro Vita Sua*, links it to the Fathers, who produced works with similar titles. Newman's own favourite, Athanasius, that untiring defender of orthodoxy whose name became a rallying cry in nineteenth-century England, wrote an *Apologia de Fuga Sua*. (The title of Coleridge's poem 'Apologia pro Vita Sua' was apparently an editorial one, given to it in 1907. See *The Complete Poetical Works of Samuel Taylor Coleridge*, ed. E. H. Coleridge [2 vols., Oxford, 1912], i. 345.)

[3] The *Apologia* is not an autobiography nor even a complete spiritual autobiography of the years between 1801 and 1845. It is primarily a work of rhetoric. For a discussion which space does not permit here of how Newman put it together, the materials he used and the dramatic framework into which he cast them, see Martin J. Svaglic, 'The Structure of Newman's *Apologia*', in *Victorian Literature: Modern Essays in Criticism*, ed. Austin Wright (New York, 1961), pp. 225–37, reprinted from *PMLA*, lxvi (1951), 138–48. See also Walter E. Houghton, *The Art of Newman's 'Apologia'* (New Haven and London, 1945).

idea whatever of giving any *point* to what I am writing,' he told Church, 'but that I did not act dishonestly.'[1] To Rogers he wrote:

I sincerely wish only to state facts, and may truly say that it, and nothing else, has been my object. So far as my character is connected with the fact of my conversion I have wished to do a service to Catholicism,—but in no other way. I say this because my friends here think that the upshot of the whole tells *against* Anglicanism; but I am clear that I have no such intention, and cannot at all divine what people generally will say about me. I say all this in fairness,—it is what has made me delicate in applying to Anglican friends.[2]

One of Newman's greatest handicaps was his own temperament, whose natural reserve had been strongly accentuated by the quest for sanctity which inspired the Oxford Movement and made anything in the nature of self-display abhorrent. 'When you see part of my publication', he confessed to Keble, 'you will wonder how I could ever get myself to write it. Well, I could not, except under some very great stimulus. I do not think I could write it, if I delayed it a month.'[3] Lack of easily accessible material and shortness of time increased his difficulty. There was an abundance of documents to be consulted—no strictly autobiographical notes, it is true, as we are told in the preface to the *Apologia*, but letters he had received from his earliest years, many copies of those he had sent, annotated and illustrated classroom journals, personal notebooks sometimes in Latin when dealing with religious and moral problems, study notes at Oxford, a journal begun in 1821.[4] Yet, though these are today all classified and available to students in the Oratory at Birmingham (and many of them have been published in the volume called *Autobiographical Writings*), in March 1864 they were only in process of being put into order; and, as we have seen, Newman had not got beyond 1836. Most of his own early books he had last read when revising the proof sheets. Friends like Church and Rogers and Keble had to be asked for letters he had sent them—'that kind of literature which more than any

---

[1] Ward, *Life*, ii. 21.　　　　[2] Ibid., p. 24.　　　　[3] Ibid., p. 22.
[4] For some of the information that follows, I am indebted to a valuable article by Henry Tristram, 'Note au bas d'un grand texte', *La France franciscaine. Recherches de théologie, philosophie, histoire*, iiie série, xxii (1939), 35–48.

other represents the abundance of the heart'[1]—as well as for criticism and advice. Above all there was the necessity which his own common sense told him and his publisher Longman never let him forget: the account had to be relatively brief, or it would not be read; and it had to be done at once, while public interest was at its height, if it was to be done at all. 'Under these circumstances', Newman wrote,

my sketch will of course be incomplete. I now for the first time contemplate my course as a whole; it is a first essay, but it will contain, I trust, no serious or substantial mistake, and so far will answer the purpose for which I write it. I purpose to set nothing down in it as certain, for which I have not a clear memory, or some written memorial, or the corroboration of some friend. There are witnesses enough up and down the country to verify, or correct, or complete it; and letters moreover of my own in abundance, unless they have been destroyed.[2]

Newman began to write soon after the appearance of Kingsley's pamphlet, certainly before the end of March. He considered for a time a series of lectures like the *Difficulties of Anglicans*, which Ambrose St. John had urged, but soon gave up the idea of a lecture platform as incongruous with the nature of the revelations he would have to make. He resolved instead to publish his story at his own expense in a series of weekly pamphlets. Longmans hesitated at first but then agreed that the novelty of the method would help to attract attention. Accordingly, the *Apologia* first appeared in seven pamphlets published on Thursdays between April 21 and June 2, 1864, with an eighth, an appendix called *Answer in Detail to Mr. Kingsley's Accusations*, appearing two weeks later on June 16.[3] Newman allowed the interval, not merely because the eighth part was longer than the others and required more time, but because he wished to consider any reply Kingsley might have made in the meantime. His failure to do so Newman considered a great tactical error.

The fact is that on medical advice Mrs. Kingsley saw to it that her run-down and overworked husband, already in a high state of tension, did not read the *Apologia* until it was complete. Then, though he had earlier hinted at 'such a revanche as will make [Newman] wince, if any English common sense is left

---

[1] *Historical Sketches*, ii. 219.   [2] *Apologia*, Appendix C, p. 407.
[3] And not on June 25, as Ward says (*Life*, ii. 28).

in him, which I doubt',[1] Kingsley decided to let the whole thing drop and 'retired . . . into silence, with a reputation permanently damaged'.[2]

The first two of Newman's pamphlets were called 'Mr. Kingsley's Method of Disputation' and 'True Mode of Meeting Mr. Kingsley'. Pamphlets III–VI (1865 edition, Chapters I to IV) were known as 'History of My Religious Opinions'. Part VII was called 'General Answer to Mr. Kingsley'. According to the account given to Wilfrid Ward by Fr. Ignatius Dudley Ryder, who succeeded Newman as Superior of the Birmingham Oratory, Newman found the 'effort of writing the weekly parts . . . overpowering. On such occasions he wrote through the night, and he has been found with his head in his hands crying like a child over the, to him, well-nigh impossibly painful task of public confession.'[3]

Newman first sketched the general plan of the work, with the principal heads of narrative and argument, and fixed it in large letters to the wall opposite his desk. He did his writing on large sheets of paper folded down the middle. Each page he divided in two and wrote on both sides, on the recto leaving the right-hand column free for his many additions and corrections, and on the verso doing the reverse so that when the sheets were unfolded, the text occupied the centre in two columns.[4] Scattered throughout the manuscript are pages not divided but written across.

Most of the manuscripts of Newman's published works have disappeared, possibly having been disposed of by printer or publisher, though this seems strange when one considers how careful Newman invariably was in keeping even the smallest records of his life. Much of the manuscript of the *Apologia* has survived, however, perhaps because what the printer received was not most of what remains at the Birmingham Oratory but a copy of this manuscript made by Newman's sometime secretary and future literary executor, Fr. William Neville.

---

[1] Quoted from a letter to his curate Frederick Stapleton by M. F. Thorp, *Charles Kingsley*, p. 159.

[2] Guy Kendall, *Charles Kingsley and His Ideas*, p. 157. This is perhaps overstated, as Kingsley's career, at least, does not appear to have suffered any damage from the episode. In 1873 he was made Canon of Westminster.

[3] Ward, *Life*, ii. 23.

[4] See Tristram, 'Note au bas d'un grand texte', p. 36.

The manuscript at the Oratory consists of the first four parts, more than half of Part VI, and several sections and scattered pages of Part VII. There are also fragments of Part V and of Part VIII. Part VI differs from most of the rest in that the pages are not divided into columns and are written on one side only. The writing, much clearer than elsewhere, is probably Fr. Neville's, whose script closely resembled Newman's. At the top of the first page of VI is written in pencil '*copy*' and 'Part 6 copy of 6th'. At the top of the page where it breaks off (1864 ed., p. 321), the same unknown hand has written 'This makes the whole of Part 6', an obvious error unless it means all that has survived of that part.

The manuscript of Part VI and a few other pages are signed occasionally in the margins with the names 'Edwards' and 'Yeowall'. If, as seems possible, these are the names of printers at the London firm of Gilbert and Rivington, which printed the *Apologia*, then these signed pages may be the only part of the final manuscript which survives. In any event, much of the present manuscript is so heavily corrected and revised as to be virtually illegible from time to time, even to those familiar with Newman's script; and it is hard to see how the most hardened printers could have worked with it. Furthermore, the manuscript differs frequently, sometimes extensively, from what actually appeared in the pamphlets of 1864. Surviving scraps show that Newman heavily revised his galley proof, sometimes at the suggestion of friends like Copeland and Keble, who received copies of it. The present edition of the *Apologia* supplies in the notes the more significant of the passages in the original manuscript which Newman later cancelled.

It was on April 10 that he began the stretches of prolonged labour he has described so vividly in letters to intimate friends. 'During the writing and reading of my Part 3', he confessed to Rogers on April 22, 'I could not get on from beginning to end for crying.'[1] On May 2 he wrote to Hope-Scott:

I never have been in such stress of brain and such pain of heart,—and I have both trials together. Say some good prayers for me. I have been writing without interruption of Sundays since Easter Monday—five weeks—and I have at least three weeks more of the same work to come. I have been constantly in tears, and constantly crying out with

[1] Ward, *Life*, ii. 19.

distress. I am sure I never could say what I am saying in cold blood, or if I waited a month. . . .[1]

One day, we learn from his diary, he worked uninterruptedly for sixteen hours on Part III and once for twenty-two on Part V. As he began in Part III to tell his own story and the details piled up, he had twice to enlarge his original plan, which called for a 'History of My Religious Opinions' first in Parts III and IV, then in III, IV, and V, and finally in the four parts from III to VI.[2] This change of plan during the course of composition may account in part for a certain confusion in the chronology of the chapters: e.g. the fact that Tract 90 is treated at the end of Part IV (to 1839), although it did not appear until 1841. However, this confusion is more apparent than real and may be explained better on thematic grounds. Tract 90 grew out of speculations that long antedated 1841, and it is part of the general case for Anglo-Catholicism that is the main subject of Part IV (1865, Ch. II).

When it was all over and peace of mind was again possible, and with the acclaim his story had received reinforcing the artist's satisfaction in a work well done, Newman could look back on his ordeal with almost childlike wonder and exhilaration. 'I never had such a time of it', he wrote to a Dominican nun. 'When I was in Oxford I have twice written a pamphlet in a night, and once in a day, but now I had writing and printing upon me at once; but with so much suffering, such profuse crying, such long spells of work . . . that it is a prodigious, awful marvel that I have got through it and that I am not simply knocked up by it.'[3] His success was a providential sign that there was still a work in the world for him to do. Henceforward he would be heard with respect and considerable sympathy. The *Apologia* meant the start of a new and final period of literary activity.

3. *The Reception of the* Apologia

Rarely has any prophecy been more quickly fulfilled than Newman's assurance that he would vanquish, not his accuser,

[1] Ward, *Life*, ii. 25.
[2] Tristram, 'Note au bas d'un grand texte', pp. 42–44.
[3] Ward, *Life*, ii. 30–31.

but his judges. Before the last part of the *Apologia* was in print, the reviews began to come in; and in spite of certain qualifications and some dissenting opinions (one or two pamphlets in Kingsley's favour appeared, and there were those who agreed with the view that T. H. Huxley expressed much later: 'That man is the slipperiest sophist I have ever met with. Kingsley was entirely right about him'[1]), most critics in the influential journals of opinion agreed that Newman had unquestionably won his point and proved himself an honest man.[2]

R. H. Hutton again led the way with two articles in the *Spectator* of June 4 and June 11. He admitted that for those neither far enough away to judge by his writings alone nor close enough to be his confidants, Newman's behaviour during the years of his uncertainty might have seemed perplexing, even to the extent of shaking one's trust in his simplicity of purpose. Yet he repeated his original view 'that there was absolutely no justification for Mr. Kingsley's rash accusation' and contended that 'it would be mere dullness of nature not to recognize freely the whole truthfulness and almost childlike candour of the autobiographic sketch now before us', which was the work of a 'great and noble mind', one 'incapable . . . of insincerity'.[3]

On June 16 *The Times* devoted three columns to the *Apologia*, affirming that 'every candid reader will acquit Dr. Newman of any dishonest intentions in his relations towards the English Church during his abode in her', a transition state being a very trying period: 'It is a situation which involves many tender considerations, and nice estimates, and intricate comparisons of

---

[1] From a letter of May 30, 1889, to Sir James Hooker. *Life and Letters of Thomas Henry Huxley* (2 vols., London, 1900), ii. 226. The principal reviewer to make this charge was James Fitzjames Stephen, brother of Leslie, whose similar views have already been referred to. In *Fraser's Magazine*, lxx (1864), pp. 265–303, Fitzjames Stephen argued that though Newman was personally honest, he had 'been brought to accept superstition by sophistry' and that the 'misapprehension of the nature of probability' vitiated his argument.

On the other hand, the *Westminster Review* held that Newman not only clearly bested Kingsley in the polemic but, though wrong in his ultimate conclusion, was logical and consistent in his progress; whereas Kingsley and similar compromisers between 'freedom and authority' were themselves guilty of sophistry. (N.S. xxvi. [1864], 137–51 and 357–77.) These are important reviews, but the nature of their argument makes brief summary impracticable.

[2] The response of the denominational journals varied pretty much according to their attitude toward Catholic theology and Rome. See V. F. Blehl, S.J., 'Early Criticism of the *Apologia*', in *Newman's 'Apologia': A Classic Reconsidered*, pp. 47–63.　　　　[3] *The Spectator*, xxxvii (1864), 655 and 683.

conflicting duties; but it is a situation which a person may be in without dishonesty, and which he may carry out without dishonesty; and Dr. Newman may claim with perfect right a decisive verdict in his favour on this question.' Perhaps the most perceptive of the critic's observations was that

. . . the accuracy and minuteness with which Dr. Newman registers all the different fluctuations of the theological barometer and conducts a doctrinal transmutation through all its stages, noting its rises and falls, its pauses and advances, till it reaches its destined completeness, unconsciously reveal in the *Apologia* an undertaking which, though doubtless accompanied with much to harass and distress, has been in some respects not other than a labour of love to him.[1]

On June 25 the *Saturday Review*, which had already castigated Kingsley, introduced its review of the *Apologia* with the remark that a

loose and offhand, and, we may venture to add, an unjustifiable imputation, cast on Dr. Newman by a popular writer more remarkable for vigorous writing than vigorous thought, has produced one of the most interesting works of the present literary age. Dr. Newman is one of the finest masters of language; his logical powers are almost unequalled, and, in one way or other, he has influenced the course of English thought more perhaps than any of his contemporaries.

It spoke of his task as to account for 'what vulgar minds will always brand as an act of desertion'. The complexity of his mind meant that it is 'not given to the gentlemen who write in religious newspapers, or to the ordinary run of pious Christians, to understand Dr. Newman; and to say that a man is receiving Protestant pay while he is teaching Popish doctrine saves thought, and gives an opportunity for coarse-minded piety to violate the ninth commandment'. The *Apologia* as a whole it found chiefly useful not as a vindication of the author's sincerity and pureness of motive, 'for such was not required', but as 'a curious and most interesting chapter in psychology', and as 'a valuable contribution from the most trustworthy source to the inner history of the Church of England in very momentous times', the cold facts of a William Palmer having 'at last been invested with life, and described with the energy of a master, by the one original genius who has risen above the heavy clouds

[1] *The Times*, Thursday, June 16, 1864, p. 12.

and fog of the Tractarian flats'. It reaffirmed that there was 'the stamp of truth in every word which Newman utters about himself', and that he was 'thoroughly and implicitly to be believed'. Newman had anatomized himself with 'dignity and pathos': the 'lofty egotism' of the work was 'inseparable perhaps from the occasion'.[1]

Of the monthly and quarterly magazines, we may take *Blackwood's*, the *Edinburgh Review*, and the *Quarterly* as examples. The first, though finding the dialectical duel 'not in any sense of the term an agreeable spectacle', devoted much of its space to an attack on Kingsley, 'entirely and wantonly the aggressor', for endangering 'higher interests than the personal reputation of a rash man'. It lamented the 'strange confusion of ideas from which, let him discuss what topic he may, Mr. Kingsley seems incapable of extricating himself'. As for Newman, it expressed the opinion that he showed a far greater yearning for truth than Mr. Kingsley in any of his works: 'We believe him to be now, and always to have been, a thoroughly honest man. We do not distrust one word of all that he has written about himself.' Kingsley was only 'a misguided clever man', but Newman was 'a fallen angel'.[2]

The *Edinburgh Review*, in an article on Whately's *Miscellaneous Remains from the Commonplace Book*, was inclined to think Whately right in holding that there was too much 'reserve' and 'economy' in the conduct of the Oxford Movement, but spoke of the *Apologia* as a 'most engaging record . . . now in the hands of every one'; and of Newman as a 'great leader of men', and of the 'honest allegiance to truth' of 'a man of honour'.[3]

Most pointed of all the reviews and in the long run perhaps the most influential was that by Samuel Wilberforce in the *Quarterly*. The writer, son of the Evangelical abolitionist and himself the Bishop of Oxford, had seen his three brothers and many of his old friends go over to Rome since Newman's conversion; his own faith in Anglicanism remained unshaken, however, and in his review he attempted to show that nothing in Newman's process of change was an argument in favour of following him. He is gentle to Kingsley, not anxious to give

[1] *The Saturday Review*, xvii (1864), 785 and 786.
[2] *Blackwood's Edinburgh Magazine*, xcvi (1864), 292, 299, 308.
[3] *The Edinburgh Review*, cxx (1864), 378 and 382.

more than 'bare justice' to Newman, and holds that 'this strange narrative' offers 'abundant reason . . . for the widely-diffused impression of that being true which it is so pleasant to find unfounded'. Nevertheless, he is quite definite about Newman's success. These pages, he says, were meant to exhibit to Newman's countrymen

. . . the whole secret of his moral and spiritual anatomy; they were intended to prove that he was altogether free from that foul and disgraceful taint of innate dishonesty, the unspoken suspicion of which in so many quarters had so long troubled him; the open utterance of which, from the lips of a popular and respectable writer, was so absolutely intolerable to him. From that imputation it is but bare justice to say he does thoroughly clear himself. The post-mortem examination of his life is complete; the hand which guided the dissecting-knife has trembled nowhere, nor shrunk from any incision. All lies perfectly open, and the foul taint is nowhere.[1]

Early in the controversy Kingsley's own master and friend, F. D. Maurice, who judged men more by the nature of their search than by the views they held, expressed the opinion that (despite 'all apparent evidence') 'Newman loves the truth in his heart of hearts, and more now than when he was an Anglican'.[2]

And how did Kingsley feel about all this? Hutton had written: '. . . we can scarcely conceive that Mr. Kingsley himself can read this apology without the profoundest personal conviction of the stedfast uprightness and true simplicity of Dr. Newman's theological career.'[3] He was very wrong. Kingsley was still convinced that Newman was alternately a knave and a fool, but he was now more prudent than to pursue the matter further. On June 8, 1864, he wrote to Alexander Macmillan a letter 'so deplorable in taste', says one of his biographers, 'that if it had not already been made public one could wish to leave it unnoticed'.[4]

Here is my ultimatum on the Newman question, which please shew (privately) to any one and every one you like, including Mr. Hutton.

I have determined to take no notice whatever of Dr. Newman's apology.

[1] *The Quarterly Review*, cxvi (1864), 544.
[2] In a letter to Dean Stanley, Apr. 19, 1864. See *The Life of Frederick Denison Maurice*, ed. Frederick Maurice (2 vols., London, 1884), ii. 478–9.
[3] *Spectator*, xxxvii (1864), 655.
[4] Kendall, p. 157. The letter was first published by Mrs. Thorp in her *Charles Kingsley* (1937).

1. I have nothing to retract, apologize for, explain. Deliberately, after 20 years of thought, I struck as hard as I could. Deliberately I shall strike again, if it so please me, though not one literary man in England approved. I know too well of what I am talking.

2. I cannot trust—I can only smile at—the autobiography of a man who (beginning with Newman's light, learning, and genius) ends in believing that he believes in the Infallibility of the Church, and in the Immaculate Conception. If I am to bandy words, it must be with sane persons.

3. I cannot be [?] weak enough to put myself a second time, by any fresh act of courtesy, into the power of one who, like a treacherous ape, lifts to you meek and suppliant eyes, till he thinks he has you within his reach, and then springs, gibbering and biting, at your face.

He goes on in this vein, ending with a wish that 'poor dear Thackeray' were alive:

He knew what I know, and would have taken a tone about this matter, which would have astonished too many literary men. He was too true a liberal to pat lies and bigotry on the back.

Give my really kind regards to Mr. Hutton, for whom I have a sincere respect.[1]

There were, of course, various objections to Newman's position as outlined in the *Apologia*. The reaction of Catholics, best indicated by the letters Newman later incorporated in the text, was immensely favourable, on the whole, but with some reservations.[2] It was hardly to be expected, however, that a group of Protestant writers in nineteenth-century England should applaud Newman's choice of creed as well as his honesty in making it. At least some indication of their views may be given here, though it will necessarily be inadequate.

Like many critics of Newman to this day, the reviewers generally attributed his conversion to faulty premises logically carried out, to various psychological factors more or less determining his conclusions, or to both. Thus to Hutton (who in later

---

[1] Thorp, *Charles Kingsley*, p. 160.

[2] Thus, the future Cardinal Vaughan read it with a mixture of pain and pleasure, the 'egotism' of the book 'disgusting him', the 'satire and contempt appealing to one's bad nature, unfortunately'. Manning, who said the book was like 'a voice from the dead', was annoyed at the parts of the work that he rightly sensed were directed against views and attitudes like his own. See Dom Cuthbert Butler, *The Life and Times of Bishop Ullathorne* (2 vols., London, 1926), i. 332; and Edward Kelly, S.J., 'The *Apologia* and the Ultramontanes', in *Newman's 'Apologia': A Classic Reconsidered*, pp. 26–46.

years moved closer to Newman's thought), all Newman's 'premises of thought were Roman Catholic from the beginning'; his logic, as displayed in the *Apologia*, registered 'the *rate*' rather than 'the track' of his advance; and, except for the relation of God to the soul, all the other great theses of Newman's theology 'seem to us to recommend themselves less as self-demonstrating, than as parts of a great system which is given on a high authority, and which he finds perfectly adapted to cope with the naturalism and anarchy of what he calls Liberal thought'. Newman's was 'the mind of a great reactionary, recoiling upon the strongest defences it can find against the decomposing power of modern thought, instead of throwing itself on that power of faith which is really greatest only in alliance with perfect freedom'.[1]

The fact that Anglo-Catholicism, at least as a co-ordinated theory, was still relatively undeveloped when Newman wrote the *Apologia*, may help to account for the agreement of *Blackwood's*, *The Times*, and the *Saturday Review* that Newman's theory of the Church was not only individual but even highly visionary from the start. Both the *Saturday Review* and *The Times* likened Newman in some respects to an Irvingite, and though the latter admitted that 'his course of change was from the first in one direction, and . . . exhibits a unity and consistency', still it felt compelled to state that the *Apologia* 'has not diminished our idea of the extraordinary wildness and visionariness of the task which he imposed upon himself and the object he fixed upon in this undertaking of Church reformation as he understood and conceived it'. Characterizing as obsolete Newman's 'fundamental idea of the theological necessity of going ahead, absolute logical development in one direction, &c.', *The Times* held that such an attitude had long been changed for 'a larger basis of judgment'.[2]

Blackwood's agreed that Newman had built up a theology of his own, to which Evangelicals and liberals were expected to subscribe, and was therefore wrong because his principles were 'indefensible *ab initio*', however perfectly they might agree with one another.[3] The *Saturday Review*, looking askance at the

---

[1] *Spectator*, xxxvii. 655 and 683. But compare these remarks with his essay 'Newman and Tennyson', *Brief Literary Criticisms* (London, 1906), pp. 192–200.

[2] Thursday, June 16, 1864, p. 12.

[3] *Blackwood's Edinburgh Magazine*, xcvi. 306 and 308.

influence of the Alexandrian Platonists and at Newman's 'mysterious view' of two and two only luminously self-evident beings, felt there was truth in the opinion that Newman had never really understood the Church of England, and spoke of his religious system as a 'piecing here and patching there'.[1]

From Bishop Wilberforce, a moderate Anglo-Catholic and not likely therefore to regard Newman's conception of the Church as visionary or obsolete nor his logic as flawless, came an interpretation almost wholly psychological. Newman's 'defection' was due to the 'peculiarities of the individual'. His mind was eminently subjective and, though honest, had no engrossing affection for abstract truth. In fact, so feeble was Newman's hold on any truth external to himself by comparison with his conception of what was passing within himself 'that the external truth was always liable to corrections which would make its essential elements harmonize with what was occurring within his own intellectual or spiritual being'. From such a condition came both an 'inexhaustible mutability in his view on all subjects' and 'a continually recurring temptation to entire scepticism as to everything external to himself'. Wilberforce saw no logical connexion between the various steps outlined in the *Apologia*: 'It was not that argument was weighed against argument: there was argument nowhere. The leaning to Rome was from the bias of his own mind, not from the strength of her cause; that bias was counteracted only by personal inclination, which a change in the atmosphere around him might at any moment reverse.' This change came with the outburst against Tract 90, which had a decisive effect on 'that sensitive, ill-understood soul', already marked by 'a noble and mounting ambition . . . struggling within him'. From that time on, '[h]is heart . . . began to eat itself'.[2] In this important review are anticipated such later interpretations of Newman as those of A. M. Fairbairn, F. L. Cross, and Walter E. Houghton.

[1] xvii. 786.

[2] *The Quarterly Review*, cxvi. 546 ff., *passim*. In a letter of May 10, 1864, W. J. Copeland called Newman's attention to perhaps the earliest of the interpretations based on the theory of Newman's 'oversensitive mind': in the *English Churchman* of Oct. 16, 1845, reprinted with editorial comment in the *British Magazine* for November of that year, pp. 530–1 and 537. Copeland's concern was with the rather confusing letter's charge that Newman was, without dishonesty, 'in heart and intention, while nominally with us . . . during the last four years a member of the Roman Communion'. (MS. *Apologia* Letters, Birmingham Oratory.)

One other note in Wilberforce's essay deserves attention, for as we have seen, it reflects a strain in English thought which has by no means disappeared: i.e. that granting Kingsley's mistakes and Newman's honesty, there still remains the question whether, as Mrs. Kingsley put it, 'the Roman Catholic priesthood are encouraged or discouraged to pursue "Truth for its own sake"'. Kingsley himself, according to his wife, always felt 'that the general position which he had taken up against the policy of the Roman Catholic Church, remained unshaken'; and in his funeral sermon for Kingsley, Dean Stanley, endorsing his view, implied that the Roman Church substituted authority for truth.[1] Wilberforce expressed the opinion that truthfulness was more likely to be found among Anglicans than among Catholics. And a biographer of Kingsley has written: 'Nor is it true, though Mrs. Kingsley has affirmed it, that "the main point of issue was the question whether the Roman Catholic priesthood are encouraged to pursue truth for its own sake", and not the personal integrity of Newman, though the former question, if really discussed on its merits, would have been far more fruitful.'[2]

With the public at large, however, the *Apologia* probably accomplished its aim even in regard to this matter. It was a triumph not only for Newman but for the Roman Church in general. As Hutton wrote in 1890, it was 'a book which, I venture to say, has done more to break down the English distrust of Roman Catholics, and to bring about a hearty good fellowship between them and the members of other Churches,

[1] See *Life and Works of Charles Kingsley*, iii. 198–9.

[2] Kendall, *Charles Kingsley and His Ideas*, p. 156. The question, both about Newman and the Roman clergy, seems to have been raised most commonly by historians. Well before Kingsley's charge, Acton doubted that Newman believed in truth for its own sake.

See Joseph L. Altholz, 'Newman and History', *Victorian Studies*, vii (Mar. 1964), 285–94. The author acknowledges in a footnote that 'Recent historians would not accept as norms Acton's ideals of scientific history and absolute truth', but maintains nevertheless that 'his viewpoint supplies a useful angle of approach for a critique of his contemporary, Newman'. We are then told that 'Newman quailed before the massive impartiality and dangerous independence of scientific history' and that his 'commitment to religion was too profound to allow him to submit to the *rival discipline* of history'. (292–4. Italics mine.) But see Owen Chadwick, *From Bossuet to Newman: The Idea of Doctrinal Development* (Cambridge, 1957), *passim*, esp. pp. 193–5; Günter Biemer, 'B. G. Niebuhr and J. H. Newman', *Newman Studien*, vi (1964), 39–54; and the letter of J. Derek Holmes in *Victorian Studies*, viii (1965), 271–7.

than all the rest of the religious literature of our time put together'.[1]

4. *The Text of the* Apologia

The *Apologia* appeared first, as we have seen, in the form of eight pamphlets. These were later corrected for minor errors and then published in book form. In this form there are three principal versions:

1. The first edition: *Apologia Pro Vita Sua: Being A Reply to a Pamphlet Entitled 'What, Then, Does Dr. Newman Mean?'* (London: Longman, Green, Longman, Roberts, and Green, 1864). This consists of the first seven pamphlets or 'parts' consecutively paged and a separately paged appendix including the eighth pamphlet, 'Answer in Detail to Mr. Kingsley's Accusations'; notes giving the Latin, French, and Italian originals of various passages translated in the preceding section; a list of Newman's works; and a postscript containing Bishop Ullathorne's testimonial letter. (430+127 pp.)

Parts I and II and the original Appendix, in which Kingsley's charges were refuted as 'blots' and numbered presumably after the Articles to a total of thirty-nine, are reprinted in Appendix C of the present edition. It should be noted that there are at least two issues of the first edition which differ very slightly in minor wording from what might be called the standard version of the 1864 text. One of these was known to Wilfrid Ward, who supplied the variant readings in his 1913 edition of the *Apologia*. Another, differing only slightly from Ward's variant issue, is in the Newberry Library, Chicago. The variant readings of both issues are supplied in the present edition. Like Wilfrid Ward, I am unable to account for these variants but would surmise that they represent wording changed early, at Newman's direction, during the printing of the original pamphlets. Some of these early pamphlets must have remained to be bound up with the rest in book form. If this theory is correct, it is possible that there are still other variant issues of the first edition.

2. The second edition: *History of My Religious Opinions* (London: Longman, Green, Longman, Roberts, and Green,

---

[1] Richard Holt Hutton, *Cardinal Newman* (London, 1891), p. 230.

1865). It consists of a brief Preface replacing the polemical Parts I and II of the first edition; five chapters (Parts III–VII, slightly revised) which form the heart of the *Apologia*; a series of Notes numbered A to G which represent a recasting of the 'Answer in Detail' so as to eliminate all reference to Kingsley, plus two new Notes: A and B, 'Liberalism' and 'Series of Saints' Lives of 1843–44', as well as a partially new one: D, 'Ecclesiastical Miracles'. There is also a section of 'Supplemental Matter', including a chronological list of the letters and papers quoted, a list of Newman's works, Bishop Ullathorne's letter, and the letters from the various groups of clergy and laity. (xxiv+379 pp.)

3. The definitive text: *Apologia Pro Vita Sua: Being a History of his Religious Opinions*, on which the present edition is based. This version, which reached its final form *c.* 1886, about four years before Newman's death, differs from the second edition only slightly in the main body of the text and is printed from the same plates. The original title returned in 1873, the title of the second edition (with 'My' changed to 'his') being used for a subtitle. The Preface was enlarged in 1869 by the addition of extracts from Parts I and II, and there were some sixty small textual changes made in various impressions after 1865, only a few of them at all significant. The principal difference is the series of 'Additional Notes' supplied by Newman between 1869 and 1879. (xxviii+395 pp.)[1]

The second edition of the *Apologia* was reprinted, usually in runs of 500 or 750 copies each, in 1869 (twice), 1873, 1874, 1875, 1876, 1878, 1879 (twice), 1881, 1882, 1883, 1885 (when Longmans acquired the copyright from Newman and the stereotype plates from Rivington), and almost yearly thereafter for many years. After 1885 Newman was paid in advance a royalty of one-fourth the retail price (6*s.*) on each new impression: e.g. £56. 5*s.* on a run of 750 copies. Previously he had paid Longmans a 10 per cent. commission on sales.[2] Newman

---

[1] A 'Letter to the Very Rev. Canon Flanagan' was added to the 1904 sixpenny edition by Newman's literary executor, Fr. William Neville. It is not reprinted in the present edition.

[2] The record of these transactions is partially preserved at the Birmingham Oratory in the correspondence of Newman with Longman and with the printing firm of Rivington. There is nothing about the revisions themselves, when they were made or why, except for Longman's concurrence—and perhaps initial suggestion—

retained the right to make small additions to and corrections in the text without charge. The last significant one he made concerned hell, which he tried to make 'less terrible' (p. 19) to the 'reason' in 1864, to the 'intellect' in 1865, and finally to the 'imagination' *c.* 1886. Save for insignificant changes in punctuation, the present edition gives all the variant readings.[1] If the first variant listed is undated, it is the reading of the 1864 edition. If the variant is dated, e.g. 64–78, it means that this is the reading in all impressions before that of 1879. As it has proved impossible thus far to assemble all the impressions in which Newman could have made his various small changes after 1865, these dates may in a few cases be only close approximations rather than exact.

The material dropped in the second edition is almost entirely concerned with Kingsley, who is no longer ever mentioned by name and is alluded to only when necessary as 'my accuser' or 'a popular writer' or included in the group of 'my accusers'. The duel with Kingsley had served its purpose in winning Newman a hearing; Newman had nothing against Kingsley personally; and the sharp thrusts, especially of Part I and of the Appendix, had pained some readers. Accordingly, Newman dropped such remarks as 'Mr. Kingsley's word of honour is about as valuable as in the jester's opinion was the Christian charity of Rowena' and 'I am in a train of thought higher and more serene than any which slanders can disturb. Away with you, Mr. Kingsley, and fly into space.' The last chapter, 'General Answer to Mr. Kingsley', became 'Position of My Mind Since 1845'.

From the 'thirty-nine blot' Appendix, which as we have seen

that the second edition be recast in a permanent literary, less polemical form. (Most of the records at Longmans were destroyed in the air raids of the Second World War.)

Another record in the Oratory files indicates that there were new impressions of the *Apologia* every year from 1865 to 1890, but this is not borne out by the Longman correspondence or by the sales figures for the book, which are given by Martin J. Svaglic in 'Newman's *Apologia*: Introduction, Notes, and Commentary', an unpublished doctoral dissertation (University of Chicago, 1949), pp. 211–13. It may be, however, that Longmans dated anew every year the stock sent out of any given impression.

[1] Wilfrid Ward's Oxford edition of 1913 included the first two editions but only a few of the changes subsequent to 1865. Ward's ingenious method of combining the two editions in the body of the text, with the aid of round and square brackets, proved distracting for many readers and so has not been followed in the present edition.

he completely recast, Newman eliminated even his answer to what the Kingsleys always regarded as a serious objection:

> Then he says that I committed an economy in placing in my original title-page, that the question between him and me, was whether 'Dr. Newman teaches that Truth is no virtue'. It was a 'wisdom of the serpentine type', since I did not add, 'for its own sake'. Now observe: First, as to the matter of fact, in the course of my Letters, which have that Title-page, I printed the words 'for its own sake', *five* times over. Next, pray, what kind of a virtue is that, which is *not* done for its own sake? So this, after all, is the Writer's idea of virtue! a something that is done for the sake of something *else*; a sort of expedience. He is honest, it seems, simply *because* honesty is 'the best policy', and on that score it is that he thinks himself virtuous. Why, 'for its own sake' enters into the very idea or definition of a virtue. Defend me from such virtuous men, as this Writer would inflict upon us! Blot thirty-six.

It is easy enough to understand why some of Newman's readers had found such passages less than edifying.

There is no doubt that the *Apologia* of 1865 is a clearer and more effective book than its predecessor. There is no very substantial difference between them, to be sure: almost half the roughly nine hundred changes in the main body of the text are in punctuation; and the rest are often so slight in nature and subtle in effect as almost to preclude formal analysis. Yet slight as most of the changes are, anyone interested in the nuances of style will find much of interest and value in the process whereby a great writer, always given to the most painstaking revisions and now no longer pressed for time, made what had already been acclaimed a masterpiece into the clearer, more vivid, and dramatic story of a still more appealing human being.[1]

5. *The* Apologia *and Newman Today*

The history of Newman's reputation parallels the intellectual development of the modern world. At the turn of the last century, when rationalism still predominated, it was customary to praise Newman for his style and charm and to pass over, if not to deplore, his thought. A verdict like Saintsbury's that he was 'one of the greatest masters of quietly exquisite prose that the

---

[1] For a discussion of these matters, see Martin J. Svaglic, 'The Revision of Newman's *Apologia*', *Modern Philology*, l (1952), 43-49.

world has ever seen'[1] was commonly rendered innocuous by a warning like Hugh Walker's that 'his brilliant logic had no sound foundation in reason' and that he was 'a conspicuous, though personally blameless and most attractive, specimen of the class of those who sink "from the van and the freemen" back "to the rear and the slaves"'.[2]

Half a century later, in a world more apt to turn for guidance to a Freud, a Kierkegaard, or a Sartre than to T. H. Huxley or John Stuart Mill, such judgements had come to seem as shallow as they were rare. Today we are witnessing the fulfilment of Dean Church's prophecy that Newman was 'a great writer, of whose genius and religious feeling Englishmen will one day be even prouder than they are now'.[3]

Almost inevitably, of course, judgements of Newman and the *Apologia* continue to be coloured to some degree by the religious or ideological bent of the judges. Ever since the appearance of Geoffrey Faber's *Oxford Apostles* in 1933, for instance, one strain in the writing on Newman has implied that the subconscious motives evident in the feminine traits of his character and the power of his attraction to Hurrell Froude are of far greater significance in his development than Newman himself or a pre-Freudian age could be expected to realize. Anglo-Catholics and some Protestants, though respecting and even venerating Newman, are likely to account for his secession more or less in terms of his sensitivity to criticism, to a feeling of what a sympathetic and scholarly biographer, F. L. Cross, has called *ressentiment* at the treatment he received in the affair of Tract 90. Roman Catholic writers stress the rational grounds for his change of creed.

If one accepts Newman's own view that 'my one paramount reason for contemplating a change is my deep, unvarying conviction that our Church is in schism, and that my salvation depends on my joining the Church of Rome',[4] as the present writer does, for the evidence of Newman's letters and later life seems to bear it out, there is no denying that many influences converged to bring him to this frame of mind. As he himself

[1] George Saintsbury, *A History of English Prose Rhythm* (London, 1912), p. 388.
[2] Hugh Walker, *The Age of Tennyson* (London, 1909), pp. 152–3.
[3] R. W. Church, *Occasional Papers* (2 vols., London, 1897), ii. 415.
[4] *Apologia*, p. 206.

said, 'things are wonderfully linked together', and it is precisely
Newman's recognition of the multiplicity of influences that
combine in every significant human decision which makes the
Apologia an unusually sophisticated book for its age. At any
rate, it seems clear enough today that Newman was almost as
much influenced by the 'bright and beautiful' Hurrell Froude as
Tennyson, say, was by Hallam—though the Freudians are too
apt to forget that like Tennyson, Newman had a well-attested
masculine as well as a feminine side to his character. And
though he himself said more than once that he was 'not conscious of resentment, or disgust, at any thing that has happened
to me',[1] he also recognized that 'it has been the recent speeches
and acts of authorities, who had so long been tolerant of Protestant error, which has given to inquiry and to theory its force
and its edge'.[2]

Still, he puts the decisive stress on 'inquiry' and 'theory',
wishing to be guided by his reason and conscience, he says, and
not by his feelings. And he gives us a clue to his development
that has not yet been followed up in the detail it requires: a
feeling that 'the reasons for which I believe as much as our
system teaches, *must* lead me to believe more, and that not to
believe more is to fall back into scepticism'.[3] Given the Anglo-
Catholic premisses Newman had come to accept before 1833, a
temperament deferential to authority, and an intellect unusually
responsive to argument from analogy and what he called
antecedent probability—it was analogy that led him to the
theory of development—is there anything really surprising or
'illogical' in a decision for Rome, let alone so surprising as to
warrant the assumption that the compelling motives of a convert
always scrupulously introspective were other than those he
adduces? Perhaps Newman could have made clearer in the
Apologia the process by which in the years from 1843 to 1845
theory or opinion gradually became certitude; but he would
have thought it beyond the power of the mind to know or words
to register more fully than he has done, 'when it is, that the
scales in the balance of opinion begin to turn, and what was a
greater probability in behalf of a belief becomes a positive doubt
against it'.[4] And here again, as the critic of the *Saturday Review*

---

[1] Ibid., p. 206.   [2] Ibid., p. 136.   [3] Ibid., p. 207.
[4] Ibid., p. 195.

recognized, he seems more sophisticated than those who expect more.

But of course such matters are incapable of final resolution in this world. The important thing is that it is far easier now for the unbeliever to see the *Apologia* as George Eliot saw it long ago: 'as the revelation of a life—how different in form from one's own, yet with how close a fellowship in its needs and burthens—I mean spiritual needs and burthens'.[1] And once he begins to read Newman, he is likely to respond to him less like Hugh Walker and more like Lionel Trilling: 'the challenge that he offers to one's assumptions is so lively and so real, his sense of the world is so subtle and coherent, and his psychological perception is so complex and shrewd that any reader who takes pleasure in endangering his own fixed ideas must be grateful for the exhilaration that Newman can give'.[2]

As for the believer, the striving of an ecumenical age toward 'a deeper understanding of the grounds of faith and the nature of religious experience' has made it easier for men of all creeds to recognize the justice of Basil Willey's verdict: 'It is because Newman contributed so largely to the deepening of that understanding that we may claim for him a place, not amongst the reactionaries or obscurantists, but among the light bearers of the nineteenth century.'[3]

For this Newman, who as another Protestant scholar has written, 'remains, and will always remain, an abiding force for all men of intellect and imagination',[4] the reader must look especially to the moving sermons, Anglican and Catholic; to the profound speculations on faith and reason which begin with the *University Sermons* and culminate in *A Grammar of Assent*; to the influential but too commonly unread *Development of Christian Doctrine*; and to that epitome of Christian humanism, *The Idea of a University*. To this perennial Newman, the *Apologia* is an admirable introduction, being the quintessence of his thought. It suffers, however, from being tied to the events, figures, and terminology of a theological history, both ancient and modern, which had already grown obscure by 1864 and

[1] *The Letters of George Eliot*, iv. 159.
[2] *The Nation*, clxii (Feb. 2, 1946), 132. Cf. John Holloway, *The Victorian Sage* (London, 1953), p. 158.
[3] *Nineteenth Century Studies* (London, 1949), p. 90.
[4] Charles Frederick Harrold, ed., *A Newman Treasury* (London, 1945), p 30.

has become infinitely more so since the virtual eclipse of theology in the educational world.

If the *Apologia* needed annotation in 1864, as William Longman implied to Newman, it needs it all the more today if the book is to be more than another widely acknowledged but largely unread classic. It is the hope of the present editor that the notes here provided—in Newman's own words when possible —may lead the reader to what Newman himself would have considered a real and not merely a notional knowledge of his remarkable odyssey. The more one thinks of the task that Newman set himself in his *Apologia*—to chart in all its complexity the spiritual evolution of a gifted and sensitive human being— the easier it becomes to understand how he could say of it without exaggeration: 'I have done various bold things in my life: this is the boldest.'[1]

6. *Acknowledgements*

So many people have been of help to me in preparing this edition that it is impossible to thank them all individually. I can only hope that those whom I do not mention by name will take the wish to do so for the deed. I am especially grateful for one kindness or another to Professors Vincent F. Blehl, S.J., Patrick Casey, Robert A. Colby, A. Dwight Culler, Howard Fulweiler, John S. Gerrietts, Edward L. Surtz, S.J., Geoffrey Tillotson, and Kathleen Tillotson, to Dr. Margaret Maison, and to Mr. D. J. Barr.

My more particular thanks for their encouragement and criticism are due to the late E. K. Brown and Morton D. Zabel and to Professor Donald F. Bond, under whose direction an earlier version of this work was prepared as a doctoral dissertation at the University of Chicago; to the Committee on Faculty Appointments of Loyola University, Chicago, for a leave of absence enabling me to revise and complete the edition; to the Librarian and staff of the Loyola and Fordham University Libraries; of the British Museum; and especially of the Newberry Library, Chicago; to Harcourt, Brace and World for permission to use in the Introduction a few passages from an essay of mine in *Newman's 'Apologia': A Classic Reconsidered,*

[1] *Apologia.* p. 91.

ed. V. F. Blehl, S.J. and F. X. Connolly; and to the Revd. Dr. F. L. Cross, Lady Margaret Professor of Divinity at Oxford, for carefully reading and making helpful suggestions about many of the notes.

My greatest debt is, of course, to the Fathers of the Birmingham Oratory, whose hospitality is by now almost legendary among students and scholars the world over. In particular I wish to thank the Revd. Charles Stephen Dessain, the present curator of the Newman collection, for generously interrupting his own work on the great new edition of the Newman letters to aid me in a variety of ways; and above all, the late Revd. Henry Tristram, his beloved predecessor, who not only introduced me to the material at the Oratory but, on reading my own work, characteristically placed at my disposal a set of magisterial notes to the *Apologia* for an edition that he had begun but put aside. Many of these notes, which are largely to the first chapter only, I have abridged and incorporated in the present edition, signing them with the initials H. T. But my debt to them is greater than I have thus indicated by reason of the wealth of material to which they directed my attention. All manuscript material, it should be added, is quoted with the kind permission of the Oratory.

In thanking the many scholars who have helped me, I am implying neither their agreement with the conclusions I have reached nor their responsibility for the deficiencies of my own work. Without their assistance, however, these latter would have been even more evident.

MARTIN J. SVAGLIC

January 1966

PREFACE

THE following History of my Religious Opinions, now that it is
detached from the context in which it originally stood, requires
some preliminary explanation; and that, not only in order to
introduce it generally to the reader, but specially to make him
understand, how I came to write a whole book about myself, and
about my most private thoughts and feelings. Did I consult
indeed my own impulses, I should do my best simply to wipe out
of my Volume, and consign to oblivion, every trace of the circumstances to which it is to be ascribed; but its original title of
'Apologia' is too exactly borne out by its matter and structure,
and these again are too suggestive of correlative circumstances,
and those circumstances are of too grave a character, to allow of
my indulging so natural a wish. And therefore, though in this
new Edition I have managed to omit nearly a hundred pages of
my original Volume, which I could safely consider to be of
merely ephemeral importance, I am even for that very reason
obliged, by way of making up for their absence, to prefix to my
Narrative some account of the provocation out of which it arose.

It is now more than twenty years that a vague impression to
my disadvantage has rested on the popular mind, as if my conduct towards the Anglican Church, while I was a member of it,
was inconsistent with Christian simplicity and uprightness. An
impression of this kind was almost unavoidable under the circumstances of the case, when a man, who had written strongly
against a cause, and had collected a party round him by virtue
of such writings, gradually faltered in his opposition to it, unsaid
his words, threw his own friends into perplexity and their proceedings into confusion, and ended by passing over to the side
of those whom he had so vigorously denounced. Sensitive then
as I have ever been of the imputations which have been so freely
cast upon me, I have never felt much impatience under them, as
considering them to be a portion of the penalty which I naturally
and justly incurred by my change of religion, even though they
were to continue as long as I lived. I left their removal to a future
day, when personal feelings would have died out, and documents

would see the light, which were as yet buried in closets or scattered through the country.

This was my state of mind, as it had been for many years, when, in the beginning of 1864, I unexpectedly found myself publicly put upon my defence, and furnished with an opportunity of pleading my cause before the world, and, as it so happened, with a fair prospect of an impartial hearing. Taken indeed by surprise, as I was, I had much reason to be anxious how I should be able to acquit myself in so serious a matter; however, I had long had a tacit understanding with myself, that, in the improbable event of a challenge being formally made to me, by a person of name, it would be my duty to meet it. That opportunity had now occurred; it never might occur again; not to avail myself of it at once would be virtually to give up my cause; accordingly, I took advantage of it, and, as it has turned out, the circumstance that no time was allowed me for any studied statements has compensated, in the equitable judgment of the public, for such imperfections in composition as my want of leisure involved.

It was in the number for January 1864, of a magazine of wide circulation, and in an Article upon Queen Elizabeth, that a popular writer took occasion formally to accuse me by name of thinking so lightly of the virtue of Veracity, as in set terms to have countenanced and defended that neglect of it which he at the same time imputed to the Catholic Priesthood. His words were these:—

'Truth, for its own sake, had never been a virtue with the Roman clergy. Father Newman informs us that it need not, and on the whole ought not to be; that cunning is the weapon which heaven has given to the Saints wherewith to withstand the brute male force of the wicked world which marries and is given in marriage. Whether his notion be doctrinally correct or not, it is at least historically so.'

These assertions, going far beyond the popular prejudice entertained against me, had no foundation whatever in fact. I never had said, I never had dreamed of saying, that truth for its own sake, need not, and on the whole ought not to be, a virtue with the Roman Clergy; or that cunning is the weapon which heaven has given to the Saints wherewith to withstand the wicked

world. To what work of mine then could the writer be referring?
In a correspondence which ensued upon the subject between him
and myself, he rested his charge against me on a Sermon of mine,
preached, before I was a Catholic, in the pulpit of my Church at
Oxford; and he gave me to understand, that, after having done
as much as this, he was not bound, over and above such a general
reference to my Sermon, to specify the passages of it, in which
the doctrine, which he imputed to me, was contained. On my
part I considered this not enough; and I demanded of him to
bring out his proof of his accusation in form and in detail, or to
confess he was unable to do so. But he persevered in his refusal
to cite any distinct passages from any writing of mine; and,
though he consented to withdraw his charge, he would not do so
on the issue of its truth or falsehood, but simply on the ground
that I assured him that I had had no intention of incurring it.
This did not satisfy my sense of justice. Formally to charge me
with committing a fault is one thing; to allow that I did not
intend to commit it, is another; it is no satisfaction to me, if a
man accuses me of *this* offence, for him to profess that he does
not accuse me *of that*; but he thought differently. Not being able
then to gain redress in the quarter, where I had a right to ask it,
I appealed to the public. I published the correspondence in the
shape of a Pamphlet, with some remarks of my own at the end,
on the course which that correspondence had taken.

This Pamphlet, which appeared in the first weeks of February,
received a reply from my accuser towards the end of March, in
another Pamphlet of 48 pages, entitled, 'What then does Dr.
Newman mean?' in which he professed to do that which I had
called upon him to do; that is, he brought together a number of
extracts from various works of mine, Catholic and Anglican,
with the object of showing that, if I was to be acquitted of the
crime of teaching and practising deceit and dishonesty, according
to his first supposition, it was at the price of my being considered
no longer responsible for my actions; for, as he expressed it,
'I had a human reason once, no doubt, but I had gambled it
away', and I had 'worked my mind into that morbid state, in
which nonsense was the only food for which it hungered'; and
that it could not be called 'a hasty or farfetched or unfounded
mistake, when he concluded that I did not care for truth for its
own sake, or teach my disciples to regard it as a virtue'; and,

though 'too many prefer the charge of insincerity to that of insipience, Dr. Newman seemed not to be of that number'.

He ended his Pamphlet by returning to his original imputation against me, which he had professed to abandon. Alluding by anticipation to my probable answer to what he was then publishing, he professed his heartfelt embarrassment how he was to believe any thing I might say in my exculpation, in the plain and literal sense of the words. 'I am henceforth', he said, 'in doubt and fear, as much as an honest man can be, concerning every word Dr. Newman may write. How can I tell, that I shall not be the dupe of some cunning equivocation, of one of the three kinds laid down as permissible by the blessed St. Alfonso da Liguori and his pupils, even when confirmed with an oath, because "then we do not deceive our neighbour, but allow him to deceive himself"? . . . How can I tell, that I may not in this Pamphlet have made an accusation, of the truth of which Dr. Newman is perfectly conscious; but that, as I, a heretic Protestant, have no business to make it, he has a full right to deny it?'

Even if I could have found it consistent with my duty to my own reputation to leave such an elaborate impeachment of my moral nature unanswered, my duty to my Brethren in the Catholic Priesthood, would have forbidden such a course. *They* were involved in the charges which this writer, all along, from the original passage in the Magazine, to the very last paragraph of the Pamphlet, had so confidently, so pertinaciously made. In exculpating myself, it was plain I should be pursuing no mere personal quarrel;—I was offering my humble service to a sacred cause. I was making my protest in behalf of a large body of men of high character, of honest and religious minds, and of sensitive honour—who had their place and their rights in this world, though they were ministers of the world unseen, and who were insulted by my Accuser, as the above extracts from him sufficiently show, not only in my person, but directly and pointedly in their own. Accordingly, I at once set about writing the *Apologia pro vitâ suâ*, of which the present Volume is a New Edition; and it was a great reward to me to find, as the controversy proceeded, such large numbers of my clerical brethren supporting me by their sympathy in the course which I was pursuing, and, as occasion offered, bestowing on me the formal and public expression of their approbation. These testimonials in my behalf, so important and so grateful to me, are, together with the Letter, sent to me with the same purpose, from my Bishop, contained in the last pages of this Volume.

This Edition differs from the first form of the Apologia as follows:—The original work consisted of seven Parts, which were published in series on consecutive Thursdays, between April 21 and June 2. An Appendix, in answer to specific allegations urged against me in the Pamphlet of Accusation, appeared on June 16. Of these Parts 1 and 2, as being for the most part directly controversial, are omitted in this Edition, excepting certain passages in them, which are subjoined to this Preface, as being necessary for the due explanation of the subsequent five Parts. These (being 3, 4, 5, 6, 7, of the Apologia) are here numbered as Chapters 1, 2, 3, 4, 5 respectively. Of the Appendix, about half has been omitted, for the same reason as has led to the omission of Parts 1 and 2. The rest of it is thrown into the shape of Notes of a discursive character, with two new ones on Liberalism and the Lives of the English Saints of 1843–4, and another, new in part, on Ecclesiastical Miracles. In the body of the work, the only addition of consequence is the letter which is found at p. 206, a copy of which has recently come into my possession.

I should add that, since writing the Apologia last year, I have seen for the first time Mr. Oakeley's 'Notes on the Tractarian Movement'. This work remarkably corroborates the substance of my Narrative, while the kind terms in which he speaks of me personally, call for my sincere gratitude.

May 2, 1865

I make these extracts from the first edition of my Apologia, Part 1, pp. 3, 20–25, and Part 2, pp. 29–31 and pp. 41–51, in order to set before the reader the drift I had in writing my Volume:—

I cannot be sorry to have forced my Accuser to bring out in fulness his charges against me. It is far better that he should discharge his thoughts upon me in my lifetime, than after I am dead. Under the circumstances I am happy in having the opportunity of reading the worst that can be said of me by a writer who has taken pains with his work and is well satisfied with it. I account it a gain to be surveyed from without by one who hates the principles which are nearest to my heart, has no personal knowledge of me to set right his misconceptions of my doctrine, and who has some motive or other to be as severe with me as he can possibly be. . . .

But I really feel sad for what I am obliged now to say. I am in warfare with him, but I wish him no ill;—it is very difficult to get up resentment towards persons whom one has never seen. It is easy enough to be irritated with friends or foes *vis-à-vis*; but, though I am writing with all my heart against what he has said of me, I am not conscious of personal unkindness towards himself. I think it necessary to write as I am writing, for my own sake, and for the sake of the Catholic Priesthood; but I wish to impute nothing worse to him than that he has been furiously carried away by his feelings. Yet what shall I say of the upshot of all his talk of my economies and equivocations and the like? What is the precise *work* which it is directed to effect? I am at war with him; but there is such a thing as legitimate warfare: war has its laws; there are things which may fairly be done, and things which may not be done. I say it with shame and with stern sorrow;—he has attempted a great transgression; he has attempted (as I may call it) to *poison the wells*. I will quote him and explain what I mean. . . . He says,—

'I am henceforth in doubt and fear, as much as any honest man can be, *concerning every word* Dr. Newman may write. *How can I tell that I shall not be the dupe of some cunning equivocation*, of one of the three kinds laid down as permissible by the blessed Alfonso da Liguori and his pupils, even when confirmed by an oath, because "then we do not deceive our neighbour, but allow him to deceive himself"? . . . It is admissible, therefore, to use words and sentences which have a double signification, and leave the hapless hearer to take which of them he may choose. *What proof have I, then, that by "mean it? I never said it!" Dr. Newman does not signify*, I did not say it, but I did mean it?'— Pp. 44, 45.

Now these insinuations and questions shall be answered in their proper places; here I will but say that I scorn and detest lying, and quibbling, and double-tongued practice, and slyness, and cunning, and smoothness, and cant, and pretence, quite as much as any Protestants hate them; and I pray to be kept from the snare of them. But all this is just now by the bye; my present subject is my Accuser; what I insist upon here is this unmanly attempt of his, in his concluding pages, to cut the ground from under my feet;—to poison by anticipation the public mind against me, John Henry Newman, and to infuse into the imaginations of my readers, suspicion and mistrust of everything that I may say in reply to him. This I call *poisoning the wells*.

'I am henceforth in *doubt and fear*', he says, 'as much as any *honest* man can be, *concerning every word* Dr. Newman may write. *How can I tell that I shall not be the dupe of some cunning equivocation?*' . . .

Well, I can only say, that, if his taunt is to take effect, I am but wasting my time in saying a word in answer to his calumnies; and this is precisely what he knows and intends to be its fruit. I can hardly get myself to protest against a method of controversy so base and cruel, lest in doing so, I should be violating my self-respect and self-possession; but most base and most cruel it is. We all know how our imagination runs away with us, how suddenly and at what a pace;—the saying, 'Caesar's wife should not be suspected', is an instance of what I mean. The habitual prejudice, the humour of the moment, is the turning-point which leads us to read a defence in a good sense or a bad. We interpret it by our antecedent impressions. The very same sentiments, according as our jealousy is or is not awake, or our aversion stimulated, are tokens of truth or of dissimulation and pretence. There is a story of a sane person being by mistake shut up in the wards of a Lunatic Asylum, and that, when he pleaded his cause to some strangers visiting the establishment, the only remark he elicited in answer was, 'How naturally he talks! you would think he was in his senses.' Controversies should be decided by the reason; is it legitimate warfare to appeal to the misgivings of the public mind and to its dislikings? Any how, if my accuser is able thus to practise upon my readers, the more I succeed, the less will be my success. If I am natural, he will tell them 'Ars est celare artem'; if I am convincing, he will suggest that I am an able logician; if I show warmth, I am acting the indignant innocent; if I am calm, I am thereby detected as a smooth hypocrite; if I clear up difficulties, I am too plausible and perfect to be true. The more triumphant are my statements, the more certain will be my defeat.

So will it be if my Accuser succeeds in his manœuvre; but I do not for an instant believe that he will. Whatever judgment my readers may eventually form of me from these pages, I am confident that they will believe me in what I shall say in the course of them. I have no misgiving at all, that they will be ungenerous or harsh towards a man who has been so long before the eyes of the world; who has so many to speak of him from personal knowledge; whose natural impulse it has ever been to speak out; who has ever spoken too much rather than too little; who would have saved himself many a scrape, if he had been wise enough to hold his tongue; who has ever been fair to the doctrines and arguments of his opponents; who has never slurred over facts and reasonings which told against himself; who has never given his name or authority to proofs which he thought unsound, or to testimony which he did not think at least plausible; who has never shrunk from confessing a fault when he felt that he had committed one; who has ever consulted for others more than for himself; who has given up much that he loved and prized and could have retained, but that he loved honesty better than name, and Truth better than dear friends. . . .

What then shall be the special imputation, against which I shall throw myself in these pages, out of the thousand and one which my Accuser directs upon me? I mean to confine myself to one, for there is only one about which I much care,—the charge of Untruthfulness. He may cast upon me as many other imputations as he pleases, and they may stick on me, as long as they can, in the course of nature. They will fall to the ground in their season.

And indeed I think the same of the charge of Untruthfulness, and select it from the rest, not because it is more formidable but because it is more serious. Like the rest, it may disfigure me for a time, but it will not stain: Archbishop Whately used to say, 'Throw dirt enough, and some will stick'; well, will stick, but not, will stain. I think he used to mean 'stain', and I do not agree with him. Some dirt sticks longer than other dirt; but no dirt is immortal. According to the old saying, Prævalebit Veritas. There are virtues indeed, which the world is not fitted to judge of or to uphold, such as faith, hope, and charity: but it can judge about Truthfulness; it can judge about the natural virtues, and Truthfulness is one of them. Natural virtues may also become supernatural; Truthfulness is such; but that does not withdraw it from the jurisdiction of mankind at large. It may be more difficult in this or that particular case for men to take cognizance of it, as it may be difficult for the Court of Queen's Bench at Westminster to try a case fairly which took place in Hindostan: but that is a question of capacity, not of right. Mankind has the right to judge of Truthfulness in a Catholic, as in the case of a Protestant, of an Italian, or of a Chinese. I have never doubted, that in my hour, in God's hour, my avenger will appear, and the world will acquit me of untruthfulness, even though it be not while I live.

Still more confident am I of such eventual acquittal, seeing that my judges are my own countrymen. I consider, indeed, Englishmen the most suspicious and touchy of mankind; I think them unreasonable, and unjust in their seasons of excitement; but I had rather be an Englishman (as in fact I am) than belong to any other race under heaven. They are as generous, as they are hasty and burly; and their repentance for their injustice is greater than their sin.

For twenty years and more I have borne an imputation, of which I am at least as sensitive, who am the object of it, as they can be, who are only the judges. I have not set myself to remove it, first, because I never have had an opening to speak, and, next, because I never saw in them the disposition to hear. I have wished to appeal from Philip drunk to Philip sober. When shall I pronounce him to be himself again? If I may judge from the tone of the public press, which represents the public voice, I have great reason to take heart at this time. I have been treated by contemporary critics in this controversy with great fairness and gentleness, and I am grateful to them for it. However, the decision of the time and mode of my defence has been taken out of my hands; and I am thankful that it has been so. I am bound now as a duty to myself, to the Catholic cause, to the Catholic Priesthood, to give account of myself without any delay, when I am so rudely and circumstantially charged with Untruthfulness. I accept the challenge; I shall do my best to meet it, and I shall be content when I have done so.

It is not my present accuser alone who entertains, and has entertained, so dishonourable an opinion of me and of my writings. It is the impression of large classes of men; the impression twenty years ago and the impression now. There has been a general feeling that I was for years where I had no right to be; that I was a 'Romanist' in Protestant livery and service; that I was doing the work of a hostile Church in the bosom of the English Establishment, and knew it, or ought to have known it. There was no need of arguing about particular passages in my writings, when the fact was so patent, as men thought it to be.

First it was certain, and I could not myself deny it, that I scouted the name 'Protestant'. It was certain again, that many of the doctrines which I professed were popularly and generally known as badges of the Roman Church, as distinguished from the faith of the Reformation. Next, how could I have come by them? Evidently, I had certain friends and advisers who did not appear; there was some underground communication between Stonyhurst or Oscott and my rooms at Oriel. Beyond a doubt, I was advocating certain doctrines, not by accident, but on an understanding with ecclesiastics of the old religion. Then men went further, and said that I had actually been received into that religion, and withal had leave given me to profess myself a Protestant still. Others went even further, and gave it out to the world, as a matter of fact, of which they themselves had the proof in their hands, that I was actually a Jesuit. And when the opinions which I advocated spread, and younger men went further than I, the feeling against me waxed stronger and took a wider range.

And now indignation arose at the knavery of a conspiracy such as this:—and it became of course all the greater in consequence of its being the received belief of the public at large, that craft and intrigue, such as they fancied they beheld with their eyes, were the very instruments to which the Catholic Church has in these last centuries been indebted for her maintenance and extension.

There was another circumstance still, which increased the irritation and aversion felt by the large classes, of whom I have been speaking,

against the preachers of doctrines, so new to them and so unpalatable;
and that was, that they developed them in so measured a way. If they
were inspired by Roman theologians, (and this was taken for granted,)
why did they not speak out at once? Why did they keep the world in
such suspense and anxiety as to what was coming next, and what was
to be the upshot of the whole? Why this reticence, and half-speaking,
and apparent indecision? It was plain that the plan of operations had
been carefully mapped out from the first, and that these men were
cautiously advancing towards its accomplishment, as far as was safe at
the moment; that their aim and their hope was to carry off a large body
with them of the young and the ignorant; that they meant gradually to
leaven the minds of the rising generation, and to open the gates of that
city, of which they were the sworn defenders, to the enemy who lay in
ambush outside of it. And when in spite of the many protestations of
the party to the contrary, there was at length an actual movement
among their disciples, and one went over to Rome, and then another,
the worst anticipations and the worst judgments which had been
formed of them received their justification. And, lastly, when men first
had said of me, 'You will see, *he* will go, he is only biding his time, he
is waiting the word of command from Rome', and, when after all, after
my arguments and denunciations of former years, at length I did leave
the Anglican Church for the Roman, then they said to each other, 'It
is just as we said: we knew it would be so.'

This was the state of mind of masses of men twenty years ago, who
took no more than an external and common sense view of what was
going on. And partly the tradition, partly the effect of that feeling,
remains to the present time. Certainly I consider that, in my own case,
it is the great obstacle in the way of my being favourably heard, as at
present, when I have to make my defence. Not only am I now a member
of a most un-English communion, whose great aim is considered to be
the extinction of Protestantism and the Protestant Church, and whose
means of attack are popularly supposed to be unscrupulous cunning
and deceit, but how came I originally to have any relations with the
Church of Rome at all? did I, or my opinions, drop from the sky? how
came I, in Oxford, *in gremio Universitatis*, to present myself to the eyes
of men in that full blown investiture of Popery? How could I dare, how
could I have the conscience, with warnings, with prophecies, with
accusations against me, to persevere in a path which steadily advanced
towards, which ended in, the religion of Rome? And how am I now to
be trusted, when long ago I was trusted, and was found wanting?

It is this which is the strength of the case of my Accuser against me;
—not the articles of impeachment which he has framed from my writings, and which I shall easily crumble into dust, but the bias of the
court. It is the state of the atmosphere; it is the vibration all around,

which will echo his bold assertion of my dishonesty; it is that pre-possession against me, which takes it for granted that, when my reasoning is convincing it is only ingenious, and that when my state-ments are unanswerable, there is always something put out of sight or hidden in my sleeve; it is that plausible, but cruel conclusion to which men are apt to jump, that when much is imputed, much must be true, and that it is more likely that one should be to blame, than that many should be mistaken in blaming him;—these are the real foes which I have to fight, and the auxiliaries to whom my Accuser makes his advances.

Well, I must break through this barrier of prejudice against me if I can; and I think I shall be able to do so. When first I read the Pamphlet of Accusation, I almost despaired of meeting effectively such a heap of misrepresentations and such a vehemence of animosity. What was the good of answering first one point, and then another, and going through the whole circle of its abuse; when my answer to the first point would be forgotten, as soon as I got to the second? What was the use of bringing out half a hundred separate principles or views for the refuta-tion of the separate counts in the Indictment, when rejoinders of this sort would but confuse and torment the reader by their number and their diversity? What hope was there of condensing into a pamphlet of a readable length, matter which ought freely to expand itself into half a dozen volumes? What means was there, except the expenditure of interminable pages, to set right even one of that series of 'single passing hints', to use my Assailant's own language, which, 'as with his finger tip he had delivered' against me?

All those separate charges had their force in being illustrations of one and the same great imputation. He had already a positive idea to illuminate his whole matter, and to stamp it with a force, and to quicken it with an interpretation. He called me a *liar*,—a simple, a broad, an intelligible, to the English public a plausible arraignment; but for me, to answer in detail charge one by reason one, and charge two by reason two, and charge three by reason three, and so on through the whole string both of accusations and replies, each of which was to be indepen-dent of the rest, this would be certainly labour lost as regards any effective result. What I needed was a corresponding antagonist unity in my defence, and where was that to be found? We see, in the case of commentators on the prophecies of Scripture, an exemplification of the principle on which I am insisting; viz. how much more powerful even a false interpretation of the sacred text is than none at all;—how a cer-tain key to the visions of the Apocalypse, for instance, may cling to the mind (I have found it so in the case of my own), because the view, which it opens on us, is positive and objective, in spite of the fullest demonstration that it really has no claim upon our reception. The

reader says, 'What else can the prophecy mean?' just as my Accuser
asks, 'What, then, does Dr. Newman mean?' ... I reflected, and I saw
a way out of my perplexity.

Yes, I said to myself, his very question is about my *meaning*; 'What
does Dr. Newman mean?' It pointed in the very same direction as that
into which my musings had turned me already. He asks what I *mean*;
not about my words, not about my arguments, not about my actions,
as his ultimate point, but about that living intelligence, by which I write,
and argue, and act. He asks about my Mind and its Beliefs and its
sentiments; and he shall be answered;—not for his own sake, but for
mine, for the sake of the Religion which I profess, and of the Priesthood
in which I am unworthily included, and of my friends and of my foes,
and of that general public which consists of neither one nor the other,
but of well-wishers, lovers of fair play, sceptical cross-questioners,
interested inquirers, curious lookers-on, and simple strangers, unconcerned yet not careless about the issue,—for the sake of all these he
shall be answered.

My perplexity had not lasted half an hour. I recognized what I had
to do, though I shrank from both the task and the exposure which it
would entail. I must, I said, give the true key to my whole life; I must
show what I am, that it may be seen what I am not, and that the
phantom may be extinguished which gibbers instead of me. I wish to
be known as a living man, and not as a scarecrow which is dressed up
in my clothes. False ideas may be refuted indeed by argument, but by
true ideas alone are they expelled. I will vanquish, not my Accuser, but
my judges. I will indeed answer his charges and criticisms on me one
by one,[1] lest any one should say that they are unanswerable, but such
a work shall not be the scope nor the substance of my reply. I will draw
out, as far as may be, the history of my mind; I will state the point at
which I began, in what external suggestion or accident each opinion
had its rise, how far and how they developed from within, how they
grew, were modified, were combined, were in collision with each other,
and were changed; again how I conducted myself towards them, and
how, and how far, and for how long a time, I thought I could hold them
consistently with the ecclesiastical engagements which I had made and
with the position which I held. I must show—what is the very truth—
that the doctrines which I held, and have held for so many years, have
been taught me (speaking humanly) partly by the suggestions of
Protestant friends, partly by the teaching of books, and partly by the
action of my own mind: and thus I shall account for that phenomenon
which to so many seems so wonderful, that I should have left 'my
kindred and my father's house' for a Church from which once I turned

---

[1] This was done in the Appendix, of which the more important parts are preserved
in the Notes. (All notes in the text itself are Newman's.—Ed.)

away with dread;—so wonderful to them! as if forsooth a Religion which has flourished through so many ages, among so many nations, amid such varieties of social life, in such contrary classes and conditions of men, and after so many revolutions, political and civil, could not subdue the reason and overcome the heart, without the aid of fraud in the process and the sophistries of the schools.

What I had proposed to myself in the course of half-an-hour, I determined on at the end of ten days. However, I have many difficulties in fulfilling my design. How am I to say all that has to be said in a reasonable compass? And then as to the materials of my narrative; I have no autobiographical notes to consult, no written explanations of particular treatises or of tracts which at the time gave offence, hardly any minutes of definite transactions or conversations, and few contemporary memoranda, I fear, of the feelings or motives under which from time to time I acted. I have an abundance of letters from friends with some copies or drafts of my answers to them, but they are for the most part unsorted; and, till this process has taken place, they are even too numerous and various to be available at a moment for my purpose. Then, as to the volumes which I have published, they would in many ways serve me, were I well up in them: but though I took great pains in their composition, I have thought little about them, when they were once out of my hands, and for the most part the last time I read them has been when I revised their last proof sheets.

Under these circumstances my sketch will of course be incomplete. I now for the first time contemplate my course as a whole; it is a first essay, but it will contain, I trust, no serious or substantial mistake, and so far will answer the purpose for which I write it. I purpose to set nothing down in it as certain, of which I have not a clear memory, or some written memorial, or the corroboration of some friend. There are witnesses enough up and down the country to verify, or correct, or complete it; and letters moreover of my own in abundance, unless they have been destroyed.

Moreover, I mean to be simply personal and historical: I am not expounding Catholic doctrine, I am doing no more than explaining myself, and my opinions and actions. I wish, as far as I am able, simply to state facts, whether they are ultimately determined to be for me or against me. Of course there will be room enough for contrariety of judgment among my readers, as to the necessity, or appositeness, or value, or good taste, or religious prudence, of the details which I shall introduce. I may be accused of laying stress on little things, of being beside the mark, of going into impertinent or ridiculous details, of sounding my own praise, of giving scandal; but this is a case above all others, in which I am bound to follow my own lights and to speak out my own heart. It is not at all pleasant for me to be egotistical; nor to be criticized for being so. It is not pleasant to reveal to high and low, young and old, what has gone on within me from my early years. It is not pleasant to be giving to every shallow or flippant disputant the advantage over me of knowing my most private thoughts, I might even say the intercourse between myself and my Maker. But I do not like to be called to my face a liar and a knave; nor should I be doing my duty to my faith or to my name, if I were to suffer it. I know I have done nothing to deserve such an insult, and if I prove this, as I hope to do, I must not care for such incidental annoyances as are involved in the process.

MY RELIGIOUS OPINIONS

CHAPTER I

HISTORY OF MY RELIGIOUS OPINIONS TO THE YEAR 1833

IT may easily be conceived how great a trial it is to me to write 5
the following history of myself; but I must not shrink from the
task. The words, 'Secretum meum mihi', keep ringing in my
ears; but as men draw towards their end, they care less for disclosures. Nor is it the least part of my trial, to anticipate that,
upon first reading what I have written, my friends may consider 10
much in it irrelevant to my purpose; yet I cannot help thinking
that, viewed as a whole, it will effect what I propose to myself in
giving it to the public.

I was brought up from a child to take great delight in reading
the Bible; but I had no formed religious convictions till I was 15
fifteen. Of course I had a perfect knowledge of my Catechism.
After I was grown up, I put on paper my recollections of the
thoughts and feelings on religious subjects, which I had at the
time that I was a child and a boy,—such as had remained on my
mind with sufficient prominence to make me then consider them 20
worth recording. Out of these, written in the Long Vacation of
1820, and transcribed with additions in 1823, I select two, which
are at once the most definite among them, and also have a bearing on my later convictions.

   1. 'I used to wish the Arabian Tales were true: my imagination 25

  1 My Religious Opinions] *not in 64*   2 Chapter I] Part III   3 To . . . 1833.]
not in 64   9-10 that . . . my friends may] that my friends may, upon . . .
written   12-13 propose . . . public.] wish it to do.   16 had a perfect] had perfect
17-19 my recollections . . . time] such recollections as I had of my thoughts and
feelings on religious subjects, at the time   19-21 a boy . . . recording.] a boy.
21-22 Out of these, written . . . 1823, I] Out of these I   25: 1. 'I used] In the
paper to which I have referred, written either in the Long Vacation of 1820, or in
October, 1823, the following notices of my school days were sufficiently prominent
in my memory for me to consider them worth recording:—'I used

ran on unknown influences, on magical powers, and talis-
mans. . . . I thought life might be a dream, or I an Angel, and
all this world a deception, my fellow-angels by a playful device
concealing themselves from me, and deceiving me with the
5 semblance of a material world.'

Again: 'Reading in the Spring of 1816 a sentence from [Dr.
Watts's] "Remnants of Time", entitled "the Saints unknown to
the world", to the effect, that "there is nothing in their figure or
countenance to distinguish them", &c., &c., I supposed he spoke
10 of Angels who lived in the world, as it were disguised.'

2. The other remark is this: 'I was very superstitious, and for
some time previous to my conversion' [when I was fifteen] 'used
constantly to cross myself on going into the dark.'

Of course I must have got this practice from some external
15 source or other; but I can make no sort of conjecture whence;
and certainly no one had ever spoken to me on the subject of the
Catholic religion, which I only knew by name. The French master
was an *émigré* Priest, but he was simply made a butt, as French
masters too commonly were in that day, and spoke English very
20 imperfectly. There was a Catholic family in the village, old
maiden ladies we used to think; but I knew nothing about them.
I have of late years heard that there were one or two Catholic
boys in the school; but either we were carefully kept from knowing this, or the knowledge of it made simply no impression on
25 our minds. My brother will bear witness how free the school was
from Catholic ideas.

I had once been into Warwick Street Chapel, with my father,
who, I believe, wanted to hear some piece of music; all that I
bore away from it was the recollection of a pulpit and a preacher,
30 and a boy swinging a censer.

When I was at Littlemore, I was looking over old copy-books
of my school days, and I found among them my first Latin verse-
book; and in the first page of it there was a device which almost
took my breath away with surprise. I have the book before me
35 now, and have just been showing it to others. I have written in
the first page, in my school-boy hand, 'John H. Newman,
February 11th, 1811, Verse Book'; then follow my first Verses.
Between 'Verse' and 'Book' I have drawn the figure of a solid
cross upright, and next to it is, what may indeed be meant for

11: 2. The other] The other   21 about them.] but their name.

a necklace, but what I cannot make out to be any thing else than a set of beads suspended, with a little cross attached. At this time I was not quite ten years old. I suppose I got these ideas from some romance, Mrs. Radcliffe's or Miss Porter's; or from some religious picture; but the strange thing is, how, among the 5 thousand objects which meet a boy's eyes, these in particular should so have fixed themselves in my mind, that I made them thus practically my own. I am certain there was nothing in the churches I attended, or the prayer books I read, to suggest them. It must be recollected that Anglican churches and prayer books 10 were not decorated in those days as I believe they are now.

When I was fourteen, I read Paine's Tracts against the Old Testament, and found pleasure in thinking of the objections which were contained in them. Also, I read some of Hume's Essays; and perhaps that on Miracles. So at least I gave my 15 Father to understand; but perhaps it was a brag. Also, I recollect copying out some French verses, perhaps Voltaire's, in denial of the immortality of the soul, and saying to myself something like 'How dreadful, but how plausible!'

When I was fifteen (in the autumn of 1816) a great change of 20 thought took place in me. I fell under the influences of a definite Creed, and received into my intellect impressions of dogma, which, through God's mercy, have never been effaced or obscured. Above and beyond the conversations and sermons of the excellent man, long dead, the Rev. Walter Mayers, of Pembroke 25 College, Oxford, who was the human means of this beginning of divine faith in me, was the effect of the books which he put into my hands, all of the school of Calvin. One of the first books I read was a work of Romaine's; I neither recollect the title nor the contents, except one doctrine, which of course I do not 30 include among those which I believe to have come from a divine source, viz. the doctrine of final perseverance. I received it at once, and believed that the inward conversion of which I was conscious (and of which I still am more certain than that I have hands and feet) would last into the next life, and that I was 35 elected to eternal glory. I have no consciousness that this belief had any tendency whatever to lead me to be careless about pleasing God. I retained it till the age of twenty-one, when it

3 these ideas] the idea   17 in denial of] against   25–26 dead, the Rev. . . . .
Oxford] dead, who was

gradually faded away; but I believe that it had some influence on my opinions, in the direction of those childish imaginations which I have already mentioned, viz. in isolating me from the objects which surrounded me, in confirming me in my mistrust
5 of the reality of material phenomena, and making me rest in the thought of two and two only absolute and luminously self-evident beings, myself and my Creator;—for while I considered myself predestined to salvation, my mind did not dwell upon others, as fancying them simply passed over, not predestined to
10 eternal death. I only thought of the mercy to myself.

The detestable doctrine last mentioned is simply denied and abjured, unless my memory strangely deceives me, by the writer who made a deeper impression on my mind than any other, and to whom (humanly speaking) I almost owe my soul,—Thomas
15 Scott of Aston Sandford. I so admired and delighted in his writings, that, when I was an under-graduate, I thought of making a visit to his Parsonage, in order to see a man whom I so deeply revered. I hardly think I could have given up the idea of this expedition, even after I had taken my degree; for the
20 news of his death in 1821 came upon me as a disappointment as well as a sorrow. I hung upon the lips of Daniel Wilson, afterwards Bishop of Calcutta, as in two sermons at St. John's Chapel he gave the history of Scott's life and death. I had been possessed of his 'Force of Truth' and Essays from a boy; his Commentary
25 I bought when I was an under-graduate.

What, I suppose, will strike any reader of Scott's history and writings, is his bold unworldliness and vigorous independence of mind. He followed truth wherever it led him, beginning with Unitarianism, and ending in a zealous faith in the Holy Trinity.
30 It was he who first planted deep in my mind that fundamental truth of religion. With the assistance of Scott's Essays, and the admirable work of Jones of Nayland, I made a collection of Scripture texts in proof of the doctrine, with remarks (I think) of my own upon them, before I was sixteen; and a few months
35 later I drew up a series of texts in support of each verse of the Athanasian Creed. These papers I have still.

Besides his unworldliness, what I also admired in Scott was his resolute opposition to Antinomianism, and the minutely

6 absolute] supreme   8–9 my mind . . . over] I thought others simply passed over   24 his 'Force . . . and Essays] his Essays   31 truth] Truth

practical character of his writings. They show him to be a true Englishman, and I deeply felt his influence; and for years I used almost as proverbs what I considered to be the scope and issue of his doctrine, 'Holiness rather than peace', and 'Growth the only evidence of life'.   5

Calvinists make a sharp separation between the elect and the world; there is much in this that is cognate or parallel to the Catholic doctrine; but they go on to say, as I understand them, very differently from Catholicism,—that the converted and the unconverted can be discriminated by man, that the justified are 10 conscious of their state of justification, and that the regenerate cannot fall away. Catholics on the other hand shade and soften the awful antagonism between good and evil, which is one of their dogmas, by holding that there are different degrees of justification, that there is a great difference in point of gravity 15 between sin and sin, that there is the possibility and the danger of falling away, and that there is no certain knowledge given to any one that he is simply in a state of grace, and much less that he is to persevere to the end:—of the Calvinistic tenets the only one which took root in my mind was the fact of heaven and hell, 20 divine favour and divine wrath, of the justified and the unjustified. The notion that the regenerate and the justified were one and the same, and that the regenerate, as such, had the gift of perseverance, remained with me not many years, as I have said already.   25

This main Catholic doctrine of the warfare between the city of God and the powers of darkness was also deeply impressed upon my mind by a work of a character very opposite to Calvinism, Law's 'Serious Call'.

From this time I have held with a full inward assent and belief 30 the doctrine of eternal punishment, as delivered by our Lord Himself, in as true a sense as I hold that of eternal happiness; though I have tried in various ways to make that truth less terrible to the imagination.

Now I come to two other works, which produced a deep im- 35 pression on me in the same Autumn of 1816, when I was fifteen

4 rather than] before   'Growth the] 'Growth is the   7 cognate or parallel]
parallel or cognate   28–29 of a character . . . Calvinism] of a very opposite
character   30 held with] given   30–31 belief the] belief to the   34 imagination]
reason 64; intellect 65–85   36 Autumn] autumn

years old, each contrary to each, and planting in me the seeds of
an intellectual inconsistency which disabled me for a long course
of years. I read Joseph Milner's Church History, and was nothing
short of enamoured of the long extracts from St. Augustine,
5 St. Ambrose, and the other Fathers which I found there. I read
them as being the religion of the primitive Christians: but simultaneously with Milner I read Newton on the Prophecies, and in
consequence became most firmly convinced that the Pope was
the Antichrist predicted by Daniel, St. Paul, and St. John. My
10 imagination was stained by the effects of this doctrine up to the
year 1843; it had been obliterated from my reason and judgment
at an earlier date; but the thought remained upon me as a sort
of false conscience. Hence came that conflict of mind, which so
many have felt besides myself;—leading some men to make a
15 compromise between two ideas, so inconsistent with each other,
—driving others to beat out the one idea or the other from their
minds,—and ending in my own case, after many years of intellectual unrest, in the gradual decay and extinction of one of
them,—I do not say in its violent death, for why should I not
20 have murdered it sooner, if I murdered it at all ?

I am obliged to mention, though I do it with great reluctance,
another deep imagination, which at this time, the autumn of
1816, took possession of me,—there can be no mistake about the
fact; viz. that it would be the will of God that I should lead a
25 single life. This anticipation, which has held its ground almost
continuously ever since,—with the break of a month now and
a month then, up to 1829, and, after that date, without any break
at all,—was more or less connected in my mind with the notion,
that my calling in life would require such a sacrifice as celibacy
30 involved; as, for instance, missionary work among the heathen,
to which I had a great drawing for some years. It also strengthened my feeling of separation from the visible world, of which
I have spoken above.

In 1822 I came under very different influences from those to
35 which I had hitherto been subjected. At that time, Mr. Whately,
as he was then, afterwards Archbishop of Dublin, for the few
months he remained in Oxford, which he was leaving for good,
showed great kindness to me. He renewed it in 1825, when he

4–5 St. Augustine, St. Ambrose, and] St. Augustine and   24 would be]
was

became Principal of Alban Hall, making me his Vice-Principal and Tutor. Of Dr. Whately I will speak presently: for from 1822 to 1825 I saw most of the present Provost of Oriel, Dr. Hawkins, at that time Vicar of St. Mary's; and, when I took orders in 1824 and had a curacy in Oxford, then, during the Long Vacations, I was especially thrown into his company. I can say with a full heart that I love him, and have never ceased to love him; and I thus preface what otherwise might sound rude, that in the course of the many years in which we were together afterwards, he provoked me very much from time to time, though I am perfectly certain that I have provoked him a great deal more. Moreover, in me such provocation was unbecoming, both because he was the Head of my College, and because, in the first years that I knew him, he had been in many ways of great service to my mind.

He was the first who taught me to weigh my words, and to be cautious in my statements. He led me to that mode of limiting and clearing my sense in discussion and in controversy, and of distinguishing between cognate ideas, and of obviating mistakes by anticipation, which to my surprise has been since considered, even in quarters friendly to me, to savour of the polemics of Rome. He is a man of most exact mind himself, and he used to snub me severely, on reading, as he was kind enough to do, the first Sermons that I wrote, and other compositions which I was engaged upon.

Then as to doctrine, he was the means of great additions to my belief. As I have noticed elsewhere, he gave me the 'Treatise on Apostolical Preaching', by Sumner, afterwards Archbishop of Canterbury, from which I was led to give up my remaining Calvinism, and to receive the doctrine of Baptismal Regeneration. In many other ways too he was of use to me, on subjects semi-religious and semi-scholastic.

It was Dr. Hawkins too who taught me to anticipate that, before many years were over, there would be an attack made upon the books and the canon of Scripture. I was brought to the same belief by the conversation of Mr. Blanco White, who also led me to have freer views on the subject of inspiration than were usual in the Church of England at the time.

2 presently: for] presently, for   5 in] at   29 was led] learned

There is one other principle, which I gained from Dr. Hawkins, more directly bearing upon Catholicism, than any that I have mentioned; and that is the doctrine of Tradition. When I was an Under-graduate, I heard him preach in the University
5 Pulpit his celebrated sermon on the subject, and recollect how long it appeared to me, though he was at that time a very striking preacher; but, when I read it and studied it as his gift, it made a most serious impression upon me. He does not go one step, I think, beyond the high Anglican doctrine, nay he does not
10 reach it; but he does his work thoroughly, and his view was in him original, and his subject was a novel one at the time. He lays down a proposition, self-evident as soon as stated, to those who have at all examined the structure of Scripture, viz. that the sacred text was never intended to teach doctrine, but only to
15 prove it, and that, if we would learn doctrine, we must have recourse to the formularies of the Church; for instance to the Catechism, and to the Creeds. He considers, that, after learning from them the doctrines of Christianity, the inquirer must verify them by Scripture. This view, most true in its outline, most fruit-
20 ful in its consequences, opened upon me a large field of thought. Dr. Whately held it too. One of its effects was to strike at the root of the principle on which the Bible Society was set up. I belonged to its Oxford Association; it became a matter of time when I should withdraw my name from its subscription-list, though I
25 did not do so at once.

It is with pleasure that I pay here a tribute to the memory of the Rev. William James, then Fellow of Oriel; who, about the year 1823, taught me the doctrine of Apostolical Succession, in the course of a walk, I think, round Christ Church meadow;
30 I recollect being somewhat impatient of the subject at the time.

It was at about this date, I suppose, that I read Bishop Butler's Analogy; the study of which has been to so many, as it was to me, an era in their religious opinions. Its inculcation of a visible Church, the oracle of truth and a pattern of sanctity, of the duties
35 of external religion, and of the historical character of Revelation, are characteristics of this great work which strike the reader at once; for myself, if I may attempt to determine what I most gained from it, it lay in two points, which I shall have an opportunity of dwelling on in the sequel; they are the underlying

10–11 in him original] original with him   30 of] on

principles of a great portion of my teaching. First, the very idea of an analogy between the separate works of God leads to the conclusion that the system which is of less importance is economically or sacramentally connected with the more momentous system,[1] and of this conclusion the theory, to which I was inclined as a boy, viz. the unreality of material phenomena, is an ultimate resolution. At this time I did not make the distinction between matter itself and its phenomena, which is so necessary and so obvious in discussing the subject. Secondly, Butler's doctrine that Probability is the guide of life, led me, at least under the teaching to which a few years later I was introduced, to the question of the logical cogency of Faith, on which I have written so much. Thus to Butler I trace those two principles of my teaching, which have led to a charge against me both of fancifulness and of scepticism.

And now as to Dr. Whately. I owe him a great deal. He was a man of generous and warm heart. He was particularly loyal to his friends, and to use the common phrase, 'all his geese were swans'. While I was still awkward and timid in 1822, he took me by the hand, and acted towards me the part of a gentle and encouraging instructor. He, emphatically, opened my mind, and taught me to think and to use my reason. After being first noticed by him in 1822, I became very intimate with him in 1825, when I was his Vice-Principal at Alban Hall. I gave up that office in 1826, when I became Tutor of my College, and his hold upon me gradually relaxed. He had done his work towards me or nearly so, when he had taught me to see with my own eyes and to walk with my own feet. Not that I had not a good deal to learn from others still, but I influenced them as well as they me, and co-operated rather than merely concurred with them. As to Dr. Whately, his mind was too different from mine for us to remain long on one line. I recollect how dissatisfied he was with an Article of mine in the London Review, which Blanco White, good-humouredly, only called Platonic. When I was diverging from him in opinion (which he did not like), I thought of dedicating my first book to him, in words to the effect that he had

5 system,[1]] *no footnote in 64*   20 acted . . . part] acted the part to me
35 in opinion] *not in 64*

---

[1] It is significant that Butler begins his work with a quotation from Origen.

not only taught me to think, but to think for myself. He left Oxford in 1831; after that, as far as I can recollect, I never saw him but twice,—when he visited the University; once in the street in 1834, once in a room in 1838. From the time that he left, I have
5 always felt a real affection for what I must call his memory: for, at least from the year 1834, he made himself dead to me. He had practically indeed given me up from the time that he became Archbishop in 1831; but in 1834 a correspondence took place between us, which, though conducted especially on his side in
10 a friendly spirit, was the expression of differences of opinion which acted as a final close to our intercourse. My reason told me that it was impossible we could have got on together longer, had he stayed in Oxford; yet I loved him too much to bid him farewell without pain. After a few years had passed, I began to
15 believe that his influence on me in a higher respect than intellectual advance, (I will not say through his fault,) had not been satisfactory. I believe that he has inserted sharp things in his later works about me. They have never come in my way, and I have not thought it necessary to seek out what would pain me
20 so much in the reading.

What he did for me in point of religious opinion, was, first, to teach me the existence of the Church, as a substantive body or corporation; next to fix in me those anti-Erastian views of Church polity, which were one of the most prominent features
25 of the Tractarian movement. On this point, and, as far as I know, on this point alone, he and Hurrell Froude intimately sympathized, though Froude's development of opinion here was of a later date. In the year 1826, in the course of a walk, he said much to me about a work then just published, called 'Letters on the
30 Church by an Episcopalian'. He said that it would make my blood boil. It was certainly a most powerful composition. One of our common friends told me, that, after reading it, he could not keep still, but went on walking up and down his room. It was ascribed at once to Whately; I gave eager expression to the con-
35 trary opinion; but I found the belief of Oxford in the affirmative to be too strong for me; rightly or wrongly I yielded to the

4 in 1834] *not in 64*   in 1838] *not in 64*   5–6 for, at least from . . . 1834,] for thenceforward   6–11 He . . . intercourse.] *not in 64*   9–10 especially . . . spirit] in the most friendly language on both sides 65–78   12 impossible we] impossible that we   12–13 longer . . . Oxford;] longer;

general voice; and I have never heard, then or since, of any disclaimer of authorship on the part of Dr. Whately.

The main positions of this able essay are these; first that Church and State should be independent of each other:—he speaks of the duty of protesting 'against the profanation of 5 Christ's kingdom, by that *double usurpation*, the interference of the Church in temporals, of the State in spirituals', p. 191; and, secondly, that the Church may justly and by right retain its property, though separated from the State. 'The clergy,' he says p. 133, 'though they ought not to be the hired servants of the 10 Civil Magistrate, may justly retain their revenues; and the State, though it has no right of interference in spiritual concerns, not only is justly entitled to support from the ministers of religion, and from all other Christians, but would, under the system I am recommending, obtain it much more effectually.' The author of 15 this work, whoever he may be, argues out both these points with great force and ingenuity, and with a thoroughgoing vehemence, which perhaps we may refer to the circumstance, that he wrote, not *in propriâ personâ*, and as thereby answerable for every sentiment that he advanced, but in the professed character of a 20 Scotch Episcopalian. His work had a gradual, but a deep effect on my mind.

I am not aware of any other religious opinion which I owe to Dr. Whately. In his special theological tenets I had no sympathy. In the next year, 1827, he told me he considered that I was 25 Arianizing. The case was this: though at that time I had not read Bishop Bull's *Defensio* nor the Fathers, I was just then very strong for that ante-Nicene view of the Trinitarian doctrine, which some writers, both Catholic and non-Catholic, have accused of wearing a sort of Arian exterior. This is the meaning 30 of a passage in Froude's Remains, in which he seems to accuse me of speaking against the Athanasian Creed. I had contrasted the two aspects of the Trinitarian doctrine, which are respectively presented by the Athanasian Creed and the Nicene. My criticisms were to the effect that some of the verses of the former 35 Creed were unnecessarily scientific. This is a specimen of a certain disdain for Antiquity which had been growing on me now for several years. It showed itself in some flippant language against the Fathers in the Encyclopædia Metropolitana, about

whom I knew little at the time, except what I had learnt as a
boy from Joseph Milner. In writing on the Scripture Miracles
in 1825–6, I had read Middleton on the Miracles of the early
Church, and had imbibed a portion of his spirit.

5   The truth is, I was beginning to prefer intellectual excellence
to moral; I was drifting in the direction of the Liberalism of the
day.[1] I was rudely awakened from my dream at the end of 1827
by two great blows—illness and bereavement.

In the beginning of 1829, came the formal break between
10 Dr. Whately and me; the affair of Mr. Peel's re-election was the
occasion of it. I think in 1828 or 1827 I had voted in the minority,
when the Petition to Parliament against the Catholic Claims was
brought into Convocation. I did so mainly on the views suggested
to me in the Letters of an Episcopalian. Also I shrank from the
15 bigoted 'two-bottle-orthodox', as they were invidiously called.
When then I took part against Mr. Peel, it was on an academical,
not at all an ecclesiastical or a political ground; and this I professed at the time. I considered that Mr. Peel had taken the
University by surprise; that his friends had no right to call upon
20 us to turn round on a sudden, and to expose ourselves to the
imputation of time-serving; and that a great University ought
not to be bullied even by a great Duke of Wellington. Also by
this time I was under the influence of Keble and Froude; who,
in addition to the reasons I have given, disliked the Duke's
25 change of policy as dictated by liberalism.

Whately was considerably annoyed at me, and he took a
humourous revenge, of which he had given me due notice beforehand. As head of a house he had duties of hospitality to men of
all parties; he asked a set of the least intellectual men in Oxford
30 to dinner, and men most fond of port; he made me one of this
party; placed me between Provost This and Principal That, and
then asked me if I was proud of my friends. However, he had a
serious meaning in his act; he saw, more clearly than I could do,
that I was separating from his own friends for good and all.

6–7 the Liberalism ... day.[1]] of liberalism. *No footnote*   10 the affair ... was]
Mr. Peel's attempted re-election was   14 in the] by the theory of the *64–78*
14 shrank from] disliked *64–78*   16 When ... academical] I took part against
Mr. Peel, on a simple academical *64*; Accordingly, I took part against Mr. Peel,
on a simple academical *65–78*   19 his friends] he

---

[1] Vide Note A, *Liberalism*, at the end of the volume.

Dr. Whately attributed my leaving his *clientela* to a wish on my part to be the head of a party myself. I do not think that this charge was deserved. My habitual feeling then and since has been, that it was not I who sought friends, but friends who sought me. Never man had kinder or more indulgent friends than I have had; but I expressed my own feeling as to the mode in which I gained them, in this very year 1829, in the course of a copy of verses. Speaking of my blessings, I said, 'Blessings of friends, which to my door *unasked, unhoped*, have come.' They have come, they have gone; they came to my great joy, they went to my great grief. He who gave took away. Dr. Whately's impression about me, however, admits of this explanation:—

During the first years of my residence at Oriel, though proud of my College, I was not quite at home there. I was very much alone, and I used often to take my daily walk by myself. I recollect once meeting Dr. Copleston, then Provost, with one of the Fellows. He turned round, and with the kind courteousness which sat so well on him, made me a bow and said, 'Nunquam minus solus, quàm cùm solus.' At that time indeed (from 1823) I had the intimacy of my dear and true friend Dr. Pusey, and could not fail to admire and revere a soul so devoted to the cause of religion, so full of good works, so faithful in his affections; but he left residence when I was getting to know him well. As to Dr. Whately himself, he was too much my superior to allow of my being at my ease with him; and to no one in Oxford at this time did I open my heart fully and familiarly. But things changed in 1826. At that time I became one of the Tutors of my College, and this gave me position; besides, I had written one or two Essays which had been well received. I began to be known. I preached my first University Sermon. Next year I was one of the Public Examiners for the B.A. degree. In 1828 I became Vicar of St. Mary's. It was to me like the feeling of spring weather after winter; and, if I may so speak, I came out of my shell; I remained out of it till 1841.

The two persons who knew me best at that time are still alive, beneficed clergymen, no longer my friends. They could tell better than any one else what I was in those years. From this time my tongue was, as it were, loosened, and I spoke spontaneously

2–3 this charge] it   14 not quite at] not at   31–32 In 1828 ... St. Mary's.]
not in 64

and without effort. One of the two, Mr. Rickards, said of me, I have been told, 'Here is a fellow who, when he is silent, will never begin to speak; and when he once begins to speak, will never stop.' It was at this time that I began to have influence,
5 which steadily increased for a course of years. I gained upon my pupils, and was in particular intimate and affectionate with two of our probationer Fellows, Robert Isaac Wilberforce (afterwards Archdeacon) and Richard Hurrell Froude. Whately then, an acute man, perhaps saw around me the signs of an incipient
10 party, of which I was not conscious myself. And thus we discern the first elements of that movement afterwards called Tractarian.

The true and primary author of it, however, as is usual with great motive-powers, was out of sight. Having carried off as a mere boy the highest honours of the University, he had turned
15 from the admiration which haunted his steps, and sought for a better and holier satisfaction in pastoral work in the country. Need I say that I am speaking of John Keble? The first time that I was in a room with him was on occasion of my election to a fellowship at Oriel, when I was sent for into the Tower, to
20 shake hands with the Provost and Fellows. How is that hour fixed in my memory after the changes of forty-two years, forty-two this very day on which I write! I have lately had a letter in my hands, which I sent at the time to my great friend, John William Bowden, with whom I passed almost exclusively my
25 Under-graduate years. 'I had to hasten to the Tower', I say to him, 'to receive the congratulations of all the Fellows. I bore it till Keble took my hand, and then felt so abashed and unworthy of the honour done me, that I seemed desirous of quite sinking into the ground.' His had been the first name which I had heard
30 spoken of, with reverence rather than admiration, when I came up to Oxford. When one day I was walking in High Street with my dear earliest friend just mentioned, with what eagerness did he cry out, 'There's Keble!' and with what awe did I look at him. Then at another time I heard a Master of Arts of my College
35 give an account how he had just then had occasion to introduce himself on some business to Keble, and how gentle, courteous, and unaffected Keble had been, so as almost to put him out of

---

1–2 One . . . told] A shrewd man, who knew me at this time, said   1 Mr. Rickards]
a shrewd man *65–82*   2 fellow] man   7 Isaac] I.   23–24 John
William Bowden] John Bowden

countenance. Then too it was reported, truly or falsely, how a
rising man of brilliant reputation, the present Dean of St. Paul's,
Dr. Milman, admired and loved him, adding, that somehow he
was strangely unlike any one else. However, at the time when
I was elected Fellow of Oriel he was not in residence, and he was 5
shy of me for years in consequence of the marks which I bore
upon me of the evangelical and liberal schools. At least so I have
ever thought. Hurrell Froude brought us together about 1828:
it is one of the sayings preserved in his 'Remains',—'Do you
know the story of the murderer who had done one good thing in 10
his life? Well; if I was ever asked what good deed I had ever
done, I should say that I had brought Keble and Newman to
understand each other.'

The Christian Year made its appearance in 1827. It is not
necessary, and scarcely becoming, to praise a book which has 15
already become one of the classics of the language. When the
general tone of religious literature was so nerveless and impotent,
as it was at that time, Keble struck an original note and woke
up in the hearts of thousands a new music, the music of a school,
long unknown in England. Nor can I pretend to analyze, in my 20
own instance, the effect of religious teaching so deep, so pure, so
beautiful. I have never till now tried to do so; yet I think I am
not wrong in saying, that the two main intellectual truths which
it brought home to me, were the same two, which I had learned
from Butler, though recast in the creative mind of my new master. 25
The first of these was what may be called, in a large sense of the
word, the Sacramental system; that is, the doctrine that material
phenomena are both the types and the instruments of real things
unseen,—a doctrine, which embraces in its fulness, not only what
Anglicans, as well as Catholics, believe about Sacraments 30
properly so called; but also the article of 'the Communion of
Saints'; and likewise the Mysteries of the faith. The connexion
of this philosophy of religion with what is sometimes called
'Berkeleyism' has been mentioned above; I knew little of Berkeley at this time except by name: nor have I ever studied him. 35

On the second intellectual principle which I gained from
Mr. Keble, I could say a great deal; if this were the place for it.
It runs through very much that I have written, and has gained

4 was strangely unlike] was unlike   29 embraces in its fulness, not only]
embraces, not only   31–32 of Saints';] of Saints' in its fulness;

for me many hard names. Butler teaches us that probability is the guide of life. The danger of this doctrine, in the case of many minds, is, its tendency to destroy in them absolute certainty, leading them to consider every conclusion as doubtful, and
5 resolving truth into an opinion, which it is safe indeed to obey or to profess, but not possible to embrace with full internal assent. If this were to be allowed, then the celebrated saying, 'O God, if there be a God, save my soul, if I have a soul!' would be the highest measure of devotion:—but who can really pray
10 to a Being, about whose existence he is seriously in doubt?

I considered that Mr. Keble met this difficulty by ascribing the firmness of assent which we give to religious doctrine, not to the probabilities which introduced it, but to the living power of faith and love which accepted it. In matters of religion, he
15 seemed to say, it is not merely probability which makes us intellectually certain, but probability as it is put to account by faith and love. It is faith and love which give to probability a force which it has not in itself. Faith and love are directed towards an Object; in the vision of that Object they live; it is that Object,
20 received in faith and love, which renders it reasonable to take probability as sufficient for internal conviction. Thus the argument from Probability, in the matter of religion, became an argument from Personality, which in fact is one form of the argument from Authority.

25   In illustration, Mr. Keble used to quote the words of the Psalm: 'I will guide thee with mine *eye*. Be ye not like to horse and mule, which have no understanding; whose mouths must be held with bit and bridle, lest they fall upon thee.' This is the very difference, he used to say, between slaves, and friends or children.
30 Friends do not ask for literal commands; but, from their knowledge of the speaker, they understand his half-words, and from love of him they anticipate his wishes. Hence it is, that in his Poem for St. Bartholomew's Day, he speaks of the 'Eye of God's word'; and in the note quotes Mr. Miller, of Worcester College,
35 who remarks in his Bampton Lectures, on the special power of Scripture, as having 'this Eye, like that of a portrait, uniformly fixed upon us, turn where we will'. The view thus suggested by Mr. Keble, is brought forward in one of the earliest of the 'Tracts for the Times'. In No. 8 I say, 'The Gospel is a Law of Liberty.

5 safe indeed to] safe to   22 from] about

We are treated as sons, not as servants; not subjected to a code of formal commandments, but addressed as those who love God, and wish to please Him.'

I did not at all dispute this view of the matter, for I made use of it myself; but I was dissatisfied, because it did not go to the 5 root of the difficulty. It was beautiful and religious, but it did not even profess to be logical; and accordingly I tried to complete it by considerations of my own, which are to be found in my University Sermons, Essay on Ecclesiastical Miracles, and Essay on Development of Doctrine. My argument is in outline 10 as follows: that that absolute certitude which we were able to possess, whether as to the truths of natural theology, or as to the fact of a revelation, was the result of an *assemblage* of concurring and converging probabilities, and that, both according to the constitution of the human mind and the will of its Maker; that 15 certitude was a habit of mind, that certainty was a quality of propositions; that probabilities which did not reach to logical certainty, might suffice for a mental certitude; that the certitude thus brought about might equal in measure and strength the certitude which was created by the strictest scientific demonstra- 20 tion; and that to possess such certitude might in given cases and to given individuals be a plain duty, though not to others in other circumstances:—

Moreover, that as there were probabilities which sufficed for certitude, so there were other probabilities which were legiti- 25 mately adapted to create opinion; that it might be quite as much a matter of duty in given cases and to given persons to have about a fact an opinion of a definite strength and consistency, as in the case of greater or of more numerous probabilities it was a duty to have a certitude; that accordingly we were bound to 30 be more or less sure, on a sort of (as it were) graduated scale of assent, viz. according as the probabilities attaching to a professed fact were brought home to us, and as the case might be, to entertain about it a pious belief, or a pious opinion, or a religious conjecture, or at least, a tolerance of such belief, or opinion or 35 conjecture in others; that on the other hand, as it was a duty to have a belief, of more or less strong texture, in given cases, so in other cases it was a duty not to believe, not to opine, not to

8 to be found] implied   18 suffice for] create   19 brought about] created   21 possess] have   24 sufficed for] sufficed to create

conjecture, not even to tolerate the notion that a professed fact was true, inasmuch as it would be credulity or superstition, or some other moral fault, to do so. This was the region of Private Judgment in religion; that is, of a Private Judgment, not formed 5 arbitrarily and according to one's fancy or liking, but conscientiously, and under a sense of duty.

Considerations such as these throw a new light on the subject of Miracles, and they seem to have led me to reconsider the view which I had taken of them in my Essay in 1825–6. I do not know 10 what was the date of this change in me, nor of the train of ideas on which it was founded. That there had been already great miracles, as those of Scripture, as the Resurrection, was a fact establishing the principle that the laws of nature had sometimes been suspended by their Divine Author, and since what had 15 happened once might happen again, a certain probability, at least no kind of improbability, was attached to the idea taken in itself, of miraculous intervention in later times, and miraculous accounts were to be regarded in connexion with the verisimilitude, scope, instrument, character, testimony, and cir- 20 cumstances, with which they presented themselves to us; and, according to the final result of those various considerations, it was our duty to be sure, or to believe, or to opine, or to surmise, or to tolerate, or to reject, or to denounce. The main difference between my Essay on Miracles in 1826 and my Essay in 1842 is 25 this: that in 1826 I considered that miracles were sharply divided into two classes, those which were to be received, and those which were to be rejected; whereas in 1842 I saw that they were to be regarded according to their greater or less probability, which was in some cases sufficient to create certitude about them, in other 30 cases only belief or opinion.

Moreover, the argument from Analogy, on which this view of the question was founded, suggested to me something besides, in recommendation of the Ecclesiastical Miracles. It fastened itself upon the theory of Church History which I had learned as 35 a boy from Joseph Milner. It is Milner's doctrine, that upon the visible Church come down from above, at certain intervals, large and temporary *Effusions* of divine grace. This is the leading idea of his work. He begins by speaking of the Day of Pentecost,

9 had taken] took   14 Author,] Author;   36 at certain intervals]
from time to time

as marking 'the first of those *Effusions* of the Spirit of God, which from age to age have visited the earth since the coming of Christ'. Vol. i. p. 3. In a note he adds that 'in the term "Effusion" there is *not* here included the idea of the miraculous or extraordinary operations of the Spirit of God'; but still it was natural for me, admitting Milner's general theory, and applying to it the principle of analogy, not to stop short at his abrupt *ipse dixit*, but boldly to pass forward to the conclusion, on other grounds plausible, that as miracles accompanied the first effusion of grace, so they might accompany the later. It is surely a natural and on the whole, a true anticipation (though of course there are exceptions in particular cases), that gifts and graces go together; now, according to the ancient Catholic doctrine, the gift of miracles was viewed as the attendant and shadow of transcendent sanctity: and moreover, since such sanctity was not of every day's occurrence, nay further, since one period of Church history differed widely from another, and, as Joseph Milner would say, there have been generations or centuries of degeneracy or disorder, and times of revival, and since one region might be in the mid-day of religious fervour, and another in twilight or gloom, there was no force in the popular argument, that, because we did not see miracles with our own eyes, miracles had not happened in former times, or were not now at this very time taking place in distant places:—but I must not dwell longer on a subject, to which in a few words it is impossible to do justice.[1]

Hurrell Froude was a pupil of Keble's, formed by him, and in turn reacting upon him. I knew him first in 1826, and was in the closest and most affectionate friendship with him from about 1829 till his death in 1836. He was a man of the highest gifts,— so truly many-sided, that it would be presumptuous in me to attempt to describe him, except under those aspects in which he came before me. Nor have I here to speak of the gentleness and tenderness of nature, the playfulness, the free elastic force and graceful versatility of mind, and the patient winning considerateness in discussion, which endeared him to those to whom he opened his heart; for I am all along engaged upon matters of

4 *not*] not   15, 16, 19 since] as   25 justice.[1]] *no footnote in 64*

---

[1] Vide note B, *Ecclesiastical Miracles*, at the end of the volume.

belief and opinion, and am introducing others into my narrative, not for their own sake, or because I love and have loved them, so much as because, and so far as, they have influenced my theological views. In this respect then, I speak of Hurrell Froude,
5 —in his intellectual aspect,—as a man of high genius, brimful and overflowing with ideas and views, in him original, which were too many and strong even for his bodily strength, and which crowded and jostled against each other in their effort after distinct shape and expression. And he had an intellect as critical
10 and logical as it was speculative and bold. Dying prematurely, as he did, and in the conflict and transition-state of opinion, his religious views never reached their ultimate conclusion, by the very reason of their multitude and their depth. His opinions arrested and influenced me, even when they did not gain my
15 assent. He professed openly his admiration of the Church of Rome, and his hatred of the Reformers. He delighted in the notion of an hierarchical system, of sacerdotal power, and of full ecclesiastical liberty. He felt scorn of the maxim, 'The Bible and the Bible only is the religion of Protestants'; and he gloried in
20 accepting Tradition as a main instrument of religious teaching. He had a high severe idea of the intrinsic excellence of Virginity; and he considered the Blessed Virgin its great Pattern. He delighted in thinking of the Saints; he had a vivid appreciation of the idea of sanctity, its possibility and its heights; and he was
25 more than inclined to believe a large amount of miraculous interference as occurring in the early and middle ages. He embraced the principle of penance and mortification. He had a deep devotion to the Real Presence, in which he had a firm faith. He was powerfully drawn to the Medieval Church, but not to the
30 Primitive.

He had a keen insight into abstract truth; but he was an Englishman to the backbone in his severe adherence to the real and the concrete. He had a most classical taste, and a genius for philosophy and art; and he was fond of historical inquiry, and
35 the politics of religion. He had no turn for theology as such. He set no sufficient value on the writings of the Fathers, on the detail or development of doctrine, on the definite traditions of the Church viewed in their matter, on the teaching of the Ecumenical

23 vivid] keen   36 set . . . on] had no appreciation of   on the detail] of the detail   37, 38 on the] of the

Councils, or on the controversies out of which they arose. He took an eager courageous view of things on the whole. I should say that his power of entering into the minds of others did not equal his other gifts; he could not believe, for instance, that I really held the Roman Church to be Antichristian. On many 5 points he would not believe but that I agreed with him, when I did not. He seemed not to understand my difficulties. His were of a different kind, the contrariety between theory and fact. He was a high Tory of the Cavalier stamp, and was disgusted with the Toryism of the opponents of the Reform Bill. He was smitten 10 with the love of the Theocratic Church; he went abroad and was shocked by the degeneracy which he thought he saw in the Catholics of Italy.

It is difficult to enumerate the precise additions to my theological creed which I derived from a friend to whom I owe so 15 much. He taught me to look with admiration towards the Church of Rome, and in the same degree to dislike the Reformation. He fixed deep in me the idea of devotion to the Blessed Virgin, and he led me gradually to believe in the Real Presence.

There is one remaining source of my opinions to be mentioned, 20 and that far from the least important. In proportion as I moved out of the shadow of that liberalism which had hung over my course, my early devotion towards the Fathers returned; and in the Long Vacation of 1828 I set about to read them chronologically, beginning with St. Ignatius and St. Justin. About 1830 a 25 proposal was made to me by Mr. Hugh Rose, who with Mr. Lyall (afterwards Dean of Canterbury) was providing writers for a Theological Library, to furnish them with a History of the Principal Councils. I accepted it, and at once set to work on the Council of Nicæa. It was to launch myself on an ocean with 30 currents innumerable; and I was drifted back first to the ante-Nicene history, and then to the Church of Alexandria. The work at last appeared under the title of 'The Arians of the Fourth Century'; and of its 422 pages, the first 117 consisted of introductory matter, and the Council of Nicæa did not appear till the 35 254th, and then occupied at most twenty pages.

I do not know when I first learnt to consider that Antiquity

1 on the] of the   2 eager courageous] eager, courageous   16 taught me to]
made me   22 of that liberalism] of liberalism   30 to launch] launching

was the true exponent of the doctrines of Christianity and the basis of the Church of England; but I take it for granted that the works of Bishop Bull, which at this time I read, were my chief introduction to this principle. The course of reading, which I
5 pursued in the composition of my volume, was directly adapted to develope it in my mind. What principally attracted me in the ante-Nicene period was the great Church of Alexandria, the historical centre of teaching in those times. Of Rome for some centuries comparatively little is known. The battle of Arianism
10 was first fought in Alexandria; Athanasius, the champion of the truth, was Bishop of Alexandria; and in his writings he refers to the great religious names of an earlier date, to Origen, Dionysius, and others, who were the glory of its see, or of its school. The broad philosophy of Clement and Origen carried me away; the
15 philosophy, not the theological doctrine; and I have drawn out some features of it in my volume, with the zeal and freshness, but with the partiality, of a neophyte. Some portions of their teaching, magnificent in themselves, came like music to my inward ear, as if the response to ideas, which, with little external to
20 encourage them, I had cherished so long. These were based on the mystical or sacramental principle, and spoke of the various Economies or Dispensations of the Eternal. I understood these passages to mean that the exterior world, physical and historical, was but the manifestation to our senses of realities greater than
25 itself. Nature was a parable: Scripture was an allegory: pagan literature, philosophy, and mythology, properly understood, were but a preparation for the Gospel. The Greek poets and sages were in a certain sense prophets; for 'thoughts beyond their thought to those high bards were given'. There had been a
30 directly divine dispensation granted to the Jews; but there had been in some sense a dispensation carried on in favour of the Gentiles. He who had taken the seed of Jacob for His elect people had not therefore cast the rest of mankind out of His sight. In the fulness of time both Judaism and Paganism had come to nought;
35 the outward framework, which concealed yet suggested the Living Truth, had never been intended to last, and it was dis-

2–3 the works ... were] Bishop Bull, whose works at this time I read, was
5 volume, was] work was   22–23 these passages] them   24 manifestation to our senses] outward manifestation   25 parable] parable[1] *Footnote*: Vid. Mr. Morris's beautiful poem with this title.   29–30 a directly divine] a divine   30 Jews; but there] Jews; there

solving under the beams of the Sun of Justice which shone behind it and through it. The process of change had been slow; it had been done not rashly, but by rule and measure, 'at sundry times and in divers manners', first one disclosure and then another, till the whole evangelical doctrine was brought into full manifesta- 5 tion. And thus room was made for the anticipation of further and deeper disclosures, of truths still under the veil of the letter, and in their season to be revealed. The visible world still remains without its divine interpretation; Holy Church in her sacraments and her hierarchical appointments, will remain, even to the end 10 of the world, after all but a symbol of those heavenly facts which fill eternity. Her mysteries are but the expressions in human language of truths to which the human mind is unequal. It is evident how much there was in all this in correspondence with the thoughts which had attracted me when I was young, and 15 with the doctrine which I have already associated with the Analogy and the Christian Year.

It was, I suppose, to the Alexandrian school and to the early Church, that I owe in particular what I definitely held about the Angels. I viewed them, not only as the ministers employed by the 20 Creator in the Jewish and Christian dispensations, as we find on the face of Scripture, but as carrying on, as Scripture also implies, the Economy of the Visible World. I considered them as the real causes of motion, light, and life, and of those elementary principles of the physical universe, which, when offered in their 25 developments to our senses, suggest to us the notion of cause and effect, and of what are called the laws of nature. This doctrine I have drawn out in my Sermon for Michaelmas day, written in 1831. I say of the Angels, 'Every breath of air and ray of light and heat, every beautiful prospect, is, as it were, the skirts of 30 their garments, the waving of the robes of those whose faces see God.' Again, I ask what would be the thoughts of a man who, 'when examining a flower, or a herb, or a pebble, or a ray of light, which he treats as something so beneath him in the scale of existence, suddenly discovered that he was in the presence of 35 some powerful being who was hidden behind the visible things

  1 Justice which shone behind] Justice behind   5 whole evangelical doctrine was] whole was   11 after all but] only   16 associated] connected   18 It was, I suppose, to] I suppose it was to   27–28 This doctrine . . . out] I have drawn out this doctrine   28–29 in 1831] not later than 1834.

he was inspecting,—who, though concealing his wise hand, was giving them their beauty, grace, and perfection, as being God's instrument for the purpose,—nay, whose robe and ornaments those objects were, which he was so eager to analyze?' and I 5 therefore remark that 'we may say with grateful and simple hearts with the Three Holy Children, "O all ye works of the Lord, &c., &c., bless ye the Lord, praise Him, and magnify Him for ever".'

Also, besides the hosts of evil spirits, I considered there was a middle race, δαιμόνια, neither in heaven, nor in hell; partially 10 fallen, capricious, wayward; noble or crafty, benevolent or malicious, as the case might be. These beings gave a sort of inspiration or intelligence to races, nations, and classes of men. Hence the action of bodies politic and associations, which is often so different from that of the individuals who compose them. Hence 15 the character and the instinct of states and governments, of religious communities and communions. I thought these assemblages had their life in certain unseen Powers. My preference of the Personal to the Abstract would naturally lead me to this view. I thought it countenanced by the mention of 'the Prince of 20 Persia' in the Prophet Daniel; and I think I considered that it was of such intermediate beings that the Apocalypse spoke, in its notice of 'the Angels of the Seven Churches'.

In 1837 I made a further development of this doctrine. I said to an intimate and dear friend, Samuel Francis Wood, in a letter 25 which came into my hands on his death, 'I have an idea. The mass of the Fathers (Justin, Athenagoras, Irenæus, Clement, Tertullian, Origen, Lactantius, Sulpicius, Ambrose, Nazianzen,) hold that, though Satan fell from the beginning, the Angels fell before the deluge, falling in love with the daughters of men. This 30 has lately come across me as a remarkable solution of a notion which I cannot help holding. Daniel speaks as if each nation had its guardian Angel. I cannot but think that there are beings with a great deal of good in them, yet with great defects, who are the animating principles of certain institutions, &c., &c. . . . Take 35 England with many high virtues, and yet a low Catholicism. It seems to me that John Bull is a spirit neither of heaven nor hell.

---

11 These beings] They   13–14 often so different] so different often   16–17 I thought . . . Powers.] I thought they were inhabited by unseen intelligences. 21–22 in its notice of] when it introduced   24 an intimate and dear] my great 35 England with] England, with

. . . Has not the Christian Church, in its parts, surrendered itself to one or other of these simulations of the truth? . . . How are we to avoid Scylla and Charybdis and go straight on to the very image of Christ?' &c., &c.

I am aware that what I have been saying will, with many men, be doing credit to my imagination at the expense of my judgment —'Hippoclides doesn't care'; I am not setting myself up as a pattern of good sense or of any thing else: I am but giving a history of my opinions, and that, with the view of showing that I have come by them through intelligible processes of thought and honest external means. The doctrine indeed of the Economy has in some quarters been itself condemned as intrinsically pernicious,—as if leading to lying and equivocation, when applied, as I have applied it in my remarks upon it in my History of the Arians, to matters of conduct. My answer to this imputation I postpone to the concluding pages of my Volume.

While I was engaged in writing my work upon the Arians, great events were happening at home and abroad, which brought out into form and passionate expression the various beliefs which had so gradually been winning their way into my mind. Shortly before, there had been a Revolution in France; the Bourbons had been dismissed: and I held that it was unchristian for nations to cast off their governors, and, much more, sovereigns who had the divine right of inheritance. Again, the great Reform Agitation was going on around me as I wrote. The Whigs had come into power; Lord Grey had told the Bishops to set their house in order, and some of the Prelates had been insulted and threatened in the streets of London. The vital question was, how were we to keep the Church from being liberalized? there was such apathy on the subject in some quarters, such imbecile alarm in others; the true principles of Churchmanship seemed so radically decayed, and there was such distraction in the councils of the Clergy. Blomfield, the Bishop of London of the day, an active and open-hearted man, had been for years engaged in diluting the high orthodoxy of the Church by the introduction

5

10

15

20

25

30

35

8–11 giving . . . means.] vindicating myself from the charge of dishonesty.— 11–16 The doctrine . . . Volume.] There is indeed another view of the Economy brought out in the course of the same dissertation on the subject, in my History of the Arians, which has afforded matter for the latter imputation; but I reserve it for the concluding portion of my Reply. [*Space left between this and next paragraph in 64.*] 22 held] believed 33 Blomfield, the Bishop] The Bishop

of members of the Evangelical body into places of influence and
trust. He had deeply offended men who agreed in opinion with
myself, by an off-hand saying (as it was reported) to the effect
that belief in the Apostolical succession had gone out with the
5 Non-jurors. 'We can count you', he said to some of the gravest
and most venerated persons of the old school. And the Evangelical party itself, with their late successes, seemed to have lost that
simplicity and unworldliness which I admired so much in Milner
and Scott. It was not that I did not venerate such men as Ryder,
10 the then Bishop of Lichfield, and others of similar sentiments,
who were not yet promoted out of the ranks of the Clergy, but
I thought little of the Evangelicals as a class. I thought they
played into the hands of the Liberals. With the Establishment
thus divided and threatened, thus ignorant of its true strength,
15 I compared that fresh vigorous Power of which I was reading in
the first centuries. In her triumphant zeal on behalf of that
Primeval Mystery, to which I had had so great a devotion from
my youth, I recognized the movement of my Spiritual Mother.
'Incessu patuit Dea.' The self-conquest of her Ascetics, the
20 patience of her Martyrs, the irresistible determination of her
Bishops, the joyous swing of her advance, both exalted and
abashed me. I said to myself, 'Look on this picture and on that';
I felt affection for my own Church, but not tenderness; I felt
dismay at her prospects, anger and scorn at her do-nothing per-
25 plexity. I thought that if Liberalism once got a footing within
her, it was sure of the victory in the event. I saw that Reformation principles were powerless to rescue her. As to leaving her,
the thought never crossed my imagination; still I ever kept before
me that there was something greater than the Established
30 Church, and that that was the Church Catholic and Apostolic,
set up from the beginning, of which she was but the local
presence and the organ. She was nothing, unless she was this.
She must be dealt with strongly, or she would be lost. There was
need of a second reformation.

35   At this time I was disengaged from College duties, and my
health had suffered from the labour involved in the composition

---

1 of members of the] of the   2 agreed in opinion with] agreed with   7 itself, with . . . seemed] itself seemed, with their late successes,   9–10 as Ryder, the]
as the   12 the Evangelicals] them   15 Power] power   32 and the
organ] and organ   34 reformation] Reformation

of my Volume. It was ready for the Press in July, 1832, though not published till the end of 1833. I was easily persuaded to join Hurrell Froude and his Father, who were going to the south of Europe for the health of the former.

We set out in December, 1832. It was during this expedition that my Verses which are in the Lyra Apostolica were written;— a few indeed before it, but not more than one or two of them after it. Exchanging, as I was, definite Tutorial work, and the literary quiet and pleasant friendships of the last six years, for foreign countries and an unknown future, I naturally was led to think that some inward changes, as well as some larger course of action, were coming upon me. At Whitchurch, while waiting for the down mail to Falmouth, I wrote the verses about my Guardian Angel, which begin with these words: 'Are these the tracks of some unearthly Friend?' and which go on to speak of 'the vision' which haunted me:—that vision is more or less brought out in the whole series of these compositions.

I went to various coasts of the Mediterranean; parted with my friends at Rome; went down for the second time to Sicily without companion, at the end of April; and got back to England by Palermo in the early part of July. The strangeness of foreign life threw me back into myself; I found pleasure in historical sites and beautiful scenes, not in men and manners. We kept clear of Catholics throughout our tour. I had a conversation with the Dean of Malta, a most pleasant man, lately dead; but it was about the Fathers, and the Library of the great church. I knew the Abbate Santini, at Rome, who did no more than copy for me the Gregorian tones. Froude and I made two calls upon Monsignore (now Cardinal) Wiseman at the Collegio Inglese, shortly before we left Rome. Once we heard him preach at a church in the Corso. I do not recollect being in a room with any other ecclesiastics, except a Priest at Castro-Giovanni in Sicily, who called on me when I was ill, and with whom I wished to hold a controversy. As to Church Services, we attended the Tenebræ, at the Sestine, for the sake of the Miserere; and that was all. My general feeling was, 'All, save the spirit of man, is divine.' I saw nothing but what was external; of the hidden life of Catholics I knew nothing. I was still more driven back into

myself, and felt my isolation. England was in my thoughts solely,
and the news from England came rarely and imperfectly. The
Bill for the Suppression of the Irish Sees was in progress, and
filled my mind. I had fierce thoughts against the Liberals.

5   It was the success of the Liberal cause which fretted me inwardly. I became fierce against its instruments and its manifestations. A French vessel was at Algiers; I would not even look at
the tricolour. On my return, though forced to stop twenty-four
hours at Paris, I kept indoors the whole time, and all that I saw
10 of that beautiful city was what I saw from the Diligence. The
Bishop of London had already sounded me as to my filling one
of the Whitehall preacherships, which he had just then put on
a new footing; but I was indignant at the line which he was
taking, and from my Steamer I had sent home a letter declining
15 the appointment by anticipation, should it be offered to me. At
this time I was specially annoyed with Dr. Arnold, though it did
not last into later years. Some one, I think, asked, in conversation
at Rome, whether a certain interpretation of Scripture was
Christian? it was answered that Dr. Arnold took it; I interposed,
20 'But is *he* a Christian?' The subject went out of my head at once;
when afterwards I was taxed with it, I could say no more in
explanation, than (what I believe was the fact) that I must have
had in mind some free views of Dr. Arnold about the Old Testament:—I thought I must have meant, 'Arnold answers for the
25 interpretation, but who is to answer for Arnold?' It was at Rome,
too, that we began the Lyra Apostolica which appeared monthly
in the British Magazine. The motto shows the feeling of both
Froude and myself at the time: we borrowed from M. Bunsen
a Homer, and Froude chose the words in which Achilles, on
30 returning to the battle, says, 'You shall know the difference, now
that I am back again.'

  Especially when I was left by myself, the thought came upon
me that deliverance is wrought, not by the many but by the few,
not by bodies but by persons. Now it was, I think, that I repeated
35 to myself the words, which had ever been dear to me from my
school days, 'Exoriare aliquis!'—now too, that Southey's beautiful poem of Thalaba, for which I had an immense liking, came

    8–9 twenty-four hours] a day   22–23 (what . . . mind] that I must have been
alluding to   24–25 meant, 'Arnold answers . . . Arnold?'] meant, 'But who is to
answer for Arnold?'

forcibly to my mind. I began to think that I had a mission. There are sentences of my letters to my friends to this effect, if they are not destroyed. When we took leave of Monsignore Wiseman, he had courteously expressed a wish that we might make a second visit to Rome; I said with great gravity, 'We have a work to do in England.' I went down at once to Sicily, and the presentiment grew stronger. I struck into the middle of the island, and fell ill of a fever at Leonforte. My servant thought that I was dying, and begged for my last directions. I gave them, as he wished; but I said, 'I shall not die.' I repeated, 'I shall not die, for I have not sinned against light, I have not sinned against light.' I never have been able quite to make out what I meant.

I got to Castro-Giovanni, and was laid up there for nearly three weeks. Towards the end of May I left for Palermo, taking three days for the journey. Before starting from my inn in the morning of May 26th or 27th, I sat down on my bed, and began to sob violently. My servant, who had acted as my nurse, asked what ailed me. I could only answer him, 'I have a work to do in England.'

I was aching to get home; yet for want of a vessel I was kept at Palermo for three weeks. I began to visit the Churches, and they calmed my impatience, though I did not attend any services. I knew nothing of the Presence of the Blessed Sacrament there. At last I got off in an orange boat, bound for Marseilles. Then it was that I wrote the lines, 'Lead, kindly light', which have since become well known. We were becalmed a whole week in the Straits of Bonifacio. I was writing verses the whole time of my passage. At length I got to Marseilles, and set off for England. The fatigue of travelling was too much for me, and I was laid up for several days at Lyons. At last I got off again, and did not stop night or day, (except a compulsory delay at Paris,) till I reached England, and my mother's house. My brother had arrived from Persia only a few hours before. This was on the Tuesday. The following Sunday, July 14th, Mr. Keble preached the Assize Sermon in the University Pulpit. It was published under the title of 'National Apostasy'. I have ever considered and kept the day, as the start of the religious movement of 1833.

12 quite . . . meant.] to make out at all what I meant. *64–78*   14 left] set off
16 violently] bitterly *64–78*   18 answer him, 'I] answer, 'I   23–26 Then it
was . . . Bonifacio.] *These sentences were transposed* 64–65   30 day, (except a
. . . till] day till *64*; day, (excepting the . . . till] *64–78*

CHAPTER II

HISTORY OF MY RELIGIOUS OPINIONS FROM 1833 TO 1839

I N spite of the foregoing pages, I have no romantic story to tell;
but I have written them, because it is my duty to tell things as
they took place. I have not exaggerated the feelings with which
I returned to England, and I have no desire to dress up the
events which followed, so as to make them in keeping with the
narrative which has gone before. I soon relapsed into the every-
day life which I had hitherto led; in all things the same, except
that a new object was given me. I had employed myself in my own
rooms in reading and writing, and in the care of a Church, before
I left England, and I returned to the same occupations when I
was back again. And yet perhaps those first vehement feelings
which carried me on, were necessary for the beginning of the
Movement; and afterwards, when it was once begun, the special
need of me was over.

When I got home from abroad, I found that already a movement had commenced, in opposition to the specific danger which
at that time was threatening the religion of the nation and its
Church. Several zealous and able men had united their counsels,
and were in correspondence with each other. The principal of
these were Mr. Keble, Hurrell Froude, who had reached home
long before me, Mr. William Palmer of Dublin and Worcester
College (not Mr. William Palmer of Magdalen, who is now a
Catholic), Mr. Arthur Perceval, and Mr. Hugh Rose.

To mention Mr. Hugh Rose's name is to kindle in the minds
of those who knew him a host of pleasant and affectionate
remembrances. He was the man above all others fitted by his
cast of mind and literary powers to make a stand, if a stand
could be made, against the calamity of the times. He was gifted
with a high and large mind, and a true sensibility of what was

great and beautiful; he wrote with warmth and energy; and he had a cool head and cautious judgment. He spent his strength and shortened his life, Pro Ecclesia Dei, as he understood that sovereign idea. Some years earlier he had been the first to give warning, I think from the University Pulpit at Cambridge, of the perils to England which lay in the biblical and theological speculations of Germany. The Reform agitation followed, and the Whig Government came into power; and he anticipated in their distribution of Church patronage the authoritative intro- duction of liberal opinions into the country. He feared that by the Whig party a door would be opened in England to the most grievous of heresies, which never could be closed again. In order under such grave circumstances to unite Churchmen together, and to make a front against the coming danger, he had in 1832 commenced the British Magazine, and in the same year he came to Oxford in the summer term, in order to beat up for writers for his publication; on that occasion I became known to him through Mr. Palmer. His reputation and position came in aid of his obvious fitness, in point of character and intellect, to become the centre of an ecclesiastical movement, if such a movement were to depend on the action of a party. His delicate health, his premature death, would have frustrated the expectation, even though the new school of opinion had been more exactly thrown into the shape of a party, than in fact was the case. But he zealously backed up the first efforts of those who were principals in it; and, when he went abroad to die, in 1838, he allowed me the solace of expressing my feelings of attachment and gratitude to him by addressing him, in the dedication of a volume of my Sermons, as the man 'who, when hearts were failing, bade us stir up the gift that was in us, and betake ourselves to our true Mother'.

But there were other reasons, besides Mr. Rose's state of health, which hindered those who so much admired him from availing themselves of his close co-operation in the coming fight. United as both he and they were in the general scope of the Movement, they were in discordance with each other from the first in their estimate of the means to be adopted for attaining it. Mr. Rose had a position in the Church, a name, and serious

---

10 country. He] country:—by 'liberal' I mean liberalism in *religion*, for questions of politics, as such, do not come into this narrative at all. He

responsibilities; he had direct ecclesiastical superiors; he had intimate relations with his own University, and a large clerical connexion through the country. Froude and I were nobodies; with no characters to lose, and no antecedents to fetter us. Rose could not go a-head across country, as Froude had no scruples in doing. Froude was a bold rider, as on horseback, so also in his speculations. After a long conversation with him on the logical bearing of his principles, Mr. Rose said of him with quiet humour, that 'he did not seem to be afraid of inferences'. It was simply the truth; Froude had that strong hold of first principles, and that keen perception of their value, that he was comparatively indifferent to the revolutionary action which would attend on their application to a given state of things; whereas in the thoughts of Rose, as a practical man, existing facts had the precedence of every other idea, and the chief test of the soundness of a line of policy lay in the consideration whether it would work. This was one of the first questions, which, as it seemed to me, on every occasion occurred to his mind. With Froude, Erastianism,—that is, the union (so he viewed it) of Church and State,—was the parent, or if not the parent, the serviceable and sufficient tool, of liberalism. Till that union was snapped, Christian doctrine never could be safe; and, while he well knew how high and unselfish was the temper of Mr. Rose, yet he used to apply to him an epithet, reproachful in his own mouth;—Rose was a 'conservative'. By bad luck, I brought out this word to Mr. Rose in a letter of my own, which I wrote to him in criticism of something he had inserted in his Magazine: I got a vehement rebuke for my pains, for though Rose pursued a conservative line, he had as high a disdain, as Froude could have, of a worldly ambition, and an extreme sensitiveness of such an imputation.

But there was another reason still, and a more elementary one, which severed Mr. Rose from the Oxford Movement. Living movements do not come of committees, nor are great ideas worked out through the post, even though it had been the penny post. This principle deeply penetrated both Froude and myself from the first, and recommended to us the course which things soon took spontaneously, and without set purpose of our own. Universities are the natural centres of intellectual movements. How could men act together, whatever was their zeal, unless they

18 on every occasion] ever   27 in his] into the

were united in a sort of individuality? Now, first, we had no
unity of place. Mr. Rose was in Suffolk, Mr. Perceval in Surrey,
Mr. Keble in Gloucestershire; Hurrell Froude had to go for his
health to Barbadoes. Mr. Palmer was indeed in Oxford; this was
an important advantage, and told well in the first months of the 5
Movement;—but another condition, besides that of place, was
required.

A far more essential unity was that of antecedents,—a common
history, common memories, an intercourse of mind with mind in
the past, and a progress and increase in that intercourse in the 10
present. Mr. Perceval, to be sure, was a pupil of Mr. Keble's;
but Keble, Rose, and Palmer, represented distinct parties, or at
least tempers, in the Establishment. Mr. Palmer had many conditions of authority and influence. He was the only really learned
man among us. He understood theology as a science; he was 15
practised in the scholastic mode of controversial writing; and,
I believe, was as well acquainted, as he was dissatisfied, with the
Catholic schools. He was as decided in his religious views, as he
was cautious and even subtle in their expression, and gentle in
their enforcement. But he was deficient in depth; and besides, 20
coming from a distance, he never had really grown into an
Oxford man, nor was he generally received as such; nor had he
any insight into the force of personal influence and congeniality
of thought in carrying out a religious theory,—a condition which
Froude and I considered essential to any true success in the stand 25
which had to be made against Liberalism. Mr. Palmer had a
certain connexion, as it may be called, in the Establishment,
consisting of high Church dignitaries, Archdeacons, London
Rectors, and the like, who belonged to what was commonly
called the high-and-dry school. They were far more opposed than 30
even he was to the irresponsible action of individuals. Of course
their *beau idéal* in ecclesiastical action was a board of safe, sound,
sensible men. Mr. Palmer was their organ and representative;
and he wished for a Committee, an Association, with rules and
meetings, to protect the interests of the Church in its existing 35
peril. He was in some measure supported by Mr. Perceval.

I, on the other hand, had out of my own head begun the
Tracts; and these, as representing the antagonist principle of
personality, were looked upon by Mr. Palmer's friends with

considerable alarm. The great point at the time with these good men in London,—some of them men of the highest principle, and far from influenced by what we used to call Erastianism,—was to put down the Tracts. I, as their editor, and mainly their author, was of course willing to give way. Keble and Froude advocated their continuance strongly, and were angry with me for consenting to stop them. Mr. Palmer shared the anxiety of his own friends; and, kind as were his thoughts of us, he still not unnaturally felt, for reasons of his own, some fidget and nervousness at the course which his Oriel friends were taking. Froude, for whom he had a real liking, took a high tone in his project of measures for dealing with bishops and clergy, which must have shocked and scandalized him considerably. As for me, there was matter enough in the early Tracts to give him equal disgust; and doubtless I much tasked his generosity, when he had to defend me, whether against the London dignitaries or the country clergy. Oriel, from the time of Dr. Copleston to Dr. Hampden, had had a name far and wide for liberality of thought; it had received a formal recognition from the Edinburgh Review, if my memory serves me truly, as the school of speculative philosophy in England; and on one occasion, in 1833, when I presented myself, with some of the first papers of the Movement, to a country clergyman in Northamptonshire, he paused awhile, and then, eyeing me with significance, asked, 'Whether Whately was at the bottom of them?'

Mr. Perceval wrote to me in support of the judgment of Mr. Palmer and the dignitaries. I replied in a letter, which he afterwards published. 'As to the Tracts,' I said to him (I quote my own words from his Pamphlet), 'every one has his own taste. You object to some things, another to others. If we altered to please every one, the effect would be spoiled. They were not intended as symbols è *cathedrâ*, but as the expression of individual minds; and individuals, feeling strongly, while on the one hand, they are incidentally faulty in mode or language, are still peculiarly effective. No great work was done by a system; whereas systems rise out of individual exertions. Luther was an individual. The very faults of an individual excite attention; he loses, but his cause (if good and he powerful-minded) gains. This is the way of things; we promote truth by a self-sacrifice.'

5 of course] not unnaturally   39 things; we] things: we

The visit which I made to the Northamptonshire Rector was
only one of a series of similar expedients, which I adopted during
the year 1833. I called upon clergy in various parts of the country, whether I was acquainted with them or not, and I attended
at the houses of friends where several of them were from time to 5
time assembled. I do not think that much came of such attempts,
nor were they quite in my way. Also I wrote various letters to
clergymen, which fared not much better, except that they advertised the fact, that a rally in favour of the Church was commencing. I did not care whether my visits were made to high Church 10
or low Church; I wished to make a strong pull in union with all
who were opposed to the principles of liberalism, whoever they
might be. Giving my name to the Editor, I commenced a series
of letters in the Record Newspaper: they ran to a considerable
length; and were borne by him with great courtesy and patience. 15
The heading given to them was, 'Church Reform'. The first was
on the revival of Church Discipline; the second, on its Scripture
proof; the third, on the application of the doctrine; the fourth
was an answer to objections; the fifth was on the benefits of
discipline. And then the series was abruptly brought to a termi- 20
nation. I had said what I really felt, and what was also in keeping
with the strong teaching of the Tracts, but I suppose the Editor
discovered in me some divergence from his own line of thought;
for at length he sent a very civil letter, apologizing for the non-
appearance of my sixth communication, on the ground that it 25
contained an attack upon 'Temperance Societies', about which
he did not wish a controversy in his columns. He added, however, his serious regret at the theological views of the Tracts.
I had subscribed a small sum in 1828 towards the first start of
the Record.   30

Acts of the officious character, which I have been describing,
were uncongenial to my natural temper, to the genius of the
Movement, and to the historical mode of its success:—they were
the fruit of that exuberant and joyous energy with which I had
returned from abroad, and which I never had before or since. 35
I had the exultation of health restored, and home regained.
While I was at Palermo and thought of the breadth of the Mediterranean, and the wearisome journey across France, I could not

16 The heading . . . was,] They were headed as being on   17 revival]
Revival   28 theological views] character

imagine how I was ever to get to England; but now I was amid familiar scenes and faces once more. And my health and strength came back to me with such a rebound, that some friends at Oxford, on seeing me, did not well know that it was I, and
5 hesitated before they spoke to me. And I had the consciousness that I was employed in that work which I had been dreaming about, and which I felt to be so momentous and inspiring. I had a supreme confidence in our cause; we were upholding that primitive Christianity which was delivered for all time by the
10 early teachers of the Church, and which was registered and attested in the Anglican formularies and by the Anglican divines. That ancient religion had well nigh faded away out of the land, through the political changes of the last 150 years, and it must be restored. It would be in fact a second Reformation:—a better
15 reformation, for it would be a return not to the sixteenth century, but to the seventeenth. No time was to be lost, for the Whigs had come to do their worst, and the rescue might come too late. Bishopricks were already in course of suppression; Church property was in course of confiscation; Sees would soon be
20 receiving unsuitable occupants. We knew enough to begin preaching upon, and there was no one else to preach. I felt as on board a vessel, which first gets under weigh, and then the deck is cleared out, and luggage and live stock stowed away into their proper receptacles.
25   Nor was it only that I had confidence in our cause, both in itself, and in its polemical force, but also, on the other hand, I despised every rival system of doctrine and its arguments too. As to the high Church and the low Church, I thought that the one had not much more of a logical basis than the other; while
30 I had a thorough contempt for the controversial position of the latter. I had a real respect for the character of many of the advocates of each party, but that did not give cogency to their arguments; and I thought, on the contrary, that the Apostolical form of doctrine was essential and imperative, and its grounds
35 of evidence impregnable. Owing to this supreme confidence, it

22 on board a] on a   23 and luggage] and the luggage   stowed] stored
22–23 the deck … stowed] clears out the deck, and stores away luggage and live
stock   *another copy of 64*   26 polemical] controversial   also, on the other
hand, I] besides, I   27 arguments too.] arguments.   30–31 controversial …
latter.] evangelical.   33 thought, on the contrary, that] thought on the other
hand that   35 this supreme confidence] this confidence

came to pass at that time, that there was a double aspect in my bearing towards others, which it is necessary for me to enlarge upon. My behaviour had a mixture in it both of fierceness and of sport; and on this account, I dare say, it gave offence to many; nor am I here defending it.   5

I wished men to agree with me, and I walked with them step by step, as far as they would go; this I did sincerely; but if they would stop, I did not much care about it, but walked on, with some satisfaction that I had brought them so far. I liked to make them preach the truth without knowing it, and encouraged them   10 to do so. It was a satisfaction to me that the Record had allowed me to say so much in its columns, without remonstrance. I was amused to hear of one of the Bishops, who, on reading an early Tract on the Apostolical Succession, could not make up his mind whether he held the doctrine or not. I was not distressed at the   15 wonder or anger of dull and self-conceited men, at propositions which they did not understand. When a correspondent, in good faith, wrote to a newspaper, to say that the 'Sacrifice of the Holy Eucharist', spoken of in the Tract, was a false print for 'Sacrament', I thought the mistake too pleasant to be corrected before   20 I was asked about it. I was not unwilling to draw an opponent on step by step, by virtue of his own opinions, to the brink of some intellectual absurdity, and to leave him to get back as he could. I was not unwilling to play with a man, who asked me impertinent questions. I think I had in my mouth the words of   25 the Wise man, 'Answer a fool according to his folly', especially if he was prying or spiteful. I was reckless of the gossip which was circulated about me; and, when I might easily have set it right, did not deign to do so. Also I used irony in conversation, when matter-of-fact-men would not see what I meant.   30

This kind of behaviour was a sort of habit with me. If I have ever trifled with my subject, it was a more serious fault. I never used arguments which I saw clearly to be unsound. The nearest approach which I remember to such conduct, but which I consider was clear of it nevertheless, was in the case of Tract 15.   35 The matter of this Tract was furnished to me by a friend, to whom I had applied for assistance, but who did not wish to be mixed up with the publication. He gave it me, that I might throw it into shape, and I took his arguments as they stood. In the chief

22 step, by virtue . . . opinions, to] step to   36 furnished] supplied

portion of the Tract I fully agreed; for instance, as to what it says about the Council of Trent; but there were arguments, or some argument, in it which I did not follow; I do not recollect what it was. Froude, I think, was disgusted with the whole Tract, 5 and accused me of *economy* in publishing it. It is principally through Mr. Froude's Remains that this word has got into our language. I think, I defended myself with arguments such as these:—that, as every one knew, the Tracts were written by various persons who agreed together in their doctrine, but not 10 always in the arguments by which it was to be proved; that we must be tolerant of difference of opinion among ourselves; that the author of the Tract had a right to his own opinion, and that the argument in question was ordinarily received; that I did not give my own name or authority, nor was asked for my personal 15 belief, but only acted instrumentally, as one might translate a friend's book into a foreign language. I account these to be good arguments; nevertheless I feel also that such practices admit of easy abuse and are consequently dangerous; but then, again, I feel also this,—that if all such mistakes were to be severely visited, 20 not many men in public life would be left with a character for honour and honesty.

This absolute confidence in my cause, which led me to the negligence or wantonness which I have been instancing, also laid me open, not unfairly, to the opposite charge of fierceness in 25 certain steps which I took, or words which I published. In the Lyra Apostolica, I have said that before learning to love, we must 'learn to hate'; though I had explained my words by adding 'hatred of sin'. In one of my first Sermons I said, 'I do not shrink from uttering my firm conviction that it would be a gain to the 30 country were it vastly more superstitious, more bigoted, more gloomy, more fierce in its religion than at present it shows itself to be.' I added, of course, that it would be an absurdity to suppose such tempers of mind desirable in themselves. The corrector of the press bore these strong epithets till he got to 'more fierce', 35 and then he put in the margin a *query*. In the very first page of the first Tract, I said of the Bishops, that, 'black event though it would be for the country, yet we could not wish them a more blessed termination of their course, than the spoiling of their goods and martyrdom'. In consequence of a passage in my work

23 negligence] imprudence

upon the Arian History, a Northern dignitary wrote to accuse me of wishing to re-establish the blood and torture of the Inquisition. Contrasting heretics and heresiarchs, I had said, 'The latter should meet with no mercy: he assumes the office of the Tempter; and, so far forth as his error goes, must be dealt with by the competent authority, as if he were embodied evil. To spare him is a false and dangerous pity. It is to endanger the souls of thousands, and it is uncharitable towards himself.' I cannot deny that this is a very fierce passage; but Arius was banished, not burned; and it is only fair to myself to say that neither at this, nor any other time of my life, not even when I was fiercest, could I have even cut off a Puritan's ears, and I think the sight of a Spanish *auto-da-fè* would have been the death of me. Again, when one of my friends, of liberal and evangelical opinions, wrote to expostulate with me on the course I was taking, I said that we would ride over him and his, as Othniel prevailed over Chushan-rishathaim, king of Mesopotamia. Again, I would have no dealings with my brother, and I put my conduct upon a syllogism. I said, 'St. Paul bids us avoid those who cause divisions; you cause divisions: therefore I must avoid you.' I dissuaded a lady from attending the marriage of a sister who had seceded from the Anglican Church. No wonder that Blanco White, who had known me under such different circumstances, now hearing the general course that I was taking, was amazed at the change which he recognized in me. He speaks bitterly and unfairly of me in his letters contemporaneously with the first years of the Movement; but in 1839, on looking back, he uses terms of me, which it would be hardly modest in me to quote, were it not that what he says of me in praise occurs in the midst of blame. He says: 'In this party [the anti-Peel, in 1829] I found, to my great surprise, my dear friend, Mr. Newman of Oriel. As he had been one of the annual Petitioners to Parliament for Catholic Emancipation, his sudden union with the most violent bigots was inexplicable to me. That change was the first manifestation of the mental revolution, which has suddenly made him one of the leading persecutors of Dr. Hampden, and the most active and influential member of that association called the Puseyite party, from which we have those very strange productions, entitled, Tracts for the Times. While stating these public

27 on] when   29–30 occurs . . . blame.] is but part of a whole account of me.

facts, my heart feels a pang at the recollection of the affectionate and mutual friendship between that excellent man and myself; a friendship, which his principles of orthodoxy could not allow him to continue in regard to one, whom he now regards as
5 inevitably doomed to eternal perdition. Such is the venomous character of orthodoxy. What mischief must it create in a bad heart and narrow mind, when it can work so effectually for evil, in one of the most benevolent of bosoms, and one of the ablest of minds, in the amiable, the intellectual, the refined John Henry
10 Newman!' (Vol. iii. p. 131.) He adds that I would have nothing to do with him, a circumstance which I do not recollect, and very much doubt.

I have spoken of my firm confidence in my position; and now let me state more definitely what the position was which I took
15 up, and the propositions about which I was so confident. These were three:—

1. First was the principle of dogma: my battle was with liberalism; by liberalism I mean the anti-dogmatic principle and its developments. This was the first point on which I was certain.
20 Here I make a remark: persistence in a given belief is no sufficient test of its truth: but departure from it is at least a slur upon the man who has felt so certain about it. In proportion, then, as I had in 1832 a strong persuasion of the truth of opinions which I have since given up, so far a sort of guilt attaches to me, not
25 only for that vain confidence, but for all the various proceedings which were the consequence of it. But under this first head I have the satisfaction of feeling that I have nothing to retract, and nothing to repent of. The main principle of the movement is as dear to me now, as it ever was. I have changed in many things:
30 in this I have not. From the age of fifteen, dogma has been the fundamental principle of my religion: I know no other religion; I cannot enter into the idea of any other sort of religion; religion, as a mere sentiment, is to me a dream and a mockery. As well can there be filial love without the fact of a father, as devotion
35 without the fact of a Supreme Being. What I held in 1816, I held in 1833, and I hold in 1864. Please God, I shall hold it to the end. Even when I was under Dr. Whately's influence, I had no temp-

18 mean] meant   23 of the truth of opinions] in beliefs   25–26 all . . . were the] my multiform conduct in   26 under this first head] here

tation to be less zealous for the great dogmas of the faith, and at various times I used to resist such trains of thought on his part as seemed to me (rightly or wrongly) to obscure them. Such was the fundamental principle of the Movement of 1833.

2. Secondly, I was confident in the truth of a certain definite religious teaching, based upon this foundation of dogma; viz. that there was a visible Church, with sacraments and rites which are the channels of invisible grace. I thought that this was the doctrine of Scripture, of the early Church, and of the Anglican Church. Here again, I have not changed in opinion; I am as certain now on this point as I was in 1833, and have never ceased to be certain. In 1834 and the following years I put this ecclesiastical doctrine on a broader basis, after reading Laud, Bramhall, and Stillingfleet and other Anglican divines on the one hand, and after prosecuting the study of the Fathers on the other; but the doctrine of 1833 was strengthened in me, not changed. When I began the Tracts for the Times I rested the main doctrine, of which I am speaking, upon Scripture, on the Anglican Prayer Book, and on St. Ignatius's Epistles. (1) As to the existence of a visible Church, I especially argued out the point from Scripture, in Tract 11, viz. from the Acts of the Apostles and the Epistles. (2) As to the Sacraments and Sacramental rites, I stood on the Prayer Book. I appealed to the Ordination Service, in which the Bishop says, 'Receive the Holy Ghost'; to the Visitation Service, which teaches confession and absolution; to the Baptismal Service, in which the Priest speaks of the child after baptism as regenerate; to the Catechism, in which Sacramental Communion is receiving 'verily and indeed the Body and Blood of Christ'; to the Commination Service, in which we are told to do 'works of penance'; to the Collects, Epistles, and Gospels, to the calendar and rubrics, portions of the Prayer Book, wherein we find the festivals of the Apostles, notice of certain other Saints, and days of fasting and abstinence.

(3.) And further, as to the Episcopal system, I founded it upon the Epistles of St. Ignatius, which inculcated it in various ways. One passage especially impressed itself upon me: speaking of

cases of disobedience to ecclesiastical authority, he says, 'A man does not deceive that Bishop whom he sees, but he practises rather with the Bishop Invisible, and so the question is not with flesh, but with God, who knows the secret heart.' I wished to act
5 on this principle to the letter, and I may say with confidence that I never consciously transgressed it. I loved to act as feeling myself in my Bishop's sight, as if it were the sight of God. It was one of my special supports and safeguards against myself; I could not go very wrong while I had reason to believe that I was
10 in no respect displeasing him. It was not a mere formal obedience to rule that I put before me, but I desired to please him personally, as I considered him set over me by the Divine Hand. I was strict in observing my clerical engagements, not only because they *were* engagements, but because I considered myself simply as
15 the servant and instrument of my Bishop. I did not care much for the Bench of Bishops, except as they might be the voice of my Church: nor should I have cared much for a Provincial Council; nor for a Diocesan Synod presided over by my Bishop; all these matters seemed to me to be *jure ecclesiastico*, but what
20 to me was *jure divino* was the voice of my Bishop in his own person. My own Bishop was my Pope; I knew no other; the successor of the Apostles, the Vicar of Christ. This was but a practical exhibition of the Anglican theory of Church Government, as I had already drawn it out myself, after various Angli-
25 can Divines. This continued all through my course; when at length, in 1845, I wrote to Bishop Wiseman, in whose Vicariate I found myself, to announce my conversion, I could find nothing better to say to him than that I would obey the Pope as I had obeyed my own Bishop in the Anglican Church. My duty to him
30 was my point of honour; his disapprobation was the one thing which I could not bear. I believe it to have been a generous and honest feeling; and in consequence I was rewarded by having all my time for ecclesiastical superior a man, whom, had I had a choice, I should have preferred, out and out, to any other Bishop
35 on the Bench, and for whose memory I have a special affection, Dr. Bagot—a man of noble mind, and as kind-hearted and as

---

3 with the] upon the *64*; with the *another copy of 64* (*Ward*)   6–7 as feeling . . .
were] in the sight of my Bishop, as if I was, as it were, in   8 supports . . .
myself;] safeguards against myself and of my supports;   24–25 myself, after
. . . Divines.] myself.

considerate as he was noble. He ever sympathized with me in my
trials which followed; it was my own fault, that I was not brought
into more familiar personal relations with him, than it was my
happiness to be. May his name be ever blessed!

And now in concluding my remarks on the second point on 5
which my confidence rested, I repeat that here again I have no
retractation to announce as to its main outline. While I am now
as clear in my acceptance of the principle of dogma, as I was in
1833 and 1816, so again I am now as firm in my belief of a visible
Church, of the authority of Bishops, of the grace of the sacra- 10
ments, of the religious worth of works of penance, as I was in
1833. I have added Articles to my Creed; but the old ones, which
I then held with a divine faith, remain.

3. But now, as to the third point on which I stood in 1833, and
which I have utterly renounced and trampled upon since,—my 15
then view of the Church of Rome;—I will speak about it as
exactly as I can. When I was young, as I have said already, and
after I was grown up, I thought the Pope to be Antichrist. At
Christmas 1824–5 I preached a sermon to that effect. But in 1827
I accepted eagerly the stanza in the Christian Year, which many 20
people thought too charitable, 'Speak *gently* of thy sister's fall.'
From the time that I knew Froude I got less and less bitter on
the subject. I spoke (successively, but I cannot tell in what order
or at what dates) of the Roman Church as being bound up with
'the *cause* of Antichrist', as being *one* of the '*many* antichrists' 25
foretold by St. John, as being influenced by 'the *spirit* of Antichrist', and as having something 'very Antichristian' or 'unchristian' about her. From my boyhood and in 1824 I considered,
after Protestant authorities, that St. Gregory I. about A.D. 600
was the first Pope that was Antichrist, though, in spite of this, 30
he was also a great and holy man; but in 1832–3 I thought the
Church of Rome was bound up with the cause of Antichrist by
the Council of Trent. When it was that in my deliberate judgment I gave up the notion altogether in any shape, that some
special reproach was attached to her name, I cannot tell; but I 35
had a shrinking from renouncing it, even when my reason so
ordered me, from a sort of conscience or prejudice, I think up to
1843. Moreover, at least during the Tract Movement, I thought

the essence of her offence to consist in the honours which she paid to the Blessed Virgin and the Saints; and the more I grew in devotion, both to the Saints and to our Lady, the more impatient was I at the Roman practices, as if those glorified creations of 5 God must be gravely shocked, if pain could be theirs, at the undue veneration of which they were the objects.

On the other hand, Hurrell Froude in his familiar conversations was always tending to rub the idea out of my mind. In a passage of one of his letters from abroad, alluding, I suppose, to 10 what I used to say in opposition to him, he observes: 'I think people are injudicious who talk against the Roman Catholics for worshipping Saints, and honouring the Virgin and images, &c. These things may perhaps be idolatrous; I cannot make up my mind about it; but to my mind it is the Carnival that is real 15 practical idolatry, as it is written, "the people sat down to eat and drink, and rose up to play".' The Carnival, I observe in passing, is, in fact, one of those very excesses, to which, for at least three centuries, religious Catholics have ever opposed themselves, as we see in the life of St. Philip, to say nothing of the 20 present day; but this we did not then know. Moreover, from Froude I learned to admire the great medieval Pontiffs; and, of course, when I had come to consider the Council of Trent to be the turning-point of the history of Christian Rome, I found myself as free, as I was rejoiced, to speak in their praise. Then, 25 when I was abroad, the sight of so many great places, venerable shrines, and noble churches, much impressed my imagination. And my heart was touched also. Making an expedition on foot across some wild country in Sicily, at six in the morning, I came upon a small church; I heard voices, and I looked in. It was 30 crowded, and the congregation was singing. Of course it was the mass, though I did not know it at the time. And, in my weary days at Palermo, I was not ungrateful for the comfort which I had received in frequenting the churches; nor did I ever forget it. Then, again, her zealous maintenance of the doctrine and the 35 rule of celibacy, which I recognized as Apostolic, and her faithful agreement with Antiquity in so many other points which were dear to me, was an argument as well as a plea in favour of the great Church of Rome. Thus I learned to have tender feelings

20 we did not then know.] he did not know.   31 mass] Mass   36 other points] points besides,

towards her; but still my reason was not affected at all. My judgment was against her, when viewed as an institution, as truly as it ever had been.

This conflict between reason and affection I expressed in one of the early Tracts, published July, 1834. 'Considering the high 5 gifts and the strong claims of the Church of Rome and its dependencies on our admiration, reverence, love, and gratitude; how could we withstand it, as we do, how could we refrain from being melted into tenderness, and rushing into communion with it, but for the words of Truth itself, which bid us prefer It to the whole 10 world? "He that loveth father or mother more than Me, is not worthy of me." How could "we learn to be severe, and execute judgment", but for the warning of Moses against even a divinely-gifted teacher, who should preach new gods; and the anathema of St. Paul even against Angels and Apostles, who should bring 15 in a new doctrine'?—*Records*, No. 24. My feeling was something like that of a man, who is obliged in a court of justice to bear witness against a friend; or like my own now, when I have said, and shall say, so many things on which I had rather be silent.

As a matter, then, of simple conscience, though it went against 20 my feelings, I felt it to be a duty to protest against the Church of Rome. But besides this, it was a duty, because the prescription of such a protest was a living principle of my own Church, as expressed not simply in a *catena*, but by a *consensus* of her divines, and by the voice of her people. Moreover, such a protest 25 was necessary as an integral portion of her controversial basis; for I adopted the argument of Bernard Gilpin, that Protestants 'were *not able* to give any *firm and solid* reason of the separation besides this, to wit, that the Pope is Antichrist'. But while I thus thought such a protest to be based upon truth, and to be a 30 religious duty, and a rule of Anglicanism, and a necessity of the case, I did not at all like the work. Hurrell Froude attacked me for doing it; and, besides, I felt that my language had a vulgar and rhetorical look about it. I believed, and really measured, my words, when I used them; but I knew that I had a temptation, 35 on the other hand, to say against Rome as much as ever I could, in order to protect myself against the charge of Popery.

And now I come to the very point, for which I have introduced the subject of my feelings about Rome. I felt such confidence in

24 not simply in] in not simply   but by a] but a   25 and by the] and the

the substantial justice of the charges which I advanced against her, that I considered them to be a safeguard and an assurance that no harm could ever arise from the freest exposition of what I used to call Anglican principles. All the world was astounded
5 at what Froude and I were saying: men said that it was sheer Popery. I answered, 'True, we seem to be making straight for it; but go on awhile, and you will come to a deep chasm across the path, which makes real approximation impossible.' And I urged in addition, that many Anglican divines had been accused of
10 Popery, yet had died in their Anglicanism;—now, the ecclesiastical principles which I professed, they had professed also; and the judgment against Rome which they had formed, I had formed also. Whatever deficiencies then had to be supplied in the existing Anglican system, and however boldly I might point
15 them out, any how that system would not in the process be brought nearer to the special creed of Rome, and might be mended in spite of her. In that very agreement of the two forms of faith, close as it might seem, would really be found, on examination, the elements and principles of an essential discor-
20 dance.

It was with this absolute persuasion on my mind that I fancied that there could be no rashness in giving to the world in fullest measure the teaching and the writings of the Fathers. I thought that the Church of England was substantially founded upon
25 them. I did not know all that the Fathers had said, but I felt that, even when their tenets happened to differ from the Anglican, no harm could come of reporting them. I said out what I was clear they had said; I spoke vaguely and imperfectly, of what I thought they said, or what some of them had said. Any how, no
30 harm could come of bending the crooked stick the other way, in the process of straightening it; it was impossible to break it. If there was any thing in the Fathers of a startling character, this would be only for a time; it would admit of explanation, or it might suggest something profitable to Anglicans; it could not
35 lead to Rome. I express this view of the matter in a passage of the Preface to the first volume, which I edited, of the Library

13–14 Whatever deficiencies ... system,] Whatever faults then the Anglican system might have,   15–16 would not . . . Rome,] was not vulnerable on the side of Rome,   21 absolute] supreme   32 this] it   33–34 explanation, or . . . Anglicans; it] explanation; it of the Fathers. Speaking of the strangeness at first sight, in the judgment of the present day, of some of their principles and opinions, I bid the reader go forward hopefully, and not indulge his criticism till he knows more about them, than he will learn at the outset. 'Since the evil', I say, 'is in the nature of the case itself, we can do no more than have patience, and recommend patience to others, and with the racer in the Tragedy, look forward steadily and hopefully to the *event*, τῷ τέλει πίστιν φέρων, when, as we trust, all that is inharmonious and anomalous in the details, will at length be practically smoothed.'

Such was the position, such the defences, such the tactics, by which I thought that it was both incumbent on us, and possible for us, to meet that onset of Liberal principles, of which we were all in immediate anticipation, whether in the Church or in the University. And during the first year of the Tracts, the attack upon the University began. In November, 1834, was sent to me by Dr. Hampden the second edition of his Pamphlet, entitled, 'Observations on Religious Dissent, with particular reference to the use of religious tests in the University'. In this Pamphlet it was maintained, that 'Religion is distinct from Theological Opinion', pp. 1, 28, 30, &c.; that it is but a common prejudice to identify theological propositions methodically deduced and stated, with the simple religion of Christ, p. 1; that under Theological Opinion were to be placed the Trinitarian doctrine, p. 27, and the Unitarian, p. 19; that a dogma was a theological opinion formally insisted on, pp. 20, 21; that speculation always left an opening for improvement, p. 22; that the Church of England was not dogmatic in its spirit, though the wording of its formularies might often carry the sound of dogmatism, p. 23.

I acknowledged the receipt of this work in the following letter:—

'The kindness which has led to your presenting me with your late Pamphlet, encourages me to hope that you will forgive me, if I take the opportunity it affords of expressing to you my very sincere and deep regret that it has been published. Such an opportunity I could not let slip without being unfaithful to my own serious thoughts on the subject.

'While I respect the tone of piety which the Pamphlet displays,

---

1–2 in . . . day] presented to the Anglican mind   13 for] to   17 Dr. Hampden] the author *64–68*   his] a *64–68*   26 opinion formally insisted] opinion insisted   29 might] may

I dare not trust myself to put on paper my feelings about the principles contained in it; tending as they do, in my opinion, altogether to make shipwreck of Christian faith. I also lament, that, by its appearance, the first step has been taken towards
5 interrupting that peace and mutual good understanding which has prevailed so long in this place, and which, if once seriously disturbed, will be succeeded by dissensions the more intractable, because justified in the minds of those who resist innovation by a feeling of imperative duty.'

10 Since that time Phaeton has got into the chariot of the sun; we, alas! can only look on, and watch him down the steep of heaven. Meanwhile, the lands, which he is passing over, suffer from his driving.

Such was the commencement of the assault of Liberalism upon
15 the old orthodoxy of Oxford and England; and it could not have been broken, as it was, for so long a time, had not a great change taken place in the circumstances of that counter-movement which had already started with the view of resisting it. For myself, I was not the person to take the lead of a party; I never
20 was, from first to last, more than a leading author of a school; nor did I ever wish to be anything else. This is my own account of the matter; and I say it, neither as intending to disown the responsibility of what was done, or as if ungrateful to those who at that time made more of me than I deserved, and did more for
25 my sake and at my bidding than I realized myself. I am giving my history from my own point of sight, and it is as follows:—I had lived for ten years among my personal friends; the greater part of the time, I had been influenced, not influencing; and at no time have I acted on others, without their acting upon me.
30 As is the custom of a University, I had lived with my private, nay, with some of my public, pupils, and with the junior fellows of my College, without form or distance, on a footing of equality. Thus it was through friends, younger, for the most part, than myself, that my principles were spreading. They heard what I
35 said in conversation, and told it to others. Under-graduates in due time took their degree, and became private tutors themselves. In their new *status*, they in turn preached the opinions,

23 or] nor   35 Under-graduates] Undergraduates   37 their] this they
in turn] in turn, they

with which they had already become acquainted. Others went down to the country, and became curates of parishes. Then they had down from London parcels of the Tracts, and other publications. They placed them in the shops of local booksellers, got them into newspapers, introduced them to clerical meetings, and 5 converted more or less their Rectors and their brother curates. Thus the Movement, viewed with relation to myself, was but a floating opinion; it was not a power. It never would have been a power, if it had remained in my hands. Years after, a friend, writing to me in remonstrance at the excesses, as he thought them, 10 of my disciples, applied to me my own verse about St. Gregory Nazianzen, 'Thou couldst a people raise, but couldst not rule.' At the time that he wrote to me, I had special impediments in the way of such an exercise of power; but at no time could I exercise over others that authority, which under the circumstances was 15 imperatively required. My great principle ever was, Live and let live. I never had the staidness or dignity necessary for a leader. To the last I never recognized the hold I had over young men. Of late years I have read and heard that they even imitated me in various ways. I was quite unconscious of it, and I think my 20 immediate friends knew too well how disgusted I should be at such proceedings, to have the heart to tell me. I felt great impatience at our being called a party, and would not allow that we were such. I had a lounging, free-and-easy way of carrying things on. I exercised no sufficient censorship upon the Tracts. 25 I did not confine them to the writings of such persons as agreed in all things with myself; and, as to my own Tracts, I printed on them a notice to the effect, that any one who pleased, might make what use he would of them, and reprint them with alterations if he chose, under the conviction that their main scope could not 30 be damaged by such a process. It was the same with me afterwards, as regards other publications. For two years I furnished a certain number of sheets for the British Critic from myself and my friends, while a gentleman was editor, a man of splendid talent, who, however, was scarcely an acquaintance of mine, and 35 had no sympathy with the Tracts. When I was Editor myself, from 1838 to 1841, in my very first number I suffered to appear

p. 62, l. 37–1 opinions, with . . . acquainted.] opinions which they had already learned themselves.   22 such proceedings] the news   24 were such.] were.   31–32 same with me afterwards] same afterwards

a critique unfavorable to my work on Justification, which had been published a few months before, from a feeling of propriety, because I had put the book into the hands of the writer who so handled it. Afterwards I suffered an article against the Jesuits to
5 appear in it, of which I did not like the tone. When I had to provide a curate for my new church at Littlemore, I engaged a friend, by no fault of his, who, before he had entered into his charge, preached a sermon, either in depreciation of baptismal regeneration, or of Dr. Pusey's view of it. I showed a similar
10 easiness as to the Editors who helped me in the separate volumes of Fleury's Church History; they were able, learned, and excellent men, but their after-history has shown, how little my choice of them was influenced by any notion I could have had of any intimate agreement of opinion between them and myself. I shall
15 have to make the same remark in its place concerning the Lives of the English Saints, which subsequently appeared. All this may seem inconsistent with what I have said of my fierceness. I am not bound to account for it; but there have been men before me, fierce in act, yet tolerant and moderate in their reasonings; at
20 least, so I read history. However, such was the case, and such its effect upon the Tracts. These at first starting were short, hasty, and some of them ineffective; and at the end of the year, when collected into a volume, they had a slovenly appearance.

It was under these circumstances, that Dr. Pusey joined us.
25 I had known him well since 1827–8, and had felt for him an enthusiastic admiration. I used to call him ὁ μέγας. His great learning, his immense diligence, his scholarlike mind, his simple devotion to the cause of religion, overcame me; and great of course was my joy, when in the last days of 1833 he showed a
30 disposition to make common cause with us. His Tract on Fasting appeared as one of the series with the date of December 21. He was not, however, I think, fully associated in the Movement till 1835 and 1836, when he published his Tract on Baptism, and started the Library of the Fathers. He at once gave to us a
35 position and a name. Without him we should have had little chance, especially at the early date of 1834, of making any serious resistance to the Liberal aggression. But Dr. Pusey was a Professor and Canon of Christ Church; he had a vast influence in consequence of his deep religious seriousness, the munificence

7 he had entered] he entered　　　35 little] no

of his charities, his Professorship, his family connexions, and his
easy relations with University authorities. He was to the Movement all that Mr. Rose might have been, with that indispensable
addition, which was wanting to Mr. Rose, the intimate friendship and the familiar daily society of the persons who had com- 5
menced it. And he had that special claim on their attachment,
which lies in the living presence of a faithful and loyal affec-
tionateness. There was henceforth a man who could be the head
and centre of the zealous people in every part of the country, who
were adopting the new opinions; and not only so, but there was 10
one who furnished the Movement with a front to the world, and
gained for it a recognition from other parties in the University.
In 1829, Mr. Froude, or Mr. Robert Wilberforce, or Mr. Newman
were but individuals; and, when they ranged themselves in the
contest of that year on the side of Sir Robert Inglis, men on 15
either side only asked with surprise how they got there, and
attached no significancy to the fact; but Dr. Pusey was, to use
the common expression, a host in himself; he was able to give
a name, a form, and a personality, to what was without him a
sort of mob; and when various parties had to meet together in 20
order to resist the liberal acts of the Government, we of the
Movement took our place by right among them.

Such was the benefit which he conferred on the Movement
externally; nor were the internal advantages at all inferior to it.
He was a man of large designs; he had a hopeful, sanguine mind; 25
he had no fear of others; he was haunted by no intellectual perplexities. People are apt to say that he was once nearer to the
Catholic Church than he is now; I pray God that he may be one
day far nearer to the Catholic Church than he was then; for I
believe that, in his reason and judgment, all the time that I knew 30
him, he never was near to it at all. When I became a Catholic,
I was often asked, 'What of Dr. Pusey?' when I said that I did
not see symptoms of his doing as I had done, I was sometimes
thought uncharitable. If confidence in his position is, (as it is,)
a first essential in the leader of a party, this Dr. Pusey possessed 35
pre-eminently. The most remarkable instance of this, was his
statement, in one of his subsequent defences of the Movement,
when moreover it had advanced a considerable way in the

13 Robert] R.   24 were...advantages] was...advantage   35–36 this...
pre-eminently.] Dr. Pusey had it.   38 moreover] too
811840   F

direction of Rome, that among its more hopeful peculiarities was its 'stationariness'. He made it in good faith; it was his subjective view of it.

Dr. Pusey's influence was felt at once. He saw that there ought
5 to be more sobriety, more gravity, more careful pains, more sense of responsibility in the Tracts and in the whole Movement. It was through him that the character of the Tracts was changed. When he gave to us his Tract on Fasting, he put his initials to it. In 1835 he published his elaborate Treatise on Baptism, which
10 was followed by other Tracts from different authors, if not of equal learning, yet of equal power and appositeness. The Catenas of Anglican divines, projected by me, which occur in the Series, were executed with a like aim at greater accuracy and method. In 1836 he advertised his great project for a Translation of the
15 Fathers:—but I must return to myself. I am not writing the history either of Dr. Pusey or of the Movement; but it is a pleasure to me to have been able to introduce here reminiscences of the place which he held in it, which have so direct a bearing on myself, that they are no digression from my narrative.

20   I suspect it was Dr. Pusey's influence and example which set me, and made me set others, on the larger and more careful works in defence of the principles of the Movement which followed in a course of years,—some of them demanding and receiving from their authors, such elaborate treatment that they
25 did not make their appearance till both its temper and its fortunes had changed. I set about a work at once; one in which was brought out with precision the relation in which we stood to the Church of Rome. We could not move a step in comfort, till this was done. It was of absolute necessity and a plain duty from the
30 first, to provide as soon as possible a large statement, which would encourage and reassure our friends, and repel the attacks of our opponents. A cry was heard on all sides of us, that the Tracts and the writings of the Fathers would lead us to become Catholics, before we were aware of it. This was loudly expressed
35 by members of the Evangelical party, who in 1836 had joined us in making a protest in Convocation against a memorable

1 its more hopeful] its hopeful *64*; its most hopeful *another copy of 64* (*Ward*)
12 divines, projected . . . Series,] divines which occur in the Series, though projected, I think, by me,   29–30 duty from the first, to] duty, to

appointment of the Prime Minister. These clergymen even then avowed their desire, that the next time they were brought up to Oxford to give a vote, it might be in order to put down the Popery of the Movement. There was another reason still, and quite as important. Monsignore Wiseman, with the acuteness 5 and zeal which might be expected from that great Prelate, had anticipated what was coming, had returned to England by 1836, had delivered Lectures in London on the doctrines of Catholicism, and created an impression through the country, shared in by ourselves, that we had for our opponents in controversy, not 10 only our brethren, but our hereditary foes. These were the circumstances, which led to my publication of 'The Prophetical office of the Church viewed relatively to Romanism and Popular Protestantism'.

This work employed me for three years, from the beginning 15 of 1834 to the end of 1836, and was published in 1837. It was composed, after a careful consideration and comparison of the principal Anglican divines of the 17th century. It was first written in the shape of controversial correspondence with a learned French Priest; then it was re-cast, and delivered in 20 Lectures at St. Mary's; lastly, with considerable retrenchments and additions, it was rewritten for publication.

It attempts to trace out the rudimental lines on which Christian faith and teaching proceed, and to use them as means of determining the relation of the Roman and Anglican systems to each 25 other. In this way it shows that to confuse the two together is impossible, and that the Anglican can be as little said to tend to the Roman, as the Roman to the Anglican. The spirit of the Volume is not so gentle to the Church of Rome, as Tract 71 published the year before; on the contrary, it is very fierce; and 30 this I attribute to the circumstance that the Volume is theological and didactic, whereas the Tract, being controversial, assumes as little and grants as much as possible on the points in dispute, and insists on points of agreement as well as of difference. A further and more direct reason is, that in my Volume I deal with 35 'Romanism' (as I call it), not so much in its formal decrees and in the substance of its creed, as in its traditional action and its authorized teaching as represented by its prominent writers;— whereas the Tract is written as if discussing the differences of the

7 by] in   16: 1836, and . . . 1837.] 1836.

Churches with a view to a reconciliation between them. There is a further reason too, which I will state presently.

But this Volume had a larger scope than that of opposing the Roman system. It was an attempt at commencing a system of 5 theology on the Anglican idea, and based upon Anglican authorities. Mr. Palmer, about the same time, was projecting a work of a similar nature in his own way. It was published, I think, under the title, 'A Treatise on the Christian Church'. As was to be expected from the author, it was a most learned, most careful 10 composition; and in its form, I should say, polemical. So happily at least did he follow the logical method of the Roman Schools, that Father Perrone in his Treatise on dogmatic theology, recognized in him a combatant of the true cast, and saluted him as a foe worthy of being vanquished. Other soldiers in that field he 15 seems to have thought little better than the *Lanzknechts* of the middle ages, and, I dare say, with very good reason. When I knew that excellent and kind-hearted man at Rome at a later time, he allowed me to put him to ample penance for those light thoughts of me, which he had once had, by encroaching on his 20 valuable time with my theological questions. As to Mr. Palmer's book, it was one which no Anglican could write but himself,— in no sense, if I recollect aright, a tentative work. The ground of controversy was cut into squares, and then every objection had its answer. This is the proper method to adopt in teaching 25 authoritatively young men; and the work in fact was intended for students in theology. My own book, on the other hand, was of a directly tentative and empirical character. I wished to build up an Anglican theology out of the stores which already lay cut and hewn upon the ground, the past toil of great divines. To do 30 this could not be the work of one man; much less, could it be at once received into Anglican theology, however well it was done. This I fully recognized; and, while I trusted that my statements of doctrine would turn out to be true and important, still I wrote, to use the common phrase, 'under correction'.

35 There was another motive for my publishing, of a personal nature, which I think I should mention. I felt then, and all along felt, that there was an intellectual cowardice in not finding a basis in reason for my belief, and a moral cowardice in not avowing

32–33 This I fully . . . still] I fully trusted that my statement of doctrine would turn out true and important; yet   37 finding] having that basis. I should have felt myself less than a man, if I did not bring it out, whatever it was. This is one principal reason why I wrote and published the 'Prophetical Office'. It was from the same feeling, that in the spring of 1836, at a meeting of residents on the subject of the struggle then proceeding against a Whig 5 appointment, when some one wanted us all merely to act on college and conservative grounds (as I understood him), with as few published statements as possible, I answered, that the person whom we were resisting had committed himself in writing, and that we ought to commit ourselves too. This again was a main 10 reason for the publication of Tract 90. Alas! it was my portion for whole years to remain without any satisfactory basis for my religious profession, in a state of moral sickness, neither able to acquiesce in Anglicanism, nor able to go to Rome. But I bore it, till in course of time my way was made clear to me. If here it be 15 objected to me, that as time went on, I often in my writings hinted at things which I did not fully bring out, I submit for consideration whether this occurred except when I was in great difficulties, how to speak, or how to be silent, with due regard for the position of mind or the feelings of others. However, I may 20 have an opportunity to say more on this subject. But to return to the 'Prophetical Office'.

I thus speak in the Introduction to my Volume:—

'It is proposed', I say, 'to offer helps towards the formation of a recognized Anglican theology in one of its departments. The 25 present state of our divinity is as follows: the most vigorous, the clearest, the most fertile minds, have through God's mercy been employed in the service of our Church: minds too as reverential and holy, and as fully imbued with Ancient Truth, and as well versed in the writings of the Fathers, as they were intellectually 30 gifted. This is God's great mercy indeed, for which we must ever be thankful. Primitive doctrine has been explored for us in every direction, and the original principles of the Gospel and the Church patiently brought to light. But one thing is still wanting: our champions and teachers have lived in stormy times: political and 35 other influences have acted upon them variously in their day, and have since obstructed a careful consolidation of their judgments. We have a vast inheritance, but no inventory of our treasures. All is given us in profusion; it remains for us to catalogue,

3 from] on   5–6 proceeding . . . when some one] proceeding, some one

sort, distribute, select, harmonize, and complete. We have more than we know how to use; stores of learning, but little that is precise and serviceable; Catholic truth and individual opinion, first principles and the guesses of genius, all mingled in the same
5 works, and requiring to be discriminated. We meet with truths overstated or misdirected, matters of detail variously taken, facts incompletely proved or applied, and rules inconsistently urged or discordantly interpreted. Such indeed is the state of every deep philosophy in its first stages, and therefore of theological
10 knowledge. What we need at present for our Church's well-being, is not invention, nor originality, nor sagacity, nor even learning in our divines, at least in the first place, though all gifts of God are in a measure needed, and never can be unseasonable when used religiously, but we need peculiarly a sound judgment,
15 patient thought, discrimination, a comprehensive mind, an abstinence from all private fancies and caprices and personal tastes,—in a word, Divine Wisdom.'

The subject of the Volume is the doctrine of the *Via Media*, a name which had already been applied to the Anglican system
20 by writers of repute. It is an expressive title, but not altogether satisfactory, because it is at first sight negative. This had been the reason of my dislike to the word 'Protestant'; viz. it did not denote the profession of any particular religion at all, and was compatible with infidelity. A *Via Media* was but a receding from
25 extremes—therefore it needed to be drawn out into a definite shape and character: before it could have claims on our respect, it must first be shown to be one, intelligible, and consistent. This was the first condition of any reasonable treatise on the *Via Media*. The second condition, and necessary too, was not in my
30 power. I could only hope that it would one day be fulfilled. Even if the *Via Media* were ever so positive a religious system, it was not as yet objective and real; it had no original any where of which it was the representative. It was at present a paper religion. This I confess in my Introduction; I say, 'Protestantism
35 and Popery are real religions . . . but the *Via Media*, viewed as an integral system, has scarcely had existence except on paper.'

20 repute] name *64–82*   22–23 viz. . . . religion] in the idea which it conveyed, it was not the profession of any religion   25–26 extremes—therefore . . . character:] extremes, therefore I had to draw it out into a shape, and a character; 26 could have] had

I grant the objection, though I endeavour to lessen it:—'It still remains to be tried, whether what is called Anglo-Catholicism, the religion of Andrewes, Laud, Hammond, Butler, and Wilson, is capable of being professed, acted on, and maintained on a large sphere of action, or whether it be a mere modification or 5 transition-state of either Romanism or popular Protestantism.' I trusted that some day it would prove to be a substantive religion.

Lest I should be misunderstood, let me observe that this hesitation about the validity of the theory of the *Via Media* 10 implied no doubt of the three fundamental points on which it was based, as I have described them above, dogma, the sacramental system, and anti-Romanism.

Other investigations which had to be followed up were of a still more tentative character. The basis of the *Via Media*, con- 15 sisting of the three elementary points, which I have just mentioned, was clear enough; but, not only had the house itself to be built upon them, but it had also to be furnished, and it is not wonderful if, after building it, both I and others erred in detail in determining what its furniture should be, what was consistent 20 with the style of building, and what was in itself desirable. I will explain what I mean.

I had brought out in the 'Prophetical Office' in what the Roman and the Anglican systems differed from each other, but less distinctly in what they agreed. I had indeed enumerated the 25 Fundamentals, common to both, in the following passage:—'In both systems the same Creeds are acknowledged. Besides other points in common, we both hold, that certain doctrines are necessary to be believed for salvation; we both believe in the doctrines of the Trinity, Incarnation, and Atonement; in original 30 sin; in the necessity of regeneration; in the supernatural grace of the Sacraments; in the Apostolical succession; in the obligation of faith and obedience, and in the eternity of future punishment',—pp. 55, 56. So much I had said, but I had not said enough. This enumeration implied a great many more points of 35 agreement than were found in those very Articles which were

1 objection, . . . 'It still] objection and proceed to lessen it. There I say, 'It still
12 described them above] described above   13 anti-Romanism.] opposition to
the Church of Rome.   14–15 Other . . . character.] Other investigations which
followed, gave a still more tentative character to what I wrote or got written.
17 house itself to] house to   19 if, after building it, both] if both   20 its] that

fundamental. If the two Churches were thus the same in fundamentals, they were also one and the same in such plain consequences as were contained in those fundamentals and in such
natural observances as outwardly represented them. It was an
5 Anglican principle that 'the abuse of a thing doth not take away
the lawful use of it'; and an Anglican Canon in 1603 had
declared that the English Church had no purpose to forsake all
that was held in the Churches of Italy, France, and Spain, and
reverenced those ceremonies and particular points which were
10 Apostolic. Excepting then such exceptional matters, as are
implied in this avowal, whether they were many or few, all these
Churches were evidently to be considered as one with the Anglican. The Catholic Church in all lands had been one from the
first for many centuries; then, various portions had followed
15 their own way to the injury, but not to the destruction, whether
of truth or of charity. These portions or branches were mainly
three:—the Greek, Latin, and Anglican. Each of these inherited
the early undivided Church *in solido* as its own possession. Each
branch was identical with that early undivided Church, and in
20 the unity of that Church it had unity with the other branches.
The three branches agreed together in *all but* their later accidental errors. Some branches had retained in detail portions of
Apostolical truth and usage, which the others had not; and these
portions might be and should be appropriated again by the
25 others which had let them slip. Thus, the middle age belonged
to the Anglican Church, and much more did the middle age of
England. The Church of the 12th century was the Church of the
19th. Dr. Howley sat in the seat of St. Thomas the Martyr;
Oxford was a medieval University. Saving our engagements to
30 Prayer Book and Articles, we might breathe and live and act and
speak, as in the atmosphere and climate of Henry III.'s day, or
the Confessor's, or of Alfred's. And we ought to be indulgent to
all that Rome taught now, as to what Rome taught then, saving
our protest. We might boldly welcome, even what we did not
35 ourselves think right to adopt. And, when we were obliged on
the contrary boldly to denounce, we should do so with pain, not
with exultation. By very reason of our protest, which we had
made, and made *ex animo*, we could agree to differ. What the

3 were] are   3–4 and . . . them.] or as outwardly represented them.
31 speak, as in] speak, in   33 to] of

members of the Bible Society did on the basis of Scripture, we could do on the basis of the Church; Trinitarian and Unitarian were further apart than Roman and Anglican. Thus we had a real wish to co-operate with Rome in all lawful things, if she would let us, and if the rules of our own Church let us; and we thought there was no better way towards the restoration of doctrinal purity and unity. And we thought that Rome was not committed by her formal decrees to all that she actually taught: and again, if her disputants had been unfair to us, or her rulers tyrannical, we bore in mind that on our side too there had been rancour and slander in our controversial attacks upon her, and violence in our political measures. As to ourselves being direct instruments in improving her belief or practice, I used to say, 'Look at home; let us first, (or at least let us the while,) supply our own shortcomings, before we attempt to be physicians to any one else.' This is very much the spirit of Tract 71, to which I referred just now. I am well aware that there is a paragraph inconsistent with it in the Prospectus to the Library of the Fathers; but I do not consider myself responsible for it. Indeed, I have no intention whatever of implying that Dr. Pusey concurred in the ecclesiastical theory, which I have been now drawing out; nor that I took it up myself except by degrees in the course of ten years. It was necessarily the growth of time. In fact, hardly any two persons, who took part in the Movement, agreed in their view of the limit to which our general principles might religiously be carried.

And now I have said enough on what I consider to have been the general objects of the various works, which I wrote, edited, or prompted in the years which I am reviewing. I wanted to bring out in a substantive form a living Church of England, in a position proper to herself, and founded on distinct principles; as far as paper could do it, as far as earnestly preaching it and influencing others towards it, could tend to make it a fact;—a living Church, made of flesh and blood, with voice, complexion, and motion and action, and a will of its own. I believe I had no

5 and if the] and the   10 tyrannical, we bore in mind that] tyrannical, that
11 controversial attacks upon] controversy with   12-13 being direct instruments]
being instruments   13 her belief or practice] the belief or practice of Rome
directly   18 inconsistent with] contrary to   19 do . . . it.] never concurred
in it.   21-22 been now drawing] been drawing   28 works, which] works
which   29 reviewing. I] reviewing; I   32 it, as far] it, and

private motive, and no personal aim. Nor did I ask for more than 'a fair stage and no favour', nor expect the work would be accomplished in my days; but I thought that enough would be secured to continue it in the future, under, perhaps, more hopeful
5 circumstances and prospects than the present.

I will mention in illustration some of the principal works, doctrinal and historical, which originated in the object which I have stated.

I wrote my Essay on Justification in 1837; it was aimed at the
10 Lutheran dictum that justification by faith only was the cardinal doctrine of Christianity. I considered that this doctrine was either a paradox or a truism,—a paradox in Luther's mouth, a truism in Melanchthon's. I thought that the Anglican Church followed Melanchthon, and that in consequence between Rome
15 and Anglicanism, between high Church and low Church, there was no real intellectual difference on the point. I wished to fill up a ditch, the work of man. In this Volume again, I express my desire to build up a system of theology out of the Anglican divines, and imply that my dissertation was a tentative Inquiry.
20 I speak in the Preface of 'offering suggestions towards a work, which must be uppermost in the mind of every true son of the English Church at this day,—the consolidation of a theological system, which, built upon those formularies, to which all clergy-men are bound, may tend to inform, persuade, and absorb into
25 itself religious minds, which hitherto have fancied, that, on the peculiar Protestant questions, they were seriously opposed to each other'.—P. vii.

In my University Sermons there is a series of discussions upon the subject of Faith and Reason; these again were the tentative
30 commencement of a grave and necessary work, viz. an inquiry into the ultimate basis of religious faith, prior to the distinction into Creeds.

In like manner in a Pamphlet, which I published in the sum-mer of 1838, is an attempt at placing the doctrine of the Real
35 Presence on an intellectual basis. The fundamental idea is con-sonant to that to which I had been so long attached: it is the denial of the existence of space except as a subjective idea of our minds.

The Church of the Fathers is one of the earliest productions

3 accomplished] done   13 Melanchthon's] Melanchthon   30 work, viz.]
work; it was

of the Movement, and appeared in numbers in the British Magazine, being written with the aim of introducing the religious sentiments, views, and customs of the first ages into the modern Church of England.

The Translation of Fleury's Church History was commenced 5 under these circumstances:—I was fond of Fleury for a reason which I express in the Advertisement; because it presented a sort of photograph of ecclesiastical history without any comment upon it. In the event, that simple representation of the early centuries had a good deal to do with unsettling me in my Anglican- 10 ism; but how little I could anticipate this, will be seen in the fact that the publication of Fleury was a favourite scheme with Mr. Rose. He proposed it to me twice, between the years 1834 and 1837; and I mention it as one out of many particulars curiously illustrating how truly my change of opinion arose, not 15 from foreign influences, but from the working of my own mind, and the accidents around me. The date, from which the portion actually translated began, was determined by the Publisher on reasons with which we were not concerned.

Another historical work, but drawn from original sources, was 20 given to the world by my old friend Mr. Bowden, being a Life of Pope Gregory VII. I need scarcely recall to those who have read it, the power and the liveliness of the narrative. This composition was the author's relaxation, on evenings and in his summer vacations, from his ordinary engagements in London. 25 It had been suggested to him originally by me, at the instance of Hurrell Froude.

The Series of the Lives of the English Saints was projected at a later period, under circumstances which I shall have in the sequel to describe. Those beautiful compositions have nothing 30 in them, as far as I recollect, simply inconsistent with the general objects which I have been assigning to my labours in these years, though the immediate occasion which led to them, and the tone in which they were written, had little that was congenial with Anglicanism. 35

At a comparatively early date I drew up the Tract on the

---

2 being] and was   10–11 me in my Anglicanism;] me;   12 publication of Fleury was] publication was   12–13 with Mr. Rose.] of Mr. Rose's.   17 date, from] date at   33–35 which led ... Anglicanism.] of them and their tone could not in the exercise of the largest indulgence be said to have an Anglican direction.

Roman Breviary. It frightened my own friends on its first appearance; and several years afterwards, when younger men began to
translate for publication the four volumes *in extenso*, they were
dissuaded from doing so by advice to which from a sense of duty
5 they listened. It was an apparent accident, which introduced me
to the knowledge of that most wonderful and most attractive
monument of the devotion of saints. On Hurrell Froude's death,
in 1836, I was asked to select one of his books as a keepsake.
I selected Butler's Analogy; finding that it had been already
10 chosen, I looked with some perplexity along the shelves as they
stood before me, when an intimate friend at my elbow said, 'Take
that.' It was the Breviary which Hurrell had had with him at
Barbadoes. Accordingly I took it, studied it, wrote my Tract
from it, and have it on my table in constant use till this day.
15   That dear and familiar companion, who thus put the Breviary
into my hands, is still in the Anglican Church. So, too, is that
early venerated long-loved friend, together with whom I edited
a work which, more perhaps than any other, caused disturbance
and annoyance in the Anglican world,—Froude's Remains; yet,
20 however judgments might run as to the prudence of publishing
it, I never heard any one impute to Mr. Keble the very shadow
of dishonesty or treachery towards his Church in so acting.
The annotated Translation of the Treatises of St. Athanasius
was of course in no sense of a tentative character; it belongs to
25 another order of thought. This historico-dogmatic work employed me for years. I had made preparations for following it up
with a doctrinal history of the heresies which succeeded to the
Arian.
I should make mention also of the British Critic. I was Editor
30 of it for three years, from July 1838 to July 1841. My writers
belonged to various schools, some to none at all. The subjects are
various,—classical, academical, political, critical, and artistic, as
well as theological, and upon the Movement none are to be
found which do not keep quite clear of advocating the cause of
35 Rome.

So I went on for years up to 1841. It was, in a human point of
view, the happiest time of my life. I was truly at home. I had

20 judgments] judgment   23 Treatises] Treatise   24 of a tentative
character] a tentative work

in one of my volumes appropriated to myself the words of Bramhall, 'Bees, by the instinct of nature, do love their hives, and birds their nests.' I did not suppose that such sunshine would last, though I knew not what would be its termination. It was the time of plenty, and, during its seven years, I tried to 5 lay up as much as I could for the dearth which was to follow it. We prospered and spread. I have spoken of the doings of these years, since I was a Catholic, in a passage, part of which I will here quote:

'From beginnings so small,' I said, 'from elements of thought 10 so fortuitous, with prospects so unpromising, the Anglo-Catholic party suddenly became a power in the National Church, and an object of alarm to her rulers and friends. Its originators would have found it difficult to say what they aimed at of a practical kind: rather, they put forth views and principles for their own 15 sake, because they were true, as if they were obliged to say them; and, as they might be themselves surprised at their earnestness in uttering them, they had as great cause to be surprised at the success which attended their propagation. And, in fact, they could only say that those doctrines were in the air; that to assert 20 was to prove, and that to explain was to persuade; and that the Movement in which they were taking part was the birth of a crisis rather than of a place. In a very few years a school of opinion was formed, fixed in its principles, indefinite and pro-gressive in their range; and it extended itself into every part of 25 the country. If we inquire what the world thought of it, we have still more to raise our wonder; for, not to mention the excitement it caused in England, the Movement and its party-names were known to the police of Italy and to the back-woodmen of America. And so it proceeded, getting stronger and stronger every 30 year, till it came into collision with the Nation, and that Church of the Nation, which it began by professing especially to serve.'

The greater its success, the nearer was that collision at hand. The first threatenings of what was coming were heard in 1838. At that time, my Bishop in a Charge made some light anim- 35 adversions, but they *were* animadversions, on the Tracts for the Times. At once I offered to stop them. What took place on the occasion I prefer to state in the words, in which I related it in

8–9 will here quote:] will quote, though there is a sentence in it that requires some limitation: 34 what was coming] the crisis

a Pamphlet addressed to him in a later year, when the blow
actually came down upon me.

'In your Lordship's Charge for 1838', I said, 'an allusion was
made to the Tracts for the Times. Some opponents of the Tracts
5 said that you treated them with undue indulgence. . . . I wrote
to the Archdeacon on the subject, submitting the Tracts entirely
to your Lordship's disposal. What I thought about your Charge
will appear from the words I then used to him. I said, "A
Bishop's lightest word *ex cathedrâ* is heavy. His judgment on a
10 book cannot be light. It is a rare occurrence." And I offered to
withdraw any of the Tracts over which I had control, if I were
informed which were those to which your Lordship had objections. I afterwards wrote to your Lordship to this effect, that "I
trusted I might say sincerely, that I should feel a more lively
15 pleasure in knowing that I was submitting myself to your Lordship's expressed judgment in a matter of that kind, than I could
have even in the widest circulation of the volumes in question".
Your Lordship did not think it necessary to proceed to such a
measure, but I felt, and always have felt, that, if ever you deter-
20 mined on it, I was bound to obey.'

That day at length came, and I conclude this portion of my
narrative, with relating the circumstances of it.

From the time that I had entered upon the duties of Public
Tutor at my College, when my doctrinal views were very differ-
25 ent from what they were in 1841, I had meditated a comment
upon the Articles. Then, when the Movement was in its swing,
friends had said to me, 'What will you make of the Articles?'
but I did not share the apprehension which their question implied. Whether, as time went on, I should have been forced, by
30 the necessities of the original theory of the Movement, to put on
paper the speculations which I had about them, I am not able to
conjecture. The actual cause of my doing so, in the beginning
of 1841, was the restlessness, actual and prospective, of those who
neither liked the *Via Media*, nor my strong judgment against
35 Rome. I had been enjoined, I think by my Bishop, to keep these
men straight, and I wished so to do: but their tangible difficulty
was subscription to the Articles; and thus the question of the
Articles came before me. It was thrown in our teeth; 'How can
you manage to sign the Articles? they are directly against

Rome.' 'Against Rome?' I made answer, 'What do you mean by "Rome"?' and then I proceeded to make distinctions, of which I shall now give an account.

By 'Roman doctrine' might be meant one of three things: 1, the *Catholic teaching* of the early centuries; or 2, the *formal* 5 *dogmas of Rome* as contained in the later Councils, especially the Council of Trent, and as condensed in the Creed of Pope Pius IV.; 3, the *actual popular beliefs and usages* sanctioned by Rome in the countries in communion with it, over and above the dogmas; and these I called 'dominant errors'. Now Protestants 10 commonly thought that in all three senses, 'Roman doctrine' was condemned in the Articles: I thought that the *Catholic teaching* was not condemned; that the *dominant errors* were; and as to the *formal dogmas*, that some were, some were not, and that the line had to be drawn between them. Thus, 1. The use of Prayers 15 for the dead was a Catholic doctrine,—not condemned in the Articles; 2. The prison of Purgatory was a Roman dogma,— which was condemned in them; but the infallibility of Ecumenical Councils was a Roman dogma,—not condemned; and 3. The fire of Purgatory was an authorized and popular error, not a 20 dogma, which was condemned.

Further, I considered that the difficulties, felt by the persons whom I have mentioned, mainly lay in their mistaking, 1, Catholic teaching, which was not condemned in the Articles, for Roman dogma which was condemned; and 2, Roman dogma, which was 25 not condemned in the Articles, for dominant error which was. If they went further than this, I had nothing more to say to them.

A further motive which I had for my attempt, was the desire to ascertain the ultimate points of contrariety between the Roman and Anglican creeds, and to make them as few as possible. I 30 thought that each creed was obscured and misrepresented by a dominant circumambient 'Popery' and 'Protestantism'.

The main thesis then of my Essay was this:—the Articles do not oppose Catholic teaching; they but partially oppose Roman dogma; they for the most part oppose the dominant errors of 35 Rome. And the problem was, as I have said, to draw the line as to what they allowed and what they condemned.

Such being the object which I had in view, what were my

16–17 condemned in the Articles;] condemned;   18 condemned in them;] condemned;   36 was, as I have said, to] was to

prospects of widening and of defining their meaning ? The prospect was encouraging; there was no doubt at all of the elasticity
of the Articles: to take a palmary instance, the seventeenth was
assumed by one party to be Lutheran, by another Calvinistic,
5 though the two interpretations were contradictory of each other;
why then should not other Articles be drawn up with a vagueness
of an equally intense character ? I wanted to ascertain what was
the limit of that elasticity in the direction of Roman dogma. But
next, I had a way of inquiry of my own, which I state without
10 defending. I instanced it afterwards in my Essay on Doctrinal
Development. That work, I believe, I have not read since I published it, and I do not doubt at all I have made many mistakes
in it;—partly, from my ignorance of the details of doctrine, as the
Church of Rome holds them, but partly from my impatience to
15 clear as large a range for the *principle* of doctrinal Development
(waiving the question of historical *fact*) as was consistent with
the strict Apostolicity and identity of the Catholic Creed. In like
manner, as regards the 39 Articles, my method of inquiry was to
leap *in medias res*. I wished to institute an inquiry how far, in
20 critical fairness, the text *could* be opened; I was aiming far more
at ascertaining what a man who subscribed it might hold than
what he must, so that my conclusions were negative rather than
positive. It was but a first essay. And I made it with the full
recognition and consciousness, which I had already expressed in
25 my Prophetical Office, as regards the *Via Media*, that I was
making only 'a first approximation to the required solution';—
'a series of illustrations supplying hints for the removal' of a
difficulty, and with full acknowledgment 'that in minor points,
whether in question of fact or of judgment, there was room for
30 difference or error of opinion', and that I 'should not be ashamed
to own a mistake, if it were proved against me, nor reluctant to
bear the just blame of it'.—Proph. Off. p. 31.

I will add, I was embarrassed in consequence of my wish to go
as far as was possible in interpreting the Articles in the direction
35 of Roman dogma, without disclosing what I was doing to the
parties whose doubts I was meeting; who, if they understood at

1 and of defining] and defining　　　5 of] to　　　　12 do not doubt at all I
have] doubt not at all that I have　　　26 the] a　　　27 for] in　　　32 it'.—
Proph. Off. p. 31.] it'.—P. 31.　　　33 I will add] In addition　　　36–p. 81, l. 3 meeting;
who, if . . . go.] meeting, who might be thereby encouraged to go still further than
at present they found in themselves any call to do.

once the full extent of the licence which the Articles admitted, might be thereby encouraged to proceed still further than at present they found in themselves any call to go.

1. But in the way of such an attempt comes the prompt objection that the Articles were actually drawn up against 'Popery', and therefore it was transcendently absurd and dishonest to suppose that Popery, in any shape,—patristic belief, Tridentine dogma, or popular corruption authoritatively sanctioned,— would be able to take refuge under their text. This premiss I denied. Not any religious doctrine at all, but a political principle, was the primary English idea of 'Popery' at the date of the Reformation. And what was that political principle, and how could it best be suppressed in England? What was the great question in the days of Henry and Elizabeth? The *Supremacy*; —now, was I saying one single word in favour of the Supremacy of the Holy See, in favour of the foreign jurisdiction? No; I did not believe in it myself. Did Henry VIII. religiously hold Justification by faith only? did he disbelieve Purgatory? Was Elizabeth zealous for the marriage of the Clergy? or had she a conscience against the Mass? The Supremacy of the Pope was the essence of the 'Popery' to which, at the time of the composition of the Articles, the Supreme Head or Governor of the English Church was so violently hostile.

2. But again I said this:—let 'Popery' mean what it would in the mouths of the compilers of the Articles, let it even, for argument's sake, include the doctrines of that Tridentine Council, which was not yet over when the Articles were drawn up, and against which they could not be simply directed, yet, consider, what was the object of the Government in their imposition? merely to get rid of 'Popery'? No; it had the further object of gaining the 'Papists'. What then was the best way to induce reluctant or wavering minds, and these, I supposed, were the majority, to give in their adhesion to the new symbol? how had the Arians drawn up their Creeds? was it not on the principle of using vague ambiguous language, which to the subscribers would seem to bear a Catholic sense, but which, when worked

11–12 of 'Popery' . . . Reformation.] at that time of 'Popery'.   13 suppressed in] kept out of   16 See, in favour of the] See, of the   21–22 of the composition of the Articles] of the Articles   29 the object] the religious object   30 get rid of] disown

out on the long run, would prove to be heterodox? Accordingly, there was great antecedent probability, that, fierce as the Articles might look at first sight, their bark would prove worse than their bite. I say antecedent probability, for to what extent that
5 surmise might be true, could only be ascertained by investigation.

3. But a consideration came up at once, which threw light on this surmise:—what if it should turn out that the very men who drew up the Articles, in the very act of doing so, had avowed, or
10 rather in one of those very Articles themselves had imposed on subscribers, a number of those very 'Papistical' doctrines, which they were now thought to deny, as part and parcel of that very Protestantism, which they were now thought to consider divine? and this was the fact, and I showed it in my Essay.

15 Let the reader observe:—the 35th Article says: 'The second Book of Homilies doth contain *a godly and wholesome doctrine, and necessary for* these times, as doth the former Book of Homilies.' Here the *doctrine* of the Homilies is recognized as godly and wholesome, and concurrence in that recognition is imposed
20 on all subscribers of the Articles. Let us then turn to the Homilies, and see what this godly doctrine is: I quoted from them to the followng effect:

1. They declare that the so-called 'apocryphal' book of Tobit is the teaching of the Holy Ghost, and is Scripture.

25 2. That the so-called 'apocryphal' book of Wisdom is Scripture, and the infallible and undeceivable word of God.

3. That the Primitive Church, next to the Apostles' time, and, as they imply, for almost 700 years, is no doubt most pure.

4. That the Primitive Church is specially to be followed.

30 5. That the Four first General Councils belong to the Primitive Church.

6. That there are Six Councils which are allowed and received by all men.

7. Again, they speak of a certain truth, and say that it is
35 declared by God's word, the sentences of the ancient doctors, and judgment of the Primitive Church.

8. Of the learned and holy Bishops and doctors of the Church

1 on] in   19 concurrence in that recognition] subscription to that proposition
34–35 truth, and say . . . declared] truth which they are enforcing, as declared *64–*
68   37–p. 83, l. 1 doctors of the Church of the first] doctors of the first

of the first eight centuries being of great authority and credit with the people.

9. Of the declaration of Christ and His Apostles and all the rest of the Holy Fathers.

10. Of the authority both of Scripture and also of Augustine. 5

11. Of Augustine, Chrysostom, Ambrose, Jerome, and about thirty other Fathers, to some of whom they give the title of 'Saint', to others of 'ancient Catholic Fathers and doctors, &c.'

12. They declare that, not only the holy Apostles and disciples 10 of Christ, but the godly Fathers also, before and since Christ, were endued without doubt with the Holy Ghost.

13. That the ancient Catholic Fathers say that the 'Lord's Supper' is the salve of immortality, the sovereign preservative against death, the food of immortality, the healthful grace.   15

14. That the Lord's Blessed Body and Blood are received under the form of bread and wine.

15. That the meat in the Sacrament is an invisible meat and a ghostly substance.

16. That the holy Body and Blood of thy God ought to be 20 touched with the mind.

17. That Ordination is a Sacrament.

18. That Matrimony is a Sacrament.

19. That there are other Sacraments besides 'Baptism and the Lord's Supper', though not 'such as' they.   25

20. That the souls of the Saints are reigning in joy and in heaven with God.

21. That alms-deeds purge the soul from the infection and filthy spots of sin, and are a precious medicine, an inestimable jewel.   30

22. That mercifulness wipes out and washes away sins, as salves and remedies to heal sores and grievous diseases.

23. That the duty of fasting is a truth more manifest than it should need to be proved.

24. That fasting, used with prayer, is of great efficacy and 35 weigheth much with God; so the Angel Raphael told Tobias.

25. That the puissant and mighty Emperor Theodosius was,

---

1 great] good   5 both of] of both   20 Blood of thy God ought] Blood
ought   25 Supper', . . . they.] Supper'.   31 sins, as] infirmity and weakness as

in the Primitive Church which was most holy and godly, excommunicated by St. Ambrose.

26. That Constantine, Bishop of Rome, did condemn Philippicus, then Emperor, not without a cause indeed, but very justly.

5   Putting altogether aside the question how far these separate theses came under the matter to which subscription was to be made, it was quite plain, that in the minds of the men who wrote the Homilies, and who thus incorporated them into the Anglican system of doctrine, there was no such nice discrimination between

10 the Catholic and the Protestant faith, no such clear recognition of formal Protestant principles and tenets, no such accurate definition of 'Roman doctrine', as is received at the present day:— hence great probability accrued to my presentiment, that the Articles were tolerant, not only of what I called 'Catholic teach-

15 ing', but of much that was 'Roman'.

4. And here was another reason against the notion that the Articles directly attacked the Roman dogmas as declared at Trent and as promulgated by Pius the Fourth:—the Council of Trent was not over, nor its Canons promulgated at the date when

20 the Articles were drawn up,[1] so that those Articles must be aiming at something else. What was that something else? The Homilies tell us: the Homilies are the best comment upon the Articles. Let us turn to the Homilies, and we shall find from first to last that, not only is not the Catholic teaching of the first

25 centuries, but neither again are the dogmas of Rome, the objects of the protest of the compilers of the Articles, but the dominant errors, the popular corruptions, authorized or suffered by the high name of Rome. The eloquent declamation of the Homilies finds its matter almost exclusively in the dominant errors. As to

30 Catholic teaching, nay as to Roman dogma, of such theology

---

4 then] the   very] most   7 that in the minds of the men] that the men
9 there was no such nice] could not have possessed that exact   10 and the
Protestant] and Protestant   no such] or have made that   11–12 no such accurate definition] or have accepted that definition   12 as] which   the present]
this   19 Canons] Decrees   20 up,[1] *no footnote in 64*   28–29 The
eloquent . . . errors.] *not in 64*   30–p. 85, l. 1 dogma, of such theology
those] dogma, those

---

[1] The Pope's Confirmation of the Council, by which its Canons became *de fide*, and his Bull *super confirmatione* by which they were promulgated to the world, are dated January 26, 1564. The Articles are dated 1562.

those Homilies, as I have shown, contained no small portion themselves.

5. So much for the writers of the Articles and Homilies;— they were witnesses, not authorities, and I used them as such; but in the next place, who were the actual authorities imposing them? I reasonably considered the authority *imponens* to be the Convocation of 1571; but here again, it would be found that the very Convocation, which received and confirmed the 39 Articles, also enjoined by Canon that 'preachers should be *careful*, that they should *never* teach aught in a sermon, to be religiously held and believed by the people, except that which is agreeable to the doctrine of the Old and New Testament, and *which the Catholic Fathers and ancient Bishops have collected* from that very doctrine'. Here, let it be observed, an appeal is made by the Convocation *imponens* to the very same ancient authorities, as had been mentioned with such profound veneration by the writers of the Homilies and the Articles, and thus, if the Homilies contained views of doctrine which now would be called Roman, there seemed to me to be an extreme probability that the Convocation of 1571 also countenanced and received, or at least did not reject, those doctrines.

6. And further, when at length I came actually to look into the text of the Articles, I saw in many cases a patent justification of all that I had surmised as to their vagueness and indecisiveness, and that, not only on questions which lay between Lutherans, Calvinists, and Zuinglians, but on Catholic questions also; and I have noticed them in my Tract. In the conclusion of my Tract I observe: The Articles are 'evidently framed on the principle of leaving open large questions on which the controversy hinges. They state broadly extreme truths, and are silent about their adjustment. For instance, they say that all necessary faith must be proved from Scripture; but do not say *who* is to prove it. They say, that the Church has authority in controversies; they do not say *what* authority. They say that it may enforce nothing beyond Scripture, but do not say *where* the remedy lies when it does. They say that works *before* grace *and* justification are worthless and worse, and that works *after* grace *and* justification

1–2 portion themselves] portion of it themselves 6 I reasonably . . . to be] I considered the *imponens* to be 17 and the] and of the 23 justification] fulfilment 28 The Articles] They

are acceptable, but they do not speak at all of works *with* God's aid *before* justification. They say that men are lawfully called and sent to minister and preach, who are chosen and called by men who have public authority *given* them in the Congregation; but
5　they do not add *by whom* the authority is to be given. They say that Councils called by *princes* may err; they do not determine whether Councils called in the name of Christ may err.'

Such were the considerations which weighed with me in my inquiry how far the Articles were tolerant of a Catholic, or even
10　a Roman interpretation; and such was the defence which I made in my Tract for having attempted it. From what I have already said, it will appear that I have no need or intention at this day to maintain every particular interpretation which I suggested in the course of my Tract, nor indeed had I then. Whether it was
15　prudent or not, whether it was sensible or not, any how I attempted only a first essay of a necessary work, an essay which, as I was quite prepared to find, would require revision and modification by means of the lights which I should gain from the criticism of others. I should have gladly withdrawn any state-
20　ment, which could be proved to me to be erroneous; I considered my work to be faulty and open to objection in the same sense in which I now consider my Anglican interpretations of Scripture to be erroneous; but in no other sense. I am surprised that men do not apply to the interpreters of Scripture generally the hard
25　names which they apply to the author of Tract 90. He held a large system of theology, and applied it to the Articles: Episcopalians, or Lutherans, or Presbyterians, or Unitarians, hold a large system of theology and apply it to Scripture. Every theology has its difficulties; Protestants hold justification by faith only,
30　though there is no text in St. Paul which enunciates it, and though St. James expressly denies it; do we therefore call Protestants dishonest? they deny that the Church has a divine mission, though St. Paul says that it is 'the Pillar and ground of Truth'; they keep the Sabbath, though St. Paul says, 'Let no man judge
35　you in meat or drink or in respect of . . . the sabbath days.' Every creed has texts in its favour, and again texts which run counter to it: and this is generally confessed. And this is what I felt keenly:—how had I done worse in Tract 90 than Anglicans, Wesleyans, and Calvinists did daily in their Sermons and their

21 open to objection] objectionable　　　23 erroneous; but] erroneous, but

publications? how had I done worse, than the Evangelical party in their *ex animo* reception of the Services for Baptism and Visitation of the Sick?[1] Why was I to be dishonest and they immaculate? There was an occasion on which our Lord gave an answer, which seemed to be appropriate to my own case, when the tumult broke out against my Tract:—'He that is without sin among you, let him first cast a stone at him.' I could have fancied that a sense of their own difficulties of interpretation would have persuaded the great party I have mentioned to some prudence, or at least moderation, in opposing a teacher of an opposite school. But I suppose their alarm and their anger overcame their sense of justice.

In the sudden storm of indignation with which the Tract was received throughout the country on its appearance, I recognize much of real religious feeling, much of honest and true principle, much of straightforward ignorant common sense. In Oxford there was genuine feeling too; but there had been a smouldering, stern, energetic animosity, not at all unnatural, partly rational, against its author. A false step had been made; now was the time for action. I am told that, even before the publication of the Tract, rumours of its contents had got into the hostile camp in an exaggerated form; and not a moment was lost in proceeding to action, when I was actually fallen into the hands of the Philistines. I was quite unprepared for the outbreak, and was

13 sudden] universal   14 received throughout the country on] received on
23 actually fallen into] actually in

---

[1] For instance, let candid men consider the form of Absolution contained in that Prayer Book, of which all clergymen, Evangelical and Liberal as well as high Church, and (I think) all persons in University office declare that 'it containeth *nothing contrary to the Word of God*'.

I challenge, in the sight of all England, Evangelical clergymen generally, to put on paper an interpretation of this form of words, consistent with their sentiments, which shall be less forced than the most objectionable of the interpretations which Tract 90 puts upon any passage in the Articles.

'Our Lord Jesus Christ, who hath left *power* to His Church to absolve all sinners who truly repent and believe in Him, of His great mercy forgive thee thine offences; and by *His authority committed to me, I absolve thee from all thy sins*, in the Name of the Father, and of the Son, and of the Holy Ghost. Amen.'

I subjoin the Roman form, as used in England and elsewhere: 'Dominus noster Jesus Christus te absolvat; et ego auctoritate ipsius te absolvo, ab omni vinculo excommunicationis et interdicti, in quantum possum et tu indiges. Deinde ego te absolvo à peccatis tuis, in nomine Patris et Filii et Spiritûs Sancti. Amen.'

startled at its violence. I do not think I had any fear. Nay, I will add, I am not sure that it was not in one point of view a relief to me.

I saw indeed clearly that my place in the Movement was lost;
5 public confidence was at an end; my occupation was gone. It was simply an impossibility that I could say any thing henceforth to good effect, when I had been posted up by the marshal on the buttery-hatch of every College of my University, after the manner of discommoned pastry-cooks, and when in every part of the
10 country and every class of society, through every organ and opportunity of opinion, in newspapers, in periodicals, at meetings, in pulpits, at dinner-tables, in coffee-rooms, in railway carriages, I was denounced as a traitor who had laid his train and was detected in the very act of firing it against the time-honoured
15 Establishment. There were indeed men, besides my own immediate friends, men of name and position, who gallantly took my part, as Dr. Hook, Mr. Palmer, and Mr. Perceval; it must have been a grievous trial for themselves; yet what after all could they do for me? Confidence in me was lost;—but I had already lost
20 full confidence in myself. Thoughts had passed over me a year and a half before in respect to the Anglican claims, which for the time had profoundly troubled me. They had gone: I had not less confidence in the power and the prospects of the Apostolical movement than before; not less confidence than before in the
25 grievousness of what I called the 'dominant errors' of Rome: but how was I any more to have absolute confidence in myself? how was I to have confidence in my present confidence? how was I to be sure that I should always think as I thought now? I felt that by this event a kind Providence had saved me from an
30 impossible position in the future.

First, if I remember right, they wished me to withdraw the Tract. This I refused to do: I would not do so for the sake of those who were unsettled or in danger of unsettlement. I would not do so for my own sake; for how could I acquiesce in a mere
35 Protestant interpretation of the Articles? how could I range myself among the professors of a theology, of which it put my teeth on edge even to hear the sound?

11 opportunity] occasion   15–16 own immediate friends] own friends
17 Perceval;] Perceval: 21 before ... which] before, which

Next they said, 'Keep silence; do not defend the Tract'; I answered, 'Yes, if you will not condemn it,—if you will allow it to continue on sale.' They pressed on me whenever I gave way; they fell back when they saw me obstinate. Their line of action was to get out of me as much as they could; but upon the point 5 of their tolerating the Tract I *was* obstinate. So they let me continue it on sale; and they said they would not condemn it. But they said that this was on condition that I did not defend it, that I stopped the series, and that I myself published my own condemnation in a letter to the Bishop of Oxford. I impute nothing 10 whatever to him, he was ever most kind to me. Also, they said they could not answer for what some individual Bishops might perhaps say about the Tract in their own charges. I agreed to their conditions. My one point was to save the Tract.

Not a line in writing was given me, as a pledge of the obser- 15 vance of the main article on their side of the engagement. Parts of letters from them were read to me, without being put into my hands. It was an 'understanding'. A clever man had warned me against 'understandings' some thirteen years before: I have hated them ever since.   20

In the last words of my letter to the Bishop of Oxford I thus resigned my place in the Movement:—

'I have nothing to be sorry for', I say to him, 'except having made your Lordship anxious, and others whom I am bound to revere. I have nothing to be sorry for, but everything to rejoice 25 in and be thankful for. I have never taken pleasure in seeming to be able to move a party, and whatever influence I have had, has been found, not sought after. I have acted because others did not act, and have sacrificed a quiet which I prized. May God be with me in time to come, as He has been hitherto! and He will 30 be if I can but keep my hand clean and my heart pure. I think I can bear, or at least will try to bear, any personal humiliation, so that I am preserved from betraying sacred interests, which the Lord of grace and power has given into my charge.'[1]

12 what some individual] what individual   15 line in] scrap of   15–16 obser-
vance] performance   16 the main article on their side] their side   19 thirteen]
six *64–78*   34 charge] *footnote added 1869*

[1] To the Pamphlets published in my behalf at this time I should add 'One Tract more', an able and generous defence of Tractarianism and No. 90, by the present Lord Houghton.

CHAPTER III

HISTORY OF MY RELIGIOUS OPINIONS FROM
1839 TO 1841

AND now that I am about to trace, as far as I can, the course of
that great revolution of mind, which led me to leave my own
home, to which I was bound by so many strong and tender ties,
I feel overcome with the difficulty of satisfying myself in my
account of it, and have recoiled from the attempt, till the near
approach of the day, on which these lines must be given to the
world, forces me to set about the task. For who can know himself,
and the multitude of subtle influences which act upon him?
And who can recollect, at the distance of twenty-five years, all
that he once knew about his thoughts and his deeds, and that,
during a portion of his life, when, even at the time, his observation, whether of himself or of the external world, was less than
before or after, by very reason of the perplexity and dismay
which weighed upon him,—when, in spite of the light given to
him according to his need amid his darkness, yet a darkness it
emphatically was? And who can suddenly gird himself to a new
and anxious undertaking, which he might be able indeed to
perform well, were full and calm leisure allowed him to look
through every thing that he had written, whether in published
works or private letters? yet again, granting that calm contemplation of the past, in itself so desirable, who could afford to be
leisurely and deliberate, while he practises on himself a cruel
operation, the ripping up of old griefs, and the venturing again
upon the 'infandum dolorem' of years, in which the stars of this
lower heaven were one by one going out? I could not in cool
blood, nor except upon the imperious call of duty, attempt what
I have set myself to do. It is both to head and heart an extreme

1 Chapter III] Part V   2–3 Opinions . . . 1841] Opinions   8 the
attempt] doing so   17–18 in spite . . . need] though it would be most un-
thankful to seem to imply that he had not all-sufficient light   19 suddenly gird
himself] gird himself suddenly   21 were . . . him] had he full and calm leisure
22 had] has   23 yet again, granting] but, on the other hand, as to 64–68
24 could] can 64–68

trial, thus to analyze what has so long gone by, and to bring out the results of that examination. I have done various bold things in my life: this is the boldest: and, were I not sure I should after all succeed in my object, it would be madness to set about it.

In the spring of 1839 my position in the Anglican Church was at its height. I had supreme confidence in my controversial *status*, and I had a great and still growing success, in recommending it to others. I had in the foregoing autumn been somewhat sore at the Bishop's Charge, but I have a letter which shows that all annoyance had passed from my mind. In January, if I recollect aright, in order to meet the popular clamour against myself and others, and to satisfy the Bishop, I had collected into one all the strong things which they, and especially I, had said against the Church of Rome, in order to their insertion among the advertisements appended to our publications. Conscious as I was that my opinions in religion were not gained, as the world said, from Roman sources, but were, on the contrary, the birth of my own mind and of the circumstances in which I had been placed, I had a scorn of the imputations which were heaped upon me. It was true that I held a large bold system of religion, very unlike the Protestantism of the day, but it was the concentration and adjustment of the statements of great Anglican authorities, and I had as much right to hold it, as the Evangelical, and more right than the Liberal party could show, for asserting their own respective doctrines. As I declared on occasion of Tract 90, I claimed, in behalf of who would in the Anglican Church, the right of holding with Bramhall a comprecation with the Saints, and the Mass all but Transubstantiation with Andrewes, or with Hooker that Transubstantiation itself is not a point for Churches to part communion upon, or with Hammond that a General Council, truly such, never did, never shall err in a matter of faith, or with Bull that man had in paradise and lost on the fall, a supernatural habit of grace, or with Thorndike that penance is a propitiation for post-baptismal sin, or with Pearson that the all-powerful name of Jesus is no

23 hold it] do so   23–24 Evangelical . . . show,] Evangelical party had, and more right than the Liberal,   24–25 for asserting] to hold   25 declared] spoke   26 who would in] who would, that he might hold in   27 Church, the . . . Bramhall] Church a comprecation with the Saints with Bramhall 32–33 had . . . fall] lost inward grace by the fall

otherwise given than in the Catholic Church. 'Two can play at that', was often in my mouth, when men of Protestant sentiments appealed to the Articles, Homilies, or Reformers; in the sense that, if they had a right to speak loud, I had the liberty to speak
5 out as well as they, and had the means, by the same or parallel appeals, of giving them tit for tat. I thought that the Anglican Church was tyrannized over by a mere party, and I aimed at bringing into effect the promise contained in the motto to the Lyra, 'They shall know the difference now.' I only asked to be
10 allowed to show them the difference.

What will best describe my state of mind at the early part of 1839, is an Article in the British Critic for that April. I have looked over it now, for the first time since it was published; and have been struck by it for this reason:—it contains the last
15 words which I ever spoke as an Anglican to Anglicans. It may now be read as my parting address and valediction, made to my friends. I little knew it at the time. It reviews the actual state of things, and it ends by looking towards the future. It is not altogether mine; for my memory goes to this,—that I had asked
20 a friend to do the work; that then, the thought came on me, that I would do it myself: and that he was good enough to put into my hands what he had with great appositeness written, and that I embodied it in my Article. Every one, I think, will recognize the greater part of it as mine. It was published two years before
25 the affair of Tract 90, and was entitled 'The State of Religious Parties'.

In this Article, I begin by bringing together testimonies from our enemies to the remarkable success of our exertions. One writer said: 'Opinions and views of a theology of a very marked
30 and peculiar kind have been extensively adopted and strenuously upheld, and are daily gaining ground among a considerable and influential portion of the members, as well as ministers of the Established Church.' Another: The Movement has manifested itself 'with the most rapid growth of the hot-bed of these evil
35 days'. Another: 'The *Via Media* is crowded with young enthusiasts, who never presume to argue, except against the propriety of arguing at all.' Another: 'Were I to give you a full list of the

4–6　had the liberty . . . tat.] had both the liberty and the means of giving them
tit for tat.　　7 was] had been　　a mere party] a party　　22–23 and that I] and I
23 in] into

works, which they have produced within the short space of five years, I should surprise you. You would see what a task it would be to make yourself complete master of their system, even in its present probably immature state. The writers have adopted the motto, "In quietness and confidence shall be your strength." 5 With regard to confidence, they have justified their adopting it; but as to quietness, it is not very quiet to pour forth such a succession of controversial publications.' Another: 'The spread of these doctrines is in fact now having the effect of rendering all other distinctions obsolete, and of severing the religious com- 10 munity into two portions, fundamentally and vehemently opposed one to the other. Soon there will be no middle ground left; and every man, and especially every clergyman, will be compelled to make his choice between the two.' Another: 'The time has gone by, when those unfortunate and deeply regretted publica- 15 tions can be passed over without notice, and the hope that their influence would fail is now dead.' Another: 'These doctrines had already made fearful progress. One of the largest churches in Brighton is crowded to hear them; so is the church at Leeds. There are few towns of note, to which they have not extended. 20 They are preached in small towns in Scotland. They obtain in Elginshire, 600 miles north of London. I found them myself in the heart of the highlands of Scotland. They are advocated in the newspaper and periodical press. They have even insinuated themselves into the House of Commons.' And, lastly, a bishop 25 in a charge:—It 'is daily assuming a more serious and alarming aspect. Under the specious pretence of deference to Antiquity and respect for primitive models, the foundations of the Protestant Church are undermined by men, who dwell within her walls, and those who sit in the Reformers' seat are traducing the 30 Reformation.'

After thus stating the phenomenon of the time, as it presented itself to those who did not sympathize in it, the Article proceeds to account for it; and this it does by considering it as a re-action from the dry and superficial character of the religious teaching 35 and the literature of the last generation, or century, and as a result of the need which was felt both by the hearts and the intellects of the nation for a deeper philosophy, and as the evidence and as the partial fulfilment of that need, to which even the chief authors of the then generation had borne witness. 40

First, I mentioned the literary influence of Walter Scott, who turned men's minds in the direction of the middle ages. 'The general need', I said, 'of something deeper and more attractive, than what had offered itself elsewhere, may be considered to have
5 led to his popularity; and by means of his popularity he re-acted on his readers, stimulating their mental thirst, feeding their hopes, setting before them visions, which, when once seen, are not easily forgotten, and silently indoctrinating them with nobler ideas, which might afterwards be appealed to as first principles.'
10 Then I spoke of Coleridge, thus: 'While history in prose and verse was thus made the instrument of Church feelings and opinions, a philosophical basis for the same was laid in England by a very original thinker, who, while he indulged a liberty of speculation, which no Christian can tolerate, and advocated
15 conclusions which were often heathen rather than Christian, yet after all instilled a higher philosophy into inquiring minds, than they had hitherto been accustomed to accept. In this way he made trial of his age, and succeeded in interesting its genius in the cause of Catholic truth.'
20 Then come Southey and Wordsworth, 'two living poets, one of whom in the department of fantastic fiction, the other in that of philosophical meditation, have addressed themselves to the same high principles and feelings, and carried forward their readers in the same direction'.
25 Then comes the prediction of this re-action hazarded by 'a sagacious observer withdrawn from the world, and surveying its movements from a distance', Mr. Alexander Knox. He had said twenty years before the date of my Article: 'No Church on earth has more intrinsic excellence than the English Church, yet
30 no Church probably has less practical influence. . . . The rich provision, made by the grace and providence of God, for habits of a noble kind, is evidence that men shall arise, fitted both by nature and ability, to discover for themselves, and to display to others, whatever yet remains undiscovered, whether in the words
35 or works of God.' Also I referred to 'a much venerated clergy-man of the last generation', who said shortly before his death, 'Depend on it, the day will come, when those great doctrines, now buried, will be brought out to the light of day, and then the effect will be fearful.' I remarked upon this, that they who

2 in] to   28 Article] writing

'now blame the impetuosity of the current, should rather turn their animadversions upon those who have dammed up a majestic river, till it has become a flood'.

These being the circumstances under which the Movement began and progressed, it was absurd to refer it to the act of two or three individuals. It was not so much a movement as a 'spirit afloat'; it was within us, 'rising up in hearts where it was least suspected, and working itself, though not in secret, yet so subtly and impalpably, as hardly to admit of precaution or encounter on any ordinary human rules of opposition. It is', I continued, 'an adversary in the air, a something one and entire, a whole wherever it is, unapproachable and incapable of being grasped, as being the result of causes far deeper than political or other visible agencies, the spiritual awakening of spiritual wants.'

To make this clear, I proceed to refer to the chief preachers of the revived doctrines at that moment, and to draw attention to the variety of their respective antecedents. Dr. Hook and Mr. Churton represented the high Church dignitaries of the last century; Mr. Perceval, the Tory aristocracy; Mr. Keble came from a country parsonage; Mr. Palmer from Ireland; Dr. Pusey from the Universities of Germany, and the study of Arabic MSS.; Mr. Dodsworth from the study of Prophecy; Mr. Oakeley had gained his views, as he himself expressed it, 'partly by study, partly by reflection, partly by conversation with one or two friends, inquirers like himself': while I speak of myself as being 'much indebted to the friendship of Archbishop Whately'. And thus I am led on to ask, 'What head of a sect is there? What march of opinions can be traced from mind to mind among preachers such as these? They are one and all in their degree the organs of one Sentiment, which has risen up simultaneously in many places very mysteriously.'

My train of thought next led me to speak of the disciples of the Movement, and I freely acknowledged and lamented that they needed to be kept in order. It is very much to the purpose to draw attention to this point now, when such extravagances as then occurred, whatever they were, are simply laid to my door, or to the charge of the doctrines which I advocated. A man cannot do more than freely confess what is wrong, say that it need not

3 has] had

be, that it ought not to be, and that he is very sorry that it should be. Now I said in the Article, which I am reviewing, that the great truths themselves, which we were preaching, must not be condemned on account of such abuse of them. 'Aberrations
5 there must ever be, whatever the doctrine is, while the human heart is sensitive, capricious, and wayward. A mixed multitude went out of Egypt with the Israelites.' 'There will ever be a number of persons', I continued, 'professing the opinions of a movement party, who talk loudly and strangely, do odd or
10 fierce things, display themselves unnecessarily, and disgust other people; persons, too young to be wise, too generous to be cautious, too warm to be sober, or too intellectual to be humble. Such persons will be very apt to attach themselves to particular persons, to use particular names, to say things merely because
15 others do, and to act in a party-spirited way.'

While I thus republish what I then said about such extravagances as occurred in these years, at the same time I have a very strong conviction that those extravagances furnished quite as much the welcome excuse for those who were jealous or shy of us,
20 as the stumbling-blocks of those who were well inclined to our doctrines. This too we felt at the time; but it was our duty to see that our good should not be evil-spoken of; and accordingly, two or three of the writers of the Tracts for the Times had commenced a Series of what they called 'Plain Sermons' with the
25 avowed purpose of discouraging and correcting whatever was uppish or extreme in our followers: to this Series I contributed a volume myself.

Its conductors say in their Preface: 'If therefore as time goes on, there shall be found persons, who admiring the innate
30 beauty and majesty of the fuller system of Primitive Christianity, and seeing the transcendent strength of its principles, *shall become loud and voluble advocates* in their behalf, speaking the more freely, *because they do not feel them deeply as founded* in divine and eternal truth, of such persons *it is our duty to declare*
35 *plainly*, that, as we should contemplate their condition with serious misgiving, *so would they be the last persons from whom we should* seek support.

'But if, on the other hand, there shall be any, who, in the silent humility of their lives, and in their unaffected reverence for

18 those extravagances] they

holy things, show that they in truth accept these principles as real and substantial, and by habitual purity of heart and serenity of temper, give proof of their deep veneration for sacraments and sacramental ordinances, those persons, *whether our professed adherents or not*, best exemplify the kind of character which the 5 writers of the Tracts for the Times have wished to form.'

These clergymen had the best of claims to use these beautiful words, for they were themselves, all of them, important writers in the Tracts, the two Mr. Kebles, and Mr. Isaac Williams. And this passage, with which they ushered their Series into the 10 world, I quoted in the Article, of which I am giving an account, and I added, 'What more can be required of the preachers of neglected truth, than that they should admit that some, who do not assent to their preaching, are holier and better men than some who do?' They were not answerable for the intemperance 15 of those who dishonoured a true doctrine, provided they protested, as they did, against such intemperance. 'They were not answerable for the dust and din which attends any great moral movement. The truer doctrines are, the more liable they are to be perverted.' 20

The notice of these incidental faults of opinion or temper in adherents of the Movement, led on to a discussion of the secondary causes, by means of which a system of doctrine may be embraced, modified, or developed, of the variety of schools which may all be in the One Church, and of the succession of 25 one phase of doctrine to another, while that doctrine is ever one and the same. Thus I was brought on to the subject of Antiquity, which was the basis of the doctrine of the *Via Media*, and by which was not to be understood a servile imitation of the past, but such a reproduction of it as is really new, while it is old. 'We 30 have good hope', I say, 'that a system will be rising up, superior to the age, yet harmonizing with, and carrying out its higher points, which will attract to itself those who are willing to make a venture and to face difficulties, for the sake of something higher in prospect. On this, as on other subjects, the proverb will apply, 35 "Fortes fortuna adjuvat".'

Lastly, I proceeded to the question of that future of the Anglican Church, which was to be a new birth of the Ancient Religion. And I did not venture to pronounce upon it. 'About

26 that doctrine] it   29 to be understood] implied   30 new] young

the future, we have no prospect before our minds whatever, good or bad. Ever since that great luminary, Augustine, proved to be the last bishop of Hippo, Christians have had a lesson against attempting to foretell, *how* Providence will prosper and' [or?]
5 'bring to an end, what it begins.' Perhaps the lately-revived principles would prevail in the Anglican Church; perhaps they would be lost in 'some miserable schism, or some more miserable compromise'; but there was nothing rash in venturing to predict that 'neither Puritanism nor Liberalism had any permanent
10 inheritance within her'.

Then I went on: 'As to Liberalism, we think the formularies of the Church will ever, with the aid of a good Providence, keep it from making any serious inroads upon the clergy. Besides, it is too cold a principle to prevail with the multitude.' But as
15 regarded what was called Evangelical Religion or Puritanism, there was more to cause alarm. I observed upon its organization; but on the other hand it had no intellectual basis; no internal idea, no principle of unity, no theology. 'Its adherents', I said, 'are already separating from each other; they will melt away
20 like a snow-drift. It has no straightforward view on any one point, on which it professes to teach, and to hide its poverty, it has dressed itself out in a maze of words. We have no dread of it at all; we only fear what it may lead to. It does not stand on intrenched ground, or make any pretence to a position; it does
25 but occupy the space between contending powers, Catholic Truth and Rationalism. Then indeed will be the stern encounter, when two real and living principles, simple, entire, and consistent, one in the Church, the other out of it, at length rush upon each other, contending not for names and words, or half-views,
30 but for elementary notions and distinctive moral characters.'

Whether the ideas of the coming age upon religion were true or false, at least they would be real. 'In the present day', I said, 'mistiness is the mother of wisdom. A man who can set down a half-a-dozen general propositions, which escape from destroying
35 one another only by being diluted into truisms, who can hold the balance between opposites so skilfully as to do without

10 her'.] her'. I suppose I meant to say that in the present age, without the aid of Apostolical principles, the Anglican Church would, in the event, cease to exist.   11 Then I went on:] *not in 64*   32 false, at least they] false, they 33–34 a half-a-dozen] half-a-dozen

fulcrum or beam, who never enunciates a truth without guarding himself against being supposed to exclude the contradictory,—who holds that Scripture is the only authority, yet that
the Church is to be deferred to, that faith only justifies, yet that
it does not justify without works, that grace does not depend on 5
the sacraments, yet is not given without them, that bishops are
a divine ordinance, yet those who have them not are in the same
religious condition as those who have,—this is your safe man
and the hope of the Church; this is what the Church is said to
want, not party men, but sensible, temperate, sober, well- 10
judging persons, to guide it through the channel of no-meaning,
between the Scylla and Charybdis of Aye and No.'

This state of things, however, I said, could not last, if men were
to read and think. They 'will not keep in that very attitude which
you call sound Church-of-Englandism or orthodox Protestan- 15
tism. They cannot go on for ever standing on one leg, or sitting
without a chair, or walking with their feet tied, or like Tityrus's
stags grazing in the air. They will take one view or another, but
it will be a consistent view. It may be Liberalism, or Erastianism,
or Popery, or Catholicity; but it will be real.' 20

I concluded the Article by saying, that all who did not wish
to be 'democratic, or pantheistic, or popish', must 'look out for
some Via Media which will preserve us from what threatens,
though it cannot restore the dead. The spirit of Luther is dead;
but Hildebrand and Loyola are alive. Is it sensible, sober, 25
judicious, to be so very angry with those writers of the day, who
point to the fact, that our divines of the seventeenth century
have occupied a ground which is the true and intelligible mean
between extremes? Is it wise to quarrel with this ground,
because it is not exactly what we should choose, had we the 30
power of choice? Is it true moderation, instead of trying to
fortify a middle doctrine, to fling stones at those who do? . . .
Would you rather have your sons and daughters members of
the Church of England or of the Church of Rome?'

And thus I left the matter. But, while I was thus speaking of 35
the future of the Movement, I was in truth winding up my
accounts with it, little dreaming that it was so to be;—while I
was still, in some way or other, feeling about for an available
Via Media, I was soon to receive a shock which was to cast out

14 keep in] keep standing in   17–18 like . . . grazing] grazing like Tityrus's stags

of my imagination all middle courses and compromises for ever. As I have said, this Article appeared in the April number of the British Critic; in the July number, I cannot tell why, there is no Article of mine; before the number for October, the event had 5 happened to which I have alluded.

But before I proceed to describe what happened to me in the summer of 1839, I must detain the reader for a while, in order to describe the *issue* of the controversy between Rome and the Anglican Church, as I viewed it. This will involve some dry 10 discussion; but it is as necessary for my narrative, as plans of buildings and homesteads are at times needed in the proceedings of our law courts.

I have said already that, though the object of the Movement was to withstand the Liberalism of the day, I found and felt this 15 could not be done by mere negatives. It was necessary for us to have a positive Church theory erected on a definite basis. This took me to the great Anglican divines; and then of course I found at once that it was impossible to form any such theory, without cutting across the teaching of the Church of Rome. 20 Thus came in the Roman controversy.

When I first turned myself to it, I had neither doubt on the subject, nor suspicion that doubt would ever come upon me. It was in this state of mind that I began to read up Bellarmine on the one hand, and numberless Anglican writers on the other. But 25 I soon found, as others had found before me, that it was a tangled and manifold controversy, difficult to master, more difficult to put out of hand with neatness and precision. It was easy to make points, not easy to sum up and settle. It was not easy to find a clear issue for the dispute, and still less by a logical 30 process to decide it in favour of Anglicanism. This difficulty, however, had no tendency whatever to harass or perplex me: it was a matter which bore not on convictions, but on proofs.

First I saw, as all see who study the subject, that a broad distinction had to be drawn between the actual state of belief 35 and of usage in the countries which were in communion with the Roman Church, and her formal dogmas; the latter did not cover the former. Sensible pain, for instance, is not implied in the

Tridentine decree upon Purgatory; but it was the tradition of the Latin Church, and I had seen the pictures of souls in flames in the streets of Naples. Bishop Lloyd had brought this distinction out strongly in an Article in the British Critic in 1825; indeed, it was one of the most common objections made to the Church of Rome, that she dared not commit herself by formal decree, to what nevertheless she sanctioned and allowed. Accordingly, in my Prophetical Office, I view as simply separate ideas, Rome quiescent, and Rome in action. I contrasted her creed on the one hand, with her ordinary teaching, her controversial tone, her political and social bearing, and her popular beliefs and practices, on the other.

While I made this distinction between the decrees and the traditions of Rome, I drew a parallel distinction between Anglicanism quiescent, and Anglicanism in action. In its formal creed Anglicanism was not at a great distance from Rome : far otherwise, when viewed in its insular spirit, the traditions of its establishment, its historical characteristics, its controversial rancour, and its private judgment. I disavowed and condemned those excesses, and called them 'Protestantism' or 'Ultra-Protestantism': I wished to find a parallel disclaimer, on the part of Roman controversialists, of that popular system of beliefs and usages in their own Church, which I called 'Popery'. When that hope was a dream, I saw that the controversy lay between the book-theology of Anglicanism on the one side, and the living system of what I called Roman corruption on the other. I could not get further than this; with this result I was forced to content myself.

These then were the *parties* in the controversy:—the Anglican *Via Media* and the popular religion of Rome. And next, as to the *issue*, to which the controversy between them was to be brought, it was this:—the Anglican disputant took his stand upon Antiquity or Apostolicity, the Roman upon Catholicity. The Anglican said to the Roman: 'There is but One Faith, the Ancient, and you have not kept to it'; the Roman retorted: 'There is but One Church, the Catholic, and you are out of it.' The Anglican urged: 'Your special beliefs, practices, modes of action, are nowhere in Antiquity'; the Roman objected: 'You do not communicate with any one Church besides your own and its offshoots, and you have discarded principles, doctrines,

sacraments, and usages, which are and ever have been received in the East and the West.' The true Church, as defined in the Creeds, was both Catholic and Apostolic; now, as I viewed the controversy in which I was engaged, England and Rome had
5 divided these notes or prerogatives between them: the cause lay thus, Apostolicity *versus* Catholicity.

However, in thus stating the matter, of course I do not wish it supposed that I allowed the note of Catholicity really to belong to Rome, to the disparagement of the Anglican Church; but I
10 considered that the special point or plea of Rome in the controversy was Catholicity, as the Anglican plea was Antiquity. Of course I contended that the Roman idea of Catholicity was not ancient and apostolic. It was in my judgment at the utmost only natural, becoming, expedient, that the whole of Christen-
15 dom should be united in one visible body; while such a unity might, on the other hand, be nothing more than a mere heartless and political combination. For myself, I held with the Anglican divines, that, in the Primitive Church, there was a very real mutual independence between its separate parts, though, from
20 a dictate of charity, there was in fact a close union between them. I considered that each See and Diocese might be compared to a crystal, and that each was similar to the rest, and that the sum total of them all was only a collection of crystals. The unity of the Church lay, not in its being a polity, but in its being a
25 family, a race, coming down by apostolical descent from its first founders and bishops. And I considered this truth brought out, beyond the possibility of dispute, in the Epistles of St. Ignatius, in which the Bishop is represented as the one supreme authority in the Church, that is, in his own place, with no one above him,
30 except as, for the sake of ecclesiastical order and expedience, arrangements had been made by which one was put over or under another. So much for our own claim to Catholicity, which was so perversely appropriated by our opponents to themselves: —on the other hand, as to our special strong point, Antiquity,
35 while, of course, by means of it, we were able to condemn most emphatically the novel claim of Rome to domineer over other Churches, which were in truth her equals, further than that, we thereby especially convicted her of the intolerable offence of

8 allowed] considered   9–10 but I considered that] but that   16 might
... mere] might be, on the other hand, a mere

having added to the Faith. This was the critical head of accusation urged against her by the Anglican disputant; and as he
referred to St. Ignatius in proof that he himself was a true
Catholic, in spite of being separated from Rome, so he triumphantly referred to the Treatise of Vincentius of Lerins upon the 5
'Quod semper, quod ubique, quod ab omnibus', in proof that
the controversialists of Rome, in spite of their possession of the
Catholic name, were separated in their creed from the Apostolical
and primitive faith.

Of course those controversialists had their own mode of 10
answering him, with which I am not concerned in this place;
here I am only concerned with the issue itself, between the one
party and the other—Antiquity *versus* Catholicity.

Now I will proceed to illustrate what I have been saying of
the *status* of the controversy, as it presented itself to my mind, 15
by extracts from my writings of the dates of 1836, 1840, and
1841. And I introduce them with a remark, which especially
applies to the paper, from which I shall quote first, of the date of
1836. That paper appeared in the March and April numbers of
the British Magazine of that year, and was entitled 'Home 20
Thoughts Abroad'. Now it will be found, that, in the discussion
which it contains, as in various other writings of mine, when I
was in the Anglican Church, the argument in behalf of Rome
is stated with considerable perspicuity and force. And at the
time my friends and supporters cried out, 'How imprudent!' 25
and, both at the time, and especially at a later date, my enemies
have cried out, 'How insidious!' Friends and foes virtually
agreed in their criticism; I had set out the cause which I was
combating to the best advantage: this was an offence; it might
be from imprudence, it might be with a traitorous design. It was 30
from neither the one nor the other; but for the following reasons.
First, I had a great impatience, whatever was the subject, of
not bringing out the whole of it, as clearly as I could; next I
wished to be as fair to my adversaries as possible; and thirdly I
thought that there was a great deal of shallowness among our 35
own friends, and that they undervalued the strength of the
argument in behalf of Rome, and that they ought to be roused
to a more exact apprehension of the position of the controversy.
At a later date (1841), when I really felt the force of the Roman

7–8 Rome, in . . . name, were] Rome were   10–11 mode of answering] answer to side of the question myself, as a difficulty which had to be met, I had a fourth reason for such frankness in argument, and that was because a number of persons were unsettled far more than I was as to the Catholicity of the Anglican Church. It was quite plain that, unless I was perfectly candid in stating what could be said against it, there was no chance that any representations, which I felt to be in its favour, or at least to be adverse to Rome, would have had any success with the persons in question. At all times I had a deep conviction, to put the matter on the lowest ground, that 'honesty was the best policy'. Accordingly, in July 1841, I expressed myself thus on the Anglican difficulty: 'This is an objection which we must honestly say is deeply felt by many people, and not inconsiderable ones; and the more it is openly avowed to be a difficulty, the better; for there is then the chance of its being acknowledged, and in the course of time obviated, as far as may be, by those who have the power. Flagrant evils cure themselves by being flagrant; and we are sanguine that the time is come when so great an evil as this is, cannot stand its ground against the good feeling and common sense of religious persons. It is the very strength of Romanism against us; and, unless the proper persons take it into their serious consideration, they may look for certain to undergo the loss, as time goes on, of some whom they would least like to be lost to our Church.' The measure which I had especially in view in this passage, was the project of a Jerusalem Bishopric, which the then Archbishop of Canterbury was at that time concocting with M. Bunsen, and of which I shall speak more in the sequel. And now to return to the Home Thoughts Abroad of the spring of 1836:—

The discussion contained in this composition runs in the form of a dialogue. One of the disputants says: 'You say to me that the Church of Rome is corrupt. What then? to cut off a limb is a strange way of saving it from the influence of some constitutional ailment. Indigestion may cause cramp in the extremities; yet we spare our poor feet notwithstanding. Surely there is such a religious *fact* as the existence of a great Catholic body, union with which is a Christian privilege and duty. Now, we English are separate from it.'

8–9 any . . . question.] their real weight duly acknowledged.   11 in July 1841]
in 1841

The other answers: 'The present is an unsatisfactory, miserable state of things, yet I can grant no more. The Church is founded on a doctrine,—on the gospel of Truth; it is a means to an end. Perish the Church, (though blessed be the promise! this cannot be,) yet let it perish *rather* than the Truth should 5 fail. Purity of faith is more precious to the Christian than unity itself. If Rome has erred grievously in doctrine, then it is a duty to separate even from Rome.'

His friend, who takes the Roman side of the argument, refers to the image of the Vine and its branches, which is found, I 10 think, in St. Cyprian, as if a branch cut from the Catholic Vine must necessarily die. Also he quotes a passage from St. Augustine in controversy with the Donatists to the same effect; viz. that, as being separated from the body of the Church, they were *ipso facto* cut off from the heritage of Christ. And he quotes St. 15 Cyril's argument drawn from the very title Catholic, which no body or communion of men has ever dared or been able to appropriate, besides one. He adds, 'Now I am only contending for the fact, that the communion of Rome constitutes the main body of the Church Catholic, and that we are split off from it, 20 and in the condition of the Donatists.'

The other replies by denying the fact that the present Roman communion is like St. Augustine's Catholic Church, inasmuch as there must be taken into account the large Anglican and Greek communions. Presently he takes the offensive, naming 25 distinctly the points, in which Rome has departed from Primitive Christianity, viz. 'the practical idolatry, the virtual worship of the Virgin and Saints, which are the offence of the Latin Church, and the degradation of moral truth and duty, which follows from these'. And again: 'We cannot join a Church, did 30 we wish it ever so much, which does not acknowledge our orders, refuses us the Cup, demands our acquiescence in image-worship, and excommunicates us, if we do not receive it and all other decisions of the Tridentine Council.'

His opponent answers these objections by referring to the 35 doctrine of 'developments of gospel truth'. Besides, 'The Anglican system itself is not found complete in those early centuries; so that the [Anglican] principle [of Antiquity] is self-destructive.' 'When a man takes up this *Via Media*, he is a mere *doctrinaire*';

24 must] are to

he is like those, 'who, in some matter of business, start up to suggest their own little crotchet, and are ever measuring mountains with a pocket ruler, or improving the planetary courses'. 'The *Via Media* has slept in libraries; it is a substitute of infancy
5 for manhood.'

It is plain, then, that at the end of 1835 or beginning of 1836, I had the whole state of the question before me, on which, to my mind, the decision between the Churches depended. It is observable that the question of the position of the Pope, whether
10 as the centre of unity, or as the source of jurisdiction, did not come into my thoughts at all; nor did it, I think I may say, to the end. I doubt whether I ever distinctly held any of his powers to be *de jure divino*, while I was in the Anglican Church;—not that I saw any difficulty in the doctrine; not that in connexion with
15 the history of St. Leo, of which I shall speak by and by, the idea of his infallibility did not cross my mind, for it did,—but after all, in my view the controversy did not turn upon it; it turned upon the Faith and the Church. This was my issue of the controversy from the beginning to the end. There was a contrariety of
20 claims between the Roman and Anglican religions, and the history of my conversion is simply the process of working it out to a solution. In 1838 I illustrated it by the contrast presented to us between the Madonna and Child, and a Calvary. The peculiarity of the Anglican theology was this,—that it 'supposed
25 the Truth to be entirely objective and detached, not' (as in the theology of Rome) 'lying hid in the bosom of the Church as if one with her, clinging to and (as it were) lost in her embrace, but as being sole and unapproachable, as on the Cross or at the Resurrection, with the Church close by, but in the background'.
30 As I viewed the controversy in 1836 and 1838, so I viewed it in 1840 and 1841. In the British Critic of January 1840, after gradually investigating how the matter lies between the Churches by means of a dialogue, I end thus: 'It would seem, that, in the above discussion, each disputant has a strong point: our strong
35 point is the argument from Primitiveness, that of Romanists from Universality. It is a fact, however it is to be accounted for, that Rome has added to the Creed; and it is a fact, however we justify ourselves, that we are estranged from the great body of

14 that in connexion] that, together   23–24 The peculiarity] I said that the
peculiarity   25–26 (as . . . Rome)] (as the Roman)

Christians over the world. And each of these two facts is at first sight a grave difficulty in the respective systems to which they belong.' Again, 'While Rome, though not deferring to the Fathers, recognizes them, and England, not deferring to the large body of the Church, recognizes it, both Rome and England 5 have a point to clear up.'

And still more strongly, in July, 1841:

'If the Note of schism, on the one hand, lies against England, an antagonist disgrace lies upon Rome, the Note of idolatry. Let us not be mistaken here; we are neither accusing Rome of 10 idolatry nor ourselves of schism; we think neither charge tenable; but still the Roman Church practises what is so like idolatry, and the English Church makes much of what is so very like schism, that without deciding what is the duty of a Roman Catholic towards the Church of England in her present state, 15 we do seriously think that members of the English Church have a providential direction given them, how to comport themselves towards the Church of Rome, while she is what she is.'

One remark more about Antiquity and the *Via Media*. As time went on, without doubting the strength of the Anglican 20 argument from Antiquity, I felt also that it was not merely our special plea, but our only one. Also I felt that the *Via Media*, which was to represent it, was to be a sort of remodelled and adapted Antiquity. This I advanced both in Home Thoughts Abroad and in the Article of the British Critic which I have 25 analyzed above. But this circumstance, that after all we must use private judgment upon Antiquity, created a sort of distrust of my theory altogether, which in the conclusion of my Volume on the Prophetical Office (1836–7) I express thus: 'Now that our discussions draw to a close, the thought, with which we entered on 30 the subject, is apt to recur, when the excitement of the inquiry has subsided, and weariness has succeeded, that what has been said is but a dream, the wanton exercise, rather than the practical conclusions of the intellect.' And I conclude the paragraph by anticipating a line of thought into which I was, in the event, 35 almost obliged to take refuge: 'After all,' I say, 'the Church is ever invisible in its day, and faith only apprehends it.' What was this, but to give up the Notes of a visible Church altogether, whether the Catholic Note or the Apostolic?

24 advanced] observe   29 Office (1836–7) I] Office I

The Long Vacation of 1839 began early. There had been a great many visitors to Oxford from Easter to Commemoration; and Dr. Pusey's party had attracted attention, more, I think, than in any former year. I had put away from me the contro-
5 versy with Rome for more than two years. In my Parochial Sermons the subject had at no time been introduced: there had been nothing for two years, either in my Tracts or in the British Critic, of a polemical character. I was returning, for the Vacation, to the course of reading which I had many years before
10 chosen as especially my own. I have no reason to suppose that the thoughts of Rome came across my mind at all. About the middle of June I began to study and master the history of the Monophysites. I was absorbed in the doctrinal question. This was from about June 13th to August 30th. It was during this
15 course of reading that for the first time a doubt came upon me of the tenableness of Anglicanism. I recollect on the 30th of July mentioning to a friend, whom I had accidentally met, how remarkable the history was; but by the end of August I was seriously alarmed.

20 I have described in a former work, how the history affected me. My stronghold was Antiquity; now here, in the middle of the fifth century, I found, as it seemed to me, Christendom of the sixteenth and the nineteenth centuries reflected. I saw my face in that mirror, and I was a Monophysite. The Church of the *Via*
25 *Media* was in the position of the Oriental communion, Rome was, where she now is; and the Protestants were the Eutychians. Of all passages of history, since history has been, who would have thought of going to the sayings and doings of old Eutyches, that *delirus senex*, as (I think) Petavius calls him, and to the enormi-
30 ties of the unprincipled Dioscorus, in order to be converted to Rome!

Now let it be simply understood that I am not writing controversially, but with the one object of relating things as they happened to me in the course of my conversion. With this view I
35 will quote a passage from the account, which I gave in 1850, of my reasonings and feelings in 1839:

'It was difficult to make out how the Eutychians or Monophysites were heretics, unless Protestants and Anglicans were

3 Dr. Pusey's party] Dr. Pusey and myself   4 than in any] than any
6 at no time] never

heretics also; difficult to find arguments against the Tridentine
Fathers, which did not tell against the Fathers of Chalcedon;
difficult to condemn the Popes of the sixteenth century, without
condemning the Popes of the fifth. The drama of religion, and
the combat of truth and error, were ever one and the same. The 5
principles and proceedings of the Church now, were those of the
Church then; the principles and proceedings of heretics then,
were those of Protestants now. I found it so,—almost fearfully;
there was an awful similitude, more awful, because so silent and
unimpassioned, between the dead records of the past and the 10
feverish chronicle of the present. The shadow of the fifth century
was on the sixteenth. It was like a spirit rising from the troubled
waters of the old world, with the shape and lineaments of the
new. The Church then, as now, might be called peremptory and
stern, resolute, overbearing, and relentless; and heretics were 15
shifting, changeable, reserved, and deceitful, ever courting
civil power, and never agreeing together, except by its aid; and
the civil power was ever aiming at comprehensions, trying to
put the invisible out of view, and substituting expediency for
faith. What was the use of continuing the controversy, or defend- 20
ing my position, if, after all, I was forging arguments for Arius
or Eutyches, and turning devil's advocate against the much-
enduring Athanasius and the majestic Leo? Be my soul with
the Saints! and shall I lift up my hand against them? Sooner
may my right hand forget her cunning, and wither outright, 25
as his who once stretched it out against a prophet of God!
anathema to a whole tribe of Cranmers, Ridleys, Latimers, and
Jewels! perish the names of Bramhall, Ussher, Taylor, Stillingfleet, and Barrow from the face of the earth, ere I should do
ought but fall at their feet in love and in worship, whose image 30
was continually before my eyes, and whose musical words were
ever in my ears and on my tongue!'

Hardly had I brought my course of reading to a close, when
the Dublin Review of that same August was put into my hands,
by friends who were more favourable to the cause of Rome than 35
I was myself. There was an article in it on the 'Anglican Claim'
by Dr. Wiseman. This was about the middle of September. It
was on the Donatists, with an application to Anglicanism. I read
it, and did not see much in it. The Donatist controversy was

37 Dr.] Bishop

known to me for some years, as has appeared already. The case
was not parallel to that of the Anglican Church. St. Augustine in
Africa wrote against the Donatists in Africa. They were a
furious party who made a schism within the African Church,
5 and not beyond its limits. It was a case of Altar against Altar, of
two occupants of the same See, as that between the Non-jurors
in England and the Established Church; not the case of one
Church against another, as of Rome against the Oriental
Monophysites. But my friend, an anxiously religious man, now,
10 as then, very dear to me, a Protestant still, pointed out the
palmary words of St. Augustine, which were contained in one
of the extracts made in the Review, and which had escaped my
observation. 'Securus judicat orbis terrarum.' He repeated these
words again and again, and, when he was gone, they kept
15 ringing in my ears. 'Securus judicat orbis terrarum'; they were
words which went beyond the occasion of the Donatists: they
applied to that of the Monophysites. They gave a cogency to the
Article, which had escaped me at first. They decided ecclesiastical questions on a simpler rule than that of Antiquity; nay, St.
20 Augustine was one of the prime oracles of Antiquity; here then
Antiquity was deciding against itself. What a light was hereby
thrown upon every controversy in the Church! not that, for the
moment, the multitude may not falter in their judgment,—not
that, in the Arian hurricane, Sees more than can be numbered
25 did not bend before its fury, and fall off from St. Athanasius,—
not that the crowd of Oriental Bishops did not need to be
sustained during the contest by the voice and the eye of St. Leo;
but that the deliberate judgment, in which the whole Church at
length rests and acquiesces, is an infallible prescription and a
30 final sentence against such portions of it as protest and secede.
Who can account for the impressions which are made on him?
For a mere sentence, the words of St. Augustine, struck me with
a power which I never had felt from any words before. To take a
familiar instance, they were like the 'Turn again Whittington'
35 of the chime; or, to take a more serious one, they were like the
'Tolle, lege,—Tolle, lege', of the child, which converted St.
Augustine himself. 'Securus judicat orbis terrarum!' By those
great words of the ancient Father, interpreting and summing up

---

1 has appeared already.] I have instanced above.   8 as of Rome] as Rome
38–p. 111, l. 1 Father, interpreting . . . theory] Father, the theory

the long and varied course of ecclesiastical history, the theory of the *Via Media* was absolutely pulverized.

I became excited at the view thus opened upon me. I was just starting on a round of visits; and I mentioned my state of mind to two most intimate friends: I think to no others. After a while, I got calm, and at length the vivid impression upon my imagination faded away. What I thought about it on reflection, I will attempt to describe presently. I had to determine its logical value, and its bearing upon my duty. Meanwhile, so far as this was certain,—I had seen the shadow of a hand upon the wall. It was clear that I had a good deal to learn on the question of the Churches, and that perhaps some new light was coming upon me. He who has seen a ghost, cannot be as if he had never seen it. The heavens had opened and closed again. The thought for the moment had been, 'The Church of Rome will be found right after all'; and then it had vanished. My old convictions remained as before.

At this time, I wrote my Sermon on Divine Calls, which I published in my volume of Plain Sermons. It ends thus:—

'O that we could take that simple view of things, as to feel that the one thing which lies before us is to please God! What gain is it to please the world, to please the great, nay even to please those whom we love, compared with this? What gain is it to be applauded, admired, courted, followed,—compared with this one aim, of "not being disobedient to a heavenly vision"? What can this world offer comparable with that insight into spiritual things, that keen faith, that heavenly peace, that high sanctity, that everlasting righteousness, that hope of glory, which they have, who in sincerity love and follow our Lord Jesus Christ? Let us beg and pray Him day by day to reveal Himself to our souls more fully, to quicken our senses, to give us sight and hearing, taste and touch of the world to come; so to work within us, that we may sincerely say, "Thou shalt guide me with Thy counsel, and after that receive me with glory. Whom have I in heaven but Thee? and there is none upon earth that I desire in comparison of Thee. My flesh and my heart faileth, but God is the strength of my heart, and my portion for ever."'

Now to trace the succession of thoughts, and the conclusions, and the consequent innovations on my previous belief, and the

general conduct, to which I was led, upon this sudden visitation.
And first, I will say, whatever comes of saying it, for I leave
inferences to others, that for years I must have had something of
an habitual notion, though it was latent, and had never led me
5 to distrust my own convictions, that my mind had not found its
ultimate rest, and that in some sense or other I was on journey.
During the same passage across the Mediterranean in which
I wrote 'Lead kindly light', I also wrote the verses, which are
found in the Lyra under the head of 'Providences', beginning,
10 'When I look back.' This was in 1833; and, since I have begun
this narrative, I have found a memorandum under the date of
September 7, 1829, in which I speak of myself, as 'now in my
rooms in Oriel College, slowly advancing &c. and led on by
God's hand blindly, not knowing whither He is taking me'.
15 But, whatever this presentiment be worth, it was no protection
against the dismay and disgust, which I felt, in consequence of
the dreadful misgiving, of which I have been relating the history.
The one question was, what was I to do ? I had to make up my
mind for myself, and others could not help me. I determined to
20 be guided, not by my imagination, but by my reason. And this
I said over and over again in the years which followed, both in
conversation and in private letters. Had it not been for this
severe resolve, I should have been a Catholic sooner than I was.
Moreover, I felt on consideration a positive doubt, on the other
25 hand, whether the suggestion did not come from below. Then I
said to myself, Time alone can solve that question. It was my
business to go on as usual, to obey those convictions to which I
had so long surrendered myself, which still had possession of
me, and on which my new thoughts had no direct bearing. That
30 new conception of things should only so far influence me, as it
had a logical claim to do so. If it came from above, it would
come again;—so I trusted,—and with more definite outlines and
greater cogency and consistency of proof. I thought of Samuel,
before 'he knew the word of the Lord'; and therefore I went, and
35 lay down to sleep again. This was my broad view of the matter,
and my *primâ facie* conclusion.

However, my new historical fact had already to a certain
point a logical force. Down had come the *Via Media* as a
definite theory or scheme, under the blows of St. Leo. My

32–33 outlines . . . proof.] outlines.   37 had already to] had to

'Prophetical Office' had come to pieces; not indeed as an argument against 'Roman errors', nor as against Protestantism, but
as in behalf of England. I had no longer a distinctive plea for
Anglicanism, unless I would be a Monophysite. I had, most
painfully, to fall back upon my three original points of belief, 5
which I have spoken so much of in a former passage,—the
principle of dogma, the sacramental system, and anti-Romanism.
Of these three, the first two were better secured in Rome than in
the Anglican Church. The Apostolical Succession, the two
prominent sacraments, and the primitive Creeds, belonged, 10
indeed, to the latter; but there had been and was far less strictness on matters of dogma and ritual in the Anglican system than
in the Roman: in consequence, my main argument for the
Anglican claims lay in the positive and special charges, which
I could bring against Rome. I had no positive Anglican theory. 15
I was very nearly a pure Protestant. Lutherans had a sort of
theology, so had Calvinists; I had none.

However, this pure Protestantism, to which I was gradually
left, was really a practical principle. It was a strong, though it
was only a negative ground, and it still had great hold on me. 20
As a boy of fifteen, I had so fully imbibed it, that I had actually
erased in my *Gradus ad Parnassum*, such titles, under the word
'Papa', as 'Christi Vicarius', 'sacer interpres', and 'sceptra
gerens', and substituted epithets so vile that I cannot bring
myself to write them down here. The effect of this early persua- 25
sion remained as, what I have already called it, a 'stain upon
my imagination'. As regards my reason, I began in 1833 to form
theories on the subject, which tended to obliterate it; yet by

3 longer] more
28–p. 115, l. 9 obliterate it; yet . . . have thrown off,—the] obliterate it. In the
first part of Home Thoughts Abroad, written in that year, after speaking of
Rome as 'undeniably the most exalted Church in the whole world', and mani-
festing, 'in all the truth and beauty of the Spirit, that side of high mental
excellence, which Pagan Rome attempted but could not realize,—high-mindedness,
majesty, and the calm consciousness of power',—I proceed to say, 'Alas! . . .
the old spirit has revived, and the monster of Daniel's vision, untamed by
its former judgments, has seized upon Christianity as the new instrument of its
impieties, and awaits a second and final woe from God's hand. Surely the
doctrine of the *Genius Loci* is not without foundation, and explains to us how the
blessing or the curse attaches to cities and countries, not to generations. Michael
is represented [in the book of Daniel] as opposed to the Prince of the kingdom
of Persia. Old Rome is still alive. The Sorceress upon the Seven Hills, in the
book of Revelation, is not the Church of Rome, but Rome itself, the bad spirit, which,

1838 I had got no further than to consider Antichrist, as not the Church of Rome, but the spirit of the old pagan city, the fourth monster of Daniel, which was still alive, and which had corrupted the Church which was planted there. Soon after this
5 indeed, and before my attention was directed to the Monophysite

in its former shape, was the animating spirit of the Fourth Monarchy.' Then I refer to St. Malachi's Prophecy which 'makes a like distinction between the City and the Church of Rome. "In the last persecution", it says "of the Holy Roman Church, Peter of Rome shall be on the throne, who shall feed his flock in many tribulations. When these are past, the City upon the Seven Hills shall be destroyed, and the awful Judge shall judge the people."' Then I append my moral. 'I deny that the distinction is unmeaning; Is it nothing to be able to look on our Mother, to whom we owe the blessing of Christianity, with affection instead of hatred ? with pity indeed, aye, and fear, but not with horror ? Is it nothing to rescue her from the hard names, which interpreters of prophecy have put upon her, as an idolatress and an enemy of God, when she is deceived rather than a deceiver ? Nothing to be able to account her priests as ordained of God, and anointed for their spiritual functions by the Holy Spirit, instead of considering her communion the bond of Satan ?' This was my first advance in rescuing, on an intelligible, intellectual basis, the Roman Church from the designation of Antichrist; it was not the Church, but the old dethroned Pagan monster, still living in the ruined city, that was Antichrist.

In a Tract in 1838, I profess to give the opinions of the Fathers on the subject, and the conclusions to which I come, are still less violent against the Roman Church, though on the same basis as before. I say that the local Christian Church of Rome has been the means of shielding the pagan city from the fulness of those judgments, which are due to it; and that, in consequence of this, though Babylon has been utterly swept from the earth, Rome remains to this day. The reason seemed to be simply this, that, when the barbarians came down, God had a people in that city. Babylon was a mere prison of the Church; Rome had received her as a guest. 'That vengeance has never fallen: it is still suspended; nor can reason be given why Rome has not fallen under the rule of God's general dealings with His rebellious creatures, except that a Christian Church is still in that city, sanctifying it, interceding for it, saving it.' I add in a note, 'No opinion, one way or the other, is here expressed as to the question, how far, as the local Church has saved Rome, so Rome has corrupted the local Church; or whether the local Church in consequence, or again whether other Churches elsewhere, may or may not be types of Antichrist.' I quote all this in order to show how Bishop Newton was still upon my mind even in 1838; and how I was feeling after some other interpretation of prophecy instead of his, and not without a good deal of hesitation.

However, I have found notes written in March, 1839, which anticipate my Article in the British Critic of October, 1840, in which I contended that the Churches of Rome and England were both one, and also the one true Church, for the very reason that they had both been stigmatized by the name of Antichrist, proving my point from the text, 'If they have called the Master of the House Beelzebub, how much more them of His household', and quoting largely from Puritans and Independents to show that, in their mouths, the Anglican Church is Antichrist and Antichristian as well as the Roman. I urged in that article that the calumny of being Antichrist is almost 'one of the notes of the true Church'; and that 'there is no medium between a Vice-Christ and Anti-Christ'; for 'it is not the *acts* that make the difference between them, but the *authority* for those acts'. This of course was a new controversy, I underwent a great change of opinion. I saw that, from the nature of the case, the true Vicar of Christ must ever to the world seem like Antichrist, and be stigmatized as such, because a resemblance must ever exist between an original and a forgery; and thus the fact of such a calumny was almost one 5 of the notes of the Church. But we cannot unmake ourselves or change our habits in a moment. Though my reason was convinced, I did not throw off, for some time after,—I could not have thrown off,—the unreasoning prejudice and suspicion, which I cherished about her at least by fits and starts, in spite of this con- 10 viction of my reason. I cannot prove this, but I believe it to have been the case from what I recollect of myself. Nor was there any thing in the history of St. Leo and the Monophysites to undo the firm belief I had in the existence of what I called the practical abuses and excesses of Rome.   15

To her inconsistencies then, to her ambition and intrigue, to her sophistries (as I considered them to be) I now had recourse in my opposition to her, both public and personal. I did so by way of a relief. I had a great and growing dislike, after the summer of 1839, to speak against the Roman Church herself or 20 her formal doctrines. I was very averse to speaking against doctrines, which might possibly turn out to be true, though at the time I had no reason for thinking they were; or against the Church, which had preserved them. I began to have misgivings, that, strong as my own feelings had been against her, yet in 25 some things which I had said, I had taken the statements of Anglican divines for granted without weighing them for myself. I said to a friend in 1840, in a letter, which I shall use presently, 'I am troubled by doubts whether as it is, I have not, in what I have published, spoken too strongly against Rome, though I 30 think I did it in a kind of faith, being determined to put myself into the English system, and say all that our divines said, whether I had fully weighed it or not.' I was sore about the great Anglican divines, as if they had taken me in, and made me say

mode of viewing the question; but we cannot unmake ourselves or change our habits in a moment. It is quite clear, that, if I dared not commit myself in 1838, to the belief that the Church of Rome was not a type of Antichrist, I could not have thrown off the

10–11 about her . . . this conviction] about her, for some time after, at least by fits and starts, in spite of the conviction   16 her . . . her] the . . . the   17 her sophistries] the sophistries of Rome   I now had] I had   21 speaking] speak

strong things, which facts did not justify. Yet I *did* still hold in substance all that I had said against the Church of Rome in my Prophetical Office. I felt the force of the usual Protestant objections against her; I believed that we had the Apostolical succes-
5 sion in the Anglican Church, and the grace of the sacraments; I was not sure that the difficulty of its isolation might not be overcome, though I was far from sure that it could. I did not see any clear proof that it had committed itself to any heresy, or had taken part against the truth; and I was not sure that it
10 would not revive into full Apostolic purity and strength, and grow into union with Rome herself (Rome explaining her doctrines and guarding against their abuse), that is, if we were but patient and hopeful. I began to wish for union between the Anglican Church and Rome, if, and when, it was possible; and
15 I did what I could to gain weekly prayers for that object. The ground which I felt to be good against her was the moral ground: I felt I could not be wrong in striking at her political and social line of action. The alliance of a dogmatic religion with liberals, high or low, seemed to me a providential direction against
20 moving towards Rome, and a better 'Preservative against Popery', than the three volumes in folio, in which, I think, that prophylactic is to be found. However, on occasions which demanded it, I felt it a duty to give out plainly all that I thought, though I did not like to do so. One such instance occurred, when
25 I had to publish a Letter about Tract 90. In that Letter, I said, 'Instead of setting before the soul the Holy Trinity, and heaven and hell, the Church of Rome does seem to me, as a popular system, to preach the Blessed Virgin and the Saints, and purgatory.' On this occasion I recollect expressing to a friend the
30 distress it gave me thus to speak; but, I said, 'How can I help saying it, if I think it ? and I *do* think it; my Bishop calls on me to say out what I think; and that is the long and the short of it.' But I recollected Hurrell Froude's words to me, almost his dying words, 'I must enter another protest against your cursing
35 and swearing. What good can it do ? and I call it uncharitable to an excess. How mistaken we may ourselves be, on many points that are only gradually opening on us!'

Instead then of speaking of errors in doctrine, I was driven,

13 began to wish] wished   16 felt to be good] felt good   20 Rome] it
21 in folio] of folio

by my state of mind, to insist upon the political conduct, the controversial bearing, and the social methods and manifestations of Rome. And here I found a matter ready to my hand, which affected me the more sensibly for the reason that it lay at our very doors. I can hardly describe too strongly my feeling upon it. 5 I had an unspeakable aversion to the policy and acts of Mr. O'Connell, because, as I thought, he associated himself with men of all religions and no religion against the Anglican Church, and advanced Catholicism by violence and intrigue. When then I found him taken up by the English Catholics, and, as I sup- 10 posed, at Rome, I considered I had a fulfilment before my eyes how the Court of Rome played fast and loose, and justified the serious charges which I had seen put down in books against it. Here we saw what Rome was in action, whatever she might be when quiescent. Her conduct was simply secular and political. 15

This feeling led me into the excess of being very rude to that zealous and most charitable man, Mr. Spencer, when he came to Oxford in January, 1840, to get Anglicans to set about praying for Unity. I myself, at that time, or soon after, drew up such prayers; their desirableness was one of the first thoughts which 20 came upon me after my shock; but I was too much annoyed with the political action of the Catholic body in these islands to wish to have any thing to do with them personally. So glad in my heart was I to see him, when he came to my rooms with Mr. Palmer of Magdalen, that I could have laughed for joy; I 25 think I did laugh; but I was very rude to him, I would not meet him at dinner, and that, (though I did not say so,) because I considered him 'in loco apostatæ' from the Anglican Church, and I hereby beg his pardon for it. I wrote afterwards with a view to apologize, but I dare say he must have thought that I 30 made the matter worse, for these were my words to him:—

'The news that you are praying for us is most touching, and raises a variety of indescribable emotions . . . . May their prayers return abundantly into their own bosoms. . . . Why then do I not meet you in a manner conformable with these first 35

3 ready to my] close at   4–5 the more sensibly for . . . doors.] most sensibly too, because it was before my eyes.   12–13 justified . . . charges] fulfilled the bad points   19 myself, at that time] myself then   20 their desirableness] it 22 Catholic body in these islands] members of the Roman Church in England 24–25 rooms with . . . Magdalen] rooms, whither Mr. Palmer of Magdalen brought him 26 did laugh;] did;   33 emotions. . . .] emotions.   34 bosoms. . . .] bosoms!

feelings ? For this single reason, if I may say it, that your acts
are contrary to your words. You invite us to a union of hearts, at
the same time that you are doing all you can, not to restore, not
to reform, not to re-unite, but to destroy our Church. You go
5 further than your principles require. You are leagued with our
enemies. "The voice is Jacob's voice, but the hands are the hands
of Esau." This is what especially distresses us; this is what we
cannot understand; how Christians, like yourselves, with the
clear view you have that a warfare is ever waging in the world
10 between good and evil, should, in the present state of England,
ally yourselves with the side of evil against the side of good. . . .
Of parties now in the country, you cannot but allow, that next to
yourselves we are nearest to revealed truth. We maintain great
and holy principles; we profess Catholic doctrines. . . . So near
15 are we as a body to yourselves in modes of thinking, as even to
have been taunted with the nicknames which belong to you;
and, on the other hand, if there are professed infidels, scoffers,
sceptics, unprincipled men, rebels, they are found among our
opponents. And yet you take part with them against us. . . . You
20 consent to act hand in hand [with these and others] for our overthrow. Alas! all this it is that impresses us irresistibly with the
notion that you are a political, not a religious party; that in order
to gain an end on which you set your hearts,—an open stage for
yourselves in England,—you ally yourselves with those who hold
25 nothing against those who hold something. This is what distresses my own mind so greatly, to speak of myself, that, with
limitations which need not now be mentioned, I cannot meet
familiarly any leading persons of the Roman Communion, and
least of all when they come on a religious errand. Break off, I
30 would say, with Mr. O'Connell in Ireland and the liberal party
in England, or come not to us with overtures for mutual prayer
and religious sympathy.'

And here came in another feeling, of a personal nature, which
had little to do with the argument against Rome, except that, in
35 my prejudice, I viewed what happened to myself in the light of
my own ideas of the traditionary conduct of her advocates and
instruments. I was very stern in the case of any interference in
our Oxford matters on the part of charitable Catholics, and of any

35 viewed . . . light of] connected it with   36 traditionary] usual   37 in
the case of] upon   38 of any] on any

attempt to do me good personally. There was nothing, indeed, at
the time more likely to throw me back. 'Why do you meddle ?
why cannot you let me alone ? You can do me no good; you
know nothing on earth about me; you may actually do me harm;
I am in better hands than yours. I know my own sincerity of 5
purpose; and I am determined upon taking my time.' Since I
have been a Catholic, people have sometimes accused me of
backwardness in making converts; and Protestants have argued
from it that I have no great eagerness to do so. It would be
against my nature to act otherwise than I do; but besides, it 10
would be to forget the lessons which I gained in the experience
of my own history in the past.

This is the account which I have to give of some savage and
ungrateful words in the British Critic of 1840 against the
controversialists of Rome: 'By their fruits ye shall know them. 15
... We see it attempting to gain converts among us by unreal
representations of its doctrines, plausible statements, bold
assertions, appeals to the weaknesses of human nature, to our
fancies, our eccentricities, our fears, our frivolities, our false
philosophies. We see its agents, smiling and nodding and duck- 20
ing to attract attention, as gipsies make up to truant boys, holding out tales for the nursery, and pretty pictures, and gilt
gingerbread, and physic concealed in jam, and sugar-plums for
good children. Who can but feel shame when the religion of
Ximenes, Borromeo, and Pascal, is so overlaid ? Who can but 25
feel sorrow, when its devout and earnest defenders so mistake its
genius and its capabilities ? We Englishmen like manliness,
openness, consistency, truth. Rome will never gain on us, till she
learns these virtues, and uses them; and then she *may* gain us,
but it will be by ceasing to be what we now mean by Rome, by 30
having a right, not to "have dominion over our faith", but to gain
and possess our affections in the bonds of the gospel. Till she
ceases to be what she practically is, a union is impossible between
her and England; but, if she does reform, (and who can presume
to say that so large a part of Christendom never can ?) then it 35
will be our Church's duty at once to join in communion with the
continental Churches, whatever politicians at home may say to it,
and whatever steps the civil power may take in consequence.
And though we may not live to see that day, at least we are

21 gipsies] gipseys   29 *may*] may

bound to pray for it; we are bound to pray for our brethren that they and we may be led together into the pure light of the gospel, and be one as we once were one. It was most touching news to be told, as we were lately, that Christians on the Continent were
5 praying together for the spiritual well-being of England. May they gain light, while they aim at unity, and grow in faith while they manifest their love! We too have our duties to them; not of reviling, not of slandering, not of hating, though political interests require it; but the duty of loving brethren still more
10 abundantly in spirit, whose faces, for our sins and their sins, we are not allowed to see in the flesh.'

No one ought to indulge in insinuations; it certainly diminishes my right to complain of slanders uttered against myself, when, as in this passage, I had already spoken in disparagement of the
15 controversialists of that religious body, to which I myself now belong.

I have thus put together, as well as I can, what has to be said about my general state of mind from the autumn of 1839 to the summer of 1841; and, having done so, I go on to narrate how
20 my new misgivings affected my conduct, and my relations towards the Anglican Church. When I got back to Oxford in October, 1839, after the visits which I had been paying, it so happened, there had been, in my absence, occurrences of an awkward character, compromising
25 me both with my Bishop and also with the authorities of the University; and this drew my attention at once to the state of the Movement party there, and made me very anxious for the future. In the spring of the year, as has been seen in the Article analyzed above, I had spoken of the excesses which were to be
30 found among persons commonly included in it:—at that time I thought little of such an evil, but the new views, which had come on me during the Long Vacation, on the one hand made me comprehend it, and on the other took away my power of effectually meeting it. A firm and powerful control was necessary to
35 keep men straight; I never had a strong wrist, but at the very

14 disparagement] condemnation   14–15 the controversialists . . . body] that class of controversialists   17 can] could   24–25 compromising me] bringing me into collision   25–26 authorities of the University] University authorities 26–27 of the Movement] of what would be considered the Movement   31 views] thoughts

time, when it was most needed, the reins had broken in my hands. With an anxious presentiment on my mind of the upshot of the whole inquiry, which it was almost impossible for me to conceal from men who saw me day by day, who heard my familiar conversation, who came perhaps for the express purpose 5 of pumping me, and having a categorical *yes* or *no* to their questions,—how could I expect to say any thing about my actual, positive, present belief, which would be sustaining or consoling to such persons as were haunted already by doubts of their own ? Nay, how could I, with satisfaction to myself, 10 analyze my own mind, and say what I held and what I did not hold ? or how could I say with what limitations, shades of difference, or degrees of belief, I still held that body of Anglican opinions which I had openly professed and taught ? how could I deny or assert this point or that, without injustice to the new 15 light, in which the whole evidence for those old opinions presented itself to my mind ?

However, I had to do what I could, and what was best, under the circumstances; I found a general talk on the subject of the Article in the Dublin Review; and, if it had affected me, it was 20 not wonderful, that it affected others also. As to myself, I felt no kind of certainty that the argument in it was conclusive. Taking it at the worst, granting that the Anglican Church had not the Note of Catholicity; yet there were many Notes of the Church. Some belonged to one age or place, some to another. 25 Bellarmine had reckoned Temporal Prosperity among the Notes of the Church; but the Roman Church had not any great popularity, wealth, glory, power, or prospects, in the nineteenth century. It was not at all certain as yet, even that we had not the Note of Catholicity; but, if not this, we had others. My first 30 business then, was to examine this question carefully, and see, whether a great deal could not be said after all for the Anglican Church, in spite of its acknowledged short-comings. This I did in an Article 'on the Catholicity of the English Church', which appeared in the British Critic of January, 1840. As to my 35 personal distress on the point, I think it had gone by February 21st in that year, for I wrote then to Mr. Bowden about the

11–12 not hold ?] not ?   12 or how could I say] or say   13 I still held] I held   13–14 of Anglican opinions] of opinions   16 light] view   29 certain as yet] certain yet   30 if not this, we] if not, we   32 whether] if

important Article in the Dublin, thus: 'It made a great impression here [Oxford]; and, I say what of course I would only say to such as yourself, it made me for a while very uncomfortable in my own mind. The great speciousness of his argument is one of
5 the things which have made me despond so much', that is, as anticipating its effect upon others.

But, secondly, the great stumbling-block lay in the 39 Articles. It was urged that here was a positive Note *against* Anglicanism: —Anglicanism claimed to hold, that the Church of England
10 was nothing else than a continuation in this country, (as the Church of Rome might be in France or Spain,) of that one Church of which in old times Athanasius and Augustine were members. But, if so, the doctrine must be the same; the doctrine of the Old Church must live and speak in Anglican formularies,
15 in the 39 Articles. Did it ? Yes, it did; that is what I maintained; it did in substance, in a true sense. Man had done his worst to disfigure, to mutilate, the old Catholic Truth; but there it was, in spite of them, in the Articles still. It was there,—but this must be shown. It was a matter of life and death to us to show it. And
20 I believed that it could be shown; I considered that those grounds of justification, which I gave above, when I was speaking of Tract 90, were sufficient for the purpose; and therefore I set about showing it at once. This was in March, 1840, when I went up to Littlemore. And, as it was a matter of life and death with
25 us, all risks must be run to show it. When the attempt was actually made, I had got reconciled to the prospect of it, and had no apprehensions as to the experiment; but in 1840, while my purpose was honest, and my grounds of reason satisfactory, I did nevertheless recognize that I was engaged in an *experi-*
30 *mentum crucis.* I have no doubt that then I acknowledged to myself that it would be a trial of the Anglican Church, which it had never undergone before,—not that the Catholic sense of the Articles had not been held or at least suffered by their framers and promulgators, not that it was not implied in the
35 teaching of Andrewes or Beveridge, but that it had never been publicly recognized, while the interpretation of the day was Protestant and exclusive. I observe also, that, though my Tract was an experiment, it was, as I said at the time, 'no *feeler*'; the event showed this; for, when my principle was not granted, I

5–6 as anticipating] as to   34 not that it was not] and was not   39 this] it

did not draw back, but gave up. I would not hold office in a
Church which would not allow my sense of the Articles. My
tone was, 'This is necessary for us, and have it we must and will,
and, if it tends to bring men to look less bitterly on the Church
of Rome, so much the better.'   5

This then was the second work to which I set myself; though
when I got to Littlemore, other things interfered to prevent my
accomplishing it at the moment. I had in mind to remove all such
obstacles as lay in the way of holding the Apostolic and Catholic
character of the Anglican teaching; to assert the right of all who 10
chose, to say in the face of day, 'Our Church teaches the Primitive Ancient faith.' I did not conceal this: in Tract 90, it is put
forward as the first principle of all, 'It is a duty which we owe
both to the Catholic Church, and to our own, to take our reformed confessions in the most Catholic sense they will admit: 15
we have no duties towards their framers.' And still more
pointedly in my Letter, explanatory of the Tract, addressed to
Dr. Jelf, I say: 'The only peculiarity of the view I advocate, if
I must so call it, is this—that whereas it is usual at this day to
make the *particular belief of their writers* their true interpreta- 20
tion, I would make the *belief of the Catholic Church such.* That
is, as it is often said that infants are regenerated in Baptism,
not on the faith of their parents, but of the Church, so in like
manner I would say that the Articles are received, not in the
sense of their framers, but (as far as the wording will admit or 25
any ambiguity requires it) in the one Catholic sense.'

A third measure which I distinctly contemplated, was the
resignation of St. Mary's, whatever became of the question of
the 39 Articles; and as a first step I meditated a retirement to
Littlemore. Littlemore was an integral part of St. Mary's Parish, 30
and between two and three miles distant from Oxford. I had
built a Church there several years before; and I went there to
pass the Lent of 1840, and gave myself up to teaching in the
Parish School, and practising the choir. At the same time, I had
in view a monastic house there. I bought ten acres of ground 35
and began planting; but this great design was never carried out.
I mention it, because it shows how little I had really the idea

---

7 interfered to prevent my] came in the way of   9 lay] were   29 the
39 Articles] the Articles   30–31 Littlemore was . . . Oxford.] *not in 64*
34 Parish School] Poor Schools   34–35 had in view] contemplated

at that time of ever leaving the Anglican Church. That I contemplated as early as 1839 the further step of giving up St. Mary's,
appears from a letter which I wrote in October, 1840, to Mr.
Keble, the friend whom it was most natural for me to consult
5 on such a point. It ran as follows:—

'For a year past a feeling has been growing on me that I
ought to give up St. Mary's, but I am no fit judge in the matter.
I cannot ascertain accurately my own impressions and convictions, which are the basis of the difficulty, and though you cannot
10 of course do this for me, yet you may help me generally, and
perhaps supersede the necessity of my going by them at all.

'First, it is certain that I do not know my Oxford parishioners;
I am not conscious of influencing them, and certainly I have no
insight into their spiritual state. I have no personal, no pastoral
15 acquaintance with them. To very few have I any opportunity
of saying a religious word. Whatever influence I exert on them
is precisely that which I may be exerting on persons out of my
parish. In my excuse I am accustomed to say to myself that I am
not adapted to get on with them, while others are. On the other
20 hand, I am conscious that by means of my position at St. Mary's,
I do exert a considerable influence on the University, whether on
Undergraduates or Graduates. It seems, then, on the whole that
I am using St. Mary's, to the neglect of its direct duties, for
objects not belonging to it; I am converting a parochial charge
25 into a sort of University office.

'I think I may say truly that I have begun scarcely any plan
but for the sake of my parish, but every one has turned, independently of me, into the direction of the University. I began
Saints'-days Services, daily Services, and Lectures in Adam de
30 Brome's Chapel, for my parishioners; but they have not come
to them. In consequence I dropped the last mentioned, having,
while it lasted, been naturally led to direct it to the instruction of
those who did come, instead of those who did not. The Weekly
Communion, I believe, I did begin for the sake of the University.
35 'Added to this the authorities of the University, the appointed
guardians of those who form great part of the attendants on my
Sermons, have shown a dislike of my preaching. One dissuades

1 at that time] then   1–2 I contemplated] I also contemplated   2 as early as
1839] even *64–68*   2–3 St. Mary's, appears] St. Mary's itself as early as 1839
64–68   3–4 to Mr. Keble, the friend] to the friend *64–68*

men from coming;—the late Vice-Chancellor threatens to take his own children away from the Church; and the present, having an opportunity last spring of preaching in my parish pulpit, gets up and preaches against doctrine with which I am in good measure identified. No plainer proof can be given of the feeling in these quarters, than the absurd myth, now a second time put forward, "that Vice-Chancellors cannot be got to take the office on account of Puseyism".

'But further than this, I cannot disguise from myself that my preaching is not calculated to defend that system of religion which has been received for 300 years, and of which the Heads of Houses are the legitimate maintainers in this place. They exclude me, as far as may be, from the University Pulpit; and, though I never have preached strong doctrine in it, they do so rightly, so far as this, that they understand that my sermons are calculated to undermine things established. I cannot disguise from myself that they are. No one will deny that most of my sermons are on moral subjects, not doctrinal; still I am leading my hearers to the Primitive Church, if you will, but not to the Church of England. Now, ought one to be disgusting the minds of young men with the received religion, in the exercise of a sacred office, yet without a commission, and against the wish of their guides and governors?

'But this is not all. I fear I must allow that, whether I will or no, I am disposing them towards Rome. First, because Rome is the only representative of the Primitive Church besides ourselves; in proportion then as they are loosened from the one, they will go to the other. Next, because many doctrines which I have held have far greater, or their only scope, in the Roman system. And, moveover, if, as is not unlikely, we have in process of time heretical Bishops or teachers among us, an evil which *ipso facto* infects the whole community to which they belong, and if, again (what there are at this moment symptoms of), there be a movement in the English Roman Catholics to break the alliance of O'Connell and of Exeter Hall, strong temptations will be placed in the way of individuals, already imbued with a tone of thought congenial to Rome, to join her Communion.

'People tell me, on the other hand, that I am, whether by sermons or otherwise, exerting at St. Mary's a beneficial influence

22 commission, and against] commission, against

on our prospective clergy; but what if I take to myself the credit of seeing further than they, and of having in the course of the last year discovered that what they approve so much is very likely to end in Romanism ?

5   'The *arguments* which I have published against Romanism seem to myself as cogent as ever, but men go by their sympathies, not by argument; and if I feel the force of this influence myself, who bow to the arguments, why may not others still more, who never have in the same degree admitted the arguments ?

10   'Nor can I counteract the danger by preaching or writing against Rome. I seem to myself almost to have shot my last arrow in the Article on English Catholicity. It must be added, that the very circumstance that I have committed myself against Rome has the effect of setting to sleep people suspicious about
15 me, which is painful now that I begin to have suspicions about myself. I mentioned my general difficulty to Rogers a year since, than whom I know no one of a more fine and accurate conscience, and it was his spontaneous idea that I should give up St. Mary's, if my feelings continued. I mentioned it again to him lately, and
20 he did not reverse his opinion, only expressed great reluctance to believe it must be so.'

Mr. Keble's judgment was in favour of my retaining my living; at least for the present; what weighed with me most was his saying, 'You must consider, whether your retiring either
25 from the Pastoral Care only, or from writing and printing and editing in the cause, would not be a sort of scandalous thing, unless it were done very warily. It would be said, "You see he can go on no longer with the Church of England, except in mere Lay Communion"; or people might say you repented of
30 the cause altogether. Till you see [your way to mitigate, if not remove this evil] I certainly should advise you to stay.' I answered as follows:—

'Since you think I *may* go on, it seems to follow that, under the circumstances, I *ought* to do so. There are plenty of reasons
35 for it, directly it is allowed to be lawful. The following considerations have much reconciled my feelings to your conclusion.

'1. I do not think that we have yet made fair trial how much the English Church will bear. I know it is a hazardous experiment,—like proving cannon. Yet we must not take it for granted

16 Rogers] A.B.   22 Mr. Keble's] My friend's *64–68*

that the metal will burst in the operation. It has borne at various times, not to say at this time, a great infusion of Catholic truth without damage. As to the result, viz. whether this process will not approximate the whole English Church, as a body, to Rome, that is nothing to us. For what we know, it may be the provi- 5 dential means of uniting the whole Church in one, without fresh schismatizing or use of private judgment.'

Here I observe, that, what was contemplated was the bursting of the *Catholicity* of the Anglican Church, that is, my *subjective idea* of that Church. Its bursting would not hurt her with the 10 world, but would be a discovery that she was purely and essentially Protestant, and would be really the 'hoisting of the engineer with his own petar'. And this was the result. I continue:—

'2. Say, that I move sympathies for Rome: in the same sense does Hooker, Taylor, Bull, &c. Their *arguments* may be against 15 Rome, but the sympathies they raise must be towards Rome, *so far* as Rome maintains truths which our Church does not teach or enforce. Thus it is a question of *degree* between our divines and me. I may, if so be, go further; I may raise sympathies *more*; but I am but urging minds in the same direction as they do. I am 20 doing just the very thing which all our doctors have ever been doing. In short, would not Hooker, if Vicar of St. Mary's, be in my difficulty?'—Here it may be objected, that Hooker could preach against Rome and I could not; but I doubt whether he could have preached effectively against Transubstantiation 25 better than I, though neither he nor I held that doctrine.

'3. Rationalism is the great evil of the day. May not I consider my post at St. Mary's as a place of protest against it? I am more certain that the Protestant [spirit], which I oppose, leads to infidelity, than that which I recommend, leads to Rome. 30 Who knows what the state of the University may be, as regards Divinity Professors in a few years hence? Any how, a great battle may be coming on, of which Milman's book is a sort of earnest. The whole of *our* day may be a battle with this spirit. May we not leave to another age *its own* evil,—to settle the 35 question of Romanism?'

I may add that from this time I had a curate at St. Mary's, who gradually took more and more of my work.

Also, this same year, 1840, I made arrangements for giving

23 objected] said   26 that doctrine] it   33 Milman's] C.D.'s

up the British Critic, in the following July, which were carried into effect at that date.

Such was about my state of mind, on the publication of Tract 90 in February 1841. I was indeed in prudence taking steps 5 towards eventually withdrawing from St. Mary's, and I was not confident about my permanent adhesion to the Anglican creed; but I was in no actual perplexity or trouble of mind. Nor did the immense commotion consequent upon the publication of the Tract unsettle me again; for I fancied I had weathered the 10 storm, as far as the Bishops were concerned: the Tract had not been condemned: that was the great point, and I made much of it.

To illustrate my feelings during this trial, I will make extracts from my letters addressed severally to Mr. Bowden and another friend, which have come into my possession.

15   1. March 15.—'The Heads, I believe, have just done a violent act: they have said that my interpretation of the Articles is an *evasion*. Do not think that this will pain me. You see, no *doctrine* is censured, and my shoulders shall manage to bear the charge. If you knew all, or were here, you would see that I have asserted 20 a great principle, and I *ought* to suffer for it:—that the Articles are to be interpreted, not according to the meaning of the writers, but (as far as the wording will admit) according to the sense of the Catholic Church.'

2. March 25.—'I do trust I shall make no false step, and hope 25 my friends will pray for me to this effect. If, as you say, a destiny hangs over us, a single false step may ruin all. I am very well and comfortable; but we are not yet out of the wood.'

3. April 1.—'The Bishop sent me word on Sunday to write a Letter to him *"instanter"*. So I wrote it on Monday: on Tuesday 30 it passed through the press: on Wednesday it was out: and to-day [Thursday] it is in London.

'I trust that things are smoothing now; and that we have made a *great step* is certain. It is not right to boast, till I am

4 February 1841] February, 1841   4–7 I was indeed . . . trouble of mind.] *not in 64*   7–8 Nor did the immense] The immense   9 Tract unsettle] Tract did not unsettle   for I fancied I had] for I had   9–10 the storm . . . concerned:] the storm: 13–14 addressed . . . possession.] to a friend, which have come into my possession. The dates are respectively March 25, April 1, and May 9. 15 March 15] *This letter not at this place in 64.*   24: 2. March 25.—'I] 1. 'I 28: 3. April 1.—'The] 2. 'The

clear out of the wood, i.e. till I know how the Letter is received
in London. You know, I suppose, that I am to stop the Tracts;
but you will see in the Letter, though I speak *quite* what I feel,
yet I have managed to take out on *my* side my snubbing's worth.
And this makes me anxious how it will be received in London.   5

'I have not had a misgiving for five minutes from the first:
but I do not like to boast, lest some harm come.'

4. April 4.—'Your letter of this morning was an exceedingly
great gratification to me; and it is confirmed, I am thankful to
say, by the opinion of others. The Bishop sent me a message   10
that my Letter had his unqualified approbation; and since that,
he has sent me a note to the same effect, only going more into
detail. It is most pleasant too to my feelings, to have such a
testimony to the substantial truth and importance of No. 90,
as I have had from so many of my friends, from those who, from   15
their cautious turn of mind, I was least sanguine about. I have
not had one misgiving myself about it throughout; and I do
trust that what has happened will be overruled to subserve the
great cause we all have at heart.'

5. May 9.—'The Bishops are very desirous of hushing   20
the matter up: and I certainly have done my utmost to co-
operate with them, on the understanding that the Tract is not
to be withdrawn or condemned.'

Upon this occasion several Catholics wrote to me; I answered
one of my correspondents in the same tone:—   25

'April 8.—You have no cause to be surprised at the discon-
tinuance of the Tracts. We feel no misgivings about it whatever,
as if the cause of what we hold to be Catholic truth would suffer
thereby. My letter to my Bishop has, I trust, had the effect of
bringing the preponderating *authority* of the Church on our   30
side. No stopping of the Tracts can, humanly speaking, stop
the spread of the opinions which they have inculcated.

'The Tracts are not *suppressed*. No doctrine or principle has
been conceded by us, or condemned by authority. The Bishop
has but said that a certain Tract is "objectionable", no reason   35
being stated. I have no intention whatever of yielding any one

8: 4. April 4.] *This letter not in 64.*   20: 5. May 9.—'The] 3. 'The   23 condemned.'] *This was followed in 64 by a paragraph beginning*: And to my friend,
Mr. Bowden, under date of March 15, 'The Heads ... Catholic Church.' (*As on*
p. 128.)   24 Upon this occasion] Upon occasion of Tract 90   25 in the
same tone] thus

point which I hold on conviction; and that the authorities of the Church know full well.'

In the summer of 1841, I found myself at Littlemore without any harass or anxiety on my mind. I had determined to put
5 aside all controversy, and I set myself down to my translation of St. Athanasius; but, between July and November, I received three blows which broke me.

1. I had got but a little way in my work, when my trouble returned on me. The ghost had come a second time. In the Arian
10 History I found the very same phenomenon, in a far bolder shape, which I had found in the Monophysite. I had not observed it in 1832. Wonderful that this should come upon me! I had not sought it out; I was reading and writing in my own line of study, far from the controversies of the day, on what is
15 called a 'metaphysical' subject; but I saw clearly, that in the history of Arianism, the pure Arians were the Protestants, the semi-Arians were the Anglicans, and that Rome now was what it was then. The truth lay, not with the *Via Media*, but with what was called 'the extreme party'. As I am not writing a work of
20 controversy, I need not enlarge upon the argument; I have said something on the subject in a Volume, from which I have already quoted.

2. I was in the misery of this new unsettlement, when a second blow came upon me. The Bishops one after another began to
25 charge against me. It was a formal, determinate movement. This was the real 'understanding'; that, on which I had acted on the first appearance of Tract 90, had come to nought. I think the words, which had then been used to me, were, that 'perhaps two or three of them might think it necessary to say something
30 in their charges'; but by this time they had tided over the difficulty of the Tract, and there was no one to enforce the 'understanding'. They went on in this way, directing charges at me, for three whole years. I recognized it as a condemnation; it was the only one that was in their power. At first I intended to
35 protest; but I gave up the thought in despair.

On October 17th, I wrote thus to a friend: 'I suppose it will be

18 was then.] was.   with what] in what   21–22 subject in a Volume, from . . . quoted.] subject, in a Volume which I published fourteen years ago.
27 the first appearance] occasion   29 three of them might] three might

necessary in some shape or other to re-assert Tract 90; else, it will seem, after these Bishops' Charges, as if it were silenced, which it has not been, nor do I intend it should be. I wish to keep quiet; but if Bishops speak, I will speak too. If the view were silenced, I could not remain in the Church, nor could 5 many others; and therefore, since it is *not* silenced, I shall take care to show that it isn't.'

A day or two after, Oct. 22, a stranger wrote to me to say, that the Tracts for the Times had made a young friend of his a Catholic, and to ask, 'would I be so good as to convert him 10 back'; I made answer:

'If conversions to Rome take place in consequence of the Tracts for the Times, I do not impute blame to them, but to those who, instead of acknowledging such Anglican principles of theology and ecclesiastical polity as they contain, set them- 15 selves to oppose them. Whatever be the influence of the Tracts, great or small, they may become just as powerful for Rome, if our Church refuses them, as they would be for our Church if she accepted them. If our rulers speak either against the Tracts, or not at all, if any number of them, not only do not favour, but 20 even do not suffer the principles contained in them, it is plain that our members may easily be persuaded either to give up those principles, or to give up the Church. If this state of things goes on, I mournfully prophesy, not one or two, but many secessions to the Church of Rome.' 25

Two years afterwards, looking back on what had passed, I said, 'There were no converts to Rome, till after the condemna- tion of No. 90.'

3. As if all this were not enough, there came the affair of the Jerusalem Bishopric; and, with a brief mention of it, I shall 30 conclude.

I think I am right in saying that it had been long a desire with the Prussian Court to introduce Episcopacy into the new Evan- gelical Religion, which was intended in that country to embrace both the Lutheran and Calvinistic bodies. I almost think I 35 heard of the project, when I was at Rome in 1833, at the Hotel of the Prussian Minister, M. Bunsen, who was most hospitable and kind, as to other English visitors, so also to my friends and my- self. The idea of Episcopacy, as the Prussian king understood it,

39 The idea of] I suppose that the idea of

was, I suppose, very different from that taught in the Tractarian
School: but still, I suppose also, that the chief authors of that
school would have gladly seen such a measure carried out in
Prussia, had it been done without compromising those prin-
5 ciples which were necessary to the being of a Church. About the
time of the publication of Tract 90, M. Bunsen and the then
Archbishop of Canterbury were taking steps for its execution,
by appointing and consecrating a Bishop for Jerusalem.
Jerusalem, it would seem, was considered a safe place for the
10 experiment; it was too far from Prussia to awaken the suscepti-
bilities of any party at home; if the project failed, it failed without harm to any one; and, if it succeeded, it gave Protestantism
a *status* in the East, which, in association with the Monophysite
or Jacobite and the Nestorian bodies, formed a political instru-
15 ment for England, parallel to that which Russia had in the
Greek Church, and France in the Latin.

Accordingly, in July 1841, full of the Anglican difficulty on the
question of Catholicity, I thus spoke of the Jerusalem scheme in
an Article in the British Critic: 'When our thoughts turn to the
20 East, instead of recollecting that there are Christian Churches
there, we leave it to the Russians to take care of the Greeks, and
the French to take care of the Romans, and we content ourselves
with erecting a Protestant Church at Jerusalem, or with helping
the Jews to rebuild their Temple there, or with becoming the
25 august protectors of Nestorians, Monophysites, and all the
heretics we can hear of, or with forming a league with the Mus-
sulman against Greeks and Romans together.'

I do not pretend, so long after the time, to give a full or exact
account of this measure in detail. I will but say that in the Act
30 of Parliament, under date of October 5, 1841, (if the copy, from
which I quote, contains the measure as it passed the Houses),
provision is made for the consecration of 'British subjects, or the
subjects or citizens of any foreign state, to be Bishops in any
foreign country, whether such foreign subjects or citizens be or
35 be not subjects or citizens of the country in which they are to
act, and . . . without requiring such of them as may be subjects
or citizens of any foreign kingdom or state to take the oaths of
allegiance and supremacy, and the oath of due obedience to the
Archbishop for the time being' . . . also 'that such Bishop or

1 was, I suppose, very] was very

Bishops, so consecrated, may exercise, within such limits, as may from time to time be assigned for that purpose in such foreign countries by her Majesty, spiritual jurisdiction over the ministers of British congregations of the United Church of England and Ireland, and over *such other Protestant* Congregations, as may 5 be desirous of placing themselves under his or their authority'.

Now here, at the very time that the Anglican Bishops were directing their censure upon me for avowing an approach to the Catholic Church not closer than I believed the Anglican formularies would allow, they were on the other hand, fraterniz- 10 ing, by their act or by their sufferance, with Protestant bodies, and allowing them to put themselves under an Anglican Bishop, without any renunciation of their errors or regard to their due reception of baptism and confirmation; while there was great reason to suppose that the said Bishop was intended to make 15 converts from the orthodox Greeks, and the schismatical Oriental bodies, by means of the influence of England. This was the third blow, which finally shattered my faith in the Anglican Church. That Church was not only forbidding any sympathy or concurrence with the Church of Rome, but it actually was 20 courting an intercommunion with Protestant Prussia and the heresy of the Orientals. The Anglican Church might have the Apostolical succession, as had the Monophysites; but such acts as were in progress led me to the gravest suspicion, not that it would soon cease to be a Church, but that, since the 16th century, 25 it had never been a Church all along.

On October 12th, I thus wrote to Mr. Bowden:—'We have not a single Anglican in Jerusalem; so we are sending a Bishop to *make* a communion, not to govern our own people. Next, the excuse is, that there are converted Anglican Jews there who 30 require a Bishop; I am told there are not half-a-dozen. But for *them* the Bishop is sent out, and for them he is a Bishop of the *circumcision*' (I think he was a converted Jew, who boasted of his Jewish descent), 'against the Epistle to the Galatians pretty nearly. Thirdly, for the sake of Prussia, he is to take under him 35 all the foreign Protestants who will come; and the political advantages will be so great, from the influence of England, that there is no doubt they *will* come. They are to sign the Confession

13 their due] the due   25–26 that, since the 16th century, it] that it   27 Mr. Bowden] a friend

of Augsburg, and there is nothing to show that they hold the doctrine of Baptismal Regeneration.

'As to myself, I shall do nothing whatever publicly, unless indeed it were to give my signature to a Protest; but I think it would be out of place in *me* to agitate, having been in a way silenced; but the Archbishop is really doing most grave work, of which we cannot see the end.'

I did make a solemn Protest, and sent it to the Archbishop of Canterbury, and also sent it to my own Bishop with the following letter:—

'It seems as if I were never to write to your Lordship, without giving you pain, and I know that my present subject does not specially concern your Lordship; yet, after a great deal of anxious thought, I lay before you the enclosed Protest.

'Your Lordship will observe that I am not asking for any notice of it, unless you think that I ought to receive one. I do this very serious act in obedience to my sense of duty.

'If the English Church is to enter on a new course, and assume a new aspect, it will be more pleasant to me hereafter to think, that I did not suffer so grievous an event to happen, without bearing witness against it.

'May I be allowed to say, that I augur nothing but evil, if we in any respect prejudice our title to be a branch of the Apostolic Church? That Article of the Creed, I need hardly observe to your Lordship, is of such constraining power, that, if *we* will not claim it, and use it for ourselves, *others* will use it in their own behalf against us. Men who learn whether by means of documents or measures, whether from the statements or the acts of persons in authority, that our communion is not a branch of the One Church, I foresee with much grief, will be tempted to look out for that Church elsewhere.

'It is to me a subject of great dismay, that, as far as the Church has lately spoken out, on the subject of the opinions which I and others hold, those opinions are, not merely not *sanctioned* (for that I do not ask), but not even *suffered*.

'I earnestly hope that your Lordship will excuse my freedom in thus speaking to you of some members of your Most Rev. and Right Rev. Body. With every feeling of reverent attachment to your Lordship,

'I am, &c.'

PROTEST

'Whereas the Church of England has a claim on the allegiance of Catholic believers only on the ground of her own claim to be considered a branch of the Catholic Church:

'And whereas the recognition of heresy, indirect as well as 5 direct, goes far to destroy such claim in the case of any religious body:

'And whereas to admit maintainers of heresy to communion, without formal renunciation of their errors, goes far towards recognizing the same: 10

'And whereas Lutheranism and Calvinism are heresies, repugnant to Scripture, springing up three centuries since, and anathematized by East as well as West:

'And whereas it is reported that the Most Reverend Primate and other Right Reverend Rulers of our Church have conse- 15 crated a Bishop with a view to exercising spiritual jurisdiction over Protestant, that is, Lutheran and Calvinist congregations in the East (under the provisions of an Act made in the last session of Parliament to amend an Act made in the 26th year of the reign of his Majesty King George the Third, intituled, "An Act 20 to empower the Archbishop of Canterbury, or the Archbishop of York for the time being, to consecrate to the office of Bishop persons being subjects or citizens of countries out of his Majesty's dominions"), dispensing at the same time, not in particular cases and accidentally, but as if on principle and universally, with any 25 abjuration of error on the part of such congregations, and with any reconciliation to the Church on the part of the presiding Bishop; thereby giving some sort of formal recognition to the doctrines which such congregations maintain:

'And whereas the dioceses in England are connected together 30 by so close an intercommunion, that what is done by authority in one, immediately affects the rest:

'On these grounds, I in my place, being a priest of the English Church and Vicar of St. Mary the Virgin's, Oxford, by way of relieving my conscience, do hereby solemnly protest against the 35 measure aforesaid, and disown it, as removing our Church from her present ground and tending to her disorganization.

'JOHN HENRY NEWMAN.
'November 11, 1841.'

7 body:] body advancing it:

Looking back two years afterwards on the above-mentioned and other acts, on the part of Anglican Ecclesiastical authorities, I observed: 'Many a man might have held an abstract theory about the Catholic Church, to which it was difficult to
5 adjust the Anglican,—might have admitted a suspicion, or even painful doubts about the latter,—yet never have been impelled onwards, had our Rulers preserved the quiescence of former years; but it is the corroboration of a present, living, and energetic heterodoxy, that realizes and makes such doubts
10 practical; it has been the recent speeches and acts of authorities, who had so long been tolerant of Protestant error, which has given to inquiry and to theory its force and its edge.'

As to the project of a Jerusalem Bishopric, I never heard of any good or harm it has ever done, except what it has done for
15 me; which many think a great misfortune, and I one of the greatest of mercies. It brought me on to the beginning of the end.

3 observed] observe   9 that] which   such doubts] them   11 has] have

CHAPTER IV

HISTORY OF MY RELIGIOUS OPINIONS FROM 1841 TO 1845

§ 1

FROM the end of 1841, I was on my death-bed, as regards my membership with the Anglican Church, though at the time I became aware of it only by degrees. I introduce what I have to say with this remark, by way of accounting for the character of this remaining portion of my narrative. A death-bed has scarcely a history; it is a tedious decline, with seasons of rallying and seasons of falling back; and since the end is foreseen, or what is called a matter of time, it has little interest for the reader, especially if he has a kind heart. Moreover, it is a season when doors are closed and curtains drawn, and when the sick man neither cares nor is able to record the stages of his malady. I was in these circumstances, except so far as I was not allowed to die in peace,—except so far as friends, who had still a full right to come in upon me, and the public world which had not, have given a sort of history to those last four years. But in consequence, my narrative must be in great measure documentary, as I cannot rely on my memory, except for definite particulars, positive or negative. Letters of mine to friends since dead have come into my hands; others have been kindly lent me for the occasion; and I have some drafts of others, and some notes which I made, though I have no strictly personal or continuous memoranda to consult, and have unluckily mislaid some valuable papers.

And first as to my position in the view of duty; it was this:—
1. I had given up my place in the Movement in my letter to the Bishop of Oxford in the spring of 1841; but 2. I could not give up my duties towards the many and various minds who had

1 Chapter IV] Part VI   2–3 Opinions From 1841 to 1845] Opinions   4 §1]
not in 64   19–21 documentary, as . . . negative.] documentary.   21–22 friends
. . . hands;] friends have come to me since their deaths;   23–24 others . . .
made] letters, and notes of my own

more or less been brought into it by me; 3. I expected or intended gradually to fall back into Lay Communion; 4. I never contemplated leaving the Church of England; 5. I could not hold office in its service, if I were not allowed to hold the Catholic
5 sense of the Articles; 6. I could not go to Rome, while she suffered honours to be paid to the Blessed Virgin and the Saints which I thought in my conscience to be incompatible with the Supreme, Incommunicable Glory of the One Infinite and Eternal; 7. I desired a union with Rome under conditions, Church with
10 Church; 8. I called Littlemore my Torres Vedras, and thought that some day we might advance again within the Anglican Church, as we had been forced to retire; 9. I kept back all persons who were disposed to go to Rome with all my might.

And I kept them back for three or four reasons; 1. because
15 what I could not in conscience do myself, I could not suffer them to do; 2. because I thought that in various cases they were acting under excitement; 3. because I had duties to my Bishop and to the Anglican Church; and 4, in some cases, because I had received from their Anglican parents or superiors direct
20 charge of them.

This was my view of my duty from the end of 1841, to my resignation of St. Mary's in the autumn of 1843. And now I shall relate my view, during that time, of the state of the controversy between the Churches.

25   As soon as I saw the hitch in the Anglican argument, during my course of reading in the summer of 1839, I began to look about, as I have said, for some ground which might supply a controversial basis for my need. The difficulty in question had affected my view both of Antiquity and Catholicity; for, while
30 the history of St. Leo showed me that the deliberate and eventual consent of the great body of the Church ratified a doctrinal decision as a part of revealed truth, it also showed that the rule of Antiquity was not infringed, though a doctrine had not been publicly recognized as so revealed, till centuries after the time of
35 the Apostles. Thus, whereas the Creeds tell us that the Church

---

4 its service] her   7 thought . . . incompatible] thought incompatible
17: 3. because] 3, while I held St. Mary's, because   24 Churches.] *no space
following in 64*   32 decision . . . truth, it] decision, it   34 so revealed] a
portion of the dogmatic foundation of the Church

is One, Holy, Catholic, and Apostolic, I could not prove that the Anglican communion was an integral part of the One Church, on the ground of its teaching being Apostolic or Catholic, without reasoning in favour of what are commonly called the Roman corruptions; and I could not defend our separation from 5 Rome and her faith without using arguments prejudicial to those great doctrines concerning our Lord, which are the very foundation of the Christian religion. The *Via Media* was an impossible idea; it was what I had called 'standing on one leg'; and it was necessary, if my old issue of the controversy was to be retained, 10 to go further either one way or the other.

Accordingly, I abandoned that old ground and took another. I deliberately quitted the old Anglican ground as untenable; though I did not do so all at once, but as I became more and more convinced of the state of the case. The Jerusalem Bishopric 15 was the ultimate condemnation of the old theory of the *Via Media*:—if its establishment did nothing else, at least it demolished the sacredness of diocesan rights. If England could be in Palestine, Rome might be in England. But its bearing upon the controversy, as I have shown in the foregoing chapter, was 20 much more serious than this technical ground. From that time the Anglican Church was, in my mind, either not a normal portion of that One Church to which the promises were made, or at least in an abnormal state; and from that time I said boldly (as I did in my Protest, and as indeed I had even intimated in 25 my Letter to the Bishop of Oxford), that the Church in which I found myself had no claim on me, except on condition of its being a portion of the One Catholic Communion, and that that condition must ever be borne in mind as a practical matter, and had to be distinctly proved. All this is not inconsistent with my 30 saying above that, at this time, I had no thought of leaving the Church of England; because I felt some of my old objections against Rome as strongly as ever. I had no right, I had no leave, to act against my conscience. That was a higher rule than any argument about the Notes of the Church. 35

Under these circumstances I turned for protection to the Note

---

3 its teaching being] its being without 14 though] but 30 is] was 31 saying above that] saying that 6 Rome and her faith without] Rome without 17–21 *Media*:—if . . . ground. From] *Media*; 31–32 the Church of England] that Church

of Sanctity, with a view of showing that we had at least one of the necessary Notes, as fully as the Church of Rome; or, at least, without entering into comparisons, that we had it in such a sufficient sense as to reconcile us to our position, and to supply
5 full evidence, and a clear direction, on the point of practical duty. We had the Note of Life,—not any sort of life, not such only as can come of nature, but a supernatural Christian life, which could only come directly from above. Thus, in my Article in the British Critic, to which I have so often referred, in
10 January, 1840 (before the time of Tract 90), I said of the Anglican Church that 'she has the note of possession, the note of freedom from party titles, the note of life,—a tough life and a vigorous; she has ancient descent, unbroken continuance, agreement in doctrine with the Ancient Church'. Presently I go on to
15 speak of sanctity: 'Much as Roman Catholics may denounce us at present as schismatical, they could not resist us if the Anglican communion had but that one note of the Church upon it,— sanctity. The Church of the day [4th century] could not resist Meletius; his enemies were fairly overcome by him, by his
20 meekness and holiness, which melted the most jealous of them.' And I continue, 'We are almost content to say to Romanists, account us not yet as a branch of the Catholic Church, though we be a branch, till we are like a branch, provided that when we do become like a branch, then you consent to acknowledge us',
25 &c. And so I was led on in the Article to that sharp attack on English Catholics, for their shortcomings as regards this Note, a good portion of which I have already quoted in another place. It is there that I speak of the great scandal which I took at their political, social, and controversial bearing; and this was a second
30 reason why I fell back upon the Note of Sanctity, because it took me away from the necessity of making any attack upon the doctrines of the Roman Church, nay, from the consideration of her popular beliefs, and brought me upon a ground on which I felt I could not make a mistake; for what is a higher guide for us in
35 speculation and in practice, than that conscience of right and wrong, of truth and falsehood, those sentiments of what is decorous, consistent, and noble, which our Creator has made a part of our original nature? Therefore I felt I could not be wrong in attacking what I fancied was a fact,—the unscrupulousness,

8 Thus, in] In

the deceit, and the intriguing spirit of the agents and representatives of Rome.

This reference to Holiness as the true test of a Church was
steadily kept in view in what I wrote in connexion with Tract
90. I say in its Introduction, 'The writer can never be party to 5
forcing the opinions or projects of one school upon another;
religious changes should be the act of the whole body. No good
can come of a change which is not a development of feelings
springing up freely and calmly within the bosom of the whole
body itself; every change in religion' must be 'attended by deep 10
repentance; changes' must be 'nurtured in mutual love; we
cannot agree without a supernatural influence'; we must come
'together to God to do for us what we cannot do for ourselves'.
In my Letter to the Bishop I said, 'I have set myself against
suggestions for considering the differences between ourselves 15
and the foreign Churches with a view to their adjustment.'
(I meant in the way of negotiation, conference, agitation, or the
like.) 'Our business is with ourselves,—to make ourselves more
holy, more self-denying, more primitive, more worthy of our
high calling. To be anxious for a composition of differences is to 20
begin at the end. Political reconciliations are but outward and
hollow, and fallacious. And till Roman Catholics renounce
political efforts, and manifest in their public measures the light
of holiness and truth, perpetual war is our only prospect.'

According to this theory, a religious body is part of the One 25
Catholic and Apostolic Church, if it has the succession and the
creed of the Apostles, with the note of holiness of life; and there
is much in such a view to approve itself to the direct common
sense and practical habits of an Englishman. However, with the
events consequent upon Tract 90, I sunk my theory to a lower 30
level. For what could be said in apology, when the Bishops and
the people of my Church, not only did not suffer, but actually
rejected primitive Catholic doctrine, and tried to eject from their
communion all who held it? after the Bishops' charges? after
the Jerusalem 'abomination?'[1] Well, this could be said; still we 35
were not nothing: we could not be as if we never had been a

29–30 with the events] with events   31 For what] What   35 'abomination?'[1]]
no footnote in 64

---

[1] Matt. xxiv. 15.

Church; we were 'Samaria'. This then was that lower level on which I placed myself, and all who felt with me, at the end of 1841.

To bring out this view was the purpose of Four Sermons
5 preached at St. Mary's in December of that year. Hitherto I had not introduced the exciting topics of the day into the Pulpit;[2] on this occasion I did. I did so, for the moment was urgent; there was great unsettlement of mind among us, in consequence of those same events which had unsettled me. One
10 special anxiety, very obvious, which was coming on me now, was, that what was 'one man's meat was another man's poison'. I had said even of Tract 90, 'It was addressed to one set of persons, and has been used and commented on by another'; still more was it true now, that whatever I wrote for the service
15 of those whom I knew to be in trouble of mind, would become on the one hand matter of suspicion and slander in the mouths of my opponents, and of distress and surprise to those on the other hand, who had no difficulties of faith at all. Accordingly, when I published these Four Sermons at the end of 1843, I
20 introduced them with a recommendation that none should read them who did not need them. But in truth the virtual condemnation of Tract 90, after that the whole difficulty seemed to have been weathered, was an enormous disappointment and trial. My Protest also against the Jerusalem Bishopric was an unavoid-
25 able cause of excitement in the case of many; but it calmed them too, for the very fact of a Protest was a relief to their impatience. And so, in like manner, as regards the Four Sermons, of which I speak, though they acknowledged freely the great scandal which was involved in the recent episcopal
30 doings, yet at the same time they might be said to bestow upon the multiplied disorders and shortcomings of the Anglican Church a sort of place in the Revealed Dispensation, and an intellectual position in the controversy, and the dignity of a great principle, for unsettled minds to take and use—a principle
35 which might teach them to recognize their own consistency, and to be reconciled to themselves, and which might absorb and dry

7 Pulpit;[2]] *no footnote in 64*   34–35 use—a principle which] use, which
36 absorb and] absorb into itself and

---

[2] Vide Note C. *Sermon on Wisdom and Innocence.*

up a multitude of their grudgings, discontents, misgivings, and questionings, and lead the way to humble, thankful, and tranquil thoughts;—and this was the effect which certainly it produced on myself.

The point of these Sermons is, that, in spite of the rigid 5 character of the Jewish law, the formal and literal force of its precepts, and the manifest schism, and worse than schism, of the Ten Tribes, yet in fact they were still recognized as a people by the Divine Mercy; that the great prophets Elias and Eliseus were sent to them; and not only so, but were sent to preach to 10 them and reclaim them, without any intimation that they must be reconciled to the line of David and the Aaronic priesthood, or go up to Jerusalem to worship. They were not in the Church, yet they had the means of grace and the hope of acceptance with their Maker. The application of all this to the Anglican Church 15 was immediate;—whether, under the circumstances, a man could assume or exercise ministerial functions, or not, might not clearly appear (though it must be remembered that England had the Apostolic Priesthood, whereas Israel had no priesthood at all), but so far was clear, that there was no call at all for an 20 Anglican to leave his Church for Rome, though he did not believe his own to be part of the One Church:—and for this reason, because it was a fact that the kingdom of Israel was cut off from the Temple; and yet its subjects, neither in a mass, nor as individuals, neither the multitudes on Mount Carmel, nor the 25 Shunammite and her household, had any command given them, though miracles were displayed before them, to break off from their own people, and to submit themselves to Judah.[3]

It is plain, that a theory such as this,—whether the marks of a divine presence and life in the Anglican Church were sufficient 30 to prove that she was actually within the covenant, or only sufficient to prove that she was at least enjoying extraordinary

10 but were sent] but sent   16–17 whether, under . . . or not] whether a man could assume or exercise ministerial functions under the circumstances, or not 18–20 (though . . . at all), but] though . . . at all; but   28 Judah.[3]] Judah.[1] n. 3 As . . . conditions] As . . . command, which implies physical conditions

---

[3] As I am not writing controversially, I will only here remark upon this argument, that there is a great difference between a command, which presupposes physical, material, and political conditions, and one which is moral. To go to Jerusalem was a matter of the body, not of the soul.

and uncovenanted mercies,—not only lowered her level in a religious point of view, but weakened her controversial basis. Its very novelty made it suspicious; and there was no guarantee that the process of subsidence might not continue, and that it might not end in a submersion. Indeed, to many minds, to say that England was wrong was even to say that Rome was right; and no ethical or casuistic reasoning whatever could overcome in their case the argument from prescription and authority. To this objection, as made to my new teaching, I could only answer that I did not make my circumstances. I fully acknowledged the force and effectiveness of the genuine Anglican theory, and that it was all but proof against the disputants of Rome; but still like Achilles, it had a vulnerable point, and that St. Leo had found it out for me, and that I could not help it;—that, were it not for matter of fact, the theory would be great indeed; it would be irresistible, if it were only true. When I became a Catholic, the Editor of the Christian Observer, Mr. Wilkes, who had in former days accused me, to my indignation, of tending towards Rome, wrote to me to ask, which of the two was now right, he or I? I answered him in a letter, part of which I here insert, as it will serve as a sort of leave-taking of the great theory, which is so specious to look upon, so difficult to prove, and so hopeless to work.

'Nov. 8, 1845. I do not think, at all more than I did, that the Anglican principles which I advocated at the date you mention, lead men to the Church of Rome. If I must specify what I mean by "Anglican principles", I should say, e.g. taking *Antiquity*, not the *existing Church*, as the oracle of truth; and holding that the *Apostolical Succession* is a sufficient guarantee of Sacramental Grace, *without union with the Christian Church throughout the world*. I think these still the firmest, strongest ground against Rome—that is, *if they can be held*' [as truths or facts]. 'They *have* been held by many, and are far more difficult to refute in the Roman controversy, than those of any other religious body.

'For myself, I found *I could not* hold them. I left them. From the time I began to suspect their unsoundness, I ceased to put

---

7 ethical or casuistic reasoning] ethical reasoning   8–9 objection, as . . . teaching, I] objection I   17 the Christian Observer, Mr. Wilkes, who] a Magazine who   32–33 *held*' [as . . . facts]. 'They] *held*. They

them forward. When I was fairly sure of their unsoundness, I gave up my Living. When I was fully confident that the Church of Rome was the only true Church, I joined her.

'I have felt all along that Bp. Bull's theology was the only theology on which the English Church could stand. I have felt, that opposition to the Church of Rome was *part* of that theology; and that he who could not protest against the Church of Rome was no true divine in the English Church. I have never said, nor attempted to say, that any one in office in the English Church, whether Bishop or incumbent, could be otherwise than in hostility to the Church of Rome.'

The *Via Media* then disappeared for ever, and a Theory, made expressly for the occasion, took its place. I was pleased with my new view. I wrote to an intimate friend, Samuel F. Wood, Dec. 13, 1841: 'I think you will give me the credit, Carissime, of not undervaluing the strength of the feelings which draw one [to Rome], and yet I am (I trust) quite clear about my duty to remain where I am; indeed, much clearer than I was some time since. If it is not presumptuous to say, I have . . . a much more definite view of the promised inward Presence of Christ with us in the Sacraments now that the outward notes of it are being removed. And I am content to be with Moses in the desert, or with Elijah excommunicated from the Temple. I say this, putting things at the strongest.'

However, my friends of the moderate Apostolical party, who were my friends for the very reason of my having been so moderate and Anglican myself in general tone in times past, who had stood up for Tract 90 partly from faith in me, and certainly from generous and kind feeling, and had thereby shared an obloquy which was none of theirs, were naturally surprised and offended at a line of argument, novel, and, as it appeared to them, wanton, which threw the whole controversy into confusion, stultified my former principles, and substituted, as they would consider, a sort of methodistic self-contemplation, especially abhorrent both to my nature and to my past professions, for the plain and honest tokens, as they were commonly received, of a divine mission in the Anglican Church. They

11 Rome.'] *no space following in 64*   12 a Theory] a new Theory
14–15 friend, Samuel F. Wood, Dec.] friend, Dec.

could not tell whither I was going; and were still further annoyed when I persisted in viewing the condemnation of Tract 90 by the public and the Bishops as so grave a matter, and when I threw about what they considered mysterious hints of 'even-
5 tualities', and would not simply say, 'An Anglican I was born, and an Anglican I will die.' One of my familiar friends, Mr. Church, who was in the country at Christmas, 1841–2, reported to me the feeling that prevailed about me; and how I felt towards it will appear in the following letter of mine, written in
10 answer:—

'Oriel, Dec. 24, 1841. Carissime, you cannot tell how sad your account of Moberly has made me. His view of the sinfulness of the decrees of Trent is as much against union of Churches as against individual conversions. To tell the truth, I never have
15 examined those decrees with this object, and have no view; but that is very different from having a deliberate view against them. Could not he say *which* they are? I suppose Transubstantiation is one. Charles Marriott, though of course he would not like to have it repeated,[4] does not scruple at that. I have not
20 my mind clear. Moberly must recollect that Palmer [of Worcester] thinks they all bear a Catholic interpretation. For myself, this only I see, that there is indefinitely more in the Fathers against our own state of alienation from Christendom than against the Tridentine Decrees.

25   'The only thing I can think of' [that I can have said of a startling character] 'is this, that there were persons who, if our Church committed herself to heresy, *sooner* than think that there was no Church any where, would believe the Roman to be the Church; and therefore would on faith accept what they
30 could not otherwise acquiesce in. I suppose, it would be no relief to him to insist upon the circumstance that there is no immediate danger. Individuals can never be answered for of course; but I should think lightly of that man, who, for some

1–2 annoyed when I persisted in viewing] annoyed, when I would view   condemnation] reception *64–78*   3–4 and when I threw] and threw   6–7 friends, Mr. Church, who] friends, who   18 Charles Marriott] A.B.   19 repeated,⁴] *no footnote in 64*   20–21 Palmer [of Worcester] thinks] Palmer thinks 25–26 of' [that . . . character] 'is] of [that I can have said] is

---

4 As things stand now, I do not think he would have objected to his opinion being generally known.

act of the Bishops, should all at once leave the Church. Now, considering how the Clergy really are improving, considering that this row is even making them read the Tracts, is it not possible we may all be in a better state of mind seven years hence to consider these matters? and may we not leave them meanwhile to the will of Providence? I *cannot* believe this work has been of man; God has a right to His own work, to do what He will with it. May we not try to leave it in His hands, and be content?

'If you learn any thing about Barter, which leads you to think that I can relieve him by a letter, let me know. The truth is this, —our good friends do not read the Fathers; they assent to us from the common sense of the case: then, when the Fathers, and we, say *more* than their common sense, they are dreadfully shocked.

'The Bishop of London has rejected a man, 1. For holding *any* Sacrifice in the Eucharist. 2. The Real Presence. 3. That there is a grace in Ordination.[5]

'Are we quite sure that the Bishops will not be drawing up some stringent declarations of faith? Is this what Moberly fears? Would the Bishop of Oxford accept them? If so, I should be driven into the Refuge for the Destitute [Littlemore]. But I promise Moberly, I would do my utmost to catch all dangerous persons and clap them into confinement there.'

Christmas Day, 1841. 'I have been dreaming of Moberly all night. Should not he and the like see, that it is unwise, unfair, and impatient to ask others, What will you do under circumstances, which have not, which may never come? Why bring fear, suspicion, and disunion into the camp about things which are merely *in posse*? Natural, and exceedingly kind as Barter's and another friend's letters were, I think they have done great harm. I speak most sincerely when I say, that there are things which I neither contemplate, nor wish to contemplate; but, when I am asked about them ten times, at length I begin to contemplate them.

18 Ordination.[5]] Ordination.[2]

---

[5] I cannot prove this at this distance of time; but I do not think it wrong to introduce here the passage containing it, as I am imputing to the Bishop nothing which the world would think disgraceful, but, on the contrary, what a large religious body would approve.

'He surely does not mean to say, that *nothing* could separate a man from the English Church, e.g. its avowing Socinianism; its holding the Holy Eucharist in a Socinian sense. Yet, he would say, it was not *right* to contemplate such things.

5　'Again, our case is [diverging] from that of Ken's. To say nothing of the last miserable century, which has given us to *start* from a much lower level and with much less to *spare* than a Churchman in the 17th century, questions of *doctrine* are now coming in; with him, it was a question of discipline.

10　'If such dreadful events were realized, I cannot help thinking we should all be vastly more agreed than we think now. Indeed, is it possible (humanly speaking) that those, who have so much the same heart, should widely differ? But let this be considered, as to alternatives. *What* communion could we join? Could the
15　Scotch or American sanction the presence of its Bishops and congregations in England, without incurring the imputation of schism, unless indeed (and is that likely?) they denounced the English as heretical?

'Is not this a time of strange providences? is it not our safest
20　course, without looking to consequences, to do simply *what we think right* day by day? shall we not be sure to go wrong, if we attempt to trace by anticipation the course of divine Providence?

'Has not all our misery, as a Church, arisen from people being
25　afraid to look difficulties in the face? They have palliated acts, when they should have denounced them. There is that good fellow, Worcester Palmer, can whitewash the Ecclesiastical Commission and the Jerusalem Bishopric. And what is the consequence? that our Church has, through centuries, ever
30　been sinking lower and lower, till good part of its pretensions and professions is a mere sham, though it be a duty to make the best of what we have received. Yet, though bound to make the best of other men's shams, let us not incur any of our own. The truest friends of our Church are they, who say boldly when her
35　rulers are going wrong, and the consequences; and (to speak catachrestically) *they* are most likely to die in the Church, who are, under these black circumstances, most prepared to leave it.

'And I will add, that, considering the traces of God's grace which surround us, I am very sanguine, or rather confident,
40　(if it is right so to speak,) that our prayers and our alms will come

up as a memorial before God, and that all this miserable confusion tends to good.

'Let us not then be anxious, and anticipate differences in
prospect, when we agree in the present.

'P.S. I think when friends' [i.e. the extreme party] 'get over 5
their first unsettlement of mind and consequent vague apprehensions, which the new attitude of the Bishops, and our feelings
upon it, have brought about, they will get contented and
satisfied. They will see that they exaggerated things. . . . Of
course it would have been wrong to anticipate what one's feelings 10
would be under such a painful contingency as the Bishops'
charging as they have done,—so it seems to me nobody's fault.
Nor is it wonderful that others' [moderate men] 'are startled'
[i.e. at my Protest, &c. &c.]; 'yet they should recollect that the
more implicit the reverence one pays to a Bishop, the more keen 15
will be one's perception of heresy in him. The cord is binding
and compelling, till it snaps.

'Men of reflection would have seen this, if they had looked
that way. Last spring, a very high churchman talked to me of
resisting my Bishop, of asking him for the Canons under which 20
he acted, and so forth; but those, who have cultivated a loyal
feeling towards their superiors, are the most loving servants, or
the most zealous protestors. If others became so too, if the
clergy of Chester denounced the heresy of their diocesan, they
would be doing their duty, and relieving themselves of the share 25
which they otherwise have in any possible defection of their
brethren.

'St. Stephen's [Day, December 26]. How I fidget! I now fear
that the note I wrote yesterday only makes matters worse by
disclosing too much. This is always my great difficulty.   30

'In the present state of excitement on both sides, I think of
leaving out altogether my reassertion of No. 90 in my Preface to
Volume 6 [of Parochial Sermons], and merely saying, "As many
false reports are at this time in circulation about him, he hopes
his well-wishers will take this Volume as an indication of his real 35
thoughts and feelings: those who are not, he leaves in God's
hand to bring them to a better mind in His own time." What do
you say to the logic, sentiment, and propriety of this?'

28 'St. Stephen's [Day, December 26].] "St. Stephen's [December 26]. 33 Volume
6 [of Parochial Sermons], and] Volume 6, and

An old friend, at a distance from Oxford, Archdeacon Robert I. Wilberforce, must have said something to me at this time, I do not know what, which challenged a frank reply; for I disclosed to him, I do not know in what words, my frightful suspicion, hitherto only known to two persons, viz. his brother Henry and Mr. Frederic Rogers,[6] that, as regards my Anglicanism, perhaps I might break down in the event,—that perhaps we were both out of the Church. I think I recollect expressing my difficulty, as derived from the Arian and Monophysite history, in a form in which it would be most intelligible to him, as being in fact an admission of Bishop Bull's; viz. that in the controversies of the early centuries the Roman Church was ever on the right side, which was of course a *primâ facie* argument in favour of Rome and against Anglicanism now. He answered me thus, under date of Jan. 29, 1842: 'I don't think that I ever was so shocked by any communication, which was ever made to me, as by your letter of this morning. It has quite unnerved me. . . . I cannot but write to you, though I am at a loss where to begin. . . . I know of no act by which we have dissevered ourselves from the communion of the Church Universal. . . . The more I study Scripture, the more am I impressed with the resemblance between the Romish principle in the Church and the Babylon of St. John. . . . I am ready to grieve that I ever directed my thoughts to theology, if it is indeed so uncertain, as your doubts seem to indicate.'

While my old and true friends were thus in trouble about me, I suppose they felt not only anxiety but pain, to see that I was gradually surrendering myself to the influence of others, who had not their own claims upon me, younger men, and of a cast of mind in no small degree uncongenial to my own. A new school of thought was rising, as is usual in doctrinal inquiries, and was sweeping the original party of the Movement aside,

1–2 An old . . . at this time,] There was one very old friend, at a distance from Oxford, afterwards a Catholic, now dead some years, who must have said something to me,   5–6 viz. . . . Mr. Frederic Rogers,[6]] *not in 64*; viz. . . . Mr. (now Sir Frederick) Rogers, *65–82*   8–14 I think . . . now.] *not in 64*   25 indicate.'] *no space following in 64*   30 mind in no small degree uncongenial] mind uncongenial   31 doctrinal inquiries] such movements   32 Movement] movement

---

6 Now Lord Blachford.

and was taking its place. The most prominent person in it, was a man of elegant genius, of classical mind, of rare talent in literary composition:—Mr. Oakeley. He was not far from my own age; I had long known him, though of late years he had not been in residence at Oxford; and quite lately, he has been taking several signal occasions of renewing that kindness, which he ever showed towards me when we were both in the Anglican Church. His tone of mind was not unlike that which gave a character to the early Movement; he was almost a typical Oxford man, and, as far as I recollect, both in political and ecclesiastical views, would have been of one spirit with the Oriel party of 1826–1833. But he had entered late into the Movement; he did not know its first years; and, beginning with a new start, he was naturally thrown together with that body of eager, acute, resolute minds who had begun their Catholic life about the same time as he, who knew nothing about the *Via Media*, but had heard much about Rome. This new party rapidly formed and increased, in and out of Oxford, and, as it so happened, contemporaneously with that very summer, when I received so serious a blow to my ecclesiastical views from the study of the Monophysite controversy. These men cut into the original Movement at an angle, fell across its line of thought, and then set about turning that line in its own direction. They were most of them keenly religious men, with a true concern for their souls as the first matter of all, with a great zeal for me, but giving little certainty at the time as to which way they would ultimately turn. Some in the event have remained firm to Anglicanism, some have become Catholics, and some have found a refuge in Liberalism. Nothing was clearer concerning them, than that they needed to be kept in order; and on me who had had so much to do with the making of them, that duty was as clearly incumbent; and it is equally clear, from what I have already said, that I was just the person, above all others, who could not undertake it. There are no friends like old friends; but of those old friends, few could help me, few could understand me, many were annoyed with me, some were angry, because I was breaking up a compact party, and some, as a matter of conscience, could not listen to me. When I looked round for those

5

10

15

20

25

30

35

3:—Mr. Oakeley] *not in original pamphlet*   9 Movement] movement
38–p. 152, l. 3 When I ... advice.] *not in 64*

whom I might consult in my difficulties, I found the very
hypothesis of those difficulties acting as a bar to their giving me
their advice. Then I said, bitterly, 'You are throwing me on
others, whether I will or no.' Yet still I had good and true
5 friends around me of the old sort, in and out of Oxford too, who
were a great help to me. But on the other hand, though I neither
was so fond (with a few exceptions) of the persons, nor of the
methods of thought, which belonged to this new school, as of
the old set, though I could not trust in their firmness of purpose,
10 for, like a swarm of flies, they might come and go, and at length
be divided and dissipated, yet I had an intense sympathy in their
object and in the direction in which their path lay, in spite of my
old friends, in spite of my old life-long prejudices. In spite of my
ingrained fears of Rome, and the decision of my reason and con-
15 science against her usages, in spite of my affection for Oxford
and Oriel, yet I had a secret longing love of Rome the Mother
of English Christianity, and I had a true devotion to the Blessed
Virgin, in whose College I lived, whose Altar I served, and whose
Immaculate Purity I had in one of my earliest printed Sermons
20 made much of. And it was the consciousness of this bias in
myself, if it is so to be called, which made me preach so earnestly
against the danger of being swayed in religious inquiry by our
sympathy rather than by our reason. And moreover, the
members of this new school looked up to me, as I have said,
25 and did me true kindnesses, and really loved me, and stood by
me in trouble, when others went away, and for all this I was
grateful; nay, many of them were in trouble themselves, and in
the same boat with me, and that was a further cause of sympathy between us; and hence it was, when the new school came on
30 in force, and into collision with the old, I had not the heart, any
more than the power, to repel them; I was in great perplexity,
and hardly knew where I stood; I took their part; and, when I
wanted to be in peace and silence, I had to speak out, and I incurred the charge of weakness from some men, and of mysterious-
35 ness, shuffling, and underhand dealing from the majority.

3 Then I] I   5–6 too, who were a great help to me. But] too. But
7 fond (with a few exceptions) of] fond of   8 school, as of] school, excepting
two or three men, as of   12 in which their path lay] of their path
16 Mother] mother 64; author *another copy of 64*   22–23 swayed in
. . . reason.] swayed by our sympathy rather than our reason in religious
inquiry.   35 majority.] *no space following in 64*

Now I will say here frankly, that this sort of charge is a matter which I cannot properly meet, because I cannot duly realize it. I have never had any suspicion of my own honesty; and, when men say that I was dishonest, I cannot grasp the accusation as a distinct conception, such as it is possible to encounter. If a man said to me, 'On such a day and before such persons you said a thing was white, when it was black', I understand what is meant well enough, and I can set myself to prove an *alibi* or to explain the mistake; or if a man said to me, 'You tried to gain me over to your party, intending to take me with you to Rome, but you did not succeed', I can give him the lie, and lay down an assertion of my own as firm and as exact as his, that not from the time that I was first unsettled, did I ever attempt to gain any one over to myself or to my Romanizing opinions, and that it is only his own coxcombical fancy which has bred such a thought in him: but my imagination is at a loss in presence of those vague charges, which have commonly been brought against me, charges, which are made up of impressions, and understandings, and inferences, and hearsay, and surmises. Accordingly, I shall not make the attempt, for, in doing so, I should be dealing blows in the air; what I shall attempt is to state what I know of myself and what I recollect, and leave to others its application.

While I had confidence in the *Via Media*, and thought that nothing could overset it, I did not mind laying down large principles, which I saw would go further than was commonly perceived. I considered that to make the *Via Media* concrete and substantive, it must be much more than it was in outline; that the Anglican Church must have a ceremonial, a ritual, and a fulness of doctrine and devotion, which it had not at present, if it were to compete with the Roman Church with any prospect of success. Such additions would not remove it from its proper basis, but would merely strengthen and beautify it: such, for instance, would be confraternities, particular devotions, reverence for the Blessed Virgin, prayers for the dead, beautiful churches, munificent offerings to them and in them, monastic houses, and many other observances and institutions, which I used to say belonged to us as much as to Rome, though Rome had appropriated them and boasted of them, by reason of our having let them slip from us. The principle, on which all this turned, is

22 to others its application.] its application to others.   35 munificent] rich

brought out in one of the Letters I published on occasion of Tract 90. 'The age is moving', I said, 'towards something; and most unhappily the one religious communion among us, which has of late years been practically in possession of this something,
5   is the Church of Rome. She alone, amid all the errors and evils of her practical system, has given free scope to the feelings of awe, mystery, tenderness, reverence, devotedness, and other feelings which may be especially called Catholic. The question then is, whether we shall give them up to the Roman Church or
10 claim them for ourselves. . . . But if we do give them up, we must give up the men who cherish them. We must consent either to give up the men, or to admit their principles.' With these feelings I frankly admit, that, while I was working simply for the sake of the Anglican Church, I did not at all mind, though I found
15 myself laying down principles in its defence, which went beyond that particular kind of defence which high-and-dry men thought perfection, and even though I ended in framing a kind of defence, which they might call a revolution, while I thought it a restoration. Thus, for illustration, I might discourse upon the 'Com-
20 munion of Saints' in such a manner, (though I do not recollect doing so,) as might lead the way towards devotion to the Blessed Virgin and the Saints on the one hand, and towards prayers for the dead on the other. In a memorandum of the year 1844 or 1845, I thus speak on this subject: 'If the Church be not defended
25 on establishment grounds, it must be upon principles, which go far beyond their immediate object. Sometimes I saw these further results, sometimes not. Though I saw them, I sometimes did not say that I saw them:—so long as I thought they were inconsistent, *not* with our Church, but only with the existing
30 opinions, I was not unwilling to insinuate truths into our Church, which I thought had a right to be there.'

To so much I confess; but I do not confess, I simply deny that I ever said any thing which secretly bore against the Church of England, knowing it myself, in order that others might un-
35 warily accept it. It was indeed one of my great difficulties and causes of reserve, as time went on, that I at length recognized in principles which I had honestly preached as if Anglican, con-

16 particular kind of defence] particular defence   17 and even though]
and though   kind] sort   22 Saints] saints   28 them:—so]
them; so

clusions favourable to the cause of Rome. Of course I did not like to confess this; and, when interrogated, was in consequence in perplexity. The prime instance of this was the appeal to Antiquity; St. Leo had overset, in my own judgment, its force as the special argument for Anglicanism; yet I was committed 5 to Antiquity, together with the whole Anglican school; what then was I to say, when acute minds urged this or that application of it against the *Via Media*? it was impossible that, in such circumstances, any answer could be given which was not unsatisfactory, or any behaviour adopted which was not mysterious. 10 Again, sometimes in what I wrote I went just as far as I saw, and could as little say more, as I could see what is below the horizon; and therefore, when asked as to the consequences of what I had said, I had no answer to give. Again, sometimes when I was asked, whether certain conclusions did not follow 15 from a certain principle, I might not be able to tell at the moment, especially if the matter were complicated; and for this reason, if for no other, because there is great difference between a conclusion in the abstract and a conclusion in the concrete, and because a conclusion may be modified in fact by a conclusion 20 from some opposite principle. Or it might so happen that my head got simply confused, by the very strength of the logic which was administered to me, and thus I gave my sanction to conclusions which really were not mine; and when the report of those conclusions came round to me through others, I had to 25 unsay them. And then again, perhaps I did not like to see men scared or scandalized by unfeeling logical inferences, which would not have troubled them to the day of their death, had they not been forced to recognize them. And then I felt altogether the force of the maxim of St. Ambrose, 'Non in dialecticâ 30 complacuit Deo salvum facere populum suum';—I had a great dislike of paper logic. For myself, it was not logic that carried me on; as well might one say that the quicksilver in the barometer changes the weather. It is the concrete being that reasons; pass a number of years, and I find my mind in a new place; how? 35 the whole man moves; paper logic is but the record of it. All the logic in the world would not have made me move faster towards

1 cause of Rome.] Roman Church.   5 as] in   14 said, I had] said, had   21–22 my head] I   22 strength] clearness   23 thus I gave] thus gave   28 troubled] touched   29 forced to recognize] made to eat

Rome than I did; as well might you say that I have arrived at the end of my journey, because I see the village church before me, as venture to assert that the miles, over which my soul had to pass before it got to Rome, could be annihilated, even though 5 I had been in possession of some far clearer view than I then had, that Rome was my ultimate destination. Great acts take time. At least this is what I felt in my own case; and therefore to come to me with methods of logic had in it the nature of a provocation, and, though I do not think I ever showed it, made 10 me somewhat indifferent how I met them, and perhaps led me, as a means of relieving my impatience, to be mysterious or irrelevant, or to give in because I could not meet them to my satisfaction. And a greater trouble still than these logical mazes, was the introduction of logic into every subject whatever, so far, 15 that is, as this was done. Before I was at Oriel, I recollect an acquaintance saying to me that 'the Oriel Common Room stank of Logic'. One is not at all pleased when poetry, or eloquence, or devotion, is considered as if chiefly intended to feed syllo- gisms. Now, in saying all this, I am saying nothing against the 20 deep piety and earnestness which were characteristics of this second phase of the Movement, in which I had taken so promi- nent a part. What I have been observing is, that this phase had a tendency to bewilder and to upset me; and, that, instead of saying so, as I ought to have done, perhaps from a sort of 25 laziness I gave answers at random, which have led to my appearing close or inconsistent.

I have turned up two letters of this period, which in a measure illustrate what I have been saying. The first was written to the Bishop of Oxford on occasion of Tract 90:

30 'March 20, 1841. No one can enter into my situation but my- self. I see a great many minds working in various directions and a variety of principles with multiplied bearings; I act for the best. I sincerely think that matters would not have gone better for the Church, had I never written. And if I write I have a choice of 35 difficulties. It is easy for those who do not enter into those difficulties to say, 'He ought to say this and not say that', but

5 had been in possession of] had had   12–13 meet . . . satisfaction.] reply.
15 this] it   21 had] have *64*; had *another copy of 64*   23 me;] me,
24–25 perhaps from a sort of laziness I gave] in a sort of easiness, for what I know,
I gave   28 was written] is what I said

things are wonderfully linked together, and I cannot, or rather I would not be dishonest. When persons too interrogate me, I am obliged in many cases to give an opinion, or I seem to be under-hand. Keeping silence looks like artifice. And I do not like people to consult or respect me, from thinking differently of my 5 opinions from what I know them to be. And again (to use the proverb) what is one man's food is another man's poison. All these things make my situation very difficult. But that collision must at some time ensue between members of the Church of opposite sentiments, I have long been aware. The time and mode 10 has been in the hand of Providence; I do not mean to exclude my own great imperfections in bringing it about; yet I still feel obliged to think the Tract necessary.'

The second is taken from the notes of a letter which I sent to Dr. Pusey in the next year: 15

'October 16, 1842. As to my being entirely with Ward, I do not know the limits of my own opinions. If Ward says that this or that is a development from what I have said, I cannot say Yes or No. It is plausible, it *may* be true. Of course the fact that the Roman Church *has* so developed and maintained, adds great 20 weight to the antecedent plausibility. I cannot assert that it is not true; but I cannot, with that keen perception which some people have, appropriate it. It is a nuisance to me to be *forced* beyond what I can fairly accept.'

There was another source of the perplexity with which at this 25 time I was encompassed, and of the reserve and mysteriousness, of which that perplexity gained for me the credit. After Tract 90 the Protestant world would not let me alone; they pursued me in the public journals to Littlemore. Reports of all kinds were circulated about me. 'Imprimis, why did I go up to Littlemore 30 at all? For no good purpose certainly; I dared not tell why.' Why, to be sure, it was hard that I should be obliged to say to the Editors of newspapers that I went up there to say my prayers; it was hard to have to tell the world in confidence, that I had a

---

6 again (to] (again to *64–68*   13 necessary.'] *Followed in 64 by this para-graph*: 'Dr. Pusey has shown me your Lordship's letters to him. I am most desirous of saying in print any thing which I can honestly say to remove false impressions created by the Tract.'   14 taken from] part of   letter which I sent] letter sent   16 and 17 Ward] A.B. *64–68*   24 accept.'] *no space following in 64*   27 that perplexity gained for me] it gave me

certain doubt about the Anglican system, and could not at that
moment resolve it, or say what would come of it; it was hard to
have to confess that I had thought of giving up my Living a
year or two before, and that this was a first step to it. It was
5 hard to have to plead, that, for what I knew, my doubts would
vanish, if the newspapers would be so good as to give me time
and let me alone. Who would ever dream of making the world
his confidant? yet I was considered insidious, sly, dishonest, if
I would not open my heart to the tender mercies of the world.
10 But they persisted: 'What was I doing at Littlemore?' Doing
there! have I not retreated from you? have I not given up my
position and my place? am I alone, of Englishmen, not to have
the privilege to go where I will, no questions asked? am I alone
to be followed about by jealous prying eyes, which take note
15 whether I go in at a back door or at the front, and who the men
are who happen to call on me in the afternoon? Cowards! if I
advanced one step, you would run away; it is not you that I fear:
'Di me terrent, et Jupiter hostis.' It is because the Bishops still
go on charging against me, though I have quite given up: it is
20 that secret misgiving of heart which tells me that they do well,
for I have neither lot nor part with them: this it is which weighs
me down. I cannot walk into or out of my house, but curious
eyes are upon me. Why will you not let me die in peace?
Wounded brutes creep into some hole to die in, and no one
25 grudges it them. Let me alone, I shall not trouble you long.
This was the keen feeling which pierced me, and, I think, these
are the very words in which I expressed it to myself. I asked, in
the words of a great motto, 'Ubi lapsus? quid feci?' One day
when I entered my house, I found a flight of Under-graduates
30 inside. Heads of Houses, as mounted patrols, walked their
horses round those poor cottages. Doctors of Divinity dived into
the hidden recesses of that private tenement uninvited, and drew
domestic conclusions from what they saw there. I had thought
that an Englishman's house was his castle; but the newspapers
35 thought otherwise, and at last the matter came before my good
Bishop. I insert his letter, and a portion of my reply to
him:—

11 there!] there?   14 take note] note down *64–68*   26 keen feeling] keen
heavy feeling   27 in which I expressed it] that I used   29 Under-
graduates] Undergraduates

'April 12, 1842. So many of the charges against yourself and your friends which I have seen in the public journals have been, within my own knowledge, false and calumnious, that I am not apt to pay much attention to what is asserted with respect to you in the newspapers.   5

'In' [a newspaper] 'however, of April 9, there appears a paragraph in which it is asserted, as a matter of notoriety, that a "so-called Anglo-Catholic Monastery is in process of erection at Littlemore, and that the cells of dormitories, the chapel, the refectory, the cloisters all may be seen advancing to perfection, 10 under the eye of a Parish Priest of the Diocese of Oxford".

'Now, as I have understood that you really are possessed of some tenements at Littlemore,—as it is generally believed that they are destined for the purposes of study and devotion,—and as much suspicion and jealousy are felt about the matter, I am 15 anxious to afford you an opportunity of making me an explanation on the subject.

'I know you too well not to be aware that you are the last man living to attempt in my Diocese a revival of the Monastic orders (in any thing approaching to the Romanist sense of the term) 20 without previous communication with me,—or indeed that you should take upon yourself to originate any measure of importance without authority from the heads of the Church,—and therefore I at once exonerate you from the accusation brought against you by the newspaper I have quoted, but I feel it never- 25 theless a duty to my Diocese and myself, as well as to you, to ask you to put it in my power to contradict what, if uncontradicted, would appear to imply a glaring invasion of all ecclesiastical discipline on *your* part, or of inexcusable neglect and indifference to my duties on *mine.*'   30

I wrote in answer as follows:—

'April 14, 1842. I am very much obliged by your Lordship's kindness in allowing me to write to you on the subject of my house at Littlemore; at the same time I feel it hard both on your Lordship and myself that the restlessness of the public mind 35 should oblige you to require an explanation of me.

'It is now a whole year that I have been the subject of incessant misrepresentation. A year since I submitted entirely to your Lordship's authority; and, with the intention of following out

30 *mine.*'] *In 1864 a space was left here and the next sentence omitted.*

the particular act enjoined upon me, I not only stopped the series of Tracts, on which I was engaged, but withdrew from all public discussion of Church matters of the day, or what may be called ecclesiastical politics. I turned myself at once to the
5 preparation for the Press of the translations of St. Athanasius to which I had long wished to devote myself, and I intended and intend to employ myself in the like theological studies, and in the concerns of my own parish and in practical works.

'With the same view of personal improvement I was led more
10 seriously to a design which had been long on my mind. For many years, at least thirteen, I have wished to give myself to a life of greater religious regularity than I have hitherto led; but it is very unpleasant to confess such a wish even to my Bishop, because it seems arrogant, and because it is committing me to a
15 profession which may come to nothing. For what have I done that I am to be called to account by the world for my private actions, in a way in which no one else is called? Why may I not have that liberty which all others are allowed? I am often accused of being underhand and uncandid in respect to the
20 intentions to which I have been alluding; but no one likes his own good resolutions noised about, both from mere common delicacy and from fear lest he should not be able to fulfil them. I feel it very cruel, though the parties in fault do not know what they are doing, that very sacred matters between me and my
25 conscience are made a matter of public talk. May I take a case parallel though different? suppose a person in prospect of marriage; would he like the subject discussed in newspapers, and parties, circumstances, &c., &c., publicly demanded of him, at the penalty of being accused of craft and duplicity?

30 'The resolution I speak of has been taken with reference to myself alone, and has been contemplated quite independent of the co-operation of any other human being, and without reference to success or failure other than personal, and without regard to the blame or approbation of man. And being a resolution of
35 years, and one to which I feel God has called me, and in which I am violating no rule of the Church any more than if I married, I should have to answer for it, if I did not pursue it, as a good Providence made openings for it. In pursuing it then I am thinking of myself alone, not aiming at any ecclesiastical or
40 external effects. At the same time of course it would be a great

comfort to me to know that God had put it into the hearts of others to pursue their personal edification in the same way, and unnatural not to wish to have the benefit of their presence and encouragement, or not to think it a great infringement on the rights of conscience if such personal and private resolutions were 5 interfered with. Your Lordship will allow me to add my firm conviction that such religious resolutions are most necessary for keeping a certain class of minds firm in their allegiance to our Church; but still I can as truly say that my own reason for any thing I have done has been a personal one, without which I 10 should not have entered upon it, and which I hope to pursue whether with or without the sympathies of others pursuing a similar course. . . .

'As to my intentions, I purpose to live there myself a good deal, as I have a resident curate in Oxford. In doing this, I 15 believe I am consulting for the good of my parish, as my population at Littlemore is at least equal to that of St. Mary's in Oxford, and the *whole* of Littlemore is double of it. It has been very much neglected; and in providing a parsonage-house at Littlemore, as this will be, and will be called, I conceive I am doing a 20 very great benefit to my people. At the same time it has appeared to me that a partial or temporary retirement from St. Mary's Church might be expedient under the prevailing excitement.

'As to the quotation from the [newspaper], which I have not seen, your Lordship will perceive from what I have said, that no 25 "monastery is in process of erection"; there is no "chapel"; no "refectory", hardly a dining-room or parlour. The "cloisters" are my shed connecting the cottages. I do not understand what "cells of dormitories" means. Of course I can repeat your Lordship's words that "I am not attempting a revival of the Monastic 30 Orders, in any thing approaching to the Romanist sense of the term", or "taking on myself to originate any measure of importance without authority from the Heads of the Church". I am attempting nothing ecclesiastical, but something personal and private, and which can only be made public, not private, by 35 newspapers and letter-writers, in which sense the most sacred and conscientious resolves and acts may certainly be made the objects of an unmannerly and unfeeling curiosity.'

37 curiosity.'] *no space following in* 64

One calumny there was which the Bishop did not believe, and of which of course he had no idea of speaking. It was that I was actually in the service of the enemy. I had forsooth been already received into the Catholic Church, and was rearing at Littlemore
5 a nest of Papists, who, like me, were to take the Anglican oaths which they disbelieved, by virtue of a dispensation from Rome, and thus in due time were to bring over to that unprincipled Church great numbers of the Anglican Clergy and Laity. Bishops gave their countenance to this imputation against me.
10 The case was simply this:—as I made Littlemore a place of retirement for myself, so did I offer it to others. There were young men in Oxford, whose testimonials for Orders had been refused by their Colleges; there were young clergymen, who had found themselves unable from conscience to go on with their
15 duties, and had thrown up their parochial engagements. Such men were already going straight to Rome, and I interposed; I interposed for the reasons I have given in the beginning of this portion of my narrative. I interposed from fidelity to my clerical engagements, and from duty to my Bishop; and from the interest
20 which I was bound to take in them, and from belief that they were premature or excited. Their friends besought me to quiet them, if I could. Some of them came to live with me at Littlemore. They were laymen, or in the place of laymen. I kept some of them back for several years from being received into the
25 Catholic Church. Even when I had given up my living, I was still bound by my duty to their parents or friends, and I did not forget still to do what I could for them. The immediate occasion of my resigning St. Mary's, was the unexpected conversion of one of them. After that, I felt it was impossible to keep my post
30 there, for I had been unable to keep my word with my Bishop.

The following letters refer, more or less, to these men, whether they were actually with me at Littlemore or not:—

1. 'March 6, 1842. Church doctrines are a powerful weapon; they were not sent into the world for nothing. God's word does
35 not return unto Him void: If I have said, as I have, that the doctrines of the Tracts for the Times would build up our Church and destroy parties, I meant, if they were used, not if they were

---

3 had forsooth been] had been   6 disbelieved . . . Rome] did not believe, and for which they got dispensation from Rome   32 were actually with] were with   33: 1. 'March 6, 1842.] 1. 1843 or 1844. *March 6 letter not in 64.*

denounced. Else, they will be as powerful against us, as they might be powerful for us.

'If people who have a liking for another, hear him called a Roman Catholic, they will say, "Then after all Romanism is no such bad thing." All these persons, who are making the cry, are fulfilling their own prophecy. If all the world agree in telling a man, he has no business in our Church, he will at length begin to think he has none. How easy is it to persuade a man of any thing, when numbers affirm it! so great is the force of imagination. Did every one who met you in the streets look hard at you, you would think you were somehow in fault. I do not know any thing so irritating, so unsettling, especially in the case of young persons, as, when they are going on calmly and unconsciously, obeying their Church and following its divines, (I am speaking from facts,) as suddenly to their surprise to be conjured not to make a leap, of which they have not a dream and from which they are far removed.'

2. 1843 or 1844. 'I did not explain to you sufficiently the state of mind of those who were in danger. I only spoke of those who were convinced that our Church was external to the Church Catholic, though they felt it unsafe to trust their own private convictions; but there are two other states of mind; 1. that of those who are unconsciously near Rome, and whose *despair* about our Church would at once develope into a state of conscious approximation, or a *quasi*-resolution to go over; 2. those who feel they can with a safe conscience remain with us *while* they are allowed to *testify* in behalf of Catholicism, i.e. as if by such acts they were putting our Church, or at least that portion of it in which they were included, in the position of catechumens.'

3. 'June 20, 1843. I return the very pleasing letter you have permitted me to read. What a sad thing it is, that it should be a plain duty to restrain one's sympathies, and to keep them from boiling over; but I suppose it is a matter of common prudence.

'Things are very serious here; but I should not like you to say so, as it might do no good. The Authorities find, that, by the Statutes, they have more than military power; and the general impression seems to be, that they intend to exert it, and put down Catholicism at any risk. I believe that by the Statutes, they can pretty nearly suspend a Preacher, as *seditiosus* or causing

18: 2.] 1.　　30: 3. 'June 20, 1843.] *This letter not in 64.*

dissension, without assigning their grounds in the particular case, nay, banish him, or imprison him. If so, all holders of preferment in the University should make as quiet an *exit* as they can. There is more exasperation on both sides at this moment, as
5 I am told, than ever there was.'

4. 'July 16, 1843. I assure you that I feel, with only too much sympathy, what you say. You need not be told that the whole subject of our position is a subject of anxiety to others beside yourself. It is no good attempting to offer advice, when perhaps
10 I might raise difficulties instead of removing them. It seems to me quite a case, in which you should, as far as may be, make up your mind for yourself. Come to Littlemore by all means. We shall all rejoice in your company; and, if quiet and retirement are able, as they very likely will be, to reconcile you to things as they
15 are, you shall have your fill of them. How distressed poor Henry Wilberforce must be! Knowing how he values you, I feel for him; but, alas! he has his own position, and every one else has his own, and the misery is that no two of us have exactly the same.

'It is very kind of you to be so frank and open with me, as you
20 are; but this is a time which throws together persons who feel alike. May I without taking a liberty sign myself, yours affectionately, &c.'

5. 'August 30, 1843. A. B. has suddenly conformed to the Church of Rome. He was away for three weeks. I suppose I must
25 say in my defence, that he promised me distinctly to remain in our Church three years, before I received him here.'

6. 'June 17, 1845. I am concerned to find you speak of me in a tone of distrust. If you knew me ever so little, instead of hearing of me from persons who do not know me at all, you would think
30 differently of me, whatever you thought of my opinions. Two years since, I got your son to tell you my intention of resigning St. Mary's, before I made it public, thinking you ought to know it. When you expressed some painful feeling upon it, I told him I could not consent to his remaining here, painful as it would be
35 to me to part with him, without your written sanction. And this you did me the favour to give.

'I believe you will find that it has been merely a delicacy on your son's part, which has delayed his speaking to you about me

6: 4.] 2.   23: 5. 'August 30, 1843.] *This letter not placed here in 64.*
27: 6. 'June 17, 1845] 3. '1845.

for two months past; a delicacy, lest he should say either too much or too little about me. I have urged him several times to speak to you.

'Nothing can be done after your letter, but to recommend him to go to A. B. (his home) at once. I am very sorry to part with 5 him.'

7. The following letter is addressed to Cardinal Wiseman, then Vicar Apostolic, who accused me of coldness in my conduct towards him:—

'April 16, 1845. I was at that time in charge of a ministerial 10 office in the English Church, with persons entrusted to me, and a Bishop to obey; how could I possibly write otherwise than I did without violating sacred obligations and betraying momentous interests which were upon me? I felt that my immediate, undeniable duty, clear if any thing was clear, was to fulfil that 15 trust. It might be right indeed to give it up, that was another thing; but it never could be right to hold it, and to act as if I did not hold it. . . . If you knew me, you would acquit me, I think, of having ever felt towards your Lordship in an unfriendly spirit, or ever having had a shadow on my mind (as far as I dare witness 20 about myself) of what might be called controversial rivalry or desire of getting the better, or fear lest the world should think I had got the worse, or irritation of any kind. You are too kind indeed to imply this, and yet your words lead me to say it. And now in like manner, pray believe, though I cannot explain it to 25 you, that I am encompassed with responsibilities, so great and so various, as utterly to overcome me, unless I have mercy from Him, who all through my life has sustained and guided me, and to whom I can now submit myself, though men of all parties are thinking evil of me.' 30

Such fidelity, however, was taken *in malam partem* by the high Anglican authorities; they thought it insidious. I happen still to have a correspondence which took place in 1843, in which the chief place is filled by one of the most eminent Bishops of the day, a theologian and reader of the Fathers, a moderate man, 35

7–8: 7. The following . . . Apostolic] 4. The following letter is addressed to a
Catholic prelate   23 worse] worst   30 me.'] *Here follows in 1864, without
intervening space:* 5. August 30, 1843. *Letter as above, p. 164.*   33 correspondence which took place in 1843, in] correspondence, in

who at one time was talked of as likely on a vacancy to succeed to the Primacy. A young clergyman in his diocese became a Catholic; the papers at once reported on authority from 'a very high quarter', that, after his reception, 'the Oxford men had
5 been recommending him to retain his living'. I had reasons for thinking that the allusion was made to me, and I authorized the Editor of a Paper, who had inquired of me on the point, to 'give it, as far as I was concerned, an unqualified contradiction';—when from a motive of delicacy he hesitated, I added 'my direct
10 and indignant contradiction'. 'Whoever is the author of it,' I continued to the Editor, 'no correspondence or intercourse of any kind, direct or indirect, has passed between Mr. S. and myself, since his conforming to the Church of Rome, except my formally and merely acknowledging the receipt of his letter, in which he
15 informed me of the fact, without, as far as I recollect, my expressing any opinion upon it. You may state this as broadly as I have set it down.' My denial was told to the Bishop; what took place upon it is given in a letter from which I copy. 'My father showed the letter to the Bishop, who, as he laid it down, said, "Ah, those
20 Oxford men are not ingenuous." "How do you mean?" asked my father. "Why," said the Bishop, "they advised Mr. B. S. to retain his living after he turned Catholic. I know that to be a fact, because A. B. told me so."' 'The Bishop,' continues the letter, 'who is perhaps the most influential man in reality on the
25 bench, evidently believes it to be the truth.' Upon this Dr. Pusey wrote in my behalf to the Bishop; and the Bishop instantly beat a retreat. 'I have the honour', he says in the autograph which I transcribe, 'to acknowledge the receipt of your note, and to say in reply that it has not been stated by me, (though such a state-
30 ment has, I believe, appeared in some of the Public Prints,) that Mr. Newman had advised Mr. B. S. to retain his living, after he had forsaken our Church. But it has been stated to me, that Mr. Newman was in close correspondence with Mr. B. S., and, being fully aware of his state of opinions and feelings, yet advised
35 him to continue in our communion. Allow me to add', he says to Dr. Pusey, 'that neither your name, nor that of Mr. Keble, was mentioned to me in connexion with that of Mr. B. S.'

1–2 on a vacancy to succeed to] to have the reversion of   6 was made to] was to
10–11 of it,' I . . . Editor, 'no] of it, no   12 passed between] passed', I continued
to the Editor, 'between   25–26 Upon this . . . behalf] Dr. Pusey too wrote for me

I was not going to let the Bishop off on this evasion, so I wrote to him myself. After quoting his Letter to Dr. Pusey, I continued, 'I beg to trouble your Lordship with my own account of the two allegations' [*close correspondence* and *fully aware*, &c.] 'which are contained in your statement, and which have led to your 5 speaking of me in terms which I hope never to deserve. 1. Since Mr. B. S. has been in your Lordship's diocese, I have seen him in Common rooms or private parties in Oxford two or three times, when I never (as far as I can recollect) had any conversation with him. During the same time I have, to the best of my 10 memory, written to him three letters. One was lately, in acknowledgment of his informing me of his change of religion. Another was last summer, when I asked him (to no purpose) to come and stay with me in this place. The earliest of the three letters was written just a year since, as far as I recollect, and it certainly was 15 on the subject of his joining the Church of Rome. I wrote this letter at the earnest wish of a friend of his. I cannot be sure that, on his replying, I did not send him a brief note in explanation of points in my letter which he had misapprehended. I cannot recollect any other correspondence between us. 20

'2. As to my knowledge of his opinions and feelings, as far as I remember, the only point of perplexity which I knew, the only point which to this hour I know, as pressing upon him, was that of the Pope's supremacy. He professed to be searching Antiquity whether the see of Rome had formerly that relation to the whole 25 Church which Roman Catholics now assign to it. My letter was directed to the point, that it was his duty not to perplex himself with arguments on [such] a question, . . . and to put it altogether aside. . . . It is hard that I am put upon my memory, without knowing the details of the statement made against me, consider- 30 ing the various correspondence in which I am from time to time unavoidably engaged. . . . Be assured, my Lord, that there are very definite limits, beyond which persons like me would never urge another to retain preferment in the English Church, nor would retain it themselves; and that the censure which has been 35 directed against them by so many of its Rulers has a very grave bearing upon those limits.' The Bishop replied in a civil letter, and sent my own letter to his original informant, who wrote to me the letter of a gentleman. It seems that an anxious lady had said

25 formerly] formally

something or other which had been misinterpreted, against her real meaning, into the calumny which was circulated, and so the report vanished into thin air. I closed the correspondence with the following Letter to the Bishop:—

5   'I hope your Lordship will believe me when I say, that statements about me, equally incorrect with that which has come to your Lordship's ears, are from time to time reported to me as credited and repeated by the highest authorities in our Church, though it is very seldom that I have the opportunity of denying

10 them. I am obliged by your Lordship's letter to Dr. Pusey as giving me such an opportunity.' Then I added, with a purpose, 'Your Lordship will observe that in my Letter I had no occasion to proceed to the question, whether a person holding Roman Catholic opinions can in honesty remain in our Church. Lest

15 then any misconception should arise from my silence, I here take the liberty of adding, that I see nothing wrong in such a person's continuing in communion with us, provided he holds no preferment or office, abstains from the management of ecclesiastical matters, and is bound by no subscription or oath to our

20 doctrines.'

This was written on March 8, 1843, and was in anticipation of my own retirement into lay communion. This again leads me to a remark:—for two years I was in lay communion, not indeed being a Catholic in my convictions, but in a state of serious doubt,

25 and with the probable prospect of becoming some day, what as yet I was not. Under these circumstances I thought the best thing I could do was to give up duty and to throw myself into lay communion, remaining an Anglican. I could not go to Rome, while I thought what I did of the devotions she sanctioned to the

30 Blessed Virgin and the Saints. I did not give up my fellowship, for I could not be sure that my doubts would not be reduced or overcome, however unlikely I might consider such an event. But I gave up my living; and, for two years before my conversion, I took no clerical duty. My last Sermon was in September, 1843;

35 then I remained at Littlemore in quiet for two years. But it was made a subject of reproach to me at the time, and is at this day, that I did not leave the Anglican Church sooner. To me this seems a wonderful charge; why, even had I been quite sure that Rome was the true Church, the Anglican Bishops would have

21 March 8] March 7   32 might consider] thought

had no just subject of complaint against me, provided I took no
Anglican oath, no clerical duty, no ecclesiastical administration.
Do they force all men who go to their Churches to believe in the
39 Articles, or to join in the Athanasian Creed? However, I was
to have other measure dealt to me; great authorities ruled it so; 5
and a great controversialist, Mr. Stanley Faber, thought it a
shame that I did not leave the Church of England as much as
ten years sooner than I did. He said this in print between the
years 1847 and 1849. His nephew, an Anglican clergyman,
kindly wished to undeceive him on this point. So, in the latter year, 10
after some correspondence, I wrote the following letter, which
will be of service to this narrative, from its chronological notes:—

'Dec. 6, 1849. Your uncle says, "If he (Mr. N.) will declare,
sans phrase, as the French say, that I have laboured under an
entire mistake, and that he was not a concealed Romanist during 15
the ten years in question," (I suppose, the last ten years of my
membership with the Anglican Church,) "or during any part of
the time, my controversial antipathy will be at an end, and I will
readily express to him that I am truly sorry that I have made
such a mistake." 20

'So candid an avowal is what I should have expected from a
mind like your uncle's. I am extremely glad he has brought it
to this issue.

'By a "concealed Romanist" I understand him to mean one,
who, professing to belong to the Church of England, in his heart 25
and will intends to benefit the Church of Rome, at the expense
of the Church of England. He cannot mean by the expression
merely a person who in fact is benefiting the Church of Rome,
while he is intending to benefit the Church of England, for that
is no discredit to him morally, and he (your uncle) evidently 30
means to impute blame.

'In the sense in which I have explained the words, I can simply
and honestly say that I was not a concealed Romanist during the
whole, or any part of, the years in question.

'For the first four years of the ten, (up to Michaelmas, 1839,) 35
I honestly wished to benefit the Church of England, at the expense of the Church of Rome:

6 great] learned *64–78*   controversialist, Mr. Stanley Faber, thought] controversialist in the North thought *64–78*   8–9 He said . . . 1849.] *not in 64*
10 So, in the latter year,] So, in 1850,   12 notes] character

'For the second four years I wished to benefit the Church of England without prejudice to the Church of Rome:

'At the beginning of the ninth year (Michaelmas, 1843) I began to despair of the Church of England, and gave up all
5 clerical duty; and then, what I wrote and did was influenced by a mere wish not to injure it, and not by the wish to benefit it:

'At the beginning of the tenth year I distinctly contemplated leaving it, but I also distinctly told my friends that it was in my contemplation.

10 'Lastly, during the last half of that tenth year I was engaged in writing a book (Essay on Development) in favour of the Roman Church, and indirectly against the English; but even then, till it was finished, I had not absolutely intended to publish it, wishing to reserve to myself the chance of changing my mind
15 when the argumentative views which were actuating me had been distinctly brought out before me in writing.

'I wish this statement, which I make from memory, and without consulting any document, severely tested by my writings and doings, as I am confident it will, on the whole, be borne out,
20 whatever real or apparent exceptions (I suspect none) have to be allowed by me in detail.

'Your uncle is at liberty to make what use he pleases of this explanation.'

I have now reached an important date in my narrative, the year
25 1843; but before proceeding to the matters which it contains, I will insert portions of my letters from 1841 to 1843, addressed to Catholic acquaintances.

1. 'April 8, 1841. . . . The unity of the Church Catholic is very near my heart, only I do not see any prospect of it in our time;
30 and I despair of its being effected without great sacrifices on all hands. As to resisting the Bishop's will, I observe that no point of doctrine or principle was in dispute, but a course of action, the publication of certain works. I do not think you sufficiently understood our position. I suppose you would obey the Holy See
35 in such a case; now, when we were separated from the Pope, his authority reverted to our Diocesans. Our Bishop is our Pope. It is our theory, that each diocese is an integral Church, inter-communion being a duty, (and the breach of it a sin,) but not

23 explanation.'] *no space following in* 64

essential to Catholicity. To have resisted my Bishop, would have been to place myself in an utterly false position, which I never could have recovered. Depend upon it, the strength of any party lies in its being *true to its theory*. Consistency is the life of a movement.

'I have no misgivings whatever that the line I have taken can be other than a prosperous one: that is, in itself, for of course Providence may refuse to us its legitimate issues for our sins.

'I am afraid, that in one respect you may be disappointed. It is my trust, though I must not be too sanguine, that we shall not have individual members of our communion going over to yours. What one's duty would be under other circumstances, what our duty ten or twenty years ago, I cannot say; but I do think that there is less of private judgment in going with one's Church, than in leaving it. I can earnestly desire a union between my Church and yours. I cannot listen to the thought of your being joined by individuals among us.'

2. 'April 26, 1841. My only anxiety is lest your branch of the Church should not meet us by those reforms which surely are *necessary*. It never could be, that so large a portion of Christendom should have split off from the communion of Rome, and kept up a protest for 300 years for nothing. I think I never shall believe that so much piety and earnestness would be found among Protestants, if there were not some very grave errors on the side of Rome. To suppose the contrary is most unreal, and violates all one's notions of moral probabilities. All aberrations are founded on, and have their life in, some truth or other—and Protestantism, so widely spread and so long enduring, must have in it, and must be witness for, a great truth or much truth. That I am an advocate for Protestantism, you cannot suppose;—but I am forced into a *Via Media*, short of Rome, as it is at present.'

3. 'May 5, 1841. While I most sincerely hold that there is in the Roman Church a traditionary system which is not necessarily connected with her essential formularies, yet, were I ever so much to change my mind on this point, this would not tend to bring me from my present position, providentially appointed in the English Church. That your communion was unassailable, would not prove that mine was indefensible. Nor would it at all affect the sense in which I receive our Articles; they would still

30 suppose;—but] suppose, but

speak against certain definite errors, though you had reformed them.

'I say this lest any lurking suspicion should be left in the mind of your friends that persons who think with me are likely, by the
5 growth of their present views, to find it imperative on them to pass over to your communion. Allow me to state strongly, that if you have any such thoughts, and proceed to act upon them, your friends will be committing a fatal mistake. We have (I trust) the principle and temper of obedience too intimately wrought
10 into us to allow of our separating ourselves from our ecclesiastical superiors because in many points we may sympathize with others. We have too great a horror of the principle of private judgment to trust it in so immense a matter as that of changing from one communion to another. We may be cast out of our communion,
15 or it may decree heresy to be truth,—you shall say whether such contingencies are likely; but I do not see other conceivable causes of our leaving the Church in which we were baptized.

'For myself, persons must be well acquainted with what I have written before they venture to say whether I have much changed
20 my main opinions and cardinal views in the course of the last eight years. That my *sympathies* have grown towards the religion of Rome I do not deny; that my *reasons* for *shunning* her communion have lessened or altered it would be difficult perhaps to prove. And I wish to go by reason, not by feeling.'

25 4. 'June 18, 1841. You urge persons whose views agree with mine to commence a movement in behalf of a union between the Churches. Now in the letters I have written, I have uniformly said that I did not expect that union in our time, and have discouraged the notion of all sudden proceedings with a view to it.
30 I must ask your leave to repeat on this occasion most distinctly, that I cannot be party to any agitation, but mean to remain quiet in my own place, and to do all I can to make others take the same course. This I conceive to be my simple duty; but, over and above this, I will not set my teeth on edge with sour grapes. I know it
35 is quite within the range of possibilities that one or another of our people should go over to your communion; however, it would be a greater misfortune to you than grief to us. If your friends wish to put a gulf between themselves and us, let them make converts, but not else. Some months ago, I ventured to say that I felt it
40 a painful duty to keep aloof from all Roman Catholics who came

with the intention of opening negotiations for the union of the Churches: when you now urge us to petition our Bishops for a union, this, I conceive, is very like an act of negotiation.'

5. I have the first sketch or draft of a letter, which I wrote to a zealous Catholic layman: it runs as follows, as far as I have preserved it, but I think there were various changes and additions:—'September 12, 1841. It would rejoice all Catholic minds among us, more than words can say, if you could persuade members of the Church of Rome to take the line in politics which you so earnestly advocate. Suspicion and distrust are the main causes at present of the separation between us, and the nearest approaches in doctrine will but increase the hostility, which, alas, our people feel towards yours, while these causes continue. Depend upon it, you must not rely upon our Catholic tendencies till they are removed. I am not speaking of myself, or of any friends of mine; but of our Church generally. Whatever *our* personal feelings may be, we shall but tend to raise and spread a *rival* Church to yours in the four quarters of the world, unless *you* do what none but you *can* do. Sympathies, which would flow over to the Church of Rome, as a matter of course, did she admit them, will but be developed in the consolidation of our own system, if she continues to be the object of our suspicions and fears. I wish, of course I do, that our own Church may be built up and extended, but still, not at the cost of the Church of Rome, not in opposition to it. I am sure, that, while you suffer, we suffer too from the separation; *but we cannot remove the obstacles*; it is with you to do so. You do not fear us; we fear you. Till we cease to fear you, we cannot love you.

'While you are in your present position, the friends of Catholic unity in our Church are but fulfilling the prediction of those of your body who are averse to them, viz. that they will be merely strengthening a rival communion to yours. Many of you say that *we* are your greatest enemies; we have said so ourselves: so we are, so we shall be, as things stand at present. We are keeping people from you, by supplying their wants in our own Church. We *are* keeping persons from you: do you wish us to keep them from you for a time or for ever? It rests with you to determine. I do not fear that you will succeed among us; you will not supplant our Church in the affections of the English nation; only

6–7 it, but . . . additions:—] it:—

through the English Church can you act upon the English nation. I wish of course our Church should be consolidated, with and through and in your communion, for its sake, and your sake, and for the sake of unity.

5   'Are you aware that the more serious thinkers among us are used, as far as they dare form an opinion, to regard the spirit of Liberalism as the characteristic of the destined Antichrist? In vain does any one clear the Church of Rome from the badges of Antichrist, in which Protestants would invest her, if she deliber-
10   ately takes up her position in the very quarter, whither we have cast them, when we took them off from her. Antichrist is described as the ἄνομος, as exalting himself above the yoke of religion and law. The spirit of lawlessness came in with the Reformation, and Liberalism is its offspring.

15   'And now I fear I am going to pain you by telling you, that you consider the approaches in doctrine on our part towards you, closer than they really are. I cannot help repeating what I have many times said in print, that your services and devotions to St. Mary in matter of fact do most deeply pain me. I am only
20   stating it as a fact.

'Again, I have nowhere said that I can accept the decrees of Trent throughout, nor implied it. The doctrine of Transubstantiation is a great difficulty with me, as being, as I think, not primitive. Nor have I said that our Articles in all respects admit
25   of a Roman interpretation; the very word "Transubstantiation" is disowned in them.

'Thus, you see, it is not merely on grounds of expedience that we do not join you. There are positive difficulties in the way of it. And, even if there were not, we shall have no divine warrant for
30   doing so, while we think that the Church of England is a branch of the true Church, and that intercommunion with the rest of Christendom is necessary, not for the life of a particular Church, but for its health only. I have never disguised that there are actual circumstances in the Church of Rome, which pain me
35   much; of the removal of these I see no chance, while we join you one by one; but if our Church were prepared for a union, she might make her terms; she might gain the cup; she might protest against the extreme honours paid to St. Mary; she might make some explanation of the doctrine of Transubstantiation. I am not

37 cup] Cup

prepared to say that a reform in other branches of the Roman Church would be necessary for our uniting with them, however desirable in itself, so that we were allowed to make a reform in our own country. We do not look towards Rome as believing that its communion is infallible, but that union is a duty.'

6. The following letter was occasioned by the present made to me of a book by the friend to whom it is written; more will be said on the subject of it presently:—

'Nov. 22, 1842. I only wish that your Church were more known among us by such writings. You will not interest us in her, till we see her, not in politics, but in her true functions of exhorting, teaching, and guiding. I wish there were a chance of making the leading men among you understand, what I believe is no novel thought to yourself. It is not by learned discussions, or acute arguments, or reports of miracles, that the heart of England can be gained. It is by men "approving themselves", like the Apostle, "ministers of Christ".

'As to your question, whether the Volume you have sent is not calculated to remove my apprehensions that another gospel is substituted for the true one in your practical instructions, before I can answer it in any way, I ought to know how far the Sermons which it comprises are *selected* from a number, or whether they are the whole, or such as the whole, which have been published of the author's. I assure you, or at least I trust, that, if it is ever clearly brought home to me that I have been wrong in what I have said on this subject, my public avowal of that conviction will only be a question of time with me.

'If, however, you saw our Church as we see it, you would easily understand that such a change of feeling, did it take place, would have no necessary tendency, which you seem to expect, to draw a person from the Church of England to that of Rome. There is a divine life among us, clearly manifested, in spite of all our disorders, which is as great a note of the Church, as any can be. Why should we seek our Lord's presence elsewhere, when He vouchsafes it to us where we are? What *call* have we to change our communion?

'Roman Catholics will find this to be the state of things in time to come, whatever promise they may fancy there is of a large

6: 6.] *Numeral omitted in 64.*   6–7 present made to me of] present of
7 book by] book, from

secession to their Church. This man or that may leave us, but there will be no general movement. There is, indeed, an incipient movement of our *Church* towards yours, and this your leading men are doing all they can to frustrate by their unwearied efforts 5 at all risks to carry off individuals. When will they know their position, and embrace a larger and wiser policy?'

§ 2

The letter which I have last inserted, is addressed to my dear friend, Dr. Russell, the present President of Maynooth. He had, 10 perhaps, more to do with my conversion than any one else. He called upon me, in passing through Oxford in the summer of 1841, and I think I took him over some of the buildings of the University. He called again another summer, on his way from Dublin to London. I do not recollect that he said a word on the 15 subject of religion on either occasion. He sent me at different times several letters; he was always gentle, mild, unobtrusive, uncontroversial. He let me alone. He also gave me one or two books. Veron's Rule of Faith and some Treatises of the Wallenburghs was one; a volume of St. Alfonso Liguori's Sermons was 20 another; and it is to those Sermons that my letter to Dr. Russell relates.

Now it must be observed that the writings of St. Alfonso, as I knew them by the extracts commonly made from them, prejudiced me as much against the Roman Church as any thing else, 25 on account of what was called their 'Mariolatry'; but there was nothing of the kind in this book. I wrote to ask Dr. Russell whether any thing had been left out in the translation; he answered that there certainly were omissions in one Sermon about the Blessed Virgin. This omission, in the case of a book 30 intended for Catholics, at least showed that such passages as are found in the works of Italian Authors were not acceptable to every part of the Catholic world. Such devotional manifestations in honour of our Lady had been my great *crux* as regards Catholicism; I say frankly, I do not fully enter into them now; I trust I do not love her the less, because I cannot enter into them. They

---

7 § 2] *Section not numbered in 64, but large space left between preceding sentence and this paragraph.* 8 The letter which I have last inserted] The last letter, which I have inserted 20 it is . . . Dr. Russell] to that the letter which I have last inserted 28 were omissions in one Sermon] was an omission of one passage

may be fully explained and defended; but sentiment and taste do not run with logic: they are suitable for Italy, but they are not suitable for England. But, over and above England, my own case was special; from a boy I had been led to consider that my Maker and I, His creature, were the two beings, luminously 5 such, *in rerum naturâ*. I will not here speculate, however, about my own feelings. Only this I know full well now, and did not know then, that the Catholic Church allows no image of any sort, material or immaterial, no dogmatic symbol, no rite, no sacrament, no Saint, not even the Blessed Virgin herself, to come 10 between the soul and its Creator. It is face to face, 'solus cum solo', in all matters between man and his God. He alone creates; He alone has redeemed; before His awful eyes we go in death; in the vision of Him is our eternal beatitude.

1. Solus cum solo:—I recollect but indistinctly what I gained 15 from the Volume of which I have been speaking; but it must have been something considerable. At least I had got a key to a difficulty; in these Sermons, (or rather heads of sermons, as they seem to be, taken down by a hearer,) there is much of what would be called legendary illustration; but the substance of them 20 is plain, practical, awful preaching upon the great truths of salvation. What I can speak of with greater confidence is the effect produced on me a little later by studying the Exercises of St. Ignatius. For here again, in a matter consisting in the purest and most direct acts of religion,—in the intercourse between God 25 and the soul, during a season of recollection, of repentance, of good resolution, of inquiry into vocation,—the soul was 'sola cum solo'; there was no cloud interposed between the creature and the Object of his faith and love. The command practically enforced was, 'My son, give Me thy heart'. The devotions then 30 to Angels and Saints as little interfered with the incommunicable glory of the Eternal, as the love which we bear our friends and relations, our tender human sympathies, are inconsistent with that supreme homage of the heart to the Unseen, which really does but sanctify and exalt, not jealously destroy, what is of 35

5 luminously] certainly   15: 1. Solus cum solo:—] 'Solus cum solo':— *no*
par. in 64   15–16 what . . . speaking; but] the effect produced upon me by
this Volume, but   17 been something considerable] been considerable   At
least] At all events   23 effect produced on] effect upon   by studying] of
24–25 For here . . . religion,—in] Here again, in a pure matter of the most direct
religion, in   35 exalt, not jealously destroy, what] exalt what

N

earth. At a later date Dr. Russell sent me a large bundle of penny or half-penny books of devotion, of all sorts, as they are found in the booksellers' shops at Rome; and, on looking them over, I was quite astonished to find how different they were from what I had
5 fancied, how little there was in them to which I could really object. I have given an account of them in my Essay on the Development of Doctrine. Dr. Russell sent me St. Alfonso's book at the end of 1842; however, it was still a long time before I got over my difficulty, on the score of the devotions paid to the Saints;
10 perhaps, as I judge from a letter I have turned up, it was some way into 1844 before I could be said fully to have got over it.

2. I am not sure that I did not also at this time feel the force of another consideration. The idea of the Blessed Virgin was as it were *magnified* in the Church of Rome, as time went on,—but
15 so were all the Christian ideas; as that of the Blessed Eucharist. The whole scene of pale, faint, distant Apostolic Christianity is seen in Rome, as through a telescope or magnifier. The harmony of the whole, however, is of course what it was. It is unfair then to take one Roman idea, that of the Blessed Virgin, out of what
20 may be called its context.

3. Thus I am brought to the principle of development of doctrine in the Christian Church, to which I gave my mind at the end of 1842. I had made mention of it in the passage, which I quoted many pages back (vide p. 105), in 'Home Thoughts
25 Abroad', published in 1836; and even at an earlier date I had introduced it into my History of the Arians in 1832; nor had I ever lost sight of it in my speculations. And it is certainly recognized in the Treatise of Vincent of Lerins, which has so often been taken as the basis of Anglicanism. In 1843 I began to con-
30 sider it attentively; I made it the subject of my last University Sermon on February 2; and the general view to which I came is stated thus in a letter to a friend of the date of July 14, 1844;— it will be observed that, now as before, my *issue* is still Creed *versus* Church:—

11 said fully to] said to   12: 2.] *Numeral omitted in 64.*   12–13 I did…
consideration.] another consideration did not also weigh with me then.   21: 3.]
Numeral omitted in 64.   23 made mention] spoken   24–25 back (vide p. 105),
in 'Home Thoughts Abroad',] back, in Home Thoughts Abroad,   25–27 and
even . . . speculations.] but it had been a favourite subject with me all along.
28 the] that celebrated   29 Anglicanism.] the Anglican theory.   30 atten-
tively] steadily   30–31 I made . . . February 2;] *not in 64*   33 Creed] Faith

'The kind of considerations which weighs with me are such as the following:—1. I am far more certain (according to the Fathers) that we *are* in a state of culpable separation, *than* that developments do *not* exist under the Gospel, and that the Roman developments are not the true ones. 2. I am far more certain, that *our* (modern) doctrines are wrong, *than* that the *Roman* (modern) doctrines are wrong. 3. Granting that the Roman (special) doctrines are not found drawn out in the early Church, yet I think there is sufficient trace of them in it, to recommend and prove them, *on the hypothesis* of the Church having a divine guidance, though not sufficient to prove them by itself. So that the question simply turns on the nature of the promise of the Spirit, made to the Church. 4. The proof of the Roman (modern) doctrine is as strong (or stronger) in Antiquity, as that of certain doctrines which both we and Romans hold: e.g. there is more of evidence in Antiquity for the necessity of Unity, than for the Apostolical Succession; for the Supremacy of the See of Rome, than for the Presence in the Eucharist; for the practice of Invocation, than for certain books in the present Canon of Scripture, &c. &c. 5. The analogy of the Old Testament, and also of the New, leads to the acknowledgment of doctrinal developments.'

4. And thus I was led on to a further consideration. I saw that the principle of development not only accounted for certain facts, but was in itself a remarkable philosophical phenomenon, giving a character to the whole course of Christian thought. It was discernible from the first years of the Catholic teaching up to the present day, and gave to that teaching a unity and individuality. It served as a sort of test, which the Anglican could not exhibit, that modern Rome was in truth ancient Antioch, Alexandria, and Constantinople, just as a mathematical curve has its own law and expression.

5. And thus again I was led on to examine more attentively what I doubt not was in my thoughts long before, viz. the concatenation of argument by which the mind ascends from its first to its final religious idea; and I came to the conclusion that there was no medium, in true philosophy, between Atheism and Catholicity, and that a perfectly consistent mind, under those circumstances in which it finds itself here below, must embrace

---

1 weighs] weigh   22: 4.] *Numeral omitted in 64.*   32: 5.] *Numeral omitted in 64.*

either the one or the other. And I hold this still: I am a Catholic by virtue of my believing in a God; and if I am asked why I believe in a God, I answer that it is because I believe in myself, for I feel it impossible to believe in my own existence (and of that

5 fact I am quite sure) without believing also in the existence of Him, who lives as a Personal, All-seeing, All-judging Being in my conscience. Now, I dare say, I have not expressed myself with philosophical correctness, because I have not given myself to the study of what metaphysicians have said on the subject;

10 but I think I have a strong true meaning in what I say which will stand examination.

6. Moreover, I found a corroboration of the fact of the logical connexion of Theism with Catholicism in a consideration parallel to that which I had adopted on the subject of development of

15 doctrine. The fact of the operation from first to last of that principle of development in the truths of Revelation, is an argument in favour of the identity of Roman and Primitive Christianity; but as there is a law which acts upon the subject-matter of dogmatic theology, so is there a law in the matter of religious

20 faith. In the first chapter of this Narrative I spoke of certitude as the consequence, divinely intended and enjoined upon us, of the accumulative force of certain given reasons which, taken one by one, were only probabilities. Let it be recollected that I am historically relating my state of mind, at the period of my life

25 which I am surveying. I am not speaking theologically, nor have I any intention of going into controversy, or of defending myself; but speaking historically of what I held in 1843–4, I say, that I believed in a God on a ground of probability, that I believed in Christianity on a probability, and that I believed in Catholicism

30 on a probability, and that these three grounds of probability, distinct from each other of course in subject matter, were still all of them one and the same in nature of proof, as being probabilities—probabilities of a special kind, a cumulative, a transcendent probability but still probability; inasmuch as He who made

35 us has so willed, that in mathematics indeed we should arrive at

9 metaphysicians] others   12: 6.] *Numeral omitted in 64.*   12–14 found . . .
parallel to] came to the conclusion which I have been stating, on reasoning of the
same nature, as   16 development in the truths of Revelation, is] development is
20 first chapter] third part   30–34 these three . . . probability;] all three were
about the same kind of probability, a cumulative, a transcendent probability, but
still probability;   35 we should arrive] we arrive

certitude by rigid demonstration, but in religious inquiry we should arrive at certitude by accumulated probabilities;—He has willed, I say, that we should so act, and, as willing it, He co-operates with us in our acting, and thereby enables us to do that which He wills us to do, and carries us on, if our will does but co-operate with His, to a certitude which rises higher than the logical force of our conclusions. And thus I came to see clearly, and to have a satisfaction in seeing, that, in being led on into the Church of Rome, I was not proceeding on any secondary or isolated grounds of reason, or by controversial points in detail, but was protected and justified, even in the use of those secondary or particular arguments, by a great and broad principle. But, let it be observed, that I am stating a matter of fact, not defending it; and if any Catholic says in consequence that I have been converted in a wrong way, I cannot help that now.

I have nothing more to say on the subject of the change in my religious opinions. On the one hand I came gradually to see that the Anglican Church was formally in the wrong, on the other that the Church of Rome was formally in the right; then, that no valid reasons could be assigned for continuing in the Anglican, and again that no valid objections could be taken to joining the Roman. Then, I had nothing more to learn; what still remained for my conversion, was, not further change of opinion, but to change opinion itself into the clearness and firmness of intellectual conviction.

Now I proceed to detail the acts, to which I committed myself during this last stage of my inquiry.

In 1843, I took two very significant steps:—1. In February, I made a formal Retractation of all the hard things which I had

1–2 we should arrive] we arrive   2–6 probabilities;—He . . . with His, to] probabilities—inasmuch as He who has willed that we should so act, co-operates with us in our acting, and thereby bestows on us   9–10 was not proceeding on any secondary or isolated] was proceeding, not by any secondary   11–12 secondary or particular arguments] secondary arguments   16–27 I have . . . inquiry.] And now I have carried on the history of my opinions to their last point, before I became a Catholic. I find great difficulty in fixing dates precisely; but it must have been some way into 1844, before I thought not only that the Anglican Church was certainly wrong, but that Rome was right. Then I had nothing more to learn on the subject. How 'Samaria' faded away from my imagination I cannot tell, but it was gone. Now to go back to the time when this last stage of my inquiry was in its commencement, which, if I dare assign dates, was towards the end of 1842. 28 significant] important and significant said against the Church of Rome. 2. In September, I resigned the Living of St. Mary's, Littlemore included:—I will speak of these two acts separately.

   1. The words, in which I made my Retractation, have given
5 rise to much criticism. After quoting a number of passages from my writings against the Church of Rome, which I withdrew, I ended thus:—'If you ask me how an individual could venture, not simply to hold, but to publish such views of a communion so ancient, so widespreading, so fruitful in Saints, I answer that I
10 said to myself, "I am not speaking my own words, I am but following almost a *consensus* of the divines of my own Church. They have ever used the strongest language against Rome, even the most able and learned of them. I wish to throw myself into their system. While I say what they say, I am safe. Such views,
15 too, are necessary for our position." Yet I have reason to fear still, that such language is to be ascribed, in no small measure, to an impetuous temper, a hope of approving myself to persons I respect, and a wish to repel the charge of Romanism.'

   These words have been, and are, again and again cited against
20 me, as if a confession that, when in the Anglican Church, I said things against Rome which I did not really believe.

   For myself, I cannot understand how any impartial man can so take them; and I have explained them in print several times. I trust that by this time their plain meaning has been satisfac-
25 torily brought out by what I have said in former portions of this Narrative; still I have a word or two to say in addition to my former remarks upon them.

   In the passage in question I apologize for *saying out* in controversy charges against the Church of Rome, which withal I
30 affirm that I fully *believed* at the time when I made them. What is wonderful in such an apology? There are surely many things a man may hold, which at the same time he may feel that he has no right to say publicly, and which it may annoy him that he has said publicly. The law recognizes this principle. In our own time, men

---

2 included] inclusive   19 again and again cited] cited again and again
24–25 their plain meaning . . . brought out] they have been sufficiently explained
26–27 in addition . . . them.] about them, which I have not said before.   28 In]
No par. in 64.   28–30 In the passage . . . made them.] I apologized in the
lines in question for saying out charges against the Church of Rome which I fully
believed to be true.   31 There are surely many] *New par. in 64:* There are many
33–34 publicly, and . . . publicly.] publicly.

have been imprisoned and fined for saying true things of a bad
king. The maxim has been held, that, 'The greater the truth, the
greater is the libel'. And so as to the judgment of society, a just
indignation would be felt against a writer who brought forward
wantonly the weaknesses of a great man, though the whole world 5
knew that they existed. No one is at liberty to speak ill of another
without a justifiable reason, even though he knows he is speaking
truth, and the public knows it too. Therefore, though I believed
what I said against the Roman Church, nevertheless I could not
religiously speak it out, unless I was really justified, not only in 10
believing ill, but in speaking ill. I did believe what I said on what
I thought to be good reasons; but had I also a just cause for
saying out what I believed? I thought I had, and it was this, viz.
that to say out what I believed was simply necessary in the controversy for self-defence. It was impossible to let it alone: the 15
Anglican position could not be satisfactorily maintained, without
assailing the Roman. In this, as in most cases of conflict, one
party was right or the other, not both; and the best defence was
to attack. Is not this almost a truism in the Roman controversy?
Is it not what every one says, who speaks on the subject at all? 20
does any serious man abuse the Church of Rome, for the sake
of abusing her, or because that abuse justifies his own religious
position? What is the meaning of the very word 'Protestantism',
but that there is a call to speak out? This then is what I said;
'I know I spoke strongly against the Church of Rome; but it was 25
no mere abuse, for I had a serious reason for doing so.'

But, not only did I think such language necessary for my
Church's religious position, but I recollected that all the great
Anglican divines had thought so before me. They had thought
so, and they had acted accordingly. And therefore I observe in 30
the passage in question, with much propriety, that I had not
used strong language simply out of my own head, but that in

8–11 Therefore, though . . . ill.] Therefore I could not speak ill against the Church
of Rome, though I believed what I said, without a good reason.   11–13 said on
. . . believed ?] said; but had I a good reason for saying it?   13–19 had, and . . .
to attack.] had; viz. I said what I believed was simply necessary in the controversy,
in order to defend ourselves; I considered that the Anglican position could not be
defended, without bringing charges against the Church of Rome.   17–18 one party
was] one was *65–82*   19–20 truism in the Roman controversy? Is] truism? is
22 that abuse] it   28 but I recollected that all] but all   30–31 I observe . . .
question] I said   32 used strong language] done it   32–p. 184, l. 1 that
in doing so I was] that I was

doing so I was following the track, or rather reproducing the teaching, of those who had preceded me.

I was pleading guilty to using violent language, but I was pleading also that there were extenuating circumstances in the
5 case. We all know the story of the convict, who on the scaffold bit off his mother's ear. By doing so he did not deny the fact of his own crime, for which he was to hang; but he said that his mother's indulgence when he was a boy, had a good deal to do with it. In like manner I had made a charge, and I had made it
10 *ex animo*; but I accused others of having, by their own example, led me into believing it and publishing it.

I was in a humour, certainly, to bite off their ears. I will freely confess, indeed I said it some pages back, that I was angry with the Anglican divines. I thought they had taken me in; I had read
15 the Fathers with their eyes; I had sometimes trusted their quotations or their reasonings; and from reliance on them, I had used words or made statements, which by right I ought rigidly to have examined myself. I had thought myself safe, while I had their warrant for what I said. I had exercised more faith than criticism
20 in the matter. This did not imply any broad misstatements on my part, arising from reliance on their authority, but it implied carelessness in matters of detail. And this of course was a fault.

But there was a far deeper reason for my saying what I said
25 in this matter, on which I have not hitherto touched; and it was this:—The most oppressive thought, in the whole process of my change of opinion, was the clear anticipation, verified by the event, that it would issue in the triumph of Liberalism. Against the Anti-dogmatic principle I had thrown my whole mind; yet
30 now I was doing more than any one else could do, to promote it. I was one of those who had kept it at bay in Oxford for so many years; and thus my very retirement was its triumph. The men who had driven me from Oxford were distinctly the Liberals; it was they who had opened the attack upon Tract 90, and it was
35 they who would gain a second benefit, if I went on to abandon the Anglican Church. But this was not all. As I have already

3 guilty . . . language, but I was] guilty; but   3-4 was pleading] pleading
10-11 having, by their own example, led] having led   12 I was . . . ears. I] But
there was more than this meant in the words which I used:—first, I   17 by
right] properly   18-19 I had thought . . . said.] *not in 64*   35 abandon]
retire from

said, there are but two alternatives, the way to Rome, and the way to Atheism: Anglicanism is the halfway house on the one side, and Liberalism is the halfway house on the other. How many men were there, as I knew full well, who would not follow me now in my advance from Anglicanism to Rome, but would 5 at once leave Anglicanism and me for the Liberal camp. It is not at all easy (humanly speaking) to wind up an Englishman to a dogmatic level. I had done so in good measure, in the case both of young men and of laymen, the Anglican *Via Media* being the representative of dogma. The dogmatic and the Anglican prin- 10 ciple were one, as I had taught them; but I was breaking the *Via Media* to pieces, and would not dogmatic faith altogether be broken up, in the minds of a great number, by the demolition of the *Via Media*? Oh! how unhappy this made me! I heard once from an eye-witness the account of a poor sailor whose legs 15 were shattered by a ball, in the action off Algiers in 1816, and who was taken below for an operation. The surgeon and the chaplain persuaded him to have a leg off; it was done and the tourniquet applied to the wound. Then, they broke it to him that he must have the other off too. The poor fellow said, 'You should 20 have told me that, gentlemen', and deliberately unscrewed the instrument and bled to death. Would not that be the case with many friends of my own? How could I ever hope to make them believe in a second theology, when I had cheated them in the first? with what face could I publish a new edition of a dogmatic 25 creed, and ask them to receive it as gospel? Would it not be plain to them that no certainty was to be found any where? Well, in my defence I could but make a lame apology; however, it was the true one, viz. that I had not read the Fathers cautiously enough; that in such nice points, as those which determine the 30 angle of divergence between the two Churches, I had made con- siderable miscalculations. But how came this about? why, the fact was, unpleasant as it was to avow, that I had leaned too much upon the assertions of Ussher, Jeremy Taylor, or Barrow, and had been deceived by them. Valeat quantum,—it was all 35 that *could* be said. This then was a chief reason of that wording of the Retractation, which has given so much offence, because

the bitterness, with which it was written, was not understood;—
and the following letter will illustrate it:—

'April 3, 1844. I wish to remark on William's chief distress,
that my changing my opinion seemed to unsettle one's confidence
in truth and falsehood as external things, and led one to be
suspicious of the new opinion as one became distrustful of the
old. Now in what I shall say, I am not going to speak in favour
of my second thoughts in comparison of my first, but against
such scepticism and unsettlement about truth and falsehood
generally, the idea of which is very painful.

'The case with me, then, was this, and not surely an unnatural
one:—as a matter of feeling and of duty I threw myself into the
system which I found myself in. I saw that the English Church
had a theological idea or theory as such, and I took it up. I read
Laud on Tradition, and thought it (as I still think it) very
masterly. The Anglican Theory was very distinctive. I admired
it and took it on faith. It did not (I think) occur to me to doubt
it; I saw that it was able, and supported by learning, and I felt
it was a duty to maintain it. Further, on looking into Antiquity
and reading the Fathers, I saw such portions of it as I examined,
fully confirmed (e.g. the supremacy of Scripture). There was only
one question about which I had a doubt, viz. whether it would
work, for it has never been more than a paper system. . . .

'So far from my change of opinion having any fair tendency
to unsettle persons as to truth and falsehood viewed as objective
realities, it should be considered whether such change is not
necessary, if truth be a real objective thing, and be made to
confront a person who has been brought up in a system *short
of* truth. Surely the *continuance* of a person, who wishes to go
right, in a wrong system, and not his *giving it up*, would be that
which militated against the objectiveness of Truth, leading, as
it would, to the suspicion, that one thing and another were
equally pleasing to our Maker, where men were sincere.

'Nor surely is it a thing I need be sorry for, that I defended the
system in which I found myself, and thus have had to unsay my
words. For is it not one's duty, instead of beginning with criticism, to throw oneself generously into that form of religion which
is providentially put before one? Is it right, or is it wrong, to
begin with private judgment? May we not, on the other hand,

3 William's] W.'s

look for a blessing *through* obedience even to an erroneous
system, and a guidance even by means of it out of it? Were
those who were strict and conscientious in their Judaism, or those
who were lukewarm and sceptical, more likely to be led into
Christianity, when Christ came? Yet in proportion to their 5
previous zeal, would be their appearance of inconsistency. Certainly, I have always contended that obedience even to an erring
conscience was the way to gain light, and that it mattered not
where a man began, so that he began on what came to hand, and
in faith; and that any thing might become a divine method of 10
Truth; that to the pure all things are pure, and have a self-
correcting virtue and a power of germinating. And though I
have no right at all to assume that this mercy is granted to me,
yet the fact, that a person in my situation *may* have it granted
to him, seems to me to remove the perplexity which my change 15
of opinion may occasion.

'It may be said,—I have said it to myself,—"Why, however,
did you *publish*? had you waited quietly, you would have
changed your opinion without any of the misery, which now is
involved in the change, of disappointing and distressing people." 20
I answer, that things are so bound up together, as to form a
whole, and one cannot tell what is or is not a condition of what.
I do not see how possibly I could have published the Tracts, or
other works professing to defend our Church, without accom-
panying them with a strong protest or argument against Rome. 25
The one obvious objection against the whole Anglican line is,
that it is Roman; so that I really think there was no alternative
between silence altogether, and forming a theory and attacking
the Roman system.'

2. And now, in the next place, as to my Resignation of St. 30
Mary's, which was the second of the steps which I took in 1843.
The ostensible, direct, and sufficient reason for my doing so was
the persevering attack of the Bishops on Tract 90. I alluded to
it in the letter which I have inserted above, addressed to one of
the most influential among them. A series of their *ex cathedrâ* 35
judgments, lasting through three years, and including a notice
of no little severity in a Charge of my own Bishop, came as near
to a condemnation of my Tract, and, so far, to a repudiation of
the ancient Catholic doctrine, which was the scope of the Tract,

30 in the next place] secondly   32 reason for] cause of

as was possible in the Church of England. It was in order to
shield the Tract from such a condemnation, that I had at the
time of its publication in 1841 so simply put myself at the
disposal of the higher powers in London. At that time, all that
5 was distinctly contemplated in the way of censure, was contained
in the message which my Bishop sent me, that the Tract was
'objectionable'. That I thought was the end of the matter. I had
refused to suppress it, and they had yielded that point. Since I
published the former portions of this Narrative, I have found
10 what I wrote to Dr. Pusey on March 24, while the matter was in
progress. 'The more I think of it,' I said, 'the more reluctant I
am to suppress Tract 90, though *of course* I will do it if the
Bishop wishes it; I cannot, however, deny that I shall feel it a
severe act.' According to the notes which I took of the letters or
15 messages which I sent to him on that and the following days, I
wrote successively, 'My first feeling was to obey without a word;
I will obey still; but my judgment has steadily risen against it
ever since.' Then in the Postscript, 'If I have done any good to
the Church, I do ask the Bishop this favour, as my reward for it,
20 that he would not insist on a measure, from which I think good
will not come. However, I will submit to him.' Afterwards, I got
stronger still and wrote: 'I have almost come to the resolution,
if the Bishop publicly intimates that I must suppress the Tract,
or speaks strongly in his charge against it, to suppress it indeed,
25 but to resign my living also. I could not in conscience act otherwise. You may show this in any quarter you please.'

All my then hopes, all my satisfaction at the apparent fulfilment of those hopes was at an end in 1843. It is not wonderful
then, that in May of that year, when two out of the three years
30 were gone, I wrote on the subject of my retiring from St. Mary's
to the same friend, whom I had consulted upon it in 1840. But
I did more now; I told him my great unsettlement of mind on
the question of the Churches. I will insert portions of two of
my letters:—

3 publication in 1841 so] publication so   5–6 was contained in the] was the
6 the Tract] it *64–82*   9 published] wrote   15 on that and the following days]
in the course of that day *64–78*   15–16 I wrote successively] I went on to say *64*;
I presently wrote to him *65–78*   21–22 got stronger still and wrote:] get stronger
still: 28 hopes was] hopes, were   29–31 year . . . 1840.] year I addressed
a letter on the subject of St. Mary's to the same friend, whom I had consulted about
retiring from it in 1840.

'May 4, 1843. . . . At present I fear, as far as I can analyze my own convictions, I consider the Roman Catholic Communion to be the Church of the Apostles, and that what grace is among us (which, through God's mercy, is not little) is extraordinary, and from the overflowings of His dispensation. I am very far 5 more sure that England is in schism, than that the Roman additions to the Primitive Creed may not be developments, arising out of a keen and vivid realizing of the Divine Depositum of Faith.

'You will now understand what gives edge to the Bishops' 10 Charges, without any undue sensitiveness on my part. They distress me in two ways:—first, as being in some sense protests and witnesses to my conscience against my own unfaithfulness to the English Church, and next, as being samples of her teaching, and tokens how very far she is from even aspiring to 15 Catholicity.

'Of course my being unfaithful to a trust is my great subject of dread,—as it has long been, as you know.'

When he wrote to make natural objections to my purpose, such as the apprehension that the removal of clerical obligations 20 might have the indirect effect of propelling me towards Rome, I answered:—

'May 18, 1843. . . . My office or charge at St. Mary's is not a mere *state*, but a continual *energy*. People assume and assert certain things of me in consequence. With what sort of sincerity 25 can I obey the Bishop? how am I to act in the frequent cases, in which one way or another the Church of Rome comes into consideration? I have to the utmost of my power tried to keep persons from Rome, and with some success; but even a year and a half since, my arguments, though more efficacious with the 30 persons I aimed at than any others could be, were of a nature to infuse great suspicion of me into the minds of lookers-on.

'By retaining St. Mary's, I am an offence and a stumbling-block. Persons are keen-sighted enough to make out what I think on certain points, and then they infer that such opinions 35 are compatible with holding situations of trust in our Church. A number of younger men take the validity of their interpretation of the Articles, &c. from me on *faith*. Is not my present position a cruelty, as well as a treachery towards the Church?

'I do not see how I can either preach or publish again, while 40

I hold St. Mary's;—but consider again the following difficulty in such a resolution, which I must state at some length.

'Last Long Vacation the idea suggested itself to me of publishing the Lives of the English Saints; and I had a conversation
5 with [a publisher] upon it. I thought it would be useful, as employing the minds of men who were in danger of running wild, bringing them from doctrine to history, and from speculation to fact;—again, as giving them an interest in the English soil, and the English Church, and keeping them from seeking
10 sympathy in Rome, as she is; and further, as tending to promote the spread of right views.

'But, within the last month, it has come upon me, that, if the scheme goes on, it will be a practical carrying out of No. 90, from the character of the usages and opinions of ante-reformation
15 times.

'It is easy to say, "Why *will* you do *any* thing? why won't you keep quiet? what business had you to think of any such plan at all?" But I cannot leave a number of poor fellows in the lurch. I am bound to do my best for a great number of people both in
20 Oxford and elsewhere. If *I* did not act, others would find means to do so.

'Well, the plan has been taken up with great eagerness and interest. Many men are setting to work. I set down the names of men, most of them engaged, the rest half engaged and probable,
25 some actually writing.' About thirty names follow, some of them at that time of the school of Dr. Arnold, others of Dr. Pusey's, some my personal friends and of my own standing, others whom I hardly knew, while of course the majority were of the party of the new Movement. I continue:—
30 'The plan has gone so far, that it would create surprise and talk, were it now suddenly given over. Yet how is it compatible with my holding St. Mary's, being what I am?'

Such was the object and the origin of the projected Series of the English Saints; and, since the publication was connected, as
35 has been seen, with my resignation of St. Mary's, I may be allowed to conclude what I have to say on the subject here, though it may read like a digression. As soon then as the first of the

10 tending] seeking   32 am ?'] *No space between paragraphs in 64.*
34 since] as   37 may] will

Series got into print, the whole project broke down. I had already anticipated that some portions of the Series would be written in a style inconsistent with the professions of a beneficed clergyman, and therefore I had given up my Living; but men of great weight went further in their misgivings than I, when they saw the Life 5 of St. Stephen Harding, and decided that it was of a character inconsistent even with its proceeding from an Anglican publisher: and so the scheme was given up at once. After the two first numbers, I retired from the Editorship, and those Lives only were published in addition, which were then already finished, or 10 in advanced preparation. The following passages from what I or others wrote at the time will illustrate what I have been saying:—

In November, 1844, I wrote thus to the author of one of them: 'I am not Editor, I have no direct control over the Series. It is T.'s work; he may admit what he pleases; and exclude what he 15 pleases. I was to have been Editor. I did edit the two first numbers. I was responsible for them, in the way in which an Editor is responsible. Had I continued Editor, I should have exercised a control over all. I laid down in the Preface that doctrinal subjects were, if possible, to be excluded. But, even then, I also set 20 down that no writer was to be held answerable for any of the Lives but his own. When I gave up the Editorship, I had various engagements with friends for separate Lives remaining on my hands. I should have liked to have broken from them all, but there were some from which I could not break, and I let them 25 take their course. Some have come to nothing; others like yours have gone on. I have seen such, either in MS. or Proof. As time goes on, I shall have less and less to do with the Series. I think the engagement between you and me should come to an end. I have any how abundant responsibility on me, and too much. 30 I shall write to T. that if he wants the advantage of your assistance, he must write to you direct.'

In accordance with this letter, I had already advertised in January 1844, ten months before it, that 'other Lives', after St. Stephen Harding, would 'be published by their respective 35 authors on their own responsibility'. This notice was repeated in

5 further in their misgivings than I, when] further, when   6–7 of a character . . . from] of such a character as to be inconsistent even with its being given to the world by   9 numbers] parts   13 the author of one] one of the authors 35 would 'be] 'will be   36 was] is

February, in the advertisement to the second number entitled
'The Family of St. Richard', though to this number, for some
reason which I cannot now recollect, I also put my initials. In the
Life of St. Augustine, the author, a man of nearly my own age,
5 says in like manner, 'No one but himself is responsible for the
way in which these materials have been used.' I have in MS.
another advertisement to the same effect, but I cannot tell
whether it ever appeared in print.

I will add, since the authors have been considered 'hot-headed
10 fanatic young men', whom I was in charge of, and whom I
suffered to do intemperate things, that, while the writer of
St. Augustine was in 1844 past forty, the author of the proposed
Life of St. Boniface, Mr. Bowden, was forty-six; Mr. Johnson,
who was to write St. Aldhelm, forty-three; and most of the others
15 were on one side or other of thirty. Three, I think, were under
twenty-five. Moreover, of these writers some became Catholics,
some remained Anglicans, and others have professed what are
called free or liberal opinions.[1]

The immediate cause of the resignation of my Living is stated
20 in the following letter, which I wrote to my Bishop:—
'August 29, 1843. It is with much concern that I inform your
Lordship, that Mr. A. B., who has been for the last year an
inmate of my house here, has just conformed to the Church of
Rome. As I have ever been desirous, not only of faithfully dis-
25 charging the trust, which is involved in holding a living in your
Lordship's diocese, but of approving myself to your Lordship,
I will for your information state one or two circumstances connected with this unfortunate event. . . . I received him on condition of his promising me, which he distinctly did, that he would
30 remain quietly in our Church for three years. A year has passed
since that time, and, though I saw nothing in him which promised that he would eventually be contented with his present
position, yet for the time his mind became as settled as one could

1 number] volume   2–3 number, for . . . recollect] volume also, for some
reason   8 ever appeared in] was ever put into   9–10 'hot-headed fanatic
young men'] hot-headed boys   12–14 in 1844 . . . and most] of the mature
age which I have stated, most   15 Three, I think, were] Three were
18 opinions.[1]] *No footnote and no space following in 64.*

[1] Vide Note D, *Lives of the English Saints.*

wish, and he frequently expressed his satisfaction at being under the promise which I had exacted of him.'

I felt it impossible to remain any longer in the service of the Anglican Church, when such a breach of trust, however little I had to do with it, would be laid at my door. I wrote in a few days 5 to a friend:

'September 7, 1843. I this day ask the Bishop leave to resign St. Mary's. Men whom you little think, or at least whom I little thought, are in almost a hopeless way. Really we may expect any thing. I am going to publish a Volume of Sermons, including 10 those Four against moving.'

I resigned my living on September the 18th. I had not the means of doing it legally at Oxford. The late Mr. Goldsmid was kind enough to aid me in resigning it in London. I found no fault with the Liberals; they had beaten me in a fair field. As to the 15 act of the Bishops, I thought, to borrow a Scriptural image from Walter Scott, that they had 'seethed the kid in his mother's milk'.

I said to a friend:—

'Victrix causa diis placuit, sed victa Catoni.'

And now I may be almost said to have brought to an end, as 20 far as is necessary for a sketch such as this is, the history both of my changes of religious opinion and of the public acts which they involved.

I had one final advance of mind to accomplish, and one final step to take. That further advance of mind was to be able hon- 25 estly to say that I was *certain* of the conclusions at which I had already arrived. That further step, imperative when such certitude was attained, was my *submission* to the Catholic Church.

This submission did not take place till two full years after the resignation of my living in September 1843; nor could I have 30

13–14 was kind enough to aid] aided   16–17 to borrow a Scriptural image from Walter Scott] as Walter Scott has applied the text   20–22 may be . . . opinion and] have brought almost to an end, as far as this sketch has to treat of them, the history both of my opinions, and   24–p. 194, l. 4 I had one final . . . lay communion with] *No par. in 64.* I had only one more advance of mind to make; and that was, to be *certain* of what I had hitherto anticipated, concluded, and believed; and this was close upon my submission to the Catholic Church. And I had only one more act to perform, and that was the act of submission itself. But two years yet intervened before the date of these final events; during which I was in lay communion in made it at an earlier day, without doubt and apprehension, that is, with any true conviction of mind or certitude.

In the interval, of which it remains to speak, viz. between the autumns of 1843 and 1845, I was in lay communion with the Church of England, attending its services as usual, and abstaining altogether from intercourse with Catholics, from their places of worship, and from those religious rites and usages, such as the Invocation of Saints, which are characteristics of their creed. I did all this on principle; for I never could understand how a man could be of two religions at once.

What I have to say about myself between these two autumns I shall almost confine to this one point,—the difficulty I was in, as to the best mode of revealing the state of my mind to my friends and others, and how I managed to reveal it.

Up to January, 1842, I had not disclosed my state of unsettlement to more than three persons, as has been mentioned above, and as is repeated in the course of the letters which I am now about to give to the reader. To two of them, intimate and familiar companions, in the Autumn of 1839: to the third, an old friend too, whom I have also named above, I suppose, when I was in great distress of mind upon the affair of the Jerusalem Bishopric. In May, 1843, I made it known, as has been seen, to the friend, by whose advice I wished, as far as possible, to be guided. To mention it on set purpose to any one, unless indeed I was asking advice, I should have felt to be a crime. If there is any thing that was abhorrent to me, it was the scattering doubts, and unsettling consciences without necessity. A strong presentiment that my existing opinions would ultimately give way, and that the grounds of them were unsound, was not a sufficient warrant for disclosing the state of my mind. I had no guarantee yet, that that presentiment would be realized. Supposing I were crossing ice, which came right in my way, which I had good reasons for considering

11–12 What . . . point,—the] What then I now have to add is of a private nature, being my preparation for the great event, for which I was waiting, in the interval between the autumns of 1843 and 1845.
And I shall confine what I have to say to this one point, the
14 reveal it.] do it. *No space following in 64.*   17 and as is] and is   the course of the letters] the letters   20 whom I have also named above, I suppose, when] when, I suppose,   22 made it known, as has been seen, to] mentioned it to
26 was abhorrent] was and is abhorrent   it was] it is

sound, and which I saw numbers before me crossing in safety, and supposing a stranger from the bank, in a voice of authority, and in an earnest tone, warned me that it was dangerous, and then was silent, I think I should be startled, and should look about me anxiously, but I think too that I should go on, till I had 5 better grounds for doubt; and such was my state, I believe, till the end of 1842. Then again, when my dissatisfaction became greater, it was hard at first to determine the point of time, when it was too strong to suppress with propriety. Certitude of course is a point, but doubt is a progress; I was not near certitude yet. 10 Certitude is a reflex action; it is to know that one knows. Of that I believe I was not possessed, till close upon my reception into the Catholic Church. Again, a practical, effective doubt is a point too, but who can easily ascertain it for himself? Who can determine when it is, that the scales in the balance of opinion begin 15 to turn, and what was a greater probability in behalf of a belief becomes a positive doubt against it?

In considering this question in its bearing upon my conduct in 1843, my own simple answer to my great difficulty had been, *Do* what your present state of opinion requires in the light of duty, 20 and let that *doing* tell: speak by *acts*. This I had done; my first *act* of the year had been in February. After three months' deliberation I had published my retractation of the violent charges which I had made against Rome: I could not be wrong in doing so much as this; but I did no more at the time: I did 25 not retract my Anglican teaching. My second *act* had been in September in the same year; after much sorrowful lingering and hesitation, I had resigned my Living. I tried indeed, before I did so, to keep Littlemore for myself, even though it was still to remain an integral part of St. Mary's. I had given to it a Church 30 and a sort of Parsonage; I had made it a Parish, and I loved it; I thought in 1843 that perhaps I need not forfeit my existing relations towards it. I could indeed submit to become the curate

5 think too that I] also   11–12 Of that I believe I was not possessed] I believe I had not that   19 had been] was   20–21 requires in the light of duty, and] requires, and   21 had done] did   22 had been in February.] was in February, 1843. 23 I had published] I published   25 more at the time: I] more: I 26–27 had been in September in the same year;] was in September;   28 I had resigned] I resigned   28–29 indeed, before I did so, to] indeed to   30–33 I had given . . . towards it.] I had made it a Parish, and I loved it; but I did not succeed in my attempt.   33 submit] bear

at will of another, but I hoped an arrangement was possible, by which, while I had the curacy, I might have been my own master in serving it. I had hoped an exception might have been made in my favour, under the circumstances; but I did not gain my
5 request. Perhaps I was asking what was impracticable, and it is well for me that it was so.

These had been my two acts of the year, and I said, 'I cannot be wrong in making them; let that follow which must follow in the thoughts of the world about me, when they see what I do.'
10 And, as time went on, they fully answered my purpose. What I felt it a simple duty to do, did create a general suspicion about me, without such responsibility as would be involved in my initiating any direct act for the sake of creating it. Then, when friends wrote me on the subject, I either did not deny or I con-
15 fessed my state of mind, according to the character and need of their letters. Sometimes in the case of intimate friends, whom I should otherwise have been leaving in ignorance of what others knew on every side of them, I invited the question.

And here comes in another point for explanation. While I was
20 fighting in Oxford for the Anglican Church, then indeed I was very glad to make converts, and, though I never broke away from that rule of my mind, (as I may call it,) of which I have already spoken, of finding disciples rather than seeking them, yet, that I made advances to others in a special way, I have no
25 doubt; this came to an end, however, as soon as I fell into misgivings as to the true ground to be taken in the controversy. For then, when I gave up my place in the Movement, I ceased from any such proceedings: and my utmost endeavour was to tranquillize such persons, especially those who belonged to the new
30 school, as were unsettled in their religious views, and, as I judged, hasty in their conclusions. This went on till 1843; but, at that date, as soon as I turned my face Romeward, I gave up, as far as ever was possible, the thought of in any respect and in any

1–3 an arrangement . . . serving it.] still that I might have been my own master there.   5 Perhaps I] Indeed, I   7 had been] were   10 And, as time went on, they] They   11 it] as   13 initiating any direct act for the sake of] taking the initiative in   15 my state of mind] it   17–18 should otherwise . . . them] seemed to leave in ignorance of what others knew about me   20 in Oxford for the Anglican Church] for the Anglican Church in Oxford   26–27 For then] Then   28 proceedings] proceeding   32–p. 197, l. 1 up, as far . . . shape] up altogether and in any shape, as far as ever was possible, the thought of shape acting upon others. Then I myself was simply my own concern. How could I in any sense direct others, who had to be guided in so momentous a matter myself? How could I be considered in a position, even to say a word to them one way or the other? How could I presume to unsettle them, as I was unsettled, when I had no means of bringing them out of such unsettlement? And, if they were unsettled already, how could I point to them a place of refuge, when I was not sure that I should choose it for myself? My only line, my only duty, was to keep simply to my own case. I recollected Pascal's words, 'Je mourrai seul.' I deliberately put out of my thoughts all other works and claims, and said nothing to any one, unless I was obliged.

But this brought upon me a great trouble. In the newspapers there were continual reports about my intentions; I did not answer them; presently strangers or friends wrote, begging to be allowed to answer them; and, if I still kept to my resolution and said nothing, then I was thought to be mysterious, and a prejudice was excited against me. But, what was far worse, there were a number of tender, eager hearts, of whom I knew nothing at all, who were watching me, wishing to think as I thought, and to do as I did, if they could but find it out; who in consequence were distressed, that, in so solemn a matter, they could not see what was coming, and who heard reports about me this way or that, on a first day and on a second; and felt the weariness of waiting, and the sickness of delayed hope, and did not understand that I was as perplexed as they were, and, being of more sensitive complexion of mind than myself, were made ill by the suspense. And they too of course for the time thought me mysterious and inexplicable. I ask their pardon as far as I was really unkind to them. There was a gifted and deeply earnest lady, who in a parabolical account of that time, has described both my conduct as she felt it, and her own feelings upon it. In a singularly graphic, amusing vision of pilgrims, who were making their way across a bleak common in great discomfort, and who were ever warned against, yet continually nearing, 'the king's highway', on the right, she says, 'All my fears and disquiets were speedily renewed by seeing the most daring of our leaders, (the same who had first forced his way through the

8 when . . . it] which I was not sure that I should choose   26 they were]
themselves   32 her own feelings upon it.] that of such as herself.

palisade, and in whose courage and sagacity we all put implicit
trust,) suddenly stop short, and declare that he would go on no
further. He did not, however, take the leap at once, but quietly
sat down on the top of the fence with his feet hanging towards the
5 road, as if he meant to take his time about it, and let himself
down easily.' I do not wonder at all that I thus seemed so unkind
to a lady, who at that time had never seen me. We were both in
trial in our different ways. I am far from denying that I was
acting selfishly both in her case and in that of others; but it was
10 a religious selfishness. Certainly to myself my own duty seemed
clear. They that are whole can heal others; but in my case it was,
'Physician, heal thyself.' My own soul was my first concern, and
it seemed an absurdity to my reason to be converted in partner-
ship. I wished to go to my Lord by myself, and in my own way,
15 or rather His way. I had neither wish, nor, I may say, thought
of taking a number with me. Moreover, it is but the truth to say,
that it had ever been an annoyance to me to seem to be the head
of a party; and that even from fastidiousness of mind, I could not
bear to find a thing done elsewhere, simply or mainly because I
20 did it myself, and that, from distrust of myself, I shrank from the
thought, whenever it was brought home to me, that I was
influencing others. But nothing of this could be known to the
world.

The following three letters are written to a friend, who had
25 every claim upon me to be frank with him, Archdeacon Manning:—it will be seen that I disclose the real state of my mind in
proportion as he presses me.

1. 'October 14, 1843. I would tell you in a few words why I
have resigned St. Mary's, as you seem to wish, were it possible
30 to do so. But it is most difficult to bring out in brief, or even *in
extenso*, any just view of my feelings and reasons.

'The nearest approach I can give to a general account of them
is to say, that it has been caused by the general repudiation of the
view, contained in No. 90, on the part of the Church. I could not
35 stand against such an unanimous expression of opinion from the
Bishops, supported, as it has been, by the concurrence, or at least
silence, of all classes in the Church, lay and clerical. If there ever

9 in her case and in that of] towards them and towards   16–22 Moreover . . .
others.] *not in 64*   22–23 the world.] others.   25–26 him, Archdeacon
Manning:] him: *64–72*   26 of my mind in] of mind to him, in

was a case, in which an individual teacher has been put aside and virtually put away by a community, mine is one. No decency has been observed in the attacks upon me from authority; no protests have been offered against them. It is felt,—I am far from denying, justly felt,—that I am a foreign material, and cannot assimi- 5 late with the Church of England.

'Even my own Bishop has said that my mode of interpreting the Articles makes them mean *any thing or nothing*. When I heard this delivered, I did not believe my ears. I denied to others that it was said. . . . Out came the charge, and the words could 10 not be mistaken. This astonished me the more, because I published that Letter to him, (how unwillingly you know,) on the understanding that *I* was to deliver his judgment on No. 90 *instead* of him. A year elapses, and a second and heavier judgment came forth. I did not bargain for this,—nor did he, but the 15 tide was too strong for him.

'I fear that I must confess, that, in proportion as I think the English Church is showing herself intrinsically and radically alien from Catholic principles, so do I feel the difficulties of defending her claims to be a branch of the Catholic Church. It 20 seems a dream to call a communion Catholic, when one can neither appeal to any clear statement of Catholic doctrine in its formularies, nor interpret ambiguous formularies by the received and living Catholic sense, whether past or present. Men of Catholic views are too truly but a party in our Church. I cannot 25 deny that many other independent circumstances, which it is not worth while entering into, have led me to the same conclusion.

'I do not say all this to every body, as you may suppose; but I do not like to make a secret of it to you.'

2. 'Oct. 25, 1843. You have engaged in a dangerous corre- 30 spondence; I am deeply sorry for the pain I shall give you.

'I must tell you then frankly, (but I combat arguments which to me, alas, are shadows,) that it is not from disappointment, irritation, or impatience, that I have, whether rightly or wrongly, resigned St. Mary's; but because I think the Church of Rome 35 the Catholic Church, and ours not part of the Catholic Church, because not in communion with Rome; and because I feel that I could not honestly be a teacher in it any longer.

'This thought came to me last summer four years. . . . I mentioned it to two friends in the autumn. . . . It arose in the first 40

instance from the Monophysite and Donatist controversies, the
former of which I was engaged with in the course of theological
study to which I had given myself. This was at a time when no
Bishop, I believe, had declared against us,[2] and when all was
5 progress and hope. I do not think I have ever felt disappointment
or impatience, certainly not then; for I never looked forward to
the future, nor do I realize it now.

'My first effort was to write that article on the Catholicity of
the English Church; for two years it quieted me. Since the sum-
10 mer of 1839 I have written little or nothing on modern controversy. . . . You know how unwillingly I wrote my letter to the
Bishop in which I committed myself again, as the safest course
under circumstances. The article I speak of quieted me till the
end of 1841, over the affair of No. 90, when that wretched Jerusa-
15 lem Bishopric (no personal matter) revived all my alarms. They
have increased up to this moment. At that time I told my secret
to another person in addition.

'You see then that the various ecclesiastical and quasi-eccle-
siastical acts, which have taken place in the course of the last two
20 years and a half, are not the *cause* of my state of opinion, but are
keen stimulants and weighty confirmations of a conviction forced
upon me, while engaged in the *course of duty*, viz. that theological
reading to which I had given myself. And this last-mentioned
circumstance is a fact, which has never, I think, come before me
25 till now that I write to you.

'It is three years since, on account of my state of opinion, I
urged the Provost in vain to let St. Mary's be separated from
Littlemore; thinking I might with a safe conscience serve the
latter, though I could not comfortably continue in so public a
30 place as a University. This was before No. 90.

'Finally, I have acted under advice, and that, not of my own
choosing, but what came to me in the way of duty, nor the advice
of those only who agree with me, but of near friends who differ
from me.

35 'I have nothing to reproach myself with, as far as I see, in the
matter of impatience; i.e. practically or in conduct. And I trust
that He, who has kept me in the slow course of change hitherto,

4 us,[2]] *no footnote in 64*

---

[2] I think Sumner, Bishop of Chester, must have done so already.

will keep me still from hasty acts, or resolves with a doubtful conscience.

'This I am sure of, that such interposition as yours, kind as it is, only does what *you* would consider harm. It makes me realize my own views to myself; it makes me see their consistency; it 5 assures me of my own deliberateness; it suggests to me the traces of a Providential Hand; it takes away the pain of disclosures; it relieves me of a heavy secret.

'You may make what use of my letters you think right.'

3. My correspondent wrote to me once more, and I replied 10 thus: 'October 31, 1843. Your letter has made my heart ache more, and caused me more and deeper sighs than any I have had a long while, though I assure you there is much on all sides of me to cause sighing and heartache. On all sides:—I am quite haunted by the one dreadful whisper repeated from so many 15 quarters, and causing the keenest distress to friends. You know but a part of my present trial, in knowing that I am unsettled myself.

'Since the beginning of this year I have been obliged to tell the state of my mind to some others; but never, I think, without being in a way obliged, as from friends writing to me as you did, 20 or guessing how matters stood. No one in Oxford knows it or here' [Littlemore], 'but one near friend whom I felt I could not help telling the other day. But, I suppose, many more suspect it.'

On receiving these letters, my correspondent, if I recollect rightly, at once communicated the matter of them to Dr. Pusey, 25 and this will enable me to describe, as nearly as I can, the way in which he first became aware of my changed state of opinion.

I had from the first a great difficulty in making Dr. Pusey understand such differences of opinion as existed between himself and me. When there was a proposal about the end of 1838 30 for a subscription for a Cranmer Memorial, he wished us both to subscribe together to it. I could not, of course, and wished him to subscribe by himself. That he would not do; he could not bear the thought of our appearing to the world in separate positions, in a matter of importance. And, as time went on, he would not 35 take any hints, which I gave him, on the subject of my growing

10: 3. My] My   14 On all sides:—I] On all sides I   22 one near friend] one friend   23 many more] very many   26 describe, as] state as 26–27 can, the . . . opinion.] can the way in which my changed state of opinion was made known to him.

inclination to Rome. When I found him so determined, I often
had not the heart to go on. And then I knew, that, from affection
to me, he so often took up and threw himself into what I said,
that I felt the great responsibility I should incur, if I put things
5 before him just as I might view them myself. And, not knowing
him so well as I did afterwards, I feared lest I should unsettle
him. And moreover, I recollected well, how prostrated he had
been with illness in 1832, and I used always to think that the
start of the Movement had given him a fresh life. I fancied that
10 his physical energies even depended on the presence of a vigorous
hope and bright prospects for his imagination to feed upon; so
much so, that when he was so unworthily treated by the authorities of the place in 1843, I recollect writing to the late Mr. Dodsworth to state my anxiety, lest, if his mind became dejected in
15 consequence, his health should suffer seriously also. These were
difficulties in my way; and then again, another difficulty was,
that, as we were not together under the same roof, we only saw
each other at set times; others indeed, who were coming in or out
of my rooms freely, and according to the need of the moment,
20 knew all my thoughts easily; but for him to know them well,
formal efforts were necessary. A common friend of ours broke it
all to him in 1841, as far as matters had gone at that time, and
showed him clearly the logical conclusions which must lie in
propositions to which I had committed myself; but somehow or
25 other in a little while, his mind fell back into its former happy
state, and he could not bring himself to believe that he and I
should not go on pleasantly together to the end. But that affectionate dream needs must have been broken at last; and two
years afterwards, that friend to whom I wrote the letters which
30 I have just now inserted, set himself, as I have said, to break it.
Upon that, I too begged Dr. Pusey to tell in private to any one
he would, that I thought in the event I should leave the Church
of England. However, he would not do so; and at the end of 1844
had almost relapsed into his former thoughts about me, if I may
35 judge from a letter of his which I have found. Nay, at the Commemoration of 1845, a few months before I left the Anglican
Church, I think he said about me to a friend, 'I trust after all we
shall keep him.'

    5 them myself.] them.   15 should] would   19 according to the need of]
and as there might be need at

In that autumn of 1843, at the time that I spoke to Dr. Pusey, I asked another friend also to communicate in confidence, to whom he would, the prospect which lay before me.

To another friend, Mr. James Hope, now Mr. Hope Scott, I gave the opportunity of knowing it, if he would, in the following Postscript to a letter:—

'While I write, I will add a word about myself. You may come near a person or two who, owing to circumstances, know more exactly my state of feeling than you do, though they would not tell you. Now I do not like that you should not be aware of this, though I see no *reason* why you should know what they happen to know. Your wishing it would *be* a reason.'

I had a dear and old friend, near his death; I never told him my state of mind. Why should I unsettle that sweet calm tranquillity, when I had nothing to offer him instead? I could not say, 'Go to Rome'; else I should have shown him the way. Yet I offered myself for his examination. One day he led the way to my speaking out; but, rightly or wrongly, I could not respond. My reason was, 'I have no certainty on the matter myself. To say "I think" is to tease and to distress, not to persuade.'

I wrote to him on Michaelmas Day, 1843: 'As you may suppose, I have nothing to write to you about, pleasant. I *could* tell you some very painful things; but it is best not to anticipate trouble, which after all can but happen, and, for what one knows, may be averted. You are always so kind, that sometimes, when I part with you, I am nearly moved to tears, and it would be a relief to be so, at your kindness and at my hardness. I think no one ever had such kind friends as I have.'

The next year, January 22, I wrote to him: 'Pusey has quite enough on him, and generously takes on himself more than enough, for me to add burdens when I am not obliged; particularly too, when I am very conscious, that there *are* burdens, which I am or shall be obliged to lay upon him some time or other, whether I will or no.'

And on February 21: 'Half-past ten. I am just up, having a bad cold; the like has not happened to me (except twice in January) in my memory. You may think you have been in my

thoughts, long before my rising. Of course you are so continually, as you well know. I could not come to see you; I am not worthy of friends. With my opinions, to the full of which I dare not confess, I feel like a guilty person with others, though I trust I
5   am not so. People kindly think that I have much to bear externally, disappointment, slander, &c. No, I have nothing to bear, but the anxiety which I feel for my friends' anxiety for me, and their perplexity. This is a better Ash-Wednesday than birthday present'; [his birthday was the same day as mine; it was Ash-
10 Wednesday that year;] 'but I cannot help writing about what is uppermost. And now, my dear B., all kindest and best wishes to you, my oldest friend, whom I must not speak more about, and with reference to myself, lest you should be angry.' It was not in his nature to have doubts: he used to look at me with anxiety,
15 and wonder what had come over me.

On Easter Monday: 'All that is good and gracious descend upon you and yours from the influences of this Blessed Season; and it will be so, (so be it!) for what is the life of you all, as day passes after day, but a simple endeavour to serve Him, from
20 whom all blessing comes? Though we are separated in place, yet this we have in common, that you are living a calm and cheerful time, and I am enjoying the thought of you. It is your blessing to have a clear heaven, and peace around, according to the blessing pronounced on Benjamin.[3] So it is, my dear B., and so may
25 it ever be.'

He was in simple good faith. He died in September of the same year. I had expected that his last illness would have brought light to my mind, as to what I ought to do. It brought none. I made a note, which runs thus: 'I sobbed bitterly over his coffin,
30 to think that he left me still dark as to what the way of truth was, and what I ought to do in order to please God and fulfil His will.' I think I wrote to Charles Marriott to say, that at that moment, with the thought of my friend before me, my strong view in favour of Rome remained just what it was. On the other hand,

8 This is] This [letter] is   11 And now, my dear B., all] And now all *64*; And now, my dear A., all *65–78*   24 Benjamin.[3]] *no footnote in 64*   is, my dear B., and] is, and *64*; is, my dear A., and *65–78*   26–27 of the same] that

---

[3] Deut. xxxiii. 12.

my firm belief that grace was to be found within the Anglican Church remained too.[4] I wrote to another friend thus:—

'Sept. 16, 1844. I am full of wrong and miserable feelings, which it is useless to detail, so grudging and sullen, when I should be thankful. Of course, when one sees so blessed an end, and 5 that, the termination of so blameless a life, of one who really fed on our ordinances and got strength from them, and sees the same continued in a whole family, the little children finding quite a solace of their pain in the Daily Prayer, it is impossible not to feel more at ease in our Church, as at least a sort of Zoar, a place 10 of refuge and temporary rest, because of the steepness of the way. Only, may we be kept from unlawful security, lest we have Moab and Ammon for our progeny, the enemies of Israel.'

I could not continue in this state, either in the light of duty or of reason. My difficulty was this: I had been deceived greatly 15 once; how could I be sure that I was not deceived a second time? I thought myself right then; how was I to be certain that I was right now? How many years had I thought myself sure of what I now rejected? how could I ever again have confidence in my-self? As in 1840 I listened to the rising doubt in favour of Rome, 20 now I listened to the waning doubt in favour of the Anglican Church. To be certain is to know that one knows; what inward test had I, that I should not change again, after that I had become a Catholic? I had still apprehension of this, though I thought a time would come, when it would depart. However, some limit 25 ought to be put to these vague misgivings; I must do my best and then leave it to a higher Power to prosper it. So, at the end of 1844, I came to the resolution of writing an Essay on Doc-trinal Development; and then, if, at the end of it, my convictions in favour of the Roman Church were not weaker, of taking the 30 necessary steps for admission into her fold.

1 within] in   2 too.[4]] too.[1]   another friend thus] a friend upon his death
17 thought myself right then] then thought myself right   21 Anglican] English
22–23 what inward test] what test   27 Power] power   27–28 at the end of 1844,
I came to the resolution of writing] I determined to write   30–31 of taking the
necessary steps for admission into her fold.] to make up my mind to seek admission
into her fold. I acted upon this resolution in the beginning of 1845, and worked at my
Essay steadily into the autumn.   n. 4 On this . . . *Church.*][1] On this subject, vid.
my Third Lecture on 'Anglican Difficulties'. *This footnote not in original pamphlet.*

[4] On this subject, vide my Third Lecture on 'Anglican Difficulties', also Note E, *Anglican Church.*

By this time the state of my mind was generally known, and I made no great secret of it. I will illustrate it by letters of mine which have been put into my hands.

'November 16, 1844. I am going through what must be gone
5 through; and my trust only is that every day of pain is so much taken from the necessary draught which must be exhausted. There is no fear (humanly speaking) of my moving for a long time yet. This has got out without my intending it; but it is all well. As far as I know myself, my one great distress is the per-
10 plexity, unsettlement, alarm, scepticism, which I am causing to so many; and the loss of kind feeling and good opinion on the part of so many, known and unknown, who have wished well to me. And of these two sources of pain it is the former that is the constant, urgent, unmitigated one. I had for days a literal ache
15 all about my heart; and from time to time all the complaints of the Psalmist seemed to belong to me.

'And as far as I know myself, my one paramount reason for contemplating a change is my deep, unvarying conviction that our Church is in schism, and that my salvation depends on my
20 joining the Church of Rome. I may use *argumenta ad hominem* to this person or that;[5] but I am not conscious of resentment, or disgust, at any thing that has happened to me. I have no visions whatever of hope, no schemes of action, in any other sphere more suited to me. I have no existing sympathies with Roman Catho-
25 lics; I hardly ever, even abroad, was at one of their services; I know none of them, I do not like what I hear of them.

'And then, how much I am giving up in so many ways! and to me sacrifices irreparable, not only from my age, when people hate changing, but from my especial love of old associations and
30 the pleasures of memory. Nor am I conscious of any feeling, enthusiastic or heroic, of pleasure in the sacrifice; I have nothing to support me here.

'What keeps me yet is what has kept me long; a fear that I am under a delusion; but the conviction remains firm under all cir-
35 cumstances, in all frames of mind. And this most serious feeling

1–3 By this . . . hands.] I told my resolution to various friends at the beginning of the year; indeed, it was at that time known generally. I wrote to a friend thus:— 'My intention, is . . . .' *Here follows letter p. 207, l. 6.*]
4 'November 16, 1844.] *This letter not in 64.*

5 Vide supr. p. 198, &c. Letter of Oct. 14, 1843, compared with that of Oct. 25.

is growing on me; viz. that the reasons for which I believe as much as our system teaches, *must* lead me to believe more, and that not to believe more is to fall back into scepticism.

'A thousand thanks for your most kind and consoling letter; though I have not yet spoken of it, it was a great gift.' 5

Shortly after I wrote to the same friend thus: 'My intention is, if nothing comes upon me, which I cannot foresee, to remain quietly *in statu quo* for a considerable time, trusting that my friends will kindly remember me and my trial in their prayers. And I should give up my fellowship some time before any thing 10 further took place.'

There was a lady, now a nun of the Visitation, to whom at this time I wrote the following letters:—

1. 'November 7, 1844. I am still where I was; I am not moving. Two things, however, seem plain, that every one is 15 prepared for such an event, next, that every one expects it of me. Few, indeed, who do not think it suitable, fewer still, who do not think it likely. However, I do not think it either suitable or likely. I have very little reason to doubt about the issue of things, but the when and the how are known to Him, from whom, I trust, 20 both the course of things and the issue come. The expression of opinion, and the latent and habitual feeling about me, which is on every side and among all parties, has great force. I insist upon it, because I have a great dread of going by my own feelings, lest they should mislead me. By one's sense of duty one must go; but 25 external facts support one in doing so.'

2. 'January 8, 1845. What am I to say in answer to your letter? I know perfectly well, I ought to let you know more of my feelings and state of mind than you do know. But how is that possible in a few words? Any thing I say must be abrupt; nothing 30 can I say which will not leave a bewildering feeling, as needing

6 Shortly after . . . thus:] *These words not in 64.*

11 place.'] *In 64 the paragraph following begins:*
One very dear friend, now no more, Charles Marriott, sent me a letter at the beginning of the next year, from which, from love of him, I quote some sentences: *Here follows in 64 the letter of Jan. 15, 1845, p. 210, l. 15.*

12–13 now a nun of the Visitation, to whom at this time I wrote] who was very anxious on the subject, and I wrote to her *64–78*   14 1. 'November 7, 1844.] 1. 'October, 1844. What can I say more to your purpose? If you will ask me any specific questions, I will answer them, as far as I am able.'   2. 'November 7, 1844.

27: 2. 'January 8, 1845.] 3. 'January 8, 1845   ¶ 27–p. 208. l. 3 What am I . . . subject.] *This paragraph omitted in 64.*

so much to explain it, and being isolated, and (as it were) un-located, and not having any thing with it to show its bearings upon other parts of the subject.

'At present, my full belief is, in accordance with your letter,
5 that, if there is a move in our Church, very few persons indeed will be partners to it. I doubt whether one or two at the most among residents at Oxford. And I don't know whether I can wish it. The state of the Roman Catholics is at present so unsatis-factory. This I am sure of, that nothing but a simple, direct call
10 of duty is a warrant for any one leaving our Church; no prefer-ence of another Church, no delight in its services, no hope of greater religious advancement in it, no indignation, no disgust, at the persons and things, among which we may find ourselves in the Church of England. The simple question is, Can *I* (it is
15 personal, not whether another, but can *I*) be saved in the English Church? am *I* in safety, were I to die to-night? Is it a mortal sin in *me*, not joining another communion?

'P.S. I hardly see my way to concur in attendance, though occasional, in the Roman Catholic chapel, unless a man has
20 made up his mind pretty well to join it eventually. Invocations are not *required* in the Church of Rome; somehow, I do not like using them except under the sanction of the Church, and this makes me unwilling to admit them in members of our Church.'

3. 'March 30. Now I will tell you more than any one knows
25 except two friends. My own convictions are as strong as I sup-pose they can become: only it is so difficult to know whether it is a call of *reason* or of conscience. I cannot make out, if I am impelled by what seems *clear*, or by a sense of *duty*. You can understand how painful this doubt is; so I have waited, hoping
30 for light, and using the words of the Psalmist, "Show some token upon me." But I suppose I have no right to wait for ever for this. Then I am waiting, because friends are most considerately bear-ing me in mind, and asking guidance for me; and, I trust, I should attend to any new feelings which came upon me, should
35 that be the effect of their kindness. And then this waiting sub-serves the purpose of preparing men's minds. I dread shocking, unsettling people. Any how, I can't avoid giving incalculable pain. So, if I had my will, I should like to wait till the summer

4 'At present, my] My   18 'P.S.] P.S. *No new paragraph in 64.*
24: 3. 'March 30.] 4. 'March 30.

of 1846, which would be a full seven years from the time that my
convictions first began to fall on me. But I don't think I shall
last so long.

'My present intention is to give up my Fellowship in October,
and to publish some work or treatise between that and Christ- 5
mas. I wish people to know *why* I am acting, as well as *what*
I am doing; it takes off that vague and distressing surprise,
"What *can* have made him?"'

4. 'June 1. What you tell me of yourself makes it plain that
it is your duty to remain quietly and patiently, till you see more 10
clearly where you are; else you are leaping in the dark.'

In the early part of this year, if not before, there was an idea
afloat that my retirement from the Anglican Church was owing
to my distress that I had been so thrust aside, without any one's
taking my part. Various measures were, I believe, talked of in 15
consequence of this surmise. Coincidently with it appeared an
exceedingly kind article about me in a Quarterly, in its April
number. The writer praised me in kind and beautiful language
far above my deserts. In the course of his remarks, he said, speaking of me as Vicar of St. Mary's: 'He had the future race of 20
clergy hearing him. Did he value and feel tender about, and
cling to his position? . . . Not at all. . . . No sacrifice to him
perhaps, he did not care about such things.'

There was a censure implied, however covertly, in these words;
and it is alluded to in the following letter, addressed to a very 25
intimate friend:—

'April 3, 1845. . . . Accept this apology, my dear Church, and
forgive me. As I say so, tears come into my eyes;—that arises
from the accident of this time, when I am giving up so much
I love. Just now I have been overset by James Mozley's article 30
in the Remembrancer; yet really, my dear Church, I have never
for an instant had even the temptation of repenting my leaving
Oxford. The feeling of repentance has not even come into my
mind. How could it? How could I remain at St. Mary's a hypocrite? how could I be answerable for souls, (and life so uncer- 35
tain,) with the convictions, or at least persuasions, which I had

9: 4.] 5.   14 my distress] the feeling *64–78*   been so thrust] so been thrust
18 kind] feeling   24–26 There was . . . friend:—] This was the occasion of my
writing to a very intimate friend the following letter:—   27 Church] C.
30 James Mozley's] A.B.'s *64*; A's *65–78*   31 Remembrancer] C.D. *64*;
Christian Remembrancer *65–78*   Church] C.

upon me? It is indeed a responsibility to act as I am doing; and I feel His hand heavy on me without intermission, who is all Wisdom and Love, so that my heart and mind are tired out, just as the limbs might be from a load on one's back. That sort of

5 dull aching pain is mine; but my responsibility really is nothing to what it would be, to be answerable for souls, for confiding loving souls, in the English Church, with my convictions. My love to Marriott, and save me the pain of sending him a line.'

10   I am now close upon the date of my reception into the Catholic Church; at the beginning of the year a letter had been addressed to me by a very dear friend, now no more, Charles Marriott. I quote some sentences from it, for the love which I bear him and the value that I set on his good word.

15   'January 15, 1845. You know me well enough to be aware, that I never see through any thing at first. Your letter to Badeley casts a gloom over the future, which you can understand, if you have understood me, as I believe you have. But I may speak out at once, of what I see and feel at once, and doubt not that I shall

20 ever feel: that your whole conduct towards the Church of England and towards us, who have striven and are still striving to seek after God for ourselves, and to revive true religion among others, under her authority and guidance, has been generous and considerate, and, were that word appropriate, dutiful, to a degree

25 that I could scarcely have conceived possible, more unsparing of self than I should have thought nature could sustain. I have felt with pain every link that you have severed, and I have asked no questions, because I felt that you ought to measure the disclosure of your thoughts according to the occasion, and the capacity of

30 those to whom you spoke. I write in haste, in the midst of engagements engrossing in themselves, but partly made tasteless, partly embittered by what I have heard; but I am willing to trust even you, whom I love best on earth, in God's Hand, in the earnest prayer that you may be so employed as is best for the Holy

35 Catholic Church.'

   9 line.'] *Here followed in 64 and 65, without intervening space, the first par.* p. 211, 'In July . . . with him.'   10–35 I am . . . Church.'] *not in 64* 11–12 at the . . . to me] and have reserved for this place some sentences from a letter addressed to me at the beginning of the year *65–68*   13 some sentences from it,] them *65–68*

In July, a Bishop thought it worth while to give out to the world that 'the adherents of Mr. Newman are few in number. A short time will now probably suffice to prove this fact. It is well known that he is preparing for secession; and, when that event takes place, it will be seen how few will go with him.'   5

I had begun my Essay on the Development of Doctrine in the beginning of 1845, and I was hard at it all through the year till October. As I advanced, my difficulties so cleared away that I ceased to speak of 'the Roman Catholics', and boldly called them Catholics. Before I got to the end, I resolved to be received, and 10 the book remains in the state in which it was then, unfinished.

One of my friends at Littlemore had been received into the Church on Michaelmas Day, at the Passionist House at Aston, near Stone, by Father Dominic, the Superior. At the beginning of October the latter was passing through London to Belgium; 15 and, as I was in some perplexity what steps to take for being received myself, I assented to the proposition made to me that the good priest should take Littlemore in his way, with a view to his doing for me the same charitable service as he had done to my friend.   20

On October the 8th I wrote to a number of friends the following letter:—

'Littlemore, October 8th, 1845. I am this night expecting Father Dominic, the Passionist, who, from his youth, has been led to have distinct and direct thoughts, first of the countries of 25 the North, then of England. After thirty years' (almost) waiting, he was without his own act sent here. But he has had little to do with conversions. I saw him here for a few minutes on St. John Baptist's day last year.

'He is a simple, holy man; and withal gifted with remarkable 30 powers. He does not know of my intention; but I mean to ask of him admission into the One Fold of Christ. . . .

'I have so many letters to write, that this must do for all who choose to ask about me. With my best love to dear Charles Marriott, who is over your head, &c., &c.   35

6–8 I had . . . October.] All this time I was hard at my Essay on Doctrinal Development.   7 beginning] first months *65–68*   8 difficulties] view *65–68*   8–9 cleared away that I ceased to speak] cleared that instead of speaking any more *64–68*   9 and] I *64–68*   12 One of my friends . . .] *This par. not in 64.*   30–31 He . . . powers.] *not in 64*   31–32 He . . . Christ. . . .] *Ends previous par. in 64.*   32 One] one

'P.S. This will not go till all is over. Of course it requires no answer.'

For a while after my reception, I proposed to betake myself to some secular calling. I wrote thus in answer to a very gracious letter of congratulation sent me by Cardinal Acton:—

'Nov. 25, 1845. I hope you will have anticipated, before I express it, the great gratification which I received from your Eminence's letter. That gratification, however, was tempered by the apprehension, that kind and anxious well-wishers at a distance attach more importance to my step than really belongs to it. To me indeed personally it is of course an inestimable gain; but persons and things look great at a distance, which are not so when seen close; and, did your Eminence know me, you would see that I was one, about whom there has been far more talk for good and bad than he deserves, and about whose movements far more expectation has been raised than the event will justify.

'As I never, I do trust, aimed at any thing else than obedience to my own sense of right, and have been magnified into the leader of a party without my wishing it or acting as such, so now, much as I may wish to the contrary, and earnestly as I may labour (as is my duty) to minister in a humble way to the Catholic Church, yet my powers will, I fear, disappoint the expectations of both my own friends, and of those who pray for the peace of Jerusalem.

'If I might ask of your Eminence a favour, it is that you would kindly moderate those anticipations. Would it were in my power to do, what I do not aspire to do! At present certainly I cannot look forward to the future, and, though it would be a good work if I could persuade others to do as I have done, yet it seems as if I had quite enough to do in thinking of myself.'

Soon, Dr. Wiseman, in whose Vicariate Oxford lay, called me to Oscott; and I went there with others; afterwards he sent me to Rome, and finally placed me in Birmingham.

I wrote to a friend:—

'January 20, 1846. You may think how lonely I am. "Obliviscere populum tuum et domum patris tui," has been in my ears for the last twelve hours. I realize more that we are leaving Littlemore, and it is like going on the open sea.'

5 congratulation sent me by Cardinal Acton:—] congratulation:—

I left Oxford for good on Monday, February 23, 1846. On the Saturday and Sunday before, I was in my house at Littlemore simply by myself, as I had been for the first day or two when I had originally taken possession of it. I slept on Sunday night at my dear friend's, Mr. Johnson's, at the Observatory. Various 5 friends came to see the last of me; Mr. Copeland, Mr. Church, Mr. Buckle, Mr. Pattison, and Mr. Lewis. Dr. Pusey too came up to take leave of me; and I called on Dr. Ogle, one of my very oldest friends, for he was my private Tutor, when I was an Undergraduate. In him I took leave of my first College, Trinity, 10 which was so dear to me, and which held on its foundation so many who had been kind to me both when I was a boy, and all through my Oxford life. Trinity had never been unkind to me. There used to be much snap-dragon growing on the walls opposite my freshman's rooms there, and I had for years taken it as 15 the emblem of my own perpetual residence even unto death in my University.

On the morning of the 23rd I left the Observatory. I have never seen Oxford since, excepting its spires, as they are seen from the railway.[6]   20

12 had] have

---

[6] At length I revisited Oxford on February 26th, 1878, after an absence of just 32 years. Vide Additional Note at the end of the volume.

CHAPTER V

POSITION OF MY MIND SINCE 1845

FROM the time that I became a Catholic, of course I have no further history of my religious opinions to narrate. In saying this, I do not mean to say that my mind has been idle, or that I have given up thinking on theological subjects; but that I have had no variations to record, and have had no anxiety of heart whatever. I have been in perfect peace and contentment; I never have had one doubt. I was not conscious to myself, on my conversion, of any change, intellectual or moral, wrought in my mind. I was not conscious of firmer faith in the fundamental truths of Revelation, or of more self-command; I had not more fervour; but it was like coming into port after a rough sea; and my happiness on that score remains to this day without interruption.

Nor had I any trouble about receiving those additional articles, which are not found in the Anglican Creed. Some of them I believed already, but not any one of them was a trial to me. I made a profession of them upon my reception with the greatest ease, and I have the same ease in believing them now. I am far of course from denying that every article of the Christian Creed, whether as held by Catholics or by Protestants, is beset with intellectual difficulties; and it is simple fact, that, for myself, I cannot answer those difficulties. Many persons are very sensitive of the difficulties of Religion; I am as sensitive of them as any one; but I have never been able to see a connexion between apprehending those difficulties, however keenly, and multiplying them to any extent, and on the other hand doubting the doctrines to which they are attached. Ten thousand difficulties do not make one doubt, as I understand the subject; difficulty and doubt are incommensurate. There of course may be difficulties in the evidence; but I am speaking of difficulties intrinsic to the

1 Chapter V] Part VII   2 Position . . . 1845] General Answer to Mr. Kingsley
7 variations] changes   8 contentment; I] contentment. I   9 to myself]
omitted in another copy of 64   10–11 change, intellectual . . . mind.] difference
of thought or of temper from what I had before. *64*   inward difference . . . before.
another copy of 64   12 Revelation] revelation   24 Religion] religion   sensitive
of them as] sensitive as   27 and on the other hand doubting] and doubting

doctrines themselves, or to their relations with each other. A man may be annoyed that he cannot work out a mathematical problem, of which the answer is or is not given to him, without doubting that it admits of an answer, or that a certain particular answer is the true one. Of all points of faith, the being of a God 5 is, to my own apprehension, encompassed with most difficulty, and yet borne in upon our minds with most power.

People say that the doctrine of Transubstantiation is difficult to believe; I did not believe the doctrine till I was a Catholic. I had no difficulty in believing it, as soon as I believed that the 10 Catholic Roman Church was the oracle of God, and that she had declared this doctrine to be part of the original revelation. It is difficult, impossible, to imagine, I grant;—but how is it difficult to believe? Yet Macaulay thought it so difficult to believe, that he had need of a believer in it of talents as eminent as Sir Thomas 15 More, before he could bring himself to conceive that the Catholics of an enlightened age could resist 'the overwhelming force of the argument against it'. 'Sir Thomas More', he says, 'is one of the choice specimens of wisdom and virtue; and the doctrine of transubstantiation is a kind of proof charge. A faith which stands 20 that test, will stand any test.' But for myself, I cannot indeed prove it, I cannot tell *how* it is; but I say, 'Why should it not be? What's to hinder it? What do I know of substance or matter? just as much as the greatest philosophers, and that is nothing at all';—so much is this the case, that there is a rising school of 25 philosophy now, which considers phenomena to constitute the whole of our knowledge in physics. The Catholic doctrine leaves phenomena alone. It does not say that the phenomena go; on the contrary, it says that they remain; nor does it say that the same phenomena are in several places at once. It deals with what no 30 one on earth knows any thing about, the material substances themselves. And, in like manner, of that majestic Article of the Anglican as well as of the Catholic Creed,—the doctrine of the Trinity in Unity. What do I know of the Essence of the Divine Being? I know that my abstract idea of three is simply incom- 35 patible with my idea of one; but when I come to the question of concrete fact, I have no means of proving that there is not a

1 doctrines themselves, or] doctrines, or   relations] compatibility   4 a certain
particular] a particular   7 and yet borne] and borne   22 should it not]
should not it

sense in which one and three can equally be predicated of the Incommunicable God.

But I am going to take upon myself the responsibility of more than the mere Creed of the Church; as the parties accusing me
5 are determined I shall do. They say, that now, in that I am a Catholic, though I may not have offences of my own against honesty to answer for, yet, at least, I am answerable for the offences of others, of my co-religionists, of my brother priests, of the Church herself. I am quite willing to accept the responsibility;
10 and, as I have been able, as I trust, by means of a few words, to dissipate, in the minds of all those who do not begin with dis-believing me, the suspicion with which so many Protestants start, in forming their judgment of Catholics, viz. that our Creed is actually set up in inevitable superstition and hypocrisy, as the
15 original sin of Catholicism; so now I will proceed, as before, identifying myself with the Church and vindicating it,—not of course denying the enormous mass of sin and error which exists of necessity in that world-wide multiform Communion,—but going to the proof of this one point, that its system is in no sense
20 dishonest, and that therefore the upholders and teachers of that system, as such, have a claim to be acquitted in their own persons of that odious imputation.

Starting then with the being of a God, (which, as I have said, is as certain to me as the certainty of my own existence, though
25 when I try to put the grounds of that certainty into logical shape I find a difficulty in doing so in mood and figure to my satisfac-tion,) I look out of myself into the world of men, and there I see a sight which fills me with unspeakable distress. The world seems simply to give the lie to that great truth, of which my whole being
30 is so full; and the effect upon me is, in consequence, as a matter of necessity, as confusing as if it denied that I am in existence myself. If I looked into a mirror, and did not see my face, I should have the sort of feeling which actually comes upon me, when I look into this living busy world, and see no reflexion of its
35 Creator. This is, to me, one of those great difficulties of this absolute primary truth, to which I referred just now. Were it not for this voice, speaking so clearly in my conscience and my heart, I should be an atheist, or a pantheist, or a polytheist when I

15 proceed] go on   17 error] ignorance   35 those] the

looked into the world. I am speaking for myself only; and I am far from denying the real force of the arguments in proof of a God, drawn from the general facts of human society and the course of history, but these do not warm me or enlighten me; they do not take away the winter of my desolation, or make the 5 buds unfold and the leaves grow within me, and my moral being rejoice. The sight of the world is nothing else than the prophet's scroll, full of 'lamentations, and mourning, and woe'.

To consider the world in its length and breadth, its various history, the many races of man, their starts, their fortunes, their 10 mutual alienation, their conflicts; and then their ways, habits, governments, forms of worship; their enterprises, their aimless courses, their random achievements and acquirements, the impotent conclusion of long-standing facts, the tokens so faint and broken of a superintending design, the blind evolution of what 15 turn out to be great powers or truths, the progress of things, as if from unreasoning elements, not towards final causes, the greatness and littleness of man, his far-reaching aims, his short duration, the curtain hung over his futurity, the disappointments of life, the defeat of good, the success of evil, physical pain, mental 20 anguish, the prevalence and intensity of sin, the pervading idolatries, the corruptions, the dreary hopeless irreligion, that condition of the whole race, so fearfully yet exactly described in the Apostle's words, 'having no hope and without God in the world', —all this is a vision to dizzy and appal; and inflicts upon the 25 mind the sense of a profound mystery, which is absolutely beyond human solution.

What shall be said to this heart-piercing, reason-bewildering fact? I can only answer, that either there is no Creator, or this living society of men is in a true sense discarded from His pres- 30 ence. Did I see a boy of good make and mind, with the tokens on him of a refined nature, cast upon the world without provision, unable to say whence he came, his birth-place or his family connexions, I should conclude that there was some mystery connected with his history, and that he was one, of whom, from one 35 cause or other, his parents were ashamed. Thus only should I be able to account for the contrast between the promise and the condition of his being. And so I argue about the world;—*if* there

3–4 society and the course of history, but] society, but   37–38 and the condition] and condition be a God, *since* there is a God, the human race is implicated in some terrible aboriginal calamity. It is out of joint with the purposes of its Creator. This is a fact, a fact as true as the fact of its existence; and thus the doctrine of what is theologically called original sin becomes to me almost as certain as that the world exists, and as the existence of God.

And now, supposing it were the blessed and loving will of the Creator to interfere in this anarchical condition of things, what are we to suppose would be the methods which might be necessarily or naturally involved in His purpose of mercy? Since the world is in so abnormal a state, surely it would be no surprise to me, if the interposition were of necessity equally extraordinary— or what is called miraculous. But that subject does not directly come into the scope of my present remarks. Miracles as evidence, involve a process of reason, or an argument; and of course I am thinking of some mode of interference which does not immediately run into argument. I am rather asking what must be the face-to-face antagonist, by which to withstand and baffle the fierce energy of passion and the all-corroding, all-dissolving scepticism of the intellect in religious inquiries? I have no intention at all of denying, that truth is the real object of our reason, and that, if it does not attain to truth, either the premiss or the process is in fault; but I am not speaking here of right reason, but of reason as it acts in fact and concretely in fallen man. I know that even the unaided reason, when correctly exercised, leads to a belief in God, in the immortality of the soul, and in a future retribution; but I am considering the faculty of reason actually and historically; and in this point of view, I do not think I am wrong in saying that its tendency is towards a simple unbelief in matters of religion. No truth, however sacred, can stand against it, in the long run; and hence it is that in the pagan world, when our Lord came, the last traces of the religious knowledge of former times were all but disappearing from those portions of the world in which the intellect had been active and had had a career.

And in these latter days, in like manner, outside the Catholic Church things are tending,—with far greater rapidity than in

---

10 purpose] object   15 a process of reason, or an argument;] an argument; 16 mode of interference] means   21 of denying] to deny   23 speaking **here** of] speaking of   27 the faculty of reason] it

that old time from the circumstance of the age,—to atheism in one shape or other. What a scene, what a prospect, does the whole of Europe present at this day! and not only Europe, but every government and every civilization through the world, which is under the influence of the European mind! Especially, for it most concerns us, how sorrowful, in the view of religion, even taken in its most elementary, most attenuated form, is the spectacle presented to us by the educated intellect of England, France, and Germany! Lovers of their country and of their race, religious men, external to the Catholic Church, have attempted various expedients to arrest fierce wilful human nature in its onward course, and to bring it into subjection. The necessity of some form of religion for the interests of humanity, has been generally acknowledged: but where was the concrete representative of things invisible, which would have the force and the toughness necessary to be a breakwater against the deluge? Three centuries ago the establishment of religion, material, legal, and social, was generally adopted as the best expedient for the purpose, in those countries which separated from the Catholic Church; and for a long time it was successful; but now the crevices of those establishments are admitting the enemy. Thirty years ago, education was relied upon: ten years ago there was a hope that wars would cease for ever, under the influence of commercial enterprise and the reign of the useful and fine arts; but will any one venture to say that there is any thing any where on this earth, which will afford a fulcrum for us, whereby to keep the earth from moving onwards?

The judgment, which experience passes whether on establishments or on education, as a means of maintaining religious truth in this anarchical world, must be extended even to Scripture, though Scripture be divine. Experience proves surely that the Bible does not answer a purpose for which it was never intended. It may be accidentally the means of the conversion of individuals; but a book, after all, cannot make a stand against the wild living intellect of man, and in this day it begins to testify, as regards its own structure and contents, to the power of that universal solvent, which is so successfully acting upon religious establishments.

Supposing then it to be the Will of the Creator to interfere in

28 passes whether on] passes on   29 or on education] or education

human affairs, and to make provisions for retaining in the world
a knowledge of Himself, so definite and distinct as to be proof
against the energy of human scepticism, in such a case,—I am
far from saying that there was no other way,—but there is
5 nothing to surprise the mind, if He should think fit to introduce
a power into the world, invested with the prerogative of infallibility in religious matters. Such a provision would be a direct,
immediate, active, and prompt means of withstanding the difficulty; it would be an instrument suited to the need; and, when
10 I find that this is the very claim of the Catholic Church, not only
do I feel no difficulty in admitting the idea, but there is a fitness
in it, which recommends it to my mind. And thus I am brought
to speak of the Church's infallibility, as a provision, adapted by
the mercy of the Creator, to preserve religion in the world, and
15 to restrain that freedom of thought, which of course in itself is
one of the greatest of our natural gifts, and to rescue it from its
own suicidal excesses. And let it be observed that, neither here
nor in what follows, shall I have occasion to speak directly of
Revelation in its subject-matter, but in reference to the sanction
20 which it gives to truths which may be known independently of
it,—as it bears upon the defence of natural religion. I say, that
a power, possessed of infallibility in religious teaching, is happily adapted to be a working instrument, in the course of human
affairs, for smiting hard and throwing back the immense energy
25 of the aggressive, capricious, untrustworthy intellect:—and in
saying this, as in the other things that I have to say, it must still
be recollected that I am all along bearing in mind my main purpose, which is a defence of myself.

I am defending myself here from a plausible charge brought
30 against Catholics, as will be seen better as I proceed. The charge
is this:—that I, as a Catholic, not only make profession to hold
doctrines which I cannot possibly believe in my heart, but that
I also believe in the existence of a power on earth, which at its
own will imposes upon men any new set of *credenda*, when it
35 pleases, by a claim to infallibility; in consequence, that my own
thoughts are not my own property; that I cannot tell that to-
morrow I may not have to give up what I hold to-day, and that
the necessary effect of such a condition of mind must be a degrad-

19–21 Revelation . . . bears] the revealed body of truths, but only as they bear
25 aggressive, capricious, untrustworthy intellect] aggressive intellect

ing bondage, or a bitter inward rebellion relieving itself in secret infidelity, or the necessity of ignoring the whole subject of religion in a sort of disgust, and of mechanically saying every thing that the Church says, and leaving to others the defence of it. As then I have above spoken of the relation of my mind towards the Catholic Creed, so now I shall speak of the attitude which it takes up in the view of the Church's infallibility.

And first, the initial doctrine of the infallible teacher must be an emphatic protest against the existing state of mankind. Man had rebelled against his Maker. It was this that caused the divine interposition: and to proclaim it must be the first act of the divinely-accredited messenger. The Church must denounce rebellion as of all possible evils the greatest. She must have no terms with it; if she would be true to her Master, she must ban and anathematize it. This is the meaning of a statement of mine which has furnished matter for one of those special accusations to which I am at present replying: I have, however, no fault at all to confess in regard to it; I have nothing to withdraw, and in consequence I here deliberately repeat it. I said, 'The Catholic Church holds it better for the sun and moon to drop from heaven, for the earth to fail, and for all the many millions on it to die of starvation in extremest agony, as far as temporal affliction goes, than that one soul, I will not say, should be lost, but should commit one single venial sin, should tell one wilful untruth, or should steal one poor farthing without excuse.' I think the principle here enunciated to be the mere preamble in the formal credentials of the Catholic Church, as an Act of Parliament might begin with a '*Whereas*'. It is because of the intensity of the evil which has possession of mankind, that a suitable antagonist has been provided against it; and the initial act of that divinely-commissioned power is of course to deliver her challenge and to defy the enemy. Such a preamble then gives a meaning to her position in the world, and an interpretation to her whole course of teaching and action.

In like manner she has ever put forth, with most energetic distinctness, those other great elementary truths, which either are an explanation of her mission or give a character to her work. She does not teach that human nature is irreclaimable, else

11–12 to proclaim . . . messenger.] the first act of the divinely accredited messenger must be to proclaim it.   15–16 statement of mine which] statement, which

wherefore should she be sent? not, that it is to be shattered and reversed, but to be extricated, purified, and restored; not, that it is a mere mass of hopeless evil, but that it has the promise upon it of great things, and even now, in its present state of disorder
5 and excess, has a virtue and a praise proper to itself. But in the next place she knows and she preaches that such a restoration, as she aims at effecting in it, must be brought about, not simply through certain outward provisions of preaching and teaching, even though they be her own, but from an inward spiritual power
10 or grace imparted directly from above, and of which she is the channel. She has it in charge to rescue human nature from its misery, but not simply by restoring it on its own level, but by lifting it up to a higher level than its own. She recognizes in it real moral excellence though degraded, but she cannot set it free
15 from earth except by exalting it towards heaven. It was for this end that a renovating grace was put into her hands; and therefore from the nature of the gift, as well as from the reasonableness of the case, she goes on, as a further point, to insist, that all true conversion must begin with the first springs of thought, and
20 to teach that each individual man must be in his own person one whole and perfect temple of God, while he is also one of the living stones which build up a visible religious community. And thus the distinctions between nature and grace, and between outward and inward religion, become two further articles in what
25 I have called the preamble of her divine commission.

Such truths as these she vigorously reiterates, and pertinaciously inflicts upon mankind; as to such she observes no halfmeasures, no economical reserve, no delicacy or prudence. 'Ye must be born again,' is the simple, direct form of words which
30 she uses after her Divine Master: 'your whole nature must be re-born; your passions, and your affections, and your aims, and your conscience, and your will, must all be bathed in a new element, and reconsecrated to your Maker,—and, the last not the least, your intellect.' It was for repeating these points of her
35 teaching in my own way, that certain passages of one of my Volumes have been brought into the general accusation which

3 of hopeless evil] of evil　　3–4 promise upon it of] promise of　　4–5 now, in its present state of disorder and excess, has] now has　　8 certain outward provisions] any outward provision　　9 they] it　　an inward] a certain inward　　10–11 of which she is the channel.] which is in her keeping.　　12 restoring it on] raising it upon

has been made against my religious opinions. The writer has said that I was demented if I believed, and unprincipled if I did not believe, in my own statement, that a lazy, ragged, filthy, story-telling beggar-woman, if chaste, sober, cheerful, and religious, had a prospect of heaven, such as was absolutely closed to an 5 accomplished statesman, or lawyer, or noble, be he ever so just, upright, generous, honourable, and conscientious, unless he had also some portion of the divine Christian graces;—yet I should have thought myself defended from criticism by the words which our Lord used to the chief priests, 'The publicans and harlots go 10 into the kingdom of God before you.' And I was subjected again to the same alternative of imputations, for having ventured to say that consent to an unchaste wish was indefinitely more heinous than any lie viewed apart from its causes, its motives, and its consequences: though a lie, viewed under the limitation of these 15 conditions, is a random utterance, an almost outward act, not directly from the heart, however disgraceful and despicable it may be, however prejudicial to the social contract, however deserving of public reprobation; whereas we have the express words of our Lord to the doctrine that 'whoso looketh on a 20 woman to lust after her, hath committed adultery with her already in his heart'. On the strength of these texts, I have surely as much right to believe in these doctrines which have caused so much surprise, as to believe in original sin, or that there is a supernatural revelation, or that a Divine Person suffered, or that 25 punishment is eternal.

Passing now from what I have called the preamble of that grant of power, which is made to the Church, to that power itself, Infallibility, I premise two brief remarks:—1. on the one hand, I am not here determining any thing about the essential seat of 30 that power, because that is a question doctrinal, not historical and practical; 2. nor, on the other hand, am I extending the direct subject-matter, over which that power of Infallibility has jurisdiction, beyond religious opinion:—and now as to the power itself.   35

3 my own statement, that] my statement that   5 such as] which   17 disgraceful and despicable it] disgraceful it   18–19 however prejudicial . . . reprobation;] *not in 64*   23–24 doctrines which have caused so much surprise, as] doctrines as   24 original sin] the doctrine of original sin   28 which is made to the Church] with which the Church is invested   29 premise] make   remarks:—1. on] remarks: on   32: 2.] *not in 64*   33 power of Infallibility has] power has

This power, viewed in its fulness, is as tremendous as the giant evil which has called for it. It claims, when brought into exercise but in the legitimate manner, for otherwise of course it is but quiescent, to know for certain the very meaning of every
5 portion of that Divine Message in detail, which was committed by our Lord to His Apostles. It claims to know its own limits, and to decide what it can determine absolutely and what it cannot. It claims, moreover, to have a hold upon statements not directly religious, so far as this,—to determine whether they
10 indirectly relate to religion, and, according to its own definitive judgment, to pronounce whether or not, in a particular case, they are simply consistent with revealed truth. It claims to decide magisterially, whether as within its own province or not, that such and such statements are or are not prejudicial to the
15 *Depositum* of faith, in their spirit or in their consequences, and to allow them, or condemn and forbid them, accordingly. It claims to impose silence at will on any matters, or controversies, of doctrine, which on its own *ipse dixit*, it pronounces to be dangerous, or inexpedient, or inopportune. It claims that, what-
20 ever may be the judgment of Catholics upon such acts, these acts should be received by them with those outward marks of reverence, submission, and loyalty, which Englishmen, for instance, pay to the presence of their sovereign, without express-ing any criticism on them on the ground that in their matter they
25 are inexpedient, or in their manner violent or harsh. And lastly, it claims to have the right of inflicting spiritual punishment, of cutting off from the ordinary channels of the divine life, and of simply excommunicating, those who refuse to submit themselves to its formal declarations. Such is the infallibility lodged in the
30 Catholic Church, viewed in the concrete, as clothed and sur-rounded by the appendages of its high sovereignty: it is, to repeat what I said above, a supereminent prodigious power sent upon earth to encounter and master a giant evil.

And now, having thus described it, I profess my own absolute
35 submission to its claim. I believe the whole revealed dogma as taught by the Apostles, as committed by the Apostles to the

3 exercise but in] exercise in   4 quiescent] dormant   to know for certain] to have for itself a sure guidance into   5 that] the   12 are simply consistent] are consistent   13 as within its own province] infallibly   15 *Depositum*] Apostolic *depositum*   23-25 expressing . . . they are] public criticism on them, as being in their matter

Church, and as declared by the Church to me. I receive it, as it is infallibly interpreted by the authority to whom it is thus committed, and (implicitly) as it shall be, in like manner, further interpreted by that same authority till the end of time. I submit, moreover, to the universally received traditions of the Church, in which lies the matter of those new dogmatic definitions which are from time to time made, and which in all times are the clothing and the illustration of the Catholic dogma as already defined. And I submit myself to those other decisions of the Holy See, theological or not, through the organs which it has itself appointed, which, waiving the question of their infallibility, on the lowest ground come to me with a claim to be accepted and obeyed. Also, I consider that, gradually and in the course of ages, Catholic inquiry has taken certain definite shapes, and has thrown itself into the form of a science, with a method and a phraseology of its own, under the intellectual handling of great minds, such as St. Athanasius, St. Augustine, and St. Thomas; and I feel no temptation at all to break in pieces the great legacy of thought thus committed to us for these latter days.

All this being considered as the profession which I make *ex animo*, as for myself, so also on the part of the Catholic body, as far as I know it, it will at first sight be said that the restless intellect of our common humanity is utterly weighed down, to the repression of all independent effort and action whatever, so that, if this is to be the mode of bringing it into order, it is brought into order only to be destroyed. But this is far from the result, far from what I conceive to be the intention of that high Providence who has provided a great remedy for a great evil,—far from borne out by the history of the conflict between Infallibility and Reason in the past, and the prospect of it in the future. The energy of the human intellect 'does from opposition grow'; it thrives and is joyous, with a tough elastic strength, under the terrible blows of the divinely-fashioned weapon, and is never so much itself as when it has lately been overthrown. It is the custom with Protestant writers to consider that, whereas there are two great principles in action in the history of religion, Authority and Private Judgment, they have all the Private

21–22 as the profession . . . myself] to be a profession *ex animo*, as on my own part *64*; as the profession . . . part *another copy of 64*

Judgment to themselves, and we have the full inheritance and the superincumbent oppression of Authority. But this is not so; it is the vast Catholic body itself, and it only, which affords an arena for both combatants in that awful, never-dying duel. It is
5 necessary for the very life of religion, viewed in its large operations and its history, that the warfare should be incessantly carried on. Every exercise of Infallibility is brought out into act by an intense and varied operation of the Reason, both as its ally and as its opponent, and provokes again, when it has done its
10 work, a re-action of Reason against it; and, as in a civil polity the State exists and endures by means of the rivalry and collision, the encroachments and defeats of its constituent parts, so in like manner Catholic Christendom is no simple exhibition of religious absolutism, but presents a continuous picture of
15 Authority and Private Judgment alternately advancing and retreating as the ebb and flow of the tide;—it is a vast assemblage of human beings with wilful intellects and wild passions, brought together into one by the beauty and the Majesty of a Superhuman Power,—into what may be called a large reforma-
20 tory or training-school, not as if into a hospital or into a prison, not in order to be sent to bed, not to be buried alive, but (if I may change my metaphor) brought together as if into some moral factory, for the melting, refining, and moulding, by an incessant, noisy process, of the raw material of human nature, so excellent,
25 so dangerous, so capable of divine purposes.

St. Paul says in one place that his Apostolical power is given him to edification, and not to destruction. There can be no better account of the Infallibility of the Church. It is a supply for a need, and it does not go beyond that need. Its object is, and its
30 effect also, not to enfeeble the freedom or vigour of human thought in religious speculation, but to resist and control its extravagance. What have been its great works? All of them in the distinct province of theology:—to put down Arianism, Eutychianism, Pelagianism, Manichæism, Lutheranism, Jansen-
35 ism. Such is the broad result of its action in the past;—and now

8–9 both as its ally and as its opponent] from within and without   9–10 again, when it has done its work, a] again a   14 but presents] but it presents 18 Majesty] majesty   20–24 as if into . . . process,] to be sent to bed, not to be buried alive, but for the melting, refining, and moulding, as in some moral factory, by an incessant noisy process, (if I may proceed to another metaphor,)   24 of the raw] the raw *another copy of 64* as to the securities which are given us that so it ever will act in time to come.

First, Infallibility cannot act outside of a definite circle of thought, and it must in all its decisions, or *definitions*, as they are called, profess to be keeping within it. The great truths of the moral law, of natural religion, and of Apostolical faith, are both its boundary and its foundation. It must not go beyond them, and it must ever appeal to them. Both its subject-matter, and its articles in that subject-matter, are fixed. And it must ever profess to be guided by Scripture and by tradition. It must refer to the particular Apostolic truth which it is enforcing, or (what is called) *defining*. Nothing, then, can be presented to me, in time to come, as part of the faith, but what I ought already to have received, and hitherto have been kept from receiving (if so) merely because it has not been brought home to me. Nothing can be imposed upon me different in kind from what I hold already,—much less contrary to it. The new truth which is promulgated, if it is to be called new, must be at least homogeneous, cognate, implicit, viewed relatively to the old truth. It must be what I may even have guessed, or wished, to be included in the Apostolic revelation; and at least it will be of such a character, that my thoughts readily concur in it or coalesce with it, as soon as I hear it. Perhaps I and others actually have always believed it, and the only question which is now decided in my behalf, is, that I have henceforth the satisfaction of having to believe, that I have only been holding all along what the Apostles held before me.

Let me take the doctrine which Protestants consider our greatest difficulty, that of the Immaculate Conception. Here I entreat the reader to recollect my main drift, which is this. I have no difficulty in receiving the doctrine; and that, because it so intimately harmonizes with that circle of recognized dogmatic truths, into which it has been recently received;—but if

---

9 fixed. And it must] fixed. Thus, in illustration, it does not extend to statements, however sound and evident, which are mere logical conclusions from the Articles of the Apostolic *Depositum*; again, it can pronounce nothing about the persons of heretics, whose works fall within its legitimate province. It must   14–15 hitherto . . . home to me.] have not actually received, (if not) merely because it has not been told me.   25–27 is, that . . . me.] is that I am henceforth to believe that I have only been holding what the Apostles held before me.   31–33 the doctrine; . . . but if] it: if

I have no difficulty, why may not another have no difficulty also? why may not a hundred? a thousand? Now I am sure that Catholics in general have not any intellectual difficulty at all on the subject of the Immaculate Conception; and that there is no reason why they should. Priests have no difficulty. You tell me that they *ought* to have a difficulty;—but they have not. Be large-minded enough to believe, that men may reason and feel very differently from yourselves; how is it that men, when left to themselves, fall into such various forms of religion, except that there are various types of mind among them, very distinct from each other? From my testimony then about myself, if you believe it, judge of others also who are Catholics: we do not find the difficulties which you do in the doctrines which we hold; we have no intellectual difficulty in that doctrine in particular, which you call a novelty of this day. We priests need not be hypocrites, though we be called upon to believe in the Immaculate Conception. To that large class of minds, who believe in Christianity after our manner,—in the particular temper, spirit, and light, (whatever word is used,) in which Catholics believe it,—there is no burden at all in holding that the Blessed Virgin was conceived without original sin; indeed, it is a simple fact to say, that Catholics have not come to believe it because it is defined, but that it was defined because they believed it.

So far from the definition in 1854 being a tyrannical infliction on the Catholic world, it was received every where on its promulgation with the greatest enthusiasm. It was in consequence of the unanimous petition, presented from all parts of the Church to the Holy See, in behalf of an *ex cathedrâ* declaration that the doctrine was Apostolic, that it was declared so to be. I never heard of one Catholic having difficulties in receiving the doctrine, whose faith on other grounds was not already suspicious. Of course there were grave and good men, who were made anxious by the doubt whether it could be formally proved to be Apostolical either by Scripture or tradition, and who accordingly, though believing it themselves, did not see how it could be defined by authority and imposed upon all Catholics as a matter

8–9 men, when left to themselves, fall] men fall, when left to themselves, 14 that doctrine in] that in   23 but that it] but it   27–28 parts of the Church to] parts to   an *ex cathedrâ* declaration] a declaration   30 the doctrine] it   31 already] really *another copy of 64*   33 formally proved to be] proved   36–p. 229, l. 1 authority . . . faith; but] authority; but of faith; but this is another matter. The point in question is, whether the doctrine is a burden. I believe it to be none. So far from it being so, I sincerely think that St. Bernard and St. Thomas, who scrupled at it in their day, had they lived into this, would have rejoiced to accept it for its own sake. Their difficulty, 5 as I view it, consisted in matters of words, ideas, and arguments. They thought the doctrine inconsistent with other doctrines; and those who defended it in that age had not that precision in their view of it, which has been attained by means of the long disputes of the centuries which followed. And in this want of 10 precision lay the difference of opinion, and the controversy.

Now the instance which I have been taking suggests another remark; the number of those (so called) new doctrines will not oppress us, if it takes eight centuries to promulgate even one of them. Such is about the length of time through which the 15 preparation has been carried on for the definition of the Immaculate Conception. This of course is an extraordinary case; but it is difficult to say what is ordinary, considering how few are the formal occasions on which the voice of Infallibility has been solemnly lifted up. It is to the Pope in Ecumenical Council 20 that we look, as to the normal seat of Infallibility: now there have been only eighteen such Councils since Christianity was,— an average of one to a century,—and of these Councils some passed no doctrinal decree at all, others were employed on only one, and many of them were concerned with only elementary 25 points of the Creed. The Council of Trent embraced a large field of doctrine certainly; but I should apply to its Canons a remark contained in that University Sermon of mine, which has been so ignorantly criticized in the Pamphlet which has been the occasion of this Volume;—I there have said that the various 30 verses of the Athanasian Creed are only repetitions in various shapes of one and the same idea; and in like manner, the Tridentine Decrees are not isolated from each other, but are occupied in bringing out in detail, by a number of separate declarations, as if into bodily form, a few necessary truths. I 35 should make the same remark on the various theological censures, promulgated by Popes, which the Church has received,

9 attained] given to it   10 disputes] controversy   10–11 in this want of precision lay] hence   29–30 been the occasion of this Volume;] led to my writing; 36–37 theological censures . . . received] Theses condemned by Popes

and on their dogmatic decisions generally. I own that at first sight those decisions seem from their number to be a greater burden on the faith of individuals than are the Canons of Councils; still I do not believe that in matter of fact they are so 5 at all, and I give this reason for it:—it is not that a Catholic, layman or priest, is indifferent to the subject, or, from a sort of recklessness, will accept any thing that is placed before him, or is willing, like a lawyer, to speak according to his brief, but that in such condemnations the Holy See is engaged, for the most 10 part, in repudiating one or two great lines of error, such as Lutheranism or Jansenism, principally ethical not doctrinal, which are divergent from the Catholic mind, and that it is but expressing what any good Catholic, of fair abilities, though unlearned, would say himself, from common and sound sense, if 15 the matter could be put before him.

Now I will go on in fairness to say what I think *is* the great trial to the Reason, when confronted with that august prerogative of the Catholic Church, of which I have been speaking. I enlarged just now upon the concrete shape and circumstances, 20 under which pure infallible authority presents itself to the Catholic. That authority has the prerogative of an indirect jurisdiction on subject-matters which lie beyond its own proper limits, and it most reasonably has such a jurisdiction. It could not act in its own province, unless it had a right to act out of it. 25 It could not properly defend religious truth, without claiming for that truth what may be called its *pomœria*; or, to take another illustration, without acting as we act, as a nation, in claiming as our own, not only the land on which we live, but what are called British waters. The Catholic Church claims, not 30 only to judge infallibly on religious questions, but to animadvert on opinions in secular matters which bear upon religion, on matters of philosophy, of science, of literature, of history, and it demands our submission to her claim. It claims to censure books, to silence authors, and to forbid discussions. In this pro- 35 vince, taken as a whole, it does not so much speak doctrinally, as enforce measures of discipline. It must of course be obeyed with-

---

1 own] acknowledge   2 those decisions] they   3 on] to   4 believe that in matter of fact they] believe in matter of fact that they   12 divergent from] foreign to   12–13 is but expressing] is expressing   26 that truth] it   34–35 In this province, taken as a whole, it] In all this it

out a word, and perhaps in process of time it will tacitly recede
from its own injunctions. In such cases the question of faith does
not come in at all; for what is matter of faith is true for all times,
and never can be unsaid. Nor does it at all follow, because there
is a gift of infallibility in the Catholic Church, that therefore 5
the parties who are in possession of it are in all their proceedings
infallible. 'O, it is excellent', says the poet, 'to have a giant's
strength, but tyrannous, to use it like a giant.' I think history
supplies us with instances in the Church, where legitimate
power has been harshly used. To make such admission is no 10
more than saying that the divine treasure, in the words of the
Apostle, is 'in earthen vessels'; nor does it follow that the substance of the acts of the ruling power is not right and expedient,
because its manner may have been faulty. Such high authorities
act by means of instruments; we know how such instruments 15
claim for themselves the name of their principals, who thus get
the credit of faults which really are not theirs. But granting all
this to an extent greater than can with any show of reason be
imputed to the ruling power in the Church, what difficulty is
there in the fact of this want of prudence or moderation more 20
than can be urged, with far greater justice, against Protestant
communities and institutions? What is there in it to make us
hypocrites, if it has not that effect upon Protestants? We are
called upon, not to profess any thing, but to submit and be
silent, as Protestant Churchmen have before now obeyed the 25
royal command to abstain from certain theological questions.
Such injunctions as I have been contemplating are laid merely
upon our actions, not upon our thoughts. How, for instance,
does it tend to make a man a hypocrite, to be forbidden to
publish a libel? his thoughts are as free as before: authoritative 30
prohibitions may tease and irritate, but they have no bearing
whatever upon the exercise of reason.

So much at first sight; but I will go on to say further, that, in
spite of all that the most hostile critic may urge about the encroachments or severities of high ecclesiastics, in times past, in 35
the use of their power, I think that the event has shown after all,

---

3 in at all;] in;   6 parties . . . their] power in possession of it is in all its
19 what difficulty is] what is   20 the fact of this want] this want   25–26 silent
. . . questions.] silent.   27 injunctions as I have been contemplating are] injunctions, as I have supposed, are   34 urge about] say upon

that they were mainly in the right, and that those whom they
were hard upon were mainly in the wrong. I love, for instance,
the name of Origen: I will not listen to the notion that so great a
soul was lost; but I am quite sure that, in the contest between
5 his doctrine and followers and the ecclesiastical power, his opponents were right, and he was wrong. Yet who can speak with
patience of his enemy and the enemy of St. John Chrysostom,
that Theophilus, bishop of Alexandria? who can admire or
revere Pope Vigilius? And here another consideration presents
10 itself to my thoughts. In reading ecclesiastical history, when I
was an Anglican, it used to be forcibly brought home to me,
how the initial error of what afterwards became heresy was the
urging forward some truth against the prohibition of authority
at an unseasonable time. There is a time for every thing, and
15 many a man desires a reformation of an abuse, or the fuller
development of a doctrine, or the adoption of a particular policy,
but forgets to ask himself whether the right time for it is come:
and, knowing that there is no one who will be doing any thing
towards its accomplishment in his own lifetime unless he does it
20 himself, he will not listen to the voice of authority, and he spoils
a good work in his own century, in order that another man, as yet
unborn, may not have the opportunity of bringing it happily to
perfection in the next. He may seem to the world to be nothing
else than a bold champion for the truth and a martyr to free
25 opinion, when he is just one of those persons whom the competent
authority ought to silence; and, though the case may not fall
within that subject-matter in which that authority is infallible, or
the formal conditions of the exercise of that gift may be wanting,
it is clearly the duty of authority to act vigorously in the case.
30 Yet its act will go down to posterity as an instance of a tyrannical interference with private judgment, and of the silencing of
a reformer, and of a base love of corruption or error; and it will
show still less to advantage, if the ruling power happens in its
proceedings to evince any defect of prudence or consideration.
35 And all those who take the part of that ruling authority will be
considered as time-servers, or indifferent to the cause of upright-

2 upon were mainly] upon mainly   5 followers and the ecclesiastical power]
his followers and ecclesiastical power   18–19 be doing any thing towards its
accomplishment] do any thing towards it   20 and he spoils] and spoils   21 in
order that] that   22 have the opportunity of bringing] bring   27 that
authority] it   30 its] that   34 evince] act with

ness and truth; while, on the other hand, the said authority may be accidentally supported by a violent ultra party, which exalts opinions into dogmas, and has it principally at heart to destroy every school of thought but its own.

Such a state of things may be provoking and discouraging at 5 the time, in the case of two classes of persons; of moderate men who wish to make differences in religious opinion as little as they fairly can be made; and of such as keenly perceive, and are honestly eager to remedy, existing evils,—evils, of which divines in this or that foreign country know nothing at all, and which 10 even at home, where they exist, it is not every one who has the means of estimating. This is a state of things both of past time and of the present. We live in a wonderful age; the enlargement of the circle of secular knowledge just now is simply a bewilderment, and the more so, because it has the promise of continuing, 15 and that with greater rapidity, and more signal results. Now these discoveries, certain or probable, have in matter of fact an indirect bearing upon religious opinions, and the question arises how are the respective claims of revelation and of natural science to be adjusted. Few minds in earnest can remain at ease without some 20 sort of rational grounds for their religious belief; to reconcile theory and fact is almost an instinct of the mind. When then a flood of facts, ascertained or suspected, comes pouring in upon us, with a multitude of others in prospect, all believers in Revelation, be they Catholic or not, are roused to consider their 25 bearing upon themselves, both for the honour of God, and from tenderness for those many souls who, in consequence of the confident tone of the schools of secular knowledge, are in danger of being led away into a bottomless liberalism of thought.

I am not going to criticize here that vast body of men, in the 30 mass, who at this time would profess to be liberals in religion; and who look towards the discoveries of the age, certain or in progress, as their informants, direct or indirect, as to what they shall think about the unseen and the future. The Liberalism which gives a colour to society now, is very different from that 35 character of thought which bore the name thirty or forty years ago. Now it is scarcely a party; it is the educated lay world. When I was young, I knew the word first as giving name to a

2 be accidentally supported] be supported   11 home, where they exist, it] home, it   37 Now it is scarcely] It is scarcely now

periodical, set up by Lord Byron and others. Now, as then, I
have no sympathy with the philosophy of Byron. Afterwards,
Liberalism was the badge of a theological school, of a dry and
repulsive character, not very dangerous in itself, though dan-
5 gerous as opening the door to evils which it did not itself either
anticipate or comprehend. At present it is nothing else than that
deep, plausible scepticism, of which I spoke above, as being the
development of human reason, as practically exercised by the
natural man.

10   The Liberal religionists of this day are a very mixed body,
and therefore I am not intending to speak against them. There
may be, and doubtless is, in the hearts of some or many of them
a real antipathy or anger against revealed truth, which it is
distressing to think of. Again; in many men of science or litera-
15 ture there may be an animosity arising from almost a personal
feeling; it being a matter of party, a point of honour, the excitement of a game, or a satisfaction to the soreness or annoyance
occasioned by the acrimony or narrowness of apologists for
religion, to prove that Christianity or that Scripture is untrust-
20 worthy. Many scientific and literary men, on the other hand, go
on, I am confident, in a straightforward impartial way, in their
own province and on their own line of thought, without any
disturbance from religious difficulties in themselves, or any wish
at all to give pain to others by the result of their investigations.
25 It would ill become me, as if I were afraid of truth of any kind,
to blame those who pursue secular facts, by means of the reason
which God has given them, to their logical conclusions: or to be
angry with science, because religion is bound in duty to take
cognizance of its teaching. But putting these particular classes
30 of men aside, as having no special call on the sympathy of the
Catholic, of course he does most deeply enter into the feelings of
a fourth and large class of men, in the educated portions of
society, of religious and sincere minds, who are simply perplexed,
—frightened or rendered desperate, as the case may be,—by the
35 utter confusion into which late discoveries or speculations have
thrown their most elementary ideas of religion. Who does not
feel for such men? who can have one unkind thought of them?
I take up in their behalf St. Augustine's beautiful words, 'Illi in

6 At present] Now   17 satisfaction to the] consequence of   23 difficulties]
opinion   28 bound in duty to] bound to   38 up in their behalf St.] up St.

vos sæviant', &c. Let them be fierce with you who have no experience of the difficulty with which error is discriminated from truth, and the way of life is found amid the illusions of the world. How many a Catholic has in his thoughts followed such men, many of them so good, so true, so noble! how often has the 5 wish risen in his heart that some one from among his own people should come forward as the champion of revealed truth against its opponents! Various persons, Catholic and Protestant, have asked me to do so myself; but I had several strong difficulties in the way. One of the greatest is this, that at the moment it is so 10 difficult to say precisely what it is that is to be encountered and overthrown. I am far from denying that scientific knowledge is really growing, but it is by fits and starts; hypotheses rise and fall; it is difficult to anticipate which of them will keep their ground, and what the state of knowledge in relation to them will 15 be from year to year. In this condition of things, it has seemed to me to be very undignified for a Catholic to commit himself to the work of chasing what might turn out to be phantoms, and, in behalf of some special objections, to be ingenious in devising a theory, which, before it was completed, might have to give 20 place to some theory newer still, from the fact that those former objections had already come to nought under the uprising of others. It seemed to be specially a time, in which Christians had a call to be patient, in which they had no other way of helping those who were alarmed, than that of exhorting them to have 25 a little faith and fortitude, and to 'beware', as the poet says, 'of dangerous steps'. This seemed so clear to me, the more I thought of the matter, as to make me surmise, that, if I attempted what had so little promise in it, I should find that the highest Catholic Authority was against the attempt, and that I should 30 have spent my time and my thought, in doing what either it would be imprudent to bring before the public at all, or what, did I do so, would only complicate matters further which were already complicated, without my interference, more than enough. And I interpret recent acts of that authority as fulfilling my 35

4 a Catholic] Catholics   has in his] have in their   6 his heart] their hearts   from among] among *another copy of 64*   his own people] themselves 14 which of them will] which will   23 specially a time] a time of all others 27–28 the more I thought of the matter, as] the more I thought, as *64*; as I thought more, as *another copy of 64*   33 further] more *another copy of 64*   34 complicated, without my interference, more] complicated more

expectation; I interpret them as tying the hands of a controversialist, such as I should be, and teaching us that true wisdom,
which Moses inculcated on his people, when the Egyptians were
pursuing them, 'Fear ye not, stand still; the Lord shall fight for
5 you, and ye shall hold your peace.' And so far from finding a
difficulty in obeying in this case, I have cause to be thankful
and to rejoice to have so clear a direction in a matter of difficulty.

But if we would ascertain with correctness the real course of a
principle, we must look at it at a certain distance, and as history
10 represents it to us. Nothing carried on by human instruments,
but has its irregularities, and affords ground for criticism, when
minutely scrutinized in matters of detail. I have been speaking
of that aspect of the action of an infallible authority, which is
most open to invidious criticism from those who view it from
15 without; I have tried to be fair, in estimating what can be said
to its disadvantage, as witnessed at a particular time in the
Catholic Church, and now I wish its adversaries to be equally
fair in their judgment upon its historical character. Can, then,
the infallible authority, with any show of reason, be said in fact
20 to have destroyed the energy of the Catholic intellect? Let it be
observed, I have not here to speak of any conflict which ecclesiastical authority has had with science, for this simple reason,
that conflict there has been none; and that, because the secular
sciences, as they now exist, are a novelty in the world, and there
25 has been no time yet for a history of relations between theology
and these new methods of knowledge, and indeed the Church
may be said to have kept clear of them, as is proved by the constantly cited case of Galileo. Here 'exceptio probat regulam':
for it is the one stock argument. Again, I have not to speak of
30 any relations of the Church to the new sciences, because my
simple question all along has been whether the assumption of
infallibility by the proper authority is adapted to make me a
hypocrite, and till that authority passes decrees on pure physical
subjects and calls on me to subscribe them, (which it never will
35 do, because it has not the power,) it has no tendency to interfere
by any of its acts with my private judgment on those points. The

16 witnessed at a particular time in] witnessed in   20 Catholic intellect?]
intellect in the Catholic Church?   21 not here to] not to   22–23 this simple
reason, that conflict there has been none; and that, because] there has been none
such, because   31 all along has been] is   35–36 to interfere by any of its
acts] by its acts to interfere

simple question is, whether authority has so acted upon the
reason of individuals, that they can have no opinion of their own,
and have but an alternative of slavish superstition or secret rebellion of heart; and I think the whole history of theology puts an
absolute negative upon such a supposition.   5

It is hardly necessary to argue out so plain a point. It is
individuals, and not the Holy See, that have taken the initiative,
and given the lead to the Catholic mind, in theological inquiry.
Indeed, it is one of the reproaches urged against the Roman
Church, that it has originated nothing, and has only served as a 10
sort of *remora* or break in the development of doctrine. And it is
an objection which I really embrace as a truth; for such I conceive to be the main purpose of its extraordinary gift. It is said,
and truly, that the Church of Rome possessed no great mind in
the whole period of persecution. Afterwards for a long while, it 15
has not a single doctor to show; St. Leo, its first, is the teacher of
one point of doctrine; St. Gregory, who stands at the very extre-
mity of the first age of the Church, has no place in dogma or
philosophy. The great luminary of the western world, is, as we
know, St. Augustine; he, no infallible teacher, has formed the   20
intellect of Christian Europe; indeed to the African Church
generally we must look for the best early exposition of Latin
ideas. Moreover, of the African divines, the first in order of time,
and not the least influential, is the strong-minded and heterodox
Tertullian. Nor is the Eastern intellect, as such, without its share 25
in the formation of the Latin teaching. The free thought of
Origen is visible in the writings of the Western Doctors, Hilary
and Ambrose; and the independent mind of Jerome has en-
riched his own vigorous commentaries on Scripture, from the
stores of the scarcely orthodox Eusebius. Heretical questionings 30
have been transmuted by the living power of the Church into
salutary truths. The case is the same as regards the Ecumenical
Councils. Authority in its most imposing exhibition, grave
bishops, laden with the traditions and rivalries of particular
nations or places, have been guided in their decisions by the   35
commanding genius of individuals, sometimes young and of

6 It is] *Not a new paragraph in 64.*   7 that have] who have *64*; which has
another copy of 64 (Ward)   8 the Catholic mind] Catholic minds   9–10 Roman
Church] Church of Rome   12 objection which I really embrace] objection, which
I embrace   21 of Christian Europe] of Europe   23–32 Moreover . . .
salutary truths.] *not in 64*

inferior rank. Not that uninspired intellect overruled the super-human gift which was committed to the Council, which would be a self-contradictory assertion, but that in that process of inquiry and deliberation, which ended in an infallible enuncia-
5 tion, individual reason was paramount. Thus Malchion, a mere presbyter, was the instrument of the great Council of Antioch in the third century in meeting and refuting, for the assembled Fathers, the heretical Patriarch of that see. Parallel to this instance is the influence, so well known, of a young deacon, St.
10 Athanasius, with the 318 Fathers at Nicæa. In mediæval times we read of St. Anselm at Bari, as the champion of the Council there held, against the Greeks. At Trent, the writings of St. Bonaventura, and, what is more to the point, the address of a Priest and theologian, Salmeron, had a critical effect on some of
15 the definitions of dogma. In some of these cases the influence might be partly moral, but in others it was that of a discursive knowledge of ecclesiastical writers, a scientific acquaintance with theology, and a force of thought in the treatment of doctrine.

There are of course intellectual habits which theology does not
20 tend to form, as for instance the experimental, and again the philosophical; but that is because it *is* theology, not because of the gift of infallibility. But, as far as this goes, I think it could be shown that physical science on the other hand, or again mathematical, affords but an imperfect training for the intellect.
25 I do not see then how any objection about the narrowness of theology comes into our question, which simply is, whether the belief in an infallible authority destroys the independence of the mind; and I consider that the whole history of the Church, and especially the history of the theological schools, gives a negative
30 to the accusation. There never was a time when the intellect of the educated class was more active, or rather more restless, than in the middle ages. And then again all through Church history from the first, how slow is authority in interfering! Perhaps a local teacher, or a doctor in some local school, hazards a proposi-

---

5–8 Thus Malchion . . . see.] *not in 64*   8–15 Parallel to . . . dogma.] Thus the writings of St. Bonaventura, and, what is more to the point, the address of a Priest and theologian, Salmeron, at Trent, had a critical effect on some of the definitions of dogmas. Parallel to this is the influence, so well known, of a young deacon, St. Athanasius, with the 318 Fathers at Nicaea. In like manner we hear of the influence of St. Anselm at Bari, and St. Thomas at Lyons.   15 some of these] the latter   16 others] the former   23–24 or again mathematical] or mathematical tion, and a controversy ensues. It smoulders or burns in one place, no one interposing; Rome simply lets it alone. Then it comes before a Bishop; or some priest, or some professor in some other seat of learning takes it up; and then there is a second stage of it. Then it comes before a University, and it may be 5 condemned by the theological faculty. So the controversy proceeds year after year, and Rome is still silent. An appeal perhaps is next made to a seat of authority inferior to Rome; and then at last after a long while it comes before the supreme power. Meanwhile, the question has been ventilated and turned over and over 10 again, and viewed on every side of it, and authority is called upon to pronounce a decision, which has already been arrived at by reason. But even then, perhaps the supreme authority hesitates to do so, and nothing is determined on the point for years: or so generally and vaguely, that the whole controversy has to be 15 gone through again, before it is ultimately determined. It is manifest how a mode of proceeding, such as this, tends not only to the liberty, but to the courage, of the individual theologian or controversialist. Many a man has ideas, which he hopes are true, and useful for his day, but he is not confident about them, and 20 wishes to have them discussed. He is willing, or rather would be thankful, to give them up, if they can be proved to be erroneous or dangerous, and by means of controversy he obtains his end. He is answered, and he yields; or on the contrary he finds that he is considered safe. He would not dare to do this, if he knew 25 an authority, which was supreme and final, was watching every word he said, and made signs of assent or dissent to each sentence, as he uttered it. Then indeed he would be fighting, as the Persian soldiers, under the lash, and the freedom of his intellect might truly be said to be beaten out of him. But this has not been 30 so:—I do not mean to say that, when controversies run high, in schools or even in small portions of the Church, an interposition may not advisably take place; and again, questions may be of that urgent nature, that an appeal must, as a matter of duty, be made at once to the highest authority in the Church; but if we 35 look into the history of controversy, we shall find, I think, the general run of things to be such as I have represented it. Zosimus treated Pelagius and Cœlestius with extreme forbearance;

14 years: or] years; or   20–21 he is not confident about them, and wishes]
he wishes   24 or on the contrary he] or he   33 advisably] rightly

St. Gregory VII. was equally indulgent with Berengarius:—by reason of the very power of the Popes they have commonly been slow and moderate in their use of it.

And here again is a further shelter for the legitimate exercise of the reason:—the multitude of nations which are within the fold of the Church will be found to have acted for its protection, against any narrowness, on the supposition of narrowness, in the various authorities at Rome, with whom lies the practical decision of controverted questions. How have the Greek traditions been respected and provided for in the later Ecumenical Councils, in spite of the countries that held them being in a state of schism! There are important points of doctrine which have been (humanly speaking) exempted from the infallible sentence, by the tenderness with which its instruments, in framing it, have treated the opinions of particular places. Then, again, such national influences have a providential effect in moderating the bias which the local influences of Italy may exert upon the See of St. Peter. It stands to reason that, as the Gallican Church has in it a French element, so Rome must have in it an element of Italy; and it is no prejudice to the zeal and devotion with which we submit ourselves to the Holy See to admit this plainly. It seems to me, as I have been saying, that Catholicity is not only one of the notes of the Church, but, according to the divine purposes, one of its securities. I think it would be a very serious evil, which Divine Mercy avert! that the Church should be contracted in Europe within the range of particular nationalities. It is a great idea to introduce Latin civilization into America, and to improve the Catholics there by the energy of French devotedness; but I trust that all European races will ever have a place in the Church, and assuredly I think that the loss of the English, not to say the German element, in its composition has been a most serious misfortune. And certainly, if there is one consideration more than another which should make us English grateful to Pius the Ninth, it is that, by giving us a Church of our own, he has prepared the way for our own habits of mind, our own manner of reasoning, our own tastes,

4-5 legitimate exercise of the] individual　　5 which are within] who are in
7 on the supposition of narrowness] if so　　19 a French element] an element
of France　　20 have in it an] have an　　29 devotedness] Religion
30 ever have] have ever　　32 misfortune] evil

and our own virtues, finding a place and thereby a sanctification, in the Catholic Church.

There is only one other subject, which I think it necessary to introduce here, as bearing upon the vague suspicions which are attached in this country to the Catholic Priesthood. It is one of which my accusers have before now said much,—the charge of reserve and economy. They found it in no slight degree on what I have said on the subject in my History of the Arians, and in a note upon one of my Sermons in which I refer to it. The principle of Reserve is also advocated by an admirable writer in two numbers of the Tracts for the Times, and of these I was the Editor.

Now, as to the Economy itself,[1] it is founded upon the words of our Lord, 'Cast not your pearls before swine'; and it was observed by the early Christians more or less, in their intercourse with the heathen populations among whom they lived. In the midst of the abominable idolatries and impurities of that fearful time, the Rule of the Economy was an imperative duty. But that rule, at least as I have explained and recommended it, in anything that I have written, did not go beyond (1) the concealing the truth when we could do so without deceit, (2) stating it only partially, and (3) representing it under the nearest form possible to a learner or inquirer, when he could not possibly understand it exactly. I conceive that to draw Angels with wings is an instance of the third of these economical modes; and to avoid the question, 'Do Christians believe in a Trinity?' by answering, 'They believe in only one God', would be an instance of the second. As to the first, it is hardly an Economy, but comes under what is called the 'Disciplina Arcani'. The second and third economical modes Clement calls *lying*; meaning that a partial truth is in some sense a lie, as is also a representative truth. And this, I think, is about the long and the short of the ground of the

6 accusers have before now said much,—the] accuser says much, the   7 They found] He founds   11–12 Times, and of these I was the Editor.] Times. 13 itself,[1] it] itself, I leave the greater part of what I have to say to an Appendix. Here I will but say that it   18 the Rule of the Economy was an imperative duty.] they could not do otherwise.   18–19 that rule] the rule of the Economy 19–20 in anything that I have written,] *not in 64*   24 Angels] angels 31 as is also] and so also is

[1] Vide Note F, *The Economy*.

accusation which has been so violently urged against me, as being a patron of the Economy.

Of late years I have come to think, as I believe most writers do, that Clement meant more than I have said. I used to think he
5 used the word 'lie' as an hyperbole, but I now believe that he, as other early Fathers, thought that, under certain circumstances, it was lawful to tell a lie. This doctrine I never maintained, though I used to think, as I do now, that the theory of the subject is surrounded with considerable difficulty; and it is not strange
10 that I should say so, considering that great English writers declare without hesitation that in certain extreme cases, as to save life, honour, or even property, a lie is allowable. And thus I am brought to the direct question of truth, and of the truthfulness of Catholic priests generally in their dealings with the
15 world, as bearing on the general question of their honesty, and of their internal belief in their religious professions.

It would answer no purpose, and it would be departing from the line of writing which I have been observing all along, if I entered into any formal discussion on this question; what I shall
20 do here, as I have done in the foregoing pages, is to give my own testimony on the matter in question, and there to leave it. Now first I will say, that, when I became a Catholic, nothing struck me more at once than the English out-spoken manner of the Priests. It was the same at Oscott, at Old Hall Green, at Ushaw;
25 there was nothing of that smoothness, or mannerism, which is commonly imputed to them, and they were more natural and unaffected than many an Anglican clergyman. The many years, which have passed since, have only confirmed my first impression. I have ever found it in the priests of this Diocese; did I
30 wish to point out a straightforward Englishman, I should instance the Bishop, who has, to our great benefit, for so many years presided over it.

And next, I was struck, when I had more opportunity of judging of the Priests, by the simple faith in the Catholic Creed
35 and system, of which they always gave evidence, and which they never seemed to feel, in any sense at all, to be a burden. And now that I have been in the Church nineteen years, I cannot recollect

11 declare without hesitation] simply declare   13 and of the] and the
15–16 and of their] and their   19 this question] the subject

hearing of a single instance in England of an infidel priest. Of course there are men from time to time, who leave the Catholic Church for another religion, but I am speaking of cases, when a man keeps a fair outside to the world and is a hollow hypocrite in his heart.   5

I wonder that the self-devotion of our priests does not strike a Protestant in this point of view. What do they gain by professing a Creed, in which, if their enemies are to be credited, they really do not believe? What is their reward for committing themselves to a life of self-restraint and toil, and perhaps to a premature   10 and miserable death? The Irish fever cut off between Liverpool and Leeds thirty priests and more, young men in the flower of their days, old men who seemed entitled to some quiet time after their long toil. There was a bishop cut off in the North; but what had a man of his ecclesiastical rank to do with the drudgery and   15 danger of sick calls, except that Christian faith and charity constrained him? Priests volunteered for the dangerous service. It was the same with them on the first coming of the cholera, that mysterious awe-inspiring infliction. If they did not heartily believe in the Creed of the Church, then I will say that the re-   20 mark of the Apostle had its fullest illustration:—'If in this life only we have hope in Christ, we are of all men most miserable.' What could support a set of hypocrites in the presence of a deadly disorder, one of them following another in long order up the forlorn hope, and one after another perishing? And such, I   25 may say, in its substance, is every Mission-Priest's life. He is ever ready to sacrifice himself for his people. Night and day, sick or well himself, in all weathers, off he is, on the news of a sick call. The fact of a parishioner dying without the Sacraments through his fault is terrible to him; why terrible, if he has not a   30 deep absolute faith, which he acts upon with a free service? Protestants admire this, when they see it; but they do not seem to see as clearly, that it excludes the very notion of hypocrisy.

Sometimes, when they reflect upon it, it leads them to remark on the wonderful discipline of the Catholic priesthood; they say   35 that no Church has so well ordered a clergy, and that in that respect it surpasses their own; they wish they could have such

6–7 a Protestant] Protestants   8 their enemies are to be credited] my assailant is to be believed   10 perhaps] after all   18 same with them on] same on 19 they] priests exact discipline among themselves. But is it an excellence which can be purchased? is it a phenomenon which depends on nothing else than itself, or is it an effect which has a cause? You cannot buy devotion at a price. 'It hath never been heard of in the land 5 of Chanaan, neither hath it been seen in Theman. The children of Agar, the merchants of Meran, none of these have known its way.' What then is that wonderful charm, which makes a thousand men act all in one way, and infuses a prompt obedience to rule, as if they were under some stern military compulsion? 10 How difficult to find an answer, unless you will allow the obvious one, that they believe intensely what they profess!

I cannot think what it can be, in a day like this, which keeps up the prejudice of this Protestant country against us, unless it be the vague charges which are drawn from our books of Moral 15 Theology; and with a short notice of the work in particular which by our accusers is especially thrown into our teeth, I shall bring these observations to a close.

St. Alfonso Liguori, then, it cannot be denied, lays down that an equivocation, (that is, a play upon words, in which one sense 20 is taken by the speaker, and another sense intended by him for the hearer,) is allowable, if there is a just cause, that is, in an extraordinary case, and may even be confirmed by an oath. I shall give my opinion on this point as plainly as any Protestant can wish; and therefore I avow at once that in this department 25 of morality, much as I admire the high points of the Italian character, I like the English rule of conduct better; but, in saying so, I am not, as will shortly be seen, saying any thing disrespectful to St. Alfonso, who was a lover of truth, and whose intercession I trust I shall not lose, though, on the matter under 30 consideration, I follow other guidance in preference to his.

Now I make this remark first:—great English authors, Jeremy Taylor, Milton, Paley, Johnson, men of very different schools of thought, distinctly say, that under certain extraordinary circumstances it is allowable to tell a lie. Taylor says:

15 a short notice] a notice 16 by our accusers is especially thrown into] my accuser especially throws in 17 shall bring] shall in a very few words bring 18 Liguori, then, it] Liguori, it 19–21 (that is . . . hearer,)] *no parentheses in 64* 21–22 an extraordinary] a special *64*; an extreme *another copy of 64*   26 rule of conduct] character   27 will shortly be] will be   32 different] distinct 33–34 extraordinary] special *64*; extreme *another copy of 64*

'To tell a lie for charity, to save a man's life, the life of a friend, of a husband, of a prince, of a useful and a public person, hath not only been done at all times, but commended by great and wise and good men. Who would not save his father's life, at the charge of a harmless lie, from persecutors or tyrants?' Again, Milton says: 'What man in his senses would deny, that there are those whom we have the best grounds for considering that we ought to deceive,—as boys, madmen, the sick, the intoxicated, enemies, men in error, thieves? I would ask, by which of the commandments is a lie forbidden? You will say, by the ninth. If then my lie does not injure my neighbour, certainly it is not forbidden by this commandment.' Paley says: 'There are falsehoods, which are not lies, that is, which are not criminal.' Johnson: 'The general rule is, that truth should never be violated; there must, however, be some exceptions. If, for instance, a murderer should ask you which way a man is gone.'

Now, I am not using these instances as an *argumentum ad hominem*; but the purpose to which I put them is this:—

1. First, I have set down the distinct statements of Taylor, Milton, Paley, and Johnson:—now, would any one give ever so little weight to these statements, in forming a real estimate of the veracity of the writers, if they now were alive? Were a man, who is so fierce with St. Alfonso, to meet Paley or Johnson to-morrow in society, would he look upon him as a liar, a knave, as dishonest and untrustworthy? I am sure he would not. Why then does he not deal out the same measure to Catholic priests? If a copy of Scavini, which speaks of equivocation as being in a just cause allowable, be found in a student's room at Oscott, not Scavini himself, but even the unhappy student, who has what a Protestant calls a bad book in his possession, is judged to be for life unworthy of credit. Are all Protestant text-books, which are used at the University, immaculate? Is it necessary to take for gospel every word of Aristotle's Ethics, or every assertion of Hey or Burnett on the Articles? Are text-books the ultimate authority, or rather are they not manuals in the hands of a lecturer, and the groundwork of his remarks? But, again, let us suppose, not the case of a student, or of a professor, but of

18 the purpose to which I put them is this] this is the use to which I put them
20 Johnson:—now] Johnson; now   29 but even the] but the   30 judged to
be for] judged for   35 rather are they not manuals] are they manuals

Scavini himself, or of St. Alfonso; now here again I ask, since you would not scruple in holding Paley for an honest man, in spite of his defence of lying, why do you scruple at holding St. Alfonso honest? I am perfectly sure that you would not scruple at Paley personally; you might not agree with him, but you would not go further than to call him a bold thinker: then why should St. Alfonso's person be odious to you, as well as his doctrine?

Now I wish to tell you why you are not afraid of Paley; because, you would say, when he advocated lying, he was taking *extreme* or *special cases*. You would have no fear of a man who you knew had shot a burglar dead in his own house, because you know you are *not* a burglar: so you would not think that Paley had a habit of telling lies in society, because in the case of a cruel alternative he thought it the lesser evil to tell a lie. Then why do you show such suspicion of a Catholic theologian, who speaks of certain extraordinary cases in which an equivocation in a penitent cannot be visited by his confessor as if it were a sin? for this is the exact point of the question.

But again, why does Paley, why does Jeremy Taylor, when no practical matter is actually before him, lay down a maxim about the lawfulness of lying, which will startle most readers? The reason is plain. He is forming a theory of morals, and he must treat every question in turn as it comes. And this is just what St. Alfonso or Scavini is doing. You only try your hand yourself at a treatise on the rules of morality, and you will see how difficult the work is. What is the *definition* of a lie? Can you give a better than that it is a sin against justice, as Taylor and Paley consider it? but, if so, how can it be a sin at all, if your neighbour is not injured? If you do not like this definition, take another; and then, by means of that, perhaps you will be defending St. Alfonso's equivocation. However, this is what I insist upon; that St. Alfonso, as Paley, is considering the different portions of a large subject, and he must, on the subject of lying, give his judgment, though on that subject it is difficult to form any judgment which is satisfactory.

---

1 since] if   3–4 holding St. Alfonso honest ?] St. Alfonso ?   6 would not go further than to call] would call   11 *extreme* or *special cases*] *special cases 64; extreme cases   another copy of 64*   17 extraordinary] special 64; extreme *another copy of 64*   21 is actually before] is before

But further still: you must not suppose that a philosopher or moralist uses in his own case the licence which his theory itself would allow him. A man in his own person is guided by his own conscience; but in drawing out a system of rules he is obliged to go by logic, and follow the exact deduction of conclusion from conclusion, and must be sure that the whole system is coherent and one. You hear of even immoral or irreligious books being written by men of decent character; there is a late writer who says that David Hume's sceptical works are not at all the picture of the man. A priest might write a treatise which was really lax on the subject of lying, which might come under the condemnation of the Holy See, as some treatises on that score have already been condemned, and yet in his own person be a rigorist. And, in fact, it is notorious from St. Alfonso's Life, that he, who has the repute of being so lax a moralist, had one of the most scrupulous and anxious of consciences himself. Nay, further than this, he was originally in the Law, and on one occasion he was betrayed into the commission of what seemed like a deceit, though it was an accident; and that was the very occasion of his leaving the profession and embracing the religious life.

The account of this remarkable occurrence is told us in his Life:—

'Notwithstanding he had carefully examined over and over the details of the process, he was completely mistaken regarding the sense of one document, which constituted the right of the adverse party. The advocate of the Grand Duke perceived the mistake, but he allowed Alfonso to continue his eloquent address to the end without interruption; as soon, however, as he had finished, he rose, and said with cutting coolness, "Sir, the case is not exactly what you suppose it to be; if you will review the process, and examine this paper attentively, you will find there precisely the contrary of all you have advanced." "Willingly," replied Alfonso, without hesitating; "the decision depends on this question—whether the fief were granted under the law of Lombardy, or under the French Law." The paper being examined, it was found that the Grand Duke's advocate was in the right. "Yes," said Alfonso, holding the paper in his hand, "I am wrong, I have been mistaken." A discovery so unexpected,

and the fear of being accused of unfair dealing filled him with consternation, and covered him with confusion, so much so, that every one saw his emotion. It was in vain that the President Caravita, who loved him, and knew his integrity, tried to con-
5 sole him, by telling him that such mistakes were not uncommon, even among the first men at the bar. Alfonso would listen to nothing, but, overwhelmed with confusion, his head sunk on his breast, he said to himself, "World, I know you now; courts of law, never shall you see me again!" And turning his back on the
10 assembly, he withdrew to his own house, incessantly repeating to himself, "World, I know you now." What annoyed him most was, that having studied and re-studied the process during a whole month, without having discovered this important flaw, he could not understand how it had escaped his observation.'
15   And this is the man, so easily scared at the very shadow of trickery, who is so flippantly pronounced to be a patron of lying.
     But, in truth, a Catholic theologian has objects in view which men in general little compass; he is not thinking of himself, but of a multitude of souls, sick souls, sinful souls, carried away by
20 sin, full of evil, and he is trying with all his might to rescue them from their miserable state; and, in order to save them from more heinous sins, he tries, to the full extent that his conscience will allow him to go, to shut his eyes to such sins, as are, though sins, yet lighter in character or degree. He knows perfectly well that,
25 if he is as strict as he would wish to be, he shall be able to do nothing at all with the run of men; so he is as indulgent with them as ever he can be. Let it not be for an instant supposed, that I allow of the maxim of doing evil that good may come; but, keeping clear of this, there is a way of winning men from
30 greater sins by winking for the time at the less, or at mere improprieties or faults; and this is the key to the difficulty which Catholic books of moral theology so often cause to the Protestant. They are intended for the Confessor, and Protestants view them as intended for the Preacher.
35   2. And I observe upon Taylor, Milton, and Paley thus: What would a Protestant clergyman say to me, if I accused him of teaching that a lie was allowable; and if, when he asked for my proof, I said in reply that such was the doctrine of Taylor and

15–16 man . . . trickery, who] man who   38–p. 249, l. 1 such was the doctrine of Taylor and Milton?] Taylor and Milton so taught?

Milton? Why, he would sharply retort, '*I* am not bound by Taylor or Milton'; and if I went on urging that 'Taylor was one of his authorities', he would answer that Taylor was a great writer, but great writers were not therefore infallible. This is pretty much the answer which I make, when I am considered in this matter a disciple of St. Alfonso.

I plainly and positively state, and without any reserve, that I do not at all follow this holy and charitable man in this portion of his teaching. There are various schools of opinion allowed in the Church: and on this point I follow others. I follow Cardinal Gerdil, and Natalis Alexander, nay, St. Augustine. I will quote one passage from Natalis Alexander:—'They certainly lie, who utter the words of an oath, without the will to swear or bind themselves: or who make use of mental reservations and *equivocations* in swearing, since they signify by words what they have not in mind, contrary to the end for which language was instituted, viz. as signs of ideas. Or they mean something else than the words signify in themselves and the common custom of speech.' And, to take an instance: I do not believe any priest in England would dream of saying, 'My friend is not here'; meaning, 'He is not in my pocket or under my shoe.' Nor should any consideration make me say so myself. I do not think St. Alfonso would in his own case have said so; and he would have been as much shocked at Taylor and Paley, as Protestants are at him.[2]

And now, if Protestants wish to know what our real teaching is, as on other subjects, so on that of lying, let them look, not at our books of casuistry, but at our catechisms. Works on pathology do not give the best insight into the form and the harmony of the human frame; and, as it is with the body, so is it with the mind. The Catechism of the Council of Trent was drawn up for the express purpose of providing preachers with subjects for their Sermons; and, as my whole work has been a defence of myself, I may here say that I rarely preach a Sermon, but I go to this beautiful and complete Catechism to get both my

25 him.²] *no footnote in 64*   33 Sermons] sermons

---

[2] Vide Note G, *Lying and Equivocation.*

matter and my doctrine. There we find the following notices
about the duty of Veracity:—

'"Thou shalt not bear false witness", &c.: let attention be
drawn to two laws contained in this commandment:—the one,
5 forbidding false witness; the other bidding, that removing all
pretence and deceits, we should measure our words and deeds by
simple truth, as the Apostle admonished the Ephesians of that
duty in these words: "Doing truth in charity, let us grow in
Him through all things."

10 'To deceive by a lie in joke or for the sake of compliment,
though to no one there accrues loss or gain in consequence,
nevertheless is altogether unworthy: for thus the Apostle admonishes, "Putting aside lying, speak ye truth." For therein is
great danger of lapsing into frequent and more serious lying,
15 and from lies in joke men gain the habit of lying, whence they
gain the character of not being truthful. And thence again, in
order to gain credence to their words, they find it necessary to
make a practice of swearing.

'Nothing is more necessary [for us] than truth of testimony,
20 in those things, which we neither know ourselves, nor can
allowably be ignorant of, on which point there is extant that
maxim of St. Augustine's; Whoso conceals the truth, and whoso
puts forth a lie, each is guilty; the one because he is not willing
to do a service, the other because he has a wish to do a mischief.

25 'It is lawful at times to be silent about the truth, but out of a
court of law; for in court, when a witness is interrogated by the
judge according to law, the truth is wholly to be brought out.

'Witnesses, however, must beware, lest, from over-confidence
in their memory, they affirm for certain, what they have not
30 verified.

'In order that the faithful may with more good will avoid the
sin of lying, the Parish Priest shall set before them the extreme
misery and turpitude of this wickedness. For, in holy writ, the
devil is called the father of a lie; for, in that he did not remain in
35 Truth, he is a liar, and the father of a lie. He will add, with the
view of ridding men of so great a crime, the evils which follow
upon lying; and, whereas they are innumerable, he will point
out [at least] the sources and the general heads of these mischiefs

2 Veracity] veracity   17 credence] credit   19 necessary [for us] than]
necessary than

and calamities, viz. 1. How great is God's displeasure and how great His hatred of a man who is insincere and a liar. 2. What little security there is that a man who is specially hated by God may not be visited by the heaviest punishments. 3. What more unclean and foul, as St. James says, than . . . that a fountain by 5 the same jet should send out sweet water and bitter? 4. For that tongue, which just now praised God, next, as far as in it lies, dishonours Him by lying. 5. In consequence, liars are shut out from the possession of heavenly beatitude. 6. That too is the worst evil of lying, that that disease of the mind is generally 10 incurable.

'Moreover, there is this harm too, and one of vast extent, and touching men generally, that by insincerity and lying faith and truth are lost, which are the firmest bonds of human society, and, when they are lost, supreme confusion follows in life, so 15 that men seem in nothing to differ from devils.

'Lastly, the Parish Priest will set those right who excuse their insincerity and allege the example of wise men, who, they say, are used to lie for an occasion. He will tell them, what is most true, that the wisdom of the flesh is death. He will exhort his 20 hearers to trust in God, when they are in difficulties and straits, nor to have recourse to the expedient of a lie.

'They who throw the blame of their own lie on those who have already by a lie deceived them, are to be taught that men must not revenge themselves, nor make up for one evil by another. . . .' 25

There is much more in the Catechism to the same effect, and it is of universal obligation; whereas the decision of a particular author in morals need not be accepted by any one.

To one other authority I appeal on this subject, which commands from me attention of a special kind, for it is the teaching 30 of a Father. It will serve to bring my work to a conclusion.

'St. Philip', says the Roman Oratorian who wrote his Life, 'had a particular dislike of affectation both in himself and others, in speaking, in dressing, or in any thing else.

'He avoided all ceremony which savoured of worldly compli- 35 ment, and always showed himself a great stickler for Christian simplicity in every thing; so that, when he had to deal with men of worldly prudence, he did not very readily accommodate himself to them.

'And he avoided, as much as possible, having any thing to do with *two-faced persons*, who did not go simply and straight-
5 forwardly to work in their transactions.

'*As for liars, he could not endure them*, and he was *continually reminding* his spiritual children, *to avoid them as they would a pestilence.*'

These are the principles on which I have acted before I was a
10 Catholic; these are the principles which, I trust, will be my stay and guidance to the end.

I have closed this history of myself with St. Philip's name upon St. Philip's feast-day; and, having done so, to whom can I more suitably offer it, as a memorial of affection and gratitude,
15 than to St. Philip's sons, my dearest brothers of this House, the Priests of the Birmingham Oratory, AMBROSE ST. JOHN, HENRY AUSTIN MILLS, HENRY BITTLESTON, EDWARD CASWALL, WILLIAM PAINE NEVILLE, and HENRY IGNATIUS DUDLEY RYDER? who have been so faithful to me; who have been so
20 sensitive of my needs; who have been so indulgent to my fail-ings; who have carried me through so many trials; who have grudged no sacrifice, if I asked for it; who have been so cheerful under discouragements of my causing; who have done so many good works, and let me have the credit of them;—with whom I
25 have lived so long, with whom I hope to die.

And to you especially, dear AMBROSE ST. JOHN; whom God gave me, when He took every one else away; who are the link between my old life and my new; who have now for twenty-one years been so devoted to me, so patient, so zealous, so tender;
30 who have let me lean so hard upon you; who have watched me so narrowly; who have never thought of yourself, if I was in question.

And in you I gather up and bear in memory those familiar affectionate companions and counsellors, who in Oxford were
35 given to me, one after another, to be my daily solace and relief; and all those others, of great name and high example, who were my thorough friends, and showed me true attachment in times long past; and also those many younger men, whether I knew

38 younger] young *another copy of 64 (Ward)*

them or not, who have never been disloyal to me by word or deed; and of all these, thus various in their relations to me, those more especially who have since joined the Catholic Church.

And I earnestly pray for this whole company, with a hope against hope, that all of us, who once were so united, and so happy in our union, may even now be brought at length, by the Power of the Divine Will, into One Fold and under One Shepherd.

May 26, 1864.
In Festo Corp. Christ.

1–2 by word or deed] by word or by deed

NOTES

NOTE A. ON PAGE 26

LIBERALISM

I HAVE been asked to explain more fully what it is I mean by 'Liberalism', because merely to call it the Anti-dogmatic Principle is to tell very little about it. An explanation is the more necessary, because such good Catholics and distinguished writers as Count Montalembert and Father
5 Lacordaire use the word in a favorable sense, and claim to be Liberals themselves. 'The only singularity', says the former of the two in describing his friend, 'was his Liberalism. By a phenomenon, at that time unheard of, this convert, this seminarist, this confessor of nuns, was just as stubborn a liberal, as in the days when he was a student and a
10 barrister.'—Life (transl.), p. 19.

I do not believe that it is possible for me to differ in any important matter from two men whom I so highly admire. In their general line of thought and conduct I enthusiastically concur, and consider them to be before their age. And it would be strange indeed if I did not read
15 with a special interest, in M. de Montalembert's beautiful volume, of the unselfish aims, the thwarted projects, the unrequited toils, the grand and tender resignation of Lacordaire. If I hesitate to adopt their language about Liberalism, I impute the necessity of such hesitation to some differences between us in the use of words or in the circumstances
20 of country; and thus I reconcile myself to remaining faithful to my own conception of it, though I cannot have their voices to give force to mine. Speaking then in my own way, I proceed to explain what I meant as a Protestant by Liberalism, and to do so in connexion with the circumstances under which that system of opinion came before me at Oxford.
25 If I might presume to contrast Lacordaire and myself, I should say, that we had been both of us inconsistent;—he, a Catholic, in calling himself a Liberal; I, a Protestant, in being an Anti-liberal; and moreover, that the cause of this inconsistency had been in both cases one and the same. That is, we were both of us such good conservatives, as to
30 take up with what we happened to find established in our respective countries, at the time when we came into active life. Toryism was the creed of Oxford; he inherited, and made the best of, the French Revolution.

When, in the beginning of the present century, not very long before my own time, after many years of moral and intellectual declension, the University of Oxford woke up to a sense of its duties, and began to reform itself, the first instruments of this change, to whose zeal and courage we all owe so much, were naturally thrown together for mutual support, against the numerous obstacles which lay in their path, and 5 soon stood out in relief from the body of residents, who, though many of them men of talent themselves, cared little for the object which the others had at heart. These Reformers, as they may be called, were for some years members of scarcely more than three or four Colleges; and their own Colleges, as being under their direct influence, of course had 10 the benefit of those stricter views of discipline and teaching, which they themselves were urging on the University. They had, in no long time, enough of real progress in their several spheres of exertion, and enough of reputation out of doors, to warrant them in considering themselves the *élite* of the place; and it is not wonderful if they were in consequence 15 led to look down upon the majority of Colleges, which had not kept pace with the reform, or which had been hostile to it. And, when those rivalries of one man with another arose, whether personal or collegiate, which befall literary and scientific societies, such disturbances did but tend to raise in their eyes the value which they had already set upon 20 academical distinction, and increase their zeal in pursuing it. Thus was formed an intellectual circle or class in the University,—men, who felt they had a career before them, as soon as the pupils, whom they were forming, came into public life; men, whom non-residents, whether country parsons or preachers of the Low Church, on coming up from 25 time to time to the old place, would look at, partly with admiration, partly with suspicion, as being an honour indeed to Oxford, but withal exposed to the temptation of ambitious views, and to the spiritual evils signified in what is called the 'pride of reason'.

Nor was this imputation altogether unjust; for, as they were following 30 out the proper idea of a University, of course they suffered more or less from the moral malady incident to such a pursuit. The very object of such great institutions lies in the cultivation of the mind and the spread of knowledge: if this object, as all human objects, has its dangers at all times, much more would these exist in the case of men, who were en- 35 gaged in a work of reformation, and had the opportunity of measuring themselves, not only with those who were their equals in intellect, but with the many, who were below them. In this select circle or class of men, in various Colleges, the direct instruments and the choice fruit of real University Reform, we see the rudiments of the Liberal party. 40

Whenever men are able to act at all, there is the chance of extreme and intemperate action; and therefore, when there is exercise of mind, there is the chance of wayward or mistaken exercise. Liberty of thought is in itself a good; but it gives an opening to false liberty. Now by

Liberalism I mean false liberty of thought, or the exercise of thought upon matters, in which, from the constitution of the human mind, thought cannot be brought to any successful issue, and therefore is out of place. Among such matters are first principles of whatever kind; and
5 of these the most sacred and momentous are especially to be reckoned the truths of Revelation. Liberalism then is the mistake of subjecting to human judgment those revealed doctrines which are in their nature beyond and independent of it, and of claiming to determine on intrinsic grounds the truth and value of propositions which rest for their recep-
10 tion simply on the external authority of the Divine Word.

Now certainly the party of whom I have been speaking, taken as a whole, were of a character of mind out of which Liberalism might easily grow up, as in fact it did; certainly they breathed around an influence which made men of religious seriousness shrink into themselves. But,
15 while I say as much as this, I have no intention whatever of implying that the talent of the University, in the years before and after 1820, was liberal in its theology, in the sense in which the bulk of the educated classes through the country are liberal now. I would not for the world be supposed to detract from the Christian earnestness, and the activity
20 in religious works, above the average of men, of many of the persons in question. They would have protested against their being supposed to place reason before faith, or knowledge before devotion; yet I do consider that they unconsciously encouraged and successfully intro-duced into Oxford a licence of opinion which went far beyond them.
25 In their day they did little more than take credit to themselves for enlightened views, largeness of mind, liberality of sentiment, without drawing the line between what was just and what was inadmissible in speculation, and without seeing the tendency of their own principles; and engrossing, as they did, the mental energy of the University, they
30 met for a time with no effectual hindrance to the spread of their in-fluence, except (what indeed at the moment was most effectual, but not of an intellectual character) the thorough-going Toryism and tradi-tionary Church-of-England-ism of the great body of the Colleges and Convocation.

35 Now and then a man of note appeared in the Pulpit or Lecture Rooms of the University, who was a worthy representative of the more religious and devout Anglicans. These belonged chiefly to the High-Church party; for the party called Evangelical never has been able to breathe freely in the atmosphere of Oxford, and at no time has been
40 conspicuous, as a party, for talent or learning. But of the old High Churchmen several exerted some sort of Anti-liberal influence in the place, at least from time to time, and that influence of an intellectual nature. Among these especially may be mentioned Mr. John Miller, of Worcester College, who preached the Bampton Lecture in the year

1817. But, as far as I know, he who turned the tide, and brought the talent of the University round to the side of the old theology, and against what was familiarly called 'march-of-mind', was Mr. Keble. In and from Keble the mental activity of Oxford took that contrary direction which issued in what was called Tractarianism. 5

Keble was young in years, when he became a University celebrity, and younger in mind. He had the purity and simplicity of a child. He had few sympathies with the intellectual party, who sincerely welcomed him as a brilliant specimen of young Oxford. He instinctively shut up before literary display, and pomp and donnishness of manner, faults 10 which always will beset academical notabilities. He did not respond to their advances. His collision with them (if it may be so called) was thus described by Hurrell Froude in his own way. 'Poor Keble!' he used gravely to say, 'he was asked to join the aristocracy of talent, but he soon found his level.' He went into the country, but his instance serves 15 to prove that men need not, in the event, lose that influence which is rightly theirs, because they happen to be thwarted in the use of the channels natural and proper to its exercise. He did not lose his place in the minds of men because he was out of their sight.

Keble was a man who guided himself and formed his judgments, not 20 by processes of reason, by inquiry or by argument, but, to use the word in a broad sense, by authority. Conscience is an authority; the Bible is an authority; such is the Church; such is Antiquity; such are the words of the wise; such are hereditary lessons; such are ethical truths; such are historical memories, such are legal saws and state maxims; such are 25 proverbs; such are sentiments, presages, and prepossessions. It seemed to me as if he ever felt happier, when he could speak or act under some such primary or external sanction; and could use argument mainly as a means of recommending or explaining what had claims on his reception prior to proof. He even felt a tenderness, I think, in spite of Bacon, 30 for the Idols of the Tribe and the Den, of the Market and the Theatre. What he hated instinctively was heresy, insubordination, resistance to things established, claims of independence, disloyalty, innovation, a critical, censorious spirit. And such was the main principle of the school which in the course of years was formed around him; nor is it easy to 35 set limits to its influence in its day; for multitudes of men, who did not profess its teaching, or accept its peculiar doctrines, were willing nevertheless, or found it to their purpose, to act in company with it.

Indeed for a time it was practically the champion and advocate of the political doctrines of the great clerical interest through the country, who 40 found in Mr. Keble and his friends an intellectual, as well as moral support to their cause, which they looked for in vain elsewhere. His weak point, in their eyes, was his consistency; for he carried his love of authority and old times so far, as to be more than gentle towards the

Catholic Religion, with which the Toryism of Oxford and of the Church of England had no sympathy. Accordingly, if my memory be correct, he never could get himself to throw his heart into the opposition made to Catholic Emancipation, strongly as he revolted from the politics and
5 the instruments by means of which that Emancipation was won. I fancy he would have had no difficulty in accepting Dr. Johnson's saying about 'the first Whig'; and it grieved and offended him that the 'Via prima salutis' should be opened to the Catholic body from the Whig quarter. In spite of his reverence for the Old Religion, I conceive that on the whole
10 he would rather have kept its professors beyond the pale of the Constitution with the Tories, than admit them on the principles of the Whigs. Moreover, if the Revolution of 1688 was too lax in principle for him and his friends, much less, as is very plain, could they endure to subscribe to the revolutionary doctrines of 1776 and 1789, which they
15 felt to be absolutely and entirely out of keeping with theological truth.

The Old Tory or Conservative party in Oxford had in it no principle or power of development, and that from its very nature and constitution: it was otherwise with the Liberals. They represented a new idea, which was but gradually learning to recognize itself, to ascertain its
20 characteristics and external relations, and to exert an influence upon the University. The party grew, all the time that I was in Oxford, even in numbers, certainly in breadth and definiteness of doctrine, and in power. And, what was a far higher consideration, by the accession of Dr. Arnold's pupils, it was invested with an elevation of character
25 which claimed the respect even of its opponents. On the other hand, in proportion as it became more earnest and less self-applauding, it became more free-spoken; and members of it might be found who, from the mere circumstance of remaining firm to their original professions, would in the judgment of the world, as to their public acts,
30 seem to have left it for the Conservative camp. Thus, neither in its component parts nor in its policy, was it the same in 1832, 1836, and 1841, as it was in 1845.

These last remarks will serve to throw light upon a matter personal to myself, which I have introduced into my Narrative, and to which my
35 attention has been pointedly called, now that my Volume is coming to a second edition.

It has been strongly urged upon me to re-consider the following passages which occur in it: 'The men who had driven me from Oxford were distinctly the Liberals; it was they who had opened the attack
40 upon Tract 90', p. 184, and 'I found no fault with the Liberals; they had beaten me in a fair field', p. 193.

I am very unwilling to seem ungracious, or to cause pain in any quarter; still I am sorry to say I cannot modify these statements. It is surely a matter of historical fact that I left Oxford upon the University proceedings of 1841; and in those proceedings, whether we look to the Heads of Houses or the resident Masters, the leaders, if intellect and influence make men such, were members of the Liberal party. Those who did not lead, concurred or acquiesced in them,—I may say, felt a satisfaction. I do not recollect any Liberal who was on my side on 5 that occasion. Excepting the Liberal, no other party, as a party, acted against me. I am not complaining of them; I deserved nothing else at their hands. They could not undo in 1845, even had they wished it, (and there is no proof they did,) what they had done in 1841. In 1845, when I had already given up the contest for four years, and my part in it had 10 passed into the hands of others, then some of those who were prominent against me in 1841, feeling (what they had not felt in 1841) the danger of driving a number of my followers to Rome, and joined by younger friends who had come into University importance since 1841 and felt kindly towards me, adopted a course more consistent with their prin- 15 ciples, and proceeded to shield from the zeal of the Hebdomadal Board, not me, but, professedly, all parties through the country,—Tractarians, Evangelicals, Liberals in general,—who had to subscribe to the Angli- can formularies, on the ground that those formularies, rigidly taken, were, on some point or other, a difficulty to all parties alike. 20

However, besides the historical fact, I can bear witness to my own feeling at the time, and my feeling was this:—that those who in 1841 had considered it to be a duty to act against me, had then done their worst. What was it to me what they were now doing in opposition to the New Test proposed by the Hebdomadal Board? I owed them no thanks 25 for their trouble. I took no interest at all, in February, 1845, in the proceedings of the Heads of Houses and of the Convocation. I felt myself *dead* as regarded my relations to the Anglican Church. My leaving it was all but a matter of time. I believe I did not even thank my real friends, the two Proctors, who in Convocation stopped by their 30 Veto the condemnation of Tract 90; nor did I make any acknowledg- ment to Mr. Rogers, nor to Mr. James Mozley, nor, as I think, to Mr. Hussey, for their pamphlets in my behalf. My frame of mind is best described by the sentiment of the passage in Horace, which at the time I was fond of quoting, as expressing my view of the relation that 35 existed between the Vice-Chancellor and myself.

'Pentheu,
Rector Thebarum, quid me perferre patique
Indignum cogas?' 'Adimam bona.' 'Nempe pecus, rem,
Lectos, argentum; tollas licet.' 'In manicis et 40
Compedibus, sævo te sub custode tenebo.' (*viz. the* 39 *Articles.*)
'*Ipse Deus, simul atque volam, me solvet.*' Opinor,
Hoc sentit: *Moriar. Mors ultima linea rerum est.*

24 now doing in opposition to] doing in the matter of *65–68*

I conclude this notice of Liberalism in Oxford, and the party which was antagonistic to it, with some propositions in detail, which, as a member of the latter, and together with the High Church, I earnestly denounced and abjured.

5   1. No religious tenet is important, unless reason shows it to be so.

> Therefore, e.g. the doctrine of the Athanasian Creed is not to be insisted on, unless it tends to convert the soul; and the doctrine of the Atonement is to be insisted on, if it does convert the soul.

2. No one can believe what he does not understand.

10   > Therefore, e.g. there are no mysteries in true religion.

3. No theological doctrine is any thing more than an opinion which happens to be held by bodies of men.

> Therefore, e.g. no creed, as such, is necessary for salvation.

4. It is dishonest in a man to make an act of faith in what he has
15 not had brought home to him by actual proof.

> Therefore, e.g. the mass of men ought not absolutely to believe in the divine authority of the Bible.

5. It is immoral in a man to believe more than he can spontaneously receive as being congenial to his moral and mental nature.

20   > Therefore, e.g. a given individual is not bound to believe in eternal punishment.

6. No revealed doctrines or precepts may reasonably stand in the way of scientific conclusions.

> Therefore, e.g. Political Economy may reverse our Lord's declarations
25 about poverty and riches, or a system of Ethics may teach that the highest condition of body is ordinarily essential to the highest state of mind.

7. Christianity is necessarily modified by the growth of civilization, and the exigencies of times.

30   > Therefore, e.g. the Catholic priesthood, though necessary in the Middle Ages, may be superseded now.

8. There is a system of religion more simply true than Christianity as it has ever been received.

> Therefore, e.g. we may advance that Christianity is the 'corn of
35 wheat' which has been dead for 1800 years, but at length will bear fruit; and that Mahometanism is the manly religion, and existing Christianity the womanish.

9. There is a right of Private Judgment: that is, there is no existing authority on earth competent to interfere with the liberty of individuals in reasoning and judging for themselves about the Bible and its contents, as they severally please.

> Therefore, e.g. religious establishments requiring subscription are 5 Anti-christian.

10. There are rights of conscience such, that every one may lawfully advance a claim to profess and teach what is false and wrong in matters, religious, social and moral, provided that to his private conscience it seems absolutely true and right.   10

> Therefore, e.g. individuals have a right to preach and practise fornication and polygamy.

11. There is no such thing as a national or state conscience.

> Therefore, e.g. no judgments can fall upon a sinful or infidel nation.

12. The civil power has no positive duty, in a normal state of things, 15 to maintain religious truth.

> Therefore, e.g. blasphemy and sabbath-breaking are not rightly punishable by law.

13. Utility and expedience are the measure of political duty.

> Therefore, e.g. no punishment may be enacted, on the ground that 20 God commands it: e.g. on the text, 'Whoso sheddeth man's blood, by man shall his blood be shed.'

14. The Civil Power may dispose of Church property without sacrilege.

> Therefore, e.g. Henry VIII, committed no sin in his spoliations.   25

15. The Civil Power has the right of ecclesiastical jurisdiction and administration.

> Therefore, e.g. Parliament may impose articles of faith on the Church or suppress Dioceses.

16. It is lawful to rise in arms against legitimate princes.   30

> Therefore, e.g. the Puritans in the 17th century, and the French in the 18th, were justifiable in their Rebellion and Revolution respectively.

17. The people are the legitimate source of power.

> Therefore, e.g. Universal Suffrage is among the natural rights of man.   35

18. Virtue is the child of knowledge, and vice of ignorance.

> Therefore, e.g. education, periodical literature, railroad travelling, ventilation, drainage, and the arts of life, when fully carried out, serve to make a population moral and happy.

5   All of these propositions, and many others too, were familiar to me thirty years ago, as in the number of the tenets of Liberalism, and, while I gave into none of them except No. 12, and perhaps No. 11, and partly No. 1, before I began to publish, so afterwards I wrote against most of them in some part or other of my Anglican works.

10   If it is necessary to refer to a work, not simply my own, but of the Tractarian school, which contains a similar protest, I should name the *Lyra Apostolica*. This volume, which by accident has been left unnoticed, except incidentally, in my Narrative, was collected together from the pages of the 'British Magazine', in which its contents originally 15 appeared, and published in a separate form, immediately after Hurrell Froude's death in 1836. Its signatures, $\alpha, \beta, \gamma, \delta, \epsilon, \zeta$, denote respectively as authors, Mr. Bowden, Mr. Hurrell Froude, Mr. Keble, Mr. Newman, Mr. Robert Wilberforce, and Mr. Isaac Williams.

    There is one poem on 'Liberalism', beginning 'Ye cannot halve the 20 Gospel of God's grace'; which bears out the account of Liberalism as above given; and another upon 'the Age to come', defining from its own point of view the position and prospects of Liberalism.

    I need hardly say that the above Note is mainly historical. How far the Liberal party of 1830–40 really held the above eighteen Theses, 25 which I attributed to them, and how far and in what sense I should oppose those Theses now, could scarcely be explained without a separate Dissertation.

17 as authors,] the authorship of *65–78*   17–18 Mr. Newman] myself *65–78*
21 given; and another] given. Another *65–68*   22 Liberalism.] Liberalism, shall be quoted *in extenso*.

> When I would search the truths that in me burn,
>   And mould them into rule and argument,
> A hundred reasons cried,—'Hast thou to learn
>   Those dreams are scattered now, those fires are spent?'
> And, did I mount to simpler thoughts, and try
>   Some theme of peace, 'twas still the same reply.
>
> Perplexed, I hoped my heart was pure of guile,
>   But judged me weak in wit, to disagree;
> But now I see, that men are mad awhile,
>   And joy the Age to come will think of me;
> 'Tis the old history:—Truth without a home,
>   Despised and slain; then, rising from the tomb.

23–27 I need . . . Dissertation.] *This paragraph appeared first in 1869.*

NOTE B. ON PAGE 33

ECCLESIASTICAL MIRACLES

T H E writer, who gave occasion for the foregoing Narrative, was very severe with me for what I had said about Miracles in the Preface to the Life of St. Walburga. I observe therefore as follows:—

Catholics believe that miracles happen in any age of the Church, though not for the same purposes, in the same number, or with the same 5 evidence, as in Apostolic times. The Apostles wrought them in evidence of their divine mission; and with this object they have been sometimes wrought by Evangelists of countries since, as even Protestants allow. Hence we hear of them in the history of St. Gregory in Pontus, and St. Martin in Gaul; and in their case, as in that of the Apostles, they 10 were both numerous and clear. As they are granted to Evangelists, so are they granted, though in less measure and evidence, to other holy men; and as holy men are not found equally at all times and in all places, therefore miracles are in some places and times more than in others. And since, generally, they are granted to faith and prayer, 15 therefore in a country in which faith and prayer abound, they will be more likely to occur, than where and when faith and prayer are not; so that their occurrence is irregular. And further, as faith and prayer obtain miracles, so still more commonly do they gain from above the ordinary interventions of Providence; and, as it is often very difficult to 20 distinguish between a providence and a miracle, and there will be more providences than miracles, hence it will happen that many occurrences will be called miraculous, which, strictly speaking, are not such, that is, not more than providential mercies, or what are sometimes called '*grazie*' or 'favours'. 25

Persons, who believe all this, in accordance with Catholic teaching, as I did and do, they, on the report of a miracle, will of necessity, the necessity of good logic, be led to say, first, 'It *may* be', and secondly, 'But I must have *good evidence* in order to believe it.'

1. It *may* be, because miracles take place in all ages; it must be 30 clearly *proved*, because perhaps after all it may be only a providential mercy, or an exaggeration, or a mistake, or an imposture. Well, this is precisely what I had said, which the writer, who has given occasion to this Volume, considered so irrational. I had said, as he quotes me, 'In this day, and under our present circumstances, we can only reply, that 35 there is no reason why they should not be.' Surely this is good logic, *provided* that miracles *do* occur in all ages; and so again I am logical

in saying, 'There is nothing, *primâ facie*, in the miraculous accounts in question, to repel a *properly taught* or religiously disposed mind.' What is the matter with this statement? My assailant does not pretend to say *what* the matter is, and he cannot; but he expresses a rude, unmeaning

5 astonishment. Accordingly, in the passage which he quotes, I observe, 'Miracles are the kind of facts proper to ecclesiastical history, just as instances of sagacity or daring, personal prowess, or crime, are the facts proper to secular history.' What is the harm of this?

2. But, though a miracle be conceivable, it has to be *proved*. *What*

10 has to be proved? (1.) That the event occurred as stated, and is not a false report or an exaggeration. (2.) That it is clearly miraculous, and not a mere providence or answer to prayer within the order of nature. What is the fault of saying this? The inquiry is parallel to that which is made about some extraordinary fact in secular history. Supposing I

15 hear that King Charles II died a Catholic, I am led to say: It *may* be, but what is your *proof*?

In my Essay on Miracles of the year 1826, I proposed three questions about a professed miraculous occurrence: 1. is it antecedently *probable*? 2. is it in its *nature* certainly miraculous? 3. has it sufficient *evidence*?

20 To these three heads I had regard in my Essay of 1842; and under them I still wish to conduct the inquiry into the miracles of Ecclesiastical History.

So much for general principles; as to St. Walburga, though I have no intention at all of denying that numerous miracles have been wrought

25 by her intercession, still, neither the Author of her Life, nor I, the Editor, felt that we had grounds for binding ourselves to the belief of certain alleged miracles in particular. I made, however, one exception; it was the medicinal oil which flows from her relics. Now as to the *verisimilitude*, the *miraculousness*, and the *fact*, of this medicinal oil.

30 1. The *verisimilitude*. It is plain there is nothing extravagant in this report of her relics having a supernatural virtue; and for this reason, because there are such instances in Scripture, and Scripture cannot be extravagant. For instance, a man was restored to life by touching the relics of the Prophet Eliseus. The sacred text runs thus: —'And Elisha

35 died, and they buried him. And the bands of the Moabites invaded the land at the coming in of the year. And it came to pass, as they were burying a man, that, behold, they spied a band of men; and they cast the man into the sepulchre of Elisha. And, when the man was let down, *and touched the bones of Elisha, he revived*, and stood upon his

40 feet.' Again, in the case of an inanimate substance, which had touched a living Saint: 'And God wrought *special miracles* by the hands of Paul; so that *from his body* were brought unto the sick *handkerchiefs or aprons*, and *the diseases departed from them*.' And again in the case of

a pool: 'An *Angel went down* at a certain season into the pool, and troubled the water; whosoever then first, after the troubling of the water, stepped in, *was made whole of whatsoever disease* he had.' 2 Kings [4 Kings] xiii. 20, 21. Acts xix. 11, 12. John v. 4. Therefore there is nothing *extravagant* in the *character* of the miracle. 5

2. Next, the *matter of fact*:—*is* there an oil flowing from St. Walburga's tomb, which is medicinal? To this question I confined myself in my Preface. Of the accounts of medieval miracles, I said that there was no *extravagance* in their *general character*, but I could not affirm that there was always *evidence* for them. I could not simply accept them 10 as *facts*, but I could not reject them in their *nature*;—they *might* be true, for they were not impossible; but they were *not proved* to be true, because there was not trustworthy testimony. However, as to St. Walburga, I repeat, I made *one* exception, the fact of the medicinal oil, since for that miracle there was distinct and successive testimony. And 15 then I went on to give a chain of witnesses. It was my duty to state what those witnesses said in their very words; so I gave the testimonies in full, tracing them from the Saint's death. I said, 'She is one of the principal Saints of her age and country.' Then I quoted Basnage, a Protestant, who says, 'Six writers are extant, who have employed themselves in 20 relating the deeds or miracles of Walburga.' Then I said that her 'renown was not the mere natural *growth* of ages, but begins with the very century of the Saint's death'. Then I observed that only two miracles seem to have been 'distinctly reported of her as occurring in her lifetime; and they were handed down apparently by tradition'. 25 Also, that such miracles are said to have commenced about A.D. 777. Then I spoke of the medicinal oil as having testimony to it in 893, in 1306, after 1450, in 1615, and in 1620. Also, I said that Mabillon seems not to have believed some of her miracles; and that the earliest witness had got into trouble with his Bishop. And so I left the matter, as a 30 question to be decided by evidence, not deciding any thing myself.

What was the harm of all this? but my Critic muddled it together in a most extraordinary manner, and I am far from sure that he knew himself the definite categorical charge which he intended it to convey against me. One of his remarks is, 'What has become of the holy oil for 35 the last 240 years, Dr. Newman does not say', p. 25. Of course I did not, because I did not know; I gave the evidence as I found it; he assumes that I had a point to prove, and then asks why I did not make the evidence larger than it was.

I can tell him more about it now: the oil still flows; I have had some 40 of it in my possession; it is medicinal still. This leads to the third head.

3. Its *miraculousness*. On this point, since I have been in the Catholic Church, I have found there is a difference of opinion. Some persons consider that the oil is the natural produce of the rock, and has ever

flowed from it; others, that by a divine gift it flows from the relics; and others, allowing that it now comes naturally from the rock, are disposed to hold that it was in its origin miraculous, as was the virtue of the pool of Bethsaida.

5 This point must be settled of course before the virtue of the oil can be ascribed to the sanctity of St. Walburga; for myself, I neither have, nor ever have had, the means of going into the question; but I will take the opportunity of its having come before me, to make one or two remarks, supplemental of what I have said on other occasions.

10 1. I frankly confess that the present advance of science tends to make it probable that various facts take place, and have taken place, in the order of nature, which hitherto have been considered by Catholics as simply supernatural.

2. Though I readily make this admission, it must not be supposed 15 in consequence that I am disposed to grant at once, that every event was natural in point of fact, which *might* have taken place by the laws of nature; for it is obvious, no Catholic can bind the Almighty to act only in one and the same way, or to the observance always of His own laws. An event which is possible in the way of nature, is certainly 20 possible too to Divine Power without the sequence of natural cause and effect at all. A conflagration, to take a parallel, may be the work of an incendiary, or the result of a flash of lightning; nor would a jury think it safe to find a man guilty of arson, if a dangerous thunderstorm was raging at the very time when the fire broke out. In like manner, upon 25 the hypothesis that a miraculous dispensation is in operation, a recovery from diseases to which medical science is equal, may nevertheless in matter of fact have taken place, not by natural means, but by a supernatural interposition. That the Lawgiver always acts through His own laws, is an assumption, of which I never saw proof. In a given case, 30 then, the possibility of assigning a human cause for an event does not *ipso facto* prove that it is not miraculous.

3. So far, however, is plain, that, till some *experimentum crucis* can be found, such as to be decisive against the natural cause or the supernatural, an occurrence of this kind will as little convince an unbeliever 35 that there has been a divine interference in the case, as it will drive the Catholic to admit that there has been no interference at all.

4. Still there is this gain accruing to the Catholic cause from the larger views we now possess of the operation of natural causes, viz. that our opponents will not in future be so ready as hitherto, to impute fraud 40 and falsehood to our priests and their witnesses, on the ground of their pretending or reporting things that are incredible. Our opponents have again and again accused us of false witness, on account of statements which they now allow are either true, or may have been true. They account indeed for the strange facts very differently from us; but still

they allow that facts they were. It is a great thing to have our characters cleared: and we may reasonably hope that, the next time our word is vouched for occurrences which appear to be miraculous, our facts will be investigated, not our testimony impugned.

5. Even granting that certain occurrences, which we have hitherto accounted miraculous, have not absolutely a claim to be so considered, nevertheless they constitute an argument still in behalf of Revelation and the Church. Providences, or what are called *grazie*, though they do not rise to the order of miracles, yet, if they occur again and again in connexion with the same persons, institutions, or doctrines, may supply a cumulative evidence of the fact of a supernatural presence in the quarter in which they are found. I have already alluded to this point in my Essay on Ecclesiastical Miracles, and I have a particular reason, as will presently be seen, for referring here to what I said in the course of it.

In that Essay, after bringing its main argument to an end, I append to it a review of 'the evidence for particular alleged miracles'. 'It does not strictly fall within the scope of the Essay,' I observe, 'to pronounce upon the truth or falsehood of this or that miraculous narrative, as it occurs in ecclesiastical history; but only to furnish such general considerations, as may be useful in forming a decision in particular cases', p. cv. However, I thought it right to go farther and 'to set down the evidence for and against certain miracles as we meet with them', ibid. In discussing these miracles separately, I make the following remarks, to which I have just been referring.

After discussing the alleged miracle of the Thundering Legion, I observe:—'Nor does it concern us much to answer the objection, that there is nothing strictly miraculous in such an occurrence, because sudden thunderclouds after drought are not unfrequent; for, I would answer, Grant me such miracles ordinarily in the early Church, and I will ask no other; grant that, upon prayer, benefits are vouchsafed, deliverances are effected, unhoped-for results obtained, sicknesses cured, tempests laid, pestilences put to flight, famines remedied, judgments inflicted, and there will be no need of analyzing the causes, whether supernatural or natural, to which they are to be referred. They may, or they may not, in this or that case, follow or surpass the laws of nature, and they may do so plainly or doubtfully, but the common sense of mankind will call them miraculous; for by a miracle is popularly meant, whatever be its formal definition, an event which impresses upon the mind the immediate presence of the Moral Governor of the world. He may sometimes act through nature, sometimes beyond or against it; but those who admit the fact of such interferences, will have little difficulty in admitting also their strictly miraculous character, if the circumstances of the case require it, and those who deny miracles to the early

Church will be equally strenuous against allowing her the grace of such intimate influence (if we may so speak) upon the course of divine Providence, as is here in question, even though it be not miraculous.'—p. cxxi.

5 And again, speaking of the death of Arius: 'But after all, was it a miracle? for, if not, we are labouring at a proof of which nothing comes. The more immediate answer to this question has already been suggested several times. When a Bishop with his flock prays night and day against a heretic, and at length begs of God to take him away, and when he *is* 10 suddenly taken away, almost at the moment of his triumph, and that by a death awfully significant, from its likeness to one recorded in Scripture, is it not trifling to ask whether such an occurrence comes up to the definition of a miracle? The question is not whether it is formally a miracle, but whether it is an event, the like of which persons, who 15 deny that miracles continue, will consent that the Church should be considered still able to perform. If they are willing to allow to the Church such extraordinary protection, it is for them to draw the line to the satisfaction of people in general, between these and strictly miraculous events; if, on the other hand, they deny their occurrence in the 20 times of the Church, then there is sufficient reason for our appealing here to the history of Arius in proof of the affirmative.'—p. clxxii.

These remarks, thus made upon the Thundering Legion and the death of Arius, must be applied, in consequence of investigations made since the date of my Essay, to the apparent miracle wrought in favour 25 of the African confessors in the Vandal persecution. Their tongues were cut out by the Arian tyrant, and yet they spoke as before. In my Essay I insisted on this fact as being strictly miraculous. Among other remarks (referring to the instances adduced by Middleton and others in disparagement of the miracle, viz. of 'a girl born without a tongue, who 30 yet talked as distinctly and easily, as if she had enjoyed the full benefit of that organ', and of a boy who lost his tongue at the age of eight or nine, yet retained his speech, whether perfectly or not,) I said, 'Does Middleton mean to say, that, if certain of men lost their tongues *at the command of a tyrant* for the *sake of their religion*, and then spoke *as* 35 *plainly* as before, nay *if only one person was so mutilated* and so gifted, it would not be a miracle?'—p. ccx. And I enlarged upon the minute details of the fact as reported to us by eye-witnesses and contemporaries. 'Out of the seven writers adduced, six are contemporaries; three, if not four, are eye-witnesses of the miracle. One reports from an eye-witness, 40 and one testifies to a fervent record at the burial-place of the subjects of it. All seven were living, or had been staying, at one or other of the two places which are mentioned as their abode. One is a Pope, a second a Catholic Bishop, a third a Bishop of a schismatical party, a fourth an emperor, a fifth a soldier, a politician, and a suspected infidel, a sixth a statesman and courtier, a seventh a rhetorician and philosopher. "He cut out the tongues by the roots", says Victor, Bishop of Vito; "I perceived the tongues entirely gone by the roots", says Æneas; "as low down as the throat", says Procopius; "at the roots", say Justinian and St. Gregory; "he spoke like an educated man, without impediment", says Victor of Vito; "with articulateness", says Æneas; "better than before"; "they talked without any impediment", says Procopius; "speaking with perfect voice", says Marcellinus; "they spoke perfectly, even to the end", says the second Victor; "the words were formed, full, and perfect", says St. Gregory'.—p. ccviii.

However, a few years ago an Article appeared in 'Notes and Queries' (No. for May 22, 1858), in which various evidence was adduced to show that the tongue is not necessary for articulate speech.

1. Col. Churchill, in his 'Lebanon', speaking of the cruelties of Djezzar Pacha, in extracting to the root the tongues of some Emirs, adds, 'It is a curious fact, however, that the tongues grow again sufficiently for the purposes of speech.'

2. Sir John Malcolm, in his 'Sketches of Persia', speaks of Zâb, Khan of Khisht, who was condemned to lose his tongue. 'This mandate,' he says, 'was imperfectly executed, and the loss of half this member deprived him of speech. Being afterwards persuaded that its being cut close to the root would enable him to speak so as to be understood, he submitted to the operation; and the effect has been, that his voice, though indistinct and thick, is yet intelligible to persons accustomed to converse with him. . . . I am not an anatomist, and I cannot therefore give a reason, why a man, who could not articulate with half a tongue, should speak when he had none at all; but the facts are as stated.'

3. And Sir John McNeill says, 'In answer to your inquiries about the powers of speech retained by persons who have had their tongues cut out, I can state from personal observation, that several persons whom I knew in Persia, who had been subjected to that punishment, spoke so intelligibly as to be able to transact important business. . . . The conviction in Persia is universal, that the power of speech is destroyed by merely cutting off the tip of the tongue; and is to a useful extent restored by cutting off another portion as far back as a perpendicular section can be made of the portion that is free from attachment at the lower surface. . . . I never had to meet with a person who had suffered this punishment, who could not speak so as to be quite intelligible to his familiar associates.'

I should not be honest, if I professed to be simply converted, by these testimonies, to the belief that there was nothing miraculous in the case of the African confessors. It is quite as fair to be sceptical on one side of the question as on the other; and if Gibbon is considered worthy of

praise for his stubborn incredulity in receiving the evidence for this miracle, I do not see why I am to be blamed, if I wish to be quite sure of the full appositeness of the recent evidence which is brought to its disadvantage. Questions of fact cannot be disproved by analogies or
5 presumptions; the inquiry must be made into the particular case in all its parts, as it comes before us. Meanwhile, I fully allow that the points of evidence brought in disparagement of the miracle are *primâ facie* of such cogency, that, till they are proved to be irrelevant, Catholics are prevented from appealing to it for controversial purposes.

NOTE C. ON PAGE 142

SERMON ON WISDOM AND INNOCENCE

THE professed basis of the charge of lying and equivocation made against me, and, in my person, against the Catholic clergy, was, as I have already noticed in the Preface, a certain Sermon of mine on 'Wisdom and Innocence', being the 20th in a series of 'Sermons on Subjects of the Day', written, preached, and published while I was an Anglican. Of this Sermon my accuser spoke thus in his Pamphlet:— 5

'It is occupied entirely with the attitude of "the world" to "Christians" and "the Church". By the world appears to be signified, especially, the Protestant public of these realms; what Dr. Newman means by Christians, and the Church, he has not left in doubt; for in the preceding Sermon he says: "But if the truth must be spoken, what are the humble monk and the holy nun, and other regulars, as they are called, but Christians after the very pattern given us in Scripture, &c." . . . This is his definition of Christians. And in the Sermon itself, he sufficiently defines what he means by "the Church", in two notes of her character, which he shall give in his own words: "What, for instance, though we grant that sacramental confession and the celibacy of the clergy do tend to consolidate the body politic in the relation of rulers and subjects, or, in other words, to aggrandize the priesthood? for how can the Church be one body without such relation?"'—Pp. 8, 9. 10 15

He then proceeded to analyze and comment on it at great length, and to criticize severely the method and tone of my Sermons generally. Among other things, he said:— 20

'What, then, did the Sermon *mean*? Why was it preached? To insinuate that a Church which had sacramental confession and a celibate clergy was the only true Church? Or to insinuate that the admiring young gentlemen who listened to him stood to their fellow-countrymen in the relation of the early Christians to the heathen Romans? Or that Queen Victoria's Government was to the Church of England what Nero's or Dioclesian's was to the Church of Rome? It may have been so. I know that men used to suspect Dr. Newman,—I have been inclined to do so myself,—of writing a whole Sermon, not for the sake of the text or of the matter, but for the sake of one single passing hint—one phrase, one epithet, one little barbed arrow, which, as he swept magnificently past on the stream of his calm eloquence, seemingly unconscious of all presences, save those unseen, he delivered unheeded, as with his finger-tip, to the very heart of an initiated hearer, never to be withdrawn again. I do not blame him for that. It is one of the highest triumphs of oratoric power, and may be employed honestly and fairly by any person who has the skill to do it honestly and fairly; but then, Why did he entitle his Sermon "Wisdom and Innocence?"' 25 30 35

'What, then, could I think that Dr. Newman *meant*? I found a preacher bidding Christians imitate, to some undefined point, the "arts" of the basest of animals, and of men, and of the devil himself. I found him, by a strange perversion of Scripture, insinuating that St. Paul's conduct and manner were

5 such as naturally to bring down on him the reputation of being a crafty deceiver. I found him—horrible to say it—even hinting the same of one greater than St. Paul. I found him denying or explaining away the existence of that Priestcraft, which is a notorious fact to every honest student of history, and justifying (as far as I can understand him) that double-dealing by which

10 prelates, in the middle age, too often played off alternately the sovereign against the people, and the people against the sovereign, careless which was in the right, so long as their own power gained by the move. I found him actually using of such (and, as I thought, of himself and his party likewise) the words "They yield outwardly; to assent inwardly were to betray the

15 faith. Yet they are called deceitful and double-dealing, because they do as much as they can, and not more than they may." I found him telling Christians that they will always seem "artificial", and "wanting in openness and manliness"; that they will always be "a mystery" to the world, and that the world will always think them rogues; and bidding them glory in what the

20 world (i.e. the rest of their countrymen), disown, and say with Mawworm, "I like to be despised."

'Now, how was I to know that the preacher, who had the reputation of being the most acute man of his generation, and of having a specially intimate acquaintance with the weaknesses of the human heart, was utterly blind to the

25 broad meaning and the plain practical result of a Sermon like this, delivered before fanatic and hot-headed young men, who hung upon his every word? that he did not foresee that they would think that they obeyed him by becoming affected, artificial, sly, shifty, ready for concealments and equivocations?' &c. &c.—Pp. 14–16.

30   My accuser asked in this passage what did the Sermon *mean*, and why was it preached. I will here answer this question; and with this view will speak, first of the *matter* of the Sermon, then of its *subject*, then of its *circumstances*.

    1. It was one of the last six Sermons which I wrote when I was an

35 Anglican. It was one of the five Sermons I preached in St. Mary's between Christmas and Easter, 1843, the year when I gave up my Living. The MS. of the Sermon is destroyed; but I believe, and my memory too bears me out, as far as it goes, that the sentence in question about Celibacy and Confession, of which this writer would make so

40 much, *was not preached at all*. The Volume, in which this Sermon is found, was published *after* that I had given up St. Mary's, when I had no call on me to restrain the expression of any thing which I might hold: and I stated an important fact about it in the Advertisement, in these words:—

45 'In preparing [these Sermons] for publication, *a few words and sentences* have in several places been *added*, which will be found to express more *of*

private or personal opinion, than it was expedient to introduce into the *instruction* delivered in Church to a parochial Congregation. Such introduction, however, seems unobjectionable in the case of compositions, which are *detached* from the sacred place and service to which they once belonged, and *submitted to the reason* and judgment of the general reader.' 5

This Volume of Sermons then cannot be criticized at all as *preachments*; they are *essays*; essays of a man who, at the time of publishing them, was *not* a preacher. Such passages, as that in question, are just the very ones which I added *upon* my publishing them; and, as I always was on my guard in the pulpit against saying any thing which looked 10 towards Rome, I shall believe that I did not preach the obnoxious sentence till some one is found to testify that he heard it.

At the same time I cannot conceive why the mention of Sacramental Confession, or of Clerical Celibacy, had I made it, was inconsistent with the position of an Anglican Clergyman. For Sacramental Confession 15 and Absolution actually form a portion of the Anglican Visitation of the Sick; and though the 32nd Article says that 'Bishops, priests, and deacons, are not *commanded* by God's law either to vow the state of single life or to abstain from marriage', and 'therefore it is *lawful* for them to marry', this proposition I did not dream of denying, nor is it 20 inconsistent with St. Paul's doctrine, which I held, that it is '*good* to abide even as he', i.e. in celibacy.

But I have more to say on this point. This writer says, 'I know that men used to suspect Dr. Newman,—I have been inclined to do so myself,—of *writing a whole Sermon, not for the sake of the text or of* 25 *the matter*, but for the sake of one simple passing hint,—one phrase, one epithet.' Now observe; can there be a plainer testimony borne to the practical character of my Sermons at St. Mary's than this gratuitous insinuation? Many a preacher of Tractarian doctrine has been accused of not letting his parishioners alone, and of teasing them with his 30 private theological notions. The same report was spread about me twenty years ago as this writer spreads now, and the world believed that my Sermons at St. Mary's were full of red-hot Tractarianism. Then strangers came to hear me preach, and were astonished at their own disappointment. I recollect the wife of a great prelate from a distance 35 coming to hear me, and then expressing her surprise to find that I preached nothing but a plain humdrum Sermon. I recollect how, when on the Sunday before Commemoration one year, a number of strangers came to hear me, and I preached in my usual way, residents in Oxford, of high position, were loud in their satisfaction that on a great occasion, 40 I had made a simple failure, for after all there was nothing in the Sermon to hear. Well, but they were not going to let me off, for all my common-sense view of duty. Accordingly they got up the charitable theory which this Writer revives. They said that there was a double

purpose in those plain addresses of mine, and that my Sermons were
never so artful as when they seemed common-place; that there were
sentences which redeemed their apparent simplicity and quietness. So
they watched during the delivery of a Sermon, which to them was too
5 practical to be useful, for the concealed point of it, which they could at
least imagine, if they could not discover. 'Men used to suspect Dr. Newman,' he says, 'of writing a *whole* Sermon, *not* for the sake of *the text
or of the matter*, but for the sake of one single passing hint, . . . *one*
phrase, *one* epithet, *one* little barbed arrow, which, as he *swept magnifi-*
10 *cently* past on the stream of his calm eloquence, *seemingly* unconscious
of all presences, save those unseen, he delivered unheeded', &c. To all
appearance, he says, I was 'unconscious of all presences.' He is not able
to deny that the '*whole* Sermon' had the *appearance* of being '*for the
sake* of the text and matter'; therefore he suggests that perhaps it wasn't.

15   2. And now as to the subject of the Sermon. The Sermons of which
the Volume consists are such as are, more or less, exceptions to the rule
which I ordinarily observed, as to the subjects which I introduced into
the pulpit of St. Mary's. They are not purely ethical or doctrinal. They
were for the most part caused by circumstances of the day or of the
20 moment, and they belong to various years. One was written in 1832,
two in 1836, two in 1838, five in 1840, five in 1841, four in 1842, seven
in 1843. Many of them are engaged on one subject, viz. in viewing the
Church in its relation to the world. By the world was meant, not simply
those multitudes which were not in the Church, but the existing body
25 of human society, whether in the Church or not, whether Catholics,
Protestants, Greeks, or Mahometans, theists or idolaters, as being ruled
by principles, maxims, and instincts of their own, that is, of an unregenerate nature, whatever their supernatural privileges might be,
greater or less, according to their form of religion. This view of the
30 relation of the Church to the world as taken apart from questions of
ecclesiastical politics, as they may be called, is often brought out in my
Sermons. Two occur to me at once; No. 3 of my Plain Sermons, which
was written in 1829, and No. 15 of my Third Volume of Parochial,
written in 1835. On the other hand, by Church I meant,—in common
35 with all writers connected with the Tract Movement, whatever their
shades of opinion, and with the whole body of English divines, except
those of the Puritan or Evangelical School,—the whole of Christendom,
from the Apostles' time till now, whatever their later divisions into
Latin, Greek, and Anglican. I have explained this view of the subject
40 above at pp. 71–73 of this Volume. When then I speak, in the particular
Sermon before us, of the members, or the rulers, or the action of 'the
Church', I mean neither the Latin, nor the Greek, nor the English,
taken by itself, but of the whole Church as one body: of Italy as one

with England, of the Saxon or Norman as one with the Caroline Church. *This* was specially the one Church, and the points in which one branch or one period differed from another were not and could not be Notes of the Church, because Notes necessarily belong to the whole of the Church every where and always.   5

This being my doctrine as to the relation of the Church to the world, I laid down in the Sermon three principles concerning it, and there left the matter. The first is, that Divine Wisdom had framed for its action laws, which man, if left to himself, would have antecedently pronounced to be the worst possible for its success, and which in all ages have been   10 called by the world, as they were in the Apostles' days, 'foolishness'; that man ever relies on physical and material force, and on carnal induce-ments,—as Mahomet with his sword and his houris, or indeed almost as that theory of religion, called, since the Sermon was written, 'muscu-lar Christianity'; but that our Lord, on the contrary, has substituted   15 meekness for haughtiness, passiveness for violence, and innocence for craft: and that the event has shown the high wisdom of such an economy, for it has brought to light a set of natural laws, unknown before, by which the seeming paradox that weakness should be stronger than might, and simplicity than worldly policy, is readily explained.   20

Secondly, I said that men of the world, judging by the event, and not recognizing the secret causes of the success, viz. a higher order of natural laws,—natural, though their source and action were supernatural, (for 'the meek inherit the earth', by means of a meekness which comes from above,)—these men, I say, concluded, that the success which they wit-   25 nessed must arise from some evil secret which the world had not mastered,—by means of magic, as they said in the first ages, by cunning as they say now. And accordingly they thought that the humility and inoffensiveness of Christians, or of Churchmen, was a mere pretence and blind to cover the real causes of that success, which Christians   30 could explain and would not; and that they were simply hypocrites.

Thirdly, I suggested that shrewd ecclesiastics, who knew very well that there was neither magic nor craft in the matter, and, from their intimate acquaintance with what actually went on within the Church, discerned what were the real causes of its success, were of course under   35 the temptation of substituting reason for conscience, and, instead of simply obeying the command, were led to do good that good might come, that is, to act *in order* to secure success, and not from a motive of faith. Some, I said, did yield to the temptation more or less, and their motives became mixed; and in this way the world in a more subtle   40 shape had got into the Church; and hence it had come to pass, that, looking at its history from first to last, we could not possibly draw the line between good and evil there, and say either that every thing was to be defended, or certain things to be condemned. I expressed the

difficulty, which I supposed to be inherent in the Church, in the following words. I said, '*Priestcraft has ever been considered the badge*, and its imputation is a kind of Note of the Church: and *in part indeed truly*, because the presence of powerful enemies, and the sense of their own
5 weakness, *has sometimes tempted Christians to the abuse, instead of the use of Christian wisdom, to be wise without being harmless*; but partly, nay, for the most part, not truly, but slanderously, and merely because the world called their wisdom craft, when it was found to be a match for its own numbers and power.'

10 Such is the substance of the Sermon: and as to the main drift of it, it was this; that I was, there and elsewhere, scrutinizing the course of the Church as a whole, as if philosophically, as an historical phenomenon, and observing the laws on which it was conducted. Hence the Sermon, or Essay as it more truly is, is written in a dry and unimpas-
15 sioned way: it shows as little of human warmth of feeling as a Sermon of Bishop Butler's. Yet, under that calm exterior there was a deep and keen sensitiveness, as I shall now proceed to show.

3. If I mistake not, it was written with a secret thought about myself. Every one preaches according to his frame of mind, at the time of
20 preaching. One heaviness especially oppressed me at that season, which this Writer, twenty years afterwards, has set himself with a good will to renew: it arose from the sense of the base calumnies which were heaped upon me on all sides. It is worth observing that this Sermon is exactly contemporaneous with the report spread by a Bishop (*vid. supr.*
25 pp. 165–6), that I had advised a clergyman converted to Catholicism to retain his Living. This report was in circulation in February 1843, and my Sermon was preached on the 19th. In the trouble of mind into which I was thrown by such calumnies as this, I gained, while I reviewed the history of the Church, at once an argument and a consolation. My
30 argument was this: if I, who knew my own innocence, was so blackened by party prejudice, perhaps those high rulers and those servants of the Church, in the many ages which intervened between the early Nicene times and the present, who were laden with such grievous accusations, were innocent also; and this reflection served to make me tender
35 towards those great names of the past, to whom weaknesses or crimes were imputed, and reconciled me to difficulties in ecclesiastical proceedings, which there were no means now of properly explaining. And the sympathy thus excited for them, re-acted on myself, and I found comfort in being able to put myself under the shadow of those who had
40 suffered as I was suffering, and who seemed to promise me their recompense, since I had a fellowship in their trial. In a letter to my Bishop at the time of Tract 90, part of which I have quoted, I said that I had ever tried to 'keep innocency'; and now two years had passed since then,

and men were louder and louder in heaping on me the very charges, which this Writer repeats out of my Sermon, of 'fraud and cunning', 'craftiness and deceitfulness', 'double-dealing', 'priestcraft', of being 'mysterious, dark, subtle, designing', when I was all the time conscious to myself, in my degree, and after my measure, of 'sobriety, self- 5 restraint, and control of word and feeling'. I had had experience how my past success had been imputed to 'secret management'; and how, when I had shown surprise at that success, that surprise again was imputed to 'deceit'; and how my honest heartfelt submission to authority had been called, as it was called in a Bishop's charge abroad, 'mystic 10 humility'; and how my silence was called an 'hypocrisy'; and my faithfulness to my clerical engagements a secret correspondence with the enemy. And I found a way of destroying my sensitiveness about these things which jarred upon my sense of justice, and otherwise would have been too much for me, by the contemplation of a large law of the Divine 15 Dispensation, and felt myself more and more able to bear in my own person a present trial, of which in my past writings I had expressed an anticipation.

For thus feeling and thus speaking this Writer compares me to 'Mawworm'. 'I found him telling Christians', he says, 'that they will always 20 seem "artificial", and "wanting in openness and manliness"; that they will always be "a mystery" to the world; and that the world will always think them rogues; and bidding them glory in what the world (that is, the rest of their fellow-countrymen) disown, and say with Mawworm, "I like to be despised". Now how was I to know that the preacher . . . 25 was utterly blind to the broad meaning and the plain practical result of a Sermon like this delivered before fanatic and hot-headed young men, who hung upon his every word?'—Fanatic and hot-headed young men, who hung on my every word! If he had undertaken to write a history, and not a romance, he would have easily found out, as I have 30 said above, that from 1841 I had severed myself from the younger generation of Oxford, that Dr. Pusey and I had then closed our theological meetings at his house, that I had brought my own weekly evening parties to an end, that I preached only by fits and starts at St. Mary's, so that the attendance of young men was broken up, that in 35 those very weeks from Christmas till over Easter, during which this Sermon was preached, I was but five times in the pulpit there. He would have found, that it was written at a time when I was shunned rather than sought, when I had great sacrifices in anticipation, when I was thinking much of myself; that I was ruthlessly tearing myself 40 away from my own followers, and that, in the musings of that Sermon, I was at the very utmost only delivering a testimony in my behalf for

10 Bishop's charge abroad] foreign Bishop's charge 65

time to come, not sowing my rhetoric broadcast for the chance of present sympathy.

Again, he says: 'I found him actually using of such [prelates], (and, as I thought, of himself and his party likewise,) the words "They yield outwardly; to assent inwardly were to betray the faith. Yet they are called deceitful and double-dealing, because they do as much as they can, not more than they may."' This too is a proof of my duplicity! Let this writer, in his dealings with some one else, go just a little further than he has gone with me; and let him get into a court of law for libel; and let him be convicted; and let him still fancy that his libel, though a libel, was true, and let us then see whether he will not in such a case 'yield outwardly', without assenting internally; and then again whether we should please him, if we called him 'deceitful and double-dealing', because 'he did as much as he could, not more than he ought to do'. But Tract 90 will supply a real illustration of what I meant. I yielded to the Bishops in outward act, viz. in not defending the Tract, and in closing the Series; but, not only did I not assent inwardly to any condemnation of it, but I opposed myself to the proposition of a condemnation on the part of authority. Yet I was then by the public called 'deceitful and double-dealing', as this Writer calls me now, 'because I did as much as I felt I could do, and not more than I felt I could honestly do'. Many were the publications of the day and the private letters, which accused me of shuffling, because I closed the Series of Tracts, yet kept the Tracts on sale, as if I ought to comply not only with what my Bishop asked, but with what he did not ask, and perhaps did not wish. However, such teaching, according to this Writer, was likely to make young men 'suspect, that truth was not a virtue for its own sake, but only for the sake of the spread of "Catholic opinions", and the "salvation of their own souls"; and that cunning was the weapon which heaven had allowed to them to defend themselves against the persecuting Protestant public.'—p. 16.

And now I draw attention to a further point. He says, 'How was I to know that the preacher . . . did not foresee, that [fanatic and hot-headed young men] would think that they obeyed him, by becoming affected, artificial, sly, shifty, ready for concealments and *equivocations*?' 'How should he know?' What! I suppose that we are to think every man a knave till he is proved not to be such. Know! had he no friend to tell him whether I was 'affected' or 'artificial' myself? Could he not have done better than impute *equivocations* to me, at a time when I was in no sense answerable for the *amphibologia* of the Roman casuists? Had he a single fact which belongs to me personally or by profession to couple my name with equivocation in 1843? 'How should he know' that I was not sly, smooth, artificial, non-natural! he should know by that common manly frankness, by which we put confidence in others, till they are proved to have forfeited it; he should know it by my own words in that very Sermon, in which I say it is best to be natural, and that reserve is at best but an unpleasant necessity. For I say there expressly:—

'I do not deny that there is something very engaging in a frank and unpre- 5 tending manner; some persons have it more than others; in *some persons it is a great grace.* But it must be recollected that I am speaking of *times of persecution and oppression* to Christians, such as the text foretells; and then surely frankness will become nothing else than indignation at the oppressor, and vehement speech, if it is permitted. Accordingly, as persons have deep 10 feelings, so they will find the necessity of self-control, lest they should say what they ought not.'

He sums up thus:

'If [Dr. Newman] would . . . persist (as in this Sermon) in dealing with matters dark, offensive, doubtful, sometimes actually forbidden, at least 15 according to the notions of the great majority of English Churchmen; if he would always do so in a tentative, paltering way, seldom or never letting the world know how much he believed, how far he intended to go; if, in a word, his method of teaching was a suspicious one, what wonder if the minds of men were filled with suspicions of him?'—p. 17. 20

Now, in the course of my Narrative, I have frankly admitted that I was tentative in such of my works as fairly allowed of the introduction into them of religious inquiry; but he is speaking of my Sermons; where, then, is his proof that in my Sermons I dealt in matters dark, offensive, doubtful, actually forbidden? He must show that I was tenta- 25 tive in my Sermons; and he has the range of eight volumes to gather evidence in. As to the ninth, my University Sermons, of course I was tentative in them; but not because 'I would seldom or never let the world know how much I believed, or how far I intended to go'; but because University Sermons are commonly, and allowably, of the 30 nature of disquisitions, as preached before a learned body; and because in deep subjects, which had not been fully investigated, I said as much as I believed, and about as far as I saw I could go; and a man cannot do more; and I account no man to be a philosopher who attempts to do more. 35

NOTE D. ON PAGE 192

SERIES OF SAINTS' LIVES OF 1843-4

I HAVE here an opportunity of preserving, what otherwise would be lost, the Catalogue of English Saints which I formed, as preparatory to the Series of their Lives which was begun in the above years. It is but a first Essay, and has many obvious imperfections; but it may be
5 useful to others as a step towards a complete hagiography for England. For instance St. Osberga is omitted; I suppose because it was not easy to learn any thing about her. Boniface of Canterbury is inserted, though passed over by the Bollandists on the ground of the absence of proof of a *cultus* having been paid to him. The Saints of Cornwall were too
10 numerous to be attempted. Among the men of note, not Saints, King Edward II is included from piety towards the founder of Oriel College. With these admissions I present my Paper to the reader.

Preparing for Publication, in Periodical Numbers, in small 8vo, The Lives of the English Saints, Edited by the Rev. John Henry Newman,
15 *B.D., Fellow of Oriel College.*

IT is the compensation of the disorders and perplexities of these latter times of the Church that we have the history of the foregoing. We indeed of this day have been reserved to witness a disorganization of the City of God, which it never entered into the minds of the early believers to imagine: but we are
20 witnesses also of its triumphs and of its luminaries through those many ages which have brought about the misfortunes which at present overshadow it. If they were blessed who lived in primitive times, and saw the fresh traces of their Lord, and heard the echoes of Apostolic voices, blessed too are we whose special portion it is to see that same Lord revealed in His Saints. The
25 wonders of His grace in the soul of man, its creative power, its inexhaustible resources, its manifold operation, all this we know, as they knew it not. They never heard the names of St. Gregory, St. Bernard, St. Francis, and St. Louis. In fixing our thoughts then, as in an undertaking like the present, on the History of the Saints, we are but availing ourselves of that solace and
30 recompense of our peculiar trials which has been provided for our need by our Gracious Master.

And there are special reasons at this time for recurring to the Saints of our own dear and glorious, most favoured, yet most erring and most unfortunate England. Such a recurrence may serve to make us love our country
35 better, and on truer grounds, than heretofore; to teach us to invest her territory, her cities and villages, her hills and springs, with sacred associations; to give us an insight into her present historical position in the course of the Divine Dispensation; to instruct us in the capabilities of the English

character; and to open upon us the duties and the hopes to which that Church is heir, which was in former times the Mother of St. Boniface and St. Ethelreda.

Even a selection or specimens of the Hagiology of our country may suffice for some of these high purposes; and in so wide and rich a field of research it 5 is almost presumptuous in one undertaking to aim at more than such a partial exhibition. The list that follows, though by no means so large as might have been drawn up, exceeds the limits which the Editor proposes to his hopes, if not to his wishes; but, whether it is allowed him to accomplish a larger or smaller portion of it, it will be his aim to complete such subjects 10 or periods as he begins before bringing it to a close. It is hardly necessary to observe that any list that is producible in this stage of the undertaking can but approximate to correctness and completeness in matters of detail, and even in the names which are selected to compose it.

He has considered himself at liberty to include in the Series such saints as 15 have been born in England, though they have lived and laboured out of it; and such, again, as have been in any sufficient way connected with our country, though born out of it; for instance, Missionaries or Preachers in it, or spiritual or temporal rulers, or founders of religious institutions or houses.

He has also included in the Series a few eminent or holy persons, who, 20 though not in the Sacred Catalogue, are recommended to our religious memory by their fame, learning, or the benefits they have conferred on posterity. These have been distinguished from the Saints by printing their names in italics.

It is proposed to page all the longer Lives separately; the shorter will be 25 thrown together in one. They will be published in monthly issues of not more than 128 pages each; and no regularity, whether of date or of subject, will be observed in the order of publication. But they will be so numbered as to admit ultimately of a general chronological arrangement.

The separate writers are distinguished by letters subjoined to each Life; 30 and it should be added, to prevent misapprehension, that, since under the present circumstances of our Church, they are necessarily of various, though not divergent, doctrinal opinions, no one is answerable for any composition but his own. At the same time, the work professing an historical and ethical character, questions of theology will be, as far as possible, thrown into the 35 back ground.

J. H. N.

Littlemore, Sept. 9, 1843.

CALENDAR OF ENGLISH SAINTS

JANUARY

1 Elvan, B. and Medwyne, C.
2 Martyrs of Lichfield.
3 Melorus, M.
4
5 Edward, K.C.

6 Peter, A.
7 Cedd, B.
8 Pega, V. Wulsin, B.
9 Adrian, A. Bertwald, Archb.
10 Sethrida, V.
11 Egwin, B.
12 Benedict Biscop, A. Aelred, A.

JANUARY

13 Kentigern, B.
14 Beuno, A.
15 Ceolulph, K. Mo.
16 Henry, Hermit. Fursey, A.
17 Mildwida, V.
18 Ulfrid or Wolfrid, M.
19 Wulstan, B. Henry, B.
20
21
22 Brithwold, B.
23 Boisil, A.
24 Cadoc, A.
25
26 Theoritgida, V.
27 Bathildis, Queen.
28
29 Gildas, A.
30
31 Adamnan, Mo. Serapion, M.

FEBRUARY

1
2 Laurence, Archb.
3 Wereburga, V.
4 Gilbert, A. Liephard, B.M.
5
6 Ina, K. Mo.
7 Augulus, B.M. Richard, K.
8 Elfleda, A. Cuthman, C.
9 Theliau, B.
10 Trumwin, B.
11
12 Ethelwold, B. of Lindisfarne.
   Cedmon, Mo.
13 Ermenilda, Q.A.
14
15 Sigefride, B.
16 Finan, B.
17
18
19
20 Ulric, H.
21
22
23 Milburga, V.
24 Luidhard, B. Ethelbert of Kent,
   K.

25 Walburga, V.A.
26
27 Alnoth, H.M.
28 Oswald, B.
29

MARCH

1 David, Archb. Swibert, B.
2 Chad, B. Willeik, C. Joavan, B.
3 Winwaloe, A.
4 Owin, Mo.
5
6 Kineburga, &c., and Tibba, VV.
   Balther, C. and Bilfrid, H.
7 Easterwin, A. William, Friar.
8 Felix, B.
9 Bosa, B.
10
11
12 Elphege, B. Paul de Leon, B.C.
13
14 Robert, H.
15 Eadgith, A.
16
17 Withburga, V.
18 Edward, K.M.
19 Alcmund, M.
20 Cuthbert, B. Herbert, B.
21
22
23 Ædelwald, H.
24 Hildelitha, A.
25 Alfwold of Sherborne, B. and
   William, M.
26
27
28
29 Gundleus, H.
30 Merwenna, A.
31

APRIL

1
2
3 Richard, B.
4
5

6

7

8

9 Frithstan, B.

10

11 Guthlake, H.

12

13 Caradoc, H.

14 *Richard of Bury, B.*

15 Paternus, B.

16

17 Stephen, A.

18

19 Elphege, Archb.

20 Adelhare, M. Cedwalla, K.

21 Anselm, Archb. Doctor.

22

23 George, M.

24 Mellitus, Archb. Wilfrid, Archb. Egbert, C.

25

26

27

28

29 Wilfrid II. Archb.

30 Erconwald, B. Suibert, B. *Maud, Q.*

MAY

1 Asaph, B. Ultan, A. Brioc, B.C.

2 Germanus, M.

3

4

5 Ethelred, K. Mo.

6 Eadbert, A.

7 John, Archb. of Beverley.

8

9

10

11 Fremund, M.

12

13

14

15

16 Simon Stock, H.

17

18 Elgiva, Q.

19 Dunstan, Archb. *B. Alcuin, A.*

20 Ethelbert, K.M.

21 Godric, H.

22 Winewald, A. Berethun, A. *Henry, K.*

23

24 Ethelburga, Q.

25 Aldhelm, B.

26 Augustine, Archb.

27 Bede, D. Mo.

28 *Lanfranc, Archb.*

29

30 Walston, C.

31 Jurmin, C.

JUNE

1 Wistan, K.M.

2

3

4 Petroc, A.

5 Boniface, Archb. M.

6 Gudwall, B.

7 Robert, A.

8 William, Archb.

9

10 Ivo, B. and Ithamar, B.

11

12 Eskill, B.M.

13

14 Elerius, A.

15 Edburga, V.

16

17 Botulph, A. John, Fr.

18

19

20 Idaberga, V.

21 Egelmund, A.

22 Alban, and Amphibolus, MM.

23 Ethelreda, V.A.

24 Bartholomew, H.

25 Adelbert, C.

26

27 John, C. of Moutier.

28

29 *Margaret, Countess of Richmond.*

30

JULY

1 Julius, Aaron, MM. Rumold, B. Leonorus, B.
2 Oudoceus, B. Swithun, B.
3 Gunthiern, A.
4 Odo, Archb.
5 Modwenna, V.A.
6 Sexburga, A.
7 Edelburga, V.A. Hedda, B. Willibald, B. Ercongota, V.
8 Grimbald, and Edgar, K.
9 *Stephen Langton, Archb.*
10
11
12

13 Mildreda, V.A.
14 Marchelm, C. Boniface, Archb.
15 Deusdedit, Archb. Plechelm, B. David, A. and Editha of Tamworth, Q.V.
16 Helier, H.M.
17 Kenelm, K.M.
18 Edburga and Edgitha of Aylesbury, VV. Frederic, B.M.
19
20
21
22
23
24 Wulfud and Ruffin, MM. Lewinna, V.M.
25
26
27 Hugh, M.
28 Sampson, B.
29 Lupus, B.
30 Tatwin, Archb. and Ermenigitha, V.
31 Germanus, B. and Neot, H.

AUGUST

1 Ethelwold, B. of Winton.
2 Etheldritha, V.
3 Walthen A.
4
5 Oswald, K.M. Thomas, Mo. M. of Dover

6
7
8 Colman, B.
9
10
11 *William of Waynfleet, B.*
12
13 Wigbert, A. Walter, A.
14 Werenfrid, C.
15
16
17
18 Helen, Empress.
19
20 Oswin, K.M.
21 Richard, B. of Andria.
22 Sigfrid, A.
23 Ebba, V.A.
24
25 Ebba, V.A.M.
26 Bregwin, Archb. *Bradwardine, Archb.*
27 Sturmius, A.
28
29 Sebbus, K.
30
31 Eanswida, V.A. Aidan, A.B. Cuthburga, Q.V.

SEPTEMBER

1
2 William, B. of Roschid. William, Fr.
3
4
5
6 Bega, A.
7 Alcmund, A. Tilhbert, A.
8
9 Bertelin, H. Wulfhilda or Vulfridis, A.
10 Otger, C.
11 *Robert Kilwardby, Archb.*
12
13
14 *Richard Fox, B.*
15

16 Ninian, B. Edith, daughter of
    Edgar, V.
17 Socrates and Stephen, MM.
18
19 Theodore, Archb.
20
21 Hereswide, Q. *Edward II. K.*
22
23
24
25 Ceolfrid, A.
26
27 *William of Wykeham, B.*
28 Lioba, V.A.
29 *B. Richard of Hampole, H.*
30 Honorius, Archb.

OCTOBER

1 Roger, B.
2 Thomas of Hereford, B.
3 Ewalds (two) MM.
4
5 *Walter Stapleton, B.*
6 Ywy, C.
7 Ositha, Q.V.M.
8 Ceneu, V.
9 Lina, V. and *Robert Grostete, B.*
10 Paulinus, Archb. John, C. of
    Bridlington.
11 Edilburga, V.A.
12 Edwin, K.
13
14 Burchard, B.
15 Tecla, V.A.
16 Lullus, Archb.
17 Ethelred, Ethelbright, MM.
18 *Walter de Merton, B.*
19 Frideswide, V. and Ethbin, A.
20
21 Ursula, V.M.
22 Mello, B.C.
23
24 Magloire, B.
25 *John of Salisbury, B.*
26 Eata, B.
27 Witta, B.
28 *B. Alfred.*

29 Sigebert, K. Elfreda, A.
30
31 Foillan, B.M.

NOVEMBER

1
2
3 Wenefred, V.M. Rumwald, C.
4 Brinstan, B. Clarus, M.
5 Cungar, H.
6 Iltut, A. and Winoc, A.
7 Willebrord, B.
8 Willehad, B. Tyssilio, B.
9
10 Justus, Archb.
11
12 Lebwin, C.
13 Eadburga of Menstrey, A.
14 Dubricius, B.C.
15 Malo, B.
16 Edmund, B.
17 Hilda, A. Hugh, B.
18
19 Ermenburga, Q.
20 Edmund, K.M. Humbert, B.M.
    Acca, B.
21
22 Paulinus, A.
23 Daniel, B.C.
24
25
26
27
28 Edwold, M.
29
30

DECEMBER

1
2 Weede, V.
3 Birinus, B. Lucius, K. and Sola,
    H.
4 Osmund, B.
5 Christina, V.
6
7
8 *John Peckham, Archb.*

DECEMBER		20	
9		21	Eadburga, V.A.
10		22	
11	Elfleda, A.	23	
12	Corentin, B.C.	24	
13	Ethelburga, Q. wife of Edwin.	25	
14		26	Tathai, C.
15		27	Gerald, A.B.
16		28	
17		29	Thomas, Archb. M.
18	Winebald, A.	30	
19		31	

N.B. *St. William*, *Austin-Friar*, *Ingulphus*, and *Peter of Blois* have not been introduced into the above Calendar, their days of death or festival not being as yet ascertained.

CHRONOLOGICAL ARRANGEMENT

SECOND CENTURY

182	Dec. 3.	Lucius, K. of the British.
	Jan. 1.	Elvan, B. and Medwyne, C. envoys from St. Lucius to Rome.

FOURTH CENTURY

300	Oct. 22.	Mello, B.C. of Rouen.
303	Apr. 23.	George, M. under Dioclesian. Patron of England.
—	June 22.	Alban and Amphibalus, MM.
—	July 1.	Julius and Aaron, MM. of Caerleon.
304	Jan. 2.	Martyrs of Lichfield.
—	Feb. 7.	Augulus, B.M. of London.
328	Aug. 18.	Helen, Empress, mother of Constantine.
388	Sept. 17.	Socrates and Stephen, M.M. perhaps in Wales.
411	Jan. 3.	Melorus, M. in Cornwall.

FIFTH CENTURY

432	Sept. 16.	Ninian, B. Apostle of the Southern Picts.
429	July 31.	Germanus, B.C. of Auxerre.
	July 29.	Lupus, B.C. of Troyes.
502	May 1.	Brioc, B.C., disciple of St. Germanus.
490	Oct. 8.	Ceneu, or Keyna, V., sister-in-law of Gundleus.
492	Mar. 29.	Gundleus, Hermit, in Wales.
	July 3.	Gunthiern, A., in Brittany.
453	Oct. 21.	Ursula, V.M. near Cologne.
bef. 500	Dec. 12.	Corentin, B.C. of Quimper.

FIFTH AND SIXTH CENTURIES

Welsh Schools

444–522 Nov. 14. Dubricius, B.C., first Bishop of Llandaff.
520   Nov. 22.   Paulinus, A. of Whitland, tutor of St. David and St. Theliau.
445–544 Mar. 1. David, Archb. of Menevia, afterwards called from him.
abt. 500 Dec. 26. Tathai, C., master of St. Cadoc.
480   Jan. 24.   Cadoc, A., son of St. Gundleus, and nephew of St. Keyna.
abt. 513 Nov. 6. Iltut, A., converted by St. Cadoc.
545   Nov. 23.   Daniel, B.C., first Bishop of Bangor.
aft. 559 Apr. 18. Paternus, B.A., pupil of St. Iltut.
573   Mar. 12.   Paul, B.C. of Leon, pupil of St. Iltut.
       Mar. 2.   Ioavan, B., pupil of St. Paul.
599   July 28.   SAMPSON, B., pupil of St. Iltut, cousin of St. Paul de Leon.
565   Nov. 15.   Malo, B., cousin of St. Sampson.
575   Oct. 24.   Magloire, B., cousin of St. Malo.
583   Jan. 29.   Gildas, A., pupil of St. Iltut.
       July 1.   Leonorus, B., pupil of St. Iltut.
604   Feb. 9.   Theliau, B. of Llandaff, pupil of St. Dubricius.
560   July 2.   Oudoceus, B., nephew to St. Theliau.
500–580 Oct. 19. Ethbin, A., pupil of St. Sampson.
516–601 Jan. 13. Kentigern, B. of Glasgow, founder of Monastery of Elwy.

SIXTH CENTURY

529   Mar. 3.   Winwaloe, A., in Brittany.
564   June 4.   Petroc., A., in Cornwall.
       July 16.   Helier, Hermit, M., in Jersey.
       June 27.   John, C. of Moutier, in Tours.
590   May 1.   Asaph, B. of Elwy, afterwards called after him.
abt. 600 June 6. Gudwall, B. of Aleth in Brittany.
       Nov. 8.   Tyssilio, B. of St. Asaph.

SEVENTH CENTURY

Part I

600   June 10.   Ivo, or Ivia, B. from Persia.
596   Feb. 24.   Luidhard, B. of Senlis, in France.
616   Feb. 24.   Ethelbert, K. of Kent.
608   May 26.   Augustine, Archb. of Canterbury, Apostle of England.
624   Apr. 24.   Mellitus, Archb. of Canterbury, ⎫
619   Feb. 2.   Laurence, Archb. of Canterbury, ⎪ Companions of St.
608   Jan. 6.   Peter, A. at Canterbury,   ⎬ Augustine.
627   Nov. 10.   Justus, Archb. of Canterbury, ⎪
653   Sept. 30. Honorius, Archb. of Canterbury,⎭
662   July 15.   Deus-dedit, Archb. of Canterbury.

SEVENTH CENTURY
PART II

642	Oct. 29.	Sigebert, K. of the East Angles.
646	Mar. 8.	Felix, B. of Dunwich, Apostle of the East Angles.
650	Jan. 16.	Fursey, A., preacher among the East Angles.
680	May 1.	Ultan, A., brother of St. Fursey.
655	Oct. 31.	Foillan, B.M., brother of St. Fursey, preacher in the Netherlands.
680	June 17.	Botulph, A., in Lincolnshire or Sussex.
671	June 10.	Ithamar, B. of Rochester.
650	Dec. 3.	Birinus, B. of Dorchester.
705	July 7.	Hedda, B. of Dorchester.
717	Jan. 11.	Egwin, B. of Worcester.

SEVENTH CENTURY
PART III

690	Sept. 19.	Theodore, Archb. of Canterbury.
709	Jan. 9.	Adrian, A. in Canterbury.
709	May 25.	Aldhelm, B. of Sherborne, pupil of St. Adrian.

SEVENTH CENTURY
PART IV

630	Nov. 3.	Winefred, V.M. in Wales.
642	Feb. 4.	Liephard, M.B., slain near Cambray.
660	Jan. 14.	Beuno, A., kinsman of St. Cadocus and St. Kentigern.
673	Oct. 7.	Osgitha, Q.V.M., in East Anglia during a Danish inroad.
630	June 14.	Elerius, A. in Wales.
680	Jan. 27.	Bathildis, Q., wife of Clovis II., king of France.
687	July 24.	Lewinna, V.M., put to death by the Saxons.
700	July 18.	Edberga and Edgitha, VV. of Aylesbury.

SEVENTH CENTURY
PART V

644	Oct. 10.	Paulinus, Archb. of York, companion of St. Augustine.
633	Oct. 12.	Edwin, K. of Northumberland.
	Dec. 13.	Ethelburga, Q., wife to St. Edwin.
642	Aug. 5.	Oswald, K.M., St. Edwin's nephew.
651	Aug. 20.	Oswin, K.M., cousin to St. Oswald.
683	Aug. 23.	Ebba, V.A. of Coldingham, half-sister to St. Oswin.
689	Jan. 31.	Adamnan, Mo. of Coldingham.

SEVENTH CENTURY
PART VI. WHITBY

650	Sept. 6.	Bega, V.A., foundress of St. Bee's, called after her.
681	Nov. 17.	Hilda, A. of Whitby, daughter of St. Edwin's nephew.

716   Dec. 11.   Elfleda, A. of Whitby, daughter of St. Oswin.
680   Feb. 12.   Cedmon, Mo. of Whitby.

SEVENTH AND EIGHTH CENTURIES
PART I

      Sept. 21.   Hereswida, Q., sister of Hilda, wife of Annas, who suc-
                    ceeded Egric, Sigebert's cousin.
654   Jan. 10.   Sethrida, V.A. of Faremoutier, St. Hereswida's daughter
                    by a former marriage.
693   Apr. 30.   Erconwald, A.B., son of Annas and St. Hereswida,
                    Bishop of London, Abbot of Chertsey, founder of
                    Barking.
677   Aug. 29.   Sebbus, K., converted by St. Erconwald.
      May 31.   Jurmin, C., son of Annas and St. Hereswida.
650   July 7.   Edelburga, V.A. of Faremoutier, natural daughter of
                    Annas.
679   June 23.   Ethelreda, Etheldreda, Etheltrudis, or Awdry, V.A.,
                    daughter of Annas and St. Hereswida.
      Mar. 17.   Withburga, V., daughter of Annas and St. Hereswida.
699   July 6.   Sexburga, A., daughter of Annas and St. Hereswida.
660   July 7.   Ercongota, or Ertongata, V.A. of Faremoutier, daughter
                    of St. Sexburga.
699   Feb. 13.   Ermenilda, Q.A., daughter of St. Sexburga, wife of
                    Wulfere.
aft. 675   Feb. 3. Wereburga, V., daughter of St. Ermenilda and Wulfere,
                    patron of Chester.
abt. 680   Feb. 27. Alnoth, H.M., bailiff to St. Wereburga.
640   Aug. 31.   Eanswida, V.A., sister-in-law of St. Sexburga, grand-
                    daughter to St. Ethelbert.
668   Oct. 17.   Ethelred and Ethelbright, MM., nephews of St. Ean-
                    swida.
      July 30.   Ermenigitha, V., niece of St. Eanswida.
676   Oct. 11.   Edilberga, V.A. of Barking, daughter of Annas and St.
                    Hereswida.
678   Jan. 26.   Theoritgida, V., nun of Barking.
aft. 713 Aug. 31. Cuthberga, Q.V., of Barking, sister of St. Ina.
700   Mar. 24.   Hildelitha, A. of Barking.
728   Feb. 6.   Ina, K. Mo. of the West Saxons.
740   May 24.   Ethelburga, Q., wife of St. Ina, nun at Barking.

SEVENTH AND EIGHTH CENTURIES
PART II

652   June 20.   Idaburga, V.
696   Mar. 6.   Kineburga, Q.A.
701   ————   Kinneswitha, V.   Daughters of King Penda.
      ————   Chidestre, V.
692   Dec. 2.   Weeda, V.A.

696	Mar. 6.	Tibba, V., their kinswoman.
	Nov. 3.	Rumwald, C., grandson of Penda.
680	Nov. 19.	Ermenburga, Q., mother to the three following.
	Feb. 23.	Milburga, V.A. of Wenlock, ⎫ Grand-daughters of
	July 13.	Mildreda, V.A. of Menstrey, ⎬ Penda.
676	Jan. 17.	Milwida, or Milgitha, V. ⎭
750	Nov. 13.	Eadburga, A. of Menstrey.

SEVENTH AND EIGHTH CENTURIES

PART III

670	July 24.	Wulfad and Ruffin, MM., sons of Wulfere, Penda's son and of St. Erminilda.
672	Mar. 2.	Chad, B. of Lichfield.
664	Jan. 7.	Cedd, B. of London.
688	Mar. 4.	Owin, Mo. of Lichfield.
689	Apr. 20	Cedwalla, K. of West Saxons.
690–725	Nov. 5.	Cungar, H. in Somersetshire.
700	Feb. 10.	Trumwin, B. of the Picts.
705	Mar. 9.	Bosa, Archb. of York.
709	Apr. 24.	Wilfrid, Archb. of York.
721	May 7.	John of Beverley, Archb. of York.
743	Apr. 29.	Wilfrid II., Archb. of York.
733	May 22.	Berethun, A. of Deirwood, disciple of St. John of Beverley.
751	May 22.	Winewald, A. of Deirwood.

SEVENTH AND EIGHTH CENTURIES

PART IV. MISSIONS

729	Apr. 24.	Egbert, C., master to Willebrord.
693	Oct. 3.	Ewalds (two), MM. in Westphalia.
690–736	Nov. 7.	Willebrord, B. of Utrecht, Apostle of Friesland.
717	Mar. 1.	Swibert, B., Apostle of Westphalia.
727	Mar. 2.	Willeik, C., successor to St. Swibert.
705	June 25.	Adelbert, C., grandson of St. Oswald, preacher in Holland.
705	Aug. 14.	Werenfrid, C., preacher in Friesland.
720	June 21.	Engelmund, A., preacher in Holland.
730	Sept. 10.	Otger, C. in Low Countries.
732	July 15.	Plechelm, B., preacher in Guelderland.
750	May 2.	Germanus, B.M. in the Netherlands.
760	Nov. 12.	Lebwin, C. in Overyssel, in Holland.
760	July 14.	Marchelm, C., companion of St. Lebwin, in Holland.
697–755	June 5.	Boniface, Archb., M. of Mentz, Apostle of Germany.
712	Feb. 7.	Richard, K. of the West Saxons.

704–790 July 7. Willibald, B. of Aichstadt, ⎫
in Franconia, ⎪ ⎫
730–760 Dec. 18. Winebald, A. of Heiden- ⎪ Children of
heim, in Suabia, ⎬ St. Richard. ⎪
779 Feb. 25. Walburga, V.A. of Heiden- ⎪
heim, ⎪
aft. 755 Sept. 28. Lioba, V.A. of Bischorsheim, ⎬
750 Oct. 15. Tecla, V.A. of Kitzingen, in Franconia, ⎪
788 Oct. 16. Lullus, Archb. of Mentz, ⎪ Companions
abt. 747 Aug. 13. Wigbert, A. of Fritzlar and Ortdorf, in ⎬ of St.
Germany, ⎪ Boniface
755 Apr. 20. Adelhare, B.M. of Erford, in Franconia, ⎪
780 Aug. 27. Sturmius, A. of Fulda, ⎪
786 Oct. 27. Witta, or Albuinus, B. of Buraberg, in ⎪
Germany, ⎪
791 Nov. 8. Willehad, B. of Bremen, and Apostle of ⎪
Saxony, ⎪
791 Oct. 14. Burchard, B. of Wurtzburg, in Franconia, ⎪
790 Dec. 3. Sola, H., near Aichstadt, in Franconia. ⎭
775 July 1. Rumold, B., Patron of Mechlin.
807 Apr. 30. Suibert, B. of Verden in Westphalia.

SEVENTH AND EIGHTH CENTURIES

PART V. LINDISFARNE AND HEXHAM

670 Jan. 23. Boisil, A. of Melros, in Scotland.
651 Aug. 31. Aidan, A.B. of Lindisfarne.
664 Feb. 16. Finan, B. of Lindisfarne.
676 Aug. 8. Colman, B. of Lindisfarne.
685 Oct. 26. Eata, B. of Hexham.
687 Mar. 20. Cuthbert, B. of Lindisfarne.
Oct. 6. Ywy, C. disciple of St. Cuthbert.
690 Mar. 20. Herbert, H. disciple of St. Cuthbert.
698 May 6. Eadbert, B. of Lindisfarne.
700 Mar. 23. Ædelwald, H. successor of St. Cuthbert, in his hermitage.
740 Feb. 12. Ethelwold, B. of Lindisfarne.
740 Nov. 20. Acca, B. of Hexham.
764 Jan. 15. Ceolulph, K. Mo. of Lindisfarne.
756 Mar. 6. Balther, H. at Lindisfarne.
Bilfrid, H. Goldsmith at Lindisfarne.
781 Sept. 7. Alchmund, B. of Hexham.
789 Sept. 7. Tilhbert, B. of Hexham.

SEVENTH AND EIGHTH CENTURIES

PART VI. WEARMOUTH AND YARROW

703 Jan. 12. Benedict Biscop, A. of Wearmouth.
685 Mar. 7. Easterwin, A. of Wearmouth.

689 Aug. 22.   Sigfrid, A. of Wearmouth.
716 Sept. 25.   Ceofrid, A. of Yarrow.
734 May 27.   Bede, Doctor, Mo. of Yarrow.
804 May 19.   *B. Alcuin, A. in France.*

EIGHTH CENTURY

710 May 5.   Ethelred, K. Mo. King of Mercia, Monk of Bardney.
719 Jan. 8.   Pega, V., sister of St. Guthlake.
714 April 11.   Guthlake, H. of Croyland.
717 Nov. 6.   Winoc, A. in Brittany.
730 Jan. 9.   Bertwald, Archb. of Canterbury.
732 Dec. 27.   Gerald, A.B. in Mayo.
734 July 30.   Tatwin, Archb. of Canterbury.
750 Oct. 19.   Frideswide, V. patron of Oxford.
762 Aug. 26.   Bregwin, Archb. of Canterbury.
700–800 Feb. 8.   Cuthman, C. of Stening in Sussex.
bef. 800 Sept. 9.   Bertelin, H. patron of Stafford.

EIGHTH AND NINTH CENTURIES

793 May 20.   Ethelbert, K.M. of the East Angles.
834 Aug. 2.   Etheldritha, or Alfreda, V., daughter of Offa, king of Mercia, nun at Croyland.
819 July 17.   Kenelm, K.M. of Mercia.
849 June 1.   Wistan, K.M. of Mercia.
838 July 18.   Frederic, Archb. M. of Utrecht.
894 Nov. 4.   Clarus, M. in Normandy.

NINTH CENTURY

PART I. DANISH SLAUGHTERS, & C.

819 Mar. 19.   Alcmund, M., son of Eldred, king of Northumbria, Patron of Derby.
870 Nov. 20.   Edmund, K.M. of the East Angles.
862 May 11.   Fremund, H.M. nobleman of East Anglia.
870 Nov. 20.   Humbert, B.M. of Elmon in East Anglia.
867 Aug. 25.   Ebba, V.A.M. of Coldingham.

NINTH CENTURY

PART II

862 July 2.   Swithun, B. of Winton.
870 July 5.   Modwenna, V.A. of Pollesworth in Warwickshire.
      Oct. 9.   Lina, V. nun at Pollesworth.
871 Mar. 15.   Eadgith, V.A. of Pollesworth, sister of King Ethelwolf.
900 Dec. 21.   Eadburga, V.A. of Winton, daughter of King Ethelwolf.
880 Nov. 28.   Edwold, H., brother of St. Edmund.

NINTH AND TENTH CENTURIES

883	July 31.	Neot, H. in Cornwall.
903	July 8.	Grimbald, A. at Winton.
900	Oct. 28.	*B. Alfred, K.*
929	April 9.	Frithstan, B. of Winton.
934	Nov. 4.	Brinstan, B. of Winton.

TENTH CENTURY

PART I

960	June 15.	Edburga, V., nun at Winton, granddaughter of Alfred.
926	July 15.	Editha, Q.V., nun of Tamworth, sister to Edburga.
921	May 18.	Algyfa, or Elgiva, Q., mother of Edgar.
975	July 8.	Edgar, K.
978	Mar. 18.	Edward, K.M. at Corfe Castle.
984	Sept. 16.	Edith, V., daughter of St. Edgar and St. Wulfhilda.
990	Sept. 9.	Wulfhilda, or Vulfrida, A. of Wilton.
980	Mar. 30.	Merwenna, V.A. of Romsey.
990	Oct. 29.	Elfreda, A. of Romsey.
1016	Dec. 5.	Christina of Romsey, V., sister of St. Margaret of Scotland.

TENTH CENTURY

PART II

961	July 4.	Odo, Archb. of Canterbury, Benedictine Monk.
960–992	Feb. 28.	Oswald, Archb. of York, B. of Worcester, nephew to St. Odo.
951–1012	Mar. 12.	Elphege the Bald, B. of Winton.
988	May 19.	Dunstan, Archb. of Canterbury.
973	Jan. 8.	Wulsin, B. of Sherbourne.
984	Aug. 1.	Ethelwold, B. of Winton.
1015	Jan. 22.	Brithwold, B. of Winton.

TENTH AND ELEVENTH CENTURIES

MISSIONS

950	Feb. 15.	Sigfride, B., apostle of Sweden.
1016	June 12.	Eskill, B.M. in Sweden, kinsman of St. Sigfride.
1028	Jan. 18.	Wolfred, M. in Sweden.
1050	July 15.	David, A., Cluniac in Sweden.

ELEVENTH CENTURY

1012	April 19.	Elphege, M. Archb. of Canterbury.
1016	May 30.	Walston, C. near Norwich.
1053	Mar. 25.	Alfwold, B. of Sherborne.

1067	Sept. 2.	William, B. of Roschid in Denmark.
1066	Jan. 5.	Edward, K.C.
1099	Dec. 4.	Osmund, B. of Salisbury.

ELEVENTH AND TWELFTH CENTURIES

1095	Jan. 19.	Wulstan, B. of Worcester.
1089	May 28.	*Lanfranc, Archb. of Canterbury.*
1109	Apr. 21.	Anselm, Doctor, Archb. of Canterbury.
1170	Dec. 29.	Thomas, Archb. M. of Canterbury.
1200	Nov. 17.	Hugh, B. of Lincoln, Carthusian Monk.

TWELFTH CENTURY
Part I

1109		*Ingulphus, A. of Croyland.*
1117	Apr. 30.	*B. Maud, Q.* Wife of Henry I.
1124	Apr. 13.	Caradoc, H. in South Wales.
1127	Jan. 16.	Henry, H. in Northumberland.
1144	Mar. 25.	William, M. of Norwich.
1151	Jan. 19.	Henry, M.B. of Upsal.
1150	Aug. 13.	Walter, A. of Fontenelle, in France.
1154	June 8.	William, Archb. of York.
1170	May 21.	Godric, H. in Durham.
1180	Oct. 25.	*John of Salisbury, B. of Chartres.*
1182	June 24.	Bartholomew, C., monk at Durham.
1189	Feb. 4.	Gilbert, A. of Sempringham.
1190	Aug. 21.	Richard, B. of Andria.
1200		*Peter de Blois, Archd. of Bath.*

TWELFTH CENTURY
Part II. Cistertian Order

1134	Apr. 17.	Stephen, A. of Citeaux.
1139	June 7.	Robert, A. of Newminster in Northumberland.
1154	Feb. 20.	Ulric, H. in Dorsetshire.
1160	Aug. 3.	Walthen, A. of Melrose.
1166	Jan. 12.	Aelred, A. of Rieval.

THIRTEENTH CENTURY
Part I

1228	July 9.	*Stephen Langton, Archb. of Canterbury.*
1242	Nov. 16.	Edmund, Archb. of Canterbury.
1253	Apr. 3.	Richard, B. of Chichester.
1282	Oct. 2.	Thomas, B. of Hereford.
1294	Dec. 3.	*John Peckham, Archb. of Canterbury.*

THIRTEENTH CENTURY

PART II. ORDERS OF FRIARS

1217	June 17.	John, Fr., Trinitarian.
1232	Mar. 7.	William, Fr., Franciscan.
1240	Jan. 31.	Serapion, Fr., M., Redemptionist.
1265	May 16.	Simon Stock, H., General of the Carmelites.
1279	Sept. 11.	*Robert Kilwardby, Archb. of Canterbury, Fr. Dominican.*

THIRTEENTH CENTURY

PART III

1239	Mar. 14.	Robert H. at Knaresboro'.
1241	Oct. 1.	Roger, B. of London.
1255	July 27.	Hugh, M. of Lincoln.
1295	Aug. 5.	Thomas, Mo., M. of Dover.
1254	Oct. 9.	*Robert Grossteste, B. of Lincoln.*
1270	July 14.	Boniface, Archb. of Canterbury.
1278	Oct. 18.	*Walter de Merton, B. of Rochester.*

FOURTEENTH CENTURY

1326	Oct. 5.	*Stapleton, B. of Exeter.*
1327	Sept. 21.	*Edward K.*
1349	Sept. 29.	*B. Richard, H. of Hampole.*
1345	Apr. 14.	*Richard of Bury, B. of Lincoln.*
1349	Aug. 26.	*Bradwardine, Archb. of Canterbury, the Doctor Pro-fundus.*
1358	Sept. 2.	William, Fr., Servite.
1379	Oct. 10.	John, C. of Bridlington.
1324–1404	Sept. 27.	*William of Wykeham, B. of Winton.*
1400		William, Fr. Austin.

FIFTEENTH CENTURY

1471	May 22.	*Henry, K. of England.*
1486	Aug. 11.	*William of Wanefleet, B. of Winton.*
1509	June 29.	*Margaret, Countess of Richmond.*
1528	Sept. 14.	*Richard Fox, B. of Winton.*

NOTE E. ON PAGE 205

THE ANGLICAN CHURCH

I HAVE been bringing out my mind in this Volume on every subject which has come before me; and therefore I am bound to state plainly what I feel and have felt, since I was a Catholic, about the Anglican Church. I said, in a former page, that, on my conversion, I was not conscious
5 of any change in me of thought or feeling, as regards matters of doctrine; this, however, was not the case as regards some matters of fact, and, unwilling as I am to give offence to religious Anglicans, I am bound to confess that I felt a great change in my view of the Church of England. I cannot tell how soon there came on me,—but
10 very soon,—an extreme astonishment that I had ever imagined it to be a portion of the Catholic Church. For the first time, I looked at it from without, and (as I should myself say) saw it as it was. Forthwith I could not get myself to see in it any thing else, than what I had so long fearfully suspected, from as far back as 1836,—a mere national institu-
15 tion. As if my eyes were suddenly opened, so I saw it—spontaneously, apart from any definite act of reason or any argument; and so I have seen it ever since. I suppose, the main cause of this lay in the contrast which was presented to me by the Catholic Church. Then I recognized at once a reality which was quite a new thing with me. Then I was
20 sensible that I was not making for myself a Church by an effort of thought; I needed not to make an act of faith in her; I had not pain- fully to force myself into a position, but my mind fell back upon itself in relaxation and in peace, and I gazed at her almost passively as a great objective fact. I looked at her;—at her rites, her ceremonial, and
25 her precepts; and I said, 'This *is* a religion'; and then, when I looked back upon the poor Anglican Church, for which I had laboured so hard, and upon all that appertained to it, and thought of our various attempts to dress it up doctrinally and esthetically, it seemed to me to be the veriest of nonentities.
30 Vanity of vanities, all is vanity! How can I make a record of what passed within me, without seeming to be satirical? But I speak plain, serious words. As people call me credulous for acknowledging Catholic claims, so they call me satirical for disowning Anglican pretensions; to them it *is* credulity, to them it *is* satire; but it is not so in me. What
35 they think exaggeration, I think truth. I am not speaking of the Angli- can Church with any disdain, though to them I seem contemptuous. To them of course it is 'Aut Cæsar aut nullus', but not to me. It may

be a great creation, though it be not divine, and this is how I judge of it. Men, who abjure the divine right of kings, would be very indignant, if on that account they were considered disloyal. And so I recognize in the Anglican Church a time-honoured institution, of noble historical memories, a monument of ancient wisdom, a momentous arm of political strength, a great national organ, a source of vast popular advantage, and, to a certain point, a witness and teacher of religious truth. I do not think that, if what I have written about it since I have been a Catholic, be equitably considered as a whole, I shall be found to have taken any other view than this; but that it is something sacred, that it is an oracle of revealed doctrine, that it can claim a share in St. Ignatius or St. Cyprian, that it can take the rank, contest the teaching, and stop the path of the Church of St. Peter, that it can call itself 'the Bride of the Lamb', this is the view of it which simply disappeared from my mind on my conversion, and which it would be almost a miracle to reproduce. 'I went by, and lo! it was gone; I sought it, but its place could no where be found', and nothing can bring it back to me. And, as to its possession of an episcopal succession from the time of the Apostles, well, it may have it, and, if the Holy See ever so decide, I will believe it, as being the decision of a higher judgment than my own; but, for myself, I must have St. Philip's gift, who saw the sacerdotal character on the forehead of a gaily-attired youngster, before I can by my own wit acquiesce in it, for antiquarian arguments are altogether unequal to the urgency of visible facts. Why is it that I must pain dear friends by saying so, and kindle a sort of resentment against me in the kindest of hearts? but I must, though to do it be not only a grief to me, but most impolitic at the moment. Any how, this is my mind; and, if to have it, if to have betrayed it, before now, in-voluntarily by my words or my deeds, if on a fitting occasion, as now, to have avowed it, if all this be a proof of the justice of the charge brought against me by my accuser of having 'turned round upon my Mother-Church with contumely and slander', in this sense, but in no other sense, do I plead guilty to it without a word in extenuation.

In no other sense surely; the Church of England has been the instrument of Providence in conferring great benefits on me;—had I been born in Dissent, perhaps I should never have been baptized; had I been born an English Presbyterian, perhaps I should never have known our Lord's divinity; had I not come to Oxford, perhaps I never should have heard of the visible Church, or of Tradition, or other Catholic doctrines. And as I have received so much good from the Anglican Establishment itself, can I have the heart or rather the want of charity, considering that it does for so many others, what it has done for me, to wish to see it overthrown? I have no such wish while it is what it is, and while we are so small a body. Not for its own sake, but for the sake

of the many congregations to which it ministers, I will do nothing
against it. While Catholics are so weak in England, it is doing our
work; and, though it does us harm in a measure, at present the balance
is in our favour. What our duty would be at another time and in other
5 circumstances, supposing, for instance, the Establishment lost its
dogmatic faith, or at least did not preach it, is another matter altogether. In secular history we read of hostile nations having long truces,
and renewing them from time to time, and that seems to be the position
which the Catholic Church may fairly take up at present in relation
10 to the Anglican Establishment.

Doubtless the National Church has hitherto been a serviceable
breakwater against doctrinal errors, more fundamental than its own.
How long this will last in the years now before us, it is impossible to
say, for the Nation drags down its Church to its own level; but still
15 the National Church has the same sort of influence over the Nation
that a periodical has upon the party which it represents, and my own
idea of a Catholic's fitting attitude towards the National Church in this
its supreme hour, is that of assisting and sustaining it, if it be in our
power, in the interest of dogmatic truth. I should wish to avoid every
20 thing (except indeed under the direct call of duty, and this is a material
exception,) which went to weaken its hold upon the public mind, or to
unsettle its establishment, or to embarrass and lessen its maintenance
of those great Christian and Catholic principles and doctrines which
it has up to this time successfully preached.

THE ECONOMY

FOR the Economy, considered as a rule of practice, I shall refer to what I wrote upon it in 1830–32, in my History of the Arians. I have shown above, pp. 35–37, that the doctrine in question had in the early Church a large signification, when applied to the divine ordinances: it also had a definite application to the duties of Christians, whether clergy or 5 laity, in preaching, in instructing or catechizing, or in ordinary intercourse with the world around them; and in this aspect I have here to consider it.

As Almighty God did not all at once introduce the Gospel to the world, and thereby gradually prepared men for its profitable reception, 10 so, according to the doctrine of the early Church, it was a duty, for the sake of the heathen among whom they lived, to observe a great reserve and caution in communicating to them the knowledge of 'the whole counsel of God'. This cautious dispensation of the truth, after the manner of a discreet and vigilant steward, is denoted by the word 15 'economy'. It is a mode of acting which comes under the head of Prudence, one of the four Cardinal Virtues.

The principle of the Economy is this; that out of various courses, in religious conduct or statement, all and each *allowable antecedently and in themselves*, that ought to be taken which is most expedient and most 20 suitable at the time for the object in hand.

Instances of its application and exercise in Scripture are such as the following:—1. Divine Providence did but gradually impart to the world in general, and to the Jews in particular, the knowledge of His will:—He is said to have 'winked at the times of ignorance among the 25 heathen'; and He suffered in the Jews divorce 'because of the hardness of their hearts'. 2. He has allowed Himself to be represented as having eyes, ears, and hands, as having wrath, jealousy, grief, and repentance. 3. In like manner, our Lord spoke harshly to the Syro-Phœnician woman, whose daughter He was about to heal, and made as if He 30 would go further, when the two disciples had come to their journey's end. 4. Thus too Joseph 'made himself strange to his brethren', and Elisha kept silence on request of Naaman to bow in the house of Rimmon. 5. Thus St. Paul circumcised Timothy, while he cried out 'Circumcision availeth not'. 35

It may be said that this principle, true in itself, yet is dangerous, because it admits of an easy abuse, and carries men away into what becomes insincerity and cunning. This is undeniable; to do evil that good may come, to consider that the means, whatever they are, justify the end, to sacrifice truth to expedience, unscrupulousness, reckless-ness, are grave offences. These are abuses of the Economy. But to call them *economical* is to give a fine name to what occurs every day, independent of any knowledge of the *doctrine* of the Economy. It is the abuse of a rule which nature suggests to every one. Every one looks out for the 'mollia tempora fandi', and for 'mollia verba' too.

Having thus explained what is meant by the Economy as a rule of social intercourse between men of different religious, or, again, political, or social views, next I will go on to state what I said in the Arians.

I say in that Volume first, that our Lord has given us the *principle* in His own words,—'Cast not your pearls before swine'; and that He exemplified it in His teaching by parables; that St. Paul expressly distinguishes between the milk which is necessary to one set of men, and the strong meat which is allowed to others, and that, in two Epistles. I say, that the Apostles in the Acts observe the same rule in their speeches, for it is a fact, that they do not preach the high doc-trines of Christianity, but only 'Jesus and the Resurrection' or 'repen-tance and faith'. I also say, that this is the very reason that the Fathers assign for the silence of various writers in the first centuries on the subject of our Lord's divinity. I also speak of the catechetical system practised in the early Church, and the *disciplina arcani* as regards the doctrine of the Holy Trinity, to which Bingham bears witness; also of the defence of this rule by Basil, Cyril of Jerusalem, Chrysostom, and Theodoret.

But next the question may be asked, whether I have said any thing in my Volume *to guard* the doctrine, thus laid down, from the abuse to which it is obviously exposed: and my answer is easy. Of course, had I had any idea that I should have been exposed to such hostile mis-representations, as it has been my lot to undergo on the subject, I should have made more direct avowals than I have done of my sense of the gravity and the danger of that abuse. Since I could not foresee when I wrote, that I should have been wantonly slandered, I only wonder that I have anticipated the charge as fully as will be seen in the follow-ing extracts.

For instance, speaking of the Disciplina Arcani, I say:—(1) 'The elementary information given to the heathen or catechumen was *in no sense undone* by the subsequent secret teaching, which was in fact but the *filling up of a bare but correct outline*', p. 58, and I contrast this with the conduct of the Manichæans 'who represented the initiatory discipline as founded on a *fiction* or hypothesis, which was to be forgotten by the learner as he made progress in the *real* doctrine of the Gospel'. (2) As to allegorizing, I say that the Alexandrians erred, whenever and as far as they proceeded 'to *obscure* the primary meaning of Scripture, and to *weaken the force of historical facts* and express declarations', p. 69. (3) And that they were 'more open to *censure*', when, on being '*urged by objections* to various passages in the history of the Old Testament, as derogatory to the divine perfections or to the 5 Jewish Saints, they had *recourse to an allegorical explanation by way of answer*', p. 71. (4) I add, '*It is impossible to defend such a procedure*, which seems to imply a *want of faith* in those who had recourse to it'; for 'God has given us *rules of right and wrong*', *ibid.* (5) Again, I say,—'The *abuse of the Economy* in *the hands of unscrupulous* 10 *reasoners*, is obvious. *Even the honest* controversialist or teacher will find it very difficult to represent, *without misrepresenting*, what it is yet his duty to present to his hearers with caution or reserve. Here the obvious rule to guide our practice is, to be careful ever to maintain *substantial truth* in our use of the economical method', pp. 79, 80. 15 (6) And so far from concurring at all hazards with Justin, Gregory, or Athanasius, I say, 'It *is plain* [they] *were justified or not* in their Economy, *according* as they did or did not *practically mislead their opponents*', p. 80. (7) I proceed, 'It is so difficult to hit the mark in these perplexing cases, that it is not wonderful, should these or other Fathers 20 have failed at times, and said more or less than was proper', *ibid.*

The Principle of the Economy is familiarly acted on among us every day. When we would persuade others, we do not begin by treading on their toes. Men would be thought rude who introduced their own religious notions into mixed society, and were devotional in a drawing- 25 room. Have we never thought lawyers tiresome who did *not* observe this polite rule, who came down for the assizes and talked law all through dinner? Does the same argument tell in the House of Commons, on the hustings, and at Exeter Hall? Is an educated gentleman never worsted at an election by the tone and arguments of some clever 30 fellow, who, whatever his shortcomings in other respects, understands the common people?

As to the Catholic Religion in England at the present day, this only will I observe,—that the truest expedience is to answer right out, when you are asked; that the wisest economy is to have no management; 35 that the best prudence is not to be a coward; that the most damaging folly is to be found out shuffling; and that the first of virtues is to 'tell truth, and shame the devil'.

NOTE G. ON PAGE 249

LYING AND EQUIVOCATION

ALMOST all authors, Catholic and Protestant, admit, that *when a just cause is present*, there is some kind or other of verbal misleading, which is not sin. Even silence is in certain cases virtually such a misleading, according to the Proverb, 'Silence gives consent'. Again, silence is
5 absolutely forbidden to a Catholic, as a mortal sin, under certain circumstances, e.g. to keep silence, when it is a duty to make a profession of faith.

Another mode of verbal misleading, and the most direct, is actually saying the thing that is not; and it is defended on the principle that
10 such words are not a lie, when there is a 'justa causa', as killing is not murder in the case of an executioner.

Another ground of certain authors for saying that an untruth is not a lie where there is a just cause, is, that veracity is a kind of justice, and therefore, when we have no duty of justice to tell truth to another, it is
15 no sin not to do so. Hence we may say the thing that is not, to children, to madmen, to men who ask impertinent questions, to those whom we hope to benefit by misleading.

Another ground, taken in defending certain untruths, *ex justâ causâ*, as if not lies, is, that veracity is for the sake of society, and that,
20 if in no case whatever we might lawfully mislead others, we should actually be doing society great harm.

Another mode of verbal misleading is equivocation or a play upon words; and it is defended on the theory that to lie is to use words in a sense which they will not bear. But an equivocator uses them in a re-
25 ceived sense, though there is another received sense, and therefore, according to this definition, he does not lie.

Others say that all equivocations are, after all, a kind of lying,— faint lies or awkward lies, but still lies; and some of these disputants infer, that therefore we must not equivocate, and others that equivoca-
30 tion is but a half-measure, and that it is better to say at once that in certain cases untruths are not lies.

Others will try to distinguish between evasions and equivocations; but though there are evasions which are clearly not equivocations, yet it is very difficult scientifically to draw the line between the one and the
35 other.

To these must be added the unscientific way of dealing with lies:— viz. that on a great or cruel occasion a man cannot help telling a lie, and he would not be a man, did he not tell it, but still it is very wrong, and he ought not to do it, and he must trust that the sin will be forgiven him, though he goes about to commit it ever so deliberately, and is sure to commit it again under similar circumstances. It is a necessary frailty, and had better not be thought about before it is incurred, and 5 not thought of again, after it is well over. This view cannot for a moment be defended, but, I suppose, it is very common.

I think the historical course of thought upon the matter has been this: the Greek Fathers thought that, when there was a *justa causa*, an untruth need not be a lie. St. Augustine took another view, though with 10 great misgiving; and, whether he is rightly interpreted or not, is the doctor of the great and common view that all untruths are lies, and that there can be *no* just cause of untruth. In these later times, this doctrine has been found difficult to work, and it has been largely taught that, though all untruths are lies, yet that certain equivocations, 15 when given in a just cause, are not untruths.

Further, there have been and all along through these later ages, other schools, running parallel with the above mentioned, one of which says that equivocations, &c. after all *are* lies, and another which says that there are untruths which are not lies. 20

And now as to the 'just cause', which is the condition, *sine quâ non*. The Greek Fathers make it such as these, self-defence, charity, zeal for God's honour, and the like.

St. Augustine seems to deal with the same 'just causes' as the Greek Fathers, even though he does not allow of their availableness as 25 depriving untruths, spoken on such occasions, of their sinfulness. He mentions defence of life and of honour, and the safe custody of a secret. Also the great Anglican writers, who have followed the Greek Fathers, in defending untruths when there is the 'just cause', consider that 'just cause' to be such as the preservation of life and property, defence 30 of law, the good of others. Moreover, their moral rights, e.g. defence against the inquisitive, &c.

St. Alfonso, I consider, would take the same view of the 'justa causa' as the Anglican divines; he speaks of it as 'quicunque finis *honestus*, ad servanda bona spiritui vel corpori utilia'; which is very much the 35 view which they take of it, judging by the instances which they give.

In all cases, however, and as contemplated by all authors, Clement of Alexandria, or Milton, or St. Alfonso, such a causa is, in fact, extreme, rare, great, or at least special. Thus the writer in the Mélanges Théologiques (Liège, 1852–3, p. 453) quotes Lessius: 'Si absque justa 40

16 given in] there is 65

causa fiat, est abusio orationis contra virtutem veritatis, et civilem consuetudinem, etsi proprie non sit mendacium.' That is, the virtue of truth, and the civil custom, are the *measure* of the just cause. And so Voit, 'If a man has used a reservation (restrictione non purè mentali)
5 without a *grave* cause, he has sinned gravely.' And so the author himself, from whom I quote, and who defends the Patristic and Anglican doctrine that there *are* untruths which are not lies, says, 'Under the name of mental reservation theologians authorize many lies, *when there is for them a grave reason* and proportionate', i.e. to their
10 character.—p. 459. And so St. Alfonso, in another Treatise, quotes St. Thomas to the effect, that if from one cause two immediate effects follow, and, if the good effect of that cause is *equal in value* to the bad effect (bonus *æquivalet* malo), then nothing hinders the speaker's intending the good and only permitting the evil. From which it will
15 follow that, since the evil to society from lying is very great, the just cause which is to make it allowable, must be very great also. And so Kenrick: 'It is confessed by all Catholics that, in the common intercourse of life, all ambiguity of language is to be avoided; but it is debated whether such ambiguity is *ever* lawful. Most theologians
20 answer in the affirmative, supposing a *grave cause* urges, and the [true] mind of the speaker can be collected from the adjuncts, though in fact it be not collected.'

However, there are cases, I have already said, of another kind, in which Anglican authors would think a lie allowable; such as when a
25 question is *impertinent*. Of such a case Walter Scott, if I mistake not, supplied a very distinct example, in his denying so long the authorship of his novels.

What I have been saying shows what different schools of opinion there are in the Church in the treatment of this difficult doctrine; and,
30 by consequence, that a given individual, such as I am, *cannot* agree with all of them, and has a full right to follow which of them he will. The freedom of the Schools, indeed, is one of those rights of reason, which the Church is too wise really to interfere with. And this applies not to moral questions only, but to dogmatic also.

35   It is supposed by Protestants that, because St. Alfonso's writings have had such high commendation bestowed upon them by authority, therefore they have been invested with a quasi-infallibility. This has arisen in good measure from Protestants not knowing the force of theological terms. The words to which they refer are the authoritative
40 decision that 'nothing in his works has been found *worthy of censure*', 'censurâ dignum'; but this does not lead to the conclusions which have been drawn from it. Those words occur in a legal document, and cannot be interpreted except in a legal sense. In the first place, the sentence is

negative; nothing in St. Alfonso's writings is positively approved; and, secondly, it is not said that there are no faults in what he has written, but nothing which comes under the ecclesiastical *censura*, which is something very definite. To take and interpret them, in the way commonly adopted in England, is the same mistake, as if one were to take the word 'Apologia' in the English sense of apology, or 'Infant' in law to mean a little child.

1. Now first as to the meaning of the above form of words viewed as a proposition. When a question on the subject was asked of the fitting authorities at Rome by the Archbishop of Besançon, the answer returned to him contained this condition, viz. that those words were to be interpreted, 'with due regard to the mind of the Holy See concerning the approbation of writings of the servants of God, ad effectum Canonizationis'. This is intended to prevent any Catholic taking the words about St. Alfonso's works in too large a sense. Before a Saint is canonized, his works are examined, and a judgment pronounced upon them. Pope Benedict XIV. says, 'The *end* or *scope* of this judgment is, that it may appear, whether the doctrine of the servant of God, which he has brought out in his writings, is free from any soever *theological censure*.' And he remarks in addition, 'It never can be said that the doctrine of a servant of God is *approved* by the Holy See, but at most it can [only] be said that it is not disapproved (non reprobatam) in case that the Revisers had reported that there is nothing found by them in his works, which is adverse to the decrees of Urban VIII., and that the judgment of the Revisers has been approved by the sacred Congregation, and confirmed by the Supreme Pontiff.' The Decree of Urban VIII. here referred to is, 'Let works be examined, whether they contain errors against faith or good morals (bonos mores), or any new doctrine, or a doctrine foreign and alien to the common sense and custom of the Church.' The author from whom I quote this (M. Vandenbroeck, of the diocese of Malines) observes, 'It is therefore clear, that the approbation of the works of the Holy Bishop touches not the truth of every proposition, adds nothing to them, nor even gives them by consequence a degree of intrinsic probability.' He adds that it gives St. Alfonso's theology an extrinsic probability, from the fact that, in the judgment of the Holy See, no proposition deserves to receive a censure; but that 'that probability will cease nevertheless in a particular case, for any one who should be convinced, whether by evident arguments, or by a decree of the Holy See, or otherwise, that the doctrine of the Saint deviates from the truth.' He adds, 'From the fact that the approbation of the works of St. Alfonso does not decide the truth of each proposition, it follows, as Benedict XIV. has remarked, that we may combat the doctrine which they contain; only, since a canonized saint is in question, who is honoured by a solemn

culte in the Church, we ought not to speak except with respect, nor to attack his opinions except with temper and modesty.'

2. Then, as to the meaning of the word *censura*: Benedict XIV. enumerates a number of 'Notes' which come under that name; he says,
5 'Out of propositions which are to be noted with theological censure, some are heretical, some erroneous, some close upon error, some savouring of heresy', and so on; and each of these terms has its own definite meaning. Thus by 'erroneous' is meant, according to Viva, a proposition which is not *immediately* opposed to a revealed proposition,
10 but only to a theological *conclusion* drawn from premises which are *de fide*; 'savouring of heresy is' a proposition, which is opposed to a theological conclusion not evidently drawn from premises which are *de fide*, but most probably and according to the common mode of theologizing;—and so with the rest. Therefore when it was said by the
15 Revisers of St. Alfonso's works that they were not 'worthy of *censure*', it was only meant that they did not fall under these particular Notes.

But the answer from Rome to the Archbishop of Besançon went further than this; it actually took pains to declare that any one who
20 pleased might follow other theologians instead of St. Alfonso. After saying that no Priest was to be interfered with who followed St. Alfonso in the Confessional, it added, 'This is said, however, without on that account judging that they are reprehended who follow opinions handed down by other approved authors.'

25 And this too I will observe,—that St. Alfonso made many changes of opinion himself in the course of his writings; and it could not for an instant be supposed that we were bound to every one of his opinions, when he did not feel himself bound to them in his own person. And, what is more to the purpose still, there are opinions, or some opinion,
30 of his which actually have been proscribed by the Church since, and cannot now be put forward or used. I do not pretend to be a well-read theologian myself, but I say this on the authority of a theological professor of Breda, quoted in the Mélanges Théol. for 1850–1. He says: 'It may happen, that, in the course of time, errors may be found
35 in the works of St. Alfonso and be proscribed by the Church, *a thing which in fact has already occurred.*'

In not ranging myself then with those who consider that it is justifiable to use words in a double sense, that is, to equivocate, I put myself under the protection of such authors as Cardinal Gerdil, Natalis
40 Alexander, Contenson, Concina, and others. Under the protection of these authorities, I say as follows:—

Casuistry is a noble science, but it is one to which I am led, neither by my abilities nor my turn of mind. Independently, then, of the difficulties of the subject, and the necessity, before forming an opinion, of knowing more of the arguments of theologians upon it than I do, I am very unwilling to say a word here on the subject of Lying and Equivocation. But I consider myself bound to speak; and therefore, in this strait, I can do nothing better, even for my own relief, than submit 5 myself, and what I shall say, to the judgment of the Church, and to the consent, so far as in this matter there be a consent, of the Schola Theologorum.

Now in the case of one of those special and rare exigencies or emergencies, which constitute the *justa causa* of dissembling or misleading, 10 whether it be extreme as the defence of life, or a duty as the custody of a secret, or of a personal nature as to repel an impertinent inquirer, or a matter too trivial to provoke question, as in dealing with children or madmen, there seem to be four courses:—

1. *To say the thing that is not.* Here I draw the reader's attention to 15 the words *material* and *formal*. 'Thou shalt not kill'; *murder* is the *formal* transgression of this commandment, but *accidental homicide* is the *material* transgression. The *matter* of the act is the same in both cases; but in the *homicide*, there is nothing more than the act, whereas in *murder* there must be the intention, &c., which constitutes the 20 formal sin. So, again, an executioner commits the material act, but not that formal killing which is a breach of the commandment. So a man, who, simply to save himself from starving, takes a loaf which is not his own, commits only the material, not the formal act of stealing, that is, he does not commit a sin. And so a baptized Christian, external 25 to the Church, who is in invincible ignorance, is a material heretic, and not a formal. And in like manner, if to say the thing which is not be in special cases lawful, it may be called a *material lie*.

The first mode then which has been suggested of meeting those special cases, in which to mislead by words has a sufficient occasion, 30 or has a *just cause*, is by a material lie.

The second mode is by an *æquivocatio*, which is not equivalent to the English word 'equivocation', but means sometimes a *play upon words*, sometimes an *evasion*: we must take these two modes of misleading separately. 35

2. *A play upon words.* St. Alfonso certainly says that a play upon words is allowable; and, speaking under correction, I should say that he does so on the ground that lying is *not* a sin against justice, that is, against our neighbour, but a sin against God. God has made words the signs of ideas, and therefore if a word denotes two ideas, we are at 40 liberty to use it in either of its senses: but I think I must be incorrect in some respect in supposing that the Saint does not recognize a lie as an injustice, because the Catechism of the Council, as I have quoted it at p. 251, says, 'Vanitate et mendacio fides ac veritas tolluntur, arctissima

vincula *societatis humanæ*; quibus sublatis, sequitur summa vitæ *con-fusio*, ut *homines nihil a dæmonibus differre videantur.*'

3. *Evasion*;—when, for instance, the speaker diverts the attention of the hearer to another subject; suggests an irrelevant fact or makes a
5 remark, which confuses him and gives him something to think about; throws dust into his eyes; states some truth, from which he is quite sure his hearer will draw an illogical and untrue conclusion, and the like.

The greatest school of evasion, I speak seriously, is the House of Commons; and necessarily so, from the nature of the case. And the
10 hustings is another.

An instance is supplied in the history of St. Athanasius: he was in a boat on the Nile, flying persecution; and he found himself pursued. On this he ordered his men to turn his boat round, and ran right to meet the satellites of Julian. They asked him, 'Have you seen Athana-
15 sius?' and he told his followers to answer, 'Yes, he is close to you.' *They* went on their course as if they were sure to come up to him, while *he* ran back into Alexandria, and there lay hid till the end of the persecution.

I gave another instance above, in reference to a doctrine of religion.
20 The early Christians did their best to conceal their Creed on account of the misconceptions of the heathen about it. Were the question asked of them, 'Do you worship a Trinity?' and did they answer, 'We wor-ship one God, and none else'; the inquirer might, or would, infer that they did not acknowledge the Trinity of Divine Persons.

25 It is very difficult to draw the line between these evasions and what are commonly called in English *equivocations*; and of this difficulty, again, I think, the scenes in the House of Commons supply us with illustrations.

4. The fourth method is *silence*. For instance, not giving the *whole*
30 truth in a court of law. If St. Alban, after dressing himself in the Priest's clothes, and being taken before the persecutor, had been able to pass off for his friend, and so gone to martyrdom without being dis-covered; and had he in the course of examination answered all ques-tions truly, but not given the whole truth, the most important truth,
35 that he was the wrong person, he would have come very near to telling a lie, for a half-truth is often a falsehood. And his defence must have been the *justa causa*, viz. either that he might in charity or for religion's sake save a priest, or again that the judge had no right to interrogate him on the subject.

40 Now, of these four modes of misleading others by the tongue, when there is a *justa causa* (supposing there can be such),—(1) a material lie, that is, an untruth which is not a lie, (2) an equivocation, (3) an evasion, and (4) silence,—First, I have no difficulty whatever in recognizing as allowable the method of *silence*.

Secondly, But, if I allow of *silence*, why not of the method of *material lying*, since half of a truth *is* often a lie? And, again, if all killing be not murder, nor all taking from another stealing, why must all untruths be lies? Now I will say freely that I think it difficult to answer this question, whether it be urged by St. Clement or by Milton; at the same time, I never have acted, and I think when it came to the point, I never should act upon such a theory myself, except in one case, stated below. This I say for the benefit of those who speak hardly of Catholic theologians, on the ground that they admit text-books which allow of equivocation. They are asked, how can we trust you, when such are your views? but such views, as I already have said, need not have any thing to do with their own practice, merely from the circumstance that they are contained in their text-books. A theologian draws out a system; he does it partly as a scientific speculation: but much more for the sake of others. He is lax for the sake of others, not of himself. His own standard of action is much higher than that which he imposes upon men in general. One special reason why religious men, after drawing out a theory, are unwilling to act upon it themselves, is this: that they practically acknowledge a broad distinction between their reason and their conscience; and that they feel the latter to be the safer guide, though the former may be the clearer, nay even though it be the truer. They would rather be in error with the sanction of their conscience, than be right with the mere judgment of their reason. And again here is this more tangible difficulty in the case of exceptions to the rule of Veracity, that so very little external help is given us in drawing the line, as to when untruths are allowable and when not; whereas that sort of killing which is not murder, is most definitely marked off by legal enactments, so that it cannot possibly be mistaken for such killing as *is* murder. On the other hand the cases of exemption from the rule of Veracity are left to the private judgment of the individual, and he may easily be led on from acts which are allowable to acts which are not. Now this remark does *not* apply to such acts as are related in Scripture, as being done by a particular inspiration, for in such cases there *is* a command. If I had my own way, I would oblige society, that is, its great men, its lawyers, its divines, its literature, publicly to acknowledge as such, those instances of untruth which are not lies, as for instance untruths in war; and then there could be no perplexity to the individual Catholic, for he would not be taking the law into his own hands.

Thirdly, as to playing upon words, or equivocation, I suppose it is from the English habit, but, without meaning any disrespect to a great Saint, or wishing to set myself up, or taking my conscience for more than it is worth, I can only say as a fact, that I admit it as little as the rest of my countrymen: and, without any reference to the right and the wrong of the matter, of this I am sure, that, if there is one thing more than another which prejudices Englishmen against the Catholic Church, it is the doctrine of great authorities on the subject of equivocation. For myself, I can fancy myself thinking it was allowable in extreme cases for me to lie, but never to equivocate. Luther said, 'Pecca fortiter.' I anathematize his formal sentiment, but there is a truth in it, when spoken of material acts.

Fourthly, I think *evasion*, as I have described it, to be perfectly allowable; indeed, I do not know, who does not use it, under circumstances; but that a good deal of moral danger is attached to its use; and that, the cleverer a man is, the more likely he is to pass the line of Christian duty.

But it may be said, that such decisions do not meet the particular difficulties for which provision is required; let us then take some instances.

1. I do not think it right to tell lies to children, even on this account, that they are sharper than we think them, and will soon find out what we are doing; and our example will be a very bad training for them. And so of equivocation: it is easy of imitation, and we ourselves shall be sure to get the worst of it in the end.

2. If an early Father defends the patriarch Jacob in his mode of gaining his father's blessing, on the ground that the blessing was divinely pledged to him already, that it was his, and that his father and brother were acting at once against his own rights and the divine will, it does not follow from this that such conduct is a pattern to us, who have no supernatural means of determining *when* an untruth becomes a *material*, and not a *formal* lie. It seems to me very dangerous, be it ever allowable or not, to lie or equivocate in order to preserve some great temporal or spiritual benefit; nor does St. Alfonso here say any thing to the contrary, for he is not discussing the question of danger or expedience.

3. As to Johnson's case of a murderer asking you which way a man had gone, I should have anticipated that, had such a difficulty happened to him, his first act would have been to knock the man down, and to call out for the police; and next, if he was worsted in the conflict, he would not have given the ruffian the information he asked, at whatever risk to himself. I think he would have let himself be killed first. I do not think that he would have told a lie.

4. A secret is a more difficult case. Supposing something has been confided to me in the strictest secrecy, which could not be revealed without great disadvantage to another, what am I to do? If I am a lawyer, I am protected by my profession. I have a right to treat with extreme indignation any question which trenches on the inviolability

of my position; but, supposing I was driven up into a corner, I think I should have a right to say an untruth, or that, under such circumstances, a lie would be *material*, but it is almost an impossible case, for the law would defend me. In like manner, as a priest, I should think it lawful to speak as if I knew nothing of what passed in confession. And I think in these cases, I do in fact possess that guarantee, that I am not going by private judgment, which just now I demanded; for society would bear me out, whether as a lawyer or as a priest, in holding that I had a duty to my client or penitent, such, that an untruth in the matter was not a lie. A common type of this permissible denial, be it *material lie* or *evasion*, is at the moment supplied to me:— an artist asked a Prime Minister, who was sitting to him, 'What news, my Lord, from France?' He answered, '*I do not know*; I have not read the Papers.'

5. A more difficult question is, when to accept confidence has not been a duty. Supposing a man wishes to keep the secret that he is the author of a book, and he is plainly asked on the subject. Here I should ask the previous question, whether any one has a right to publish what he dare not avow. It requires to have traced the bearings and results of such a principle, before being sure of it; but certainly, for myself, I am no friend of strictly anonymous writing. Next, supposing another has confided to you the secret of his authorship:—there are persons who would have no scruple at all in giving a denial to impertinent questions asked them on the subject. I have heard a great man in his day at Oxford, warmly contend, as if he could not enter into any other view of the matter, that, if he had been trusted by a friend with the secret of his being author of a certain book, and he were asked by a third person, if his friend was not (as he really was) the author of it, he ought, without any scruple and distinctly, to answer that he did not know. He had an existing duty towards the author; he had none towards his inquirer. The author had a claim on him; an impertinent questioner had none at all. But here again I desiderate some leave, recognized by society, as in the case of the formulas 'Not at home', and 'Not guilty', in order to give me the right of saying what is a *material* untruth. And moreover, I should here also ask the previous question, Have I any right to accept such a confidence? have I any right to make such a promise? and, if it be an unlawful promise, is it binding when it cannot be kept without a lie? I am not attempting to solve these difficult questions, but they have to be carefully examined. And now I have said more than I had intended on a question of casuistry.

SUPPLEMENTAL MATTER

I

LETTERS AND PAPERS OF THE AUTHOR USED IN THE COURSE OF THIS WORK

II

CARDINAL NEWMAN'S WORKS

Schools. 10. Universities. 11. Northmen and Normans. 12. Medieval Oxford. 13. Convocation of Canterbury. Crown 8vo. 6s. each. (*Longmans.*)

5. THEOLOGICAL

24. THE ARIANS OF THE FOURTH CENTURY. Cabinet Edition, crown 8vo. 6s. Cheap Edition, 3s. 6d. (*Longmans.*)

25, 26. ANNOTATED TRANSLATION OF ATHANASIUS. 2 vols. Crown 8vo. 15s. (*Longmans.*)

27. TRACTS. 1. Dissertatiunculæ. 2. On the Text of the Seven Epistles of St. Ignatius. 3. Doctrinal Causes of Arianism. 4. Apollinarianism. 5. St. Cyril's Formula. 6. Ordo de Tempore. 7. Douay Version of Scripture. (*Burns and Oates.*)

6. POLEMICAL

28, 29. THE VIA MEDIA OF THE ANGLICAN CHURCH. 2 vols. with Notes. Vol. I. Prophetical Office of the Church. Vol. II. Occasional Letters and Tracts. Crown 8vo. 6s. each. (*Longmans.*)

30, 31. CERTAIN DIFFICULTIES FELT BY ANGLICANS IN CATHOLIC TEACHING CONSIDERED. 2 vols. Vol. I. Twelve Lectures. Vol. II. Letters to Dr. Pusey concerning the Bl. Virgin, and to the Duke of Norfolk in Defence of the Pope and Council. Vol. 1, 7s. 6d.; Vol. 2, 5s. 6d. (*Longmans.*)

32. PRESENT POSITION OF CATHOLICS IN ENGLAND. Crown 8vo. 7s. 6d. (*Longmans.*)

33. APOLOGIA PRO VITÂ SUÂ. Cabinet Edition, crown 8vo. 6s. Cheap Edition, 3s. 6d. (*Longmans.*)

7. LITERARY

34. VERSES ON VARIOUS OCCASIONS. Cabinet Edition, crown 8vo. 6s. Cheap Edition, 3s. 6d. (*Longmans.*)

35. LOSS AND GAIN. (*Burns and Oates.*)

36. CALLISTA. Cabinet Edition, crown 8vo. 6s. Cheap Edition, 3s. 6d. (*Longmans.*)

37. THE DREAM OF GERONTIUS. 16mo. 6d. sewed, 1s. cloth. (*Longmans.*)

[This list, here given as it stood shortly after Newman's death in 1890, appeared in a variety of forms in different impressions of the *Apologia.* Two more volumes, *Sermon Notes* and *Meditations and Devotions*, were later issued to complete the standard edition of Newman's works, published by Longmans.—Ed.]

III

LETTER OF APPROBATION AND ENCOURAGEMENT
FROM THE BISHOP OF THE DIOCESE OF BIRMING-
HAM, DR. ULLATHORNE

'Bishop's House, June 2, 1864

'My dear Dr. Newman,—

'It was with warm gratification that, after the close of the Synod yesterday, I listened to the Address presented to you by the clergy of the diocese, and to your impressive reply. But I should have been little satisfied with the part of the silent listener, except on the understanding with myself that I also might afterwards express to you my own sentiments in my own way.

'We have now been personally acquainted, and much more than acquainted, for nineteen years, during more than sixteen of which we have stood in special relation of duty towards each other. This has been one of the singular blessings which God has given me amongst the cares of the Episcopal office. What my feelings of respect, of confidence, and of affection have been towards you, you know well, nor should I think of expressing them in words. But there is one thing that has struck me in this day of explanations, which you could not, and would not, be disposed to do, and which no one could do so properly or so authentically as I could, and which it seems to me is not altogether uncalled for, if every kind of erroneous impression that some persons have entertained with no better evidence than conjecture is to be removed.

'It is difficult to comprehend how, in the face of facts, the notion should ever have arisen that during your Catholic life, you have been more occupied with your own thoughts than with the service of religion and the work of the Church. If we take no other work into consideration beyond the written productions which your Catholic pen has given to the world, they are enough for the life's labour of another. There are the Lectures on Anglican Difficulties, the Lectures on Catholicism in England, the great work on the Scope and End of University Education, that on the Office and Work of Universities, the Lectures and Essays on University Subjects, and the two Volumes of Sermons; not to speak of your contributions to the Atlantis, which you founded, and to other periodicals; then there are those beautiful offerings to Catholic literature, the Lectures on the Turks, Loss and Gain, and Callista, and though last, not least, the Apologia, which is destined to put many idle rumours to rest, and many unprofitable surmises; and yet all these productions represent but a portion of your labour, and that in the second half of your period of public life.

'These works have been written in the midst of labour and cares of another kind, and of which the world knows very little. I will specify four of these undertakings, each of a distinct character, and any one of which would have made a reputation for untiring energy in the practical order.

'The first of these undertakings was the establishment of the congregation of the Oratory of St. Philip Neri—that great ornament and accession to the force of English Catholicity. Both the London and the Birmingham Oratory must look to you as their founder and as the originator of their characteristic excellences; whilst that of Birmingham has never known any other presidency.

'No sooner was this work fairly on foot than you were called by the highest authority to commence another, and one of yet greater magnitude and difficulty, the founding of a University in Ireland. After the Universities had been lost to the Catholics of these kingdoms for three centuries, every thing had to be begun from the beginning: the idea of such an institution to be inculcated, the plan to be formed that would work, the resources to be gathered, and the staff of superiors and professors to be brought together. Your name was then the chief point of attraction which brought these elements together. You alone know what difficulties you had to conciliate and what to surmount, before the work reached that state of consistency and promise, which enabled you to return to those responsibilities in England which you had never laid aside or suspended. And here, excuse me if I give expression to a fancy which passed through my mind.

'I was lately reading a poem, not long published, from the MSS. De Rerum Natura, by Neckham, the foster-brother of Richard the Lion-hearted. He quotes an old prophecy, attributed to Merlin, and with a sort of wonder, as if recollecting that England owed so much of its literary learning to that country; and the prophecy says that after long years Oxford will pass into Ireland—"Vada boum suo tempore transibunt in Hiberniam." When I read this, I could not but indulge the pleasant fancy that in the days when the Dublin University shall arise in material splendour, an allusion to this prophecy might form a poetic element in the inscription on the pedestal of the statue which commemorates its first Rector.

'The original plan of an Oratory did not contemplate any parochial work, but you could not contemplate so many souls in want of pastors without being prompt and ready at the beck of authority to strain all your efforts in coming to their help. And this brings me to the third and the most continuous of those labours to which I have alluded. The mission in Alcester Street, its church and schools, were the first work of the Birmingham Oratory. After several years of close and hard work, and a considerable call upon the private resources of the Fathers who had established this congregation, it was delivered over to other hands, and the Fathers removed to the district of Edgbaston, where up to that time nothing Catholic had appeared. Then arose under your direction the large convent of the Oratory, the church expanded by degrees into its present capaciousness, a numerous congregation has gathered and grown in it; poor schools and other pious institutions have grown up in connexion with it, and, moreover, equally at your expense and that of your brethren, and, as I have reason to know, at much inconvenience, the Oratory has relieved the other clergy of Birmingham all this while by constantly doing the duty in the poor-house and gaol of Birmingham.

'More recently still, the mission and the poor school at Smethwick owe their existence to the Oratory. And all this while the founder and father of these religious works has added to his other solicitudes the toil of frequent preaching, of attendance in the confessional, and other parochial duties.

'I have read on this day of its publication the seventh part of the Apologia, and the touching allusion in it to the devotedness of the Catholic clergy to the poor in seasons of pestilence reminds me that when the cholera raged so dreadfully at Bilston, and the two priests of the town were no longer equal to the number of cases to which they were hurried day and night, I asked you to lend me two fathers to supply the place of other priests whom I wished to send as a further aid. But you and Father St. John preferred to take the place of danger which I had destined for others, and remained at Bilston till the worst was over.

'The fourth work which I would notice is one more widely known. I refer to the school for the education of the higher classes, which at the solicitation of many friends you have founded and attached to the Oratory. Surely after reading this bare enumeration of work done, no man will venture to say that Dr. Newman is leading a comparatively inactive life in the service of the Church.

'To spare, my dear Dr. Newman, any further pressure on those feelings with which I have already taken so large a liberty, I will only add one word more for my own satisfaction. During our long intercourse there is only one subject on which, after the first experience, I have measured my words with some caution, and that has been where questions bearing on ecclesiastical duty have arisen. I found some little caution necessary, because you were always so prompt and ready to go even beyond the slightest intimation of my wish or desires.

'That God may bless you with health, life, and all the spiritual good which you desire, you and your brethren of the Oratory, is the earnest prayer now and often of,

'My dear Dr. Newman,

'Your affectionate friend and faithful servant

in Christ,

'+ W. B. ULLATHORNE.'

LETTERS OF APPROBATION AND ENCOURAGEMENT
FROM CLERGY AND LAITY

I T requires some words of explanation why I allow myself to sound my own praises so loudly, as I am doing by adding to my Volume the following Letters, written to me last year by large bodies of my Catholic brethren, Priests, and Laymen, in the course or on the conclusion of the publication of my Apologia. I have two reasons for doing so.   5

1. It seems hardly respectful to them, and hardly fair to myself, to practise self-denial in a matter, which after all belongs to others as well as to me. Bodies of men become authorities by the fact of being bodies, over and above the personal claims of the individuals who constitute them. To have received such unusual Testimonials in my favour, as I   10 have to produce, and then to have let both those Testimonials and the generous feelings which dictated them be wasted, and come to nought, would have been a rudeness of which I could not bear to be guilty. Far be it from me to show such ingratitude to those who were especially 'friends in need'. I am too proud of their approbation not to publish it to the world.   15

2. But I have a further reason. The belief obtains extensively in the country at large, that Catholics, and especially the Priesthood, disavow the mode and form, in which I am accustomed to teach the Catholic faith, as if they were not generally recognized, but something special and peculiar to myself; as if, whether for the purposes of controversy,   20 or from the traditions of an earlier period of my life, I did not exhibit Catholicism pure and simple, as the bulk of its professors manifest it. Such testimonials, then, as now follow, from as many as 558 priests, that is, not far from half of the clergy of England, secular and religious, from the Bishop and clergy of a diocese at the Antipodes, and from so   25 great and authoritative a body as the German Congress assembled last year at Würzburg, scatter to the winds a suspicion, which it is not less painful, I am persuaded, to numbers of those Protestants who entertain it, than it is injurious to me who have to bear it.

I. THE DIOCESE OF WESTMINSTER

The following Address was signed by 110 of the Westminster clergy,   30 including all the Canons, the Vicars General, a great number of secular priests, and five Doctors in theology; Fathers of the Society of

11 let both those Testimonials and] suffered the honours conferred on me, and 65   12 them be wasted, and come] them, to be wasted, and to come 65

Jesus, Fathers of the Order of St. Dominic, of St. Francis, of the Oratory, of the Passion, of Charity, Oblates of St. Charles, and Marists.

'London, March 15, 1864.

'Very Reverend and Dear Sir,

'We, the undersigned Priests of the Diocese of Westminster, tender to you our respectful thanks for the service you have done to religion, as well as to the interests of literary morality, by your Reply to the calumnies of [a popular writer of the day.]

'We cannot but regard it as a matter of congratulation that your assailant should have associated the cause of the Catholic Priesthood with the name of one so well fitted to represent its dignity, and to defend its honour, as yourself.

'We recognize in this latest effort of your literary power one further claim, besides the many you have already established, to the gratitude and veneration of Catholics, and trust that the reception which it has met with on all sides may be the omen of new successes which you are destined to achieve in the vindication of the teaching and principles of the Church.

'We are,
'Very Reverend and Dear Sir,
'Your faithful and affectionate Servants in Christ.'
(The Subscriptions follow.)

'To the Very Rev.
'John Henry Newman, D.D.'

II. THE ACADEMIA OF CATHOLIC RELIGION

'London, April 19, 1864.

'Very Rev. and Dear Sir,

'The Academia of Catholic Religion, at their meeting held to-day, under the Presidency of the Cardinal Archbishop, have instructed us to write to you in their behalf.

'As they have learned, with great satisfaction, that it is your intention to publish a defence of Catholic Veracity, which has been assailed in your person, they are precluded from asking you that that defence might be made by word of mouth, and in London, as they would otherwise have done.

'Composed, as the Academia is, mainly of Laymen, they feel that it is not out of their province to express their indignation that your opponent should have chosen, while praising the Catholic Laity, to do so at the expense of the Clergy, between whom and themselves, in this as in all other matters, there exists a perfect identity of principle and practice.

'It is because, in such a matter, your cause is the cause of all Catholics, that we congratulate ourselves on the rashness of the opponent that has thrown the defence of that cause into your hands.

'We remain,
'Very Reverend and Dear Sir,
'Your very faithful Servants,
'JAMES LAIRD PATTERSON,⎱ *Secretaries*
'EDW. LUCAS,⎰

'To the Very Rev. John Henry Newman, D.D.,
'Provost of the Birmingham Oratory.'

The above was moved at the meeting by Lord PETRE, and seconded by the Hon. CHARLES LANGDALE.

III. THE DIOCESE OF BIRMINGHAM

In this Diocese there were in 1864, according to the Directory of the year, 136 Priests.

'June 1, 1864.

'Very Reverend and Dear Sir,

'In availing ourselves of your presence at the Diocesan Synod to offer you our hearty thanks for your recent vindication of the honour of the Catholic Priesthood, We, the Provost and Chapter of the Cathedral, and the Clergy, Secular and Regular, of the Diocese of Birmingham, cannot forego the assertion of a special right, as your neighbours and colleagues, to express our veneration and affection for one whose fidelity to the dictates of conscience, in the use of the highest intellectual gifts, has won even from opponents unbounded admiration and respect.

'To most of us you are personally known. Of some, indeed, you were, in years long past, the trusted guide, to whom they owe more than can be expressed in words; and all are conscious that the ingenuous fulness of your answer to a false and unprovoked accusation, has intensified their interest in the labours and trials of your life. While, then, we resent the indignity to which you have been exposed, and lament the pain and annoyance which the manifestation of yourself must have cost you, we cannot but rejoice that, in the fulfilment of a duty, you have allowed neither the unworthiness of your assailant to shield him from rebuke, nor the sacredness of your inmost motives to deprive that rebuke of the only form which could at once complete his discomfiture, free your own name from the obloquy which prejudice had cast upon it, and afford invaluable aid to honest seekers after Truth.

'Great as is the work which you have already done, Very Reverend Sir, permit us to express a hope that a greater yet remains for you to accomplish. In an age and in a country in which the very foundations of religious faith are exposed to assault, we rejoice in numbering among our brethren one so well qualified by learning and experience to defend that priceless deposit of Truth, in obtaining which you have counted as gain the loss of all things most dear and precious. And we esteem ourselves happy in being able to offer you that support and encouragement which the assurance of our unfeigned admiration and regard may be able to give you under your present trials and future labours.

'That you may long have strength to labour for the Church of God and the glory of His Holy Name is, Very Reverend and Dear Sir, our heartfelt and united prayer.'

(The Subscriptions follow.)

'To the Very Rev. John Henry Newman, D.D.'

IV. THE DIOCESE OF BEVERLEY

The following Address, as is stated in the first paragraph, comes from more than 70 Priests:—

'Hull, May 9, 1864.

'Very Rev. and Dear Dr. Newman,

'At a recent meeting of the clergy of the Diocese of Beverley, held in York, at which upwards of seventy priests were present, special attention was called to your correspondence with [a popular writer]; and such was the enthusiasm with which your name was received—such was the admiration expressed of the dignity with which you had asserted the claims of the Catholic Priesthood in England to be treated with becoming courtesy and respect—and such was the strong and all-pervading sense of the invaluable service which you had thus rendered, not only to faith and morals, but to good manners so far as regarded religious controversy in this country, that I was requested, as Chairman, to become the voice of the meeting, and to express to you as strongly and as earnestly as I could, how heartily the whole of the clergy of this diocese desire to thank you for services to religion as well-timed as they are in themselves above and beyond all commendation, services which the Catholics of England will never cease to hold in most grateful remembrance. God, in His infinite wisdom and great mercy, has raised you up to stand prominently forth in the glorious work of re-establishing in this country the holy faith which in good old times shed such lustre upon it. We all lament that, in the order of nature, you have so few years before you in which to fight against false teaching that good fight in which you have been so victoriously engaged of late. But our prayers are that you may long be spared, and may possess to the last all your vigour, and all that zeal for the advancement of our holy faith, which imparts such a charm to the productions of your pen.

'I esteem it a great honour and a great privilege to have been deputed, as the representative of the clergy of the Diocese of Beverley, to tender you the fullest expression of our most grateful thanks, and the assurance of our prayers for your health and eternal happiness.

'I am,

'Very Rev. and Dear Sir,

'With sentiments of profound respect,

'Yours most faithfully in Christ,

'M. TRAPPES.

'The Very Rev. Dr. Newman.'

V. AND VI. THE DIOCESES OF LIVERPOOL AND SALFORD

The Secular Clergy of Liverpool amounted in 1864 to 103, and of Salford to 76.

'Preston, July 27, 1864.

'Very Rev. and Dear Sir,

'It may seem, perhaps, that the Clergy of Lancashire have been slow to address you; but it would be incorrect to suppose that they have been indifferent spectators of the conflict in which you have been recently engaged. This is the first opportunity that has presented itself, and they gladly avail themselves of their annual meeting in Preston to tender to you the united expression of their heartfelt sympathy and gratitude.

'The atrocious imputation, out of which the late controversy arose, was felt as a personal affront by them, one and all, conscious as they were, that it was mainly owing to your position as a distinguished Catholic ecclesiastic, that the charge was connected with your name.

'While they regret the pain you must needs have suffered, they cannot help rejoicing that it has afforded you an opportunity of rendering a new and most important service to their holy religion. Writers, who are not overscrupulous about the truth themselves, have long used the charge of untruthfulness as an ever ready weapon against the Catholic Clergy. Partly from the frequent repetition of this charge, partly from a consciousness that, instead of under-valuing the truth, they have ever prized it above every earthly treasure, partly, too, from the difficulty of obtaining a hearing in their own defence, they have generally passed it by in silence. They thank you for coming forward as their champion: your own character required no vindication. It was their battle more than your own that you fought. They know and feel how much pain it has caused you to bring so prominently forward your own life and motives, but they now congratulate you on the completeness of your triumph, as admitted alike by friend and enemy.

'In addition to answering the original accusation, you have placed them under a new obligation, by giving to all, who read the English language, a work which, for literary ability and the lucid exposition of many difficult and abstruse points, forms an invaluable contribution to our literature.

'They fervently pray that God may give you health and length of days, and, if it please Him, some other cause in which to use for His glory the great powers bestowed upon you.

'Signed on behalf of the Meeting,
'THOS. PROVOST COOKSON.

'The Very Rev. J. H. Newman.'

VII. THE DIOCESE OF HEXHAM

The Secular Priests on Mission in 1864 in this Diocese were 64.

'Durham, Sept. 22, 1864.

'My Dear Dr. Newman,

'At the annual meeting of the Clergy of the Diocese of Hexham and Newcastle, held a few days ago at Newcastle-upon-Tyne, I was commissioned by them to express to you their sincere sympathy, on account of the slanderous accusations, to which you have been so unjustly exposed. We are fully aware that these foul calumnies were intended to injure the character of the whole body of the Catholic Clergy, and that your distinguished name was singled out, in order that they might be more effectually propagated. It is well that these poisonous shafts were thus aimed, as no one could more triumphantly repel them. The "Apologia pro Vitâ suâ" will, if possible, render still more illustrious the name of its gifted author, and be a lasting monument of the victory of truth, and the signal overthrow of an arrogant and reckless assailant.

'It may appear late for us now to ask to join in your triumph, but as the Annual Meeting of the Northern Clergy does not take place till this time, it is the first occasion offered us to present our united congratulations, and to declare to you, that by none of your brethren are you more esteemed and venerated, than by the Clergy of the Diocese of Hexham and Newcastle.

'Wishing that Almighty God may prolong your life many more years for the defence of our holy religion and the honour of your brethren,

'I am, dear Dr. Newman,

'Yours sincerely in Jesus Christ,

'RALPH PROVOST PLATT, V. G.

The Very Rev. J. H. Newman.'

VIII. THE CONGRESS OF WÜRZBURG

'September 15, 1864.

'Sir,

'The undersigned, President of the Catholic Congress of Germany assembled in Würzburg, has been commissioned to express to you, Very Rev. and Dear Sir, its deep-felt gratitude for your late able defence of the Catholic Clergy, not only of England, but of the whole world, against the attacks of its enemies.

'The Catholics of Germany unite with the Catholics of England in testifying to you their profound admiration and sympathy, and pray that the Almighty may long preserve your valuable life.

'The above Resolution was voted by the Congress with acclamation.

'Accept, very Rev. and Dear Sir, the expression of the high consideration with which I am

'Your most obedient servant,

'(Signed) ERNEST BARON MOIJ DE SONS.

'The Very Rev. J. H. Newman.'

IX. THE DIOCESE OF HOBART TOWN

'Hobart Town, Tasmania, November 22, 1864.

'Very Rev. and Dear Sir,

'By the last month's post we at length received your admirable book, entitled, "Apologia pro Vitâ suâ", and the pamphlet, "What then does Dr. Newman mean?"

'By this month's mail, we wish to express our heartfelt gratification and delight for being possessed of a work so triumphant in maintaining truth, and so overwhelming in confounding arrogance and error, as the "Apologia".

'No doubt, your adversary, resting on the deep-seated prejudice of our fellow-countrymen in the United Kingdom, calculated upon establishing his own fame as a keen-sighted polemic, as a shrewd and truth-loving man, upon the fallen reputation of one, who, as he would demonstrate,—yes, that he would,—set little or no value on truth, and who, therefore, would deservedly sink into obscurity, henceforward rejected and despised!

'Aman of old erected a gibbet at the gate of the city, on which an unsuspecting and an unoffending man, one marked as a victim, was to be exposed to the gaze and derision of the people, in order that his own dignity and fame might be exalted; but a divine Providence ordained otherwise. The history of the judgment that fell upon Aman, has been recorded in Holy Writ, it is to be presumed, as a warning to vain and unscrupulous men, even in our days. There can be no doubt, a moral gibbet, full "fifty cubits high", had been prepared some time, on which you were to be exposed, for the pity at least, if not for the scorn and derision of so many, who had loved and venerated you through life!

'But the effort made in the forty-eight pages of the redoubtable pamphlet, "What then does Dr. Newman Mean?"—the production of a bold, unscrupulous man, with a coarse mind, and regardless of inflicting pain on the feelings of another, has failed,—marvellously failed,—and he himself is now exhibited not only in our fatherland, but even at the Antipodes, in fact wherever the English language is spoken or read, as a shallow pretender, one quite incompetent to treat of matters of such undying interest as those he presumed to interfere with.

'We fervently pray the Almighty, that you may be spared to His Church for many years to come,—that to Him alone the glory of this noble work may be given,—and to you the reward in eternal bliss!

'And from this distant land we beg to convey to you, Very Rev. and Dear Sir, the sentiments of our affectionate respect, and deep veneration.'

(The Subscriptions follow, of the Bishop Vicar-General
and eighteen Clergy.)

'The Very Rev. Dr. Newman,
&c. &c. &c.'

ADDITIONAL NOTES

NOTE ON PAGE 24

CORRESPONDENCE WITH ARCHBISHOP WHATELY
IN 1834

ON application of the Editor of Dr. Whately's Correspondence, the following four letters were sent to her for publication: they are here given entire. It will be observed that they are of the same date as my letter to Dr. Hampden at p. 61.

I

'Dublin, October 25, 1834.

'My dear Newman,

'A most shocking report concerning you has reached me, which indeed carries such an improbability on the face of it that you may perhaps wonder at my giving it a thought; and at first I did not, but finding it repeated from different quarters, it seems to me worth contradicting for the sake of your character. Some Oxford undergraduates, I find, openly report that when I was at Oriel last spring you absented yourself from chapel on purpose to avoid receiving the Communion along with me; and that you yourself declared this to be the case.

'I would not notice every idle rumour; but this has been so confidently and so long asserted that it would be a satisfaction to me to be able to declare its falsity as a fact, from your authority. I did indeed at once declare my utter unbelief; but then this has only the weight of my opinion; though an opinion resting I think on no insufficient grounds. I did not profess to rest my disbelief on our long, intimate, and confidential friendship, which would make it your right and your duty—if I did any thing to offend you or any thing you might think materially wrong—to remonstrate with me;—but on your general character; which I was persuaded would have made you incapable, even had no such close connexion existed between us, of conduct so unchristian and inhuman. But, as I said, I should like for your sake to be able to contradict the report from your own authority.

'Ever yours very truly,

'R. WHATELY.'

2

'Oriel College, October 28, 1834.

'My dear Lord,

'My absence from the Sacrament in the College Chapel on the Sunday you were in Oxford, was occasioned solely and altogether by my having it on that day in St. Mary's; and I am pretty sure, if I may trust my memory, that I did not even know of your Grace's presence there, till after the Service. Most certainly such knowledge would not have affected my attendance. I need not say, this being the case, that the report of my having made any statement on the subject is quite unfounded; indeed, your letter of this morning is the first information I have had in any shape of the existence of the report.

'I am happy in being thus able to afford an explanation as satisfactory to you, as the kind feelings which you have ever entertained towards me could desire;—yet, on honest reflection, I cannot conceal from myself, that it was generally a relief to me, to see so little of your Grace, when you were at Oxford: and it is a greater relief now to have an opportunity of saying so to yourself. I have ever wished to observe the rule, never to make a public charge against another behind his back, and, though in the course of conversation and the urgency of accidental occurrences it is sometimes difficult to keep to it, yet I trust I have not broken it, especially in your own case: i.e. though my most intimate friends know how deeply I deplore the line of ecclesiastical policy adopted under your archiepiscopal sanction, and though in society I may have clearly shown that I have an opinion one way rather than the other, yet I have never in my intention, never (as I believe) at all, spoken of your Grace in a serious way before strangers;—indeed mixing very little in general society, and not overapt to open myself in it, I have had little temptation to do so. Least of all should I so forget myself as to take undergraduates into my confidence in such a matter.

'I wish I could convey to your Grace the mixed and very painful feelings, which the late history of the Irish Church has raised in me:—the union of her members with men of heterodox views, and the extinction (without ecclesiastical sanction) of half her Candlesticks, the witnesses and guarantees of the Truth and trustees of the Covenant. I willingly own that both in my secret judgment and my mode of speaking concerning you to my friends, I have had great alternations and changes of feeling,—defending, then blaming your policy, next praising your own self and protesting against your measures, according as the affectionate remembrances which I had of you rose against my utter aversion of the secular and unbelieving policy in which I considered the Irish Church to be implicated. I trust I shall never be forgetful of the kindness you uniformly showed me during your residence in Oxford: and anxiously hope that no duty to Christ and His Church may ever interfere with the expression of my sense of it. However, on the present opportunity, I am conscious to myself, that I am acting according to the dictates both of duty and gratitude, if I beg your leave to state my persuasion, that the perilous measures in which your Grace has acquiesced are but the legitimate offspring of those principles, difficult to describe in few words, with which your reputation is especially associated; principles which bear upon the very fundamentals of all argument and investigation, and affect almost every doctrine and every maxim by which our faith or our conduct is to be guided. I can feel no reluctance to confess, that, when I first was noticed by your Grace, gratitude to you and admiration of your powers wrought upon me; and, had not something from within resisted, I should certainly have adopted views on religious and social duty, which seem to my present judgment to be based in the pride of reason and to tend towards infidelity, and which in your own case nothing but your Grace's high religious temper and the unclouded faith of early piety has been able to withstand.

'I am quite confident, that, however you may regard this judgment, you will give me credit, not only for honesty, but for a deeper feeling in thus laying it before you.

'May I be suffered to add, that your name is ever mentioned in my prayers, and to subscribe myself

'Your Grace's very sincere friend and servant,

'J. H. NEWMAN.'

3

'Dublin, November 3, 1834.

'My dear Newman,

'I cannot forbear writing again to express the great satisfaction I feel in the course I adopted; which has, eventually, enabled me to contradict a report which was more prevalent and more confidently upheld than I could have thought possible: and which, while it was perhaps likely to hurt my character with some persons, was injurious to yours in the eyes of the best men. For what idea must any one have had of religion—or at least of your religion—who was led to think there was any truth in the imputation to you of such uncharitable arrogance!

'But it is a rule with me, not to cherish, even on the strongest assertions, any belief or even suspicion, to the prejudice of any one whom I have any reason to think well of, till I have carefully inquired, and dispassionately heard both sides. And I think if others were to adopt the same rule, I should not myself be quite so much abused as I have been.

'I am well aware indeed that one cannot expect all, even good men, to think alike on every point, even after they shall have heard both sides; and that we may expect many to judge, after all, very harshly of those who do differ from them: for, God help us! what will become of men if they receive no more mercy than they show to each other! But at least, if the rule were observed, men would not condemn a brother on mere vague popular rumour, about principles (as in my case) "difficult to describe in few words", and with which his "reputation is associated". My own reputation I know is associated, to a very great degree, with what are in fact calumnious imputations, originated in exaggerated, distorted, or absolutely false statements, for which even those who circulate them, do not, for the most part, pretend to have any ground except popular rumour: like the Jews at Rome; "as for this way, we know that it is every where spoken against".

'For I have ascertained that a very large proportion of those who join in the outcry against my works, confess, or even boast, that they have never read them. And in respect of the measure you advert to—the Church Temporalities Act—(which of course I shall not now discuss), it is curious to see how many of those who load me with censure for acquiescing in it, receive with open arms, and laud to the skies, the Primate; who was consulted on the measure—as was natural, considering his knowledge of Irish affairs, and his influence—long before me; and gave his consent to it; differing from Ministers only on a point of detail, whether the revenues of six Sees, or of ten, should be alienated.

'Of course, every one is bound ultimately to decide according to his own judgment; nor do I mean to shelter myself under his example: but only to point out what strange notions of justice those have, who acquit with applause the leader, and condemn the follower in the same individual transaction.

'Far be it from any servant of our Master, to feel surprise or anger at being thus treated: it is only an admonition to me to avoid treating others in a similar manner; and not to "judge another's servant", at least without a fair hearing.

'You do me no more than justice, in feeling confident that I shall give you credit both for "honesty and for a deeper feeling" in freely laying your opinions before me: and besides this, you might have been no less confident, from your own experience, that, long since—whenever it was that you changed your judgment respecting me—if you had freely and calmly remonstrated with me on any point where you thought me going wrong, I should have listened to you with that readiness and candour and deference, which as you well know, I always showed, in the times when "we took sweet counsel together, and walked in the house of God as friends";—when we consulted together about so many practical measures, and about almost all the principal points in my publications.

'I happen to have before me a letter from you just eight years ago, in which, after saying that "there are few things you wish more sincerely than to be known as a friend of mine", and attributing to me, in the warmest and most flattering terms, a much greater share in the forming of your mind than I could presume to claim, you bear a testimony, in which I do most heartily concur, to the *freedom* at least of our *intercourse*, and the readiness and respect with which you were listened to. Your words are: "Much as I owe to Oriel in the way of mental improvement, to none, as I think, do I owe so much as to yourself. I know who it was first gave me heart to look about me after my election, and taught me to think correctly, and—strange office for an instructor—to rely upon myself. Nor can I forget that it has been at your kind suggestion, that I have since been led to employ myself in the consideration of several subjects, which I cannot doubt have been very beneficial to my mind."

'If in all this I was erroneous,—if I have misled you, or any one else, into "the pride of reason", or any other kind of pride,—or if I have entertained, or led others into, any wrong opinions, I can only say I sincerely regret it. And again I rejoice if I have been the means of contributing to form in any one that "high religious temper and unclouded faith" of which I not only believe, with you, that they are able to withstand tendencies towards infidelity, but also, that *without* them, no correctness of abstract opinions is worth much. But what I meant to point out, is, that there was plainly nothing to preclude you from offering friendly admonition (when your view of my principles changed), with a full confidence of being at least patiently and kindly listened to.

'I for my part could not bring myself to find relief in escaping the society of an old friend,—with whom I had been accustomed to frank discussion,—on account of my differing from him as to certain principles, whether through a change of *his* views, or (much more) of *my own*,—till at least I had made full trial of private and affectionate remonstrance and free discussion. Even a "man that is a heretic", we are told, even a ruler of a Church is not to reject, till after repeated admonitions.

'But though your regard for me does not show itself such as I think mine would have been under similar circumstances, I will not therefore reject what remains of it. Let us pray for each other that it may please God to enlighten whichever of us is, on any point, in error, and recall him to the truth; and that at any rate we may hold fast that charity, without which all knowledge, and all faith, that could remove mountains, will profit us nothing.

'I fear you will read with a jaundiced eye,—if you venture to read it at all —any publication of mine; but "for auld lang syne" I take advantage of a frank to enclose you my last two addresses to my clergy.

'Very sincerely yours,

'Rd. WHATELY.'

4

'Oriel, November 11, 1834.

'My dear Lord,

'The remarks contained in your last letter do not come upon me by surprise, and I can only wish that I may be as able to explain myself to you, as I do with a clear and honest conscience to myself. Your Grace will observe that the letter of mine from which you make an extract, was written when I *was* in habits of intimacy with you, in which I have not been of late years. It does not at all follow, because I could then speak freely to you, that I might at another time. Opportunity is the chief thing in such an office as delivering to a superior an opinion about himself. Though I never concealed my opinion from you, I have never been forward. I have spoken when place and time admitted, when my opinion was asked, when I was called to your side and was made your counsellor. No such favourable circumstances have befallen me of late years,—if I must now state in explanation what in truth has never occurred to me in *this fulness*, till now I am called to reflect upon my own conduct and to account for an apparent omission. I have spoken the first opportunity you have given me; and I am persuaded good very seldom comes of *volunteering* a remonstrance.

'Again, I cannot doubt for an instant that you have long been aware in a measure that my opinions differed from your Grace's. You knew it when at Oxford, for you often found me differing from you. You must have felt it, at the time you left Oxford for Dublin. You must have known it from hearsay in consequence of the book I have published. What indeed can account for my want of opportunities to speak to you freely my mind, but the feeling on your part, (which, if existing, is nothing but a fair reason,) that my views are different from yours?

'And that difference is certainly of no recent date. I tacitly allude to it in the very letter you quote—in which, I recollect well that the words "strange office for an instructor,—*to rely upon myself*", were intended to convey to you that, much as I valued (and still value) your great kindness and the advantage of your countenance to me at that time, yet even then I did not fall in with the line of opinions which you had adopted. In them I never acquiesced. Doubtless I may have used at times sentiments and expressions, which I should not now use; but I believe these had no root in my mind, and as such they were mere idle words which I ought ever to be ashamed of, because they *were* idle. But the opinions to which I especially alluded in my former letter as associated by the world with your Grace's name under the title of "Liberal", (but not, as you suppose, received by me on the world's authority,) are those which may be briefly described as the Anti-superstition notions; and to these I do not recollect ever assenting. Connected with these I would instance the undervaluing of Antiquity, and resting on one's own reasonings, judgments, definitions, &c., rather than authority and precedent; and I think I gave very little in to this;—for a very short time too (if at all), in to the notion that the State, as such, had nothing to do with religion. On the other hand, whatever I held then deliberately, I believe I hold now; though perhaps I may not consider them as points of such prominent importance, or with precisely the same bearing as I did then:—as the abolition of the Jewish Sabbath, the unscripturalness of the doctrine of imputed righteousness (i.e. our Lord's active obedience)—the mistakes of the so-called Evangelical system, the independence of the Church; the genius of the Gospel as a Law of Liberty, and the impropriety of forming geological theories from Scripture. Of course every one changes in opinion between twenty and thirty; doubtless, I have changed; yet I am not conscious that I have so much *changed*, as made up my mind on points on which I had no opinion. E.g. I had no opinion about the Catholic Question till 1829. No one can truly say I was ever *for* the Catholics; but I was not against them. In fact I did not enter into the state of the question at all.

'Then as to my change of judgment as to the character of your Grace's opinions, it is natural that, when two persons pursue different lines from the same point, they should not discover their divergence for a long while; especially if there be any kind feeling in the one towards the other. It was not for a very long time that I discovered that your opinions were (as I now think them) but part of intellectual views, so different from your own inward mind and character, so peculiar in themselves, and (if you will let me add) so dangerous. For a long time I thought them to be but different; for a longer, to be but in parts dangerous; but their full character in this respect came on me almost on a sudden. I heard at Naples the project of destroying the Irish Sees, and at first indignantly rejected the notion, which some one suggested, that your Grace had acquiesced in it. I thought I recollected correctly your Grace's opinion of the inherent rights of the Christian Church, and I thought you never would allow men of this world so to insult it. When I returned to England, all was over. I was silent on the same principle that you are silent about it in your letter; that it was not the time for speaking; and I only felt, what I hinted at when I wrote last, a bitter grief, which prompted me, when the act was irretrievable, to hide myself from you. However, I have spoken, with whatever pain to myself, the first opportunity you have given me.

'I might appeal to my conscience without fear in proof of the delight it would give me at this time to associate my name with yours, and to stand forward as your friend and defender, however humble. I should hope you know me enough to be sure, that, however great my faults are, I have no fear of man such as to restrain me, if I could feel I had a call that way. But may God help me, as I will ever strive to fulfil my first duty, the defence of His Church, and of the doctrine of the old Fathers, in opposition to all the innovations and profanities which are rising round us.

'My dear Lord,

'Ever yours most sincerely and gratefully,

'J. H. NEWMAN.

'P.S. I feel much obliged by your kindness in sending me your Addresses to your clergy, which I value highly for your Grace's sake.'

NOTE ON PAGE 89

EXTRACT OF A LETTER FROM THE REV. E. SMEDLEY, EDITOR OF THE 'ENCYCLOPÆDIA METROPOLITANA'

WHEN I urged on one occasion an 'understanding' I had had with the publishers of the 'Encyclopædia', he answered, June 5, 1828, 'I greatly dislike the word "understanding", which is always *misunderstood*, and which occasions more mischief than any other in our language, unless it be its cousin-german "delicacy".'

NOTE ON PAGE 169

EXTRACT OF A LETTER OF THE LATE REV. FRANCIS A. FABER, OF SAUNDERTON

A LETTER of Mr. F. Faber's to a friend has just now (March, 1878) come into my hands, in which he says, 'I have had a long correspondence with Newman on the subject of my uncle's saying he was "a concealed Roman Catholic" long before he left us. It ends in my uncle making an *amende*.'

NOTE ON PAGES 176-8

I HAVE said above, 'Dr. Russell had, perhaps, more to do with my conversion than any one else. He called on me in passing through Oxford in the summer of 1843; and I think I took him over some of the buildings of the University. He called again another summer, on his way from Dublin to London. I do not recollect that he said a word on the subject of religion on either occasion. He sent me at different times several letters. . . . He also gave me one or two books; Veron's Rule of Faith and some Treatises of the Wallenburghs was one; a volume of St. Alfonso Liguori's sermons was another. . . . At a later date Dr. Russell sent me a large bundle of penny or halfpenny books of devotion', &c.

On this passage I observe first that he told me, on one occasion of my seeing him since the publication of the 'Apologia', that I was so far in error, that he had called on me at Oxford once only, not twice. He was quite positive on the point; it was when he was, I believe, on his way to Rome to escape a bishopric.

Secondly, my own mistake has led to some vagueness or inaccuracy in the statements made by others. In a friendly notice of Dr. Russell upon his death, it is said, in the 'Times':—

'Personally he was unknown to the leaders of the movement, but his reputation stood high in Oxford. He was often applied to for information and suggestion on the points arising in the Tractarian controversy. Through a formal call made by him on Dr. Newman a correspondence arose, which resulted in the final determination of the latter to join the Roman Catholic Church.'

On this I remark—(1) that in 1841-5, Dr. Russell was not well known in Oxford, and it cannot be said that then 'his reputation stood high' there; (2) that he never was 'applied to for information' by any one of us, as far as my knowledge goes; and (3) that his call on me in 1841(3?) was in no sense 'formal'; I had not expected it; I think he introduced himself, though he may have had a letter from Dr. Wiseman; and no 'correspondence' arose in consequence. He may perhaps have sent me three letters, independent of each other, in five years; and, as far as I know, he was unaware of his part in my conversion, till he saw my notice of it in the 'Apologia'.

NOTE ON PAGE 209

EXTRACT OF A LETTER FROM THE REV. JOHN KEBLE TO THE AUTHOR

'Nov. 18, 1844.—I hope I shall not annoy you if I copy out for you part of a letter which I had the other day from Judge Coleridge:—

'"I was struck with part of a letter from A. B., expressing a wish that Newman should know how warmly he was loved, honoured, and sympathized with by large numbers of Churchmen, so that he might not feel solitary, or, as it were, cast out. What think you of a private address, carefully guarded against the appearance of making him the head of a party, but only assuring him of gratitude, veneration, and love?" &c., &c.

'I thought I would just let you understand how such a person as Coleridge feels.'

NOTE ON PAGE 213

EXTRACT FROM THE 'TIMES' NEWSPAPER ON THE AUTHOR'S VISIT TO OXFORD IN FEBRUARY, 1878

'THE Very Rev. Dr. Newman has this week revisited Oxford for the first time since 1845. He has been staying with the Rev. S. Wayte, President of Trinity College, of which society Dr. Newman was formerly a scholar, and has recently been elected an Honorary Fellow. On Tuesday evening Dr. Newman met a number of old friends at dinner at the President's lodgings, and on the following day he paid a long visit to Dr. Pusey at Christ Church. He also spent a considerable time at Keble College, in which he was greatly interested. In the evening Dr. Newman dined in Trinity College Hall at the high table, attired in his academical dress, and the scholars were invited to meet him afterwards. He returned to Birmingham on Thursday morning.'

NOTE ON PAGE 265

THE MEDICINAL OIL OF ST. WALBURGA

I HAVE received the following on the subject of the oil of St. Walburga from a German friend, the Rev. Corbinian Wandinger, which is a serviceable addition to what is said upon it in Note B. He says:—

'In your "Apologia", 2nd Edition, p. 302, you say you neither have, nor ever have had, the means of going into the question of the miraculousness of the oil of St. Walburga. By good chance, there has arisen a contest not long ago between two papers, a catholic and a free-thinking one, about this very question, from which I collected materials. Afterwards I asked Professor Suttner, of Eichstädt, if the defender of the miraculousness might be fully and in every point trusted, and I was answered he might, since he was nobody else but the parson of St. Walburga, Rev. Mr. Brudlacher.

'You know all the older literature of the oil of St. Walburga, therefore I restrict myself to statements of a later date than 1625.

'First of the attempts to explain the oil as a natural produce of the rock.

'Some thought of ordinary rock-oil. But the slightest experiment proves that origin, properties, and effect of the oil of St. Walburga and petroleum have nothing common with each other.

'Others thought of a salt-rock, and of solution of the salt particles. But the marble slab from which the oil drops is of Jura-chalk, and in the whole Jura is not a single particle of salt to be found, and the liquor itself does not in the least savour of salt; besides that, if this were the case, the stone must have crumbled into pieces long since, whilst it is quite massive still.

'Others thought of humour in the air, or the so-called sweating of the stones. But why does the slab which bears the holy relics alone sweat? and, why do all others beside, above, beneath it, in and out of the altar-cave, though being of the same nature, remain perfectly dry? Why should it sweat, the whole church being so dry that not a single humid spot of a hand's breadth is visible? Why does this slab not sweat except within a certain period, that is from October 12, the anniversary of depositing, to February 25, the day of the death of St. Walburga? And why does it remain dry at every other time, even at the most humid temperature of the air possible, and in the wettest years, for instance, 1866? Besides, what other stone, and be it in the deepest cave, will sweat during four or five months a quantity of liquor from six to ten Mass (a Mass = 1·07 French Litres)? If these naturalists are asked all this, then they, too, are at the end of their wits.

'To this point I add two facts which may be proved beyond any doubt; the one by unquestionable historical records, the other by still living eye-witnesses. When under Bishop Friedrich von Parsberg the interdict was inflicted on the city of Eichstädt, during all the year 1239 not a single drop of liquor became visible on the coffin-plate of St. Walburga. The contrary fact was stated on June 7, 1835. The cave was opened on this day by chance, passengers longing to see it. To their astonishment they found the stone so profusely dropping with oil, that the golden vase fixed underneath was full to the brim, whereas at this season never had been observed there any fluid. Some weeks later arrived the long-wished-for royal decree which sanctioned the reopening of the convent of St. Walburga; it was signed on that very 7th of June, 1835, by his Majesty King Louis I.

'Moreover, let one try to gather water which is dropping from sweating stone, or glass, or metal, and let him see if it will be pure and limpid, or rather muddy, filthy, and cloudy. The oil of St. Walburga on the contrary, is and remains so limpid and crystal, that a bottle, which had been filled and officially sealed at the reopening of the cave after the Swedish invasion, 1645, preserves to this day the oil so very clear and clean as if it had been filled yesterday; an occurrence never to be observed even on the purest spring-water, according to the testimony of the royal circuit-physician (K. Bezirk-sarz).

'To this testimony of a naturalist may be added that of a much higher authority. The renowned naturalist, Von Oken, surely an unquestionable expert, came one day, while he was Professor in the University of Munich, to Eichstädt on the special purpose to investigate this extraordinary phenomenon. The cave was opened to him, he received every information he wished for, and having seen and examined everything, he pronounced publicly without any reluctance that he could not explain the matter in a natural way. He took of the liquor to Munich in order to subject it to a chemical analysis, and declared then by writing the result of his researches to be that he could take it neither for natural water, nor oil, and that, in general, he was not able to explain the phenomenon as being in accordance with the laws of nature.

'Let me add the testimony of a historical authority. Mr. Sax, counsellor of the government (K. Regierungsrath), in his history of the diocese and city of Eichstädt, after he has spoken of the origin, the properties, and the effect of the oil of St. Walburga, concludes that "they are of such a singular kind, that they not only exceed far the province of extraordinary nature-phenomena, but that they, in spite of the constant discrediting and slandering by bullying free-thinkers, preserved the great confidence of the catholic people even in far distant countries.'

'Now of the miracles. There are related by the people many thousands, but, of course, few of them are attested. In the Pastoral paper of Eichstädt, 1857, page 207, I read that Anton Ernest, Bishop of Brünn, in Moravia, announces, under Nov. 1, 1857, to the Bishop of Eichstädt, the recovery of a girl in the establishment of the sisters of charity from blindness, and sends, in order to attest the fact, the following document, which I am to translate literally:—

'"In the name of the indivisible Trinity. We, Anton Ernest, by God's and the Holy See's grace, Bishop of Brünn. After we had received, first by the curate of the establishment of the Daughters of Christian Charity in this place, and then also from other quarters, the notice that a girl in the aforesaid establishment had regained the use of her eyes miraculously in the very moment when she had a vial, containing oil of St. Walburga, offered to her, brought to her mouth and kissed, we thought it to be our duty to research scrupulously into the fact, and to put it beyond all doubt in the way of a special commission, by hearing of witnesses and a trial at the place of the fact, if there be truth, and how much of it, in the supposed miraculous healing.

'"About the report of this commission and the adjoined testimony of the physician, we have then, as prescribes the Holy Council of Trent (Sess. 25), collected the judgments of our theologians and other pious men; and as these all were quite in accordance, and the fact itself with all its circumstances lay before us quite clear and open, we have, after invocation of assistance of the Holy Ghost, pronounced, judged, and decided as follows:—

'"The instantaneous removal of the most pertinacious eyelid-cramp (Augenlied-krampf), which Matilda Makara during many months had hindered in the use of her eyes and kept in blindness, and the simultaneous recurrence of the full eye-sight, phlogistic appearances still remaining in the eyes, which occurred when Matilda Makara on Nov. 7, 1856, had a vial with the oil of St. Walburga brought, full of confidence, to her mouth and kissed, must be acknowledged to be a fact which, besides the order of nature, has been effected by God's grace, and is therefore a miracle.

'"And that the memory of this Divine favour may be preserved, that to God eternal thanks may be given, the confidence of the faithful may be incited and nourished, this devotion to the great wonder-worker St. Walburga may be promoted, we order that this aforegoing decision shall be affixed in the chapel of the Daughters of Christian Charity in this place, that it shall be preserved for all times to come, and that the 7th Nov. shall be celebrated as a holiday every year in this aforesaid establishment.

'"Given in our Episcopal Residence at Brünn,

'"Nov. 1, 1857,

'"(L. S.)   ANTON ERNEST, Bishop."

'A second record about St. Walburga I find in the Eichstädt Pastoral paper, 1858, page 192, from which I take the following: "The Superioress of the Convent of St. Walburga had received in summer 1858 the notice of a miraculous cure written by the Superioress of the Convent of St. Leonard-sur-Mer, Sussex. At request for an authenticated report, John Bamber, chaplain of the Convent of the Holy Infant at St. Leonard-sur-Mer, wrote about the following: 'Sister Walburga had been ill fifteen months, of which five bedridden. The physician pronounced the malady to be incurable. Large exterior tumour, frequent (thrice or four times a day) vomitings were caused by the diseased pylorus. The matter was hopeless, when the Superioress on April 27 thought of using the oil of St. Walburga. The chaplain brought it on the tongue of the sick sister, and in the same moment she had a burning feeling which seemed to her to descend, and to affect especially the sick part. In a few minutes the inner smart ceased, the tumour fell off, she felt recovered. Next morning she rose, assisted at the holy mass, communicated, ate with good appetite. She was quite recovered, but somewhat feeble, as people always are after a great disease. The physician, a Protestant, abode by his opinion the malady to be incurable, acknowledged, however, the healing. His words were: "I believe the healing to be effected by the oil of St. Walburga, but how, I don't know." As a Protestant he refused to give testimony that the operation of the oil had been miraculous.'"

'The report is authenticated by Thomas, Bishop of Southwark.

'Freising, Bayern,
'September 13, 1873.'

NOTE ON PAGE 280

BONIFACE OF CANTERBURY

WHEN I made the above reference in 1865 to Boniface of Canterbury, I was sure I had seen among my books some recent authoritative declaration on the subject of his *cultus* in opposition to the Bollandists; but I did not know where to look for it. I have now found in our Library (Concess. Offic. t. 2) what was in my mind. It consists of five documents proceeding from the Sacred Congregation of Rites, with the following title:—

'Emo ac Revmo Domino Card. Lambruschini Relatore, Taurinen. Approbationis cultûs ab immemorabili tempore præstiti B. Bonifacio à Subaudiâ

Archiepiscopi Cantuarien. Instante serenissimo Rege Sardiniæ Carolo Alberto Romæ, 1838.'

Also Dr. Grant, Bishop of Southwark, has kindly supplied me with the following extract from the Correspondance de Rome, 24 November, 1851, adding 'St. Boniface of Canterbury or of Savoy was beatified *æquipollenter* by Gregory XVI.':—

'Le B. Boniface de Savoie, xi de ce nome, petit-fils d'Humbert iii, Archevêque de Cantorbéry. Confirmation de son culte, également à la demande du Roi Charles Albert, 7 Sept. 1838. D'abord moine parmi les Chartreux, puis Archevêque de Cantorbéry, consacré par Innocent IV. au Concile Général de Lyons; il occupa le siége 25 ans. Mort en 1270 pendant un voyage en Savoie. Son corps porté à Haucatacombe; concours des populations; miracles; son corps retrouvé intact trois siècles après sa mort. Son nom dans les livres liturgiques. Sa fête célébrée sans aucune interruption. Sur la relation de Card. Lambruschini, la S. C. des Rites le 1 Sept. 1838, décida qu'il constait de cas exceptionnel aux décrets d'Urbain VIII. p. 410.'

APPENDIX A

MR. KINGSLEY AND DR. NEWMAN

A CORRESPONDENCE ON THE QUESTION 'WHETHER
DR. NEWMAN TEACHES THAT TRUTH IS NO VIRTUE?'

ADVERTISEMENT

To prevent misconception, I think it necessary to observe,
that, in my Letters here published, I am far indeed from
implying any admission of the truth of Mr. Kingsley's
accusations against the Catholic Church, although I have
abstained from making any formal protest against them.
The object which led to my writing at all, has also led me,
in writing, to turn my thoughts in a different direction.

J. H. N.

January 31, 1864

CORRESPONDENCE, &c.

I

Extract from a Review of Froude's History of England, vols. vii. *and* viii., *in* Macmillan's Magazine *for January,* 1864, *signed* 'C. K.'

PAGES 216, 217

'THE Roman religion had, for some time past, been making men not better men, but worse. We must face, we must conceive honestly for ourselves, the deep demoralization which had been brought on in Europe by the dogma that the Pope of Rome had the power of creating right and wrong; that not only truth and falsehood, but morality and immorality, depended on his setting his seal to a bit of parchment. From the time that indulgences were hawked about in his name, which would insure pardon for any man, *"etsi matrem Dei violavisset"*, the world in general began to be of that opinion. But the mischief was older and deeper than those indulgences. It lay in the very notion of the dispensing power. A deed might be a crime, or no crime at all—like Henry the Eighth's marriage of his brother's widow—according to the will of the Pope. If it suited the interest or caprice of the old man of Rome *not* to say the word, the doer of a certain deed would be burned alive in hell for ever. If it suited him, on the other hand, to say it, the doer of the same deed would go, sacramentis munitus, to endless bliss. What rule of morality, what eternal law of right and wrong, could remain in the hearts of men born and bred under the shadow of so hideous a deception?

'And the shadow did not pass at once, when the Pope's authority was thrown off. Henry VIII. evidently thought that if the Pope could make right and wrong, perhaps he could do so likewise. Elizabeth seems to have fancied, at one weak moment, that the Pope had the power of making her marriage with Leicester right, instead of wrong.

'Moreover, when the moral canon of the Pope's will was gone, there was for a while no canon of morality left. The average morality of Elizabeth's reign was not so much low, as capricious, self-willed, fortuitous; magnificent one day in virtue, terrible the next in vice. It was not till more than one generation had grown up and died with the Bible in their hands, that Englishmen and Germans began to understand (what Frenchmen and Italians did not understand) that they were to be judged by the everlasting laws of a God who was no respecter of persons.

'So, again, of the virtue of truth. Truth, for its own sake, had never been a virtue with the Roman clergy. Father Newman informs us that it need not, and on the whole ought not to be; that cunning is the weapon which Heaven has given to the saints wherewith to withstand the brute male force of the wicked world which marries and is given in marriage. Whether his notion be doctrinally correct or not, it is at least historically so.

'Ever since Pope Stephen forged an epistle from St. Peter to Pepin, King of the Franks, and sent it with some filings of the saint's holy chains, that he might bribe him to invade Italy, destroy the Lombards, and confirm to him the "Patrimony of St. Peter"; ever since the first monk forged the first charter of his monastery, or dug the first heathen Anglo-Saxon out of his barrow, to make him a martyr and a worker of miracles, because his own minster did not "draw" as well as the rival minster ten miles off;—ever since this had the heap of lies been accumulating, spawning, breeding fresh lies, till men began to ask themselves whether truth was a thing worth troubling a practical man's head about, and to suspect that tongues were given to men, as claws to cats and horns to bulls, simply for purposes of offence and defence.'

II

DR. NEWMAN *to* MESSRS. MACMILLAN AND CO.

The Oratory, Dec. 30, 1863.

GENTLEMEN,

I do not write to you with any controversial purpose, which would be preposterous; but I address you simply because of your special interest in a Magazine which bears your name.

That highly respected name you have associated with a Magazine, of which the January number has been sent to me by this morning's post, with a pencil mark calling my attention to page 217.

There, apropos of Queen Elizabeth, I read as follows:—

'Truth, for its own sake, had never been a virtue with the Roman clergy. Father Newman informs us that it need not, and on the whole ought not to be; that cunning is the weapon which Heaven has given to the saints wherewith to withstand the brute male force of the wicked world which marries and is given in marriage. Whether his notion be doctrinally correct or not, it is at least historically so.'

There is no reference at the foot of the page to any words of mine, much less any quotation from my writings, in justification of this statement.

I should not dream of expostulating with the writer of such a passage, nor with the editor who could insert it without appending evidence in proof of its allegations. Nor do I want any reparation from either of them. I neither complain of them for their act, nor should I thank them if they reversed it. Nor do I even write to you with any desire of troubling you to send me an answer. I do but wish to draw the attention of your-selves, as gentlemen, to a grave and gratuitous slander, with which I feel confident you will be sorry to find associated a name so eminent as yours.

I am, Gentlemen,
Your obedient Servant,
(Signed)   JOHN H. NEWMAN.

III

The REV. CHARLES KINGSLEY *to* DR. NEWMAN

Eversley Rectory, January 6, 1864.

REVEREND SIR,

I have seen a letter of yours to Mr. Macmillan, in which you complain of some expressions of mine in an article in the January number of Macmillan's Magazine.

That my words were just, I believed from many passages of your writings; but the document to which I expressly referred was one of your Sermons on 'Subjects of the Day', No. XX., in the volume published in 1844, and entitled 'Wisdom and Innocence'.

It was in consequence of that Sermon, that I finally shook off the strong influence which your writings exerted on me; and for much of which I still owe you a deep debt of gratitude.

I am most happy to hear from you that I mistook (as I understand from your letter) your meaning; and I shall be most happy, on your showing me that I have wronged you, to retract my accusation as publicly as I have made it.

I am, Reverend Sir,
Your faithful Servant,
(Signed)   CHARLES KINGSLEY.

IV

DR. NEWMAN *to the* REV. CHARLES KINGSLEY

The Oratory, Birmingham,
January 7, 1864.

REVEREND SIR,

I have to acknowledge your letter of the 6th, informing me that you are the writer of an article in Macmillan's Magazine, in which I am mentioned, and referring generally to a Protestant sermon of mine, of seventeen pages, published by me, as Vicar of St. Mary's, in 1844, and treating of the bearing of the Christian towards the world, and of the character of the reaction of that bearing upon him; and also, referring to my works *passim*; in justification of your statement, categorical and definite, that 'Father Newman informs us that truth for its own sake need not, and on the whole ought not to be, a virtue with the Roman clergy'.

I have only to remark, in addition to what I have already said with great sincerity to Messrs. Macmillan and Co., in the letter of which you speak, and to which I refer you, that, when I wrote to them, no person whatever, whom I had ever seen or heard of, had occurred to me as the author of the statement in question. When I received your letter, taking upon yourself the authorship, I was amazed.

I am, Reverend Sir,
Your obedient Servant,
(Signed)   JOHN H. NEWMAN.

V

DR. NEWMAN *to* X. Y., ESQ.[1]

The Oratory, January 8, 1864.

DEAR SIR,

I thank you for the friendly tone of your letter of the 5th just received, and I wish to reply to it with the frankness which it invites. I have heard from Mr. Kingsley, avowing himself, to my extreme astonishment, the author of the passage about which I wrote to Messrs. Macmillan. No one, whose name I had ever heard, crossed my mind as the writer in their Magazine: and, had any one said that it was Mr. Kingsley, I should have laughed in his face. Certainly, I saw the initials at the end; but, you must recollect, I live out of the world; and, I must own, if Messrs. Macmillan will not think the confession rude, that, as far as I remember, I never before saw even the outside of their Magazine. And so of the Editor: when I saw his name on the cover, it conveyed to me absolutely no idea whatever. I am not defending myself, but merely stating what was the fact; and as to the article, I said to myself, 'Here is a young scribe, who is making himself a cheap reputation by smart hits at safe objects.'

All this will make you see, not only how I live out of the world, but also how wanton I feel it to have been in the parties concerned thus to let fly at me. Were I in active controversy with the Anglican body, or

---

[1] A gentleman who interposed between Mr. Kingsley and Dr. Newman.

any portion of it, as I have been before now, I should consider untrue assertions about me to be in a certain sense a rule of the game, as times go, though God forbid that I should indulge in them myself in the case of another. I have never been very sensitive of such attacks; rarely taken notice of them. Now, when I have long ceased from controversy, they continue: they have lasted incessantly from the year 1833 to this day. They do not ordinarily come in my way: when they do, I let them pass through indolence. Sometimes friends send me specimens of them; and sometimes they are such as I am bound to answer, if I would not compromise interests which are dearer to me than life. The January number of the Magazine was sent to me, I know not by whom, friend or foe, with the passage on which I have animadverted, emphatically, not to say indignantly, scored against. Nor can there be a better proof that there was a call upon me to notice it, than the astounding fact that you can so calmly (excuse me) 'confess plainly' of yourself, as you do, 'that you had read the passage, and did not even think that I or any of my communion would think it unjust.'

Most wonderful phenomenon! An educated man, breathing English air, and walking in the light of the nineteenth century, thinks that neither I nor any members of my communion feel any difficulty in allowing that 'Truth for its own sake need not, and on the whole ought not to be, a virtue with the Roman clergy'; nay, that they are not at all surprised to be told that 'Father Newman had informed' the world, that such is the standard of morality acknowledged, acquiesced in, by his co-religionists! But, I suppose, in truth, there is nothing at all, however base, up to the high mark of Titus Oates, which a Catholic may not expect to be believed of him by Protestants, however honourable and hard-headed. However, dismissing this natural train of thought, I observe on your avowal as follows; and I think what I shall say will commend itself to your judgment as soon as I say it.

I think you will allow then, that there is a broad difference between a virtue, considered in itself as a principle or rule, and the application or limits of it in human conduct. Catholics and Protestants, in their view of the substance of the moral virtues, agree, but they carry them out variously in detail; and in particular instances, and in the case of particular actors or writers, with but indifferent success. Truth is the same in itself and in substance to Catholic and Protestant; so is purity: both virtues are to be referred to that moral sense which is the natural possession of us all. But when we come to the question in detail, whether this or that act in particular is conformable to the rule of truth, or again to the rule of purity; then sometimes there is a difference of opinion between individuals, sometimes between schools, and some-times between religious communions. I, on my side, have long thought, even before I was a Catholic, that the Protestant system, as such, leads to a lax observance of the rule of purity; Protestants think that the Catholic system, as such, leads to a lax observance of the rule of truth. I am very sorry that they should think so, but I cannot help it; I lament their mistake, but I bear it as I may. If Mr. Kingsley had said no more than this, I should not have felt it necessary to criticize such an ordinary remark. But, as I should be committing a crime, heaping dirt upon my soul, and storing up for myself remorse and confusion of face at a future day, if I applied my abstract belief of the latent sensuality of Protestantism, on *à priori* reasoning, to individuals, to living persons, to authors and men of name, and said (not to make disrespectful allusion to the living) that Bishop Van Mildert, or the Rev. Dr. Spry, or Dean Milner, or the Rev. Charles Simeon 'informs us that chastity for its own sake need not be, and on the whole ought not to be, a virtue with the Anglican clergy', and then, when challenged for the proof, said, '*Vide* Van Mildert's Bampton Lectures and Simeon's Skeleton Sermons *passim*'; and, as I should only make the matter still worse, if I pointed to flagrant instances of paradoxical divines or of bad clergy-men among Protestants, as, for instance, to that popular London preacher at the end of last century who advocated polygamy in print; so, in like manner, for a writer, when he is criticizing definite historical facts of the sixteenth century, which stand or fall on their own merits, to go out of his way to have a fling at an unpopular name, living but 'down', and boldly to say to those who know no better, who know nothing but what he tells them, who take their tradition of historical facts from him, who do not know *me*,—to say of *me*, 'Father Newman *informs* us that Truth for its own sake *need not be, and on the whole ought not to be*, a virtue with the Roman clergy', and to be thus brilliant and antithetical (save the mark!) in the very cause of Truth, is a pro-ceeding of so special a character as to lead me to exclaim, after the pattern of the celebrated saying, 'O Truth, how many lies are told in thy name!'

Such being the state of the case, I think I shall carry you along with me when I say, that, if there is to be any explanation in the Magazine of so grave an inadvertence, it concerns the two gentlemen who are responsible for it, of what complexion that explanation shall be. For me, it is not I who ask for it; I look on mainly as a spectator, and shall praise or blame, according to my best judgment, as I see what they do. Not that, in so acting, I am implying a doubt of all that you tell me of them; but 'handsome is, that handsome does'. If they set about proving their point, or, should they find that impossible, if they say so, in either case I shall call them *men*. But,—bear with me for harbouring a suspicion which Mr. Kingsley's letter to me has inspired,—if they propose merely to smooth the matter over by publishing to the world that I have 'complained', or that 'they yield to my letters, expostulations, representations, explanations', or that 'they are quite ready to be convinced of their mistake, if I will convince them', or that 'they have profound respect for me, but really they are not the only persons who have gathered from my writings what they have said of me', or that 'they are unfeignedly surprised that I should visit in their case what I have passed over in the case of others', or that 'they have ever had a true sense of my good points, but cannot be expected to be blind to my faults', if this be the sum total of what they are to say, and they ignore the fact that the *onus probandi* of a very definite accusation lies upon them, and that they have no right to throw the burden upon others, then, I say with submission, they had better let it all alone, as far as I am concerned, for a half-measure settles nothing.

January 10.—I will add, that any letter addressed to me by Mr. Kingsley, I account public property; not so, should you favour me with any fresh communication yourself.

> I am, Dear Sir,
> Yours faithfully,
> (Signed)   JOHN H. NEWMAN.

VI

The REV. CHARLES KINGSLEY *to* DR. NEWMAN

Eversley Rectory, January 14, 1864.

REVEREND SIR,

I have the honour to acknowledge your answer to my letter.

I have also seen your letter to Mr. X. Y. On neither of them shall I make any comment, save to say, that, if you fancy that I have attacked you because you were, as you please to term it, 'down', you do me a great injustice; and also, that the suspicion expressed in the latter part of your letter to Mr. X. Y., is needless.

The course, which you demand of me, is the only course fit for a gentleman; and, as the tone of your letters (even more than their language) make me feel, to my very deep pleasure, that my opinion of the meaning of your words was a mistaken one, I shall send at once to Macmillan's Magazine the few lines which I inclose.

You say, that you will consider my letters as public. You have every right to do so.

> I remain, Reverend Sir,
> Yours faithfully,
> (Signed)   C. KINGSLEY.

VII

[This will appear in the next number]

'To the Editor of Macmillan's Magazine

'Sir,

'In your last number I make certain allegations against the teaching of the Rev. Dr. Newman, which were founded on a Sermon of his, entitled "Wisdom and Innocence", (the sermon will be fully described, as to[1] . . .).

'Dr. Newman has, by letter, expressed in the strongest terms, his denial of the meaning which I have put upon his words.

'No man knows the use of words better than Dr. Newman; no man, therefore, has a better right to define what he does, or does not, mean by them.

'It only remains, therefore, for me to express my hearty regret at having so seriously mistaken him; and my hearty pleasure at finding him on the side of Truth, in this, or any other, matter.

(Signed)   CHARLES KINGSLEY.'

VIII

Dr. Newman *to the* Rev. Charles Kingsley

The Oratory, January 17, 1864.

Reverend Sir,

Since you do no more than announce to me your intention of inserting in Macmillan's Magazine the letter, a copy of which you are so good as to transcribe for me, perhaps I am taking a liberty in making any remarks to you upon it. But then, the very fact of your showing it to me seems to invite criticism; and so sincerely do I wish to bring this painful matter to an immediate settlement, that, at the risk of being officious, I avail myself of your courtesy to express the judgment which I have carefully formed upon it.

I believe it to be your wish to do me such justice as is compatible with your duty of upholding the consistency and quasi-infallibility which is necessary for a periodical publication; and I am far from expecting any thing from you which would be unfair to Messrs. Macmillan and Co. Moreover, I am quite aware, that the reading public, to whom your letter is virtually addressed, cares little for the

---

[1] Here follows a word or half-word, which neither I nor any one else to whom I have shown the MS. can decypher. I have at pp. 348–349 filled in for Mr. Kingsley what I understood him to mean by 'fully'.—J. H. N.

wording of an explanation, provided it be made aware of the fact that an explanation has been given.

Nevertheless, after giving your letter the benefit of both these considerations, I am sorry to say I feel it my duty to withhold from it the approbation which I fain would bestow.

Its main fault is, that, quite contrary to your intention, it will be understood by the general reader to intimate, that I have been confronted with definite extracts from my works, and have laid before you my own interpretations of them. Such a proceeding I have indeed challenged, but have not been so fortunate as to bring about.

But besides, I gravely disapprove of the letter as a whole. The grounds of this dissatisfaction will be best understood by you, if I place in parallel columns its paragraphs, one by one, and what I conceive will be the popular reading of them.

This I proceed to do.

> I have the honour to be,
> Reverend Sir,
> Your obedient Servant,
> (Signed)   JOHN H. NEWMAN.

Mr. Kingsley's Letter.	*Unjust, but too probable, popular rendering of it.*
1. Sir,—In your last number I made certain allegations against the teaching of the Rev. Dr. Newman, which were founded on a Sermon of his, entitled 'Wisdom and Innocence', preached by him as Vicar of St. Mary's, and published in 1844.	
2. Dr. Newman has, by letter, expressed in the strongest terms his denial of the meaning which I have put upon his words.	2. I have set before Dr. Newman, as he challenged me to do, extracts from his writings, and he has affixed to them what he conceives to be their legitimate sense, to the denial of that in which I understood them.
3. No man knows the use of words better than Dr. Newman; no man, therefore, has a	3. He has done this with the skill of a great master of verbal fence, who knows, as

better right to define what he does, or does not, mean by them.

4. It only remains, therefore, for me to express my hearty regret at having so seriously mistaken him, and my hearty pleasure at finding him on the side of truth, in this or any other matter.

well as any man living, how to insinuate a doctrine without committing himself to it.

4. However, while I heartily regret that I have so seriously mistaken the sense which he assures me his words were meant to bear, I cannot but feel a hearty pleasure also, at having brought him, for once in a way, to confess that after all truth is a Christian virtue.

IX

REV. CHARLES KINGSLEY *to* DR. NEWMAN

Eversley Rectory, January 18, 1864.

REVEREND SIR,

I do not think it probable that the good sense and honesty of the British Public will misinterpret my apology, in the way in which you expect.

Two passages in it, which I put in in good faith and good feeling, may, however, be open to such a bad use, and I have written to Messrs. Macmillan to omit them; viz. the words, 'No man knows the use of words better than Dr. Newman'; and those, 'My hearty pleasure at finding him in the truth (*sic*) on this or any other matter.'

As to your Art. 2, it seems to me, that, by referring publicly to the Sermon on which my allegations are founded, I have given, not only you, but every one an opportunity of judging of their injustice. Having done this, and having frankly accepted your assertion that I was mistaken, I have done as much as one English gentleman can expect from another.

I have the honour to be,
Reverend Sir,
Your obedient Servant,
(Signed)   CHARLES KINGSLEY.

X

DR. NEWMAN *to* MESSRS. MACMILLAN & CO.

The Oratory, January 22, 1864.

GENTLEMEN,

Mr. Kingsley, the writer of the paragraph to which I called your attention on the 30th of last month, has shown his wish to recall words, which I considered a great affront to myself, and a worse insult to the Catholic priesthood. He has sent me the draft of a Letter which he proposes to insert in the February number of your Magazine; and, when I gave him my criticisms upon it, he had the good feeling to withdraw two of its paragraphs.

However, he did not remove that portion of it, to which, as I told him, lay my main objection.

That portion ran as follows:—

'Dr. Newman has by letter expressed in the strongest terms his denial of the meaning which I have put upon his words.'

My objection to this sentence, which (with the addition of a reference to a Protestant sermon of mine, which he says formed the ground of his assertion, and of an expression of regret at having mistaken me) constitutes, after the withdrawal of the two paragraphs, the whole of his proposed letter, I thus explained to him:—

'Its [the proposed letter's] main fault is, that, quite contrary to your intention, it will be understood by the general reader to intimate, that I have been confronted with definite extracts from my works, and have laid before you my own interpretation of them. Such a proceeding I have indeed challenged, but have not been so fortunate as to bring about.'

In answer to this representation, Mr. Kingsley wrote to me as follows:—

'It seems to me, that, by referring publicly to the sermon, on which my allegations are founded, I have given, not only you, but every one, an opportunity of judging of their injustice. Having done this, and having frankly accepted your assertion that I was mistaken, I have done as much as one English gentleman can expect from another.'

I received this reply the day before yesterday. It disappointed me, for I had hoped that, with the insertion of a letter from him in your Magazine for February, there would have been an end of the whole matter. However, I have waited forty-eight hours, to give time for his explanation to make its full, and therefore its legitimate impression on my mind. After this interval, I find my judgment of the passage just what it was.

Moreover, since sending to Mr. Kingsley that judgment, I have received a letter from a friend at a distance, whom I had consulted, a man about my own age, who lives out of the world of theological controversy and contemporary literature, and whose intellectual habits especially qualify him for taking a clear and impartial view of the force of words. I put before him the passage in your January number, and the writer's proposed letter in February;[1] and I asked him whether I might consider the letter sufficient for its purpose, without saying a word to show him the leaning of my own mind. He answers:

[1] Viz. as it is given above, p. 347.—J. H. N.

'In answer to your question, whether Mr. Kingsley's proposed reparation is sufficient, I have no hesitation in saying, Most decidedly not. Without attempting to quote any passage from your writings which justifies in any manner the language which he has used in his review, he leaves it to be inferred that the representation, which he has given of your statements and teaching in the sermon to which he refers, is the fair and natural and primary sense of them, and that it is only by your declaring that you did not mean what you really and in effect said, that he finds that he had made a false charge.'

This opinion thus given came to me, I repeat, *after* I had sent to Mr. Kingsley the letter of objection, of which I have quoted a portion above. You will see that, though the two judgments are independent of each other, they in substance coincide.

It only remains for me then to write to you again; and, in writing to you now, I do no more than I did on the 30th of December. I bring the matter before you, without requiring from you any reply.

I am, Gentlemen,
Your obedient Servant,
(Signed)   JOHN H. NEWMAN.

XI

Letter of Explanation from Mr. KINGSLEY, *as it stands in Macmillan's Magazine for February,* 1864, p. 368

TO THE EDITOR OF MACMILLAN'S MAGAZINE

SIR,

In your last number I made certain allegations against the teaching of Dr. John Henry Newman, which I thought were justified by a Sermon of his, entitled 'Wisdom and Innocence' (Sermon 20 of 'Sermons bearing on Subjects of the Day'). Dr. Newman has by letter expressed, in the strongest terms, his denial of the meaning which I have put upon his words. It only remains, therefore, for me to express my hearty regret at having so seriously mistaken him.

Yours faithfully,
(Signed)   CHARLES KINGSLEY.

Eversley, January 14, 1864.

XII

Reflections on the above

I shall attempt a brief analysis of the foregoing correspondence; and I trust that the wording which I shall adopt will not offend against the gravity due both to myself and to the occasion. It is impossible to do justice to the course of thought evolved in it without some familiarity of expression.

Mr. Kingsley begins then by exclaiming,—'O the chicanery, the wholesale fraud, the vile hypocrisy, the conscience-killing tyranny of Rome! We have not far to seek for an evidence of it. There's Father Newman to wit: one living specimen is worth a hundred dead ones. He, a Priest writing of Priests, tells us that lying is never any harm.'

I interpose: 'You are taking a most extraordinary liberty with my name. If I have said this, tell me when and where.'

Mr. Kingsley replies: 'You said it, Reverend Sir, in a Sermon which you preached, when a Protestant, as Vicar of St. Mary's, and published in 1844; and I could read you a very salutary lecture on the effects which that Sermon had at the time on my own opinion of you.'

I make answer: 'Oh . . . *Not*, it seems, as a Priest speaking of Priests; —but let us have the passage.'

Mr. Kingsley relaxes: 'Do you know, I like your *tone*. From your *tone* I rejoice, greatly rejoice, to be able to believe that you did not mean what you said.'

I rejoin: '*Mean* it! I maintain I never *said* it, whether as a Protestant or as a Catholic.'

Mr. Kingsley replies: 'I waive that point.'

I object: 'Is it possible! What? waive the main question! I either said it or I didn't. You have made a monstrous charge against me; direct, distinct, public. You are bound to prove it as directly, as distinctly, as publicly;—or to own you can't.'

'Well,' says Mr. Kingsley, 'if you are quite sure you did not say it, I'll take your word for it; I really will.'

My *word*! I am dumb. Somehow I thought that it was my *word* that happened to be on trial. The *word* of a Professor of lying, that he does not lie!

But Mr. Kingsley re-assures me: 'We are both gentlemen,' he says: 'I have done as much as one English gentleman can expect from another.'

I begin to see: he thought me a gentleman at the very time that he said I taught lying on system. After all, it is not I, but it is Mr. Kingsley who did not mean what he said. 'Habemus confitentem reum.'

So we have confessedly come round to this, preaching without practising; the common theme of satirists from Juvenal to Walter Scott! 'I left Baby Charles and Steenie laying his duty before him', says King James of the reprobate Dalgarno: 'O Geordie, jingling Geordie, it was grand to hear Baby Charles laying down the guilt of dissimulation, and Steenie lecturing on the turpitude of incontinence.'

While I feel then that Mr. Kingsley's February explanation is miserably insufficient in itself for his January enormity, still I feel also that the Correspondence, which lies between these two acts of his, constitutes a real satisfaction to those principles of historical and literary justice to which he has given so rude a shock.

Accordingly, I have put it into print, and make no further criticism on Mr. Kingsley.

J. H. N.

APPENDIX B

'WHAT, THEN, DOES DR. NEWMAN MEAN?'

A REPLY TO A PAMPHLET LATELY PUBLISHED
BY DR. NEWMAN

by

The Reverend Charles Kingsley

'It is not more than a hyperbole to say, that, in certain cases, a lie is the nearest approach to truth.'

NEWMAN, *Sermons on the Theory of Religious Belief, page 343*

A REPLY TO A PAMPHLET

by Charles Kingsley

'WHAT, THEN, DOES DR. NEWMAN MEAN?'

DR. NEWMAN has made a great mistake. He has published a correspondence between himself and me, with certain 'Reflexions' and a title-page, which cannot be allowed to pass without a rejoinder.

Before commenting on either, I must give a plain account of the circumstances of the controversy, which seem to have been misunderstood in several quarters. In the January number of *Macmillan's Magazine*, I deliberately and advisedly made use of these words:—

'Truth, for its own sake, had never been a virtue with the Roman clergy. Father Newman informs us that it need not, and, on the whole, ought not to be; that cunning is the weapon which Heaven has given to the saints wherewith to withstand the brute male force of the wicked world which marries and is given in marriage.' This accusation I based upon a considerable number of passages in Dr. Newman's writings, and especially on a sermon entitled 'Wisdom and Innocence', and preached by Dr. Newman as Vicar of St. Mary's, and published as No. XX. of his 'Sermons on Subjects of the Day'.

Dr. Newman wrote, in strong but courteous terms, to Messrs. Macmillan and Co. complaining of this language as a slander. I at once took the responsibility on myself, and wrote to Dr. Newman.

I had been informed (by a Protestant) that he was in weak health, that he wished for peace and quiet, and was averse to controversy; I therefore felt some regret at having disturbed him; and this regret was increased by the moderate and courteous tone of his letters, though they contained, of course, much from which I differed. I addressed to him the following letter, of which, as I trust every English gentleman will feel, I have no reason to be ashamed:—

REVEREND SIR,

I have seen a letter of yours to Mr. Macmillan, in which you complain of some expressions of mine in an article in the January number of *Macmillan's Magazine*.

That my words were just, I believed from many passages of your writings; but the document to which I expressly referred was one of your sermons on 'Subjects of the Day', No. XX. in the volume published in 1844, and entitled 'Wisdom and Innocence'.

It was in consequence of that sermon that I finally shook off the strong influence which your writings exerted on me, and for much of which I still owe you a deep debt of gratitude.

I am most happy to hear from you that I mistook (as I understand from your letter) your meaning; and I shall be most happy, on your showing me that I have wronged you, to retract my accusation as publicly as I have made it.

I am, Rev. Sir,

Your faithful servant,

CHARLES KINGSLEY.

I received a very moderate answer from Dr. Newman, and a short correspondence ensued, which ended in my inserting in the February number of *Macmillan's Magazine* the following apology:—

To the Editor of 'MACMILLAN'S MAGAZINE'

SIR,

In your last number I made certain allegations against the teaching of Dr. John Henry Newman, which I thought were justified by a sermon of his, entitled 'Wisdom and Innocence' (Sermon XX. of 'Sermons bearing on Subjects of the Day'). Dr. Newman has, by letter, expressed in the strongest terms his denial of the meaning which I have put upon his words. It only remains, therefore, for me to express my hearty regret at having so seriously mistaken him.

Yours faithfully,

CHARLES KINGSLEY.

My object had been throughout to avoid war, because I thought Dr. Newman wished for peace. I therefore dropped the question of the meaning of 'many passages of his writings', and confined myself to the sermon entitled 'Wisdom and Innocence', simply to give him an opportunity of settling the dispute on that one ground.

But whether Dr. Newman lost his temper, or whether he thought that he had gained an advantage over me, or whether he wanted a more complete apology than I chose to give, whatever, I say, may have been his reasons, he suddenly changed his tone of courtesy and dignity for one of which I shall only say that it shows sadly how the atmosphere of the Romish priesthood has degraded his notions of what is due to himself; and when he published (as I am much obliged to him for doing) the whole correspondence, he appended to it certain reflexions, in which he attempted to convict me of not having believed the accusation which I had made.

There remains for me, then, nothing but to justify my mistake, as far as I can.

I am, of course, precluded from using the sermon entitled 'Wisdom and Innocence' to prove my words. I have accepted Dr. Newman's denial that it means what I thought it did; and Heaven forbid that I should withdraw my word once given, at whatever disadvantage to myself. But more. I am informed by those from whose judgment on such points there is no appeal, that, '*en hault courage*' and strict honour, I am also precluded, by the terms of my explanation, from using any other of Dr. Newman's past writings to prove my assertion. I have declared Dr. Newman to have been an honest man up to the 1st of February, 1864. It was, as I shall show, only Dr. Newman's fault that I ever thought him to be anything else. It depends entirely on Dr. Newman whether he shall sustain the reputation which he has so recently acquired. If I give him thereby a fresh advantage in this argument, he is most welcome to it. He needs, it seems to me, as many advantages as possible. But I have a right, in self-justification, to put before the public so much of that sermon, and of the rest of Dr. Newman's writings, as will show why I formed so harsh an opinion of them and him, and why I still consider that sermon (whatever may be its meaning) as most dangerous and misleading. And I have a full right to do the same by those 'many passages of Dr. Newman's writings' which I left alone at first, simply because I thought that Dr. Newman wished for peace.

First, as to the sermon entitled 'Wisdom and Innocence'. It must be remembered always that it is not a Protestant, but a Romish sermon. It is occupied entirely with the attitude of 'the world' to 'Christians' and 'the Church'. By the world appears to be signified, especially, the Protestant public of these realms. What Dr. Newman means by Christians, and the Church, he has not left in doubt; for in the preceding sermon (XIX. p. 328) he says: 'But, if the truth must be spoken, what are the humble monk, and the holy nun, and other regulars, as they are called, but Christians after the very pattern given us in Scripture? What have they done but this—continue in the world the Christianity of the Bible? Did our Saviour come on earth suddenly, as He will one day visit, in whom would He see the features of the Christians He and His apostles left behind them, but in them? Who but these give up home and friends, wealth and ease, good name and liberty of will, for the kingdom of heaven? Where shall we find the image of St. Paul, or St. Peter, or St. John, or of Mary the mother of Mark, or of Philip's daughters, but in those who, whether they remain in seclusion, or are sent over the earth, have calm faces, and sweet plaintive voices, and spare frames, and gentle manners, and hearts weaned from the world, and wills subdued; and for their meekness meet with insult, and for their purity with slander, and for their gravity with suspicion, and for their courage with cruelty. . . .' This is his definition of Christians. And in the sermon itself he sufficiently defines what he means by 'the Church' in two 'notes' of her character, which he shall give in his own words (Sermon XX. p. 346):—'What, for instance, though we grant that sacramental confession and the celibacy of the clergy do tend to consolidate the body politic in the relation of rulers and subjects, or, in other words, to aggrandise the priesthood? for how can the Church be one body without such relation?' . . .

Monks and nuns the only perfect Christians; sacramental confession and the celibacy of the clergy notes of the Church; the laity in relation to the clergy of subjects to rulers. What more? If I, like others, on the strength of Dr. Newman's own definitions, gave to his advice to Christians concerning 'wisdom', 'prudence', 'silence', the meaning which they would have in the mouth of a Romish teacher—St. Alfonso da Liguori, for instance—whom can Dr. Newman blame for the mistake, save himself?

But to the sermon itself; the text of which is from Matthew x. 16. It begins by stating that the Church has been always helpless and persecuted, in proportion to its purity. Dr. Newman then asks, how Christians are to defend themselves if they might not fight? and answers, 'They were allowed the arms, that is, the arts, of the defenceless.' He shows how the weaker animals are enabled to defend themselves by various means, among which he enumerates 'natural cunning, which enables them to elude or even to destroy their enemies'. He goes on to show how the same holds good in our own species, in the case of 'a captive, effeminate race'; of 'slaves'; of 'ill-used and oppressed children'; of the 'subjects of a despot'. 'They exercise the inalienable right of self-defence in such methods as they best may; only, since human nature is unscrupulous, guilt or innocence is all the same to them, if it works their purpose.'

He goes on to point out the analogy between these facts and the conduct fit for Christians. 'The servants of Christ are forbidden to defend themselves by violence; but they are not forbidden other means: direct means are not allowed, but others are even commanded. For instance, foresight, "beware of men": avoidance, "when they persecute you in one city, flee into another": prudence and skill, as in the text, "Be ye wise as serpents".'

The mention of the serpent reminds him of the serpent in Paradise; and he says, 'Considering that the serpent was chosen by the enemy of mankind as the instrument of his temptations in Paradise, it is very remarkable that Christ should choose it as the pattern of wisdom for His followers. It is as if He appealed to the whole world of sin, and to the bad arts by which the feeble gain advantages over the strong. It is as if He set before us the craft and treachery, the perfidy of the slave, and bade us extract a lesson even from so great an evil. It is as if the more we are forbidden violence, the more we are exhorted to prudence;

as if it were our bounden duty to rival the wicked in endowments of mind, and to excel them in their exercise.'

Dr. Newman then goes on to assert, that 'if there be one reproach more than another which has been cast upon' the Church, 'it is that of fraud and cunning'. He quotes the imputations of craftiness and deceitfulness thrown upon St. Paul, and even of 'deceit' upon our Lord himself. He then says that 'Priestcraft has ever been considered the badge, and its imputation is a kind of note, of the Church'. He asserts that the accusation has been, save in a few exceptions, unfounded; and that 'the words "craft" and "hypocrisy" are but the version of "wisdom" and "harmlessness" in the language of the world'. 'It is remarkable, however, that not only is harmlessness the corrective of wisdom, securing it against the corruption of craft and deceit, as stated in the text: but innocence, simplicity, implicit obedience to God, tranquillity of mind, contentment, these and the like virtues are in themselves a sort of wisdom; I mean, they produce the same results as wisdom, because God works for those who do not work for themselves; and thus they especially incur the charge of craft at the hands of the world, because they pretend to so little, yet effect so much. This circumstance admits dwelling on.'

He then goes on to mention seven heads:—

'First, sobriety, self-restraint, control of word and feeling, which religious men exercise, have about them an appearance of being artificial, because they are not natural; and of being artful, because artificial'; and adds shortly after, that 'those who would be holy and blameless, the sons of God, find so much in the world to unsettle and defile them, that they are necessarily forced upon a strict self-restraint, lest they should receive injury from such intercourse with it as is unavoidable; and this self-restraint is the first thing which makes holy persons seem wanting in openness and manliness'. Next he points out that 'religious men are a mystery to the world; and being a mystery, they will in mere self-defence be called by the world mysterious, dark, subtle, designing'. Next, that 'it is very difficult to make the world understand the difference between an outward obedience and an inward assent'. He then instances the relations between the early Christians and the heathen magistrates; and adds, that 'when religious men outwardly conform, on the score of duty, to the powers that be, the world is easily led into the mistake that they have renounced their opinions, as well as submitted their actions; and it feels or affects surprise, to find that their opinions remain; and it considers, or calls this, an inconsistency, or a duplicity': with more to the same purpose.

Next, the silent resignation of Christians is set forth as a cause of the world's suspicion; and 'so is their confidence, in spite of their apparent weakness, their cause will triumph'.

Another cause of the world's suspicion is, the unexpected success of religious men.

Another, that the truth has in itself the power of spreading, with instruments, 'making the world impute' to secret management that uniformity, which is nothing but the echo of the One Living and True Word.

Another, that when Christians prosper, contrary to their own expectations, 'it looks like deceit to show surprise, and to disclaim the work themselves'.

And lastly, because God works for Christians, and they are successful, when they only mean to be dutiful. 'But what duplicity does the world think it, to speak of conscience, or honour, or propriety, or delicacy, or to give other tokens of personal motives, when the event seems to show that a calculation of results has been the actuating principle at bottom. It is God who designs, but His servants seem designing. . . .'

Dr. Newman then goes on to point out how 'Jacob is thought worldly wise in his dealings with Laban, whereas he was a "plain man", simply obedient to the angel'. . . . 'Moses is sometimes called sagacious and shrewd in his measures or his law, as if wise acts might not come from the source of wisdom.' . . . 'Bishops have been called hypocritical in submitting and yet opposing themselves to the civil power, in a matter of plain duty, if a popular movement was the consequence; and then hypocritical again, if they did their best to repress it. And, in like manner, theological doctrines or ecclesiastical usages are styled politic if they are but salutary; as if the Lord of the Church, who has willed her sovereignty, might not effect it by secondary causes. What, for instance, though we grant that sacramental confession and the celibacy of the clergy do tend to consolidate the body politic in the relation of rulers and subjects, or, in other words, to aggrandise the priesthood? For how can the Church be one body without such relation; and why should not He, who has decreed that there should be unity, take measures to secure it?'

The reason of these suspicions on the part of the world is then stated to be, that 'men do not like to hear of the interposition of Providence in the affairs of the world; and they invidiously ascribe ability and skill to His agents, to escape the thought of an Infinite Wisdom and an Almighty Power. . . '.

The sermon then closes with a few lines of great beauty, in that style which has won deservedly for Dr. Newman the honour of being the most perfect orator of this generation; but they have no reference to the question in hand, save the words, 'We will glory in what they disown.'

I have tried conscientiously to give a fair and complete digest of this, to me, very objectionable and dangerous sermon. I have omitted no passage in which Dr. Newman guards himself against the conclusions which I drew from it; and none, I verily believe, which is required for the full understanding of its general drift. I have abstained from all comment as I went on, in order not to prejudice the minds of my readers. But I must now turn round and ask, whether the mistake into which Dr. Newman asserts me to have fallen was not a very reasonable one; and whether the average of educated Englishmen, in reading that sermon, would not be too likely to fall into the same? I put on it, as I thought, the plain and straightforward signification. I find I am wrong; and nothing is left for me but to ask, with some astonishment, What, then, did the sermon mean? Why was it preached? To insinuate that a Church which had sacramental confession and a celibate clergy was the only true Church? Or to insinuate that the admiring young gentlemen who listened to him stood to their fellow-countrymen in the relation of the early Christians to the heathen Romans? Or that Queen Victoria's Government was to the Church of England what Nero's or Diocletian's was to the Church of Rome? It may have been so. I know that men used to suspect Dr. Newman—I have been inclined to do so myself—of writing a whole sermon, not for the sake of the text or of the matter, but for the sake of one single passing hint—one phrase, one epithet, one little barbed arrow which, as he swept magnificently past on the stream of his calm eloquence, seemingly unconscious of all presences, save those unseen, he delivered unheeded, as with his finger-tip, to the very heart of an initiated hearer, never to be withdrawn again. I do not blame him for that. It is one of the highest triumphs of oratoric power, and may be employed honestly and fairly, by any person who has the skill to do it honestly and fairly. But then—Why did he entitle his sermon 'Wisdom and Innocence'?

What, then, could I think that Dr. Newman meant? I found a preacher bidding Christians imitate, to some undefined point, the 'arts' of the basest of animals and of men, and even of the Devil himself. I found him, by a strange perversion of Scripture, insinuating that St. Paul's conduct and manner were such as naturally to bring down on him the reputation of being a crafty deceiver. I found him—horrible to have to say it—even hinting the same of One greater than St. Paul. I found him denying or explaining away the existence of that priest-craft which is a notorious fact to every honest student of history; and justifying (as far as I can understand him) that double-dealing by which prelates, in the middle age, too often played off alternately the sovereign against the people and the people against the sovereign, careless which was in the right, as long as their own power gained by the move. I found him actually using of such (and, as I thought, of himself and his party likewise) the words, 'They yield outwardly; to assent inwardly were to betray the faith. Yet they are called deceitful and double-dealing, because they do as much as they can, and not more than they may.' I found him telling Christians that they will always seem 'artificial', and 'wanting in openness and manliness'; that they will always be 'a mystery' to the world, and that the world will always think them rogues; and bidding them glory in what the world (*i.e.* the rest of their fellow-countrymen) disown, and say with Mawworm, 'I like to be despised.'

Now how was I to know that the preacher, who had the reputation of being the most acute man of his generation, and of having a specially intimate acquaintance with the weaknesses of the human heart, was utterly blind to the broad meaning and the plain practical result of a sermon like this, delivered before fanatic and hot-headed young men, who hung over his every word? That he did not foresee that they would think that they obeyed him, by becoming affected, artificial, sly, shifty, ready for concealments and equivocations? That he did not foresee that they, hearing his words concerning priestcraft and double-dealing, and being engaged in the study of the Mediæval Church, would consider the same chicanery allowed to them which they found practised but too often by the Mediæval Church? or even go to the Romish casuists, to discover what amount of cunning did or did not come under Dr. Newman's one passing warning against craft and deceit? In a word, that he did not foresee that the natural result of the sermon on the minds of his disciples would be, to make them suspect that truth was not a virtue for its own sake, but only for the sake of the spread of 'catholic opinions', and the 'salvation of their own souls'; and that cunning was the weapon which Heaven had allowed to them to defend themselves against the persecuting Protestant public?

All England stood round in those days, and saw that this would be the outcome of Dr. Newman's teaching. How was I to know that he did not see it himself?

And as a fact, his teaching had this outcome. Whatever else it did, it did this. In proportion as young men absorbed it into themselves, it injured their straightforwardness and truthfulness. The fact is notorious to all England. It spread misery and shame into many an English home. The net practical result of Dr. Newman's teachings on truthfulness cannot be better summed up than by one of his own disciples, Mr. Ward, who, in his 'Ideal of a Christian Church', page 382, says thus:—

'Candour is rather an intellectual than a moral virtue, and by no means either universally or distinctively characteristic of the saintly mind.'

Dr. Newman ought to have told his disciple, when he wrote those words, that he was on the highroad to the father of lies; and he ought to have told the world, too, that such was his opinion; unless he wished it to fall into the mistake into which I fell—namely, that he had wisdom enough to know the practical result of his words, and therefore meant what they seemed to say.

Dr. Newman has nothing to blame for that mistake, save his own method. If he would (while a member of the Church of England) persist (as in this sermon) in dealing with matters dark, offensive, doubtful, sometimes actually forbidden, at least according to the notions of the great majority of English Churchmen; if he would always do so in a tentative, paltering way, seldom or never letting the world know how much he believed, how far he intended to go; if, in a word, his method of teaching was a suspicious one, what wonder if the minds of men were filled with suspicions of him? What wonder if they said of him (as he so naïvely, in one of his letters, expresses his fear that they will say again), 'Dr. Newman has the skill of a great master of verbal fence, who knows, as well as any man living, how to insinuate a doctrine without committing himself to it?' If he told the world, as he virtually does in this sermon, 'I know that my conduct looks like cunning; but it is only the "arts" of the defenceless': what wonder if the world answered, 'No. It is what it seems. That is just what we call cunning; a habit of mind which, once indulged, is certain to go on from bad to worse, till the man becomes—like too many of the mediæval clergy who indulged in it—utterly untrustworthy.' Dr. Newman, I say, has no one to blame but himself. The world is not so blind but that it will soon find out an honest man if he will take the trouble of talking and acting like one. No one would have suspected him to be a dishonest man, if he had not perversely chosen to assume a style which (as he himself confesses) the world always associates with dishonesty.

When, therefore, Dr. Newman says (p. 344 of his pamphlet) that 'he supposes, in truth, there is nothing at all, however base, up to the high mark of Titus Oates, which a Catholic may not expect to be believed of him by Protestants, however honourable and hard-headed', he is stating a mere phantom of his own brain. It is not so. I do not believe it ever was so. In the days when Jesuits were inciting fanatics to assassinate Queen Elizabeth, and again in the days of the Gunpowder Plot, there was deservedly a very strong feeling against Romish priests, and against a few laymen who were their dupes; and it was the recollection of that which caused the 'Titus Oates' tragedy, which Dr. Newman so glibly flings in our teeth, omitting (or forgetting) that Oates' villany would have been impossible without the preceding villanies of Popish fanatics, and that he was unmasked, condemned, and punished by the strong and great arm of British law. But there was never, I believe, even in the worst times, any general belief that Catholics, simply as such, must be villains.

There is none now. The Catholic laity of these realms are just as much respected and trusted as the Protestants, when their conduct justifies that respect and trust, as it does in the case of all save a few wild Irish; and so are the Romish priests, as long as they show themselves good and honest men, who confine themselves to the care of their flock. If there is (as there is) a strong distrust of certain Catholics, it is restricted to the proselytizing priests among them; and especially to those who, like Dr. Newman, have turned round upon their mother-Church (I had almost said their mother-country) with contumely and slander. And I confess, also, that this public dislike is very rapidly increasing, for reasons which I shall leave Dr. Newman and his advisers to find out for themselves.

I go on now to other works of Dr. Newman, from which (as I told him in my first letter) I had conceived an opinion unfavourable to his honesty.

I shall be expected to adduce, first and foremost, the too-notorious No. 90 of 'Tracts for the Times'. I shall not do so. On reading that tract over again, I have been confirmed in the opinion which I formed of it at first, that, questionable as it was, it was not meant to be consciously dishonest; that some few sayings in it were just and true; that many of its extravagances were pardonable, as the natural fruit of a revulsion against the popular cry of those days, which called on clergymen to interpret the Articles only in their Calvinistic sense, instead of including under them (as their wise framers intended) not only the Calvinistic, but the Anglican form of thought. There were pages in it which shocked me, and which shock me still. I will instance the commentaries on the 5th, on the 7th, on the 9th, and on the 12th Articles; because in them Dr. Newman seemed to me trying to make the Articles say the very thing which (I believe) the Articles were meant not to say. But I attributed to him no intentional dishonesty. The fullest licence of interpretation should be given to every man who is bound by the letter of a document. The *animus imponentium* should be heard of as little as possible, because it is almost certain to become merely the *animus interpretantium*. And more: Every excuse was to be made for a man struggling desperately to keep himself in what was, in fact, his right place, to remain a member of the Church of England, where Providence had placed him, while he felt himself irresistibly attracted towards Rome. But I saw in that tract a fearful danger for the writer. It was but too probable, that if he continued to demand of that subtle brain of his, such *tours de force* as he had all but succeeded in performing, when he tried to show that the Article against 'the sacrifice of masses' 'did not speak against the mass itself', he would surely end in one or other of two misfortunes. He would either destroy his own sense of honesty— *i.e.* conscious truthfulness—and become a dishonest person; or he would destroy his common sense—*i.e.* unconscious truthfulness, and become the slave and puppet seemingly of his own logic, really of his own fancy, ready to believe anything, however preposterous, into which he could, for the moment, argue himself. I thought, for years past, that he had become the former; I now see that he has become the latter.

I beg pardon for saying so much about myself. But this is a personal matter between Dr. Newman and me, and I say what I say simply to show, not Dr. Newman, but my fellow-Protestants, that my opinion of him was not an 'impulsive' or 'hastily-formed one'. I know his writings of old, and now. But I was so far just to him, that No. 90, which made all the rest of England believe him a dishonest man, had not the same effect on me.

But again—

I found Dr. Newman, while yet (as far as could be now discovered) a member of the Church of England, aiding and abetting the publication of certain 'Lives of the English Saints', of which I must say, that no such public outrage on historic truth, and on plain common sense, has been perpetrated in this generation. I do not intend to impute to any of the gentlemen who wrote these lives—and more than one of whom, I believe, I knew personally—the least deliberate intention to deceive. They said what they believed; at least, what they had been taught to believe that they ought to believe. And who had taught them? Dr. Newman can best answer that question. He had, at least, that power over them, and in those days over hundreds more, which genius can always command. He might have used it well. He might have made those 'Lives of Saints', what they ought to have been, books to turn the hearts of the children to the Fathers, and to make the present generation acknowledge and respect the true sanctity which there was, in spite of all mistakes, in those great men of old—a sanctity founded on true virtue and true piety, which required no tawdry super-structure of lying and ridiculous wonders. He might have said to the author of the 'Life of St. Augustine', when he found him, in the heat and haste of youthful fanaticism, outraging historic truth and the law of evidence: 'This must not be. Truth for its own sake is a more precious thing than any purpose, however pious and useful, which we may have in hand.' But when I found him allowing the world to accept, as notoriously sanctioned by him, such statements as are found in that life, was my mistake a hasty, or far-fetched, or unfounded one, when I concluded that he did not care for truth for its own sake, or teach his disciples to regard it as a virtue? I found that 'Life of St. Augustine' saying, that though the pretended visit of St. Peter to England wanted historic evidence, 'yet it has undoubtedly been received as a pious opinion by the Church at large, as we learn from some often-quoted words of St. Innocent I. (who wrote A.D. 416), that St. Peter was instrumental in the conversion of the West generally. And this sort of argument, though it ought to be kept quite distinct from documentary and historic proof, and will form no substitute for such proof with those who stipulate for something like legal accuracy in inquiries of this nature, will not be without its effect upon devout minds, accustomed to rest in the thought of God's watchful guardianship over His church.'. . . And much more in the same tone, which is worthily, and consistently summed up by the question: 'On what evidence do we put faith in the existence of St. George, the patron of England? Upon such, assuredly, as an acute critic or skilful pleader might easily scatter to the winds; the belief of prejudiced or credulous witnesses; the unwritten record of empty pageants and bauble decorations. On the side of scepticism might be exhibited a powerful array of suspicious legends and exploded acts. Yet, after all, what Catholic is there but would count it a profaneness to question the existence of St. George?'

When I found Dr. Newman allowing his disciples—members, even then, of the Protestant Church of England—in page after page, in Life after Life, to talk nonsense of this kind, which is not only sheer Popery, but saps the very foundation of historic truth, was it so wonderful that I conceived him to have taught and thought like them?

But more. I found, that although the responsibility of these Saints' Lives was carefully divided and guarded by anonymousness, and by Dr. Newman's advertisement in No. 1, that the different lives would be 'published by their respective authors on their own responsibility', yet that Dr. Newman had, in what I must now consider merely a moment of amiable weakness, connected himself formally with one of the most offensive of these Lives, and with its most ridiculous statements. I speak of the 'Life of St. Walburga'. There is, in all the Lives, the same tendency to repeat childish miracles, to waive the common laws of evidence, to say to the reader, 'You must believe all or nothing.' But some of them, the writers, for instance, of Vol. IV., which contains, among others, a charming life of St. Neot—treat the stories openly as legends and myths, and tell them as they stand, without asking the reader, or themselves, to believe them altogether. The method is harmless enough, if the legends had stood alone; but dangerous enough, when they stand side by side with stories told in earnest, like that of St. Walburga. In that, not only has the writer expatiated upon some of the most nauseous superstitions of the middle age, but Dr. Newman has, in a preface signed with his initials, solemnly set his seal to the same.

The writer—an Oxford scholar, and, as far as I know, then a professed member of the Church of England—dares to tell us of such miracles as these:—

How a little girl, playing with a ball near the monastery, was punished for her over-fondness for play, by finding the ball stick to her hand, and, running to St. Walburga's shrine to pray, had the ball immediately taken off.

How a woman who would spin on festival-days in like manner found her distaff cling to her hand, and had to beg of St. Walburga's bone, before she could get rid of it.

How a man who came into the church to pray, 'irreverently kept his rough gauntlets, or gloves, on his hands, as he joined them in the posture of prayer'. How they were miraculously torn off, and then, when he repented, 'restored by a miracle'. 'All these', says the writer, 'have the character of a gentle mother correcting the idleness and faults of careless and thoughtless children with tenderness.'

'But the most remarkable and lasting miracle, attesting the holy Walburga's sanctity, is that which reckons her among the saints who are called "Elæophori", or "unguentiferous", becoming, almost in a literal sense, olive-trees in the courts of God. These are they from whose bones a holy oil distils. That oil of charity and gentle mercy which graced them while alive, and fed in them the flame of universal love at their death, still permeates their bodily remains.' After quoting the names of male saints who have possessed this property, the author goes on to detail how this holy oil fell, in drops, sometimes the size of a hazel-nut, sometimes of a pea, into the silver bowl beneath the stone slab. How, when the state of Aichstadt was laid under an interdict, the holy oil ceased, 'until the Church regained its rights', and so forth, and so forth; and then, returning to his original image, metaphor, illustration, proof, or whatever else it may be called by reasoners such as he and Dr. Newman, he says that the same flow of oil or dew is related of this female saint and that—women whose souls, like that of Walburga, were touched 'with true compassion; whose bosom, like hers, melted by divine love, was filled with the milk of human kindness', &c. I can quote no more. I really must recollect that my readers and I are living in the nineteenth century.

And to all this stuff and nonsense, more materialist than the dreams of any bone-worshipping Buddhist, Dr. Newman puts a preface, in which he says of the question whether the 'miracles recorded in these narratives' (*i.e.* in the whole series, this being only No. II.), especially those contained in the life of St. Walburga, 'are to be received as matter of fact'; that 'in this day, and under our present circumstances, we can only reply, that there is no reason why they should not be. They are the kind of facts proper to ecclesiastical history, just as instances of sagacity or daring, personal prowess, or crime, are the facts proper to secular history.' Verily, his idea of 'secular history' is almost as degraded as his idea of 'ecclesiastical'.

He continues: 'There is nothing, then, *primâ facie*, in the miraculous accounts in question to repel a properly-taught or religiously-disposed mind': only, it has the right of rejecting or accepting them according to the evidence. No doubt; for (as he himself confesses) Mabillon, like many sensible Romanists, has found some of these miracles too strong for his 'acute nostril', and has, therefore, been reproved by Basnage for 'not fearing for himself, and warning the reader'.

But what evidence Dr. Newman requires, he makes evident at once. He, at least, will 'fear for himself', and swallow the whole as it comes.

'As to the miracles ascribed to St. Walburga, it must be remembered that she is one of the principal saints of her age and country'; and then he goes on to quote the authorities for these miracles. They begin nearly 100 years after her death, with one Wolfhard, a monk. Then follows, more than 400 years after, Philip, Bishop of Aichstadt, the disinterested witness who tells the story of the holy oil ceasing during the interdict, who tells the world how, 'From her virgin limbs, *maxime pectoralibus*, flows this sacred oil, which, by the grace of God and the intercession of the blessed Virgin Walburga, illuminates the blind, makes the deaf hear', &c., and of which he says that he himself once drank a whole cup, and was cured forthwith. Then come the nuns of this same place, equally disinterested witnesses, after the invention of printing; then one Rader, in 1615; and one Gretser, in 1620. But what has become of the holy oil for the last 240 years, Dr. Newman does not say.

In his 'Lectures on the present position of Catholics in England, addressed to the brothers of the Oratory', in 1851, he has again used the same line of sophism. Argument I cannot call it, while such a sentence as this is to be found:—(p. 295) 'Is the tower of London shut against sight-seers, because the coats of mail or pikes there may have half legendary tales connected with them? Why, then, may not the country people come up in joyous companies, singing and piping, to see the holy coat at Treves ?' To see, forsooth! To worship, Dr. Newman would have said, had he known (as I take for granted he does not) the facts of that imposture. He himself, meanwhile, seems hardly sure of the authenticity of the holy coat. He (p. 298) 'does not see why it may not have been what it professes to be'. It may 'have been' so, no doubt, but it certainly is not so now; for the very texture and material of the thing prove it to be spurious. However, Dr. Newman 'firmly believes that portions of the true Cross are at Rome and elsewhere, that the crib of Bethlehem is at Rome', &c. And more than all; he thinks it 'impossible to withstand the evidence which is brought for the lique-faction of the blood of St. Januarius, at Naples, and for the motion of the eyes of the pictures of the Madonna in the Roman States.'

How art thou fallen from heaven, O Lucifer, son of the Morning!

But when I read these outrages upon common sense, what wonder if I said to myself, 'This man cannot believe what he is saying?'

I believe I was wrong. I have tried, as far as I can, to imagine to myself Dr. Newman's state of mind; and I see now the possibility of a man's working himself into that pitch of confusion, that he can persuade himself, by what seems to him logic, of anything whatsoever which he wishes to believe; and of his carrying self-deception to such perfection that it becomes a sort of frantic honesty, in which he is utterly unconscious, not only that he is deceiving others, but that he is deceiving himself.

But I must say, If this be 'historic truth', what is historic falsehood? If this be honesty, what is dishonesty? If this be wisdom, what is folly?

I may be told, But this is Roman Catholic doctrine. You have no right to be angry with Dr. Newman for believing it. I answer, this is not Roman Catholic doctrine, any more than belief in miraculous appearances of the Blessed Virgin, or the miracle of the stigmata, on which two matters I shall say something hereafter. No Roman Catholic, as far as I am aware, is bound to believe these things. Dr. Newman has believed them of his own free will. He is anxious, it would seem, to show his own credulity. He has worked his mind, it would seem, into that morbid state, in which nonsense is the only food for which it hungers. Like the sophists of old, he has used reason to destroy reason. I had thought that, like them, he had preserved his own reason, in order to be able to destroy that of others. But I was unjust to him, as he says. While he tried to destroy others' reason, he was at least fair enough to destroy his own. That is all that I can say. Too many prefer the charge of insincerity to that of insipience—Dr. Newman seems not to be of that number.

But more. In connexion with this said life of St. Walburga, Dr. Newman has done a deed, over which I might make merry, if that were my wish. But I am not a wit, like Dr. Newman.

In page 77, we find the following wonderful passage: 'Illuminated men . . . to them the evil influence of Satanic power is horribly discernible . . . and the only way to express their keen perception of it is to say, that they see upon the countenances of the slaves of sin, the marks, and lineaments, and stamp of the evil one; and they smell with their nostrils the horrible fumes which arise from their vices and uncleansed hearts, driving good angels from them in dismay, and attracting and delighting devils. It is said of the holy Sturme, a disciple and companion of Winfred, that in passing a horde of unconverted Germans, as they were bathing and gambolling in a stream, he was so overpowered by the intolerable scent which arose from them, that he nearly fainted away. And no doubt such preternatural discernments are sometimes given to saints'—and a religious reason is given for it which I shall not quote. I should be ashamed to use the sacred name in the same page with such materialist nonsense.

Now this 'no doubt' seemed as convincing to Dr. Newman as to the author. The fly which his disciple had heedlessly cast over the turbid waters of his brain was too fine to be resisted; and he rose at it, heavily but surely, and has hooked himself past remedy. For into his lectures, given before the Catholic University of Ireland, published in 1859, he has inserted, at page 96, on the authority of 'an Oxford writer', the whole passage which relates to St. Sturme, word for word.

I thought, when I was in my former mind as to Dr. Newman, that he had gone out of his way to tell this fable, in order to intimate to the young gentlemen who had the blessing of his instructions, that they need care nothing for 'truth for its own sake', in the investigation of a miracle, but take it on any anonymous authority, provided only it made for the Catholic faith. And when I saw that I was wrong, I was sorely puzzled as to why my old friend St. Sturme (against whom I do not say a word) had thus been dragged unceremoniously into a passage on National Literature, which had nothing whatsoever to do with him. But I am not bound to find motives for Dr. Newman's eccentricities.

But now comes the worst part of the matter. Dr. Newman has been taken in. There is no miracle. There never was any in the original document. There is none in Mabillon who quotes it. It is a sheer invention of the ardent Oxford writer.

The story appears first in the Life of St. Sturme, by his contemporary and friend St. Eigils. It may be found in Pertz's 'Monumenta Critica'; and a most charming sketch of mediæval missionary life it is; all the more so because one can comfortably believe every word of it, from its complete freedom (as far as I recollect) from signs and wonders.

The original passage sets forth how St. Sturme rides on his donkey, and wishing for a place where to found Fulda Abbey, came to a ford where the Sclavonians (not Germans, as the Oxford writer calls them) were bathing, on the way to the fair at Mentz, '*whose naked bodies the animal on which he rode fearing, began to tremble, and the man of God himself shuddered (exhorruit) at their evil smell*'. They mocked him, and went about to hurt him; but Divine providence kept them back, and he went on in safety.

That is all. There is not a hint of a miracle. A horde of dirty savages, who had not, probably, washed for a twelve-month, smelt very strong, and St. Sturme had a nose. As for his 'nearly fainting away', that is a 'devout imagination'.

Really, if Dr. Newman or the 'Oxford writer' had been monks of more than one Roman Catholic nation, one might have excused their seeing something quite miraculous in any man's being shocked at his fellow-creatures' evil smell; but in Oxford gentlemen, accustomed to the use of soap and water, it is too bad.

Besides, to impute a miracle in this case, is clearly to put the saint, in virtue, below his own donkey; for while the saint was only shocked at the odour, the donkey did what the saint should have done (in imitation of many other saints before and since), and expressed his horror at the impropriety of the *déshabille* of the 'miscreants'. Unless we are to understand a miracle—and why not?—in the donkey's case likewise; not indeed expressed, but understood as a matter of course by 'properly-taught and religiously-disposed minds'; and piously hold that the virtue of the saint (which seems, from monkish writings, to be some kind of gas or oil) diffused itself through the saddle into the inmost recesses of the donkey's frame, and imbued him for the moment, through the merits of St. Sturme, with a preternatural and angelic modesty?

Which if we shall believe, we shall believe something not a whit more ridiculous than many a story told in these hapless volumes.

What can I say, again, of Dr. Newman's 'Lectures on Anglican Difficulties', published in 1850, save what I have said already? That if I, like hundreds more, have mistaken his meaning and intent, he must blame not me, but himself. If he will indulge in subtle paradoxes, in rhetorical exaggerations; if, whenever he touches on the question of truth and honesty, he will take a perverse pleasure in saying something shocking to plain English notions, he must take the consequences of his own eccentricities.

He tells us, for instance, in Lecture VIII. that the Catholic Church 'holds it better for sun and moon to drop from heaven, for the earth to fail, and for all the many millions on it to die of starvation in extremest agony, as far as temporal affliction goes, than that one soul, I will not say should be lost, but should commit one single venial sin, should tell one wilful untruth, or should steal one poor farthing without excuse'. And this in the face of those permissions to deception, which may be seen formalized and detailed in the works of the Romish casuists, and especially in those of the great Liguori, whose books have received the public and solemn sanction of the Romish see. In one only way can Dr. Newman reconcile this passage with the teaching of his Church; namely, by saying that the licence given to equivocation, even on oath, is so complete, that to tell a downright lie is the most superfluous and therefore most wanton of all sins.

But how will he reconcile it with the statement with which we meet a few pages on, that the Church 'considers consent, though quick as thought, to a single unchaste wish as indefinitely more heinous than any lie that can possibly be fancied; that is when viewed, of course, in itself, and apart from its causes, motives, and consequences?' Heaven forbid that any man should say that such consent is anything save a great and mortal sin: but how can we reconcile this statement with the former one, save by the paradox, that it is a greater crime to sin like an animal, than like the Devil the Father of Lies?

Indeed, the whole teaching of this lecture and the one following it concerning such matters is, I confess, so utterly beyond my comprehension, that I must ask, in blank astonishment, What does Dr. Newman mean? He assures us so earnestly and indignantly that he is an honest man, believing what he says, that we in return are bound, in honour and humanity, to believe him; but still—What does he mean?

He says: 'Take a mere beggar woman, lazy, ragged, and filthy, and not over-scrupulous of truth—(I do not say she has arrived at perfection)—but if she is chaste, sober, and cheerful, and goes to her religious duties (and I am not supposing at all an impossible case), she will, in the eyes of the Church, have a prospect of heaven, quite closed and refused to the State's pattern-man, the just, the upright, the generous, the honourable, the conscientious, if he be all this, not from a supernatural power (I do not determine whether this is likely to be the fact, but I am contrasting views and principles)—not from a supernatural power, but from mere natural virtue.' (Lecture viii. p. 207.)

I must ask again, What does Dr. Newman mean by this astounding passage? What I thought that he meant, when I first read it, some twelve years ago, may be guessed easily enough. I said, This man has no real care for truth. Truth for its own sake is no virtue in his eyes, and he teaches that it need not be. I do not say that now: but this I say, that Dr. Newman, for the sake of exalting the magical powers of his Church, has committed himself unconsciously to a statement which strikes at the root of all morality. If he answer, that such is the doctrine of his Church concerning 'natural virtues', as distinguished from 'good works performed by God's grace', I can only answer, So much the worse for his Church. The sooner it is civilized off the face of the earth, if this be its teaching, the better for mankind. For as for his theory that it may be a 'natural virtue', I value it as little as I trust every honest Englishman will do. I hold it to be utterly antiscriptural; to border very closely (in theological language) on the Pelagian heresy. Every good gift and every perfect gift comes down from God above. Without Him no man does a right deed, or thinks a right thought; and when Dr. Newman says otherwise, he is doing his best (as in this passage) to make the 'State's pattern-man' an atheist, as well as to keep the beggar-woman a lying barbarian. What Dr. Newman may have meant to teach by these words, I cannot say; but what he has taught practically is patent. He has taught the whole Celtic Irish population, that as long as they are chaste (which they cannot well help being, being married almost before they are men and women) and sober (which they cannot well help being, being too poor to get enough whisky to make them drunk), and 'go to their religious duties'—an expression on which I make no comment—they may look down upon the Protestant gentry who send over millions to feed them in famine; who found hospitals and charities to which they are admitted freely; who try to introduce among them capital, industry, civilization, and, above all, that habit of speaking the truth, for want of which they are what they are and are likely to remain such, as long as they have Dr. Newman for their teacher—that they may look down, I say, on the Protestant gentry as cut off from God, and without hope of heaven, because they do their duty by mere 'natural virtue'.

And Dr. Newman has taught them, too, in the very same page,[1] that they may confess 'to the priest thefts which would sentence the penitent to transportation if brought into a court of justice; but which the priest knows too' (and it is to be remembered that the priest is bound to conceal his knowledge of the crime), 'in the judgment of the Church, might be pardoned on the man's private contrition, without any confession at all'.

If I said that Dr. Newman has, in this page, justified, formally and deliberately, some of the strongest accusations brought by the Exeter Hall party against the Irish priests, I should be answered (and possibly with temporary success) by some of those ingenious special pleadings with which, in spite of plain fact and universal public opinion, black is made to appear, if not white, yet still grey enough to do instead. But this I will say, that if the Roman Catholic hierarchy in these realms had had any sense of their own interests (as far as standing well with the British nation is concerned), they would, instead of sending the man who wrote those words to teach in an Irish Catholic university, have sent him to their furthest mission among the savages of the South Seas.

The next lecture, the ninth, contains matter more liable still to be mistaken; and equally certain, mistaken or not, to shock common sense. It is called, 'The Religious Character of Catholic Countries no Prejudice to the Sanctity of the Church.' By the religious character, we find, is meant what we should call the irreligious character—the tendency to profanity, blasphemy, imposture, stealing, lying. These are not my accusations, but Dr. Newman's. He details them all with charming *naïveté*, and gives (as we shall see) most picturesque and apposite instances. But this, he holds 'is no prejudice to the sanctity of the Church', because the Church considers that 'faith and works are separable', and that all these poor wretches, though they have not works, have at least faith, 'caused directly by a supernatural influence from above', and are, therefore, unless I have lost utterly the clue to the intent of Dr. Newman's sophistries, *ipso facto* infinitely better off than Protestants. What he means by the separableness of faith and works is clear enough. A man, he says, 'may be gifted with a simple, undoubting,

[1] p. 207.

cloudless, belief that Christ is in the Blessed Sacrament, and yet commit the sacrilege of breaking open the tabernacle, and carrying off
the consecrated particles for the sake of the precious vessel containing
them'.

At which most of my readers will be inclined to cry: 'Let Dr.
Newman alone, after that. What use in arguing with a man who has
argued himself into believing that? He had a human reason once,
no doubt: but he has gambled it away, and left no common ground on
which he and you, or we either, can meet him.'

True: so true, that I never would have written these pages, save
because it was my duty to show the world, if not Dr. Newman, how the
mistake of his not caring for truth arose; and specially how this very
lecture fostered that mistake. For in it, after using the blasphemy and
profanity which he confesses to be so common in Catholic countries,
as an argument for, and not against, the 'Catholic Faith', he takes a
seeming pleasure in detailing instances of dishonesty on the part of
Catholics, as if that were the very form of antinomianism which was
most strongly and perpetually present to his mind, and which needed
most to be palliated and excused. 'The feeble old woman, who first
genuflects before the Blessed Sacrament, and then steals her neighbour's handkerchief or prayer-book, who is intent on his devotions'—
she is very wrong, no doubt: but 'she worships, and she sins: she kneels
because she believes; she steals because she does not love. She may
be out of God's grace; she is not altogether out of His sight.'

Heaven forbid that we should deny those words. That, at least, is
a doctrine common to Romanist and to Protestant: but while Dr.
Newman, with a kind of desperate audacity, will dig forth such scandals
as notes of the 'Catholic Church', he must not wonder at his motive for
so doing being mistaken.

His next instance is even more wanton and offensive, and so curious
that I must quote it at length:—

'You come out again and mix in the idle and dissipated throng, and
you fall in with a man in a palmer's dress, selling false relics, and a
credulous circle of customers buying them as greedily, as though they
were the supposed French laces and India silks of a pedlar's basket.
One simple soul has bought of him a cure for the rheumatism or ague,
which might form a case of conscience. It is said to be a relic of St.
Cuthbert, but only has virtue at sunrise, and when applied with three
crosses to the head, arms, and feet. You pass on to encounter a rude son
of the Church, more like a showman than a religious, recounting to the
gaping multitude some tale of a vision of the invisible world, seen by
Brother Augustine of the Friar Minors, or by a holy Jesuit preacher
who died in the odour of sanctity, and sending round his bag to collect
pence for the souls in purgatory; and of some appearance of Our Lady

(the like of which has really been before and since), but on no authority except popular report, and in no shape but that which popular caprice has given it. You go forward, and you find preparations proceeding for a great pageant or mystery; it is a high festival, and the incorporated trades have each undertaken their special religious celebration. The plumbers and glaziers are to play the Creation; the barbers the call of Abraham; and at night is to be the grandest performance of all, the Resurrection and Last Judgment, played by the carpenters, masons, and blacksmiths. Heaven and hell are represented,—saints, devils, and living men; and the *chef d'œuvre* of the exhibition is the display of fireworks to be let off as the *finale*. "How unutterably profane!" again you cry. Yes, profane to you, my dear brother—profane to a population which only half believes; not profane to those who believe wholly, who one and all have a vision within which corresponds with what they see, which resolves itself into, or rather takes up into itself, the external pageant, whatever be the moral condition of each individual composing the mass. They gaze, and in drinking in the exhibition with their eyes they are making one continuous and intense act of faith' (Lecture IX. 236, 237).

The sum of which is, that for the sake of the 'one continuous and intense act of faith' which the crowd is performing, 'the rude son of the Church, more like a showman than a religious'—in plain English, the brutal and lying monk, is allowed to continue his impostures without interruption; and the moral which Dr. Newman draws is, that though his miraculous appearance of our Lady may be a lie, yet 'the like thereof has been before and since'.

After which follows a passage—of which I shall boldly say, that I trust that it will arouse in every English husband, father, and brother, who may read these words, the same feelings which it roused in me; and express my opinion, that it is a better compliment to Dr. Newman to think that he did not believe what he said, than to think that he did believe it:—

'You turn to go home, and in your way you pass through a retired quarter of the city. Look up at those sacred windows; they belong to the Convent of the Perpetual Adoration, or to the poor Clares, or to the Carmelites of the Reform of St. Theresa, or to the Nuns of the Visitation. Seclusion, silence, watching, adoration, is their life day and night. The Immaculate Lamb of God is ever before the eyes of the worshippers; or, at least, the invisible mysteries of faith ever stand out, as if in bodily shape, before their mental gaze. Where will you find such a realized heaven upon earth? Yet that very sight has acted otherwise on the mind of a weak sister; and the very keenness of her faith and wild desire of approaching the object of it has led her to fancy or to feign that she has received that singular favour vouchsafed only to a few elect souls; and she points to God's wounds, as imprinted on her hand, and feet, and side, though she herself has been instrumental in their formation' (Lecture IX. 237, 238).

There are occasions on which courtesy or reticence is a crime, and this one of them. A poor girl, cajoled, flattered, imprisoned, starved, maddened, by such as Dr. Newman and his peers, into that degrading and demoralising disease, hysteria, imitates on her own body, from that strange vanity and deceit which too often accompany the complaint, the wounds of our Lord; and all that Dr. Newman has to say about the matter is, to inform us that the gross and useless portent is 'a singular favour vouchsafed only to a few elect souls'. And this is the man who, when accused of countenancing falsehood, puts on first a tone of plaintive and startled innocence, and then one of smug self-satisfaction —as who should ask, 'What have I said? What have I done? Why am I upon my trial?' On his trial? If he be on his trial for nothing else, he is on his trial for those words; and he will remain upon his trial as long as Englishmen know how to guard the women whom God has committed to their charge. If the British public shall ever need informing that Dr. Newman wrote that passage, I trust there will be always one man left in England to inform them of the fact, for the sake of the ladies of this land.

Perhaps the most astounding specimens of Dr. Newman's teaching are to be found, after all, in the two sermons which end his 'Discourses addressed to Mixed Congregations', published in 1849; 'The Glories of Mary for the sake of her Son'; and 'On the fitness of the Glories of Mary'. Of the mis-quotations of Scripture, of the sophisms piled on sophisms, of these two sermons, I have no room wherein to give specimens. All I ask is, that they should be read; read by every man who thinks it any credit to himself to be a rational being. But two culminating wonders of these two sermons I must point out. The first is the assertion that the Blessed Virgin 'had been inspired, the first of womankind, to dedicate her virginity to God'. As if there had not been Buddhist nuns (if not others) centuries before Christianity. As if (allowing the argument that they dedicated their virginity to a false God) there were the slightest historic proof that the Blessed Virgin dedicated hers before the Incarnation. The second is in a sermon which professes to prove logically the 'fitness' of the Immaculate Conception, and is filled (instead of logic) with traditions which are utterly baseless. I allude to the assertion that 'the world'—*i.e.* all who do not belong to the Romish Church—'blasphemes' Mary. I make no comment. All I ask, again, of my readers is, to read these two sermons.

But what, after all, does Dr. Newman teach concerning truth? What he taught in 1843, and what he (as far as I can see) teaches still, may be seen in his last sermon in a volume entitled 'Chiefly on the Theory of

Religious Belief', called a sermon 'On the Theory of Developments in Religious Doctrine'. I beg all who are interested in this question to read that sermon (which I had overlooked till lately); and to judge for themselves whether I exaggerate when I say that it tries to undermine the grounds of all rational belief for the purpose of substituting blind superstition. As examples:—speaking of 'certain narratives of martyr-doms', and 'alleged miracles', he says (p. 345): 'If the alleged facts did not occur, they ought to have occurred, if I may so speak.' Historic truth is thus sapped; and physical truth fares no better. 'Scripture says (p. 350) that the sun moves, and that the earth is stationary; and science that the earth moves, and the sun is comparatively at rest. How can we determine which of these statements is the very truth, till we know what motion is? If our idea of motion be but an accident of our present senses neither proposition is true, and both are true; neither true philosophically, both true for certain purposes in the system in which they are respectively found; and physical science will have no better meaning when it says that the earth moves, than plain astronomy when it says that the earth is still.'

Quorsum hæc? What is the intent of this seemingly sceptic method, pursued through page after page? To tell us that we can know nothing certainly, and therefore must take blindly what 'The Church' shall choose to teach us. For the Church, it would seem, is not bound to tell us, indeed cannot tell us, the whole truth. We are to be treated like children, to whom (at least to those with whom Dr. Newman has come in con-tact) it is necessary to (p. 343) 'dispense and "divide" the word of truth, if we would not have it changed, as far as they are concerned, into a word of falsehood'. 'And so, again, as regards savages, or the ignorant, or weak, or narrow-minded, our representations must take a certain form, if we are to gain admission into their minds at all, and to reach them.'

This method of teaching by half-truths Dr. Newman calls 'economy'; and justifies it (if I understand his drift), by the instances of 'mythical representations', legends, and so forth, 'which, if they did not occur, ought to have occurred'. 'Many a theory or view of things',—he goes on—(p. 345) 'on which an institution is founded, or a party held together, is of the same kind. Many an argument, used by zealous and earnest men, has this economical character, being not the very ground on which they act (for they continue in the same course, though it be refuted), yet, in a certain sense, a representation of it, a proximate description of their feelings in the shape of argument, on which they can rest, to which they can recur when perplexed, and appeal when they are questioned.' After which startling words, Dr. Newman says—and it is really high time—'In this reference to accommodation or economy in human affairs, I do not meddle with the question of casuistry, viz. which of such artifices, as it may be called, are innocent, or where the "line is to be drawn".'

A hasty reader might say, that herein is an open justification of equivocation and dishonest reticence. But he would be mistaken. The whole sermon is written in so tentative a style, that it would be rash and wrong to say that Dr. Newman intends to convey any lesson by it, save that the discovery of truth is an impossibility. Only once, and in a note, he speaks out. P. 342.

'Hence it is not more than an hyperbole to say that, in certain cases, a lie is the nearest approach to truth. This seems the meaning, for instance, of St. Clement, when he says "He (the Christian) both thinks and speaks the truth, unless when, at any time, in the way of treatment, as a physician toward his patients, so for the welfare of the sick he will be false, or will tell a falsehood, as the sophists speak."'

If St. Clement said that, so much the worse for him. He was a great and good man. But he might have learned from his Bible that no lie was of the truth, and that it is ill stealing the devil's tools to do God's work withal.

Be that as it may. What Dr. Newman teaches is clear at last, and I see now how deeply I have wronged him. So far from thinking truth for its own sake to be no virtue, he considers it a virtue so lofty, as to be unattainable by man, who must therefore, in certain cases, take up with what-it-is-no-more-than-a-hyperbole-to-call lies; and who, if he should be so lucky as to get any truth into his possession, will be wise in 'economizing' the same, and 'dividing it', so giving away a bit here and a bit there, lest he should waste so precious a possession.

That this is Dr. Newman's opinion at present, there can be no manner of doubt. What he has persuaded himself to believe about St. Walburga's oil, St. Sturme's nose, St. Januarius' blood, and the winking Madonna's eyes, proves sufficiently that he still finds, in certain cases, what-it-is-no-more-than-a-hyperbole-to-call lies, the nearest approach which he can make to truth; while, as to the right of economizing and dividing truth, I shall shortly bring forward two instances of his having done so to such an extent, that very little of poor truth remains after the dismemberment.

And yet I do not call this conscious dishonesty. The man who wrote that sermon was already past the possibility of such a sin. It is simple credulity, the child of scepticism. Credulity, frightened at itself, trying to hide its absurdity alike from itself and from the world by quibbles and reticences which it thinks prudent and clever; and, like the hunted ostrich, fancying that because it thrusts its head into the sand, its whole body is invisible.

And now, I have tried to lead my readers along a path to which some of them, I fear, have objected.

They have fallen, perhaps, into the prevailing superstition that cleverness is synonymous with wisdom. They cannot believe that (as is too certain) great literary, and even barristerial ability, may co-exist with almost boundless silliness: but I can find no other explanation of the phenomena than that which I have just given. That Dr. Newman thinks that there is no harm in 'economy', and 'dividing the truth', is evident; for he has employed it again in his comments on the correspondence. He has employed twice, as the most natural and innocent thing possible, those 'arts of the defenceless' which require so much delicacy in the handling, lest 'liberal shepherds give a grosser name', and call them cunning, or even worse.

I am, of course, free to make my own comments on them, as on all other words of Dr. Newman's printed since the 1st of February, 1864, on which day my apology was published. I shall certainly take the sense of the British public on the matter. Though Dr. Newman may be 'a mystery' to them, as he says 'religious men' always are to the world, yet they possess quite common sense enough to see what his words are, even though his intention be, as it is wont to be, obscure.

They recollect the definitions of the 'Church' and 'Christians', on the ground of which I called Sermon XX. a Romish sermon?

Dr. Newman does not apply to it that epithet. He called it, in his letter to me of the 7th of January (published by him), a 'Protestant' one. I remarked that, but considered it a mere slip of the pen. Besides, I have now nothing to say to that letter. It is to his 'Reflexions' in page 352 which are open ground to me, that I refer. In them he deliberately repeats the epithet 'Protestant': only he, in an utterly imaginary conversation, puts it into my mouth, 'which you preached when a Protestant'. I call the man who preached that sermon a Protestant? I should have sooner called him a Buddhist. At that very time he was teaching his disciples to scorn and repudiate that name of Protestant, under which, for some reason or other, he now finds it convenient to take shelter. If he forgets, the world does not, the famous article in the *British Critic* (the then organ of his party), of three years before—July, 1841—which, after denouncing the name of Protestant, declared the object of the party to be none other than the 'Unprotestantising' the English Church.

But Dr. Newman convicts himself. In the sermon before, as I have shown, monks and nuns are spoken of as the only true Bible Christians, and in the sermon itself a celibate clergy is made a note of the Church. And yet Dr. Newman goes on to say that he was not then 'a priest, speaking of priests'. Whether he were a priest himself matters little to the question; but if he were not speaking of priests, and those Romish ones, when he spoke of a celibate clergy, of whom was he speaking? But there is no use in wasting words on this 'economical' statement of

Dr. Newman's. I shall only say that there are people in the world whom it is very difficult to help. As soon as they are got out of one scrape, they walk straight into another.

But Dr. Newman has made, in my opinion, another and a still greater mistake. He has committed, on the very title-page of his pamphlet, an 'economy' which some men will consider a very serious offence. He has there stated that the question is, 'Whether Dr. Newman teaches that truth is no virtue.' He has repeated this misrepresentation in a still stronger form at page 352, where he has ventured to represent me as saying 'Dr. Newman tells us that lying is never any harm.' He has economized the very four words of my accusation, which make it at least a reasonable one; namely—'*For its own sake.*'

I never said what he makes me say, or anything like it. I never was inclined to say it. Had I ever been, I should be still more inclined to say it now.

But Dr. Newman has shown 'wisdom' enough of that serpentine type which is his professed ideal in what he has done, and has been so economic of truth, and 'divided' the truth so thoroughly, that really there is very little of it left.

For while no one knew better than he the importance of the omission, none knew better that the public would not do so; that they would never observe it; that, if I called their attention to it, they would smile, and accuse me of word-splitting and raising metaphysical subtleties. Yes, Dr. Newman is a very economical person. So, when I had accused him and the Romish clergy of teaching that 'truth is no virtue, for its own sake', he simply economized the last four words, and said that I accused him and them of teaching that 'truth is no virtue'.

This, in Dr. Newman, the subtle dialectician, is, indeed, an 'enormity', as he chooses to call my accusation of him. No one better knows the value of such limitations. No one has, sometimes fairly, sometimes unfairly, made more use of them. No man, therefore, ought to have been more careful of doing what he has done.

Dr. Newman tries, by cunning sleight-of-hand logic, to prove that I did not believe the accusation when I made it. Therein he is mistaken. I did believe it, and I believed, also, his indignant denial. But when he goes on to ask, with sneers, Why I should believe his denial, if I did not consider him trustworthy in the first instance?—I can only answer, I really do not know. There is a great deal to be said for that view, now that Dr. Newman has become (one must needs suppose) suddenly, and since the 1st of February, 1864, a convert to the economic views of St. Alfonso da Liguori and his compeers. I am henceforth in doubt and fear, as much as an honest man can be, concerning every word Dr. Newman may write. How can I tell that I shall not be the dupe of some cunning equivocation, of one of the three kinds laid down

as permissible by the blessed St. Alfonso da Liguori and his pupils
even when confirmed with an oath, because 'then we do not deceive our
neighbour, but allow him to deceive himself'?[1]—The whole being
justified by the example of Christ, 'who answered, "I go not up to this
feast," *subintelligendo*, "openly"'. 'For', say the casuists, 'if there were
no such restrictions (on the telling of truth), there would be no means
of concealing secrets, which one could not open without loss or inconvenience; but this would be no less pernicious to human society than a
lie itself.' It is admissible, therefore, to use words and sentences which
have a double signification, and leave the hapless hearer to take which
of them he may choose. What proof have I, then, that by '*mean* it! I
never *said* it'! Dr. Newman does not signify, 'I did not say it: but I
did mean it'?

Or again, how can I tell that I may not in this pamphlet have made
an accusation, of the truth of which Dr. Newman is perfectly conscious;
but that as I, a heretic Protestant, have no business to make it, he has
a full right to deny it? For what says Neyraguet, after the blessed
St. Alfonso da Liguori? That 'a criminal or witness, being interrogated
by a judge contrary to law, may swear that he knows not of the crime;
meaning, that he knows not of a crime of which he may be lawfully
questioned.'

These are hard words. If Dr. Newman shall complain of them, I can
only remind him of the fate which befel the stork caught among the
cranes, even though the stork had not done all he could to make himself like a crane, as Dr. Newman has, by 'economizing' on the very
title-page of his pamphlet.

I know perfectly well that truth—'veracity', as they call it—is a
virtue with the Romish moralists; that it is one of the cardinal virtues,
the daughters of justice, like benevolence, courtesy, gratitude, and so
forth; and is proved to be such because there is a *naturalis honestas* in
it, and also that without it society could not go on. Lying, on the other
hand, though not one of the seven 'capital' sins, which are pride,
avarice, luxury (unchastity), gluttony, anger, envy, and acedia (luke-
warmness), is yet held to be always a sin, when direct. It is proved to be
such from Scripture, from the fathers, and from natural reason, because
'truth is an essential perfection of the Divine nature'. So far well. But
a lie is a venial sin, if it 'neither hurts our neighbour or God gravely, or
causes a grave scandal'; as no lie told in behalf of the Catholic faith can
well do, though one wise Pope laid it down that it was a sin to tell a lie,
even for the sake of saving a soul. But though it were a sin, the fact of
its being a venial one seems to have gained for it, as yet, a very slight

---

[1] I quote from Scavini, tom. ii. page 232, of the Paris edition, and from Neyraguet,
p. 141, two compendiums of Liguori which are (or were lately) used, so I have every
reason to believe—one at Oscott, the other at Maynooth.

penance. Meanwhile, as a thousand venial sins can never make one mortal one, a man may be a habitual liar all his life long, without falling into mortal sin. Moreover, though 'formal simulation', when 'one signifies by outward act something different to what he has in his mind', is illicit, as a lie, yet 'material simulation', or stratagem, is not so. 'For when one does something, not intending the deception of another, but some end of his own, then it is allowable on cause; although, from other circumstances, men might conjecture that the act was done for another end. So Joshua fled lawfully, not meaning fear, but that he might draw the enemy further from the city of Hai.' From which one can gather, that Romish casuists allow the same stratagems to man against his neighbours, in peaceable society, which Protestant public opinion allows (and that with a growing compunction) only to officers in war, against the enemies of their country. Considering this fact, and the permission of equivocation, even on oath, it is somewhat difficult to expect that the Romish moralists, at least, hold truth to be a virtue for its own sake, or to deny that they teach cunning to be the weapons of the weak against the strong.

Yes—I am afraid that I must say it once more—Truth is not honoured among these men for its own sake. There are, doubtless, pure and noble souls among them, superior, through the grace of God, to the official morality of their class: but in their official writings, and in too much of their official conduct, the great majority seem never, for centuries past, to have perceived that truth is the capital virtue, the virtue of all virtues, without which all others are hollow and rotten; and with which there is hope for a man's repentance and conversion, in spite of every vice, if only he remains honest. They have not seen that facts are the property not of man, to be 'economized' as man thinks fit, but of God, who ordereth all things in heaven and earth; and that therefore not only every lie, but every equivocation, every attempt at deception, is a sin, not against man, but against God; they have not seen that no lie is of the truth, and that God requires truth, not merely in outward words, but in the inward parts; and that therefore the first and most absolute duty of every human being is to speak and act the exact truth; or if he wish to be silent, to be silent, courageously and simply, and take the risk, trusting in God to protect him, as long as he remains on God's side in the universe, by scorning to sully his soul by stratagem or equivocation. Had they seen this; had they not regarded truth as a mere arbitrary command of God, which was not binding in doubtful cases, they would never have dared to bargain with God as to how little truth He required of men; and to examine and define (to the injury alike of their own sense of honour, and that of their hearers) how much deception He may be reasonably supposed to allow.

Is this last Dr. Newman's view of truth? I hope not. I hope that he, educated as an English gentleman and Oxford scholar, is at variance with the notions formally allowed by the most popular and influential modern Doctor of his Church. But that there is some slight difference between his notions of truth and ours he has confessed—in a letter to 'X. V. Esqre,'[1] which he has printed in his 'Correspondence'. For there he says (p. 344): 'I think that you will allow that there is a broad difference between a virtue, considered as a principle or rule, and the applications and limits of it in human conduct. Catholics and Protestants, in their view of the substance of the moral virtues, agree; but they carry them out variously in detail.' He then gives us to understand, that this is the case as to truth; that Catholics differ from Protestants as to 'whether this or that act in particular is conformable to the rule of truth'.

I beg to say, that in these words Dr. Newman has made another great mistake. He has calumniated, as far as my experience goes, the Catholic gentry of these realms. I am proud to say, as far as I have had the honour and pleasure of their acquaintance, that there is no difference whatsoever, of detail or other, between their truthfulness and honour, and the truthfulness and honour of the Protestant gentry among whom they live, respected and beloved, in spite of all religious differences, simply because they are honest gentlemen and noble ladies. But if Dr. Newman will limit his statement to the majority of the Romish priesthood, and to those hapless Irish Celts over whom they rule, then we will willingly accept it as perfectly correct. There is a very wide difference in practical details between their notions of truth and ours; and what that difference is, I have already pointed out. It is notorious enough in facts and practice. It may be seen at large by any one who chooses to read the Romish Moral Theologians. And if Dr. Newman, as a Catholic priest, includes himself in his own statement, that is his act, not mine.

And so I leave Dr. Newman, only expressing my fear, that if he continues to 'economize' and 'divide' the words of his adversaries as he has done mine, he will run great danger of forfeiting once more his reputation for honesty.

CHARLES KINGSLEY

---

[1] ['X. V.' for 'X. Y.', so in first and third editions of Kingsley's pamphlet.]

APPENDIX C

APOLOGIA PRO VITA SUA

BEING A REPLY TO A PAMPHLET ENTITLED
'WHAT, THEN, DOES DR. NEWMAN MEAN?'

'Commit thy way to the Lord, and trust in Him, and He
will do it. And He will bring forth thy justice as the light,
and thy judgment as the noon-day.'

By JOHN HENRY NEWMAN, D.D.

MR. KINGSLEY'S METHOD OF DISPUTATION

I CANNOT be sorry to have forced Mr. Kingsley to bring out in fulness his charges against me. It is far better that he should discharge his thoughts upon me in my lifetime, than after I am dead. Under the circumstances I am happy in having the opportunity of reading the worst that can be said of me by a writer who has taken pains with his work and is well satisfied with it. I account it a gain to be surveyed from without by one who hates the principles which are nearest to my heart, has no personal knowledge of me to set right his misconceptions of my doctrine, and who has some motive or other to be as severe with me as he can possibly be.

And first of all, I beg to compliment him on the motto in his Title-page; it is felicitous. A motto should contain, as in a nutshell, the contents, or the character, or the drift, or the *animus* of the writing to which it is prefixed. The words which he has taken from me are so apposite as to be almost prophetical. There cannot be a better illustration than he thereby affords of the aphorism which I intended them to convey. I said that it is not more than an hyperbolical expression to say that in certain cases a lie is the nearest approach to truth. Mr. Kingsley's pamphlet is emphatically one of such cases as are contemplated in that proposition. I really believe, that his view of me is about as near an approach to the truth about my writings and doings, as he is capable of taking. He has done his worst towards me; but he has also done his best. So far well; but, while I impute to him no malice, I unfeignedly think, on the other hand, that, in his invective against me, he as faithfully fulfils the other half of the proposition also.

This is not a mere sharp retort upon Mr. Kingsley, as will be seen, when I come to consider directly the subject, to which the words of his motto relate. I have enlarged on that subject in various passages of my publications; I have said that minds in different states and circumstances cannot understand one another, and that in all cases they must be instructed according to their capacity, and, if not taught step by step, they learn only so much the less; that children do not apprehend the thoughts of grown people, nor savages the instincts of civilization, nor blind men the perceptions of sight, nor pagans the doctrines of Christianity, nor men the experiences of Angels. In the same way, there are people of matter-of-fact, prosaic minds, who cannot take in the fancies of poets; and others of shallow, inaccurate minds, who cannot take in the ideas of philosophical inquirers. In a Lecture of mine I have illus - trated this phenomenon by the supposed instance of a foreigner, who, after reading a commentary on the principles of English Law, does not get nearer to a real apprehension of them than to be led to accuse Englishmen of considering that the Queen is impeccable and infallible, and that the Parliament is omnipotent. Mr. Kingsley has read me from beginning to end in the fashion in which the hypothetical Russian read Blackstone; not, I repeat, from malice, but because of his intellectual build. He appears to be so constituted as to have no notion of what goes on in minds very different from his own, and moreover to be stone-blind to his ignorance. A modest man or a philosopher would have scrupled to treat with scorn and scoffing, as Mr. Kingsley does in my own instance, principles and convictions, even if he did not acquiesce in them himself, which had been held so widely and for so long,—the beliefs and devotions and customs which have been the religious life of millions upon millions of Christians for nearly twenty centuries,—for this in fact is the task on which he is spending his pains. Had he been a man of large or cautious mind, he would not have taken it for granted that cultivation must lead every one to see things precisely as he sees them himself. But the narrow-minded are the more prejudiced by very reason of their narrowness. The Apostle bids us 'in malice be children, but in understanding be men'. I am glad to recognize in Mr. Kingsley an illustration of the first half of this precept; but I should not be honest, if I ascribed to him any sort of fulfilment of the second.

I wish I could speak as favourably either of his drift or of his method of arguing, as I can of his convictions. As to his drift, I think its ulti-mate point is an attack upon the Catholic Religion. It is I indeed, whom he is immediately insulting,—still, he views me only as a representative, and on the whole a fair one, of a class or caste of men, to whom, conscious as I am of my own integrity, I ascribe an excellence superior to mine. He desires to impress upon the public mind the con-viction that I am a crafty, scheming man, simply untrustworthy; that, in becoming a Catholic, I have just found my right place; that I do but justify and am properly interpreted by the common English notion of Roman casuists and confessors; that I was secretly a Catholic when I was openly professing to be a clergyman of the Established Church; that so far from bringing, by means of my conversion, when at length it openly took place, any strength to the Catholic cause, I am really a burden to it,—an additional evidence of the fact, that to be a pure, german, genuine Catholic, a man must be either a knave or a fool.

These last words bring me to Mr. Kingsley's method of disputation, which I must criticize with much severity;—in his drift he does but follow the ordinary beat of controversy, but in his mode of arguing he is actually dishonest.

He says that I am either a knave or a fool, and (as we shall see by and by) he is not quite sure which, probably both. He tells his readers that on one occasion he said that he had fears I should 'end in one or other of two misfortunes'. 'He would either', he continues, 'destroy his own sense of honesty, i.e. conscious truthfulness—and become a dishonest person; or he would destroy his common sense, i.e. unconscious truthfulness, and become the slave and puppet seemingly of his own logic, really of his own fancy. . . . I thought for years past that he had become the former; I now see that he has become the latter. 'pp. 365–6. Again, 'When I read these outrages upon common sense, what wonder if I said to myself, "This man cannot believe what he is saying "?' p. 369. Such has been Mr. Kingsley's state of mind till lately, but now he considers that I am possessed with a spirit of 'almost boundless silliness', of 'simple credulity, the child of scepticism', of 'absurdity' (pp. 379–80), of a 'self-deception which has become a sort of frantic honesty' (p. 370). And as to his fundamental reason for this change, he tells us, he really does not know what it is (p. 381). However, let the reason be what it will, its upshot is intelligible enough. He is enabled at once, by this professed change of judgment about me, to put forward one of these alternatives, yet to keep the other in reserve;—and this he actually does. He need not commit himself to a definite accusation against me, such as requires definite proof and admits of definite refutation; for he has two strings to his bow;—when he is thrown off his balance on the one leg, he can recover himself by the use of the other. If I demonstrate that I am not a knave, he may exclaim, 'Oh, but you are a fool!' and when I demonstrate that I am not a fool, he may turn round and retort, 'Well, then, you are a knave.' I have no objection to reply to his arguments in behalf of either alternative, but I should have been better pleased to have been allowed to take them one at a time.

But I have not yet done full justice to the method of disputation, which Mr. Kingsley thinks it right to adopt. Observe this first:—He means by a man who is 'silly' not a man who is to be pitied, but a man who is to be *abhorred*. He means a man who is not simply weak and incapable, but a moral leper; a man who, if not a knave, has every thing bad about him except knavery; nay, rather, has together with every other worst vice, a spice of knavery to boot. *His* simpleton is one who has become such, in judgment for his having once been a knave. *His* simpleton is not a born fool, but a self-made idiot, one who has drugged and abused himself into a shameless depravity; one, who, without any misgiving or remorse, is guilty of drivelling superstition, of reckless violation of sacred things, of fanatical excesses, of passionate inanities, of unmanly audacious tyranny over the weak, meriting the wrath of fathers and brothers. This is that milder judgment, which he seems to pride himself upon as so much charity; and, as he expresses it, he 'does not know' why. This is what he really meant in his letter to me of January 14, when he withdrew his charge of my being dishonest. He said, 'The *tone* of your letters, even more than their language, makes me feel, *to my very deep pleasure*',—what? that you have gambled away your reason, that you are an intellectual sot, that you are a fool in a frenzy. And in his Pamphlet, he gives us this explanation why he did not say this to my face, viz. that he had been told that I was 'in weak health', and was 'averse to controversy', p. 356. He 'felt some regret for having disturbed me'.

But I pass on from these multiform imputations, and confine myself to this one consideration, viz. that he has made any fresh imputation upon me at all. He gave up the charge of knavery; well and good: but where was the logical necessity of his bringing another? I am sitting at home without a thought of Mr. Kingsley; he wantonly breaks in upon me with the charge that I had '*informed*' the world 'that Truth for its own sake *need not* and on the whole *ought not to be* a virtue with the Roman clergy'. When challenged on the point he cannot bring a fragment of evidence in proof of his assertion, and he is convicted of false witness by the voice of the world. Well, I should have thought that he had now nothing whatever more to do. 'Vain man!' he seems to make answer, 'what simplicity in you to think so! If you have not broken one commandment, let us see whether we cannot convict you of the breach of another. If you are not a swindler or forger, you are guilty of arson or burglary. By hook or by crook you shall not escape. Are *you* to suffer or *I*? What does it matter to you who are going off the stage, to receive a slight additional daub upon a character so deeply stained already? But think of me, the immaculate lover of Truth, so observant (as I have told you p. 358) of "*hault courage* and strict honour",—and (*aside*)— "and not as this publican"—do you think I can let you go scot free instead of myself? No; *noblesse oblige*. Go to the shades, old man, and boast that Achilles sent you thither.'

But I have not even yet done with Mr. Kingsley's method of disputation. Observe secondly:—when a man is said to be a knave or a fool, it is commonly meant that he is *either* the one *or* the other; and that,— either in the sense that the hypothesis of his being a fool is too absurd to be entertained; or, again, as a sort of contemptuous acquittal of one, who after all has not wit enough to be wicked. But this is not at all what Mr. Kingsley proposes to himself in the antithesis which he suggests to his readers. Though he speaks of me as an utter dotard and fanatic, yet all along, from the beginning of his Pamphlet to the end, he insinuates, he proves from my writings, and at length in his last pages he openly pronounces, that after all he was right at first, in thinking me a conscious liar and deceiver.

Now I wish to dwell on this point. It cannot be doubted, I say, that, in spite of his professing to consider me as a dotard and driveller, on the ground of his having given up the notion of my being a knave, yet it is the very staple of his Pamphlet that a knave after all I must be. By insinuation, or by implication, or by question, or by irony, or by sneer, or by parable, he enforces again and again a conclusion which he does not categorically enunciate.

For instance (1) P. 362. 'I know that men *used to suspect Dr. Newman*, I have been inclined to do so myself, of writing a whole sermon . . . for the sake of one single passing hint, one phrase, one epithet, one little barbed arrow which . . . he delivered unheeded, as with his finger tip, to the very heart of an initiated hearer, *never to be withdrawn again.*'

(2) P. 363. 'How *was* I to know that the preacher, who had the reputation of being the most *acute* man of his generation, and of having a specially intimate acquaintance with the weaknesses of the human heart, was utterly blind to the broad meaning and the plain practical result of a sermon like this, delivered before fanatic and hot-headed young men, who hung upon his every word? That he did not *foresee* that they would think that they obeyed him, *by becoming affected, artificial, sly, shifty, ready for concealments and equivocations?*'

(3) P. 364. 'No one *would have* suspected him to be a dishonest man, if he had not perversely chosen *to assume a style* which (as he himself confesses) the world always associates with dishonesty.'

(4) P. 372. '*If* he will indulge in subtle paradoxes, in rhetorical exaggerations; if, *whenever he touches on the question of truth and honesty*, he will take a perverse pleasure in saying something shocking to plain English notions, he *must take the consequences of his own eccentricities.*'

(5) P. 375. 'At which most of my readers will be inclined to cry: "Let Dr. Newman alone, after that. . . . He had a human reason once, no doubt: but he has gambled it away.' . . . True: so true, &c.'

(6) P. 375. He continues: 'I should never have written these pages, save because it was my duty to show the world, if not Dr. Newman, how the mistake (!) of his *not caring* for truth arose.'

(7) P. 377. 'And this is the man, who when accused of countenancing falsehood, puts on first a tone of *plaintive* (!) and startled innocence, and then one of smug self-satisfaction—as who should ask, "What have I said? What have I done? Why am I on my trial?"'

(8) P. 379. 'What Dr. Newman teaches is clear at last, and *I see now*

how deeply I have wronged him. So far from thinking truth for its own sake to be no virtue, *he considers it a virtue so lofty as to be unattainable by man.*'

(9) Pp. 380–1. 'There is no use in wasting words on this "economical" statement of Dr. Newman's. I shall only say that there are people in the world whom it is very difficult to *help*. As soon as they are got out of one scrape, they walk straight into another.'

(10) P. 381. 'Dr. Newman has shown "wisdom" enough of that *serpentine* type which is his professed ideal. . . . Yes, Dr. Newman is a very economical person.'

(11) P. 381. 'Dr. Newman *tries*, by *cunning sleight-of-hand logic*, to prove that I did not believe the accusation when I made it.'

(12) P. 382. 'These are hard words. If Dr. Newman shall complain of them, I can only remind him of the fate which befel the stork caught among the cranes, *even though* the stork had *not* done all he could to make himself like a crane, *as Dr. Newman has*, by "economising" on the very title-page of his pamphlet.'

These last words bring us to another and far worse instance of these slanderous assaults upon me, but its place is in a subsequent page.

Now it may be asked of me, 'Well, why should not Mr. Kingsley take a course such as this? It was his original assertion that Dr. Newman was a professed liar, and a patron of lies; he spoke somewhat at random; granted; but now he has got up his references and he is proving, not perhaps the very thing which he said at first, but something very like it, and to say the least quite as bad. He is now only aiming to justify morally his original assertion; why is he not at liberty to do so?'

Why should he *not* now insinuate that I am a liar and a knave! he had of course a perfect right to make such a charge, if he chose; he might have said, 'I was virtually right, and here is the proof of it', but this he has not done, but on the contrary has professed that he no longer draws from my works, as he did before, the inference of my dishonesty. He says distinctly, p. 369, 'When I read these outrages upon common sense, what wonder if I said to myself, "This man cannot believe what he is saying?" *I believe I was wrong.*' And in p. 373, 'I said, This man has no real care for truth. Truth for its own sake is no virtue in his eyes, and he teaches that it need not be. *I do not say that now.*' And in p. 379, 'I do not call this conscious dishonesty; the man who wrote that sermon *was already past the possibility* of such a sin.'

Why should he *not*! because it is on the ground of my not being a knave that he calls me a fool; adding to the words just quoted, '[My readers] have fallen perhaps into the prevailing superstition that cleverness is synonymous with wisdom. They cannot believe that (as is too certain) great literary and even barristerial ability may co-exist with almost boundless silliness.'

Why should he *not*! because he has taken credit to himself for that high feeling of honour which refuses to withdraw a concession which once has been made; though, (wonderful to say!) at the very time that he is recording this magnanimous resolution, he lets it out of the bag that his relinquishment of it is only a profession and a pretence; for he says, p. 358: 'I have accepted Dr. Newman's denial that [the Sermon] means what I thought it did; and *heaven forbid*' (oh!) 'that I should withdraw my word once given, *at whatever disadvantage to myself.*' Disadvantage! but nothing can be advantageous to him which is *untrue*; therefore in proclaiming that the concession of my honesty is a disadvantage to him, he thereby implies unequivocally that there is some probability still, that I am *dis*honest. He goes on, 'I am informed by those from whose judgment on such points there is no appeal, that *"en hault courage"*, and strict honour, I am also *precluded*, by the *terms* of my explanation, from using any other of Dr. Newman's past writings to prove my assertion.' And then, 'I have declared Dr. Newman to have been an honest man up to the 1st of February, 1864; it was, as I shall show, only Dr. Newman's fault that I ever thought him to be any thing else. It depends entirely on Dr. Newman whether he shall *sustain* the reputation which he has so recently acquired,' (by diploma of course from Mr. Kingsley.) 'If I give him thereby a fresh advantage in this argument, he is *most welcome* to it. He needs, it seems to me, *as many advantages as possible.*'

What a princely mind! How loyal to his rash promise, how delicate towards the subject of it, how conscientious in his interpretation of it! I have no thought of irreverence towards a Scripture Saint, who was actuated by a very different spirit from Mr. Kingsley's, but somehow since I read his Pamphlet words have been running in my head, which I find in the Douay version thus; 'Thou hast also with thee Semei the son of Gera, who cursed me with a grievous curse when I went to the camp, but I swore to him, saying, I will not kill thee with the sword. Do not thou hold him guiltless. But thou art a wise man and knowest what to do with him, and thou shalt bring down his grey hairs with blood to hell.'

Now I ask, Why could not Mr. Kingsley be open? If he intended still to arraign me on the charge of lying, why could he not say so as a man? Why must he insinuate, question, imply, and use sneering and irony, as if longing to touch a forbidden fruit, which still he was afraid would burn his fingers, if he did so? Why must he 'palter in a double sense', and blow hot and cold in one breath? He first said he considered me a patron of lying; well, he changed his opinion; and as to the logical ground of this change, he said that, if any one asked him what it was, he could only answer that *he really did not know*. Why could not he change back again, and say he did not know why? He had quite a right to do so; and then his conduct would have been so far straightforward and unexceptionable. But no;—in the very act of professing to believe in my sincerity, he takes care to show the world that it is a profession and nothing more. That very proceeding which at p. 362 he lays to my charge, (whereas I detest it,) of avowing one thing and thinking another, that proceeding he here exemplifies himself; and yet, while indulging in practices as offensive as this, he ventures to speak of his sensitive admiration of 'hault courage and strict honour!' 'I forgive you, Sir Knight,' says the heroine in the Romance, 'I forgive you as a Christian.' 'That means', said Wamba, 'that she does not forgive him at all.' Mr. Kingsley's word of honour is about as valuable as in the jester's opinion was the Christian charity of Rowena. But here we are brought to a further specimen of Mr. Kingsley's method of disputation, and having duly exhibited it, I shall have done with him.

It is his last, and he has intentionally reserved it for his last. Let it be recollected that he professed to absolve me from his original charge of dishonesty up to February 1. And further, he implies that, *at the time when he was writing*, I had not *yet* involved myself in any fresh acts suggestive of that sin. He says that I have had a great *escape* of conviction, that he hopes I shall take warning, and act more cautiously. 'It depends entirely', he says, 'on *Dr. Newman, whether* he shall *sustain* the reputation which he has so recently acquired' (p. 358). Thus, in Mr. Kingsley's judgment, I was *then*, when he wrote these words, *still* innocent of dishonesty, for a man cannot sustain what he actually has not got; *only he could not be sure of my future.* Could not be sure! Why at this very time he had already noted down valid proofs, as he thought them, that I *had* already forfeited the character which he contemptuously accorded to me. He had cautiously said '*up to* February 1st', *in order* to reserve the Title-page and last three pages of my Pamphlet, which were not published till February 12th, and out of these four pages, which he had *not* whitewashed, he had *already* forged charges against me of dishonesty at the very time that he implied that as yet there was nothing against me. When he gave me that plenary condonation, as it seemed to be, he had already done his best that I should never enjoy it. He knew well at p. 358, what he meant to say at pp. 381 and 382. At best indeed I was only out upon ticket of leave; but that ticket was a pretence; he had made it forfeit when he gave it. But he did not say so at once, first, because between p. 358 and p. 381 he meant to talk a great deal about my idiotcy and my frenzy, which would have been simply out of place, had he proved me too soon to be a knave again; and next, because he meant to exhaust all those insinuations about my knavery in the past, which 'strict honour' did not permit him to countenance, in order thereby to give colour and force to his direct charges of knavery in the present, which 'strict honour' *did* permit him to handsel. So in the fifth act he gave a start, and found to his horror that, in my miserable four pages, I had committed the 'enormity' of an 'economy', which in matter of fact he had got by heart before he began the play. Nay, he suddenly found two, three, and (for what he knew) as many as four profligate economies in that Title-page and those Reflections, and he uses the language of distress and perplexity at this appalling discovery.

Now why this *coup de théâtre*? The reason soon breaks on us. Up to February 1, he could not categorically arraign me for lying, and therefore could not involve me, (as was so necessary for his case,) in the popular abhorrence which is felt for the casuists of Rome: but, as soon as ever he could openly and directly pronounce (saving his 'hault courage and strict honour') that I am guilty of three or four new economies, then at once I am made to bear, not only my own sins, but the sins of other people also, and, though I have been condoned the knavery of my antecedents, I am guilty of the knavery of a whole priesthood instead. So the hour of doom for Semei is come, and the wise man knows what to do with him;—he is down upon me with the odious names of 'St. Alfonso da Liguori', and 'Scavini' and 'Neyraguet', and 'the Romish moralists', and their 'compeers and pupils', and I am at once merged and whirled away in the gulph of notorious quibblers, and hypocrites, and rogues.

But we have not even yet got at the real object of the stroke, thus reserved for his *finale*. I really feel sad for what I am obliged now to say. I am in warfare with him, but I wish him no ill;—it is very difficult to get up resentment towards persons whom one has never seen. It is easy enough to be irritated with friends or foes, *vis-à-vis*; but, though I am writing with all my heart against what he has said of me, I am not conscious of personal unkindness towards himself. I think it necessary to write as I am writing, for my own sake, and for the sake of the Catholic Priesthood; but I wish to impute nothing worse to Mr. Kingsley than that he has been furiously carried away by his feelings. But what shall I say of the upshot of all this talk of my economies and equivocations and the like? What is the precise *work* which it is directed to effect? I am at war with him; but there is such a thing as legitimate warfare: war has its laws; there are things which may fairly be done, and things which may not be done. I say it with shame and with stern sorrow;—he has attempted a great transgression; he has attempted (as I may call it) to *poison the wells*. I will quote him and explain what I mean.

'Dr. Newman tries, by cunning sleight-of-hand logic, to prove that I did not believe the acccusation when I made it. Therein he is mistaken. I did believe it, and I believed also his indignant denial. But when he goes on to ask with sneers, why I should believe his denial, if I did not consider him trustworthy in the first instance? I can only answer, I really do not know. There is a *great deal* to be said for *that* view, *now that* Dr. Newman has become (one must needs suppose) *suddenly* and *since* the 1st of February, 1864, a convert to the *economic* views of St. Alfonso da Liguori and his compeers. I am *henceforth* in doubt and *fear*, as much as any honest man can be, *concerning every word* Dr. Newman may write. *How can I tell that I shall not be the dupe of some cunning equivocation*, of one of the three kinds laid down as permissible by the blessed Alfonso da Liguori and his pupils, even when confirmed by an oath, because "then we do not deceive our neighbour, but allow him to deceive himself?" . . . It is admissible, therefore, to use words and sentences which have a double signification, and leave the hapless hearer to take which of them he may choose. *What proof have I, then, that by "mean it? I never said it!" Dr. Newman does not signify*, I did not say it, but I did mean it?'—Pp. 381, 382.

Now these insinuations and questions shall be answered in their proper places; here I will but say that I scorn and detest lying, and quibbling, and double-tongued practice, and slyness, and cunning, and smoothness, and cant, and pretence, quite as much as any Protestants hate them; and I pray to be kept from the snare of them. But all this is just now by the bye; my present subject is Mr. Kingsley; what I insist upon here, now that I am bringing this portion of my discussion to a close, is this unmanly attempt of his, in his concluding pages, to cut the ground from under my feet;—to poison by anticipation the public mind against me, John Henry Newman, and to infuse into the imaginations of my readers, suspicion and mistrust of everything that I may say in reply to him. This I call *poisoning the wells*.

'I am henceforth in *doubt and fear*', he says, 'as much as any *honest* man can be, *concerning every word* Dr. Newman may write. *How can I tell that I shall not be the dupe of some cunning equivocation?* . . . What proof have I, that by "mean it? I never said it!" Dr. Newman does not signify, "I did not say it, but I did mean it?"'

Well, I can only say, that, if his taunt is to take effect, I am but wasting my time in saying a word in answer to his foul calumnies; and this is precisely what he knows and intends to be its fruit. I can hardly get myself to protest against a method of controversy so base and cruel, lest in doing so, I should be violating my self-respect and self-possession; but most base and most cruel it is. We all know how our imagination runs away with us, how suddenly and at what a pace;—the saying, 'Cæsar's wife should not be suspected', is an instance of what I mean. The habitual prejudice, the humour of the moment, is the turning-point which leads us to read a defence in a good sense or a bad. We interpret it by our antecedent impressions. The very same sentiments, according as our jealousy is or is not awake, or our aversion stimulated, are tokens of truth or of dissimulation and pretence. There is a story of a sane person being by mistake shut up in the wards of a Lunatic Asylum, and that, when he pleaded his cause to some strangers visiting the establishment, the only remark he elicited in answer was, 'How naturally he talks! you would think he was in his senses.' Controversies should be decided by the reason; is it legitimate warfare to appeal to the misgivings of the public mind and to its dislikings? Any how, if Mr. Kingsley is able thus to practise upon my readers, the more I succeed, the less will be my success. If I am natural, he will tell them, 'Ars est celare artem'; if I am convincing, he will suggest that I am an able logician; if I show warmth, I am acting the indignant innocent; if I am calm, I am thereby detected as a smooth hypocrite; if I clear up difficulties, I am too plausible and perfect to be true. The more triumphant are my statements, the more certain will be my defeat.

So will it be if Mr. Kingsley succeeds in his manœuvre; but I do not for an instant believe that he will. Whatever judgment my readers may eventually form of me from these pages, I am confident that they will believe me in what I shall say in the course of them. I have no misgiving at all, that they will be ungenerous or harsh with a man who has been so long before the eyes of the world; who has so many to speak of him from personal knowledge; whose natural impulse it has ever been to speak out; who has ever spoken too much rather than too little; who would have saved himself many a scrape, if he had been wise enough to hold his tongue; who has ever been fair to the doctrines and arguments of his opponents; who has never slurred over facts and reasonings which told against himself; who has never given his name or authority to proofs which he thought unsound, or to testimony which he did not think at least plausible; who has never shrunk from confessing a fault when he felt that he had committed one; who has ever consulted for others more than for himself; who has given up much that he loved and prized and could have retained, but that he loved honesty better than name, and Truth better than dear friends.

And now I am in a train of thought higher and more serene than any which slanders can disturb. Away with you, Mr. Kingsley, and fly into space. Your name shall occur again as little as I can help, in the course of these pages. I shall henceforth occupy myself not with you, but with your charges.

TRUE MODE OF MEETING
MR. KINGSLEY

WHAT shall be the special imputation, against which I shall throw myself in these pages, out of the thousand and one which my accuser directs upon me? I mean to confine myself to one, for there is only one about which I much care,—the charge of Untruthfulness. He may cast upon me as many other imputations as he pleases, and they may stick on me, as long as they can, in the course of nature. They will fall to the ground in their season.

And indeed I think the same of the charge of Untruthfulness, and I select it from the rest, not because it is more formidable, but because it is more serious. Like the rest, it may disfigure me for a time, but it will not stain: Archbishop Whately used to say, 'Throw dirt enough, and some will stick'; well, will stick, but not stain. I think he used to mean 'stain', and I do not agree with him. Some dirt sticks longer than other dirt; but no dirt is immortal. According to the old saying, Prævalebit Veritas. There are virtues indeed, which the world is not fitted to judge about or to uphold, such as faith, hope, and charity: but it can judge about Truthfulness; it can judge about the natural virtues, and Truthfulness is one of them. Natural virtues may also become supernatural; Truthfulness is such; but that does not withdraw it from the jurisdiction of mankind at large. It may be more difficult in this or that particular case for men to take cognizance of it, as it may be difficult for the Court of Queen's Bench at Westminster to try a case fairly, which took place in Hindoostan; but that is a question of capacity, not of right. Mankind has the right to judge of Truthfulness in the case of a Catholic, as in the case of a Protestant, of an Italian, or of a Chinese. I have never doubted, that in my hour, in God's hour, my avenger will appear, and the world will acquit me of untruthfulness, even though it be not while I live.

Still more confident am I of such eventual acquittal, seeing that my judges are my own countrymen. I think, indeed, Englishmen the most suspicious and touchy of mankind; I think them unreasonable and unjust in their seasons of excitement; but I had rather be an Englishman (as in fact I am) than belong to any other race under heaven. They are as generous, as they are hasty and burly; and their repentance for their injustice is greater than their sin.

For twenty years and more I have borne an imputation, of which I am at least as sensitive, who am the object of it, as they can be, who are only the judges. I have not set myself to remove it, first, because I never have had an opening to speak, and, next, because I never saw in them the disposition to hear. I have wished to appeal from Philip drunk to Philip sober. When shall I pronounce him to be himself again? If I may judge from the tone of the public press, which represents the public voice, I have great reason to take heart at this time. I have been treated by contemporary critics in this controversy with great fairness and gentleness, and I am grateful to them for it. However, the decision of the time and mode of my defence has been taken out of my hands; and I am thankful that it has been so. I am bound now as a duty to myself, to the Catholic cause, to the Catholic Priesthood, to give account of myself without any delay, when I am so rudely and circumstantially charged with Untruthfulness. I accept the challenge; I shall do my best to meet it, and I shall be content when I have done so.

I confine myself then, in these pages, to the charge of Untruthfulness; and I hereby cart away, as so much rubbish, the impertinences, with which the Pamphlet of Accusation swarms. I shall not think it necessary here to examine, whether I am 'worked into a pitch of confusion', or have 'carried self-deception to perfection', or am 'anxious to show my credulity', or am 'in a morbid state of mind', or 'hunger for nonsense as my food', or 'indulge in subtle paradoxes' and 'rhetorical exaggerations', or have 'eccentricities' or teach in a style 'utterly beyond' my Accuser's 'comprehension', or create in him 'blank astonishment', or 'exalt the magical powers of my Church', or have 'unconsciously committed myself to a statement which strikes at the root of all morality', or 'look down on the Protestant gentry as without hope of heaven', or 'had better be sent to the furthest' Catholic 'mission among the savages of the South seas', than 'to teach in an Irish Catholic University', or have 'gambled away my reason', or adopt 'sophistries', or have published 'sophisms piled upon sophisms', or have in my sermons 'culminating wonders', or have a 'seemingly sceptical method', or have 'barristerial ability' and 'almost boundless silliness', or 'make great mistakes', or am 'a subtle dialectician', or perhaps have 'lost my temper', or 'misquote Scripture', or am 'anti-scriptural', or 'border very closely on the Pelagian heresy'.—Pp. 370, 372, 373, 374, 375, 377, 378, 380, 381, 357, 377, 373.

These are all impertinences; and the list is so long that I am almost sorry to have given them room which might be better used. However, there they are, or at least a portion of them; and having noticed them thus much, I shall notice them no more.

Coming then to the subject, which is to furnish the staple of my publication, the question of my Truthfulness, I first direct attention to the passage which the Act of Accusation contains at p. 358 and p. 380. I shall give my reason presently, why I begin with it.

My accuser is speaking of my Sermon on Wisdom and Innocence, and he says, 'It must be *remembered always* that it is not a Protestant, but a Romish sermon.'—P. 358.

Then at p. 380 he continues, 'Dr. Newman does not apply to it that epithet. He called it in his letter to me of the 7th of January, (published by him,) a "Protestant" one. I remarked that, but considered it a mere slip of the pen. Besides, I have now nothing to say to that letter. It is to his "Reflections", in p. 352, which are open ground to me, that I refer. In them he deliberately repeats the epithet "Protestant": only he, in an utterly imaginary conversation, puts it into my mouth, "which you preached when a Protestant". I call the man who preached that Sermon a Protestant? I should have sooner called him a Buddhist. *At that very time he was teaching his disciples to scorn* and repudiate that name of Protestant, under which, for some reason or other, he *now finds it convenient to take shelter*. If *he* forgets, the world does not, the famous article in the British Critic (the then organ of his party) of three years before, July 1841, which, after denouncing the name of Protestant, declared the object of the party to be none other than the *"unprotestantising"* the English Church.'

In this passage my accuser asserts or implies, 1. that the Sermon, on which he originally grounded his slander against me in the January No. of the Magazine, was really and in matter of fact a 'Romish' Sermon; 2. that I ought in my Pamphlet to have acknowledged this fact; 3. that I didn't. 4. That I actually called it instead a Protestant Sermon. 5. That at the time when I published it, twenty years ago, I should have denied that it was a Protestant Sermon. 6. By consequence, I should in that denial have avowed that it was a 'Romish' Sermon; 7. and therefore, not only, when I was in the Established Church, was I guilty of the dishonesty of preaching what at the time I knew to be a 'Romish' Sermon, but now too, in 1864, I have committed the additional dishonesty of calling it a Protestant Sermon. If my accuser does not mean this, I submit to such reparation as I owe him for my mistake, but I cannot make out that he means any thing else.

Here are two main points to be considered; 1. I in 1864 have called it a Protestant Sermon. 2. He in 1844 and now has styled it a Popish Sermon. Let me take these two points separately.

1. Certainly, when I was in the English Church, I *did* disown the word 'Protestant', and that, even at an earlier date than my Accuser names; but just let us see whether this fact is any thing at all to the purpose of his accusation. Last January 7th I spoke to this effect: 'How can you prove that *Father* Newman informs us of a certain thing about the Roman Clergy', by referring to a *Protestant* Sermon of the Vicar

of St. Mary's? My Accuser answers me thus: 'There's a quibble! why, *Protestant* is *not* the word which you would have used when at St. Mary's, and yet you use it now!' Very true; I do; but what on earth does this matter to my *argument*? how does this word 'Protestant', which I used, tend in any degree to make my argument a quibble? What word *should* I have used twenty years ago instead of 'Protestant?' 'Roman' or 'Romish?' by no manner of means.

My accuser indeed says that 'it must always be remembered that it is not a Protestant *but* a Romish Sermon'. He implies, and, I suppose, he thinks, that not to be a Protestant is to be a Roman; he may say so, if he pleases, but so did not say that large body who have been called by the name of Tractarians, as all the world knows. The movement proceeded on the very basis of denying that position which my Accuser takes for granted that I allowed. It ever said, and it says now, that there is something *between* Protestant and Romish; that there is a 'Via Media' which is neither the one nor the other. Had I been asked twenty years ago, what the doctrine of the Established Church was, I should have answered, 'Neither Romish *nor* Protestant, *but* "Anglican" or "Anglo-catholic".' I should never have granted that the Sermon was Romish; I should have denied, and that with an internal denial, quite as much as I do now, that it was a Roman or Romish Sermon. Well then, substitute the word 'Anglican' or 'Anglo-catholic' for 'Protestant' in my question, and see if the argument is a bit the worse for it,—thus: 'How can you prove that *Father* Newman informs us a certain thing about the Roman Clergy, by referring to an *Anglican* or *Anglo-catholic* Sermon of the Vicar of St. Mary's?' The cogency of the argument remains just where it was. What have I gained in the argument, what has he lost, by my having said, not 'an Anglican Sermon', but 'a Protestant Sermon?' What dust then is he throwing into our eyes!

For instance: in 1844 I lived at Littlemore; two or three miles distant from Oxford; and Littlemore lies in three, perhaps in four, distinct parishes, so that of particular houses it is difficult to say, whether they are in St. Mary's, Oxford, or in Cowley, or in Iffley, or in Sandford, the line of demarcation running even through them. Now, supposing I were to say in 1864, that 'twenty years ago I did not live in Oxford, *because* I lived out at Littlemore, in the parish of Cowley'; and if upon this there were letters of mine produced dated Littlemore, 1844, in one of which I said that 'I lived, not in Cowley, but at Littlemore, in St. Mary's parish', how would that prove that I contradicted myself, and that therefore after all I must be supposed to have been living in Oxford in 1844? The utmost that would be proved by the discrepancy, such as it was, would be, that there was some confusion either in me, or in the state of the fact as to the limits of the parishes. There would be no confusion about the place or spot of my residence. I should be saying in 1864, 'I did not live in Oxford twenty years ago, because I lived at Littlemore in the Parish of Cowley.' I should have been saying in 1844, 'I do not live in Oxford, because I live in St. Mary's, Littlemore.' In either case I should be saying that my *habitat* in 1844 was *not* Oxford, but Littlemore; and I should be giving the same reason for it. I should be proving an *alibi*. I should be naming the same place for the *alibi*; but twenty years ago I should have spoken of it as St. Mary's, Littlemore, and to-day I should have spoken of it as Littlemore in the Parish of Cowley.

And so as to my Sermon; in January, 1864, I called it a *Protestant* Sermon, and not a Roman; but in 1844 I should, if asked, have called it an *Anglican* Sermon, and not a Roman. In both cases I should have denied that it was Roman, and that on the ground of its being something else; though I should have called that something else, then by one name, now by another. The doctrine of the *Via Media* is a *fact*, whatever name we give to it; I, as a Roman Priest, find it more natural and usual to call it Protestant: I, as an Oxford Vicar, thought it more exact to call it Anglican; but, whatever I then called it, and whatever I now call it, I mean one and the same object by my name, and therefore not another object,—viz. not the Roman Church. The argument, I repeat, is sound, whether the *Via Media* and the Vicar of St. Mary's be called Anglican or Protestant.

This is a specimen of what my Accuser means by my 'Economies'; nay, it is actually one of those special two, three, or four, committed after February 1, which he thinks sufficient to connect me with the shifty casuists and the double-dealing moralists, as he considers them, of the Catholic Church. What a 'Much ado about nothing!'

2. But, whether or no he can prove that I in 1864 have committed any logical fault in calling my Sermon on Wisdom and Innocence a Protestant Sermon, he is and has been all along, most firm in the belief himself that a Romish Sermon it is; and this is the point on which I wish specially to insist. It is for this cause that I made the above extract from his Pamphlet, not merely in order to answer him, though, when I had made it, I could not pass by the attack on me which it contains. I shall notice his charges one by one by and by; but I have made this extract here in order to insist and to dwell on this phenomenon—viz. that he does consider it an undeniable fact, that the Sermon is 'Romish', —meaning by 'Romish' not 'savouring of Romish doctrine' merely, but 'the work of a real Romanist, of a conscious Romanist'. This belief it is which leads him to be so severe on me, for now calling it 'Protestant'. He thinks that, whether I have committed any logical self-contradiction or not, I am very well aware that, when I wrote it, I ought to have been elsewhere, that I was a conscious Romanist, teaching Romanism;—or if he does not believe this himself, he wishes others

to think so, which comes to the same thing; certainly I prefer to consider that he thinks so himself, but, if he likes the other hypothesis better, he is welcome to it.

He believes then so firmly that the Sermon was a 'Romish Sermon', that he pointedly takes it for granted, before he has adduced a syllable of proof of the matter of fact. He *starts* by saying that it is a fact to be 'remembered'. 'It *must* be *remembered always'*, he says, 'that it is not a Protestant, but a Romish Sermon', p. 358. Its Romish parentage is a great truth for the memory, not a thesis for inquiry. Merely to refer his readers to the Sermon is, he considers, to secure them on his side. Hence it is that, in his letter of January 18, he said to me, 'It seems to me, that, by *referring* publicly to the Sermon on which my allegations are founded, I have given every one *an opportunity of judging of their injustice'*, that is, an opportunity of seeing that they are transparently just. The notion of there being a *Via Media*, held all along by a large party in the Anglican Church, and now at least not less than at any former time, is too subtle for his intellect. Accordingly, he thinks it was an allowable figure of speech,—not more, I suppose, than an 'hyperbole',—when referring to a Sermon of the Vicar of St. Mary's in the Magazine, to say that it was the writing of a Roman Priest; and as to serious arguments to prove the point, why, they may indeed be necessary, as a matter of form, in an Act of Accusation, such as his Pamphlet, but they are superfluous to the good sense of any one who will only just look into the matter himself.

Now, with respect to the so-called arguments which he ventures to put forward in proof that the Sermon is Romish, I shall answer them, together with all his other arguments, in the latter portion of this Reply; here I do but draw the attention of the reader, as I have said already, to the phenomenon itself, which he exhibits, of an unclouded confidence that the Sermon is the writing of a virtual member of the Roman communion, and I do so because it has made a great impression on my own mind, and has suggested to me the course that I shall pursue in my answer to him.

I say, he takes it for granted that the Sermon is the writing of a virtual or actual, of a conscious Roman Catholic; and is impatient at the very notion of having to prove it. Father Newman and the Vicar of St. Mary's are one and the same: there has been no change of mind in him; what he believed then he believes now, and what he believes now he believed then. To dispute this is frivolous; to distinguish between his past self and his present is subtlety, and to ask for proof of their identity is seeking opportunity to be sophistical. This writer really thinks that he acts a straightforward honest part, when he says 'A Catholic Priest informs us in his Sermon on Wisdom and Innocence preached at St. Mary's', and he thinks that I am the shuffler and quibbler when I forbid him to do so. So singular a phenomenon in a man of undoubted ability has struck me forcibly, and I shall pursue the train of thought which it opens.

It is not he alone who entertains, and has entertained, such an opinion of me and my writings. It is the impression of large classes of men; the impression twenty years ago and the impression now. There has been a general feeling that I was for years where I had no right to be; that I was a 'Romanist' in Protestant livery and service; that I was doing the work of a hostile Church in the bosom of the English Establishment, and knew it, or ought to have known it. There was no need of arguing about particular passages in my writings, when the fact was so patent, as men thought it to be.

First it was certain, and I could not myself deny it, that I scouted the name 'Protestant'. It was certain again, that many of the doctrines which I professed were popularly and generally known as badges of the Roman Church, as distinguished from the faith of the Reformation. Next, how could I have come by them? Evidently, I had certain friends and advisers who did not appear; there was some underground communication between Stonyhurst or Oscott and my rooms at Oriel. Beyond a doubt, I was advocating certain doctrines, not by accident, but on an understanding with ecclesiastics of the old religion. Then men went further, and said that I had actually been received into that religion, and withal had leave given me to profess myself a Protestant still. Others went even further, and gave it out to the world, as a matter of fact, of which they themselves had the proof in their hands, that I was actually a Jesuit. And when the opinions which I advocated spread, and younger men went further than I, the feeling against me waxed stronger and took a wider range.

And now indignation arose at the knavery of a conspiracy such as this:—and it became of course all the greater, in consequence of its being the received belief of the public at large, that craft and intrigue, such as they fancied they beheld with their own eyes, were the very instruments to which the Catholic Church has in these last centuries been indebted for her maintenance and extension.

There was another circumstance still, which increased the irritation and aversion felt by the large classes, of whom I have been speaking, as regards the preachers of doctrines, so new to them and so unpalatable; and that was, that they developed them in so measured a way. If they were inspired by Roman theologians, (and this was taken for granted,) why did they not speak out at once? Why did they keep the world in such suspense and anxiety as to what was coming next, and what was to be the upshot of the whole? Why this reticence, and half-speaking, and apparent indecision? It was plain that the plan of operations had been carefully mapped out from the first, and that these men were cautiously advancing towards its accomplishment, as far as was safe at the moment; that their aim and their hope was to carry off a large body with them of the young and the ignorant; that they meant gradually to leaven the minds of the rising generation, and to open the gate of that city, of which they were the sworn defenders, to the enemy who lay in ambush outside of it. And when in spite of the many protestations of the party to the contrary, there was at length an actual movement among their disciples, and one went over to Rome, and then another, the worst anticipations and the worst judgments which had been formed of them received their justification. And, lastly, when men first had said of me, 'You will see, *he* will go, he is only biding his time, he is waiting the word of command from Rome', and, when after all, after my arguments and denunciations of former years, at length I did leave the Anglican Church for the Roman, then they said to each other, 'It is just as we said: I told you so.'

This was the state of mind of masses of men twenty years ago, who took no more than an external and common-sense view of what was going on. And partly the tradition, partly the effect of that feeling, remains to the present time. Certainly I consider that, in my own case, it is the great obstacle in the way of my being favourably heard, as at present, when I have to make my defence. Not only am I now a member of a most un-English communion, whose great aim is considered to be the extinction of Protestantism and the Protestant Church, and whose means of attack are popularly supposed to be unscrupulous cunning and deceit, but besides, how came I originally to have any relations with the Church of Rome at all? did I, or my opinions, drop from the sky? how came I, in Oxford, *in gremio Universitatis*, to present myself to the eyes of men in that full-blown investiture of Popery? How could I dare, how could I have the conscience, with warnings, with prophecies, with accusations against me, to persevere in a path which steadily advanced towards, which ended in, the religion of Rome? And how am I now to be trusted, when long ago I was trusted, and was found wanting?

It is this which is the strength of the case of my Accuser against me;—not his arguments in themselves, which I shall easily crumble into dust, but the bias of the court. It is the state of the atmosphere; it is the vibration all around which will more or less echo his assertion of my dishonesty; it is that prepossession against me, which takes it for granted that, when my reasoning is convincing it is only ingenious, and that when my statements are unanswerable, there is always something put out of sight or hidden in my sleeve; it is that plausible, but cruel conclusion to which men are so apt to jump, that when much is imputed, something must be true, and that it is more likely that one should be to blame, than that many should be mistaken in blaming him;—these are the real foes which I have to fight, and the auxiliaries to whom my Accuser makes his court.

Well, I must break through this barrier of prejudice against me, if I can; and I think I shall be able to do so. When first I read the Pamphlet of Accusation, I almost despaired of meeting effectively such a heap of misrepresentation and such a vehemence of animosity. What was the good of answering first one point, and then another, and going through the whole circle of its abuse; when my answer to the first point would be forgotten, as soon as I got to the second? What was the use of bringing out half a hundred separate principles or views for the refutation of the separate counts in the Indictment, when rejoinders of this sort would but confuse and torment the reader by their number and their diversity? What hope was there of condensing into a pamphlet of a readable length, matter which ought freely to expand itself into half a dozen volumes? What means was there, except the expenditure of interminable pages, to set right even one of that series of 'single passing hints', to use my Assailant's own language, which, 'as with his finger tip, he had delivered' against me?

All those separate charges of his had their force in being illustrations of one and the same great imputation. He had a positive idea to illuminate his whole matter, and to stamp it with a form, and to quicken it with an interpretation. He called me a *liar*,—a simple, a broad, an intelligible, to the English public a plausible arraignment; but for me, to answer in detail charge one by reason one, and charge two by reason two, and charge three by reason three, and so to proceed through the whole string both of accusations and replies, each of which was to be independent of the rest, this would be certainly labour lost as regards any effective result. What I needed was a corresponding antagonist unity in my defence, and where was that to be found? We see, in the case of commentators on the prophecies of Scripture, an exemplification of the principle on which I am insisting; viz. how much more powerful even a false interpretation of the sacred text is than none at all;—how a certain key to the visions of the Apocalypse, for instance, may cling to the mind—(I have found it so in my own case),—mainly because they are positive and objective, in spite of the fullest demonstration that they really have no claim upon our belief. The reader says, 'What else can the prophecy mean?' just as my Accuser asks, 'What, then, does Dr. Newman mean?' . . . I reflected, and I saw a way out of my perplexity.

Yes, I said to myself, his very question is about my *meaning*; 'What does Dr. Newman mean?' It pointed in the very same direction as that into which my musings had turned me already. He asks what I *mean*; not about my words, not about my arguments, not about my actions, as his ultimate point, but about that living intelligence, by which I write, and argue, and act. He asks about my Mind and its Beliefs and its Sentiments; and he shall be answered;—not for his own sake, but for mine, for the sake of the Religion which I profess, and of the Priesthood in which I am unworthily included, and of my friends and of my foes, and of that general public which consists of neither one nor the other, but of well-wishers, lovers of fair play, sceptical cross-questioners, interested inquirers, curious lookers-on, and simple strangers, unconcerned yet not careless about the issue.

My perplexity did not last half an hour. I recognized what I had to do, though I shrank from both the task and the exposure which it would entail. I must, I said, give the true key to my whole life; I must show what I am that it may be seen what I am not, and that the phantom may be extinguished which gibbers instead of me. I wish to be known as a living man, and not as a scarecrow which is dressed up in my clothes. False ideas may be refuted indeed by argument, but by true ideas alone are they expelled. I will vanquish, not my Accuser, but my judges. I will indeed answer his charges and criticisms on me one by one, lest any one should say that they are unanswerable, but such a work shall not be the scope nor the substance of my reply. I will draw out, as far as may be, the history of my mind; I will state the point at which I began, in what external suggestion or accident each opinion had its rise, how far and how they were developed from within, how they grew, were modified, were combined, were in collision with each other, and were changed; again how I conducted myself towards them, and how, and how far, and for how long a time, I thought I could hold them consistently with the ecclesiastical engagements which I had made and with the position which I filled. I must show,—what is the very truth,—that the doctrines which I held, and have held for so many years, have been taught me (speaking humanly) partly by the suggestions of Protestant friends, partly by the teaching of books, and partly by the action of my own mind: and thus I shall account for that phenomenon which to so many seems so wonderful, that I should have left 'my kindred and my father's house' for a Church from which once I turned away with dread;—so wonderful to them! as if forsooth a Religion which has flourished through so many ages, among so many nations, amid such varieties of social life, in such contrary classes and conditions of men, and after so many revolutions, political and civil, could not subdue the reason and overcome the heart, without the aid of fraud and the sophistries of the schools.

What I had proposed to myself in the course of half an hour, I determined on at the end of ten days. However, I have many difficulties in fulfilling my design. How am I to say all that has to be said in a reasonable compass? And then as to the materials of my narrative; I have no autobiographical notes to consult, no written explanations of particular treatises or of tracts which at the time gave offence, hardly any minutes of definite transactions or conversations, and few contemporary memoranda, I fear, of the feelings or motives under which from time to time I acted. I have an abundance of letters from friends with some copies or drafts of my answers to them, but they are for the most part unsorted, and, till this process has taken place, they are even too numerous and various to be available at a moment for my purpose. Then, as to the volumes which I have published, they would in many ways serve me, were I well up in them; but though I took great pains in their composition, I have thought little about them, when they were at length out of my hands, and, for the most part, the last time I read them has been when I revised their proof sheets.

Under these circumstances my sketch will of course be incomplete. I now for the first time contemplate my course as a whole; it is a first essay, but it will contain, I trust, no serious or substantial mistake, and so far will answer the purpose for which I write it. I purpose to set nothing down in it as certain, for which I have not a clear memory, or some written memorial, or the corroboration of some friend. There are witnesses enough up and down the country to verify, or correct, or complete it; and letters moreover of my own in abundance, unless they have been destroyed.

Moreover, I mean to be simply personal and historical: I am not expounding Catholic doctrine, I am doing no more than explaining myself, and my opinions and actions. I wish, as far as I am able, simply to state facts, whether they are ultimately determined to be for me or against me. Of course there will be room enough for contrariety of judgment among my readers, as to the necessity, or appositeness, or value, or good taste, or religious prudence of the details which I shall introduce. I may be accused of laying stress on little things, of being beside the mark, of going into impertinent or ridiculous details, of sounding my own praise, of giving scandal; but this is a case above all others, in which I am bound to follow my own lights and to speak out my own heart. It is not at all pleasant for me to be egotistical; nor to be criticized for being so. It is not pleasant to reveal to high and low, young and old, what has gone on within me from my early years. It is not pleasant to be giving to every shallow or flippant disputant the advantage over me of knowing my most private thoughts, I might even say the intercourse between myself and my Maker. But I do not like to be called to my face a liar and a knave: nor should I be doing my duty to my faith or to my name, if I were to suffer it. I know I have done nothing to deserve such an insult; and if I prove this, as I hope to do, I must not care for such incidental annoyances as are involved in the process.

APPENDIX

ANSWER IN DETAIL TO MR. KINGSLEY'S ACCUSATIONS

In proceeding now, according to the engagement with which I entered upon my undertaking, to examine in detail the Pamphlet which has been written against me, I am very sorry to be obliged to say, that it is as slovenly and random and futile in its definite charges, as it is iniquitous in its method of disputation. And now I proceed to show this without any delay; and shall consider in order,

1. My Sermon on the Apostolical Christian.
2. My Sermon on Wisdom and Innocence.
3. The Anglican Church.
4. The Lives of the English Saints.
5. Ecclesiastical Miracles.
6. Popular Religion.
7. The Economy.
8. Lying and Equivocation.

I

My Sermon on 'The Apostolical Christian', being the 19th of 'Sermons on Subjects of the Day'

This writer says, 'What Dr. Newman means by Christians . . . he has not left in doubt'; and then, quoting a passage from this Sermon which speaks of 'the humble monk and the holy nun' being 'Christians after the very pattern given us in Scripture', he observes, 'This is his *definition* of Christians.'—p. 358.

This is not the case. I have neither given a definition, nor implied one, nor intended one; nor could I, either now or in 1843–4, or at any time, allow of the particular definition he ascribes to me. As if all Christians must be monks or nuns!

What I have said is, that monks and nuns are patterns of Christian perfection; and that Scripture itself supplies us with this pattern. Who can deny this? Who is bold enough to say that St. John Baptist, who, I suppose, is a Scripture Character, is not a pattern-monk; and that Mary, who 'sat at our Lord's feet', was not a pattern-nun? and 'Anna too, who served God with fastings and prayers night and day?' Again, what is meant but this by St. Paul's saying, 'It is good for a man not to touch a woman?' and, when speaking of the father or guardian of a young girl, 'He that giveth her in marriage doeth well; but he that giveth her not in marriage doeth better?' And what does St. John mean but to praise virginity, when he says of the hundred forty and four thousand on Mount Sion, 'These are they which were not defiled with women, for they are virgins'? And what else did our Lord mean, when He said, 'There be eunuchs who have made themselves eunuchs for the kingdom of heaven's sake. He that is able to receive it, let him receive it'?

He ought to know his logic better: I have said that 'monks and nuns find their pattern in Scripture': he adds, *Therefore* I hold all Christians are monks and nuns.

This is Blot *one*.

Now then for Blot *two*.

'Monks and nuns the *only* perfect Christians . . . what more?'—p. 359.

A second fault in logic. I said no more than that monks and nuns were perfect Christians: he adds, *Therefore* 'monks and nuns are the *only* perfect Christians'. Monks and nuns are *not* the only perfect Christians; I never thought so or said so, now or at any other time.

P. 380. 'In the Sermon . . . monks and nuns are spoken of as the *only true* Bible Christians.' This, again, is not the case. What I said is, that 'monks and nuns are Bible Christians': it does not follow, nor did I mean, that 'all Bible Christians are monks and nuns'. Bad logic again. Blot *three*.

2

My Sermon on 'Wisdom and Innocence', being the 20th of 'Sermons on Subjects of the Day'

This writer says, p. 358, about my Sermon 20, 'By the world appears to be signified, especially, the Protestant public of these realms.'

He also asks, p. 362, 'Why was it preached? . . . to insinuate, that the admiring young gentlemen, who listened to him, stood to their fellow-countrymen in the relation of the early Christians to the heathen Romans? or that Queen Victoria's Government was to the Church of England, what Nero's or Diocletian's was to the Church of Rome? It may have been so.'

May or may not, it wasn't. He insinuates, what not even with his little finger does he attempt to prove. Blot *four*.

He asserts, p. 359, that I said in the Sermon in question, that 'Sacramental Confession and the celibacy of the clergy are "notes" of the

Church'. And, just before, he puts the word 'notes' in inverted commas, as if it was mine. That is, he garbles. It is *not* mine. Blot *five*.

He says that I '*define* what I mean by the Church in two "notes" of her character'. I do not define, or dream of defining.

1. He says that I teach that the celibacy of the clergy enters into the *definition* of the Church. I do no such thing; that is the blunt truth. Define the Church by the celibacy of the clergy! why, let him read 1 Tim. iii.; there he will find that bishops and deacons are spoken of as married. How, then, could I be the dolt to say or imply that the celibacy of the clergy was a part of the definition of the Church? Blot *six*.

And again in p. 380, 'In the Sermon a celibate clergy is made a note of the Church.' Thus the untruth is repeated. Blot *seven*.

2. And now for Blot *eight*. Neither did I say that 'Sacramental confession' was 'a note of the Church'. Nor is it. Nor could I with any cogency have brought this as an argument against the Church of England, for the Church of England has retained Confession, nay, Sacramental Confession. No fair man can read the form of Absolution in the Anglican Prayer in the Visitation of the Sick, without seeing that that Church *does* sanction and provide for Confession and Absolution. If that form does not contain the profession of a grave Sacramental act, words have no meaning. The form is almost in the words of the Roman form; and, by the time that this Clergyman has succeeded in explaining it away, he will have also got skill enough to explain away the Roman form; and if he did but handle my words with that latitude with which he interprets his own formularies, he would prove that, instead of my being superstitious and frantic, I was the most Protestant of preachers and the most latitudinarian of thinkers. It would be charity in him, in his reading of my words, to use some of that power of evasion, of which he shows himself such a master in his dealing with his own Prayer Book. Yet he has the assurance at p. 362 to ask, 'Why was the Sermon preached? to insinuate that a Church which had sacramental confession and a celibate clergy was the only true Church?'

'Why?' I will tell the reader, *why*; and with this view will speak, first of the contents of the Sermon, then of its subject, then of its circumstances.

1. It was one of the last six Sermons which I wrote when I was an Anglican. It was one of the five Sermons I preached in St. Mary's between Christmas and Easter, 1843, the year when I gave up my Living. The MS. of the Sermon is destroyed; but I believe, and my memory too bears me out, as far as it goes, that the sentence in question

about Celibacy and Confession *was not preached at all*. The Volume, in which this Sermon is found, was published *after* that I had given up St. Mary's, when I had no call on me to restrain the expression of any thing which I might hold: and I state an important fact about it in the Advertisement, which this truth-loving writer *suppresses*. Blot *nine*.

My words, which stared him in the face, are as follows:—'In preparing [these Sermons] for publication, *a few words and sentences* have in several places been *added*, which will be found to express more of *private or personal opinion*, than it was expedient to introduce into the *instruction* delivered in Church to a parochial Congregation. Such introduction, however, seems unobjectionable in the case of compositions, which are *detached* from the sacred place and service to which they once belonged, and *submitted to the reason* and judgment of the general reader.'

This Volume of Sermons then cannot be criticized at all as *preachments*; they are *essays*; essays of a man who, at the time of publishing them, was *not* a preacher. Such passages, as that in question, are just the very ones which I added *upon* my publishing them. I always was on my guard in the pulpit of saying any thing which looked towards Rome; and therefore all his rhetoric about my 'disciples', 'admiring young gentlemen who listened to me', 'fanatic and hot-headed young men, who hung upon my every word', becomes simple rubbish.

I have more to say on this point. This writer says, p. 362, 'I know that men used to suspect Dr. Newman,—I have been inclined to do so myself,—of *writing a whole Sermon, not for the sake of the text or of the matter*, but for the sake of one simple passing hint,—one phrase, one epithet.' Can there be a plainer testimony borne to the practical character of my Sermons at St. Mary's than this gratuitous insinuation? Many a preacher of Tractarian doctrine has been accused of not letting his parishioners alone, and of teasing them with his private theological notions. You would gather from the general tone of this Writer that that was my way. Every one who was in the habit of hearing me, knows that it wasn't. This Writer either knows nothing about it, and then he ought to be silent; or he does know, and then he ought to speak the truth. Others spread the same report twenty years ago as he does now, and the world believed that my Sermons at St. Mary's were full of red-hot Tractarianism. Then strangers came to hear me preach, and were astonished at their own disappointment. I recollect the wife of a great prelate from a distance coming to hear me, and then expressing her surprise to find that I preached nothing but a plain humdrum Sermon. I recollect how, when on the Sunday before Commemoration one year, a number of strangers came to hear me, and I preached in my usual way, residents in Oxford, of high position, were loud in their satisfaction that on a great occasion, I had made a simple failure, for after all there was nothing in the Sermon to hear. Well, but they were not going to let me off, for all my common-sense view of duty. Accordingly, they got up the charitable theory which this Writer revives. They said that there was a double purpose in those plain addresses of mine, and that my Sermons were never so artful as when they seemed common-place; that there were sentences which redeemed their apparent simplicity and quietness. So they watched during the delivery of a Sermon, which to them was too practical to be useful, for the concealed point of it, which they could at least imagine, if they could not discover. 'Men used to suspect Dr. Newman', he says, 'of writing a *whole* Sermon, *not* for the sake of *the text or of the matter*, but for the sake of . . . *one* phrase, *one* epithet, *one* little barbed arrow, which, as he *swept magnificently* past on the stream of his calm eloquence, *seemingly* unconscious of all presences, save those unseen, he delivered unheeded', &c., p. 362. To all appearance, he says, I was 'unconscious of all presences'; so this kind Writer supplies the true interpretation of this unconsciousness. He is not able to deny that 'the *whole* Sermon' had the *appearance* of being '*for the sake* of the text and matter'; therefore he suggests that perhaps it wasn't. And then he emptily talks of the 'magnificent sweep of my eloquence', and my 'oratoric power'. Did he forget that the Sermon of which he thus speaks can be read by others as well as him? Now, the sentences are as short as Aristotle's, and as grave as Bishop Butler's. It is written almost in the condensed style of Tract 90. Eloquence there is none. I put this down as Blot *ten*.

2. And now as to the subject of the Sermon. The series of which the Volume consists are such Sermons as are, more or less, exceptions to the rule which I ordinarily observed, as to the subjects which I introduced into the pulpit of St. Mary's. They are not purely ethical or doctrinal. They were for the most part caused by circumstances of the day or of the time, and they belong to various years. One was written in 1832, two in 1836, two in 1838, five in 1840, five in 1841, four in 1842, seven in 1843. Many of them are engaged on one subject, viz. in viewing the Church in its relation to the world. By the world was meant, not simply those multitudes which were not in the Church, but the existing body of human society, whether in the Church or not, whether Catholics, Protestants, Greeks, or Mahometans, theists or idolaters, as being ruled by principles, maxims, and instincts of their own, that is, of an unregenerate nature, whatever their supernatural privileges might be, greater or less, according to their form of religion. This view of the relation of the Church to the world as taken apart from questions of ecclesiastical politics, as they may be called, is often brought out in my Sermons. Two occur to me at once; No. 3 of my Plain Sermons, which was written in 1829, and No. 15 of my Third Volume, written in 1835.

Then, on the other hand, by Church I meant,—in common with all writers connected with the Tract Movement, whatever their shades of opinion, and with the whole body of English divines, except those of the Puritan or Evangelical School,—the whole of Christendom, from the Apostles' time till now, whatever their later divisions into Latin, Greek, and Anglican. I have explained this view of the subject above at pp. 71–73 of this Volume. When then I speak, in the particular Sermon before us, of the members, or the rulers, or the action of 'the Church', I mean neither the Latin, nor the Greek, nor the English, taken by itself, but of the whole Church as one body: of Italy as one with England, of the Saxon or Norman as one with the Caroline Church. *This* was specially the one Church, and the points in which one branch or one period differed from another were not and could not be Notes of the Church, because Notes necessarily belonged to the whole of the Church every where and always.

This being my doctrine as to the relation of the Church to the world, I laid down in the Sermon three principles concerning it, and there left the matter. The first is, that Divine Wisdom had framed for its action, laws which man, if left to himself, would have antecedently pronounced to be the worst possible for its success, and which in all ages have been called by the world, as they were in the Apostles' days, 'foolishness'; that man ever relies on physical and material force, and on carnal inducements,—as Mahomet with his sword and his houris, or indeed almost as that theory of religion, called, since the Sermon was written, 'muscular Christianity'; but that our Lord, on the contrary, has substituted meekness for haughtiness, passiveness for violence, and innocence for craft: and that the event has shown the high wisdom of such an economy, for it has brought to light a set of natural laws, unknown before, by which the seeming paradox that weakness should be stronger than might, and simplicity than worldly policy, is readily explained.

Secondly, I said that men of the world, judging by the event, and not recognizing the secret causes of the success, viz. a higher order of natural laws,—natural, though their source and action were supernatural, (for 'the meek inherit the earth', by means of a meekness which comes from above,)—these men, I say, concluded, that the success which they witnessed must arise from some evil secret which the world had not mastered,—by means of magic, as they said in the first ages, by cunning as they say now. And accordingly they thought that the humility and inoffensiveness of Christians, or of Churchmen, was a mere pretence and blind to cover the real causes of that success, which Christians could explain and would not; and that they were simply hypocrites.

Thirdly, I suggested that shrewd ecclesiastics, who knew very well that there was neither magic nor craft in the matter, and, from their intimate acquaintance with what actually went on within the Church, discerned what were the real causes of its success, were of course under the temptation of substituting reason for conscience, and, instead of simply obeying the command, were led to do good that good might come, that is, to act *in order* to their success, and not from a motive of faith. Some, I said, did yield to the temptation more or less, and their motives became mixed; and in this way the world in a more subtle shape has got into the Church; and hence it has come to pass, that, looking at its history from first to last, we cannot possibly draw the line between good and evil there, and say either that every thing is to be defended, or some things to be condemned. I expressed the difficulty, which I supposed to be inherent in the Church, in the following words. I said, '*Priestcraft has ever been considered the badge*, and its imputation is a kind of Note of the Church; and *in part indeed truly*, because the presence of powerful enemies, and the sense of their own weakness, *has sometimes tempted Christians to the abuse, instead of the use of Christian wisdom, to be wise without being harmless*; but partly, nay, for the most part, not truly, but slanderously, and merely because the world called their wisdom craft, when it was found to be a match for its own numbers and power.' This passage he has partly garbled, partly omitted. Blot *eleven*.

Such is the substance of the Sermon: and as to the main drift of it, it was this; that I was, there and elsewhere, scrutinizing the course of the Church as a whole, as if philosophically, as an historical phenomenon, and observing the laws on which it was conducted. Hence the Sermon, or Essay as it more truly is, is written in a dry and unimpassioned way: it shows as little of human warmth of feeling, I repeat, as a Sermon of Bishop Butler's. Yet, under that calm exterior there was a deep and keen sensitiveness, as I shall now proceed to show.

3. If I mistake not, it was written with a secret thought about myself. Every one preaches according to his frame of mind, at the time of preaching. One heaviness especially oppressed me at that season, which this Writer, twenty years afterwards, has set himself with a good will to renew: it arose from the sense of the base calumnies which were thrown upon me on all sides. In this trouble of mind I gained, while I reviewed the history of the Church, at once an argument and a consolation. My argument was this: if I, who knew my own innocence, was so blackened by party prejudice, perhaps those high rulers and those servants of the Church, in the many ages which intervened between the early Nicene times and the present, who were laden with such grievous accusations, were innocent also; and this reflection served to make me tender towards those great names of the past, to whom weaknesses or crimes were imputed, and reconciled me to difficulties in ecclesiastical proceedings, which there were no means now of properly explaining. And the sym-

pathy thus excited for them, re-acted on myself, and I found comfort in being able to put myself under the shadow of those who had suffered as I was suffering, and who seemed to promise me their recompense, since I had a fellowship in their trial. In a letter to my Bishop at the time of Tract 90, part of which I have quoted, I said that I had ever tried to 'keep innocency'; and now two years had passed since then, and men were louder and louder in heaping on me the very charges, which this Writer repeats out of my Sermon, of 'fraud and cunning', 'craftiness and deceitfulness', 'double-dealing', 'priestcraft', of being 'mysterious, dark, subtle, designing', when I was all the time conscious to myself, in my degree, and after my measure, of 'sobriety, self-restraint, and control of word and feeling'. I had had experience how my past success had been imputed to 'secret management'; and how, when I had shown surprise at that success, that surprise again was imputed to 'deceit'; and how my honest heartfelt submission to authority had been called, as it was called in a colonial Bishop's charge, 'mystic humility'; and how my silence was called an 'hypocrisy'; and my faithfulness to my clerical engagements a secret correspondence with the enemy. And I found a way of destroying my sensitiveness about these things which jarred upon my sense of justice, and otherwise would have been too much for me, by the contemplation of a large law of the Divine Dispensation, and found myself more and more able to bear in my own person a present trial, of which in my past writings I had expressed an anticipation.

For thus feeling and thus speaking this Writer has the charitableness and the decency to call me 'Mawworm'. 'I found him telling Christians', he says, 'that they will always seem "artificial", and "wanting in openness and manliness"; that they will always be "a mystery" to the world; and that the world will always think them rogues; and bidding them glory in what the world (that is, the rest of their fellow-countrymen) disown, and say with Mawworm, "I like to be despised." . . . How was I to know that the preacher . . . was utterly blind to the broad meaning and the plain practical result of a Sermon like this delivered before fanatic and hot-headed young men, who hung upon his every word?'— p. 363. Hot-headed young men! why, man, you are writing a Romance. You think the scene is Alexandria or the Spanish main, where you may let your imagination play revel to the extent of inveracity. It is good luck for me that the scene of my labours was not at Moscow or Damascus. Then I might be one of your ecclesiastical Saints, of which I sometimes hear in conversation, but with whom, I am glad to say, I have no personal acquaintance. Then you might ascribe to me a more deadly craft than mere quibbling and lying; in Spain I should have been an Inquisitor, with my rack in the background; I should have had a concealed dagger in Sicily; at Venice I should have brewed poison; in Turkey I should have been the Sheik-el-Islam with my bowstring; in

Khorassan I should have been a veiled Prophet. 'Fanatic young men!' Why he is writing out the list of a Dramatis Personæ; 'guards, conspirators, populace', and the like. He thinks I was ever moving about with a train of Capulets at my heels. 'Hot-headed fanatics, who hung on my every word!' If he had taken to write a history, and not a play, he would have easily found out, as I have said, that from 1841 I had severed myself from the younger generation of Oxford, that Dr. Pusey and I had then closed our theological meetings at his house, that I had brought my own weekly evening parties to an end, that I preached only by fits and starts at St. Mary's, so that the attendance of young men was broken up, that in those very weeks from Christmas till over Easter, during which this Sermon was preached, I was but five times in the pulpit there. He would have known, that it was written at a time when I was shunned rather than sought, when I had great sacrifices in anticipation, when I was thinking much of myself; that I was ruthlessly tearing myself away from my own followers, and that, in the musings of that Sermon, I was at the very utmost only delivering a testimony in my behalf for time to come, not sowing my rhetoric broadcast for the chance of present sympathy. Blot *twelve*.

I proceed: he says at p. 362, 'I found him actually using of such [prelates], (and, as I thought, of himself and his party likewise,) the words "They yield outwardly; to assent inwardly were to betray the faith. Yet they are called deceitful and double-dealing, because they do as much as they can, not more than they may."' This too is a proof of my duplicity! Let this writer go with some one else, just a little further than he has gone with me; and let him get into a court of law for libel; and let him be convicted; and let him still fancy that his libel, though a libel, was true, and let us then see whether he will not in such a case 'yield outwardly', without assenting internally; and then again whether we should please him, if we called him 'deceitful and double-dealing', because 'he did as much as he could, not more than he ought to do'. But Tract 90 will supply a real illustration of what I meant. I yielded to the Bishops in outward act, viz. in not defending the Tract, and in closing the Series; but, not only did I not assent inwardly to any condemnation of it, but I opposed myself to the proposition of a condemnation on the party of authority. Yet I was then by the public called 'deceitful and double-dealing', as this Writer calls me now, 'because I did as much as I felt I could do, and not more than I felt I could honestly do'. Many were the publications of the day and the private letters which accused me of shuffling, because I closed the Series of Tracts, yet kept the Tracts on sale, as if I ought to comply not only with what my Bishop asked, but with what he did not ask, and perhaps did not wish. However, such teaching, according to this Writer, was likely to make young men suspect, that truth was not a virtue for its own sake, but only for the sake of 'the spread of Catholic opinions', and the 'salvation of their own souls'; and that 'cunning was the weapon which heaven had allowed to them to defend themselves against the persecuting Protestant public'.—p. 363. Blot *thirteen*.

And now I draw attention to another point. He says at p. 363, 'How was I to know that the preacher . . . did not foresee, that [fanatic and hot-headed young men] would think that they obeyed him, by becoming affected, artificial, sly, shifty, ready for concealments and *equivocations?*' 'How should he know!' What! I suppose that we are to think every man a knave till he is proved not to be such. Know! had he no friend to tell him whether I was 'affected' or 'artificial' myself? Could he not have done better than impute *equivocations* to me, at a time when I was in no sense answerable for the *amphibologia* of the Roman casuists? Has he a single fact which belongs to me personally or by profession to couple my name with equivocation in 1843? 'How should he know' that I was not sly, smooth, artificial, non-natural! he should know by that common manly frankness, if he had it, by which we put confidence in others, till they are proved to have forfeited it; he should know it by my own words in that very Sermon, in which I say it is best to be natural, and that reserve is at best but an unpleasant necessity. I say, 'I do not deny that there is something very engaging in a frank and unpretending manner; some persons have it more than others; in *some persons it is a great grace*. But it must be recollected that I am speaking of *times of persecution and oppression* to Christians, such as the text foretells; and then surely frankness will become nothing else than indignation at the oppressor, and vehement speech, if it is permitted. Accordingly, as persons have deep *feelings*, so they will find the necessity of self-control, lest they should say what they ought not.' He omits these words. I call, then, this base insinuation that I taught equivocation, Blot the *fourteenth*.

Lastly, he sums up thus: 'If [Dr. Newman] would . . . persist (as in this Sermon) in dealing with matters dark, offensive, doubtful, sometimes actually forbidden, at least according to the notions of the great majority of English Churchmen; if he would always do so in a tentative, paltering way, seldom or never letting the world know how much he believed, how far he intended to go; if, in a word, his method of teaching was a suspicious one, what wonder if the minds of men were filled with suspicions of him?'—p. 364.

Now first he is speaking of my Sermons; where, then, is his proof that in my Sermons I dealt in matters dark, offensive, doubtful, actually forbidden? he has said nothing in proof that I had not been able flatly to deny.

'Forbidden according to the notions of the great majority of English Churchmen.' I should like to know what opinions, beyond those which relate to the Creed, *are* held by the 'majority of English Churchmen':— are his own? is it not perfectly well known, that 'the great majority' think of him and his views with a feeling which I will not describe, because it is not necessary for my argument? So far is certain, that he has not the majority with him.

'In a tentative, paltering way.' The word 'paltering' I reject, as vague; as to 'tentative', he must show that I was tentative in my Sermons; and he has eight volumes to look through. As to the ninth, my University Sermons, of course I was 'tentative'; but not because 'I would seldom or never let the world know how much I believed, or how far I intended to go'; but because in deep subjects, which had not been fully investigated, I said as much as I believed, and about as far as I saw I could go; and a man cannot do more; and I account no man to be a philosopher who attempts to do more. How long am I to have the office of merely negativing assertions which are but supported by former assertions, in which John is ever helping Tom, and the elephant stands upon the tortoise? This is Blot *fifteen*.

3

The Anglican Church

This Writer says:—'If there is, as there is, a strong distrust of certain Catholics, it is restricted to the proselytizing priests among them; and especially to those, who, like Dr. Newman, have turned round upon their mother Church, (I had almost said their mother country,) with contumely and slander.'—p. 365.

No one has a right to make a charge, without at least an attempt to prove what he says; but this Writer is consistent with himself. From the time that he first spoke of me in the Magazine, *when* has he ever even professed to give evidence of any sort for any one of his charges, from his own sense of propriety, and without being challenged on the point? After the sentence which I have been quoting, and another like it, he coolly passes on to Tract 90! Blot *sixteen*; but I shall dwell on it awhile, for its own sake.

Now I have been bringing out my mind in this Volume on every subject which has come before me; and therefore I am bound to state plainly what I feel and have felt, since I was a Catholic, about the Anglican Church. I said, in a former page, that, on my conversion, I was not conscious of any change in me of thought or feeling, as regards matters of doctrine; this, however, was not the case as regards some matters of fact, and, unwilling as I am to give offence to religious Anglicans, I am bound to confess that I felt a great change in my view of the Church of England. I cannot tell how soon there came on me,— but very soon,—an extreme astonishment that I had ever imagined it to be a portion of the Catholic Church. For the first time, I looked at it from without, and (as I should myself say) saw it as it was. Forthwith I could not get myself to see in it any thing else, than what I had so long fearfully suspected, from as far back as 1836,—a mere national institution. As if my eyes were suddenly opened, so I saw it—spontaneously, apart from any definite act of reason or any argument; and so I have seen it ever since. I suppose, the main cause of this lay in the contrast which was presented to me by the Catholic Church. Then I recognized at once a reality which was quite a new thing with me. Then I was sensible that I was not making for myself a Church by an effort of thought; I needed not to make an act of faith in her; I had not painfully to force myself into a position, but my mind fell back upon itself in relaxation and in peace, and I gazed at her almost passively as a great objective fact. I looked at her;—at her rites, her ceremonial, and her precepts; and I said, 'This *is* a religion'; and then, when I looked back upon the poor Anglican Church, for which I had laboured so hard, and upon all that appertained to it, and thought of our various attempts to dress it up doctrinally and esthetically, it seemed to me to be the veriest of nonentities. Vanity of vanities, all is vanity! How can I make a record of what passed within me, without seeming to be satirical? But I speak plain, serious words. As people call me credulous for acknowledging Catholic claims, so they call me satirical for disowning Anglican pretensions; to them it *is* credulity, to them it *is* satire; but it is not so in me. What they think exaggeration, I think truth. I am not speaking of the Anglican Church in any disdain, though to them I seem contemptuous. To them of course it is 'Aut Cæsar aut nullus', but not to me. It may be a great creation, though it be not divine, and this is how I judge of it. Men, who abjure the divine right of kings, would be very indignant, if on that account they were considered disloyal. And so I recognize in the Anglican Church a time-honoured institution, of noble historical memories, a monument of ancient wisdom, a momentous arm of political strength, a great national organ, a source of vast popular advantage, and, to a certain point, a witness and teacher of religious truth. I do not think that, if what I have written about it since I have been a Catholic, be equitably considered as a whole, I shall be found to have taken any other view than this; but that it is something sacred, that it is an oracle of revealed doctrine, that it can claim a share in St. Ignatius or St. Cyprian, that it can take the rank, contest the teaching, and stop the path of the Church of St. Peter, that it can call itself 'the Bride of the Lamb', this is the view of it which simply disappeared from my mind on my conversion, and which it would be almost a miracle to reproduce. 'I went by, and lo! it was gone; I sought it, but its place could no where be found'; and nothing can bring it back to me. And, as to its possession of an episcopal succession from the time of the Apostles, well, it may have it, and, if the Holy See ever so decided, I will believe it, as being the decision of a higher judgment than my own; but, for myself, I must have St. Philip's gift, who saw the sacerdotal character on the forehead of a gaily-attired youngster, before I can by my own wit acquiesce in it, for antiquarian arguments are altogether unequal to the urgency of visible facts. Why is it that I must pain dear friends by saying so, and kindle a sort of resentment against me in the kindest of hearts? but I must, though to do it be not only a grief to me, but most impolitic at the moment. Any how, this is my mind; and, if to have it, if to have betrayed it, before now, involuntarily by my words or my deeds, if on a fitting occasion, as now, to have avowed it, if all this be a proof of the justice of the charge brought against me of having 'turned round upon my Mother-Church with contumely and slander', in this sense, but in no other sense, do I plead guilty to it without a word in extenuation.

In no other sense surely; the Church of England has been the instrument of Providence in conferring great benefits on me; had I been born in Dissent, perhaps I should never have been baptized; had I been born an English Presbyterian, perhaps I should never have known our Lord's divinity; had I not come to Oxford, perhaps I never should have heard of the visible Church, or of Tradition, or other Catholic doctrines. And as I have received so much good from the Anglican Establishment itself, can I have the heart, or rather the want of charity, considering that it does for so many others, what it has done for me, to wish to see it overthrown? I have no such wish while it is what it is, and while we are so small a body. Not for its own sake, but for the sake of the many congregations to which it ministers, I will do nothing against it. While Catholics are so weak in England, it is doing our work; and, though it does us harm in a measure, at present the balance is in our favour. What our duty would be at another time and in other circumstances, supposing, for instance, the Establishment lost its dogmatic faith, or at least did not preach it, is another matter altogether. In secular history we read of hostile nations having long truces, and renewing them from time to time, and that seems to be the position the Catholic Church may fairly take up at present in relation to the Anglican Establishment.

Doubtless the National Church has hitherto been a serviceable breakwater against doctrinal errors, more fundamental than its own. How long this will last in the years now before us, it is impossible to say, for the Nation drags down its Church to its own level; but still the National Church has the same sort of influence over the Nation that a periodical has upon the party which it represents, and my own idea of a Catholic's fitting attitude towards the National Church in this its supreme hour, is that of assisting and sustaining it, if it be in our power, in the interest of dogmatic truth. I should wish to avoid every thing, except under the direct call of duty, which went to weaken its hold upon the public mind, or to unsettle its establishment, or to embarrass and lessen its maintenance of those great Christian and Catholic principles and doctrines which it has up to this time successfully preached.

I say, 'except under the call of duty'; and this exception, I am obliged to admit, is not a slight one; it is one which necessarily places a bar to any closer relation between it and ourselves, than that of an armed truce. For, in the first place, it stands to reason that even a volume, such as this has been, exerts an influence adverse to the Establishment,—at least in the case of many minds; and this I cannot avoid, though I have sincerely attempted to keep as wide of controversy in the course of it, as ever I could. And next I cannot deny, what must be ever a very sore point with Anglicans, that, if any Anglican comes to me after careful thought and prayer, and with deliberate purpose, and says, 'I believe in the Holy Catholic Church, and that your Church and yours alone is it, and I demand admittance into it', it would be the greatest of sins in me to reject such a man, as being a distinct contravention of our Lord's maxim, 'Freely ye have received, freely give.'

I have written three volumes which may be considered controversial; Loss and Gain in 1847; Lectures on Difficulties felt by Anglicans in submitting to the Catholic Church in 1850; and Lectures on the present Position of Catholics in England in 1851. And though I have neither time nor need to go into the matter minutely, a few words will suffice for some general account of what has been my object and my tone in these works severally.

Of these three, the Lectures on the 'Position of Catholics' have nothing to do with the Church of England, as such; they are directed against the Protestant or Ultra-Protestant Tradition on the subject of Catholicism since the time of Queen Elizabeth, in which parties indeed in the Church of England have largely participated, but which cannot be confused with Anglican teaching itself. Much less can that Tradition be confused with the doctrine of the Laudian or of the Tractarian School. I owe nothing to Protestantism; and I spoke against it even when I was an Anglican, as well as in these Catholic Lectures. If I spoke in them against the Church Established, it was because, and so far as, at the time when they were delivered, the Establishment took a violent part against the Catholic Church, on the basis of the Protestant Tradition. Moreover, I had never as an Anglican been a lover of the actual Establishment; Hurrell Froude's Remains, in which it is called an 'incubus' and 'Upas Tree', will stand in evidence, as for him, so for me; for I was one of the Editors. What I said even as an Anglican, it is not strange that I said when I was not. Indeed I have been milder in my thoughts of the Establishment ever since I have been a Catholic than before, and for an obvious reason;—when I was an Anglican, I viewed it as repressing a higher doctrine than its own; and now I view it as keeping out a lower and more dangerous.

Then as to my Lectures on Anglican Difficulties. Neither were these formally directed against the National Church. They were addressed to the 'Children of the Movement of 1833', to impress upon them, that, whatever was the case with others, their duty at least was to become Catholics, since Catholicism was the real scope and issue of that Movement. 'There is but one thing', I say, 'that forces me to speak. . . . It will be a miserable thing for you and for me, if I have been instrumental in bringing you but half-way, if I have co-operated in removing your invincible ignorance, but am able to do no more.'—p. 5. Such being the drift of the Volume, the reasoning directed against the Church of England goes no further than this, that it had no claims whatever on such of its members as were proceeding onwards with the Movement into the Catholic Church.

Lastly, as to Loss and Gain: it is the story, simply ideal, of the conversion of an Oxford man. Its drift is to show how little there is in Anglicanism to satisfy and retain a young and earnest heart. In this Tale, all the best characters are sober Church-of-England people. No Tractarians proper are introduced: and this is noted in the Advertisement: 'No *proper* representative is intended in this Tale, of the religious opinions, which had lately so much influence in the University of Oxford.' There *could* not be such in the Tale, without the introduction of friends, which was impossible in its very notion. But, since the scene was to be laid during the very years, and at the head-quarters, of Tractarianism, some expedient was necessary in order to meet what was a great difficulty. My expedient was the introduction of what may be called Tractarians *improper*; and I took them the more readily, because, though I knew that such there were, I knew none of them personally. I mean such men as I used to consider of 'the gilt-gingerbread school', from whom I expected little good, persons whose religion lay in ritualism or architecture, and who 'played at Popery' or at Anglicanism. I repeat I knew no such men, because it is one thing to desire fine churches and ceremonies, (which of course I did myself,) and quite another thing to desire these and nothing else; but at that day there was in some quarters, though not in those where I had influence, a strong movement in the esthetic direction. Doubtless I went too far in my apprehension of such a movement: for one of the best, and most devoted and hard-working Priests I ever knew was the late Father

Hutchison, of the London Oratory, and I believe it was architecture that directed his thoughts towards the Catholic Church. However, I had in my mind an external religion which was inordinate; and, as the men who were considered instances of it, were personally unknown to me, even by name, I introduced them, under imaginary representatives, in Loss and Gain, and that, in order to get clear of Tractarians proper; and of the three men, whom I have introduced, the Anglican is the best. In like manner I introduced two 'gilt-gingerbread' young ladies, who were ideal, absolutely, utterly, without a shred of concrete existence about them; and I introduced them with the remark that they were 'really kind charitable persons', and *'by no means* put forth as *a type* of a class', that 'among such persons were to be found the gentlest spirits and the tenderest hearts', and that 'these sisters had open hands, if they had not wise heads', but that 'they did not know much of matters ecclesiastical, and they knew less of themselves'.

It has been said, indeed, I know not to what extent, that I introduced my friends or partisans into the Tale; this is utterly untrue. Only two cases of this misconception have come to my knowledge, and I at once denied each of them outright; and I take this opportunity of denying generally the truth of all other similar charges. No friend of mine, no one connected in any way with the Movement, entered into the composition of any one of the characters. Indeed, putting aside the two instances which have been distinctly brought before me, I have not even any sort of suspicion who the persons are, whom I am thus accused of introducing.

Next, this writer goes on to speak of Tract 90; a subject of which I have treated at great length in a former passage of this narrative, and, in consequence, need not take up again now.

4

Series of Lives of the English Saints

I have given the history of this publication above at pp. 190–192. It was to have consisted of almost 300 Lives, and I was to have been the Editor. It was brought to an end, before it was well begun, by the act of friends who were frightened at the first Life printed, the Life of St. Stephen Harding. Thus I was not responsible except for the first two numbers; and the Advertisements distinctly declared this. I had just the same responsibility about the other Lives, that my assailant had, and not a bit more. However, it answers his purpose to consider me responsible.

Next, I observe, that his delusion about 'hot-headed fanatic young men' continues: here again I figure with my strolling company. 'They said', he observes, 'what they believed; at least, what they had been taught to believe that they ought to believe. And who had taught them? Dr. Newman can best answer that question', p. 366. Well, I will do what I can to solve the mystery.

Now as to the juvenile writers in the proposed series. One was my friend Mr. Bowden, who in 1843 was a man of 46 years old; he was to have written St. Boniface. Another was Mr. Johnson, a man of 42; he was to have written St. Aldhelm. Another was the author of St. Augustine: let us hear something about him from this writer:—

'Dr. Newman', he says, 'might have said to the Author of the Life of St. Augustine, when he found him, in *the heat and haste of youthful fanaticism*, outraging historic truth and the law of evidence, "This must not be."'—p. 366.

Good. This juvenile was past 40,—well, say 39. Blot *seventeen*. 'This must not be.' This is what I ought to have said, it seems! And then, you see, I have not the talent, and never had, of some people, for lecturing my equals, much less men twenty years older than myself.

But again, the author of St. Augustine's Life distinctly says in his Advertisement, '*No one but himself* is responsible for the way in which these materials have been used.' Blot *eighteen*.

Thirty-three Lives were actually published. Out of the whole number this writer notices *three*. Of these one is 'charming'; therefore I am not to have the benefit of it. Another 'outrages historic truth and the law of evidence'; therefore 'it was notoriously sanctioned by Dr. Newman'. And the third was 'one of the most offensive', and Dr. Newman must have formally connected himself with it in 'a moment of amiable weakness'.—p. 367. What even-handed justice is here! Blot *nineteen*.

But to return to the juvenile author of St. Augustine:—'I found', says this writer, 'the Life of St. Augustine saying, that, though the pretended visit of St. Peter to England wanted *historic evidence*, "yet it has undoubtedly been received as a *pious opinion* by the Church at large, as we learn from the often-quoted words of St. Innocent I. (who wrote A.D. 416) that St. Peter was instrumental in the conversion of the West generally".'—p. 366. He brings this passage against me (with which, however, I have nothing more to do than he has) as a great misdemeanour; but let us see what his criticism is worth. 'And this sort of argument', continues the passage, 'though it ought to be kept *quite distinct from* documentary and historic proof, will *not be without its effect* on devout minds', &c. I should have thought this a very sober doctrine, viz. that we must not confuse together two things quite distinct from each other, criticism and devotion, proof and opinion,—that a *devout* mind will hold *opinions* which it cannot demonstrate by 'historic *proof*'. What, I ask, is the harm of saying this? Is *this* my Assailant's definition of opinion, 'a thing which *can* be proved?' I cannot answer for him, but I can answer for men in general. Let him read Sir David Brewster's 'More Worlds than One';—this principle, which is so shocking to my assailant, is precisely the argument of Sir David's book; he tells us that the plurality of worlds *cannot* be *proved*, but *will* be *received* by religious men. He asks, p. 229, '*If* the stars are *not* suns, for what conceivable *purpose* were they created?' and then he lays down dogmatically, p. 254, 'There is no *opinion*, *out of* the region of *pure demonstration*, more universally *cherished* than the doctrine of the Plurality of worlds.' And in his Title-page he styles this 'opinion' 'the *creed* of the philosopher and the *hope* of the Christian'. If Brewster may bring devotion into Astronomy, why may not my friend bring it into History? and that the more, when he actually declares that it ought to be kept *quite distinct* from history, and by no means assumes that he is an historian because he is a hagiographer; whereas, somehow or other, Sir David does seem to me to show a zeal greater than becomes a *savant*, and to assume that he himself is a theologian because he is an astronomer. This writer owes Sir David as well as me an apology. Blot *twenty*.

He ought to wish his original charge against me in the Magazine dead and buried; but he has the good sense and good taste to revive it again and again. This is one of the places which he has chosen for it. Let him then, just for a change, substitute Sir David Brewster for me in his sentence; Sir David has quite as much right to the compliment as I have, as far as this Life of St. Augustine is concerned. Then he will be saying, that, because Sir David teaches that the belief in more worlds than one is a pious opinion, and not a demonstrated fact, he 'does not care for truth for its own sake, or teach men to regard it as a virtue', p. 366. Blot *twenty-one*.

However, he goes on to give in this same page one other evidence of my disregard of truth. The author of St. Augustine's Life also asks the following question: '*On what evidence* do we put faith in the existence of St. George, the patron of England? Upon such, assuredly, as an acute *critic or skilful pleader* might easily scatter to the winds; the belief of prejudiced or credulous witnesses, the unwritten record of empty pageants and bauble decorations. On the side of scepticism might be exhibited a powerful array of suspicious legends and exploded acts. Yet, *after all, what Catholic is there but would count it a profaneness to question the existence of St. George?*' On which my assailant observes, 'When I found Dr. Newman allowing his disciples . . . in page after page, in Life after Life, to talk nonsense of this kind which is not only sheer Popery, *but saps the very foundation of historic truth*, was it so wonderful that I conceived him to have taught and thought like them?' p. 367, that is, to have taught lying.

Well and good; here again take a parallel; not St. George, but Lycurgus.

Mr. Grote says: 'Plutarch begins his biography of Lycurgus with the following ominous words: "Concerning the lawgiver Lycurgus, we can assert *absolutely nothing*, which is not controverted. There are different stories in respect to his birth, his travels, his death, and also his mode of proceeding, political as well as legislative: least of all is the time in which he lived agreed on." And this exordium *is but too well borne out* by the unsatisfactory nature of the accounts which we read, not only in Plutarch himself, but in those other authors, out of whom we are obliged to make up our idea of the memorable Lycurgian system.'—Greece, vol. ii. p. 455. But Bishop Thirlwall says, 'Experience proves that *scarcely any amount of variation*, as to the time or circumstances of a fact, in the authors who record it, *can be a sufficient ground* for doubting its reality.'—Greece, vol. i. p. 332.

Accordingly, my assailant is virtually saying of the latter of these two historians, 'When I found the Bishop of St. David's talking nonsense of this kind, which saps the very foundation of historic truth', was it 'hasty or far-fetched' to conclude 'that he did not care for truth for its own sake, or teach his disciples to regard it as a virtue?' p. 366. Nay, further, the Author of St. Augustine is no more a disciple of mine, than the Bishop of St. David's is of my Assailant's, and therefore the parallel will be more exact if I accuse this Professor of History of *teaching* Dr. Thirlwall not to care for truth, as a virtue, for its own sake. Blot *twenty-two*.

It is hard on me to have this dull, profitless work, but I have pledged myself;—so now for St. Walburga.

Now will it be believed that this Writer suppresses the fact that the miracles of St. Walburga are treated by the author of her Life as mythical? yet that is the tone of the whole composition. This Writer can notice it in the Life of St. Neot, the first of the three Lives which he criticizes; these are his words: 'Some of them, the writers, for instance, of Volume 4, which contains, among others, a charming life of St. Neot, treat the stories openly as legends and myths, and tell them as they stand, without asking the reader, or themselves, to believe them altogether. The method is harmless enough, if the legends had stood alone; but dangerous enough, when they stand side by side with stories told in earnest, like that of St. Walburga.'—p. 367.

Now, first, that the miraculous stories *are* treated, in the Life of St. Walburga, as legends and myths. Throughout, the miracles and extraordinary occurrences are spoken of as 'said' or 'reported'; and the suggestion is made that, even though they occurred, they might have been after all natural. Thus, in one of the very passages which my Assailant quotes, the author says, 'Illuminated men feel the privileges of Christianity, and to them the evil influence of Satanic power is horribly discernible, like the Egyptian darkness which could be felt; and *the only way to express* their keen perception of it is *to say*, that they *see* upon the countenances of the slaves of sin, the marks, and lineaments, and stamp of the evil one; and [that] they *smell* with their nostrils the horrible fumes that arise from their *vices* and un- cleansed *heart*', &c., p. 78. This introduces St. Sturme and the gambol- ling Germans; what does it mean but that 'the intolerable scent' was nothing physical, or strictly miraculous, but the horror, parallel to physical distress, with which the Saint was affected, from his knowledge of the state of their souls? My assailant is a lucky man, if mental pain has never come upon him with a substance and a volume, as forcible as if it were bodily.

And so in like manner, the Author of the Life says, as this writer actually has quoted him, 'a story *was told and believed*', p. 94. 'One evening, *says her history*', p. 87. 'Another incident *is thus related*', p. 88. 'Immediately, *says* Wülfhard', p. 91. 'A vast number of other cases are *recorded*', p. 92. And there is a distinct intimation that they may be myths, in a passage which this Assailant himself quotes, 'All these have the *character* of a gentle mother correcting the idleness and faults of careless and thoughtless children with tenderness.'—p. 95. I think the criticism which he makes upon this Life is one of the most wanton passages in his Pamphlet. The Life is beautifully written, full of poetry, and, as I have said, bears on its very surface the profession of a legen- dary and mythical character. Blot *twenty-three*.

In saying all this, I have no intention whatever of implying that miracles did not illustrate the Life of St. Walburga; but neither the Author nor I have bound ourselves to the belief of certain instances in particular. My Assailant, in the passage which I just now quoted from him, made some distinction, which was apparently intended to save St. Neot, while it condemned St. Walburga. He said that legends are 'dangerous enough, when they stand side by side with stories told in earnest like St. Walburga'. He will find he has here Dr. Milman against him, as he has already had Sir David Brewster, and the Bishop of St. David's. He accuses me of having 'outraged historic truth and the law of evidence', because friends of mine have considered that, though opinions need not be convictions, nevertheless that legends may be con- nected with history: now, on the contrary, let us hear the Dean of St. Paul's:—

'*History*, to be *true*, must condescend to speak the language of *legend*;

the *belief* of the times is *part* of the *record* of the times; and, though there may occur what may baffle its more calm and searching philosophy, *it must not disdain* that which was the primal, almost universal, motive of human life.'—Latin. Christ., vol. i, p. 388. Dr. Milman's decision justifies me in putting this down as Blot *twenty-four*.

However, there is one miraculous account for which this writer makes me directly answerable, and with reason; and with it I shall conclude my reply to his criticisms on the 'Lives of the English Saints'. It is the medicinal oil which flows from the relics of St. Walburga.

Now, as I shall have occasion to remark under my next Head, these two questions among others occur, in judging of a miraculous story; viz. whether the matter of it is extravagant, and whether it is a fact. And first, it is plain there is nothing extravagant in this report of the relics having a supernatural virtue; and for this reason, because there are such instances in Scripture, and Scripture cannot be extravagant. For instance, a man was restored to life by touching the relics of the Prophet Eliseus. The sacred text runs thus:—'And Elisha died, and they buried him. And the bands of the Moabites invaded the land at the coming in of the year. And it came to pass, as they were burying a man, that, behold, they spied a band of men; and they cast the man into the sepulchre of Elisha. And, when the man was let down, *and touched the bones of Elisha, he revived*, and stood upon his feet.' Again, in the case of an inanimate substance, which had touched a living Saint: 'And God wrought *special miracles* by the hands of Paul; so that *from his body* were brought unto the sick *handkerchiefs or aprons*, and *the diseases departed from them*.' And again in the case of a pool: '*An Angel went down* at a certain season into the pool, and troubled the water; whosoever then first, after the troubling of the water, stepped in, *was made whole of whatsoever disease* he had.' 2 Kings [4 Kings] xiii. 20, 21. Acts xix. 11, 12. John v. 4. Therefore there is nothing *extravagant* in the *character* of the miracle.

The main question then (I do not say the only remaining question, but the main question) is the *matter of fact*:—*is* there an oil flowing from St. Walburga's tomb, which is medicinal? To this question I confined myself in the Preface to the Volume. Of the accounts of medieval miracles, I said that there was no *extravagance* in their *general character*, but I could not affirm that there was always *evidence* for them. I could not simply accept them as *facts*, but I could not reject them in their *nature*; they *might* be true, for they were not impossible: but they were *not proved* to be true, because there was not trustworthy testimony. However, as to St. Walburga, I made *one* exception, the fact of the medicinal oil, since for that miracle there was distinct and successive testimony. And then I went on to give a chain of witnesses. It was my duty to state what those witnesses said in their very words; and I did so; they were in Latin, and I gave them in Latin. One of them speaks of the 'sacrum oleum' flowing 'de membris ejus virgineis, maximè tamen pectoralibus'; and I so printed it;—if I had left it out, this sweet-tempered Writer would have accused me of an 'economy'. I gave the testimonies in full, tracing them from the Saint's death. I said, 'She is one of the principal Saints of her age and country.' Then I quoted Basnage, a Protestant, who says, 'Six writers are extant, who have employed themselves in relating the deeds or miracles of Walburga.' Then I said that her 'renown was not the mere natural *growth* of ages, but begins with the very century of the Saint's death'. Then I observed that only two miracles seem to have been 'distinctly reported of her as occurring in her lifetime; and they were handed down apparently by tradition'. Also, that they are said to have commenced about A.D. 777. Then I spoke of the medicinal oil as having testimony to it in 893, in 1306, after 1450, in 1615, and in 1620. Also, I said that Mabillon seems not to have believed some of her miracles; and that the earliest witness had got into trouble with his Bishop. And so I left it, as a question to be decided by evidence, not deciding any thing myself.

What was the harm of all this? but my Critic has muddled it together in a most extraordinary manner, and I am far from sure that he knows himself the definite categorical charge which he intends it to convey against me. One of his remarks is, 'What has become of the holy oil for the last 240 years, Dr. Newman does not say', p. 369. Of course I did not, because I did not know; I gave the evidence as I found it; he assumes that I had a point to prove, and then asks why I did not make the evidence larger than it was. I put this down as Blot *twenty-five*.

I can tell him more about it now; the oil still flows; I have had some of it in my possession; it is medicinal; some think it is so by a natural quality, others by a divine gift. Perhaps it is on the confines of both.

5

Ecclesiastical Miracles

What is the use of going on with this Writer's criticism upon me, when I am confined to the dull monotony of exposing and oversetting him again and again, with a persistence, which many will think merciless, and few will have the interest to read? Yet I am obliged to do so, lest I should seem to be evading difficulties.

Now as to Miracles. Catholics believe that they happen in any age of the Church, though not for the same purposes, in the same number, or with the same evidence, as in Apostolic times. The Apostles wrought them in evidence of their divine mission; and with this object they have

been sometimes wrought by Evangelists of countries since, as even
Protestants allow. Hence we hear of them in the history of St. Gregory
in Pontus, and St. Martin in Gaul; and in their case, as in that of the
Apostles, they were both numerous and clear. As they are granted to
Evangelists, so are they granted, though in less measure and evidence,
to other holy men; and as holy men are not found equally at all times
and in all places, therefore miracles are in some places and times more
than in others. And since, generally, they are granted to faith and
prayer, therefore in a country in which faith and prayer abound, they
will be more likely to occur, than where and when faith and prayer are
not; so that their occurrence is irregular. And further, as faith and
prayer obtain miracles, so still more commonly do they gain from above
the ordinary interventions of Providence; and, as it is often very difficult
to distinguish between a providence and a miracle, and there will be
more providences than miracles, hence it will happen that many occurrences will be called miraculous, which, strictly speaking, are not such,
and not more than providential mercies, or what are sometimes called
'graces' or 'favours'.

Persons, who believe all this, in accordance with Catholic teaching,
as I did and do, they, on the report of a miracle, will of necessity, the
necessity of good logic, be led to say, first, 'It *may* be', and secondly,
'But I must have *good evidence* in order to believe it.' It *may* be, because
miracles take place in all ages; it must be clearly *proved*, because perhaps after all it may be only a providential mercy, or an exaggeration,
or a mistake, or an imposture. Well, this is precisely what I have said,
which this Writer considers so irrational. I have said, as he quotes me,
p. 368, 'In this day, and under our present circumstances, we can only
reply, that there is no reason why they should not be.' Surely this is good
logic, *provided* that miracles *do* occur in all ages; and so again is it
logical to say, 'There is nothing, *primâ facie*, in the miraculous accounts
in question, to repel a *properly taught* or religiously disposed mind.'
What is the matter with this statement? My assailant does not pretend
to say *what* the matter is, and he cannot; but he expresses a rude,
unmeaning astonishment. Next, I stated *what* evidence there is for the
miracles of which I was speaking; what is the harm of that? He observes, 'What evidence Dr. Newman requires, he makes evident at
once. He at least will fear for himself, and swallow the whole as it
comes.'—p. 369. What random abuse is this, or, to use *his own words*
of me just before, what 'stuff and nonsense'! What is it I am 'swallowing'? 'the whole' what? the evidence? or the miracles? I have swal-
lowed neither, nor implied any such thing. Blot *twenty-six*.

But to return: I have just said that a Catholic's state of mind, of
logical necessity, will be, 'It *may* be a miracle, but it has to be *proved*.'

What has to be proved? 1. That the event occurred as stated, and is not a false report or an exaggeration. 2. That it is clearly miraculous, and not a mere providence or answer to prayer within the order of nature. What is the fault of saying this? The inquiry is parallel to that which is made about some extraordinary fact in secular history. Supposing I hear that King Charles II. died a Catholic, I should say, 1. It *may* be. 2. What is your *proof*? Accordingly, in the passage which this writer quotes, I observe, 'Miracles are the kind of facts proper to ecclesiastical history, just as instances of sagacity or daring, personal prowess, or crime, are the facts proper to secular history.' What is the harm of this? But this writer says, 'Verily his [Dr. Newman's] idea of secular history is almost as degraded as his idea of ecclesiastical', p. 368, and he ends with this muddle of an *Ipse dixit*! Blot *twenty-seven*.

In like manner, about the Holy Coat at Treves, he says of me, 'Dr. Newman . . . seems *hardly sure* of the authenticity of the Holy Coat.' Why *need* I be, more than I am sure that Richard III. murdered the little princes? If I have not *means* of making up my mind one way or the other, surely my most logical course is '*not* to be sure'. He continues, 'Dr. Newman "does not see *why it may not have been* what it professes to be".' Well, is not that just what this Writer would say of a great number of the facts recorded in secular history? is it not what he would be obliged to say of much that is told us about the armour and other antiquities in the Tower of London? To this I alluded in the passage from which he quotes; but he has *garbled* that passage, and I must show it. He quotes me to this effect: 'Is the Tower of London shut against sight-seers because the coats of mail or pikes there may have half-legendary tales connected with them? why then may not the country people come up in joyous companies, singing and piping, to *see* the holy coat at Treves?' On this he remarks, 'To *see*, forsooth! to *worship*, Dr. Newman would have said, had he known (as I take for granted he does not) the facts of that imposture.' Here, if I understand him, he implies that the people came up, not only to see, but to worship, and that I have slurred over the fact that their coming was an act of religious homage, that is, what *he* would call 'worship'. Now, will it be believed that, so far from concealing this, I had carefully stated it in the sentence immediately preceding, and *he suppresses it*? I say, 'The world pays civil honour to it [a jewel said to be Alfred's] on the probability; we pay *religious honour* to relics, if so be, on the probability. Is the Tower of London', I proceed, 'shut', &c. Blot *twenty-eight*.

These words of mine, however, are but one sentence in a long argument, conveying the Catholic view on the subject of ecclesiastical miracles; and, as it is carefully worked out, and very much to the present point, and will save me doing over again what I could not do better or more fully now, if I set about it, I shall make a very long extract from the Lecture in which it occurs, and so bring this Head to an end.

The argument, I should first observe, which is worked out, is this, that Catholics set out with a definite religious tenet as a first principle, and Protestants with a contrary one, and that on this account it comes to pass that miracles are credible to Catholics and incredible to Protestants.

'We affirm that the Supreme Being has wrought miracles on earth ever since the time of the Apostles; Protestants deny it. Why do we affirm, why do they deny? We affirm it on a first principle, they deny it on a first principle; and on either side the first principle is made to be decisive of the question. . . . Both they and we start with the miracles of the Apostles; and then their first principle or presumption against our miracles is this, "What God did once, He is *not* likely to do again"; while our first principle or presumption for our miracles is this; "What God did once, He *is* likely to do again." They say, It cannot be supposed He will work *many* miracles; we, It cannot be supposed He will work *few*.

'The Protestant, I say, laughs at the very idea of miracles or supernatural powers as occurring at this day; his first principle is rooted in him; he repels from him the idea of miracles; he laughs at the notion of evidence; one is just as likely as another; they are all false. Why? because of his first principle, There are no miracles since the Apostles. Here, indeed, is a short and easy way of getting rid of the whole subject, not by reason, but by a first principle which he calls reason. Yes, it *is* reason, granting his first principle is true; it is not reason, supposing his first principle is false.

'There is in the Church a vast tradition and testimony about miracles; how is it to be accounted for? If miracles *can* take place, then the *fact* of the miracle will be a natural explanation of the *report*, just as the fact of a man dying accounts satisfactorily for the news that he is dead; but the Protestant cannot so explain it, because he thinks miracles cannot take place; so he is necessarily driven, by way of accounting for the report of them, to impute that report to fraud. He cannot help himself. I repeat it; the whole mass of accusations which Protestants bring against us under this head, Catholic credulity, imposture, pious frauds, hypocrisy, priestcraft, this vast and varied superstructure of imputation, you see, all rests on an assumption, on an opinion of theirs, for which they offer no kind of proof. What then, in fact, do they say more than this, *If* Protestantism be true, you Catholics are a most awful set of knaves? Here, at least, is a most sensible and undeniable position.

'Now, on the other hand, let me take our own side of the question, and consider how we ourselves stand relatively to the charge made against us. Catholics, then, hold the mystery of the Incarnation; and the Incarnation is the most stupendous event which ever can take place on earth; and after it and henceforth, I do not see how we can scruple at any miracle on the mere ground of its being unlikely to happen. . . . When we start with assuming that miracles are not unlikely, we are putting forth a position which lies embedded, as it were, and involved in the great revealed fact of the Incarnation. So much is plain on starting; but more is plain too. Miracles are not only not unlikely, but they are positively likely; and for this simple reason, because for the most part, when God begins, He goes on. We conceive, that when He first did a miracle, He began a series; what He commenced, He continued: what has been, will be. Surely this is good and clear reasoning. To my own mind, certainly, it is incomparably more difficult to believe that the Divine Being should do one miracle and no more, than that He should do a thousand; that He should do one great miracle only, than that He should do a multitude of lesser besides. . . . If the Divine Being does a thing once, He is, judging by human reason, likely to do it again. This surely is common sense. If a beggar gets food at a gentleman's house once, does he not send others thither after him? If you are attacked by thieves once, do you forthwith leave your windows open at night? . . . Nay, suppose you yourselves were once to see a miracle, would you not feel the occurrence to be like passing a line? would you, in consequence of it, declare, "I never will believe another if I hear of one?" would it not, on the contrary, predispose you to listen to a new report? . . .

'When I hear the report of a miracle, my first feeling would be of the same kind as if it were a report of any natural exploit or event. Supposing, for instance, I heard a report of the death of some public man; it would not startle me, even if I did not at once credit it, for all men must die. Did I read of any great feat of valour, I should believe it, if imputed to Alexander or Cœur de Lion. Did I hear of any act of baseness, I should disbelieve it, if imputed to a friend whom I knew and loved. And so in like manner were a miracle reported to me as wrought by a Member of Parliament, or a Bishop of the Establishment, or a Wesleyan preacher, I should repudiate the notion: were it referred to a saint, or the relic of a saint, or the intercession of a saint, I should not be startled at it, though I might not at once believe it. And I certainly should be right in this conduct, supposing my First Principle be true. Miracles to the Catholic are historical facts, and nothing short of this; and they are to be regarded and dealt with as other facts; and as natural facts, under circumstances, do not startle Protestants, so supernatural, under circumstances, do not startle the Catholic. They may or may not have taken place in particular cases; he may be unable to determine which; he may have no distinct evidence; he may suspend his judgment, but he will say "It is very possible"; he never will say "I cannot believe it."

'Take the history of Alfred; you know his wise, mild, beneficent, yet daring character, and his romantic vicissitudes of fortune. This great king has a number of stories, or, as you may call them, legends told of him. Do you believe them all? no. Do you, on the other hand, think them incredible? no. Do you call a man a dupe or a blockhead for believing them? no. Do you call an author a knave or a cheat who records them? no. You go into neither extreme, whether of implicit faith or of violent reprobation. You are not so extravagant; you see that they suit his character, they may have happened: yet this is so romantic, that has so little evidence, a third is so confused in dates or in geography, that you are in matter of fact indisposed towards them. Others are probably true, others certainly. Nor do you force every one to take your view of particular stories; you and your neighbour think differently about this or that in detail, and agree to differ. There is in the museum at Oxford, a jewel or trinket said to be Alfred's; it is shown to all comers; I never heard the keeper of the museum accused of hypocrisy or fraud for showing, with Alfred's name appended, what he might or might not himself believe to have belonged to that great king; nor did I ever see any party of strangers who were looking at it with awe, regarded by any self-complacent bystander with scornful compassion. Yet the curiosity is not to a certainty Alfred's. The world pays civil honour to it on the probability; we pay religious honour to relics, if so be, on the probability. Is the Tower of London shut against sight-seers, because the coats of mail and pikes there may have half-legendary tales connected with them? why then may not the country people come up in joyous companies, singing and piping, to see the Holy Coat at Treves? There is our Queen again, who is so truly and justly popular; she roves about in the midst of tradition and romance; she scatters myths and legends from her as she goes along; she is a being of poetry, and you might fairly be sceptical whether she had any personal existence. She is always at some beautiful, noble, bounteous work or other, if you trust the papers. She is doing alms-deeds in the Highlands; she meets beggars in her rides at Windsor; she writes verses in albums, or draws sketches, or is mistaken for the housekeeper by some blind old woman, or she runs up a hill as if she were a child. Who finds fault with these things? he would be a cynic, he would be white-livered, and would have gall for blood, who was not struck with this graceful, touching evidence of the love her subjects bear her. Who could have the head, even if he had the heart, who could be so cross and peevish, who could be so solemn and perverse, as to say that some of these stories *may* be simple lies, and all of them might have stronger evidence than they carry with them? Do you think she is displeased at them? Why then should He, the Great Father, who once walked the earth, look sternly on the unavoidable mistakes of His own subjects and children in their devotion to Him and His? Even granting they mistake some cases in particular, from the infirmity of human nature and the contingencies of evidence, and fancy there is or has been a miracle here and there when there is not, though a tradition, attached to a picture, or to a shrine, or a well, be very doubtful, though one relic be sometimes mistaken for another, and St. Theodore stands for St. Eugenius or St. Agathocles, still, once take into account our First Principle, that He is likely to continue miracles among us, which is as good as the Protestant's, and I do not see why He should feel much displeasure with us on account of this, or should cease to work wonders in our behalf. In the Protestant's view, indeed, who assumes that miracles never are, our thaumatology is one great falsehood; but that is *his* First Principle, as I have said so often, which he does not prove but assume. If *he*, indeed, upheld *our* system, or *we* held *his* principle, in either case he or we should be impostors; but though we should be partners to a fraud if we thought like Protestants, we surely are not if we think like Catholics.

'Such then is the answer I make to those who would urge against us the multitude of miracles recorded in our Saints' Lives and devotional works, for many of which there is little evidence, and for some next to none. We think them true in the same sense in which Protestants think the history of England true. When they say *that*, they do not mean to say that there are no mistakes, but no mistakes of consequence, none which alter the general course of history. Nor do they mean they are equally sure of every part; for evidence is fuller and better for some things than for others. They do not stake their credit on the truth of Froissart or Sully, they do not pledge themselves for the accuracy of Doddington or Walpole, they do not embrace as an Evangelist Hume, Sharon Turner, or Macaulay. And yet they do not think it necessary, on the other hand, to commence a religious war against all our historical catechisms, and abstracts, and dictionaries, and tales, and biographies, through the country; they have no call on them to amend and expurgate books of archæology, antiquities, heraldry, architecture, geography, and statistics, to rewrite our inscriptions, and to establish a censorship on all new publications for the time to come. And so as regards the miracles of the Catholic Church; if, indeed, miracles never can occur, then, indeed, impute the narratives to fraud; but till you prove they are not likely, we shall consider the histories which have come down to us true on the whole, though in particular cases they may be exaggerated or unfounded. Where, indeed, they can certainly be proved to be false, there we shall be bound to do our best to get rid of them; but till that is clear, we shall be liberal enough to allow others to use their private judgment in their favour, as we use ours in their disparagement. For myself, lest I appear in any way to be shrinking from a determinate judgment on the claims of some of those miracles and relics, which Protestants are so startled at, and to be hiding particular questions in what is vague and general, I will avow distinctly, that, *putting out of the question* the *hypothesis of unknown laws of nature* (which is an evasion from the force of any proof), I think it impossible to *withstand the evidence* which is brought for the liquefaction of the blood of St. Januarius at Naples, and for the motion of the eyes of the pictures of the Madonna in the Roman States. I *see no reason to doubt* the material of the Lombard crown at Monza; and I *do not see why* the Holy Coat at Treves may not have been what it professes to be. I *firmly believe* that portions of the True Cross are at Rome and elsewhere, that the Crib of Bethlehem is at Rome, and the bodies of St. Peter and St. Paul also. . . . Many men when they hear an educated man so speak, will at once impute the avowal to insanity, or to an idiosyncrasy, or to imbecility of mind, or to decrepitude of powers, or to fanaticism, or to hypocrisy. They have a right to say so, if they will; and we have a right to ask them why they do not say it of those who bow down before the Mystery of mysteries, the Divine Incarnation?'

In my Essay on Miracles of the year 1826, I proposed three questions about a professed miraculous occurrence, 1. is it antecedently *probable?* 2. is it in its *nature* certainly miraculous? 3. has it sufficient *evidence?* These are the three heads under which I still wish to conduct the inquiry into the miracles of Ecclesiastical History.

6

Popular Religion

This Writer uses much rhetoric against a Lecture of mine, in which I bring out, as honestly as I can, the state of countries which have long received the Catholic Faith, and hold it by the force of tradition, universal custom, and legal establishment; a Lecture in which I give pictures, drawn principally from the middle ages, of what, considering the corruption of the human race generally, that state is sure to be,— pictures of its special sins and offences, *sui generis*, which are the result of that Faith when it is separated from Love or Charity, or of what Scripture calls a 'dead faith', of the Light shining in darkness, and the truth held in unrighteousness. The nearest approach which this Writer is able to make towards stating what I have said in this Lecture, is to state the very reverse. Observe: we have already had some instances of the haziness of his ideas concerning the 'Notes of the Church'. These

Notes are, as any one knows who has looked into the subject, certain great and simple characteristics, which He who founded the Church has stamped upon her in order to draw both the reason and the imagination of men to her, as being really a divine work, and a religion distinct from all other religious communities; the principal of these Notes being that she is Holy, One, Catholic, and Apostolic, as the Creed says. Now, to use his own word, he has the incredible 'audacity' to say, that I have declared, not the divine characteristics of the Church, but the sins and scandals in her, to be her Notes,—as if I made God the Author of evil. He says distinctly, 'Dr. Newman, with a kind of desperate audacity, *will* dig forth such *scandals* as *Notes* of the Catholic Church.' This is what I get at his hands for my honesty. Blot *twenty-nine*.

Again, he says, '[Dr. Newman uses] the blasphemy and profanity which he confesses to be so common in Catholic countries, as an argument *for*, and not *against* the "Catholic Faith".'—p. 375. That is, because I admit that profaneness exists in the Church, therefore I consider it a token of the Church. Yes, certainly, just as our national form of cursing is an evidence of the being of a God, and as a gallows is the glorious sign of a civilized country,—but in no other way. Blot *thirty*.

What is it that I really say? I say as follows: Protestants object that the communion of Rome does not fulfil satisfactorily the expectation which we may justly form concerning the True Church, as it is delineated in the four Notes, enumerated in the Creed; and among others, e.g. in the Note of sanctity; and they point, in proof of what they assert, to the state of Catholic countries. Now, in answer to this objection, it is plain what I might have done, if I had not had a conscience. I might have denied the fact. I might have said, for instance, that the middle ages were as virtuous, as they were believing. I might have denied that there was any violence, any superstition, any immorality, any blasphemy during them. And so as to the state of countries which have long had the light of Catholic truth, and have degenerated. I might have admitted nothing against them, and explained away every thing which plausibly told to their disadvantage. I did nothing of the kind; and what effect has this had upon this estimable critic? 'Dr. Newman takes a seeming pleasure', he says, 'in detailing instances of dishonesty on the part of Catholics'. —p. 375. Blot *thirty-one*. Any one who knows me well, would testify that my 'seeming pleasure', as he calls it, at such things, is just the impatient sensitiveness, which relieves itself by means of a definite delineation of what is so hateful to it.

However, to pass on. All the miserable scandals of Catholic countries, taken at the worst, are, as I view the matter, no argument against the Church itself; and the reason which I give in the Lecture is, that, according to the proverb, Corruptio optimi est pessima. The Jews could sin in a way no other contemporary race could sin, for theirs was a sin against light; and Catholics can sin with a depth and intensity with which Protestants cannot sin. There will be more blasphemy, more hatred of God, more of diabolical rebellion, more of awful sacrilege, more of vile hypocrisy in a Catholic country than any where else, because there is in it more of sin against light. Surely, this is just what Scripture says, 'Woe unto thee, Chorazin! woe unto thee, Bethsaida!' And, again, surely what is told us by religious men, say by Father Bresciani, about the present unbelieving party in Italy, fully bears out the divine text: 'If, after they have escaped the pollutions of the world . . . they are again entangled therein and overcome, the latter end is worse with them than the beginning. For it had been better for them not to have known the way of righteousness, than, after they have known it, to turn from the holy commandments delivered unto them.'

And what is true of those who thus openly oppose themselves to the truth, as it was true of the Evil One in the beginning, will in an analogous way be true in the case of all sin, be it of a heavier or lighter character, which is found in a Catholic country:—sin will be strangely tinged or dyed by religious associations or beliefs, and will exhibit the tragical inconsistencies of the excess of knowledge over love, or of much faith with little obedience. The mysterious battle between good and evil will assume in a Catholic country its most frightful shape, when it is not the collision of two distinct and far-separated hosts, but when it is carried on in hearts and souls, taken one by one, and when the eternal foes are so intermingled and interfused that to human eyes they seem to coalesce into a multitude of individualities. This is in course of years, the real, the hidden condition of a nation, which has been bathed in Christian ideas, whether it be a young vigorous race, or an old and degenerate; and it will manifest itself socially and historically in those characteristics, sometimes grotesque, sometimes hideous, sometimes despicable, of which we have so many instances, medieval and modern, both in this hemisphere and in the western. It is, I say, the necessary result of the intercommunion of divine faith and human corruption.

But it has a light side as well as a dark. First, much which seems profane, is not in itself profane, but in the subjective view of the Protestant beholder. Scenic representations of our Lord's Passion are not profane to a Catholic population; in like manner, there are usages, customs, institutions, actions, often of an indifferent nature, which will be necessarily mixed up with religion in a Catholic country, because all things whatever are so mixed up. Protestants have been sometimes shocked, most absurdly as a Catholic rightly decides, at hearing that Mass is sometimes said for a good haul of fish. There is no sin here, but only a difference from Protestant customs. Other phenomena of a Catholic nation are at most mere extravagances. And then as to what

is really sinful, if there be in it fearful instances of blasphemy or superstition, there are also special and singular fruits and exhibitions of
sanctity; and, if the many do not seem to lead better lives for all their
religious knowledge, at least they learn, as they can learn nowhere else,
how to repent thoroughly and to die well.

The visible state of a country, which professes Catholicism, need not
be the measure of the spiritual result of that Catholicism, at the Eternal
Judgment Seat; but no one could say that that visible state was a Note
that Catholicism was divine.

All this I attempted to bring out in the Lecture of which I am speaking; and that I had some success, I am glad to infer from the message
of congratulation upon it, which I received at the time, from a foreign
Catholic layman, of high English reputation, with whom I had not the
honour of a personal acquaintance. And having given the key to the
Lecture, which the Writer so wonderfully misrepresents, I pass on to
another head.

7

The Economy

For the subject of the Economy, I shall refer to my discussion upon
it in my History of the Arians, after one word about this Writer. He
puts into his Title-page these words from a Sermon of mine: 'It is not
more than an hyperbole to say, that, in certain cases, a lie is the nearest
approach to truth.' This Sermon he attacks; but I do not think it
necessary to defend it here, because any one who reads it, will see that
he is simply incapable of forming a notion of what it is about. It treats
of subjects which are entirely out of his depth; and, as I have already
shown in other instances, and observed in the beginning of this Volume,
he illustrates in his own person the very thing that shocks him, viz. that
the nearest approach to truth, in given cases, is a lie. He does his best
to make something of it, I believe; but he gets simply perplexed. He
finds that it annihilates space, robs him of locomotion, almost scoffs at
the existence of the earth, and he is simply frightened and cowed. He
can but say 'the man who wrote that sermon was already past the
possibility of conscious dishonesty', p. 379. Perhaps it is hardly fair, after
such a confession on his part of being fairly beat, to mark down a blot;
however, let it be Blot *thirty-two*.

Then again, he quotes from me thus: 'Many a theory or view of
things, on which an institution is founded, or a party held together, is
of the same kind (economical). Many an argument, used by zealous and
earnest men, has this economical character, being not the very ground
on which they act (for they continue in the same course, though it be

refuted) yet in a certain sense, a representation of it, a proximate description of their feelings, in the shape of argument, on which they can rest, to which they can recur when perplexed, and appeal when they are questioned.' He calls these 'startling words', p. 378. Yet here again he illustrates their truth; for in his own case, he has acted on them in this very controversy with the most happy exactness. Surely he referred to my Sermon on Wisdom and Innocence, when called on to prove me a liar, as 'a proximate description of his feelings about me, in the shape of argument', and he has 'continued in the same course, though it has been refuted'. Blot *thirty-three*.

Then, as to 'a party being held together by a mythical representation', or economy. Surely 'Church and King', 'Reform', 'Non-intervention', are such symbols; or let this Writer answer Mr. Kinglake's question in his 'Crimean War', 'Is it true that . . . great armies were gathering, and that for the sake of the *Key* and the *Star* the peace of the nations was brought into danger?' Blot *thirty-four*.

In the beginning of this work, pp. 399–403, I refuted his gratuitous accusation against me at p. 380, founded on my calling one of my Anglican Sermons a Protestant one: so I have nothing to do but to register it here as Blot *thirty-five*.

Then he says that I committed an economy in placing in my original title-page, that the question between him and me, was whether 'Dr. Newman teaches that Truth is no virtue.' It was a 'wisdom of the serpentine type', since I did not add, 'for its own sake'. Now observe: First, as to the matter of fact, in the course of my Letters, which bore that Title-page, I printed the words 'for its own sake', *five* times over. Next, pray, what kind of a virtue is that, which is *not* done for its own sake? So this, after all, is this Writer's idea of virtue! a something that is done for the sake of something *else*; a sort of expedience! He is honest, it seems, simply *because* honesty is 'the best policy', and on that score it is that he thinks himself virtuous. Why, 'for its own sake' enters into the very idea or definition of a virtue. Defend me from such virtuous men, as this Writer would inflict upon us! Blot *thirty-six*.

These Blots are enough just now; so I proceed to a brief sketch of what I held in 1833 upon the Economy, as a rule of practice. I wrote this two months ago; perhaps the composition is not quite in keeping with the run of this Appendix; and it is short; but I think it will be sufficient for my purpose:—

The doctrine of the *Economia*, had, as I have shown, pp. 36–39, a large signification when applied to the divine ordinances; it also had a definite application to the duties of Christians, whether clergy or laity, in preaching, in instructing or catechizing, or in ordinary intercourse with the world around them.

As Almighty God did not all at once introduce the Gospel to the world, and thereby gradually prepared men for its profitable reception, so, according to the doctrine of the early Church, it was a duty, for the sake of the heathen among whom they lived, to observe a great reserve and caution in communicating to them the knowledge of 'the whole counsel of God'. This cautious dispensation of the truth, after the manner of a discreet and vigilant steward, is denoted by the word 'economy'. It is a mode of acting which comes under the head of Prudence, one of the four Cardinal Virtues.

The principle of the Economy is this; that out of various courses, in religious conduct or statement, all and each *allowable antecedently and in themselves*, that ought to be taken which is most expedient and most suitable at the time for the object in hand.

Instances of its application and exercise in Scripture are such as the following:—1. Divine Providence did but gradually impart to the world in general, and to the Jews in particular, the knowledge of His will:— He is said to have 'winked at the times of ignorance among the heathen'; and He suffered in the Jews divorce 'because of the hardness of their hearts'. 2. He has allowed Himself to be represented as having eyes, ears, and hands, as having wrath, jealousy, grief and repentance. 3. In like manner, our Lord spoke harshly to the Syro-Phœnician woman, whose daughter He was about to heal, and made as if He would go further, when the two disciples had come to their journey's end. 4. Thus too Joseph 'made himself strange to his brethren', and Elisha kept silence on request of Naaman to bow in the house of Rimmon. 5. Thus St. Paul circumcised Timothy, while he cried out 'Circumcision availeth not.'

It may be said that this principle, true in itself, yet is dangerous, because it admits of an easy abuse, and carries men away into what becomes insincerity and cunning. This is undeniable; to do evil that good may come, to consider that the means, whatever they are, justify the end, to sacrifice truth to expedience, unscrupulousness, recklessness, are grave offences. These are abuses of the Economy. But to call them *economical* is to give a fine name to what occurs every day, independent of any knowledge of the *doctrine* of the Economy. It is the abuse of a rule which nature suggests to every one. Every one looks out for the 'mollia tempora fandi', and 'mollia verba' too.

Having thus explained what is meant by the Economy as a rule of social intercourse between men of different religious, or, again, political, or social views, next I go on to state what I said in the Arians.

I say in that Volume first, that our Lord has given us the *principle* in His own words,—'Cast not your pearls before swine'; and that He exemplified it in His teaching by parables; that St. Paul expressly distinguishes between the milk which is necessary to one set of men, and the strong meat which is allowed to others, and that, in two Epistles. I say, that the Apostles in the Acts observe the same rule in their speeches, for it is a fact, that they do not preach the high doctrines of Christianity, but only 'Jesus and the resurrection' or 'repentance and faith'. I also say, that this is the very reason that the Fathers assign for the silence of various writers in the first centuries on the subject of our Lord's divinity. I also speak of the catechetical system practised in the early Church, and the *disciplina arcani* as regards the doctrine of the Holy Trinity, to which Bingham bears witness; also of the defence of this rule by Basil, Cyril of Jerusalem, Chrysostom, and Theodoret.

And next the question may be asked, whether I have said any thing in my Volume *to guard* the doctrine, thus laid down, from the abuse to which it is obviously exposed: and my answer is easy. Of course, had I had any idea that I should have been exposed to such hostile misrepresentations, as it has been my lot to undergo on the subject, I should have made more direct avowals than I have done of my sense of the gravity and the danger of that abuse. Since I could not foresee when I wrote, that I should have been wantonly slandered, I only wonder that I have anticipated the charge as fully as will be seen in the following extracts.

For instance, speaking of the Disciplina Arcani, I say:—(1) 'The elementary information given to the heathen or catechumen was *in no sense undone* by the subsequent secret teaching, which was in fact but the *filling up of a bare but correct outline*', p. 58, and I contrast this with the conduct of the Manichæans 'who represented the initiatory discipline as founded on a *fiction* or hypothesis, which was to be forgotten by the learner as he made progress in the *real* doctrine of the Gospel'. (2) As to allegorizing, I say that the Alexandrians erred, whenever and as far as they proceeded 'to *obscure* the primary meaning of Scripture, and to *weaken the force of historical facts* and express declarations', p. 69. (3) And that they were 'more open to *censure*', when, on being '*urged by objections* to various passages in the history of the Old Testament, as derogatory to the divine perfections or to the Jewish Saints, they had *recourse to an allegorical explanation by way of answer*', p. 71. (4) I add, '*It is impossible to defend such a procedure*, which seems to imply a *want of faith* in those who had recourse to it'; for 'God has given us *rules of right and wrong*', *ibid.* (5) Again, I say, —'The *abuse of the Economy* in *the hands of unscrupulous reasoners*, is obvious. *Even the honest* controversialist or teacher will find it very difficult to represent, *without misrepresenting*, what it is yet his duty to present to his hearers with caution or reserve. Here the obvious rule to guide our practice is, to be careful ever to maintain *substantial truth* in our use of the economical method', pp. 79, 80. (6) And so far from concurring at all hazards with Justin, Gregory, or Athanasius, I say, 'It *is plain* [they] *were justified or not* in their Economy, *according* as they did or did not *practically mislead their opponents*', p. 80. (7) I proceed, 'It is so difficult to hit the mark in these perplexing cases, that it is not wonderful, should these or other Fathers have failed at times, and said more or less than was proper', *ibid.*

The Principle of the Economy is familiarly acted on among us every day. When we would persuade others, we do not begin by treading on their toes. Men would be thought rude who introduced their own religious notions into mixed society, and were devotional in a drawing-room. Have we never thought lawyers tiresome who came down for the assizes and talked law all through dinner? Does the same argument tell in the House of Commons, on the hustings, and at Exeter Hall? Is an educated gentleman never worsted at an election by the tone and arguments of some clever fellow, who, whatever his shortcomings in other respects, understands the common people?

As to the Catholic Religion in England at the present day, this only will I observe,—that the truest expedience is to answer right out, when you are asked; that the wisest economy is to have no management; that the best prudence is not to be a coward; that the most damaging folly is to be found out shuffling; and that the first of virtues is to 'tell truth, and shame the devil'.

8

Lying and Equivocation

This writer says, 'Though [a lie] be a sin, the fact of its being a venial one seems to have gained for it as yet a very slight penance.'—p. 382. Yet he says also that Dr. Newman takes 'a perverse pleasure in eccentricities', because I say that 'it is better for sun and moon to drop from heaven than that one soul should tell one wilful untruth'.—p. 372. That is, he first accuses us without foundation of making light of a lie; and, when he finds that we don't, then he calls us inconsistent. I have noticed these words of mine, and two passages besides, which he quotes, above at pp. 221–223. Here I will but observe on the subject of venial sin generally, that he altogether forgets our doctrine of Purgatory. This punishment may last till the day of judgment; so much for duration; then as to intensity, let the image of fire, by which we denote it, show what we think of it. Here is the expiation of venial sins. Yet Protestants, after the manner of this Writer, are too apt to play fast and loose; to blame us because we hold that sin may be venial, and to blame us again when we tell them what we think will be its punishment. Blot *thirty-seven.*

At the end of his Pamphlet he makes a distinction between the Catholic clergy and gentry in England, which I know the latter consider to be very impertinent; and he makes it apropos of a passage in one of my original letters in January. He quotes me as saying that 'Catholics differ from Protestants, as to whether this or that act in particular is conformable to the rule of truth', p. 384; and then he goes on to observe, that I have 'calumniated the Catholic gentry', because 'there is no difference whatever, of detail or other, between their truthfulness and honour, and the truthfulness and honour of the Protestant gentry among whom they live'. But again he has garbled my words; they run thus:

'Truth is the same in itself and in substance, to Catholic and Protestant; so is purity; both virtues are to be referred to that moral sense which is the natural possession of us all. But, when we come to the question in detail, whether this or that act in particular is conformable to the rule of truth, or again to the rule of purity, then *sometimes* there is a difference of opinion *between individuals, sometimes between schools*, and *sometimes* between religious communions.' I knew indeed perfectly well, and I confessed that '*Protestants* think that the Catholic system, as such, leads to a lax observance of the rule of truth'; but I added, 'I am very sorry that they should think so', and I never meant myself to grant that all Protestants were on the strict side, and all Catholics on the lax. Far from it; there is a stricter party as well as a laxer party among Catholics, there is a laxer party as well as a stricter party among Protestants. I have already spoken of Protestant writers who in certain cases allow of lying, I have also spoken of Catholic writers who do not allow of equivocation; when I wrote 'a difference of opinion between individuals', and 'between schools', I meant between Protestant and Protestant, and particular instances were in my mind. I did not say then, or dream of saying, that Catholics, priests and laity, were lax on the point of lying, and that Protestants were strict, any more than I meant to say that all Catholics were pure, and all Protestants impure; but I meant to say that, whereas the rule of Truth is one and the same both to Catholic and Protestant, nevertheless some Catholics were lax, some strict, and again some Protestants were strict, some lax; and I have already had opportunities of recording my own judgment on which side this Writer is *himself*, and therefore he may keep his forward vindication of 'honest gentlemen and noble ladies', who, in spite of their priests, are still so truthful, till such time as he can find a worse assailant of them than I am, and they no better champion of them than himself. And as to the Priests of England, those who know them, as he does *not*, will pronounce them no whit inferior in this great virtue to the gentry, whom he says that he *does*; and I cannot say more. Blot *thirty-eight*.

Lastly, this Writer uses the following words, which I have more than once quoted, and with a reference to them I shall end my remarks upon him. 'I am henceforth', he says, 'in doubt and fear, as much *as an honest man can be*, concerning every word Dr. Newman may write. How can I tell that I shall not be the dupe of some cunning equivocation, of one of the three kinds, laid down as permissible by the blessed St. Alfonso da Liguori and his pupils, even when confirmed with an oath . . . ?'
I will tell him why he need not fear; because he has *left out* one very important condition in the statement of St. Alfonso,—and very applicable to my own case, even if I followed St. Alfonso's view of the subject. St. Alfonso says 'ex justâ causâ'; but our 'honest man', as he styles himself, has *omitted these words*; which are a key to the whole question. Blot *thirty-nine*. Here endeth our 'honest man'. Now for the subject of Lying.

Almost all authors, Catholic and Protestant, admit, that *when a just cause is present*, there is some kind or other of verbal misleading, which is not sin. Even silence is in certain cases virtually such a misleading, according to the Proverb, 'Silence gives consent'. Again, silence is absolutely forbidden to a Catholic, as a mortal sin, under certain circumstances, e.g. to keep silence, instead of making a profession of faith.
Another mode of verbal misleading, and the most direct, is actually saying the thing that is not; and it is defended on the principle that such words are not a lie, when there is a 'justa causa', as killing is not murder in the case of an executioner.
Another ground of certain authors for saying that an untruth is not a lie where there is a just cause, is, that veracity is a kind of justice, and therefore, when we have no duty of justice to tell truth to another, it is no sin not to do so. Hence we may say the thing that is not, to children, to madmen, to men who ask impertinent questions, to those whom we hope to benefit by misleading.
Another ground taken in defending certain untruths, *ex justâ causâ*, as if not lies, is that veracity is for the sake of society, and, if in no case we might lawfully mislead others, we should actually be doing society great harm.
Another mode of verbal misleading is equivocation or a play upon words; and it is defended on the view that to lie is to use words in a sense which they will not bear. But an equivocator uses them in a received sense, though there is another received sense, and therefore, according to this definition, he does not lie.

Others say that all equivocations are, after all, a kind of lying, faint lies or awkward lies, but still lies; and some of these disputants infer, that therefore we must not equivocate, and others that equivocation is but a half-measure, and that it is better to say at once that in certain cases untruths are not lies.

Others will try to distinguish between evasions and equivocations; but they will be answered, that, though there are evasions which are clearly not equivocations, yet that it is difficult scientifically to draw the line between them.

To these must be added the unscientific way of dealing with lies, viz. that on a great or cruel occasion a man cannot help telling a lie, and he would not be a man, did he not tell it, but still it is wrong and he ought not to do it, and he must trust that the sin will be forgiven him though he goes about to commit it. It is a frailty, and had better not be anticipated, and not thought of again, after it is once over. This view cannot for a moment be defended, but, I suppose, it is very common.

And now I think the historical course of thought upon the matter has been this: the Greek Fathers thought that, when there was a *justa causa*, an untruth need not be a lie. St. Augustine took another view, though with great misgiving; and, whether he is rightly interpreted or not, is the doctor of the great and common view that all untruths are lies, and that there can be *no* just cause of untruth. In these later times, this doctrine has been found difficult to work, and it has been largely taught that, though all untruths are lies, yet that certain equivocations, when there is a just cause, are not untruths.

Further, there have been and all along through these later ages, other schools, running parallel with the above mentioned, one of which says that equivocations, &c. after all *are* lies, and another which says that there are untruths which are not lies.

And now as to the 'just cause', which is the condition, *sine quâ non*. The Greek Fathers make them such as these, self-defence, charity, zeal for God's honour, and the like.

St. Augustine seems to deal with the same 'just causes' as the Greek Fathers, even though he does not allow of their availableness as depriving untruths, spoken with such objects, of their sinfulness. He mentions defence of life and of honour, and the safe custody of a secret. Also the Anglican writers, who have followed the Greek Fathers, in defending untruths when there is the 'just cause', consider that just cause to be such as the preservation of life and property, defence of law, the good of others. Moreover, their moral rights, e.g. defence against the inquisitive, &c.

St. Alfonso, I consider, would take the same view of the 'justa causa' as the Anglican divines; he speaks of it as 'quicunque finis *honestus*, ad servanda bona spiritui vel corpori utilia'; which is very much the view which they take of it, judging by the instances which they give.

In all cases, however, and as contemplated by all authors, Clement of Alexandria, or Milton, or St. Alfonso, such a causa is, in fact, extreme, rare, great, or at least special. Thus the writer in the Mélanges Théologiques (Liège, 1852–3, p. 453) quotes Lessius: 'Si absque justa causa fiat, est abusio orationis contra virtutem veritatis, et civilem consuetudinem, etsi proprie non sit mendacium.' That is, the virtue of truth, and the civil custom are the *measure* of the just cause. And so Voit, 'If a man has used a reservation (restrictione non purè mentali) without a *grave* cause, he has sinned gravely.' And so the author himself, from whom I quote, and who defends the Patristic and Anglican doctrine that there *are* untruths which are not lies, says, 'Under the name of mental reservation theologians authorize many lies, *when there is for them a grave reason* and proportionate' i.e. to their character.— p. 459. And so St. Alfonso, in another Treatise, quotes St. Thomas to the effect, that, if from one cause two immediate effects follow, and, if the good effect of that cause is *equal in value* to the bad effect (bonus *æquivalet* malo), then nothing hinders that the good may be intended and the evil permitted. From which it will follow that, since the evil to society from lying is very great, the just cause which is to make it allowable, must be very great also. And so Kenrick: 'It is confessed by all Catholics that, in the common intercourse of life, all ambiguity of language is to be avoided; but it is debated whether such ambiguity is ever lawful. Most theologians answer in the affirmative, supposing a *grave cause* urges, and the [true] mind of the speaker can be collected from the adjuncts, though in fact it be not collected.'

However, there are cases, I have already said, of another kind, in which Anglican authors would think a lie allowable; such as when a question is *impertinent*. Accordingly, I think the best word for embracing all the cases which would come under the 'justa causa', is, not 'extreme', but 'special', and I say the same as regards St. Alfonso; and therefore, above in pp. 244 and 246, whether I speak of St. Alfonso or Paley, I should have used the word 'special', or 'extraordinary', not 'extreme'.

What I have been saying shows what different schools of opinion there are in the Church in the treatment of this difficult doctrine; and, by consequence, that a given individual, such as I am, *cannot* agree with all, and has a full right to follow which he will. The freedom of the Schools, indeed, is one of those rights of reason, which the Church is too wise really to interfere with. And this applies not to moral questions only, but to dogmatic also.

It is supposed by Protestants that, because St. Alfonso's writings have had such high commendation bestowed upon them by authority, therefore they have been invested with a quasi-infallibility. This has arisen in good measure from Protestants not knowing the force of theological terms. The words to which they refer are the authoritative decision that 'nothing in his works has been found *worthy of censure*', 'censurâ dignum'; but this does not lead to the conclusions which have been drawn from it. Those words occur in a legal document, and cannot be interpreted except in a legal sense. In the first place, the sentence is negative; nothing in St. Alfonso's writings is positively approved; and secondly it is not said that there are no faults in what he has written, but nothing which comes under the ecclesiastical *censurâ*, which is something very definite. To take and interpret them, in the way commonly adopted in England, is the same mistake, as if one were to take the word 'Apologia' in the English sense of apology, or 'Infant' in law to mean a little child.

1. Now first as to the meaning of the form of words viewed as a proposition. When they were brought before the fitting authorities at Rome by the Archbishop of Besançon, the answer returned to him contained the condition that those words were to be interpreted, 'with due regard to the mind of the Holy See concerning the approbation of writings of the servants of God, ad effectum Canonizationis'. This is intended to prevent any Catholic taking the words about St. Alfonso's works in too large a sense. Before a Saint is canonized, his works are examined and a judgment pronounced upon them. Pope Benedict XIV. says, 'The *end* or *scope* of this judgment is, that it may appear, whether the doctrine of the servant of God, which he has brought out in his writings, is free from any soever *theological censure*.' And he remarks in addition, 'It never can be said that the doctrine of a servant of God is *approved* by the Holy See, but at most it can [only] be said that it is not disapproved (non reprobatam) in case that the Revisers had reported that there is nothing found by them in his works, which is adverse to the decrees of Urban VIII., and that the judgment of the Revisers has been approved by the sacred Congregation, and confirmed by the Supreme Pontiff.' The Decree of Urban VIII. here referred to is, 'Let works be examined, whether they contain errors against faith or good morals (bonos mores), or any new doctrine, or a doctrine foreign and alien to the common sense and custom of the Church.' The author from whom I quote this (M. Vandenbroeck, of the diocese of Malines) observes, 'It is therefore clear, that the approbation of the works of the Holy Bishop touches not the truth of every proposition, adds nothing to them, nor even gives them by consequence a degree of intrinsic probability.' He adds that it gives St. Alfonso's theology an extrinsic probability, from the fact that, in the judgment of the Holy See, no

proposition deserves to receive a censure; but that 'that probability will cease nevertheless in a particular case, for any one who should be convinced, whether by evident arguments, or by a decree of the Holy See, or otherwise, that the doctrine of the Saint deviates from the truth'. He adds, 'From the fact that the approbation of the works of St. Alfonso does not decide the truth of each proposition, it follows, as Benedict XIV. has remarked, that we may combat the doctrine which they contain; only, since a canonized saint is in question, who is honoured by a solemn *culte* in the Church, we ought not to speak except with respect, nor to attack his opinions except with temper and modesty.'

2. Then, as to the meaning of the word *censura*: Benedict XIV. enumerates a number of 'Notes' which come under that name; he says, 'Out of propositions which are to be noted with theological censure, some are heretical, some erroneous, some close upon error, some savouring of heresy', and so on; and each of these terms has its own definite meaning. Thus by 'erroneous' is meant, according to Viva, a proposition which is not *immediately* opposed to a revealed proposition, but only to a theological *conclusion* drawn from premisses which are *de fide*; 'savouring of heresy', when a proposition is opposed to a theological conclusion not evidently drawn from premisses which are *de fide*, but most probably and according to the common mode of theologizing, and so with the rest. Therefore when it was said by the Revisers of St. Alfonso's works that they were not 'worthy of *censure*', it was only meant that they did not fall under these particular Notes.

But the answer from Rome to the Archbishop of Besançon went further than this; it actually took pains to declare that any one who pleased might follow other theologians instead of St. Alfonso. After saying that no Priest was to be interfered with who followed St. Alfonso in the Confessional, it added, 'This is said, however, without on that account judging that they are reprehended who follow opinions handed down by other approved authors.'

And this too, I will observe, that St. Alfonso made many changes of opinion himself in the course of his writings; and it could not for an instant be supposed that we were bound to every one of his opinions, when he did not feel himself bound to them in his own person. And, what is more to the purpose still, there are opinions, or some opinion, of his which actually has been proscribed by the Church since, and cannot now be put forward or used. I do not pretend to be a well-read theologian myself, but I say this on the authority of a theological professor of Breda, quoted in the Mélanges Théol. for 1850-1. He says: 'It may happen, that, in the course of time, errors may be found in the works of St. Alfonso and be proscribed by the Church, *a thing which in fact has already occurred.*'

In not ranging myself then with those who consider that it is justifiable to use words in a double sense, that is, to equivocate, I put myself, first, under the protection of Cardinal Gerdil, who, in a work lately published at Rome, has the following passage, which I owe to the kindness of a friend:

Gerdil

'In an oath one ought to have respect to the intention of the party swearing, and the intention of the party to whom the oath is taken. Whoso swears binds himself in virtue of the words, not according to the sense he retains in his own mind, but in *the sense according to which he perceives that they are understood by him to whom the oath is made.* When the mind of the one is discordant with the mind of the other, if this happens by deceit or cheat of the party swearing, he is bound to observe the oath according to the right sense (sana mente) of the party receiving it; but, when the discrepancy in the sense comes of misunderstanding, without deceit of the party swearing, in that case he is not bound, except to that to which he had in mind to wish to be bound. It follows hence, that *whoso uses mental reservation or equivocation in the oath*, in order to deceive the party to whom he offers it, *sins most grievously*, and is always bound to observe the oath *in the sense in which he knew that his words were* taken by the other party, according to the decision of St. Augustine, "They are perjured, who, having kept the words, have deceived the expectations of those to whom the oath was taken." He who swears externally, without the inward intention of swearing, commits a most grave sin, and remains all the same under the obligation to fulfil it. . . . In a word, all that is contrary to good faith, is iniquitous, and by introducing the name of God the iniquity is aggravated by the guilt of sacrilege.'

Natalis Alexander

'They certainly lie, who utter the words of an oath, and without the will to swear or bind themselves; or who *make use of mental reservations and equivocations* in swearing, since they signify by words what they have not in mind, contrary to the end for which language was instituted, viz. as signs of ideas. Or they mean something else than the words signify in themselves, and the common custom of speech, and the circumstances of persons and business-matters; and thus they abuse words which were instituted for the cherishing of society.'

Contenson

'Hence is apparent how worthy of condemnation is the temerity of those half-taught men, who give a colour to lies and *equivocations* by the words and instances of Christ. Than whose doctrine, which is an art of deceiving, nothing can be more pestilent. And that, both because what you do not wish done to yourself, you should not do to another; now the patrons of equivocations and mental reservations would not like to be themselves deceived by others, &c. . . . and also because St. Augustine, &c. . . . In truth, as there is no pleasant living with those whose language we do not understand, and, as St. Augustine teaches, a man would more readily live with his dog than with a foreigner, less pleasant certainly is our converse with those who make use of frauds artificially covered, over-reach their hearers by deceits, address them insidiously, observe the right moment, and catch at words to their purpose, by which truth is hidden under a covering; and so on the other hand nothing is sweeter than the society of those, who both love and speak the naked truth, . . . without their mouth professing one thing and their mind hiding another, or spreading before it the cover of double words. Nor does it matter that they colour their lies with the name of *equivocations or mental reservations.* For Hilary says, "The sense, not the speech, makes the crime."'

Concina allows of what I shall presently call *evasions*, but nothing beyond, if I understand him; but he is most vehement against mental reservation of every kind, so I quote him.

Concina

'That mode of speech, which some theologians call pure mental reservation, others call reservation not simply mental; that language which to me is lying, to the greater part of recent authors is only amphibological. . . . I have discovered that nothing is adduced by more recent theologians for the lawful use of *amphibologies* which has not been made use of already by the ancients, whether philosophers or some Fathers, in defence of lies. Nor does there seem to me other difference when I consider their respective grounds, except that the ancients frankly called those modes of speech lies, and the more recent writers, not a few of them, call them amphibological, equivocal, and *material.*'

In another place he quotes Caramuel, so I suppose I may do so too, for the very reason that his theological reputation does not place him on the side of strictness. Concina says, 'Caramuel himself, who bore away the palm from all others in relaxing the evangelical and natural law, says,

Caramuel

"I have aninnate aversion to mental reservations. If they are contained within the bounds of piety and sincerity, then they are not necessary; . . . but if [otherwise] they are the destruction of human society and sincerity, and are to be condemned as pestilent. Once admitted, they open the way to all lying, all perjury. And the whole difference in the matter is, that what yesterday was called a lie, changing, not its nature and malice, but its name, is to-day entitled 'mental reservation'; and this is to sweeten poison with sugar, and to colour guilt with the appearance of virtue."

St. Thomas

'When the sense of the party swearing, and of the party to whom he swears, is not the same, if this proceeds from the deceit of the former, the oath ought to be kept according to the right sense of the party to whom it is made. But if the party swearing does not make use of deceit, then he is bound according to his own sense.'

St. Isidore

'With whatever artifice of words a man swears, nevertheless God who is the witness of his conscience, so takes the oath as he understands it, to whom it is sworn. And he becomes twice guilty, who both takes the name of God in vain, and deceives his neighbour.'

St. Augustine

'I do not question that this is most justly laid down, that the promise of an oath must be fulfilled, not according to the words of the party taking it, but according to the expectation of the party to whom it is taken, of which he who takes it is aware.'

And now, under the protection of these authorities, I say as follows:—
Casuistry is a noble science, but it is one to which I am led, neither by my abilities nor my turn of mind. Independently, then, of the difficulties of the subject, and the necessity, before forming an opinion, of knowing more of the arguments of theologians upon it than I do, I am very unwilling to say a word here on the subject of Lying and Equivocation. But I consider myself bound to speak; and therefore, in this strait, I can do nothing better, even for my own relief, than submit myself and what I shall say to the judgment of the Church, and to the consent, so far as in this matter there be a consent, of the Schola Theologorum.

Now, in the case of one of those special and rare exigencies or emergencies, which constitute the *justa causa* of dissembling or misleading, whether it be extreme as the defence of life, or a duty as the custody of a secret, or of a personal nature as to repel an impertinent inquirer, or a matter too trivial to provoke question, as in dealing with children or madmen, there seem to be four courses:—

1. *To say the thing that is not.* Here I draw the reader's attention to the words *material* and *formal*. 'Thou shalt not kill'; *murder* is the *formal* transgression of this commandment, but *accidental homicide* is the *material* transgression. The *matter* of the act is the same in both cases; but in the *homicide*, there is nothing more than the act, whereas in *murder* there must be the intention, &c. which constitutes the formal sin. So, again, an executioner commits the material act, but not that formal killing which is a breach of the commandment. So a man, who, simply to save himself from starving, takes a loaf which is not his own, commits only the material, not the formal act of stealing, that is, he does not commit a sin. And so a baptized Christian, external to the Church, who is in invincible ignorance, is a material heretic, and not a formal. And in like manner, if to say the thing which is not be in special cases lawful, it may be called a *material lie*.

The first mode then which has been suggested of meeting those special cases, in which to mislead by words has a sufficient object, or has a *just cause*, is by a material lie.

The second mode is by an *æquivocatio*, which is not equivalent to the English word 'equivocation', but means sometimes a *play upon words*, sometimes an *evasion*.

2. *A play upon words.* St. Alfonso certainly says that a play upon words is allowable; and, speaking under correction, I should say that he does so on the ground that lying is *not* a sin against justice, that is, against our neighbour, but a sin against God; because words are the signs of ideas, and therefore if a word denotes two ideas, we are at liberty to use it in either of its senses: but I think I must be incorrect here in some respect, because the Catechism of the Council, as I have quoted it at p. 251, says, 'Vanitate et mendacio fides ac veritas tolluntur, arctissima vincula *societatis humanæ*; quibus sublatis, sequitur summa vitæ *confusio*, ut *homines nihil a dæmonibus differre videantur*.'

3. *Evasion*;—when, for instance, the speaker diverts the attention of the hearer to another subject; suggests an irrelevant fact or makes a remark, which confuses him and gives him something to think about; throws dust into his eyes; states some truth, from which he is quite sure his hearer will draw an illogical and untrue conclusion, and the like. Bishop Butler seems distinctly to sanction such a proceeding, in a passage which I shall extract below.

The greatest school of evasion, I speak seriously, is the House of Commons; and necessarily so, from the nature of the case. And the hustings is another.

An instance is supplied in the history of St. Athanasius: he was in a boat on the Nile, flying persecution; and he found himself pursued.

On this he ordered his men to turn his boat round, and ran right to meet the satellites of Julian. They asked him, Have you seen Athanasius? and he told his followers to answer, 'Yes, he is close to you.' *They* went on their course, and *he* ran into Alexandria, and there lay hid till the end of the persecution.

I gave another instance above, in reference to a doctrine of religion. The early Christians did their best to conceal their Creed on account of the misconceptions of the heathen about it. Were the question asked of them, 'Do you worship a Trinity?' and did they answer, 'We worship one God, and none else'; the inquirer might, or would, infer that they did not acknowledge the Trinity of Divine Persons.

It is very difficult to draw the line between these evasions, and what are commonly called in English *equivocations*; and of this difficulty, again, I think, the scenes in the House of Commons supply us with illustrations.

4. The fourth method is *silence*. For instance, not giving the *whole* truth in a court of law. If St. Alban, after dressing himself in the Priest's clothes, and being taken before the persecutor, had been able to pass off for his friend, and so gone to martyrdom without being discovered; and had he in the course of examination answered all questions truly, but not given the whole truth, the most important truth, that he was the wrong person, he would have come very near to telling a lie, for a half-truth is often a falsehood. And his defence must have been the *iusta causa*, viz. either that he might in charity or for religion's sake save a priest, or again that the judge had no right to interrogate him on the subject.

Now, of these four modes of misleading others by the tongue, when there is a *justa causa* (supposing there can be such),—a material lie, that is an untruth which is not a lie, an equivocation, an evasion, and silence,—First, I have no difficulty whatever in recognizing as allowable the method of *silence*.

Secondly, But, if I allow of *silence*, why not of the method of *material lying*, since half of a truth *is* often a lie? And, again, if all killing be not murder, nor all taking from another stealing, why must all untruths be lies? Now I will say freely that I think it difficult to answer this question, whether it be urged by St. Clement or by Milton; at the same time, I never have acted, and I think, when it came to the point, I never should act upon such a theory myself, except in one case, stated below. This I say for the benefit of those who speak hardly of Catholic theologians, on the ground that they admit text-books which allow of equivocation. They are asked, how can we trust you, when such are your views? but such views, as I already have said, need not have any thing to do with their own practice, merely from the circumstance that they are contained in their text-books. A theologian draws out a system; he does it partly as a scientific speculation: but much more for the sake of others. He is lax for the sake of others, not of himself. His own standard of action is much higher than that which he imposes upon men in general. One special reason why religious men, after drawing out a theory, are unwilling to act upon it themselves, is this: that they practically acknowledge a broad distinction between their reason and their conscience; and that they feel the latter to be the safer guide, though the former may be the clearer, nay even though it be the truer. They would rather be wrong with their conscience, than right with their reason. And again here is this more tangible difficulty in the case of exceptions to the rule of Veracity, that so very little external help is given us in drawing the line, as to when untruths are allowable and when not; whereas that sort of killing which is not murder, is most definitely marked off by legal enactments, so that it cannot possibly be mistaken for such killing as *is* murder. On the other hand the cases of exemption from the rule of Veracity are left to the private judgment of the individual, and he may easily be led on from acts which are allowable to acts which are not. Now this remark does *not* apply to such acts as are related in Scripture, as being done by a particular inspiration, for in such cases there *is* a command. If I had my own way, I would oblige society, that is, its great men, its lawyers, its divines, its literature, publicly to acknowledge, as such, those instances of untruth which are not lies, as for instance, untruths in war; and then there could be no danger in them to the individual Catholic, for he would be acting under a rule.

Thirdly, as to playing upon words, or equivocation, I suppose it is from the English habit, but, without meaning any disrespect to a great Saint, or wishing to set myself up, or taking my conscience for more than it is worth, I can only say as a fact, that I admit it as little as the rest of my countrymen: and, without any reference to the right and the wrong of the matter, of this I am sure, that, if there is one thing more than another which prejudices Englishmen against the Catholic Church, it is the doctrine of great authorities on the subject of equivocation. For myself, I can fancy myself thinking it was allowable in extreme cases for me to lie, but never to equivocate. Luther said, 'Pecca fortiter.' I anathematize the formal sentiment, but there is a truth in it, when spoken of material acts.

Fourthly, I think *evasion*, as I have described it, to be perfectly allowable; indeed, I do not know, who does not use it, under circumstances; but that a good deal of moral danger is attached to its use; and that, the cleverer a man is, the more likely he is to pass the line of Christian duty.

But it may be said, that such decisions do not meet the particular difficulties for which provision is required; let us then take some instances.

1. I do not think it right to tell lies to children, even on this account, that they are sharper than we think them, and will soon find out what we are doing; and our example will be a very bad training for them. And so of equivocation: it is easy of imitation, and we ourselves shall be sure to get the worst of it in the end.

2. If an early Father defends the patriarch Jacob in his mode of gaining his father's blessing, on the ground that the blessing was divinely pledged to him already, that it was his, and that his father and brother were acting at once against his own rights and the divine will, it does not follow from this that such conduct is a pattern to us, who have no supernatural means of determining *when* an untruth becomes a *material*, and not a *formal* lie. It seems to me very dangerous, be it allowable or not, to lie or equivocate in order to preserve some great temporal or spiritual benefit, nor does St. Alfonso here say any thing to the contrary, for he is not discussing the question of danger or expedience.

3. As to Johnson's case of a murderer asking you which way a man had gone, I should have anticipated that, had such a difficulty happened to him, his first act would have been to knock the man down, and to call out for the police; and next, if he was worsted in the conflict, he would not have given the ruffian the information he asked, at whatever risk to himself. I think he would have let himself be killed first. I do not think that he would have told a lie.

4. A secret is a more difficult case. Supposing something has been confided to me in the strictest secrecy, which could not be revealed without great disadvantage to another, what am I to do? If I am a lawyer, I am protected by my profession. I have a right to treat with extreme indignation any question which trenches on the inviolability of my position; but, supposing I was driven up into a corner, I think I should have a right to say an untruth, or that, under such circumstances, a lie would be *material*, but it is almost an impossible case, for the law would defend me. In like manner, as a priest, I should think it lawful to speak as if I knew nothing of what passed in confession. And I think in these cases, I do in fact possess that guarantee, that I am not going by private judgment, which just now I demanded; for society would bear me out, whether as a lawyer or as a priest, that I had a duty to my client or penitent, such, that an untruth in the matter was not a lie. A common type of this permissible denial, be it *material lie* or *evasion*, is at the moment supplied to me: an artist asked a Prime Minister, who was sitting to him, 'What news, my Lord, from France ?' He answered, '*I do not know*; I have not read the Papers.'

5. A more difficult question is, when to accept confidence has not been a duty. Supposing a man wishes to keep the secret that he is the author of a book, and he is plainly asked on the subject. Here I should

ask the previous question, whether any one has a right to publish what he dare not avow. It requires to have traced the bearings and results of such a principle, before being sure of it; but certainly, for myself, I am no friend of strictly anonymous writing. Next, supposing another has confided to you the secret of his authorship: there are persons who would have no scruple at all in giving a denial to impertinent questions asked them on the subject. I have heard a great man in his day at Oxford, warmly contend, as if he could not enter into any other view of the matter, that, if he had been trusted by a friend with the secret of his being author of a certain book, and he were asked by a third person, if his friend was not (as he really was) the author of it, he ought without any scruple and distinctly to answer that he did not know. He had an existing duty towards the author; he had none towards his inquirer. The author had a claim on him; an impertinent questioner had none at all. But here again I desiderate some leave, recognized by society, as in the case of the formulas 'Not at home', and 'Not guilty', in order to give me the right of saying what is a *material* untruth. And moreover, I should here also ask the previous question, Have I any right to accept such a confidence? have I any right to make such a promise? and, if it be an unlawful promise, is it binding at the expense of a lie? I am not attempting to solve these difficult questions, but they have to be carefully examined.

As I put into print some weeks ago various extracts from authors relating to the subject which I have been considering, I conclude by inserting them here, though they will not have a very methodical appearance.

For instance, St. Dorotheus: 'Sometimes the *necessity* of some matter urges (incumbit), which, unless you somewhat conceal and dissemble it, will turn into a greater trouble.' And he goes on to mention the case of saving a man who has committed homicide from his pursuers: and he adds that it is not a thing that can be done often, but once in a long time.

St. Clement in like manner speaks of it only as a necessity, and as a necessary medicine.

Origen, after saying that God's commandment makes it a plain duty to speak the truth, adds, that a man, 'when necessity urges', may avail himself of a lie, as medicine, that is, to the extent of Judith's conduct towards Holofernes; and he adds that that necessity may be the obtaining of a great good as Jacob hindered his father from giving the blessing to Esau against the will of God.

Cassian says, that the use of a lie, in order to be allowable, must be like the use of hellebore, which is itself poison, unless a man has a fatal disease on him. He adds, 'Without the condition of an extreme necessity, it is a present ruin.'

St. John Chrysostom defends Jacob on the ground that his deceiving his father was not done for the sake of temporal gain, but in order to fulfil the providential purpose of God; and he says, that, as Abraham was not a murderer, though he was minded to kill his son, so an untruth need not be a lie. And he adds, that often such a deceit is the greatest possible benefit to a man who is deceived, and therefore allowable. Also St. Hilary, St. John Climacus, &c., in Thomassin, Concina, the *Mélanges*, &c.

Various modern Catholic divines hold this doctrine of the 'material lie' also. I will quote three passages in point.

Cataneo: 'Be it then well understood, that the obligation to veracity, that is, of conforming our words to the sentiments of our mind, is founded principally upon the necessity of human intercourse, for which reason they (i.e. words) ought not and cannot be lawfully opposed to this end, so just, so necessary, and so important, without which, the world would become a Babylon of confusion. And this would in a great measure be really the result, as often as a man should be unable to defend secrets of high importance, and other evils would follow, even worse than confusion, in their nature destructive of this very intercourse between man and man for which speech was instituted. Every body must see the advantage a hired assassin would have, if supposing he did not know by sight the person he was commissioned to kill, I being asked by the rascal at the moment he was standing in doubt with his gun cocked, were obliged to approve of his deed by keeping silence, or to hesitate, or lastly to answer "Yes, that is the man." [Then follow other similar cases.] In such and similar cases, in which your sincerity is unjustly assailed, when no other way more prompt or more efficacious presents itself, and when it is not enough to say, "I do not know", let such persons be met openly with a downright resolute "No" without thinking upon any thing else. For such a "No" is conformable to the universal opinion of men, who are the judges of words, and who certainly have not placed upon them obligations to the injury of the Human Republic, nor even entered into a compact to use them in behalf of rascals, spies, incendiaries, and thieves. I repeat that such a "No" is conformable to the universal mind of man, and with this mind your own mind ought to be in union and alliance. Who does not see the manifest advantage which highway robbers would derive, were travellers when asked if they had gold, jewels, &c., obliged either to invent tergiversations or to answer "Yes, we have"? Accordingly in such circumstances that "No" which you utter [see Card. Pallav. lib. iii. c. xi. n. 23, de Fide, Spe, &c.] remains deprived of its proper meaning, and is like a piece of coin, from which by the command of the government the current value has been withdrawn, so that by using it you become in no sense guilty of lying.'

Bolgeni says, 'We have therefore proved satisfactorily, and with more than moral certainty, that an *exception* occurs to the general law of not speaking untruly, viz. when it is impossible to observe a certain other precept, more important, *without* telling a lie. Some persons indeed say, that in the cases of impossibility which are above drawn out, what is said is *not* a lie. But a man who thus speaks confuses ideas and denies the essential characters of things. What is a lie? It is "locutio contra mentem"; this is its common definition. But in the cases of impossibility, a man speaks *contra mentem*; that is clear and evident. Therefore he tells a lie. Let us distinguish between the lie and the sin. In the above cases, the man really tells a lie, but this lie is not a sin, by reason of the existing impossibility. To say that in those cases no one has a right to ask, that the words have a meaning according to the common consent of men, and the like, as is said by certain authors in order in those cases to exempt the lie from sin, this is to commit oneself to frivolous excuses, and to subject oneself to a number of retorts, when there is the plain reason of the above-mentioned fact of impossibility.'

And the Author in the *Mélanges Théologiques*: 'We have then gained this truth, and it is a conclusion of which we have not the smallest doubt, that if the intention of deceiving our neighbour is essential to a lie, it is allowable in certain cases to say what we know to be false, as, e.g. to escape from a great danger. . . .

'But, let no one be alarmed, it is never allowable to lie; in this we are in perfect agreement with the whole body of theologians. The only point in which we differ from them is in what we mean by a lie. They call that a lie which is not such in our view, or rather, if you will, what in our view is only a material lie they account to be both formal and material.'

Now to come to Anglican authorities.

Taylor: 'Whether it can in any case be lawful to tell a lie? To this I answer, that the Holy Scriptures of the Old and New Testament do indefinitely and severely forbid lying. Prov. xiii. 5; xxx. 8. Ps. v. 6. John viii. 44. Col. iii. 9. Rev. xxi. 8. 27. Beyond these things, nothing can be said in condemnation of lying.

'*But then* lying is to be understood to be *something said or written to the hurt of our neighbour*, which cannot be understood otherwise than to differ from the mind of him that speaks. "A lie is petulantly or from a desire of hurting, to say one thing, or to signify it by gesture, and to think another thing":[1] so Melanchthon, "To lie is to deceive our neighbour to his hurt." For *in this sense* a lie is naturally or *intrinsically* evil; that is, to speak a lie *to our neighbour* is naturally evil . . . *not* because it is different from an eternal truth. . . . A lie is an *injury* to our neighbour. . . . There is in mankind a universal *contract* implied in all their

---

[1] 'Mendacium est petulanter, aut cupiditate nocendi, aliud loqui, seu gestu significare, et aliud sentire.'

intercourses. . . . *In justice* we are bound to speak, so as that our neighbour do not lose his *right*, which by our speaking we give him to the truth, that is, in our heart. And of a lie, *thus defined*, which is *injurious* to our neighbour, so long as his *right* to truth remains, it is that St. Austin affirms it to be simply unlawful, and that it can in no case be permitted, nisi forte regulas quasdam daturus es. . . . If a lie be *unjust*, it can never become lawful; but, *if it can be separate from injustice* then it may be *innocent*. Here then I consider,

'This right, though it be regularly and commonly belonging to all men, yet it may be *taken away* by a superior right intervening; or it may be lost, or it may be hindered, or it may cease, upon a greater reason.

'Therefore upon this account it was lawful for the children of Israel to borrow jewels of the Egyptians, *which supposes a promise of restitution, though they intended not to pay them back again.* God gave commandment so to spoil them, and the Egyptians were divested of their *rights,* and *were to be used like enemies.*

'*It is lawful to tell a lie to children or to madmen*; because they, having no powers of judging, have no *right* to truth; but then, *the lie must be charitable and useful. . . . If a lie be told,* it must be such as is *for their good* . . . and so do physicians to their patients. . . . This and the like were so usual, so permitted to physicians, that it grew to a proverb, "You lie like a doctor";[1] which yet was always to be understood in the way of charity, and with honour to the profession. . . . To tell a lie for charity, to save a man's life, the life of a friend, of a husband, of a prince, of a useful and a public person, hath not only been done at all times, but commended by great and wise and good men. . . . Who would not save his father's life . . . at the charge of a *harmless lie*, from the rage of persecutors or tyrants? . . . When the telling of a truth will certainly be the cause of evil to a man, though he have right to truth, yet it must not be given to him to his harm. . . . *Every* truth is no more *justice*, than every restitution of a straw to the right owner is a duty. "Be not over-righteous", says Solomon. . . . If it be objected, that we must not tell a lie for God, therefore much less for our brother, I answer, that it does not follow; for God needs not a lie, *but our brother does.* . . . *Deceiving* the enemy by the stratagem of actions or *words,* is *not properly lying*; for this supposes a conversation, of law or peace, trust or *promise* explicit or implicit. A lie is a deceiving of a *trust or confidence.*'—Taylor, vol. xiii. pp. 351–371, ed. Heber.

It is clear that Taylor thought that veracity was one branch of justice; a social virtue; under the second table of the law, not under the first; only binding, when those to whom we speak have a claim of justice upon us, which ordinarily all men have. Accordingly, in cases where a neigh-

[1] Mentiris ut medicus.

bour has no claim of justice upon us, there is no opportunity of exercising veracity, as, for instance, when he is mad, or is deceived by us for his own advantage. And hence, in such cases, a lie is *not really* a lie, as he says in one place, 'Deceiving the enemy is *not properly* lying.' Here he seems to make that distinction common to Catholics; viz. between what they call a *material* act and a *formal* act. Thus Taylor would maintain, that to say the thing that is not to a madman, has the *matter* of a lie, but the man who says it as little tells a formal lie, as the judge, sheriff, or executioner murders the man whom he certainly kills by forms of law.

. Other English authors take precisely the same view, viz. that veracity is a kind of justice,—that our neighbour generally has a *right* to have the truth told him; but that he may forfeit that right, or lose it for the time, and then to say the thing that is not to him is no sin against veracity, that is, no lie. Thus Milton says,[1] 'Veracity is a virtue, by which we speak true things to him *to whom it* is equitable, and concerning what things it is suitable for the *good of our neighbour*. . . . All dissimulation is not wrong, for it is not necessary for us always openly to bring out the truth; that only is blamed which is *malicious*. . . . I do not see why that cannot be said of lying which can be said of homicide and other matters, which are not weighed so much by the *deed* as by *the object and end of acting*. *What man in his senses will deny* that there are those whom we have the best of grounds for considering that we ought to deceive,— as boys, madmen, the sick, the intoxicated, enemies, men in error, thieves? . . . Is it a point of conscience not to deceive them? . . . I would ask, by which of the commandments is a lie forbidden? You will say, by the ninth. Come, read it out, and you will agree with me. For whatever is here forbidden comes under the head of injuring one's neighbour. If then any lie does *not* injure one's neighbour, certainly it is not forbidden by this commandment. It is on this ground that, by the judgment of theologians, we shall acquit so many holy men of lying. Abraham, who said to his servants that he would return with his son; . . . the wise man understood that it did not matter to his servants to know [that his son would not return], and that it was at the moment expedient for himself that they should not know. . . . Joseph would be a man of many lies if the common definition of lying held; [also] Moses, Rahab, Ehud, Jael, Jonathan.' Here again veracity is due only on the score of *justice* towards the person whom we speak with; and, if he has *no claim* upon us to speak the truth, we *need* not speak the truth to him.

And so, again, Paley: '*A lie is a breach of promise*; for whoever seriously addresses his discourse to another tacitly promises to speak the truth, because he knows that the truth is expected. Or the *obligation* of

[1] The Latin original is given at the end of the Appendix.

veracity may be made out from the direct ill consequences of lying to social happiness. . . . There are *falsehoods* which are not *lies*; *that is, which are not criminal.*' (Here, let it be observed, is the same distinction as in Taylor between *material* and *formal* untruths.) '1. When no one is deceived. . . . 2. When the person to whom you speak has no *right* to know the truth, or, more properly, when little or no inconveniency results from the want of confidence in such cases, as *where you tell a falsehood to a madman* for his own advantage; to a robber, to conceal your property; to an assassin, to defeat or divert him from his purpose. . . . It is upon this principle that, by the laws of war, it is allowable to deceive an enemy by feints, false colours, spies, false intelligence. . . . Many people indulge, in serious discourse, a habit of fiction or exaggeration. . . . So long as . . . their narratives, though false, are *inoffensive*, it may seem a superstitious regard to truth to censure them *merely for truth's sake.*' Then he goes on to mention reasons *against* such a practice, adding, 'I have seldom known any one who deserted truth in trifles that could be trusted in matters of importance.'—Works, vol. iv. p. 123.

Dr. Johnson, who, if any one, has the reputation of being a sturdy moralist, thus speaks:—

'We talked', says Boswell, 'of the casuistical question,—whether it was allowable at any time to depart from *truth*.' Johnson. 'The general rule is, that truth should never be violated; because it is of the utmost importance to the comfort of life, that we should have a full security by mutual faith; and occasional inconveniences should be willingly suffered, that we may preserve it. There must, however, be some exceptions. If, for instance, a murderer should ask you which way a man is gone, you may tell him what is not true, because you are under a previous obligation not to betray a man to a murderer.' Boswell. 'Supposing the person who wrote Junius were asked whether he was the author, might he deny it?' Johnson. 'I don't know what to say to this. If you were *sure* that he wrote Junius, would you, if he denied it, think as well of him afterwards? Yet it may be urged, that what a man has no right to ask, you may refuse to communicate; and there is no other effectual mode of preserving a secret, and an important secret, the discovery of which may be very hurtful to you, but a flat denial; for if you are silent, or hesitate, or evade, it will be held equivalent to a confession. But stay, sir; here is another case. Supposing the author had told me confidentially that he had written Junius, and I were asked if he had, I should hold myself at liberty to deny it, as being under a previous promise, express or implied, to conceal it. Now what I ought to do for the author, may I not do for myself? But I deny the lawfulness of telling a lie to a sick man for fear of alarming him. You have no business with consequences; you are to tell the truth. Besides, you are not sure what effect your telling him that he is in danger may have; it may bring his distemper to a crisis, and that may cure him. Of all lying I have the greatest abhorrence of this, because I believe it has been frequently practised on myself.'—Boswell's Life, vol. iv. p. 277.

There are English authors who allow of mental reservation and equivocation; such is Jeremy Taylor.

He says, 'In the same cases in which it is lawful to tell a lie, in the same cases it is lawful to use a mental reservation.'—Ibid. p. 374.

He says, too, 'When the things are true in *several senses*, the not explicating in *what sense* I mean the words is not a criminal reservation. . . . But 1. this liberty is not to be used by inferiors, but by superiors only; 2. not by those that are interrogated, but by them which speak voluntarily; 3. not by those which speak of duty, but which speak of grace and kindness.'—Ibid. p. 378.

Bishop Butler, the first of Anglican authorities, writing in his grave and abstract way, seems to assert a similar doctrine in the following passage:—

'Though veracity, as well as justice, is to be our rule of life, it must be added, otherwise a snare will be laid in the way of some plain men, that the use of common forms of speech generally understood, cannot be falsehood; and, in general, that there can be no designed falsehood without designing to deceive. It must likewise be observed, that, *in numberless cases, a man may be under the strictest obligations to what he foresees will deceive, without his intending it.* For *it is impossible not to foresee,* that the words and actions of men in different ranks and employments, and of different educations, *will perpetually be mistaken by each other*; and it cannot but be so, whilst they will judge with the utmost carelessness, as they daily do, *of what they are not perhaps enough informed to be competent judges of,* even though they considered it with great attention.'—*Nature of Virtue,* fin. These last words seem in a measure to answer to the words in Scavini, that an equivocation is permissible, because 'then we do not deceive our neighbour, but allow him to deceive himself'. In thus speaking, I have not the slightest intention of saying any thing disrespectful to Bishop Butler; and still less of course to St. Alfonso.

And a third author, for whom I have a great respect, as different from the above two as they are from each other, bears testimony to the same effect in his 'Comment on Scripture', Thomas Scott. He maintains indeed that Ehud and Jael were divinely directed in what they did; but they could have no divine direction for what was in itself wrong.

Thus on Judges iii. 15–21:

' "And Ehud said, I have a secret errand unto thee, O king; I have a message from God unto thee, and Ehud thrust the dagger into his belly." Ehud, indeed', says Scott, 'had a secret errand, a message from God unto him; *but it was of a far different nature than Eglon expected'*. And again on Judges iv. 18–21:

' "And Jael said, Turn in, my lord, fear not. And he said to her, When any man doth inquire, Is there any man here? thou shalt say, No. Then Jael took a nail, and smote the nail into his temple." Jael', says Scott, 'is not said to have promised Sisera that she would deny his being there; she would give him shelter and refreshment, but not utter a falsehood to oblige him.'

NOTES

The following are the originals of some of the passages translated under this last Head:—

Gerdil

'Nel giuramento si dee riguardare l'intenzione di chi giura, e l'intenzione di quello a cui si presta il giuramento. Chicunque giura si obbliga in virtù delle parole non secondo il senso ch'egli si ritiene in mente, ma nel senso secondo cui egli cognosce che sono intese da quello a cui si fa il giuramento. Allorchè la mente dell'uno è discordante dalla mente dell'altro, se ciò avviene per dolo e inganno del giurante, questi è obbligato ad osservare il giuramento secondo la sana mente di chi la ha ricevuto; ma quando la discrepanza nel senso proviene da mala intelligenza senza dolo di chi giura, in quel caso egli non è obbligato se non a ciò che avea in mente di volersi obbligare. Da ciò segue che chiunque usa restrizione mentale o equivocazione nel giuramento per ingannare la parte cui egli lo presta, pecca gravissimamente, ed è sempre obbligato ad osservare il giuramento nel senso in cui egli sapea che le sue parole erano prese dall'altro, secondo la decisione di S. Agostino (epist. 224) "Perjuri sunt qui servatis verbis, expectationem eorum quibus juratum est deceperunt." Chi giura esternamente senza interna intenzione di giurare, commette gravissimo peccato, e rimane con tutto ciò nell'obbligo di adimperlo. . . . In somma tutto che è contrario alla buona fede, è iniquo, e facendovi intervenire il nome di Dio si aggrava l'iniquità colla reità del sacrilegio.' — Opusc. Theolog. Rom. 1851, p. 28.

Natalis Alexander

'Perjurium est mendacium juramento firmatum. Illos vero mentiri compertum est, qui juramenti verba proferunt, et jurare vel obligare se nolunt, aut qui restrictiones mentales et æquivocationes jurando adhibent, siquidem verbis significant quod in mente non habent, contra finem propter quem institutæ sunt voces, ut videlicet sint signa conceptuum. Vel aliud volunt quàm verba significent secundum se et secundum communem loquendi morem, et personarum ac negotiorum circumstantias; atque ita verbis ad societatem fovendam institutis abutuntur.'—Theol. Lib. iv. c. iv. Art. 3. Reg. 11.

Contenson

'Atque ex his apparet quam damnanda sit eorum semidoctorum temeritas, qui mendacia et æquivocationes verbis et exemplis Christi præcolorant. Quorum doctrinâ, quæ ars fallendi est, nihil pestilentius esse potest. Tum quia quod tibi non vis fieri, alteri ne feceris; sed æquivocationum, ac restrictionum mentalium patroni æquo animo non paterentur se ab aliis illudi: ergo illud œcumenicum naturæ principium nulli ignotum, omnibus quamlibet barbaris implantatum violant. Tum quia urget argumentum Augustinus, etc. . . . Sanè sicut ægrè cum illis convivimus, quorum linguam non intelligimus; et authore Augustino, lib. 19, de Civit. "Libentiùs vivit homo cum cane suo, quam cum homine alieno": ægriùs certè cum illis conversamur qui fraudes artificio tectas adhibent, audientes circumveniunt dolis, insidiis eos petunt, tempus observant, verbaque idonea aucupantur, quibus veritas veluti quodam involucro obtegitur: sicut è contra nihil eorum convictu suavius, qui ab omni simulandi studio longe absentes, sincero animo, candido ingenio, aperta voluntate præditi sunt, oderunt artes, nudam veritatem tam amant, quam loquuntur: quorum denique manus linguæ, lingua cordi, cor rationi, ratio Deo congruit, et tota vita unius faciei est, unius et coloris: nec aliud os præ se fert, aliud animus celat, et verborum duplicium velo obtendit. Certe tolerabilior erat Babylonica confusio, in qua invicem loquentes se minimè intelligebant, eorum convictu, qui non se intelligunt, nisi ut sese mutuo decipiant.

'Nec obest quod nomine æquivocationum, vel restrictionum mentalium mendacia fucent. Nam ut ait Hilarius lib. 2. de Trinit., "Sensus, non sermo, fit crimen. O ubi simplicitas Christiana, quæ regulâ illâ Legislatoris sui Christi contenta est: Sit sermo vester, Est est, Non non!" O ubi est mulier illa virilis totam Probabilistarum æquivocationibus veniam dantium nationem confusura! quæ referente Hieronymo *epist.* 49, nec ad gravissimos torturarum et diræ mortis cruciatus vitandos æquivocationum usum septies icta advocavit.'—Theol. vii. p. 30.

Concina

'Cardo disputationis Augustinianæ, in duobus recensitis libris, potissimum in eo vertitur, ut rationes præbeantur pro veritatis occultatione in negotiis summi momenti . . . Augustinus nulla reperire remedia potuit præter hæc: Primum est silentium . . . Alterum est aperta et invicta significatio. . . . Nullam aliam viam occultandi veritatem agnovit, —non restrictiones internas, non materiales locutiones, non verborum amphibolias, non alia juniorum inventa.'—Theol. T. iii. p. 278. Lib. v. in Decal. Diss. 3. c. 5. prop. 2d.

'. . . Hæc autem omnium scopulorum, et difficultatum origo: quia cum non possit rectæ disputationi locus esse, nisi id pateat de quo est disputandum; certas et claras notiones æquivocationum, amphibologiarum, et mentalium restrictionum præfinire minime possumus, attentis recentiorum distinctiunculis, effugiis, et thecnis, quæ rem hanc maxime implicatam efficiunt. Has ambages ut evitarem, cursum inceptum abrumpere, telamque redordiri, atque retexere decrevi: idque consilii cepi, ut primum omnium de mendacio sermonem institutam.

Illud namque commodi mihi peracta controversiæ tractatio attulit, ut deprehenderim, nihil a recentioribus Theologis pro licito amphibologiarum usu efferri quod prius ab antiquis tum Philosophis, tum Patribus aliquibus usurpatum non fuerit in mendaciorum patrocinium. Nec aliud discrimen mihi utrorumque fundamenta perpendenti occurrit, nisi quod antiqui eas locutiones quas recentiorum Theologorum non pauci amphibologicas, æquivocas, et *materiales* vocant, ingenua sinceritate mendacia appellaverint.'—Diss. iii. De Juram. Dol. etc.

Caramuel

'. . . Est mihi', inquit, 'innata aversio contra restrictiones mentales. Si enim continentur inter terminos pietatis, et sinceritatis, necessariæ non sunt. Nam omnia quæ ipsæ præstare possunt, præstabunt consignificantes circumstantiæ. Quod si tales dicantur, ut etiam ibi admittendæ sint, ubi desunt circumstantiæ significantes (ignoscant mihi earumdem auctores, et propugnatores) tollunt humanam societatem, et securitatem, et tamquam pestiferæ damnandæ sunt. Quoniam semel admissæ aperiunt omni mendacio, omni perjurio viam. Et tota differentia in eo erit ut quod heri vocabatur mendacium, naturam, et malitiam non mutet, sed nomen, ita ut hodie jubeatur Restrictio mentalis nominari; quod est virus condire saccharo, et scelus specie virtutis colorare.'— Apud Concinam Theol. Diss. iii. De Juram. Dol. etc.

S. Thomas

'Quando non est eadem jurantis intentio, et ejus cui jurat, si hoc proveniat ex dolo jurantis, debet juramentum servari secundum sanum intellectum ejus, cui juramentum præstatur. Si autem jurans dolum non adhibeat, obligatur secundum intentionem jurantis.'—Apud Nat. Alex.

S. Isidorus

'Quacunque arte verborum quisquis juret, Deus tamen qui conscientiæ testis est, ita hoc accipit, sicut ille, cui juratur, intelligit. Dupliciter autem reus fit, qui et Dei nomen in vanum assumit, et proximum dolo capit.'—Apud Nat. Alex.

S. Augustinus

'Illud sanè rectissime dici non ambigo, non secundum verba jurantis, sed secundum expectationem illius cui juratur, quam novit ille qui jurat, fidem jurationis impleri. Nam verba difficillimè comprehendunt,

maxime breviter, sententiam cujus a jurante fides exigitur. Unde perjuri
sunt, qui servatis verbis, expectationem eorum, quibus juratum est,
deceperunt: et perjuri non sunt, qui etiam verbis non servatis, illud
quod ab eis cum jurarent expectatum est, impleverunt.'—Apud Natal.
Alex.

Cattaneo

'Sappiasi dunque, che l'obbligo della veracità, cioè, di conformare le
parole ai sentimenti dell'animo nostro, egli è principalmente fondato
nella necessità del commercio umano; onde elle non devono giammai
nè possono lecitamente opporsi a questo fine, si giusto, si necessario,
e si importante; tolto il quale, diverebbe il mondo una Babilonia
di confusione. E ciò accaderebbe in gran parte, ogni qual volta non
si potessero custodire, ne difendere i segreti d'alta importanza, e ne
seguissero altri mali anche peggiori, distruttivi di lor natura di questo
stesso commercio, per cui è stato istituito il parlare. Ognun vede,
quanto tornerebbe in acconcio ad un mandatario, se non conoscendo
la persona, che deve uccidere, io da lui interrogato, mentre il traditore
sta dubbioso coll'archibugio già alzato, dovessi, o approvar col silenzio,
o titubare, o rispondergli, "Si egli è il tale." . . . In somiglianti casi, ne
quali viene ingiustamente assalita la vostra sincerità, quando non
sovvenga altro mezzo più pronto, e più efficace, e quando non basti dire
"no'l so"; piantisi pure in faccia a costoro un "No" franco e risoluto,
senza pensar ad altro. Imperocchè un tal "no" egli è conforme alla
mente universale degli uomini, i quali sono arbitri delle parole, e
certamente non le hanno obligate a danno della Republica umana, nè
hanno già mai pattuito di usarle in prò di furbi, di spie, d'incendarii,
di masnadieri, e di ladri. Torno a dire, che quel No egli è conforme alla
mente universale degli uomini, e a questa mente deve esser unita e
collegata anche la vostra. Chi non vede l'utile manifesto, che ne trar-
rebbero gli assassini di strada, se i passaggieri interrogati se abbian
seco oro, o gemme dovissero, o tergiversare, o rispondere, "si che
l'abbiamo"; adunque, in tali congiunture, quel "No", che voi proferite
(Card. Pallav., lib. iii. c. xi. n. 23 de fide, spe, &c.) resta privo del suo
significato e resta appunto agguisa di una moneta, a cui per volere del
Principio, sia stato tolto il valore, con cui prima correva; onde in niun
modo voi siete reo di menzogna.' Lezione xliv. Prima Parte.

Bolgeni

'Abbiamo dunque bene, e con certezza più che morale, provata una
eccezione da porsi alla legge generale di non mentire, cioè, quando non
si possa osservare qualche altro precetto più importante se non col dir
bugia. Dicono alcuni che nei casi della impossibilità sopra esposta non
è bugia, quello che si dice. Ma chi dice così, confonde le idee, e nega

l'essenza della cose. Che cosa è la bugia ? *Est locutio contra mentem*: così la definiscono tutti. *Atqui* nei casi della impossibilità sovra esposta si parla *contra mentem*: ciò è chiaro ed evidente. Dunque si dice bugia. Distinguiamo la bugia dal peccato. Nei casi detti si dice realmente bugia; ma questa *bugia* non è *peccato* per ragione della impossibilità. Il dire che in quei casi niuno ha diritto d'interrogare; che le parole significano secondo la convenzione comune fra gli uomini; e cose simili, che da alcuni Autori si dicono per esimere da peccato la bugia in quei casi: questo è un attaccarsi a ragioni frivole, e soggette a molte repliche quando si ha la ragione evidente della citata impossibilità.'—Il Possesso, c. 48.

Author in the Mélanges Théologiques

'Il reste donc acquis, et nous n'avons pas le moindre doute sur la vérité de cette conclusion, que si l'intention de tromper le prochain, est essentielle au mensonge, il sera permis de dire ce qu'on sait être faux, en certain cas, comme pour éviter un grand danger. . . . Au reste, que personne ne s'effraie, il ne sera jamais permis de mentir, et en cela nous sommes d'accord avec tous les théologiens: nous nous eloignons d'eux en ce seul point qu'ils appellent *mensonge*, ce qui ne l'est pas pour nous, ou si l'on veut, ils regardent comme mensonge formel et matériel ce qui pour nous est seulement un mensonge matériel.'—Mélanges Théologiques, vime Série, p. 442.

Milton

'*Veracitas* est Virtus qua ei cui æquum est, et quibus de rebus convenit ad bonum proximi, vera dicimus. Psal. xv. 2. Prov. xii. 21, 17; xx. 6. Zech. viii. 16. Eph. iv. 25.

'Huic opponitur dissimulatio vitiosa. Nam omnis non improbatur: non enim semper vera palam expromere necesse habemus; ea tantum reprehenditur quæ malitiosa est.

'Secundo opponitur mendacium. Psal. v. 7. xii. 2, 3. Prov. xiii. 5; xix. 5. Joan viii. 44. Apoc. xxii. 15. Mendacio itaque ne Dei quidem causa est utendum. Job xiii. 7.

'Mendacium vulgo definitur, quo *falsum anima fallendi verbis factisve significatur*. Sed quoniam sæpe usu venit, ut non solum vera dissimulare aut reticere, sed etiam fallendi animo falsa dicere, utile ac salutare proximo sit, danda opera est, ut mendacium quid sit melius definiamus. Neque enim video cur non idem de mendacio, quod de homicidio aliisque rebus, de quibus infra dicetur, nunc dici possit, quæ non tam facto, quam objecto et fine agendi ponderanda sunt. Esse enim quos jure optimo fallendos putemus, quis sanus negaverit ? quid enim pueros, quid furentes, quid ægrotos, quid ebrios, quid hostes, quid fallentes, quid latrones ? (certe juxta illud tritum, *Cui nullum est jus, ei nulla fit injuria:*) an illos ne fallamus religio erit ? per hanc tamen definitionem ne illos quidem dictis aut factis fallere licebit. Certe si gladium, aliamve rem quam apud me sanus deposuerit, eidem furenti non reddiderim, cur veritatem non depositam, ei ad quem veritas minime pertineat, male usuro expromam ? Enimvero si quidquid cuicunque interroganti respondetur fallendi animo, mendacium est censendum, profecto sanctis viris et prophetis nihil familiarius erat quam mentiri.

'Quid si igitur mendacium hoc modo definiamus ? *Mendacium* est cum *quis dolo malo aut veritatem depravat, aut falsum dicit ei, quicunque is sit, cui dicere veritatem ex officio debuerat.* Sic diabolus serpens primus erat mendax, Gen. iii. 4. et Cain, cap. iv. 9. et Sara, cap. xviii. 15. angelis enim merito offensis non satisfecit ingenua confessione: et Abrahamus, cap. xii. 13. et cap. xx. illud enim de Sara tanquam sorore figmentum, ut ipse didicisse poterat in Ægypto, quamvis incolumitatem vitæ sibi proposuerat solam, homines tamen inscientes in errorem et alieni cupiditatem induxit: et Davides fugiens, 1 Sam. xxi. 3. debebat enim non celasse Abimelecum quo loco res suæ apud regem essent, neque tantum periculum hospiti creare: sic Ananias et Sapphira, Act. v., mentiti sunt.

'Ex hac definitione, 1mo, haud secus atque ex altera, patet, parabolas, hyperbolas, apologos, ironias mendacia non esse: hæc enim omnia non fallendi sed erudiendi studio adhibentur. 1 Regum xviii. 27. et xxii. 15. 2do, si fallendi vocem significatione debita sumamus, neminem quidem fallere poterimus, quin eum eadem opera lædamus. Quem igitur nullo modo lædimus, sed vel juvamus, vel ab injuria aut inferenda aut patienda prohibemus, eum certe ne falso quidem millies dicto revera fallimus, sed vero potius beneficio necopinantem afficimus, 3^{tio}, dolos et strategemata in bello, modo absit perfidia aut perjurium, non esse mendacia omnes concedunt: quæ concessio alteram definitionem plane destruit. Vix enim ullæ insidiæ aut doli in bello strui possunt, quin palam idque summo fallendi studio dicantur multa quæ falsissima sunt: unde per illam definitionem mendacio absolvi nequeunt. Hanc igitur potius ob causam licere strategemata dicendum erit, etiam cum mendacio conjuncta, eo quod, si quis est cui verum dicere officii nostri non sit, nihil certe interest an illi, quoties expedit, etiam falsum dicamus: nec video cur hoc in bello magis quam in pace liceat, præsertim quoties injuriam aut periculum a nobismetipsis aut a proximo salutari et probo quodam mendacio depellere licet.

'Quæ igitur testimonia scripturæ contra mendacium proferuntur, de eo intelligenda sunt mendacio, quod aut Dei gloriam aut nostrum proximive bonum imminuere videatur. Hujusmodi sunt, præter ea quæ supra citavimus, Lev. xix. Ps. ci. 7. Prov. vi. 16, 17. Jer. ix. 5. His atque aliis hujusmodi locis veritatem dicere jubemur: at cui ? non hosti, non furioso, non violento, non sicario; sed proximo, quîcum scilicet pax et justa societas nobis intercedit. Jam vero si veritatem soli proximo dicere jubemur, profecto iis qui nomen proximi non merentur, ne falsum quidem, quoties opus est, dicere vetamur. Qui aliter sentit, ex eo libens quærerem, quonam decalogi præcepto prohibeatur mendacium ? respondebit certissime, nono. Age, recitet modo, et mecum sentiet: quidquid enim hic prohibetur, id proximum lædere ostenditur; siquod igitur mendacium non lædit proximum, sub hoc certe mandato nequaquam prohibetur.

'Hinc tot sanctissimos viros theologorum fere judicio mendacii reos merito absolvemus: Abrahamum, Gen. xxii. 5. cum dixit servis suis se reversurum cum filio; fallendi tamen animo, nequid illi suspicarentur; cum ipse persuasus esset mactatum ibi filium se relicturum; nam nisi ita sibi persuasisset, quid hoc magnopere tentationis erat ? sed intellexit vir sapiens nihil interesse servorum hoc ut scirent, sibi expedire in præsentia ne scirent. Rebeccam et Jacobum, Gen. xxvii., prudenti enim astutia et cautione aditum sibi muniebant ad jus illud hæreditatis quod alter vili vendiderat; ad jus, inquam, et oraculo et redemptione jam suum. At patri imposuit: immo potius errori patris, qui amore præpostero in Esauum ferebatur, tempestive occurrit. Josephum, Gen. xlii. 7, etc. multorum sane mendaciorum hominem, si vulgari illa definitione stetur: quam multa enim dixit non vera, eo animo ut fratres falleret ? dolo tamen fratribus non malo, sed utilissimo. Obstetrices Hebræas, Exod. i. 19, etc., comprobante etiam Deo; fefellerant enim Pharaonem, non læserant tamen, sed beneficio potius affecerant, dum male faciendi facultatem ademerunt. Mosen, Exod. iii., etiam a Deo jussum iter tridui a Pharaone petere, quasi ad rem divinam faciendam in deserto; eo licet consilio petentem ut Pharaoni verba daret; non causam enim pro causa, vel fictam saltem pro vera profectionis afferebat. Universum populum Israeliticum, Exod. xi. et xii., ab eodem Deo jussum aurum, vasa, vestemque pretiosam ab Ægyptiis mutuam petere; et pollicitum sine dubio reddere: fallendi tamen animo; quidni enim et Dei hostes et hospitii violatores et spoliatores jamdiu suos ? Raabbam, Jos. ii. 4, 5. splendide mentitam, nec sine fide; fallebat enim quos Deus falli voluit, populares licet suos, et magistratus: quos voluit ille salvos conservabat; civile officium religioni recte posthabuit. Ehudem, qui duplici mendacio Eglonem fefellit, Judic. iii. 19, 20. nec injuria tamen, quippe hostem; idque Dei non injussu. Jaelem, quæ confugientem ad se Siseram blanditiis perdidit, Judic. iv. 18, 19. hostem licet Dei magis quam suum: quamquam id non mendacio, sed pia fraude factum vult Junius, quasi quidquam interesset. Jonathanem, dum rogatus ab amico Davide causam ejus absentiæ fictam refert patri, 1 Sam. xx. 6, 28. malebat enim innocentis saluti quam patris crudelitati officiosum se esse; et majoris

erat momenti ad charitatem ut innocentis amici consuleretur vitæ, inter-
posito licet mendacio, quam ut patri ad maleficium exequendum veritatis inutili confessione mos gereretur. Hos atque alios tot viros sanctissimos vulgari illa definitione mendacii condemnatos, vetuli ex limbo
quodam patrum disquisitio hæc veritatis accuratior educit.'

EDITOR'S NOTES

ABBREVIATIONS AND REFERENCES
USED IN NOTES

ALL references to Newman's works other than the *Apologia* are to the standard edition: 39 vols. London: Longmans, Green, and Company, 1898–1903. Index by Joseph Rickaby, S.J. Titles are given in full in the first reference, after which are commonly employed the following abbreviations, which are mostly those of Rickaby:

Apo.   *Apologia pro Vita Sua*
Ari.   *The Arians of the Fourth Century*
Ath.   *Select Treatises of St. Athanasius* (2 vols.)
D.A.   *Discussions and Arguments*
Dev.   *Development of Christian Doctrine*
Diff.   *Difficulties of Anglicans* (2 vols.)
Essays   *Essays Critical and Historical* (2 vols.)
G.A.   *Grammar of Assent*
H.S.   *Historical Sketches* (3 vols.)
Idea   *Idea of a University*
L.G.   *Loss and Gain*
Letters   *Letters and Correspondence.* Edited, at Cardinal Newman's request, by Anne Mozley (2 vols.)
Mir.   *Two Essays on Miracles*
Mix.   *Discourses to Mixed Congregations*
O.S.   *Sermons Preached on Various Occasions*
P.P.   *Present Position of Catholics in England*
P.S.   *Parochial and Plain Sermons* (8 vols.)
S.S.D.   *Sermons on Subjects of the Day*
U.S.   *Oxford University Sermons*
V.M.   *Via Media* (2 vols.)
V.V.O.   *Verses on Various Occasions*

In addition, the following abbreviations are used for other important works:

A.W.   *John Henry Newman Autobiographical Writings.* Edited with Introductions by Henry Tristram of the Oratory. (London and New York: Sheed & Ward, 1957.)
Corr.   *Correspondence of John Henry Newman with John Keble and Others: 1839–1845.* Edited at the Birmingham Oratory. (London: Longmans, Green & Company, 1917.)
H.T.   Unpublished notes to the *Apologia* by Henry Tristram.
Letters and Diaries *The Letters and Diaries of John Henry Newman.* Edited at the Birmingham Oratory with notes and an introduction

by Charles Stephen Dessain of the same Oratory. (London: Thomas Nelson & Sons Ltd., 1961–.) Much of the material now quoted from Oratory MSS. will be available in later volumes of this series, which began with Vol. XI.

Life   *The Life of John Henry Cardinal Newman,* by Wilfrid Ward. 2 vols. (London: Longmans, Green & Company, 1912.)

Nédoncelle   *Apologia pro Vita Sua.* Translated by L. Michelin-Delimoges, with an Introduction and Notes by Maurice Nédoncelle. (Paris: Bloud & Gay, 1939.)

The most useful standard reference works have been *The Dictionary of National Biography,* the *Dictionnaire de Théologie Catholique, The Oxford Dictionary of the Christian Church,* and the *New Schaff-Herzog Encyclopedia of Religious Knowledge.*

Notes are numbered by page and line: e.g. 15. 9 means p. 15, l. 9. Because the notes are so numerous it has seemed pointless to number them in Newman's text. It is the editor's hope that the reader will find a note for virtually every passage in the text proper about which a question might arise in his mind. If he is already informed about the subject Newman is discussing, he will at least be spared the distraction of a call to read the obvious. Newman's Biblical quotations, it might be added here, are ordinarily from the King James or Authorized Version in passages taken from his Anglican works, and from the Douay version or Vulgate otherwise. In some cases, however, they are not precisely from either version and appear to have been quoted from memory.

15. 3 **'Secretum meum mihi'** 'My secret is my own' (Isa. xxiv. 16, Newman's transl., *Sermons Preached on Various Occasions,* p. 230). A phrase dear to St. Philip Neri (1515–95), founder of the Roman Congregation of the Oratory, the first English branch of which Newman established in 1848. 'He exhorted them [his spiritual children] to pray God, if he gave them any virtue or any gift, to keep it concealed even from themselves, that so they might the more readily preserve themselves in humility. . . . If ever they said anything which redounded to their own credit, he immediately reproved them, saying, "*Secretum meum mihi, secretum meum mihi*", thus giving them to understand that they ought not to publish or divulge to all persons the inspirations which the Lord sent them, or the favours His Divine Majesty might vouchsafe to them.' See Pietro Bacci, *The Life of St. Philip Neri,* transl. F. W. Faber (2 vols., London, 1847), i. 298.

15. 24 **my later convictions** E.g. on his philosophical idealism, though this was more apparent than real. See *Apologia pro Vita Sua,* pp. 18, 23, 29, 36.

16. 7 **Remnants** Best known for his hymns and free paraphrases of psalm like 'O God, our help in ages past', Isaac Watts (1674–1748) was a learned Independent minister and a liberal Calvinist. Newman is quoting from *Remnants of Time Employed in Prose and Verse,* section xvii: 'Out of the millions of mankind that spread over the earth in every age, the great God

has been pleased to take some into his own family, has given them a heavenly and divine nature, and made them his sons and daughters. But he has set no outward mark of glory upon them; there is nothing in their figure or in their countenance to distinguish them from the rabble of mankind . . . Divine Wisdom has appointed the other world for the place of their full discovery. . . .' (*The Works of The Rev. Isaac Watts, D.D.* [9 vols., Leeds, 1813], ix. 487. See also Samuel Johnson's *Lives of the English Poets.*)

16. 11 **I was very superstitious** 'Superstition is a faith which falls below that standard of religion which God has given, whatever it is.' (*University Sermons*, p. 244.) Even in its grosser forms, it is marked by a sense of awe and remorse before the unseen powers that Newman regarded as more salutary than the scepticism of the Enlightenment, which resisted the knowledge of such powers and threatened all religious belief. 'They who are not superstitious without the Gospel, will not be religious with it: and I would that even in us, who have the Gospel, there were more of superstition than there is; for much is it to be feared that our security about ourselves arises from defect in self-knowledge rather than in fulness of faith, and that we appropriate to ourselves promises which we cannot read.' (Ibid., p. 118.)

On the question of Newman's 'credulity', see Charles Frederick Harrold, *John Henry Newman* (London and New York, 1945), pp. 363–8.

16. 18 **an *émigré* Priest** Lechmere's MS. 'Reminiscences of Ealing School', in the cardinal's room at the Birmingham Oratory, gives the names of two French masters as Mr. Le Dieu L. and Mr. Le Dieu F. Their names have not been traced in any list of priests who found refuge in England after the French Revolution, however; and it may be that Newman was wrong in thinking that one was a priest. (H. T.)

16. 20 **the village** Ham, about nine miles south-west of London, near Hampton Court, where at Grey's Court Newman passed much of his childhood. See Wilfrid Ward, *The Life of John Henry Cardinal Newman* (2 vols., London, 1912), i. 29.

16. 23 **the school** Great Ealing School near London, which Newman attended for eight and a half years from May 1808.

16. 25 **My brother** Francis William Newman (1805–97) was as concerned with religion as his older brother, but his development proceeded in an opposite direction. After taking a double First at Oxford in 1826, he was elected Fellow of Balliol, but soon came under nonconformist influences and resigned in 1830, unwilling to accept the Thirty-nine Articles. He then went to Persia with some friends as a lay missionary for the Plymouth Brethren, returning home to obtain more volunteers in 1833, at the time of his brother's arrival from Italy. His critical rationalism made him more and more dubious about traditional theology and the possibility of a 'book revelation', however, and he never returned to such work.

An ethical idealism replaced historic Christianity for him, and he took great interest in social and political questions, becoming a friend of Mazzini, an advocate of women's suffrage, an opponent of vaccination and vivisection, and a vegetarian. He won fame as Professor of Latin at University College, London, and wrote widely on linguistic, mathematical, social, historical, and religious questions. George Eliot called him 'our blessed St. Francis', and John Sterling made him the guardian of his eldest son. Matthew Arnold, who attacked his translation of Homer as lacking in nobility, appears to have regarded him as a liberal faddist who wished to advance the modern spirit while utterly lacking the method of doing so.

See F. W. Newman, *Phases of Faith* (1850), a spiritual autobiography, and *Contributions, Chiefly to the Early History of the Late Cardinal Newman* (1891), a rather unpleasant little book intended to counterbalance the great tributes accorded the cardinal throughout England after his death in 1890. See also I. Giberne Sieveking, *Memoir and Letters of Francis W. Newman* (London, 1909), Wm. Robbins, *The Newman Brothers* (London, 1966), and Lionel Trilling, *Matthew Arnold* (New York, 1939), pp. 167–78. According to the *Memoir*, 'Francis Newman returned to his earlier faith in Christianity a few years before his death', but the evidence (pp. 342–6) is ambiguous.

16. 27 **Warwick Street Chapel** A chapel off Regent Street, then attached to the Bavarian Embassy and known today as the Church of Our Lady of the Assumption and St. Gregory. It is the only remaining Catholic embassy chapel of penal times.

16. 28 **all that I bore away** But compare Charles Reding in *Loss and Gain*: '. . . when I was a boy I was once, by chance, in a Roman Catholic Chapel; and I really never saw such devotion in my life—the people all on their knees, and most earnestly attentive to what was going on.' (p. 143.)

16. 31 **Littlemore** A village two miles south-east of Oxford, then partly in the parish of St. Mary's, Oxford. Newman gave catechetical instruction there in 1829 and built a chapel in 1836. As the Oxford Movement advanced toward its crisis, he stayed there more and more frequently, making it his head-quarters after April 1842, and being received there into the Roman Church in October 1845. The 'parsonage house' or retreat centre that Newman established there in a row of cottages has in recent years been acquired and restored by the Birmingham Oratory. The chapel and Newman's room and library are open to the public as a museum. See *Apo.*, pp. 123 and 157–62; and *Historical Sketches*, iii. 325–6.

17. 4 **Mrs. Radcliffe's or Miss Porter's** Ann Radcliffe (1764–1823), author of such Gothic novels as *The Mysteries of Udolpho* (1794) and *The Italian, or the Confessional of the Black Penitents* (1797); and either Jane Porter (1776–1850) or her sister Anna Maria (1780–1832), both writers of popular romances like Jane's *Thaddeus of Warsaw* (1803) and *The Scottish Chiefs* (1810) and Anna Maria's *The Hungarian Brothers* (1807) and *Don Sebastian, or the House of Braganza* (1809).

Although Catholic backgrounds of a sort are common to the work of all three writers, it seems more likely from the date of February 11, 1811, on the Verse Book that the rosary in Newman's drawing was prompted by memories of Warwick Street Chapel, which he had visited January 27, 1811, to judge from the entry of that date in the diary preserved at the Birmingham Oratory in the first manuscript volume of his 'Autographic Remains': 'Sunday—went to Westminster Abbey, and R.C. Chapel.'

17. 12 **Paine's Tracts** Thomas Paine's *Age of Reason*, the first two parts of which appeared in 1795 and the third in 1811, contains his strictures on the Old and New Testaments, the theme of which he thus indicates:
'Did the book, called the Bible, excell in purity of ideas and expression, all the books that are now extant in the world, I would not take it for my rule of faith, as being the word of God; because the possibility would nevertheless exist of my being imposed upon. But when I see throughout the greatest part of this book, scarcely anything but a history of the grossest vices, and a collection of the most paltry and contemptible tales, I cannot dishonour my Creator by calling it by his name.' (*The Age of Reason; Being an Investigation of True and Fabulous Theology* [Paris and London, 1795], pp. 19–20.)

17. 13 **found pleasure** '. . . when a person for the first time hears the arguments and speculations of unbelievers, and feels what a very novel light they cast upon what he has hitherto accounted most sacred, it cannot be denied that, unless he is shocked and closes his ears and heart to them, he will have a sense of expansion and elevation.' (*U.S.*, p. 284.)

17. 15 **on Miracles** David Hume's famous essay on miracles was first published in 1748 in his *Philosophical Essays Concerning Human Understanding* and was much controverted thereafter as a highly dangerous attack on the Christian religion. Newman sums up Hume's position as follows: 'It is argued by Hume against the actual occurrence of the Jewish and Christian miracles, that, whereas "it is experience only which gives authority to human testimony, and it is the same experience which assures us of the laws of nature", therefore, "when these two kinds of experience are contrary" to each other, "we are bound to subtract the one from the other"; and, in consequence, since we have no experience of a violation of natural laws, and much experience of the violation of truth, "we may establish it as a maxim that no human testimony can have such force as to prove a miracle, and make it a just foundation for any such system of religion".' (*A Grammar of Assent*, p. 306, citing the 1770 edition of Hume's works, iii. 178.) Newman's answer follows. See also J. M. Cameron, 'The Night Battle: Newman and Empiricism', *Victorian Studies*, iv (1960), 99–117, reprinted in his *The Night Battle: Essays* (London, 1962).

17. 17 **perhaps Voltaire's** Probably not, as Voltaire, though something of an agnostic on the question, had hopes for immortality. See his essay 'The Soul' in *The Works of Voltaire* (42 vols., Paris and London, 1901), xxxvii. 152–8; and 'To M. Genonville':

> And shall its existence (like bodies) soon cease?
> I know not, but I have good hope it will brave
> Death, the ruins of time and the jaws of the grave;
> And that an intelligent substance so pure,
> The Almighty intended should always endure.

(Ibid. xxxvi. 235. Translated by William F. Fleming.)

Abbé Nédoncelle suggests as a possibility these lines in *Traité de l'âme*:

> Sois sans crainte et sans espérance,
> Que ton sort ne te trouble pas,
> Que devient-on dans le trépas?
> Ce qu'on fut avant la naissance.

(1785 edition of the complete works, xxxii. 236.) But he thinks that Newman probably has Voltaire confused with one of the Encyclopedists.

17. 20 **autumn of 1816** More precisely, from August 1 to December 21. The change coincided with a reversal in his father's economic status and with his own illness. In the financial crisis after Waterloo his father's London bank was forced to close its doors on March 8, 1816; and after managing to pay his creditors Mr. Newman then took charge of a brewery in Alton, Hampshire, where he moved his family in October. Meanwhile his son remained at Ealing school: 'How the wisdom and goodness of God is discerned—I was going from school half a year sooner . . . my staying arose from 8th of March. . . . Thereby I was left at school by myself, my friends gone away—(That is, it was a time of reflection, and when the influences of Mr. Mayers would have room to act upon me. Also, I was terrified at the heavy hand of God which came down upon me.)' The 'heavy hand' presumably refers to one of the 'three great illnesses' of his life: 'The first keen, terrible one, when I was a boy of 15 . . . made me a Christian, with experiences before and after, awful, and known only to God.'

See Sean O'Faolain, *Newman's Way* (London and New York, 1952), p. 46; and *John Henry Newman: Autobiographical Writings*, ed. Henry Tristram (London and New York, 1957), pp. 150 and 268.

17. 20 **a great change of thought** Although Newman was deeply influenced by Evangelicalism, his was not an emotional conversion of the Evangelical kind, going through the stages of 'conviction of sin, terror, despair, news of the free and full salvation, apprehension of Christ, sense of pardon, assurance of salvation, joy and peace, and so on to final perseverance'. (*A.W.*, pp. 79–80 and 172.) Newman was never a complete Evangelical, as many of that party told him after the publication of the *Apologia*. The nature of his experience may be glimpsed in a fragment of his Early Journals: 'The reality of conversion:—as cutting at the root of doubt, providing a chain between God and the soul. (i.e. with every link complete) I know I am right. How do you know it? I know I know. How? I know I know I know &c. &c. (vide Grammar of Assent p 195–7 ed. 4).' (*A.W.*, p. 150.)

Before his conversion, something like the following seems to have been his frame of mind: 'I recollect (in 1815 I believe) thinking I should like to be virtuous, but not religious. . . . Nor did I see the *meaning* of loving God. I recollect contending against Mr. Mayers in favour of Pope's "Essay on Man".' (*A.W.*, p. 169.)

On his conversion he came to hold 'four doctrines . . . as if certain truths, viz. those of the Holy Trinity, of the Incarnation, of Predestination, and of the Lutheran "apprehension of Christ" . . . .' (*A.W.*, p. 81.) See Stephen Dessain, 'Newman's First Conversion', *Newman Studien*, ed. Heinrich Fries and Werner Becker (Nürnberg, 1957), iii. 37–53; and Louis Bouyer, *Newman, His Life and Spirituality* (London, 1958), pp. 9–29.

17.25 **the Rev. Walter Mayers** (1790–1828) was Newman's strongly Evangelical classical master at the school of Dr. Nicholas in Ealing. In 1823 Mayers became curate of Worton in Oxfordshire, where he took pupils and spent the rest of his short life. It was at Worton that Newman preached his first sermon, June 23, 1824; on April 2, 1828, he preached there a sermon on the death of Mayers, the manuscript being headed 'On the death of a very dear friend'. The only public record of his career appears to be an 1831 volume, *Sermons by the late Rev. Walter Mayers, A.M. formerly of Pembroke College, Oxford. To which is annexed, A Brief Memoir of his Life.* (H. T.)

Mayers gave Newman such devotional works as Law's *Serious Call to a Devout and Holy Life* and Doddridge's *Rise and Progress of Religion in the Soul.* As a parting gift he gave him Bishop Beveridge's austere *Private Thoughts on Religion.* Nearly sixty years later Newman wrote the following memorandum in his copy of *Private Thoughts*: 'This work is not mentioned in my *Apologia*, because I am speaking there of the formation of my doctrinal opinions, and I do not think they were influenced by it. I had fully and eagerly taken up Calvinism into my religion before it came into my hands. But no book was more dear to me, or exercised a more powerful influence over my devotion and my habitual thoughts. In my private memoranda I even wrote in its style.' See *Correspondence of John Henry Newman with John Keble and Others* (London, 1917), pp. 113–17; also F. W. Newman's *Contributions*, p. 15, and *Phases of Faith*, p. 1.

17. 29 **a work of Romaine's** William Romaine (1714–95) followed the Whitefield or Calvinist side of the Evangelical revival and won fame as a dynamic preacher and the ablest exponent of the most rigorous Calvinist doctrine. His views may be found in *The Life of Faith* (1764), *The Walk of Faith* (1771), and *The Triumph of Faith* (1795). Professor Harrold (*John Henry Newman*, p. 378) has called attention to Romaine's eloquent treatment of the doctrine of final perseverance in chapters vi, x, and xi of *The Triumph of Faith*; and he adds:

'Newman is more indebted to Romaine than is generally realized; the famous sermon on the "Neglect of Divine Calls and Warnings" (Discourse II in *Discourses to Mixed Congregations*) would seem to owe a direct debt to Romaine's sermon on "The Duty of Watchfulness Enforced" (*Works*, London, 1796, v. 359–84). Newman's early Evangelical stress on fear of eternal punishment likewise reminds one of Romaine's "Future Rewards and Punishments" (*Works*, vi. 61–109).'

17. 32 **final perseverance** The Calvinist doctrine that the elect, those predestined by God's absolute and inscrutable decree to eternal happiness, cannot permanently lose divine favour and so are assured of salvation. Newman later came to regard the doctrine as unscriptural and morally dangerous, leading for many to antinomianism. (See note 18. 38.)

18. 6 **the thought of two and two only** Perhaps the best comment on this famous passage is Newman's sermon 'The Individuality of the Soul': 'Nothing

is more difficult than to realize that every man has a distinct soul, that every one of all the millions who live or have lived, is as whole and independent a being in himself, as if there were no one else in the whole world but he. . . .

'. . . survey some populous town: Crowds are pouring through the streets; some on foot, some in carriages; while the shops are full, and the houses too, could we see into them. Every part of it is full of life. Hence we gain a general idea of splendour, magnificence, opulence, and energy. But what is the truth? why, that every being in that great concourse is his own centre and all things about him are but shades, but a "vain shadow", in which he "walketh and disquieteth himself in vain". He has his own hopes and fears, desires, judgments, and aims; he is everything to himself, and no one else is really anything. No one outside of him can really touch him, can touch his soul, his immortality; he must live with himself for ever. He has a depth within him unfathomable, an infinite abyss of existence; and the scene in which he bears part for a moment is but like a gleam of sunshine upon its surface.' (*Parochial and Plain Sermons*, iv. 80–83; see also *P.S.* i. 20, and v. 325–6.)

18. 11 **The detestable doctrine** Not final perseverance, as Geoffrey Faber says (*Oxford Apostles* [London, 1933], p. 18), but predestination to eternal death. Faber then finds it hard to reconcile Newman's acceptance with Scott's denial of the doctrine. The fact is that Scott accepted both doctrines. (H. T.)

18. 11 **denied and abjured** Too strong a statement of Scott's view: 'I speak not of *reprobation* or *preterition*: they who are not elected, are passed by; which is nearly all that the New Testament teaches us on the subject: and, though Calvin and others have abundantly supplied this supposed deficiency, a majority of those called modern Calvinists, especially among the Evangelical clergy, choose to adhere to the reserve of the Scripture, even if reproached for so doing.'

Again: 'But we find nowhere in Scripture so particular an account given concerning the non-elect. God would do them no wrong, but would not exert omnipotent power in new creating them to holiness, but determined to have them to walk in their own ways. It was a negative decree, a determine not effectually to interfere.' (*Remarks on the Refutation of Calvinism by George Tomline* [2 vols., London, 1811], i. 718–19, and ii. 159.) But as Fr. Tristram has written, 'if the divine intervention or interference is essential, it would seem that, whether we call it reprobation or preterition, for the individual the result is identical'.

18. 14 **Thomas Scott** (1747–1821) was a poor farm labourer who studied hard, became a clergyman for selfish reasons in 1773, and finally, under the influence of John Newton, whom he succeeded in 1781 as curate of Olney, a convert from Arminianism to Calvinism. His progress from Unitarianism is recounted in *The Force of Truth* (1779), a gentle and very popular little autobiography. His great work, *The Holy Bible with . . . Notes* (4 vols., 1788–92) became perhaps the most widely read edition of the Bible in English. It was *the* commentary for Evangelicals, as Scott was 'the commentator'. His *Essays on the Most Important Subjects in Religion* appeared in 1793. He died in the village of Aston Sandford, about sixteen miles east of Oxford, where he had been vicar since 1801.

Although Newman had begun to shake off his doctrinal influence by 1825, the influence on him of Scott in various ways can scarcely be overestimated. Among the tendencies of Scott which apparently left their impress are an insistence on the importance of conscience as our guide, which dominates *The Force of Truth*; a sense of the dangers of reliance on mere intellect; and an exaltation of faith over metaphysical speculation. There are even influences in style, as one may readily see by comparing the conclusion of *The Force of Truth* and that of Newman's *Development of Christian Doctrine*. It is also entirely possible that it was *The Force of Truth* which suggested to Newman that he put his answer to Kingsley into autobiographical form.

18. 21 **Daniel Wilson** (1778–1858) was the strongly Evangelical minister of St. John's Chapel, Bedford Row, Bloomsbury, from 1812 to 1824. In 1832 he became Bishop of Calcutta and Metropolitan of India, one of the first Evangelicals to become a bishop. He vehemently opposed the Oxford Movement.

Scott died April 16, 1821, at Aston Sandford. Wilson preached a funeral sermon at the neighbouring parish of Haddenham, Aston Sandford's church being too small for the occasion. He also delivered two sermons in his Bedford Row chapel, near Newman's home at 17 Southampton Street. Newman was in residence there from April 4 to May 12.

18. 32 **Jones of Nayland** William Jones (1726–1800) was a theologian who resided at Nayland, Suffolk, of which he accepted perpetual curacy in 1777. He was responsible for the founding in May 1793 of the *British Critic*, a quarterly destined to play a large part in the Oxford Movement and which Newman edited from 1838 to 1841. Jones was regarded as a leader in the school forming a link between the Non-jurors and the Tractarians. Newman owned the ninth edition (1814) of his *Catholic Doctrine of the Trinity proved by above an Hundred short and clear Arguments, expressed in the terms of the Holy Scripture*, first published at Oxford in 1756. Newman's edition also contains *A Letter to the Common People, an answer to some popular arguments against the Trinity*, first added to the third edition, 1767.

18. 36 **Athanasian Creed** Sometimes known as the 'Quicunque Vult', from its opening words, it is a statement of brief propositions intended to express unmistakably the trinity of persons in God and the twofold nature in the one Divine Person of Jesus Christ. (See *G.A.*, pp. 125–41.) Widely used in Western Christendom, the creed is of uncertain date and authorship. It was once thought to have grown out of the controversies of St. Athanasius (*c.* 295–373) with the Arians, who held that Christ was a creature, of a different substance from the Father, though of a very high order of perfection. In 325 the Council of Nicaea condemned this doctrine as heretical, but it was difficult to overcome and never entirely disappeared. The Athanasian Creed is now thought to have been written between 381 and 428, however, possibly by St. Ambrose, in connexion with the heresy of Apollinarianism, which denied the complete manhood of Christ.

With the growth of deism, Arian or Unitarian or Socinian views came to the fore in England and spread rapidly. In 1813 the penal laws against

Unitarianism were repealed. The ensuing controversies help to explain Newman's lifelong devotion to Athanasius, the defender of orthodoxy. Although
acceptance of the Athanasian Creed is enjoined in Article VIII of the Thirty-
nine Articles, the vigorous anathematizing of dissenters from the Trinitarian
position led to many attempts to alter the creed or drop it from services. It is
printed before the Litany in the Book of Common Prayer and periodically
replaces the Apostles' Creed at Morning Prayer. In the 1870s Broad Churchmen like Dean Stanley led a fight to modify its use, but Dr. Pusey and Dean
Liddon successfully opposed them. See F. Warre Cornish, *The English
Church in the Nineteenth Century* (2 vols., London, 1910), ii. 160–6. The
Athanasian Creed does not appear in the American edition of the Book of
Common Prayer.

18. 36 **These papers I have still** 'He seems to have destroyed them at a
later date.' (H. T.)

18. 38 **Antinomianism** An early heretical belief that Christians were free
from the necessity of observing a moral law. Johannes Agricola (*c.* 1494–
1566) helped to revive it by carrying the principle of justification by faith to
the extreme of teaching that although the unregenerate remained under the
law, the regenerate were exempt from its observation. This view was taken
up in some high Calvinist circles in England and gave rise to controversy in
the seventeenth and eighteenth centuries. It has been called 'Calvinism run
to seed'.

Thomas Scott came up against it both in theory and practice among the
2,000 or more inhabitants of Olney, 'almost all Calvinists, even the most
debauched of them', who 'in an awful manner, have learnt to abuse gospel-
notions, to stupify their consciences, vindicate their sloth and wickedness, and
shield off conviction'. (Quoted by H. T. from p. 207 of *The Life of the
Rev. Thomas Scott*, by his son John [1822].) See also Essay XV of Scott's
Essays on the Most Important Subjects of Religion and Robert Browning's
'Johannes Agricola in Meditation'.

19. 4 **Holiness rather than peace** Cf. Newman's Private Journal for
September 16, 1824: 'Those who make comfort the great subject of their
preaching seem to mistake the end of their ministry. *Holiness* is the great end.
There must be a struggle and a trial here. Comfort is a cordial, but no one
drinks cordials from morning to night.' (*A.W.*, p. 172.) According to Fr.
Tristram, Newman had obtained Scott's *Essays* the previous month.

19. 4 **Growth the only evidence of life** Cf. Newman's *Development of
Christian Doctrine*, p. 40: 'In a higher world it is otherwise, but here below
to live is to change, and to be perfect is to have changed often.'

19. 22 **the regenerate and the justified** In Lutheran and Calvinist doctrine, which teaches the total depravity of fallen man's nature, if a man is
regenerate or spiritually reborn or one of the elect, a fact Evangelicals hold
he may come to know through the experience of conversion, he is justified or
pleasing to God. Christ's merits are imputed to him to cover his sins, these
being regarded as a kind of moral infirmity over which the will is powerless.

(It is commonly emphasized, however, that good works are a sign of a saving faith.) The Reformers themselves were in disagreement about the precise efficacy of baptism.

The Catholic doctrine, upheld in general by the Book of Common Prayer and the High Church party, is that man's regeneration or first justification results from the sacrament of baptism, which takes away the guilt of sin and opens a channel for God's special aid or grace; but this is not sufficient to assure salvation. If a man does not co-operate with this grace by attempting to live a good life, he may die in the guilt of sin and therefore unpleasing to God or unjustified.

The Evangelicals, variously influenced by Luther and Calvin, denied baptismal regeneration in the sense described, although the Prayer Book, which is based on medieval sources, affirms it. As a result, the doctrine was much controverted after the rise of the Evangelicals, belief in baptismal regeneration becoming a badge of the Tractarians. Newman's attempt to reconcile the various positions may be found in his *Lectures on Justification*. See also Maisie Ward, *Young Mr. Newman* (London, 1948), pp. 102–4; R. D. Middleton, *Newman at Oxford* (London, 1950), pp. 129–34; and Louis Bouyer, *Newman*, pp. 170–3.

19. 29 **William Law** (1686–1761), Non-juror and defender of Christianity against eighteenth-century rationalism, was a contemplative man of mystical tendencies. His *Serious Call to a Devout and Holy Life* (1729) was widely read and influenced, among many others, the two Wesleys, Dr. Johnson (who regarded it as the book which first caused him to think in earnest), Edward Gibbon, and Thomas Scott. In *The Force of Truth* the latter describes it as 'a very uncomfortable book' to anyone 'brought under a serious concern for his soul, and deep conviction of sin'. Leslie Stephen in *D.N.B.* suggests that the singular literary merit of William Law has been too little recognized.

20. 3 **Joseph Milner** (1744–97), headmaster of the Latin school at Hull and a popular preacher, was one of the founders of the Evangelical movement in the Church of England. His five-volume *History of the Church of Christ* (York, 1794–1809), completed by his brother Isaac, is principally concerned with biographies of devout men rather than history of a more formal, doctrinal type. In this respect it is like Newman's *Church of the Fathers* (1840).

20. 7 **Thomas Newton** (1704–82), Bishop of Bristol and editor of Milton's poems, on the death of his father and wife in 1754, found consolation in composing his *Dissertations on the Prophecies, which have been remarkably fulfilled, and are at this time fulfilling in the world*. Completed in 1758, the work was ridiculed by Dr. Johnson and is dismissed by Leslie Stephen as 'a summary of the ordinary replies to Collins and other deists of no real value'. (See *Boswell's Life of Johnson*, ed. G. B. Hill, rev. L. F. Powell [6 vols., Oxford, 1934–50], iv. 286, and *D.N.B.* xiv [1909], 405.) Maisie Ward gives extracts (*Young Mr. Newman*, pp. 26–30) showing why Newman could find the dissertations 'extremely ingenious and also *satisfying*' and indicating that Newton's attacks on devotion to the Blessed Virgin and the saints probably had considerable influence on Newman.

Newman means, of course, that he found it difficult to reconcile the Catholic and more and more clearly papal character of the early Church, whose heroes he so greatly admired, with the view popularized by the Reformation which made the Pope 'the man of sin' leading the forces of Antichrist. He devoted much thought to the problem. See especially Tract 83, 'The Patristical Idea of Antichrist' (1838) in *Discussions and Arguments*, pp. 44–108; and 'The Protestant Idea of Antichrist' (1840), reprinted from the *British Critic* in *Essays Critical and Historical*, ii. 112–85. In the latter Newton is dismissed (pp. 134–45) after being described as 'the main source, we suppose, of that anti-Roman opinion on the subject of Antichrist, now afloat among us, as far as men have an opinion'.

20. 9 **the Antichrist predicted** See Dan. vii. 7 ff.; 2 Thess. ii. 3 ff.; 1 John ii. 18, 22; and especially Apoc. xvii and xviii, which according to Newman (*Via Media*, ii. 219–22) are the two chapters on which especially rests the supposed evidence of the Scripture against Rome.

20. 22 **another deep imagination** At the end of this sentence there follows in the incomplete manuscript of the *Apologia* at the Birmingham Oratory this passage: 'This anticipation has held its ground almost continuously ever since, and it has been closely connected with that feeling of dissociation from scenes about me, of which I have already spoken. I had a strong persuasion that offences against the rule of purity were each of them visited sharply and surely from above. I have still extant prayers and memoranda of the years 1816 and 1821, showing my distress at the thought of going to dances or to the theatre.

'This imagination, which I will speak of once for all, and then dismiss, was not founded on the Catholic belief of the moral superiority of the single life over the married, which I did not hold till many years afterwards when I was taught it by Hurrell Froude. It arose from my feeling of separation from the visible world, and it was connected with a notion that my mission in life would require such a sacrifice as it involved. When I was first on the Oriel foundation it was associated in my mind with missionary employment or with duties at Oxford. In 1824, on my Father's death, I find this remark: "When I die, shall I be followed to the grave by my children? my Mother the other day said she hoped to live to see me married; but *I* think I shall either die in a College walls [*sic*] or a missionary in a foreign land." And in 1827, in some verses which I wrote for a friend's Album, after comparing myself to the "snapdragon fringing the wall opposite the rooms in which I spent my first solitary three weeks at College in June 1817" I express a hope that I may "in College cloister live and die". Afterwards what had been a mere anticipation, became a preference. The idea had been obscured in my mind, for a month now, and a month then, in the years previous to February 1829; but from that date I have had the continuous will and resolution, with divine aid, to live and die single. I determined to be "a pilgrim pale in Paul's stern girdle bound".

'I will add that in looking over these details of past years, I accidentally have found the following written the same year under date of September 1829, [I wrote this] "In my rooms at Oriel, slowly advancing &c. and led on by God's hand blindly, not knowing whither He is taking me. Even so."'

For a good discussion of Newman and the idea of virginity, see Meriol Trevor, *Newman: The Pillar of the Cloud* (London, 1961), pp. 88–96.

20. 34 **In 1822** Newman entered Trinity College, Oxford, in June 1817, took his B.A. degree in 1820, and was elected Fellow of Oriel in 1822. Under John Eveleigh, Provost from 1787 to 1814, and Edward Copleston, Provost from 1814 to 1827, Oriel, by reforming its examination system and substituting tea for the large quantities of port then normally consumed in Common Rooms, had become the foremost college in the University. The group dominating Oriel consisted of eight or nine liberals known as Noetics, of whom only Copleston, Whately, and Hawkins were in residence on Newman's election.

The term Noetic 'will not convey much meaning to the general public, but to students of Aristotle's "Ethics", as, of course, the Oriel men were, it conveyed a very definite meaning indeed: a Noetic was a man who exercised his highest faculties, as opposed to those who let them lie dormant; and the description certainly applied to those to whom the title was given'. J. H. Overton, *The English Church in the Nineteenth Century* (London, 1894), p. 117. See also *Apo.*, pp. 254–6; W. Tuckwell, *Pre-Tractarian Oxford* (London, 1909), containing eight sketches of leading Noetics; Mark Pattison, *Memoirs* (London, 1885), pp. 78–80; R. W. Church, *The Oxford Movement* (London, 1891), pp. 139 ff.; and A. Dwight Culler, *The Imperial Intellect* (New Haven and London, 1955), pp. 35–45.

21. 3 **Dr. Hawkins** Edward Hawkins (1789–1882) became Fellow of Oriel in 1813; Vicar of St. Mary's, the University's unofficial church, in 1823; and Provost of Oriel in 1828, a position in which he remained active until 1874, when he became Canon of Rochester and left the government of Oriel to a Vice-Provost. He was known first as something of a liberal reformer, but he later became a bitter opponent of the secularizing reforms beginning at Oxford in the 1850s.

In 1831 he deprived his tutors, Newman, Hurrell Froude, and Robert Wilberforce, of pupils, disagreeing with their view that lectures should be remodelled to provide closer moral as well as intellectual relations between tutor and pupil. Pattison (*Memoirs*, pp. 83 ff.) dates the decline of Oriel from this time, Hawkins being unable to replace such skilled tutors, and the intellectual leadership of the University passing to Balliol.

Hawkins later became a bitter enemy of what he considered the disloyalty and dishonesty of the Tractarians, taking a leading part in the fight against Tract 90. See J. W. Burgon's *Lives of Twelve Good Men* (2 vols., London, 1888), i. 374–465. Burgon describes the mind of Hawkins as 'essentially legal in its texture', with a passion for accuracy of statement. He had originally wanted to be a lawyer but thought he could do more for his mother, a widow with ten children, by taking orders.

On June 6, 1864, Hawkins, who had resumed correspondence with Newman some years earlier, wrote to him: 'I have read with the deepest interest your Apologia, the first six parts of it at least; and I cannot forbear troubling you with a line to express my great pleasure in your expression of such very kind feelings towards myself and others among your old friends. You may be quite assured that, much as I have deplored your separation from us, my affectionate regard for you has remained undiminished.' (MS. *Apologia* Letters, in Birmingham Oratory Archives.)

See also *A.W.*, pp. 77 and 96–107; and Culler, *The Imperial Intellect*, pp. 62–74.

21. 28 **John Bird Sumner** (1780–1862) became Bishop of Chester in 1828 and Archbishop of Canterbury in 1848. Of Evangelical tendencies, he and his brother Charles, Bishop of Winchester, opposed the Tractarians. There is some irony in the fact that J. B. Sumner's *Apostolical Preaching Considered in an Examination of St. Paul's Epistles* (1815, rev. 1817, and very popular thereafter) should have led Newman to receive the doctrine of baptismal regeneration; for it was Sumner who, as Archbishop of Canterbury, though holding the doctrine himself, concurred with the judgement of the Privy Council in the once famous Gorham case of 1850 that a clergyman of the Church of England need not believe in it. This decision was followed by many conversions to Rome, including that of Archdeacon, later Cardinal, Manning; and it led to Newman's lectures of 1850 on the *Difficulties of Anglicans*. See *Diff*. i. 28 for Newman's remarks on Sumner's interpretation; and C. C. J. Webb, *Religious Thought in the Oxford Movement* (London, 1933), pp. 102–10.

21. 36 **Joseph Blanco White** (1775–1841), an Oriel Noetic, was born of Irish and Spanish parentage, became a Catholic priest in Spain, and then drifted into scepticism. In 1810 he came to England, became an Anglican clergyman, and wrote *Evidences against Catholicism* (1825). Oxford made him an M.A., and in October 1826 he settled at Oriel College to pursue his studies. Through his influence on colleagues like Whately and R. D. Hampden, he is sometimes considered a founder of modern Latitudinarianism in the Church of England. He and Newman had a special bond in their love of music, often playing Beethoven together in impromptu violin concerts. In 1828 he became editor of the short-lived *London Review*, to which Newman contributed. His knowledge of Catholicism and scholastic philosophy had a special interest for his companions: to Pusey and Hurrell Froude, for example, he explained the use of the Breviary. In 1832, after Whately had become Archbishop of Dublin, White left Oriel to join him, veered towards rationalism again, became separated from Whately and his Oriel friends, and ended as a Unitarian.

Belief in 'plenary inspiration' of Scripture was then still widely held in England; i.e. that the entire text, in fact, word, and plan, was directly inspired of God. For White's views on the untenability of verbal inspiration, see *The Life of The Rev. Joseph Blanco White Written by Himself with Portions of His Correspondence*, ed. J. H. Thom (3 vols., London, 1845), i. 274–84. See also Ward's *Life of Newman*, i. 80–82, and ii. 76, 349; and Newman's *Present Position of Catholics in England*, pp. 142–60; *Diff*. i. 93; *Essays*, i. 27–29, 74–79, and 112.

22. 5 **his celebrated sermon** Preached on May 31, 1818, it was published in 1819 as *A Dissertation upon the Use and Importance of Unauthoritative Tradition as an Introduction to the Christian Doctrines*. How greatly it influenced Newman may be seen in Tract 85, 'Holy Scripture in Relation to

the Catholic Creed' (reprinted in *D.A.*), in which the ideas outlined here 'in the *Apologia* are refined and enlarged into one of the most significant documents of the Oxford Movement. Hawkins also discussed the subject in his Bampton Lectures of 1840. Both the sermon and extracts from these lectures were reprinted in 1889 in consequence of J. W. Burgon's allusions in *Lives of Twelve Good Men*, i. 392–4.

22. 22 **the Bible Society** The British and Foreign Bible Society, which Newman joined in 1824, was founded by the Evangelicals in 1804. It held the Protestant view that the Bible alone, as interpreted by the individual judgement, was a sufficient guide to faith; and with this, Hawkins's view of Tradition as the teacher and Scripture as the verifier was incompatible. Newman resigned on June 8, 1830. See *Letters*, i. 200; and *V.M.* ii. 4–6 and 13.

22. 27 **Rev. William James** became Fellow of Oriel in 1809. One of Newman's examiners for the Oriel Fellowship in 1822, he recommended Newman's appointment. See *Letters*, i. 62.

22. 28 **The Doctrine of Apostolical Succession** is that the bishops who govern the Church derive their authority from consecration by other bishops in a line extending back to the first bishops, the Apostles, themselves commissioned by Christ to rule the Church. The Tractarians made this Catholic belief, then no longer widely held in the Church of England, the basis of the Oxford Movement in order better to resist the encroachments of the state in matters of religion by arguing that since the Church was not made by the State, the State had no power to unmake it. (See Tracts 1 and 19.)

Evangelicals, like perhaps the majority of Anglicans since Hooker, accepted the episcopal system but regarded it more as a matter of custom and convenience than as divinely ordained. Hence it is natural that in 1823 the Evangelical-minded Newman was 'somewhat impatient of the subject'. A somewhat different version of how he came to learn the doctrine is given in his letter to Keble of November 21, 1844, where he refers to being 'first taught the doctrine . . . of Apostolic Succession by Hurrell Froude . . . in 1829 (after James on "Episcopacy" in 1823). . . .' (*Corr.*, p. 351.)

22. 31 **Butler's *Analogy*** Joseph Butler (1692–1752), Bishop of Durham, published his *Analogy of Religion, Natural and Revealed, to the Constitution and Course of Nature* in 1736. One of the greatest and most original works in English theology, it came to have a tremendous influence on thinkers of many schools; and for Newman its importance is profound. Butler regarded the conscience as a supreme faculty of self-evident authority; and he held, against the Deists, that probability alone is sufficient to establish an obligation to believe or act recognized by the conscience. He argued that difficulties in Revelation should no more destroy belief in Christianity than difficulties in nature destroy belief in the divine origin of the natural system. Not that either Butler or Newman confined their proofs for Christianity to analogy: 'The argument from Analogy is mainly negative, but argument which tends to prove must be positive. Butler does not prove Christianity to be true by his famous argument, but he removes a great obstacle of a *prima facie* character to listening to the proofs of Christianity.' (*G.A.*, Note II, 497.)

It is the second part of the *Analogy* which shows the similarity between the workings of nature and the facts of Revelation. The tendency to read nature as an allegory of religious truth, so common in Newman, goes back in Christian history to the Alexandrian Platonist Fathers of the third and fourth centuries, of whom Origen (*c.* 185–245) was the most famous. For the allegorizing of Scripture and nature by Origen and others, see Tract 89, 'On the Mysticism of the Early Fathers of the Church', by John Keble. See also Klaus Dick, 'Das Analogieprinzip bei John Henry Newman und seine Quelle in Joseph Butler's "Analogy"', *Newman Studien*, v (1962), 9–228.

23. 4 **the more momentous system** The freely translated quotation from Origen referred to in the footnote occurs in Butler's Introduction to the *Analogy*: 'He who believes the Scripture to have proceeded from Him Who is the Author of Nature, may well expect to find the same sort of difficulties in it, as are found in the constitution of Nature.' For the Greek of Origen and a discussion of Butler's source, see *The Analogy of Religion*, ed. J. H. Bernard (London, 1900), § 6, p. 4 and n. 6.

23. 7 **the distinction between matter itself and its phenomena** But he was making the distinction at least as early as 1834. See *Letters*, ii. 36: 'As to Berkeley, I do not know enough to talk, but it seems to me, while a man holds the moral governance of God as *existing in and through his conscience*, it matters not whether he believe his senses or not. For, at least, he will hold the external world as a *divine* intimation, a scene of trial whether a reality or not—just as a child's game may be a trial. I have tried to say this in the "Arians", ch. 1, § 3. . . . To what extent Berkeley denied the existence of the external world I am not aware; nor do I mean to go so far myself (far from it) as to deny the existence of matter, though I should deny that *what we saw* was more than accidents of it, and say that space perhaps is but a condition of the objects of sense, not a reality.' See *Arians*, p. 75.

23. 10 **Probability is the guide of life** See *The Analogy*, § 3 (ed. Bernard, p. 2).

23. 16 **Dr. Whately** Richard Whately (1787–1863) became a Fellow of Oriel in 1813, when John Keble was the other successful candidate. Insular and with little historical knowledge, he was averse to theological speculation and relied on logic and the Bible for his religion. As a teacher he skilfully employed the Socratic method and delighted in using young men as his intellectual 'anvils'. In 1825 he became Principal of Alban Hall, then a kind of Botany Bay of the University, and quickly raised the standards. In 1826 he published his *Elements of Logic*, which became famous and in the composition of which Newman had assisted him. In 1829 he became Professor of Political Economy and in 1831 Archbishop of Dublin.

The sceptical temper in which Whately approached religious problems was altogether foreign to the reverential spirit inculcated by Keble and the Tractarians, and Whately's views became increasingly rationalistic and hostile to the Catholic tendencies of the Oxford Movement. In 1836 he persuaded the Prime Minister to appoint R. D. Hampden as Regius Professor of Divinity. The widespread opposition to the appointment as amounting to an endorsement of Hampden's depreciation of the traditional creeds of faith was led by the Tractarians; and this embittered Whately, who considered the charge against Hampden unfair. He later supported the movement to censure Newman's Tract 90 in Convocation. For Newman's relations with Whately, see the correspondence of 1834 referred to below, which Newman added to the text of the *Apologia* in 1869 (pp. 326–32) after it was published only in part in 1868 in a one-volume edition, abridged and with some additions, of the *Life and Correspondence of Richard Whately, D.D., late Archbishop of Dublin* (2 vols., 1866), by his daughter Jane.

There is evidence that as Newman the Roman Catholic began to experience difficulties with the ultramontane conservatives, he came to appreciate anew the virtues of Whately. See the moving tribute he wrote for the Catholic *Weekly Register* on Whately's death, *A.W.*, pp. 84–85. See also ibid., pp. 66–70; Middleton, *Newman at Oxford*, pp. 40–47; and Culler, *The Imperial Intellect*, pp. 38–43.

23. 33 an Article of mine 'Poetry with Reference to Aristotle's Poetics', which appeared in the first number of the *London Review*, January 1829. Newman later admitted that White's objection was not unfounded, the article ignoring 'one of the essential conditions of the idea of Poetry, its relation to the affections—and that, in consequence, as it would seem, of confusing the function and aim of Poetry with its formal object'. (*Essays*, i. 29.) Geoffrey Tillotson thinks such an admission unnecessary, however. See his article 'Newman's Essay on Poetry' in *Newman Centenary Essays* (London, 1945), pp. 178–200, esp. p. 189. See also *Letters*, i. 172.

24. 4 once in a room in 1838 Newman apparently called on Whately, having had him sounded beforehand and finding that he was 'pretty tame'. The visit passed off well, he being 'so good-hearted a man'. (See letter to Bowden, September 21, 1838, in *Letters*, ii. 238.) On September 24 Whately returned the call. In Letters, i. 124, 1837 is a slip for 1838. (H. T.)

24. 6 he made himself dead to me This was true even in Dublin when Newman was Rector of the Catholic University in the 1850s. On October 15, 1863, Newman wrote to a correspondent who wished him to write reminiscences of Whately at Oriel: '. . . I never saw him in Dublin. I would have gladly called on him; but both friends who saw him then, and those who did not, advised me not to do so. He took up a position of simple antagonism to me.' (H. T.)

24. 17 sharp things in his later works See, for example, his characterization of Newman as a stifler of doubt, likely to end up with 'little or no conviction' of the truth of his religion, in *The Scripture Doctrine concerning the Sacraments* (London, 1857), pp. 93–99.

24. 22 to teach me the existence of the Church See *Corr.*, p. 351: 'When I was first taught the doctrine . . . of "the Church" by Whately in 1825'. Fr. Tristram notes that the influence of Whately's teaching was soon evident. On November 19, 1826, Newman preached a sermon in St. Clement's 'On the One, Catholic, Apostolic Church', to which he appended a note: 'This is one of the first, if not the first, declarations I made of High Church principles, Dec. 10, 1859. J. H. N. Vid., however, the Sermons on the Visible Church &c. a year before. J. H. N.'

24. 23 **anti-Erastian views** The term *Erastian* is derived from the name of a German physician and controversialist, Thomas Lüber, or Erastus (1524–83), whose position it does not, perhaps, fairly represent. It is a common term in English church history, especially after 1688. 'What is really meant by a "Church", is a religious body which has jurisdiction over its members, or which governs itself; whereas, according to the doctrine of Erastus, it has no such jurisdiction, really is not a body at all, but is simply governed by the State, and is one department of the State's operations.' (*Diff*. i. 198. See also ibid. i. 101–3, where the 'heresy of Erastus' is said to be the doctrine especially opposed by the Oxford Movement.)

24. 28 **in the course of a walk, he said** i.e. Froude, not Whately.

25. 1 **any disclaimer** Whately never did affirm or deny authorship, but no one seems to have doubted that it was his work. For Newman's later objection that the book asserts a position for the Church without giving it any real function, see *Diff*. i. 203–15. See also *D.A*., pp. 360–1; Yngve Brilioth, *The Anglican Revival* (London, 1925), pp. 84–86; and *Life of Archbishop Whately*, 2nd ed., p. 43 n.

25. 21 **At this point in the MS. of the *Apologia*,** Newman quotes several passages from Whately's book, pp. 42, 97, 115–16, and 129: e.g. 'It was in truth Satan who first proposed an alliance between the Christian Church and the State by offering temporal advantages in exchange for giving up some of the things that be God's' (p. 97); and regarding the voice of the state in the naming of bishops: 'An English bishop did not dare to ordain an American to officiate in a country not under British dominion, without asking and obtaining permission of his government, which had just as much to do with the business as the government of Abyssinia' (p. 129).

25. 24 **his special theological tenets**— When Whately's *Logic* appeared, Newman was pained to find added an appendix in which theological subjects were introduced. 'In these', he goes on to say in a letter to William Monsell dated October 10, 1852, 'I had always differed from him, even to his face. . . . When I first knew him in 1822 . . . my religious views were what are called Evangelical. He, more than any one else, broke me of these, but I never took up his . . . perhaps his view concerning the Persons of the Blessed Trinity was that all that they were said to be in Revelation was only *relatively to us*; as if there were not really and absolutely any Trinity in the Godhead. What his view really was, I am not prepared to say; I am told he has published a very orthodox sermon on the subject.' Elsewhere in the same letter Newman says that Whately 'disclaimed the doctrines both of Imputed Sin and Imputed Righteousness: I disclaimed the latter, but could not digest his denial of the former'. See *Letters and Diaries*, xv (1964), 177.

25. 25 **I was Arianizing** Reviewing the year 1827 in his Private Journal, Newman wrote: 'At Easter I had to preach the usual sermon in the College

chapel, and got into some little controversy about it. The Provost Copleston liking it, recommended it to Whately (part of it was on the divinity of Christ) who accused it of Arianism. Hawkins thought it dangerous, and Blanco White thought it systematized more than Scripture does. So it must have been faulty more or less.* *(It took, without knowing it, Bull's doctrine of the "Subordinatio Filii". Whately, Hawkins, and Blanco White, were all verging then towards Sabellianism themselves.)' See *A.W.*, p. 211. The manuscript of the sermon, containing pencilled objections by Whately and White and a note in ink by Hawkins, survives at the Birmingham Oratory. Sabellianism was a third-century heretical belief also known as modalist Monarchianism, to the effect that 'in the Godhead the only differentiation was a mere succession of modes or operations'. (*O.D.C.C.*)

25. 27 **Bull's** *Defensio Defensio Fidei Nicaenae* (1685), by George Bull (1634–1710), Bishop of St. David's, is one of the great works of Anglican theology. It was written to prove against the Jesuit scholar Petavius that the orthodox doctrine of the Trinity was fully developed before the Council of Nicaea in 325, and it maintains in effect that 'the Nicene Creed is the natural key for interpreting the body of ante-Nicene theology'. (*Dev.*, p. 134. See also *V.M.* i. 60–63, and *The Arians of the Fourth Century*, pp. 416–22.)

25. 31 **a passage in Froude's Remains** *Remains of the Late Reverend Richard Hurrell Froude, M.A.* is a collection of Froude's sermons, letters, journals, etc., edited by Newman and Keble. The first part, in two volumes, appeared in London in 1838; the second, also in two, in 1839. Froude's strong criticism of the Reformers aroused hostility to the Tractarians. For the passage referred to, see pt. i, vol. i, p. 245.

26. 3 **Middleton on the Miracles** Conyers Middleton (1683–1750), a clergyman and biting controversialist who in 1749 published a work which denied the credibility of miracles after the Apostolic age and attributed accounts of them to the character of the narrators and the credulity of their audience. The title is *A Free Inquiry into the Miraculous Powers which are Supposed to have Subsisted in the Christian Church from the Earliest Ages through Several Successive Centuries*. For some more or less 'flippant' language by Newman (the essays have been revised) and a summary of Middleton's approach, see 'The Miracles of Scripture' in *Two Essays on Biblical and on Ecclesiastical Miracles*, pp. 28–29 and 40–43.

26. 4 **spirit** At this point in the manuscript of the *Apologia* appears the following cancelled passage:

'In these same years this new spirit showed itself in a different way; in what is commonly called donnishness. On this account I got into disfavour with my pupils at Alban Hall, and one of them, of some age, long dead, gave me a lesson which I never forgot. I believe it did me permanent good. I had given as a subject of an essay "Know thyself"; and he wrote about "stiff and stately distance, strict etiquette in the exterior forms of address, great punctiliousness in balancing the quantity and quality of discourse, to be addressed to each relatively to his standing, and an immoderate share of vanity to gloss over the odium and contempt which all sensible persons entertain and might express for these seeming insults on their situation, and these encroachments on a privilege only tolerated in despotic princes". "If", he continued, "the 'know thyself' is profitable to all as a means of edification, let it be instilled on [*sic*] those who come under the force of the preceding remarks. Let it place a mirror before them to reflect their persons and characters such as they really are, and such as they are discerned to be by others &c. By such observance those who have passed their time in closets may impart the fruits of their solitary inquiries at once to instruct and command esteem, and prove to those who have lived in the world that they are at least their equals in true good breeding."'

26. 8 **illness and bereavement** In November 1827 Newman suffered a breakdown similar to the one which had kept him from obtaining college honours in 1820. On January 5, 1828, his favourite and youngest sister, Mary (born November 9, 1809), died suddenly, presumably of a heart attack. For Newman's own graphic account of these important events, see *A.W.*, pp. 210–13 and 268. See also Bouyer's *Newman*, pp. 96–115, and Culler's *Imperial Intellect*, pp. 58–62.

26. 10 **the affair of Mr. Peel's re-election** Robert Peel (1788–1850), then Home Secretary in the Cabinet of the Duke of Wellington, had long been known for his opposition to Catholic Emancipation on anti-Erastian grounds. He feared for the Church of England under a Parliament influenced by those who opposed the Establishment, and in 1827 he had resigned from the Canning Government on this very issue. He felt obliged to change his stand in 1828, however, when civil war seemed certain to follow refusal of a seat in Parliament to the newly elected leader of the Catholic forces in Ireland, Daniel O'Connell. To die-hard Tories, this reversal became known as the 'Great Betrayal'.

In February 1829 Peel conscientiously offered his resignation, but allowed his supporters to nominate him for re-election. By 755 votes to 609 he lost to Sir Robert Inglis at Oxford, which he had represented since 1817. He was elected for Westbury, however, and proceeded to carry emancipation through. See *Memoirs by The Right Honorable Sir Robert Peel* (2 vols., London, 1857), i. 338; and Newman's account in *H.S.* iii. 231–2.

26. 12 **the Petition** Such a petition had long been presented annually; and even in 1829, when Peel's letter offering his resignation was read in Convocation, it was carried 164–48. (Peel's *Memoirs*, i. 318.) Newman's being in the minority in 1828 or 1827 suggests that he was then still influenced by Hawkins and the Liberals, who supported Catholic Emancipation.

26. 15 **'two-bottle-orthodox'** In an appendix to an 1866 French edition of the *Apologia*, describing the High Church party of the Establishment as distinct from Evangelicals, Liberals, and Tractarians or Apostolicals, Newman writes: '. . . amongst ecclesiastics who enjoy great revenues and have not much to do (such as the members of the Cathedral chapters), many have long since deteriorated in the pursuit of their personal advantage. Those who held high positions in great towns have been led to adopt the habits of a great position and of external display, and have boasted a formal orthodoxy which

was cold and almost entirely devoid of interior life. These self-indulgent pastors have for a long time been nicknamed "two-bottle orthodox", as though their greatest religious zeal manifested itself in the drinking of port wine to the health of "the Church and King". The pompous dignitaries of great town parishes have also been surnamed the "high and dry" school or Church.' (*Apologia*, ed. Wilfrid Ward [London, 1913], pp. xxvi–xxvii.)

26. 19 **his friends had no right to call upon us** In his letter of congratulation on the *Apologia* (MS. *Apo.* Letters, June 6, 1864), Hawkins corrected Newman on this point as implying that Peel himself 'sought to be re-elected. But it was not so. I was myself one of those who thought that the University ought not to be deprived of his services; and we chose to act without his consent, first forming committees here and in London for his re-election, and then requesting him not to prevent our getting him returned if we could. He consented to this, but almost with reluctance. He had certainly no idea himself of anything but simple resignation. He took no part in the movement in his favour, except just so far as not to prevent it by getting himself returned for another place where he had already secured a seat. You will find all the correspondence on the subject in the 1st Volume of his *Memoir* (1856), p. 312.'

27. 7 **a copy of verses** See 'A Thanksgiving' in *Verses on Various Occasions*, p. 45.

27. 10 **to my great grief** After this phrase and before the next sentence, the manuscript originally read, 'but as I did not make a canvass to get them, so I could not pay any price to retain them: He who gave took away; I was not heartless in acquiescing in their loss; nor had I manœuvred in securing their adhesion'.

27. 14 **very much alone** See the letter of June 21, 1836, to his sister Harriett. *Letters*, ii. 175.

27. 16 **Dr. Copleston** Edward Copleston (1776–1849) was the chief defender of the Oxford ideal of a liberal education against the attacks of the pragmatic-minded *Edinburgh Review*. (See his *Reply to the Calumnies of the Edinburgh Review against Oxford*, 1810; and Newman's deeply indebted *Idea of a University*, especially pp. 156–8, 167–9, and 369–71.) After a career as Professor of Poetry from 1802 to 1812 and Provost of Oriel from 1814 to 1827, Copleston was in the latter year made Bishop of Llandaff and Dean of St. Paul's. A leading Noetic, he strongly opposed the Tractarians.

27. 18 **'Nunquam minus solus...'** Never less alone than when alone. See Cicero, *De Officiis*, III. i. 1; and *De re publica*, I. xvii. 27.

27. 19 **from 1823 ... Dr. Pusey** See *A.W.*, pp. 74–76.

27. 28 **one or two Essays** Besides the articles on Aristotle and on miracles already referred to, Newman had written several essays, including 'The Personal and Literary Character of Cicero' (1824) and 'Apollonius of Tyana' (1826) for the *Encyclopaedia Metropolitana*, both reprinted in *H.S.* i. Fr. Tristram lists also an article on Duncan's Travels in the *British Review*

and London Critical Journal for May 1824; and one on Cooper's Crisis and Robinson's Acts for the *Theological Review* of June 1825.

27. 30 **my first University Sermon** 'The Philosophical Temper, First Enjoined by the Gospel', preached July 2, 1826. See *University Sermons*, pp. 1–15. University Sermons were preached by (1) Select Preachers, who had in their official period of two years five or six turns; (2) M.A.'s in their turn, perhaps once in a lifetime; (3) preachers by appointment of the Vice-Chancellor, who had a certain number of turns: e.g. Sunday afternoons in Lent; (4) preachers by appointment of the colleges in succession, generally by their Bursars, on Saints' days if they did not fall on Sundays. Newman's invitation came from the Vice-Chancellor. (H. T.)

27. 34 **I remained out of it till 1841** To these words the manuscript originally added, 'and then, as I think, I went back for good'.

28. 1 **Mr. Rickards** Samuel Rickards (1796–1865), Fellow of Oriel, became curate of Ulcombe, Kent, in 1822. For a time, especially in 1826 and 1827, he and Newman were close friends (*Letters*, i. 119 ff.), Newman relieving Rickards and occupying his house; but Rickards was one of the first to become alarmed at the Catholic tendencies of the Tracts and warn against them (*Letters*, i. 427–32). In 1832 he became rector of Stowlangtoft, Suffolk, where he spent the rest of his life, 'very fierce' against his old friend, according to a letter of Newman to W. J. Copeland, August 28, 1865.

The second of the estranged friends was Henry Woodgate (d. 1874), rector of Belbroughton, near Birmingham. On reading this passage of the *Apologia*, he was pained and wrote to Newman, whereupon they resumed friendly relations. Newman dedicated *Discussions and Arguments* to him. See Henry Tristram, *Newman and His Friends* (London, 1933), pp. 194–9.

28. 7 **probationer Fellows** i.e. in their first year, before final approval, after which they could hold their fellowships for life or until marriage. Wilberforce and Froude were elected Fellows of Oriel in March 1826. See *Letters*, i. 115, 134–40.

28.7 **Robert Isaac Wilberforce** (1802–57) was the second son of William Wilberforce, the philanthropist and leader of the Evangelicals. After the disagreement with Hawkins over the duties of a tutor, he left Oxford in 1831. In 1841 he was appointed Archdeacon of the East Riding. Meanwhile he wrote much on theological subjects and gained a scholarly reputation. Disturbed, like his close friend Manning, by the Gorham judgement of 1850, he wrote *An Inquiry into the Principles of Church Authority* in 1854 and entered the Roman Catholic Church. His brothers Henry and William also became Catholics. Another brother, Samuel, who became Bishop of Oxford in 1845, later wrote of Robert: '. . . in the theological literature of our Church his name can never be forgotten; nor of all who left us was there one who took with him a truer, purer, more loving, or more humble spirit'. (Quoted by F. Legge in *D.N.B.* from Samuel Wilberforce's *Essays* [London, 1874], i. 346.)

28. 12 The beautiful tributes to Keble and Froude which follow, the men chiefly responsible for turning Newman away from Noetic rationalism and towards Catholic conceptions of sanctity and church authority, are prime illustrations of the personal, concrete character of the Newmanian apologetic. It was above all their goodness of character which assured Newman's sympathetic interest in their religious views. So it was with the Church Fathers: 'Dogma and proof are in them at the same time hagiography.' (*H.S.* ii. 223.) In 'Personal Influence the Means of Propagating the Truth' (1832, *U.S.*, no. 5), we are told that even in the world men 'persuade themselves, with little difficulty, to scoff at principles, to ridicule books, to make sport of the names of good men; but they cannot bear their presence: it is holiness embodied in personal form, which they cannot steadily confront and bear down: so that the silent conduct of a conscientious man secures for him from beholders a feeling different in kind from any which is created by the mere versatile and garrulous Reason'.

And, significantly, Newman goes on to say: 'And if such be the personal influence excited by the Teacher of Truth over the mixed crowd of men whom he encounters, what (think we) will be his power over that select number . . . who have already, in a measure, disciplined their hearts after the law of holiness, and feel themselves, as it were, individually addressed by the invitation of his example?' (pp. 92 and 95.)

28. 12 **The true and primary author of it . . . Keble** But see *Diff.* i. 36, where Hurrell Froude, without being named, is called 'one, who, if any, is the author of the movement altogether'. Cf. Church, *Oxford Movement*, pp. 30–31.

28. 17 **John Keble** (1792–1866) was educated first by his father, the Revd. John Keble, vicar of Coln St. Aldwyn, a few miles from Fairford, Gloucestershire. His father prepared him for what proved a brilliant career at Corpus Christi, Oxford, and from 1811 as Fellow of Oriel; and he taught him the Catholic traditions of the Caroline divines (including such doctrines as the Real Presence, the authority of the visible church, and the apostolical succession), to the fuller realization of which in the Anglican church, Keble devoted his life with great success.

Despite a multitude of academic honours in classics, mathematics, and English, he remained wholly unaffected, retaining the charm of innocence and serenity. In 1816 he was ordained a priest and in 1817 became a tutor at Oriel. In 1823, on leaving Oxford to help his ailing father, he gave himself to the humble duties of a country priest. Always preferring moral to merely intellectual excellence, he had much to do with shaping the Tractarian ethos. As curate of Southrop, near Fairford, he extended an invitation to read with him during the long vacation of 1823 to such pupils as Isaac Williams, R. I. Wilberforce, and Hurrell Froude; and from this meeting the Oxford Movement may be said to have taken its ultimate origin.

Following the extraordinary success of his book of religious poetry, *The Christian Year* (1827), he became Professor of Poetry (non-resident) at Oxford, succeeding H. H. Milman and holding the chair from 1831 to 1841.

In 1836, soon after the death of his father, he became vicar of Hursley, near Winchester, where he spent the rest of his life.

Among his other works are an edition of Hooker (3 vols., 1836); eight of the *Tracts for the Times*: nos. 4, 13, 40, 52, 54, 57, 60, and 89; his Oxford lectures on poetry, published in 1841 as *De Poeticae Vi Medica* and dedicated to Wordsworth (see M. H. Abrams, *The Mirror and the Lamp* [New York and London, 1953], *passim*, esp. pp. 144–8); *Lyra Innocentium* (1846), a book of poems inspired by the idea of baptismal regeneration and written to solace himself during the crisis of Newman's conversion; and a *Life of Thomas Wilson, Bishop of Sodor and Man* (2 vols., 1863).

See the biographies of Keble by J. T. Coleridge (Oxford and London, 1869), K. Ingram (London, 1933), and Georgina Battiscombe (London, 1963); *Apo.*, pp. 257–8 and Newman's essay 'John Keble, Fellow of Oriel', in *Essays*, ii. 421–53; *The Autobiography of Isaac Williams, B.D.* (London, 1892), pp. 12–30; Christopher Dawson, *The Spirit of the Oxford Movement* (London and New York, 1933), pp. 12–24; and Owen Chadwick, *The Mind of the Oxford Movement* (London, 1960), pp. 30–42.

28. 19 **the Tower** A room in the tower above the Oriel gateway where candidates for fellowships were examined viva voce before the assembled Fellows and to which they were later summoned to be informed of their election.

28. 20 **How is that hour fixed in my memory** On Newman's extraordinarily graphic memory for persons, places, anniversaries, and other events of emotional significance, one of his great literary assets, see Fernande Tardivel, *La Personnnalité littéraire de Newman* (Paris, 1937), pp. 125–31.

28. 21 **forty-two this very day** April 12, 1822 and 1864.

28. 23 **John William Bowden** (1798–1844) was Newman's oldest and, before Froude, most intimate friend at Oxford: 'men used to mistake our names and call us by each other's', wrote Newman in 1844. Bowden later became a Commissioner of Stamps and married Elizabeth Swinburne, aunt of the future poet. He contributed to the *Lyra Apostolica*, *Tracts for the Times* (nos. 5, 29, 30, 56, and 58), and the *British Critic* and wrote a *Life and Pontificate of Gregory VII*. For Newman's sketch of his career, see *Essays*, ii. 318–19. See also *Apo.*, pp. 203–4; *Corr.*, pp. 331–3; and Henry Tristram, *Newman and His Friends*, pp. 54–60.

29. 3 **Dr. Milman** Henry Hart Milman (1791–1868), then known especially for his narrative poems and historical dramas, became Dean of St. Paul's in 1849. For his effect as a historian on Newman, see *Apo.*, p. 127 and editor's note. See also *Idea*, p. 85, Milman being the 'living dignitary' criticized there.

29. 5 **not in residence** Newman's memory is apparently at fault here as he was elected in 1822 and Keble did not resign his tutorship till the end of Hilary Term, 1823, going out of residence on his mother's death in May. (H. T.)

29. 9 **in his 'Remains'** Pt. i, vol. i, p. 438: 'With his death in prospect.' Abbé Nédoncelle has suggested that this is the story of a thief saved at the

last hour thanks to one good deed he had performed, perhaps an analogue to the story of the 'good thief' on the cross.

However, in another connexion, H. J. Ayliffe in *Notes and Queries*, clxi. (July 4, 1931), 12, refers to John Wesley's citing in a sermon on everlasting punishment a fabulous story taken from an Eastern writer of a Turkish king who after much wickedness did one good thing—seeing a poor man fall into a pit, he kicked him out of it and saved his life. When the king was eventually damned for his wickedness, the foot with which he had saved the man's life was permitted to lie out of the flames of hell. See Sermon LXXIII, 'Of Hell', *The Works of John Wesley, A.M.* (3rd ed., 14 vols., London, 1829), vi. 387.

29. 14 **The Christian Year . . . in 1827** It was a collection in two small octavo volumes of 103 short poems for Sundays and other days of liturgical importance, and for occasional ceremonies like the administration of various sacraments. On the urging of father and friends, Keble published it (anonymously), hoping, as he says in the Advertisement to the first edition, to bring the reader's 'thoughts and feelings into more entire unison with those recommended and exemplified in the Prayer Book', and to encourage 'a sober standard of feeling in matters of practical religion'. It attained phenomenal popularity, going through 109 editions by 1867. For Newman's characterization of the poems, see *Essays*, ii. 441–2. Froude's reaction improved on publication, but he first felt that Keble had not 'taken much pains to interest and guide the feeling of people who feel acutely' nor 'given much attention to that dreary visionary existence which they make themselves very uncomfortable by indulging in, and which I should have hoped it was the peculiar province of religious poetry to sober down into practical piety'. (*Remains*, i. 1. 184 and 219.)

29. 31 **the article of 'the Communion of Saints'** The Communion of Saints is part of the ninth article of the Apostles' Creed. Its meaning has been the subject of much dispute, but the traditional view is that it refers to the union in Christ of all the faithful, living and dead, who assist one another, especially by prayer. Anglican formularies forbade the direct invocation of saints in prayer, however, and Newman was careful to observe them. For the various interpretations of the article, see J. N. D. Kelly, *Early Christian Creeds* (London, 1950), pp. 388–97.

29. 34 **Berkeleyism** The philosophical system of Bishop George Berkeley (1685–1753), outlined especially in *A Treatise Concerning the Principles of Human Knowledge* (1710). Berkeley held that external objects exist only as they are perceived by a subject; that the world itself is an unsubstantial appearance held in existence by the perception of an Infinite Mind—or God— a system of signs by which He speaks to us. For Newman's views on Berkeley and idealism, see the passage from *Letters*, ii. 36 cited in note 23. 7.

30. 7 **the celebrated saying** Attributed to a common soldier before the battle of Blenheim. See the correspondence in *Notes and Queries*, clxxxvi (1944), 120 and 210.

30. 11–33. 15 **I considered that . . . and moreover** At this point the manuscript contains the following cancelled passage:

'This is a kind of philosophy, which Mr. Keble, and men like him, would never dream of deducing from the great Anglican philosophy. He would say with the whole Christian world that the notion of anything but an absolute assent to the being and attributes of the Almighty is an absurdity; yet at the same time, what, I say, would Mr. Keble insist on more than on the distinction of faith and demonstration? Yet what is this but to come round to the academic interpretation of Butler which I have just now been giving? for faith, because it is not demonstration, is thereby confessed to be an opinion, or a sentiment, and nothing more. And then again, it is almost too plain to prove, that Scripture does contrast faith and demonstration, as in the words, "Blessed are they who have not seen and yet have believed." How then can probability be the guide of life, or faith the root of religion, without running into that sort of semi-scepticism so natural to educated men? The theory which I hoped to maintain in order to meet this difficulty, was that absolute certitude may be the result of concurring and convergent probabilities. It requires a treatise to do justice to this view: there are great and obvious difficulties in maintaining it. I considered that certainty was *not* possible, but certitude *was*. Certitude was a state of mind, certainty the quality of a proposition. It was the law of our minds, or to speak more religiously, it was the will of our Creator, that probabilities which did not rise to logical certainty, should create mental certitude; that, though the mathematician demonstrated, and the philosopher or historian went by presumption and evidence, yet that the results of each process, though different when regarded as conclusions, might be the same when regarded as assents. It was the will of the Creator that in particular subject matters absolute beliefs should be the natural, the imperative effect of probabilities in reasoning. Even granting, for argument sake, that every subject matter was in itself capable of a scientific treatment; that the truths of natural theology, and that the evidence (not of course of the *matter*) of Revelation, might be proved by that rigid process which we use in physical astronomy or in philology; yet did our Creator mean the human family to wait for a thousand years hence, not to speak of the thousands of years past, before any member of it made a true act of devotion, a prayer, or a thanksgiving? Was all worship to be monopolized by the Angels who see His face? Impossible! Another mode of arriving at certitude must have been given to us.

'Accordingly, I considered that He, in His superintending providence, took man by man, each in his own way, a way which cannot be analysed or generalized by science, and supplied the means of certitude suitable to each; that He blessed and completed the probabilities afforded to each, giving in each case a perfection to a process in itself imperfect; that neither the means nor the measure of truth which fitted one man fitted another; that the object of religious certitude was ever truth and could not be falsehood, for it was effected under the guidance of the God of truth; but that it might be fuller truth or scantier; and that no man could judge his brother because he held less truth than he held himself, though he might condemn the falsehood whatever it might be which his brother mixed up with his measure of truth, and this because none of us know, how much of the "whole counsel of God" was intended for this individual man or that, or whether he had gone to the full in using those probabilities which led to that particular portion of truth, known only to the Creator which the Creator intended for him. Moreover as there were probabilities which led to certitude, so there were probabilities, which led only to opinion; and as there was a religious mode of arriving at certitude, so there was a religious mode of arriving at opinion; and as certitudes about particular objects might be the duty of particular individuals, so also the particular opinions might be their duty also. This is the doctrine which in one shape or other lies at the bottom of most of my University Sermons, of my Essay on Ecclesiastical Miracles, and of my Essay on Development of Doctrine.

'In these volumes I have supposed that the sort of Probability, which has the greatest influence in advancing us to religious beliefs, certain or probable, is antecedent:—presumption, as it may be called, or the likely, or *verisimile* as distinct from evidence. Here again many objections start up at once, and demand a broad answer: but I pass them over. My doctrine was that imperfect, half-beliefs, opinions in the instance of persons, who had the corresponding sufficient probabilities supplied to them, might be as much a duty as absolute faith might in other cases or to other men be a duty; moreover, that, even when it was not duty, it was allowable, as is seen daily in matters not religious, when men use their freedom in taking very different views from each other about reports which come to them of events or actions. Such fainter and less effectual probabilities, were either large principles, or particular evidence, which pointed towards conclusions which they did not reach. Moreover, it was plain that such half beliefs in religion were much more numerous than certitudes, and were imperative, or allowable, or idle, or superstitious, according to the particular case and the particular person. This was the region of private judgment in religion.

'Such doctrine led me at once to consider the ecclesiastical miracles in a new light, which I had not possessed when I wrote my Essay in 1825-6. That there had been already great miracles, as those of Scripture, as the Resurrection, was a fact establishing the principle that the laws of nature had sometimes been superseded by their Divine author; and, since what had happened once, might happen again, a certain vague probability attached to any report of Miracles wrought under conditions which might be fairly called more or less similar to those of Scripture: a probability greater or less, with greater or less claims upon our reception, leading to a pious belief, or a pious opinion, or a sufferance of the report, or on the other hand to a superstition. And again, as we must all be tolerant towards each other as regards our respective certitudes, so we must be tolerant too in the case of our mutual pious beliefs and opinions.

'I cannot tell when I first came to apply this mode of reasoning to the ecclesiastical miracles; it must be observed that what I had learned as a boy from Joseph Milner, seemed to defend the doctrine that such miraculous agency did continue beyond the age of the Apostles. Milner's doctrine is that, upon the visible Church, come from time to time, large and temporary effusions of divine grace. This is the leading idea of his work. He begins by speaking of the day of Pentecost, as marking "the first of those *effusions* of the Spirit of God, which from age to age have visited the earth", since the coming of Christ. Vol. i, p. 3. In a note he adds that "in the term Effusion there is not here included the idea of the miraculous or extraordinary operations of the Spirit of God"; but still, it was natural for me, going by analogy, not to be startled at the notion, that, as miracles accompanied the first effusion of grace, so they might accompany the later. It is a natural, and on the whole, a true anticipation (though of course there are exceptions in particular cases) that gifts and graces go together; now the Catholic doctrine mainly viewed the gift of miracles as the attendant and shadow of transcendent sanctity:' . . .

(Transcribed by H. T.)

30. 23 **an argument from Personality** Answering a question of Fr. H. J. Coleridge about the meaning of this remark, Newman wrote on June 24, 1864: '. . . I believe I must say that I allude to Keble's conversation more than to any thing that he wrote—or perhaps to such passages in the *Christian Year* as that to which I refer. He considered that religious truth came to us as from the mouth of our Lord; and what would be called doubt was an imperfect hearing, as if one heard from a distance. And as we were, at this time of the world at a distance from Him, of course we heard indistinctly, and faith was not a clear or confident knowledge or certainty, but a sort of loving guess. This after all is little more than *practical* certainty, and Bishop Butler seems to encourage it. Then my own theory (which I have since found is pretty much the same as Amort's) was intended to show how we could be *certain* on probabilities.' (From a copy in Birmingham Oratory Personal Collection.)

30. 26 **'I will guide thee . . .'** Ps. xxxii (Vulg. xxxi). 8, 9.

30. 33 **Poem for St. Bartholomew's Day**

> Eye of God's word! where'er we turn
> Ever upon us! thy keen gaze
> Can all the depths of sin discern,
> Unravel every bosom's maze.

See *The Christian Year* (2 vols. in 1, Oxford, 1827), p. 148.

30. 34 **Mr. Miller, of Worcester College** John Miller (1787–1858), Fellow of Worcester and a close friend of Keble, delivered the Bampton Lectures for 1817, *The Adaptation of Holy Scripture to the Real State of Human Nature*, and in 1820 wrote *A Christian Guide for Plain People*, both of which influenced Keble deeply. See J. T. Coleridge, *A Memoir of the Rev. John Keble* (Oxford and London, 1869), pp. 22–29.

30. 35 **Bampton Lectures** Eight lectures given at St. Mary's by an M.A. of Oxford or Cambridge as an 'exposition and defence of the Christian faith as expressed in the Creeds, on the authority of Scripture and the Fathers'. The series, endowed by the Revd. John Bampton (1690–1751), Canon of Salisbury, was delivered annually from 1780 to 1895, when it became biennial. (*O.D.C.C.*)

31. 4 **I made use of it myself** See *U.S.*, p. 193 and 236, *Dev.*, p. 328, and *D.A.*, p. 251.

32. 9 **my Essay in 1825–6** This essay, 'The Life of Apollonius Tyanaeus', and that of 1842 mentioned below, which was originally prefixed to a translation of Fleury's *Ecclesiastical History*, were combined in 1870 as *Two Essays on Biblical and on Ecclesiastical Miracles*. See *Apo.*, p. 264.

33. 26 **Hurrell Froude** Richard Hurrell Froude (1803–36) was the son of an archdeacon and brother of the historian James Anthony Froude, who wrote of him that he never saw anyone 'in whom the excellences of intellect and character were combined in fuller measure'. He was educated at Oriel, elected Fellow in 1826, made tutor in 1827, and ordained in 1829. He soon became Newman's closest friend, winning his sympathy for the ideas of Froude's master and good friend Keble and thus proving for a time the pivotal figure of the Oxford Movement.

Beneath the bold athlete and the explosive talker was a deeply religious ascetic who practised a rigid self-discipline. In 1831 he developed symptoms of tuberculosis and spent the winter of 1832–3 with Newman in southern Europe. He returned through France and came into contact with the party of Lammenais, Lacordaire, and Montalembert, then in the pages of *L'Avenir* leading the opposition to the Erastianizing Gallican Church. Through their influence, Christopher Dawson believes, he was probably led to the radical position he took in England, where he favoured the repeal of Praemunire and even Disestablishment, if necessary, to secure freedom of action for the church. Froude attended the Hadleigh conference of July 1833 which helped to launch the Tractarian Movement, but in November he was compelled to leave England once more for his health.

He remained in the West Indies till May 1835, lecturing for a time at Codrington College, Barbados. He kept in close touch with Newman, however, rallying his spirits and serving as a counterbalance to the more cautious temper represented especially by William Palmer of Worcester. He died in his home at Dartington on February 28, 1836. Newman's feelings may be gathered from the twelve lines he added to his poem 'The Separation of Friends' (*V.V.O.*, p. 196); from his letter to Bowden of March 2, 1836 (*Letters*, ii. 155–6); and perhaps especially from the moving lines he wrote in the back of his diary in 1837, when he was preparing Froude's *Remains* for publication, a farewell till the day when the character of Froude would be made known to all: 'Vale dilectissime, desideratissime, usque ad illum Diem qui te, paucissimis notum, omnibus patifaciet qui fueris.'

See Louise Imogen Guiney, *Hurrell Froude, Memoranda and Comments* (London, 1904); Newman's sketch prefaced to the first volume of the *Remains*; Christopher Dawson, *The Spirit of the Oxford Movement, passim*; R. W. Church, *The Oxford Movement* (London, 1891), pp. 50–56; Sister M. Regina, O.P., *Hurrell Froude*, an unpublished doctoral dissertation (Loyola University, Chicago, 1960); and Meriol Trevor, *Newman: The Pillar of the Cloud*, *passim*, esp. pp. 78–81, 88–89, and 178–82.

34. 18 **the maxim** William Chillingworth thus sums up his view of the essence of Protestantism in a once famous controversial work, *The Religion of Protestants a Safe Way to Salvation* (1638). Chillingworth himself was not a literalist in his interpretation of Scripture, however, but a High Churchman

whose remark has been remembered apart from its context and therefore commonly misunderstood. See *Anglicanism. The Thought and Practice of the Church of England, Illustrated from the Religious Literature of the Seventeenth Century*: compiled and edited by Paul Elmer More and Frank Leslie Cross (London, 1935), pp. 103–13.

34. 28 **the Real Presence** i.e. of Christ in the Eucharist, since the Reformation considered by and large in England a symbolic commemoration of the Last Supper, the Presence when admitted being regarded as a spiritual presence in the heart of the believer rather than an actual presence in the sacrament itself. Though individual Anglicans of the Caroline tradition retained the ancient belief, without accepting what they, like Newman himself as an Anglican, considered the unwarranted Roman Catholic doctrine of transubstantiation (see *Apo.*, p. 174), it was commonly associated only with Rome. In 1843 Pusey was suspended from preaching for two years for upholding the doctrine in a university sermon. As the Anglo-Catholic party grew stronger, however, its acceptance became more common and is today widespread. For Newman's exposition and defence of Froude's view, written in 1838 to answer an attack on the *Remains* by the Revd. Godfrey Faussett, Lady Margaret Professor of Divinity, see *V.M.* ii. 222–51. The notes Newman added for the new edition of his works give also a succinct presentation of the doctrine as held in the Roman Church.

34. 38 **Ecumenical Councils** Meetings of bishops representing the whole Christian world. In the Church of England the decisions of the first four councils have been generally accepted: (1) Nicaea i. 325; (2) Constantinople i. 381; (3) Ephesus, 431; (4) Chalcedon, 451. According to Article XXI of the Thirty-nine Articles, however, General Councils 'may err, and sometimes have erred, even in things pertaining unto God. Wherefore things ordained by them as necessary to salvation have neither strength nor authority, unless it may be declared that they be taken out of Holy Scripture.' The Orthodox Church accepts the first seven councils as ecumenical; and the Roman Catholic, which holds that such meetings must be called by or with the approval of the Pope, recognizes twenty-one such councils.

35. 22 **liberalism** See Note A, *Apo.*, pp. 254 ff., especially the series of propositions pp. 260–2. See also pp. 233–4 for the development of the word in Newman's lifetime till it had become synonymous with the 'deep, plausible scepticism' of the 'educated lay world'.

35. 23 **the Fathers** A term rather elastic in scope, but in general those theologians of the first six centuries after Christ who, by their writings and their holy lives, took a leading part in developing and maintaining orthodox Christian belief: e.g. Clement of Rome, Ignatius of Antioch, etc. They, too, were popularly associated with Roman Catholicism, or at least with a Christianity being gradually corrupted; and for a variety of reasons they were disregarded or even ridiculed by sceptics and latitudinarians, Whately among them. Thus, in spite of the precedent they had in many great Anglican divines, the tendency of the Tractarians to regard the Fathers as the authoritative

exponents of Christian doctrine was derided or feared in rationalist and strongly Protestant circles.

His own family found Newman's interest somewhat puzzling. In 1826 Jemima Newman could write to her brother: 'Mary desires her love, and begs that the next time you write you will be so kind as to enlighten her on the uses of reading the Fathers.' (*Letters*, i. 119.) For the chronology and results of Newman's reading of the Fathers, see *Diff*. i. 370–4: '. . . the writings of the Fathers, so far from prejudicing at least one man against the modern Catholic Church, have been simply and solely the one intellectual cause of his having renounced the religion in which he was born and submitted himself to her.' (p. 367.)

35. 25 **beginning with St. Ignatius and St. Justin** But his Diary for June 23, 1828, reads: 'began the Patres Apostolici with Barnabas.' (Barnabas was a missionary companion of St. Paul, the epistle attributed to him being classed among the pseudepigrapha.)

Of the life of St. Ignatius little is known for certain. However, he was bishop of the important church of Antioch, was condemned, sent to Rome, and martyred during the reign of Trajan (98–117). During his journey he wrote seven epistles to various churches which are a major source of our knowledge of early Christian doctrine and episcopal organization. See *G.A.*, pp. 478–80, and 'The Theology of the Seven Epistles of St. Ignatius', *Essays*, i. 222–62.

St. Justin Martyr (*c.* 105–*c.* 163), Platonic philosopher and convert, was born in Palestine and martyred at Rome. He is the first important Christian apologist, eager to defend Christians from charges made against them in the days of Antoninus Pius and Marcus Aurelius and to show that Christianity deserved the attention of the cultivated pagan (First and Second *Apology*) and of the Jew (*Dialogue with Tryphon the Jew*).

35. 26 **a proposal was made** See *Letters*, i. 210–11. Newman undertook a history of the councils on the understanding that it was to be introductory to a work on the Articles which he had projected.

35. 26 **Hugh Rose . . . with Mr. Lyall** For Rose, see p. 44 and editor's note. William Rowe Lyall (1788–1857) took his B.A. degree at Cambridge in 1810, conducted the *British Critic* during 1816–17, and reorganized the *Encyclopaedia Metropolitana* in 1820. He wrote several works on Scripture and from 1832 to 1846 edited, with Rose, fourteen volumes of the Theological Library Newman refers to. In 1845 he became Dean of Canterbury.

35. 33 **at last appeared** *The Arians of the Fourth Century*, published November 5, 1833, advanced what was then a novel thesis: that the origins of the Arian heresy were at Antioch rather than Alexandria and in Aristotelian rather than Platonic philosophy. At the same time Newman undoubtedly saw a parallel between the Alexandrian church then and the Anglican church of his own day. See Brilioth, *The Anglican Revival*, p. 116.

35. 34 **of its 422 pages** First edition. 117 is apparently a misprint for 217. Newman grew dissatisfied with the book, which he said hit 'no mark at all'.

(Ward, *Life*, ii. 576.) However, the German ecclesiastical historian Döllinger thought it 'a model in its kind' (ibid. i. 444); and as Bouyer has said, the many citations from the ancient writers are 'carefully digested and deeply pondered', with Newman's faith in an ever living Catholic Church informing the whole, a faith he would now try to reinfuse into Anglicanism. (*Newman*, p. 162.)

36. 3 **the works of Bishop Bull** Newman read the *Defensio Fidei Nicaenae* in the summer of 1831 and the *Harmonia Apostolica* in that of 1835. See *Diff*. i. 372.

36. 7 **the great Church of Alexandria** With its Greek, Egyptian, and Jewish population, Alexandria was highly syncretic in its intellectual tendencies. Its principal schools were neo-Platonic, eclectic, and Christian. During the early third century, under the leadership of men like Pantaenus, Clement, Origen, and Dionysius, the Christian school became the foremost of its kind in the world. It was notably successful in appealing to and converting educated unbelievers. The catholicity of its Christian humanism had a great appeal for Newman, but he dissociated himself from its theological doctrine, which led to heretical views on such questions as the nature of Christ (Origen apparently subordinating the Son to the Father), the pre-existence of souls, and the final redemption of those in hell. During the fourth century the catechetical school declined and disappeared. For the view that the 'school' had a briefer and less formal existence than heretofore believed, see F. L. Cross, *Early Christian Fathers* (London, 1960), pp. 116–34. See also *Arians*, pp. 39–99.

36. 10 **Athanasius** (296–373) attended the Council of Nicaea in 325 as the secretary of the Bishop of Alexandria and himself became bishop in 328, vigorously upholding the divinity of Christ against the Arians and fighting for the acceptance of the Nicene Creed. Seventeen of the forty-six years of his episcopate were spent in exile, thanks principally to the friends of Arius. Devoted to the mysteries of the Trinity and the Incarnation, he 'impressed an image on the Church, which, through God's mercy, shall not be effaced while time lasts'. (*U.S.*, p. 97.) For Athanasius, known as the 'Father of Orthodoxy', Newman had a very special regard. To the Library of the Fathers he contributed a translation of *Select Treatises of S. Athanasius . . . in Controversy with the Arians* (2 vols., 1842, 1844), with a series of learned and valuable notes. A revised edition, with the notes in alphabetical order as a kind of theological glossary, appeared in 1881. See also Newman's 'Causes of the Rise and Successes of Arianism', in *Tracts Theological and Historical*.

36. 12 **Dionysius,** Bishop of Alexandria from 248 to 265, was the successor of Heraclas, who was long thought to have followed Origen as head of the catechetical school. See *Letters*, ii. 44 and 54.

36. 15 **I have drawn out some features of it** See *Arians*, pp. 49–99, where he discusses (1) the Disciplina Arcani; (2) the allegorical method; (3) the economy; (4) the dispensation of paganism; and (5) the influence of Platonism.

36. 17 **Some portions of their teaching** For Newman's debt to the Alexandrians and a documentation from original sources of the following remarks, see Charles F. Harrold, 'Newman and the Alexandrian Platonists', *Modern Philology*, xxxvii (1939–40), 279–91.

36. 28 **'thoughts beyond their thought . . .'** See No. XXVII, 'Third Sunday in Lent', in Keble's *Christian Year*:

> 'As little children lisp, and tell of Heaven,
> So thoughts beyond their thought to those high Bards were given.'

37. 3 **'at sundry times . . .'** Heb. i. 1, 2 (Douay):

> 'God, who, at sundry times and in divers manners, spoke in times past to the fathers by the prophets, last of all,
> 'In these days hath spoken to us by his Son. . . .'

37. 22 **carrying on . . . the Economy of the Visible World** See *P.S.* ii. 358–68; *P.S.* iv. 200–13; and *Sermon Notes*, p. 166.

37. 29 **'Every breath of air . . .'** *P.S.* ii. 362.

38. 6 **the Three Holy Children** Shadrach, Meschach, and Abednego, cast into a fiery furnace by the King of Babylon but saved by an angel who drove out the flame. See Dan. iii.

38. 12 **races, nations, and classes of men** See *Sermons on the Subjects of the Day*, pp. 82–84, and *Idea*, p. 308.

38. 19 **the Prince of Persia** Dan. x. 13. Interpreted by such Fathers as Jerome and Chrysostom as being the Guardian Angel of the realm—like Michael, the protector of Israel and of the Church. According to Fr. Tristram, Newman, in assigning such beings to a 'middle race', deviated from the traditional view, which held that every race was committed to the care of a particular angel.

38. 22 **'the Angels of the Seven Churches'** The Churches to which St. John was writing. See Apoc. i. 9–20. 'The Greek Fathers saw in them the heavenly guardians of the Churches; the Latin Fathers, including S. Augustine, identified them with the Bishops, or the *presbyterium*, as a body. Both views lie open to objection. A modern view is that the Angel stood for the spirit or "character", to use Newman's word, of the Church personified.' (H. T.)

38. 24 **Samuel Francis Wood** (1810–43), younger brother of Sir Charles Wood, first Viscount Halifax, was a pupil of Newman at Oriel. He was an ardent Tractarian, and Newman felt his early death as a great loss. See *Letters*, ii. 369.

38. 26 **The mass of the Fathers** For extensive documentation from the works of the Fathers Newman cites, see G. Bareille, 'Angélologie d'apres les Pères', *Dictionnaire de Théologie Catholique*, i, cols. 1192–1222, esp. cols. 1195–6; and C. Dodgson's edition of Tertullian's *Apologetic and Practical Treatises* in Pusey's Library of the Fathers (Oxford, 1842), p. 54, note c.

38. 28 the Angels fell before the deluge Gen. vi. 2. 'The accepted reading here is not angels, but sons of God, as in Douay version, A.V., R.V. They were identified with the children of Enos, son of Seth, son of Adam; and it was explained that this title was given them on account of their piety, their father being the first "to call upon the name of the Lord" (Gen. iv. 26); whereas the descendants of Cain are described as the daughters of men.

'But as Newman says, there is a very strong patristic tradition that the sons of God were angels; and in fact several codices of the Septuagint actually bore the reading "the angels of God". This is now the generally accepted interpretation, since it is natural to expect a race of demigods as the result of the union of spiritual with human beings, whereas the mere intermixture of races could not be supposed to have such an outcome. Newman's "idea" seems to be curiously in line with this explanation, for the text of Genesis does not suggest that these demigods, "the mighty men of old, men of renown" (Gen. vi. 4) were creatures of unmixed wickedness.' (H. T.)

38. 36 John Bull For Newman on the English character, see especially 'Who's to Blame', in *D.A.*, pp. 306–62.

39. 7 'Hippoclides doesn't care' A proverbial expression in classical times from Herodotus (vi. 126–9), who tells how Clisthenes, tyrant of Sicyon, refused the hand of his daughter to Hippoclides, the suitor he had hitherto favoured, when that young man brought to a climax his extraordinary behaviour at the pre-nuptial party by standing on his head and using his legs for arms. 'You have danced away your wife', he was told, and immediately replied, 'Hippoclides doesn't care.'

39. 14 my remarks See *Arians*, pp. 71–74, and *Apo.*, Note F, p. 299. The manuscript contains a lengthy cancelled passage on the Economy, the substance of which is in Note F.

39. 21 a Revolution in France July 27–29, 1830, when Charles X, last of the Bourbons, after proclaiming a series of repressive ordinances, was dethroned in favour of the 'Citizen King', Louis Philippe. For Newman it meant 'the triumph of irreligion. . . . The effect of this miserable French affair will be great in England.' See letter to Froude of July 28, 1830, *Letters*, i. 204–5.

39. 22 I held that it was unchristian Newman's early political thought is a blend of the conservatism of Burke, which dominated Oxford, with the Non-juring principle taught in the Anglican Homily on Wilful Disobedience (1569) that 'rebellion of subjects against their prince was in every conceivable instance a grievous sin'. (*Dictionary of English Church History*.) How his attitude was liberalized by experience and necessity is recounted by Alvan S. Ryan, 'The Development of Newman's Political Thought', *The Review of Politics*, vii (1945), 210–40. See also Terence Kenny, *The Political Thought of John Henry Newman* (London, 1957).

39. 26 Lord Grey had told the Bishops Earl Grey and the Whigs came to power in November 1830, and finally managed to carry through the Great Reform Bill in June 1832. By continuing to side with the Tory opposition in the House of Lords, the bishops had alienated public opinion; but they were fearful—those who were not mere party men—of the kind of church reform sure to follow in the wake of the Bill. A commission had already been appointed to inquire into such ecclesiastical abuses as pluralism, nepotism, etc. Men like Palmer, Rose, Newman, and Keble feared that a reformed Parliament, including Radicals, Dissenters, and Roman Catholics, would act without regard for the welfare of the Church of England as part of the Church Catholic. (*Letters*, i. 208–9.)

But Lord Grey had not actually 'told the Bishops to set their house in order'. On October 3, 1831, on moving the second reading of the Reform Bill, he appealed to them not to vote against it. He took note of the Bill against pluralities already introduced by the Primate as showing 'prudent forethought', adding that the prelates 'appear to have felt . . . that it is necessary for them to set their house in order, and prepare to meet the coming storm'. But the bishops voted against the Bill by twenty-one votes to two, Grey's words were repeated in a garbled fashion, and his supposed injunction to the bishops to 'set their house in order' became a watchword of a campaign of abuse against various bishops in the following autumn. See G. M. Trevelyan, *Lord Grey of the Reform Bill* (London, 1920), pp. 306–8.

On the need for reform, see Elie Halévy, *A History of the English People in 1815* (London, 1924), pp. 342–52; and S. C. Carpenter, *Church and People, 1789–1889* (London, 1933), chaps. iii and iv. On the insulting of bishops, see Carpenter, pp. 58 and 94, and Trevelyan, pp. 316–17.

39. 33 **Blomfield** Charles James Blomfield (1786–1857), Fellow of Trinity College, Cambridge, was Bishop of London from 1828 to 1856. He was an active supporter of church reform and a great builder of churches, but proved somewhat inconsistent in his theological positions. He gave no support to the Tractarians and later became hostile, especially to the ritual movement.

40. 4 **belief in the Apostolical succession had gone out** But as Newman himself wrote in 1868, 'The Apostolical Succession, its necessity, and its grace, is not an Anglican tradition, though it is a tradition found in the Anglican Church. By contrast, our Lord's divinity *is* an Anglican tradition—every one, high and low, holds it.' (*Essays*, ii. 109–10.)

40. 5 **Non-jurors** Eight bishops, 400 clergy, and a small number of the laity who refused the oath of allegiance to William and Mary in 1689 because they felt themselves bound in conscience by their oath to James II, towards whom they adopted the traditional Anglican attitude of passive obedience rather than rebellion. Maintaining the Catholic tradition of the Caroline divines and fearful that a proposed Bill of Comprehension would destroy the succession, the clergy (including such famous names as Archbishop Sancroft and Bishop Ken) ignored the Government, consecrated their own successors until 1741, and thus perpetuated a line that finally died out in the early nineteenth century. They were the precursors of the Tractarians, who greatly admired their religious seriousness, devotion to principle, and anti-Erastian policy. At the same time, by their withdrawal from public life, they eased the way for the latitudinarianism which dominated the Church of England in the eighteenth century. See *H.S.* iii. 378, and *Diff.* i. 220–4.

40. 6 the Evangelical party ... seemed to have lost See Church, *The Oxford Movement*, pp. 11–14, and J. H. Overton, *The English Church in the Nineteenth Century (1800–1833)*, London, 1894, pp. 92–104. On the Evangelical movement in general, see Ford K. Brown, *Fathers of the Victorians* (Cambridge, 1961).

40. 9 Ryder Henry Dudley Ryder (1777–1836) became Bishop of Lichfield in 1824. After first opposing the Evangelicals, he openly espoused their cause in 1811 and, as Bishop of Gloucester in 1815, was the first Evangelical raised to the episcopate. He won a high reputation for holiness and zeal. One of his ten sons, George Dudley Ryder, was a pupil of Newman at Oriel and was received into the Roman Church with his wife and two sons in 1846. See *Apo.*, p. 252, and J. H. Overton, *The English Church in the Nineteenth Century (1800–1833)*, p. 90.

40. 17 that Primeval Mystery the doctrine of the Trinity.

40. 19 'Incessu patuit Dea.' The goddess was revealed in her step. (*Aeneid* i. 405.)

40. 22 'Look on this picture. . . .' Hamlet, III. iv. 53.

41. 6 Verses which are in the Lyra The *Lyra Apostolica* is a collection of 179 poems, of which 109 are by Newman, the rest by Keble (46), Isaac Williams (9), Hurrell Froude (8), J. W. Bowden (6), and R. I. Wilberforce (1). They appeared first in the *British Magazine* between June 1, 1833, and September 1, 1836, and were published in a small volume toward the end of 1836. Most of Newman's poems were subsequently reprinted in *V.V.O.* See *Apo.*, Note A, p. 262.

41. 13 verses about my Guardian Angel 'Angelic Guidance', December 3, 1832. *V.V.O.*, p. 73. For this stage of the journey, see *Letters*, i. 248–50.

41. 25 the Dean of Malta The bishop at that time was F. X. Caruana, appointed 1831, who, it would seem, was also Dean. (H. T.) See *Letters*, i. 295.

41. 27 Abbate Santini Fortunato Santini (1778–1862), composer and eminent authority on church music, of which he had a great collection. A friend of Mendelssohn, he did much to make German music known in Italy. See *Grove's Dictionary of Music and Musicians*, 5th edition, ed. Eric Blom (London, 1954), p. 404; and *Letters and Diaries*, xii (1962), 130.

41. 28 Monsignore (now Cardinal) Wiseman Nicholas Wiseman (1802–65), who was to play so large a part in Newman's life, won early renown as a linguist, theologian, and Roman Catholic controversialist. Of Spanish-Irish parentage, he was born at Seville and educated in England and Rome, where he was ordained in 1825. In 1828 he became rector of the newly reconstituted English College for theological students, entertaining there many celebrated visitors. He returned permanently to England in 1840 and decisively influenced Newman by an article in the *Dublin Review* (*Apo.*, pp. 109–11), a quarterly he had founded in 1836.

In 1850 Pius IX made him a cardinal and first Archbishop of Westminster in the newly organized English Catholic hierarchy. See Wilfrid Ward, *The Life and Times of Cardinal Wiseman* (2 vols., London, 1900); and Brian Fothergill, *Nicholas Wiseman* (London, 1963). Whatever its accuracy as a portrait, Browning's 'Bishop Blougram's Apology' is thought to have been written with Wiseman in mind.

The calls on Froude and Newman were made April 3 and 6, 1833, 'to find out whether they would take us in on any terms to which we could twist our consciences, and we found to our dismay that not one step could be gained without swallowing the Council of Trent as a whole . . . I own it has altogether changed my notions of the Roman Catholics, and made me wish for the total overthrow of their system. I think that the only τόπος now is "the ancient Church of England", and as an explanation of what one means, "Charles the First and the Nonjurors" '. See Froude's *Remains*, i. 1, 306–8, including Newman's comment on this passage; and E. A. Knox, *The Tractarian Movement, 1833–1845* (London, 1933), pp. 102–9, for the view that the visits were more significant than Newman has indicated.

41. 31 I do not recollect . . . other ecclesiastics In the margin of a copy of the *Apologia*, according to Fr. Tristram, Newman has written, 'This is not literally correct.' In a letter to his mother dated April 5, 1833 (*Letters*, i. 332–3), he says that 'we have fallen in, more or less, with a number of interesting Irish and English priests. I regret that we could form no intimate acquaintance with them.'

41. 34 Tenebrae, at the Sestine i.e. the Sistine Chapel. Tenebrae (L., *darkness*) was the public chanting on Wednesday, Thursday, and Friday evening of Holy Week of the Matins and Lauds for the Divine Office of the following days. This was accompanied by the gradual extinction of candles— hence the name of the service, which was especially known for the mournful chanting of the Lamentations of the Prophet Jeremias and of the fourth penitential psalm (Vulg., Ps. l), the Miserere. See *Letters*, i. 334. The public service was eliminated in recent reforms of the Roman Catholic Easter Liturgy.

42. 3 The Bill for the Suppression of the Irish Sees The various provisions of this 'act to alter and amend the laws relating to the temporalities of the Church in Ireland' included a graduated tax on clerical incomes above £200 a year, the proceeds to be used for the upkeep of churches, thus relieving the mostly Catholic ratepayers from the obnoxious 'vestry cess'; and the gradual extinction of two out of four Irish archbishoprics and eight out of eighteen bishoprics. Dioceses were to be consolidated rather than actually suppressed. Some peers like Bishop Blomfield and the Duke of Wellington supported the Bill reluctantly as the lesser of two evils, but others like the Duke of Cumberland and Bishop Philpotts of Exeter charged that it was contrary to the coronation oath. It was carried in August 1833, and widely regarded by the High Church group as another major step in an offensive against the Establishment, particularly because it at one time included an appropriation clause whereby some £60,000 a year of expected surplus revenue could be applied by Parliament to whatever use it chose. In 1854 Newman referred to the Irish Sees as 'mere pieces of patronage and occasions for jobbing'. (*H.S.* iii. 69.) See George C. Brodrick and J. K. Fotheringham, *The History of England (1801–1837)* (London, 1906), pp. 322–5; and Overton, *The English Church in the Nineteenth Century*, pp. 320–1.

42. 12 **Whitehall preacherships** The Banqueting House of Inigo Jones survived a fire which destroyed the royal palace at Whitehall in the reign of William III. It was converted into a chapel, and George III established there a series of preacherships under the supervision of the Bishop of London as Dean of the Royal Chapels. Newman preached there several times in 1828. In *Letters*, i. 164, he thus comments on the entry of July 25, 1828, in his 'Notes': 'Sent letter to the Bishop of London (Howley) accepting Whitehall preachership.'

'[N.B. This is quite consistent with what is said in my "Apologia". At this time there were twelve preachers from each University. I agreed to be one of these, but when Blomfield soon after became Bishop of London he turned all twenty-four out, and began a plan of one (or two?) from each University, and it was one of these (preacherships) which he sounded me about, and which I conditionally accepted.]' For Newman's ironic letter declining the appointment if it were actually offered, see *Letters*, i. 252.

42. 13 **indignant at the line which he was taking** *Apo.*, pp. 39–40. The original manuscript reading of the present sentence is: 'As I was sea sick on the Steamer, I sent a letter home, containing my refusal of the place of Whitehall Preacher, which I had reason to believe the Bishop of London would offer me, from indignation at the line he was taking.'

42. 16 **Dr. Arnold** Thomas Arnold (1795–1842), the famous headmaster of Rugby and father of Matthew Arnold. An Oriel Noetic who was later to attack the Tractarians in an *Edinburgh Review* article of 1836 (called by the editor 'The Oxford Malignants'), he disbelieved in the supernatural foundation and character of the Church, but wished to preserve what he considered the essence of Christian revelation. In 1833 he aroused great opposition by his pamphlet, *Principles of Church Reform*, a kind of liberalized version of Hooker in which the Establishment was to be made truly national by admitting all groups except Jews, Roman Catholics, and Quakers. (See Carpenter, *Church and People*, pp. 60–67.) For Arnold's reasons, see A. P. Stanley, *The Life and Correspondence of Thomas Arnold, D.D.*, 4th ed. (2 vols., London, 1845), ii. 352–75, *passim*. For Newman's ironical comments, written at Rome, on Arnold's scheme, see *Letters*, i. 329; also i. 332, and ii. 42.

42. 20 **'But is *he* a Christian?'** See Arnold Whitridge, *Dr. Arnold of Rugby* (London, 1928), p. 170 n. Newman later explained this remark as merely indicating dissent from Arnold's approximation to the sceptical views on the Old Testament of the historian Niebuhr; but in one of his Roman letters he characterized what he had heard of the contents of Arnold's pamphlet on church reform as 'atrocious'. (*Letters*, i. 332.)

42. 25 **It was at Rome, too, that we began the Lyra** Isaac Williams (*Autobiography*, pp. 57–65) has a different account, implying that Newman

was something of a late-comer to the project who insisted on being manager. But this cannot be reconciled with Newman's letter to H. J. Rose of March 16, 1833, in J. W. Burgon's *Lives of Twelve Good Men*, i. 171–2. See also i. 167.

42. 28 **M. Bunsen** Baron Christian C. J. Bunsen (1791–1860), German scholar and diplomat, well versed in the Fathers and theological questions in general, represented Prussia at the Holy See from 1823 to 1839. He proved especially helpful to visiting Englishmen. In 1841 he was sent to London as minister plenipotentiary and envoy extraordinary of Frederick William IV, playing a leading part in the establishment of the Anglo-Prussian bishopric at Jerusalem, which was intended to serve as a basis for a larger union between the German Evangelical and Anglican churches. For its decisive effect on Newman, see *Apo.*, pp. 131–6.

42. 30 **'You shall know the difference . . .'** A rather vigorous translation of the *Iliad* xviii. 125.

42. 33 **deliverance is wrought, not by the many** A Calvinistic sense of the small number but great importance of the elect (see *Apo.*, pp. 47–48) is an obvious link between Newman and the Victorian prophet of religion without theology, Carlyle. For even deeper ones, as well as the significant differences, see Jefferson B. Fletcher, 'Newman and Carlyle: an Unrecognized Affinity', *Atlantic Monthly*, xcv (1905), 669–79; and Henry Tristram, 'Two Leaders: Newman and Carlyle', *The Cornhill Magazine*, N.S. lxv (1928), 367–82.

Newman tried to steer a middle course between personal 'influence' and 'discipline' or organization. See 'Rise and Progress of Universities', *H.S.* iii. 60–76. His Christian social sense kept him from the excesses which overtook Carlyle's individualism. See Werner Stark, 'The Social Philosopher', *Newman Centenary Essays*, pp. 155–77.

42. 36 **'Exoriare aliquis!'** *Exoriare aliquis nostris ex ossibus ultor*: May some avenger arise from my dead bones! (*Aeneid* iv. 625.) The words of Dido asking vengeance for the desertion of Aeneas.

42. 37 **Thalaba** Newman once called Robert Southey's *Thalaba the Destroyer* (1801) 'the most sublime of English poems—I don't know Spenser— I mean morally sublime'. (*Essays*, i. 16.) It is the tale of a young Arab who sets out to avenge his father, murdered by the powers of evil who were really seeking Thalaba himself, their destined conqueror. With single-minded devotion to God and His Prophet and with the aid of the talisman Faith, he eludes the snares of the devils and finally reaches their abode. With his father's sword, he destroys them. The poem abounds in passages certain to appeal to a person of Newman's temperament:

> 'Son of Hodeirah, thou art chosen forth
> To do the will of heaven;
> To avenge thy Father's death,
> The murder of thy race,
> To work the mightiest enterprize

That mortal man hath wrought.
Live! and remember Destiny
Hath marked thee from mankind!'
(1801 ed., i. 62–63.)

According to Newman's Oratorian colleague, Fr. Ignatius Dudley Ryder, *Thalaba* was Newman's 'picture of what he trusted the Movement and his share in the Movement would have been'. (Ward, *Life*, ii. 355.) Newman's own account of *Thalaba* may be found in the transcribed notes of an 1849 lecture 'On the Characteristics of True Poetry', reprinted in Tardivel, *La Personnalité Littéraire*, pp. 387–92, from *The Tablet* of July 21, 1849.

43. 2 sentences of my letters to my friends In a letter of June 8, 1844, he said to Keble: '. . . from Rome I wrote to some one, I think Christie, saying I thought I was to be made something of in His Hands, though, if not, the happier for me.' (*Corr.*, p. 315; cf. *Letters*, i. 163.)

43. 5 I said with great gravity But see *Letters*, i. 376: 'This, indeed, I had said to Dr. Wiseman at Rome, but though sincerely said, the words were not pointedly said; but in answer to the question how long we stayed there, I said that we had work at home. I wish I could see my letter to Christie; I must ask him for it.' It seems clear that Newman is heightening or shaping the past somewhat in the light of his later history.

43. 8 a fever at Leonforte Newman had returned to Sicily on April 19 against the advice of the Froudes instead of going back with them to England. He came to regard the illness which struck him on May 2 as a punishment for wilfulness and one of the great crises of his life. He often discussed it with others and wrote a detailed account of it containing some of his most vivid description and mordant self-analysis. For the complete version of this document (Miss Mozley omitted some of the franker passages in her edition of the *Letters*), see *A.W.*, pp. 121–38.

After his illness, surrender to God's will, as expressed in his famous 'Lead, Kindly Light', became the foundation of his spirituality. In preparing notes for Newman's future biographer, the Oratorian Fr. Ignatius Ryder singled out as a dominant characteristic '*his passivity*, making no attempt to fashion the course of his life, but waiting on Providence'. See Henry Tristram, 'With Newman at Prayer', *Newman Centenary Essays*, p. 105; Bouyer, *Newman*, pp. 139–50; and Culler, *The Imperial Intellect*, pp. 85–87.

43. 9 my last directions To notify Froude. *A.W.*, p. 127.

43. 10 I repeated, '. . . I have not sinned' Another example of a histrionic heightening in memory. See the various accounts in *Letters*, i. 358; i. 367 (*A.W.*, p. 127); and *Corr.*, p. 315.

43. 11 I never have been able quite to make out what I meant. Newman had by then perhaps forgotten what he had written to Froude on September 10, 1830, in the aftermath of the July Revolution in France: 'As to the present times I have found several parallels for them in the world's history. My best is the Ante-diluvian times—which were an exhibition of intellectual infidelity in its functions of indifferentism and concession, a union of the Church and the world—a sin against light—vid. Gen. vi. 2 Matt. xxiv. 38–41—Jude 3, 14 &c.' (MS. R. H. Froude Letters, Birmingham Oratory.)

43. 22 **I knew nothing of the Presence of the Blessed Sacrament there** This and a similar remark about his inability to recognize the Mass (*Apo.*, p. 58) are difficult to understand. It is true that Catholicism was by Newman's day little known in England; yet Newman had read widely, was especially interested in religious subjects, had opportunities for frequent conversation with a former priest like Blanco White, and had visited churches in Rome.

43. 34 **Assize Sermon** The arrival of the assizes in a town was attended with great ceremony, including a service at the principal church. Keble was named by the Vice-Chancellor as preacher for the summer assizes at Oxford in 1833; and on Sunday, July 14, with the impending Irish church reform in mind, he preached his sermon. See Church, *Oxford Movement*, pp. 82–83.

According to a letter of Froude to J. F. Christie, July 22, 1833, 'Keble has been preaching such a Sermon on National Apostacy [*sic*] before the Judges one of whom was a Socinian. It is in the press now, & will be out in a day or two. He calls the Ministers Libertines & the Parliament Erastians, & implies that the Bps are such a set that he hardly knows whether we ought to remain in communion with them: he does [not] say this last, but only implies it, so don't quote him for it. . . . I am going to Rose in an hour or two to concert measures. . . .' (R. H. Froude Letters, Birmingham Oratory.)

43. 35 **I have ever considered and kept the day, as the start of the religious movement of 1833.** See *Letters*, i. 380, and *Corr.*, p. 316, indicating that Newman held to this idea at least as early as the sermon's publication about ten days later; and the letter quoted in note 43. 34 seems to imply that Froude felt the same way. However, others did not attach such significance to the sermon at the time. See F. L. Cross, *John Henry Newman* (London, 1933), Appendix IV, 'The Myth of July 14, 1833', pp. 162–3.

44. 24 **William Palmer of Dublin** (1803–85) was a learned theologian and controversialist who opposed Dissent, Arnoldian liberalism, and Roman Catholicism. After taking his B.A. degree at Trinity College, Dublin, in 1824, he became a clergyman and went to Oxford, where he took an M.A. in 1829 and became a Fellow of Worcester College in 1831. His writings on English and primitive liturgies brought him into contact with Keble, Rose, and Froude; but he was wary of the Tractarian group almost from the start, preferring to defend the Establishment by the cautious petitions of the Association of Friends of the Church, which resulted from the meeting of Rose, Froude, Perceval, and Palmer on July 25, 1833. His most important book was his *Treatise on the Church of Christ* (2 vols., 1838), expounding the 'Branch Theory' that the Church of England was a member co-ordinate with the Greek and Roman Churches of the one Church Catholic. For Newman's reactions, see *Essays*, i. 179–221, and ii. 454–5.

The conservative Palmer took alarm at the vigorous approach of the early Tracts and contributed only part of one (no. 15) himself, but he was unsuccessful in an attempt to have them stopped or censored by the leaders. He later defended Newman in the affair of Tract 90; but he was convinced that the younger Tractarians, led by W. G. Ward and Frederick Oakeley, who in the early forties propagated their views in the *British Critic*, were heading straight for Rome. Accordingly, in 1843, he published his *Narrative of Events connected with the Publication of Tracts for the Times*, attacking the Ward group and, by calling forth Ward's frankly pro-Roman *Ideal of a Christian Church* in 1844, bringing the Oxford Movement to a crisis in 1845. Enlarged in 1883, Palmer's *Narrative* remains an important source for the early history of the Movement. See J. M. Rigg, 'William Palmer', *D.N.B.* xv (1909), 168–70.

44. 25 **William Palmer of Magdalen** (1811–79) was a theologian and student of ecclesiastical history and archaeology. A Fellow and tutor at Magdalen College, he defended Tract 90 and attacked the plan for an Anglican bishopric at Jerusalem. In 1840 and 1841 he visited Russia to secure the rights of Anglicans to intercommunion, but failed, the Russian Church rejecting the Anglican claim to Catholicity. He continued his attempts to enter the Orthodox Church, especially after the Gorham judgement of 1850, but refused to be unconditionally rebaptized. He later went to Rome and was received into the Roman Catholic Church in 1855, living in Rome for the rest of his life. After his death, Newman, his close friend, edited his *Notes of a Visit to the Russian Church in the Years 1840, 1841*. See Maisie Ward, *Young Mr. Newman*, pp. 377–9.

44. 26 **Arthur Perceval** (1799–1853), educated at Oriel and then Fellow of All Souls, became rector of East Horsley in Surrey in 1824 and chaplain to George IV in 1826, continuing as chaplain to William IV and Victoria. Bishop Blomfield of London at one time attempted to shield the queen from hearing Perceval's High Church views; and according to the *O.D.C.C.*, Queen Victoria deprived him of his chaplaincy because of his opposition to the Gorham judgement. To Perceval, it was Rome and not the Church of England which was in schism. In 1841 he published a defence of Newman against the attacks on Tract 90, and in 1842 his *Collection of Papers connected with the Theological Movement of 1833*. In an appendix to the 1866 French edition of the *Apologia*, classifying the writers named in his work, Newman lists Rose, Hook (p. 88), and Perceval with the party of the High or Established Church but Palmer of Worcester with the Anglo-Catholics. See *Apo.*, ed. Ward, p. xxx.

44. 26 **Hugh James Rose** (1795–1838), educated at Trinity College, Cambridge, was a clergyman, Greek scholar, and High Church apologist. A year in Germany introduced him to the new rationalistic theology and Biblical criticism, which he attacked as Select Preacher at Cambridge in sermons published as *The State of the Protestant Religion in Germany* (1825). In 1830 he became rector of Hadleigh in Suffolk, and in 1832 he founded the *British Magazine* as an organ for High Church views, meeting Newman, Palmer, Keble, Froude, and Perceval during a visit to Oxford in search of contributors. The conversations of Palmer, Froude, Perceval, and Rose at his rectory in

Hadleigh from July 25 to 29, 1833, mark the beginning of the Oxford Movement as a concerted effort. Rose himself took little direct part in the subsequent Tractarian campaign. His health was never good; and in October 1838 he left for Italy, dying at Florence in December. To Rose, Newman dedicated the fourth volume of *P.S.* See *Essays*, ii. 99–100; *Letters*, ii. 30–31; Burgon, *Lives of Twelve Good Men*, i. 116–283; and Tristram, *Newman and His Friends*, pp. 75–78.

46. 27 **I got a vehement rebuke** According to Burgon (*Lives*, i. 228), '*that* rebuke elicited an apology, truly honourable to him who penned it'. In a note he adds: 'The former is dated March 24, 1834 (81 Pall Mall); the latter March 30th (Oriel College).' But Newman's letter of March 30 as given in *Letters*, ii. 28–29 (it is only a draft) does not merit this description. Probably the first part has been omitted.

46. 32 **Living movements do not come of committees** Cf. *P.S.* i. 287–8: 'It is plain every great change is effected by the few, not by the many; by the resolute, undaunted, zealous few. . . . One or two men, of small outward pretensions, but with their hearts in their work, these do great things.'

46. 34 **even though it had been the penny post** In 1833 postal rates outside London varied from 4*d*. to 1*s*. 8*d*. for a single sheet weighing less than one ounce, the average rate being 9*d*. inland. The publication of Rowland Hill's *Post Office Reform* in 1837, proposing a flat rate of 1*d*. per half-ounce, led to the passing of a penny postage act on August 17, 1839. It went into effect January 10, 1840, and postage stamps were introduced the following May.

48. 4 **mainly their author** According to the list of contributors in H. P. Liddon's *Life of E. B. Pusey, D.D.* (4 vols., London, 1893–7), iii. 473–80, Newman wrote or edited one-third of the Tracts: nos. 1, 2, 3, 6, 7, 8, 10, 11, 15 (in part), 19, 20, 21, 31, 33, 34, 38, 41, 45, 47, 71, 73, 74, 75, 76, 79, 82, 83, 85, 88, and 90.

But compare Appendix D, pp. 491–2, in Burgon's *Lives*, i. Burgon credits Froude with no. 8 and does not list 31 or 74 among Newman's. However, Newman himself claims no. 8, *Apo.*, p. 30. For this and other reasons, Liddon appears the more reliable authority.

According to a study by Professor Howard W. Fulweiler, not yet published, of the ninety Tracts, 'eighteen are reprints of the writings of earlier English divines: twelve (nos. 37, 39, 42, 44, 46, 48, 50, 53, 55, 62, 65, 70) from Bishop Wilson; two from Bishop Cosin (nos. 27 and 28); one from Bishop Bull (no. 64); and one from Archbishop Ussher (no. 72). Four more of the tracts were 'Catenae' or chains of evidence from a large number of English ecclesiastical or theological writers on specific problems; they are nos. 74, 76, 78, and 81.

'The first forty-six tracts were gathered together at the end of 1834 and published as Volume I of the series, which carried the general title, *Tracts for the Times*. The remaining tracts, which appeared in the succeeding years, were collected in four more volumes. Tracts 89 and 90 were published separately. Although they are almost always bound with the first five volumes, they are not really a part of them. The individual tracts were printed at various times in London for J. G. and F. Rivington and J. H. Parker, Oxford.'

48. 17 **Dr. Hampden**   See note 53. 36.

48. 19 **if my memory serves me truly**   Yes, in October 1821, in a review of Part II of Dugald Stewart's *General View of the Progress of Metaphysical, Ethical, and Political Science, since the Revival of Letters*: 'Oriel College . . . a distinguished Society, which, besides its other merits, is at present the school of Speculative Philosophy in England.' (xxxv. 254, n. * .)

49. 13 **a series of letters in the Record**   Five letters on 'Church Reform' appeared between September and November 1833. They are not reprinted in Newman's *Works*. For a summary and discussion, see E. A. Knox, *The Tractarian Movement* (2nd ed., London, 1934), pp. 124–9. This work is written from the Evangelical viewpoint and is generally unfavourable to Newman.

49. 26 **Temperance Societies**   Many attempts were then being made to lessen the widespread consumption of spirits, not only in England but in America and various parts of Europe as well. By 1830, for example, there were at least thirty local temperance societies in England alone, and in 1831 the British and Foreign Temperance Society was founded. In 1830 an Act allowing virtual free trade in the lesser evil of beer had been passed. It was greeted by Sydney Smith with the remark: 'The New Beer Bill has begun its operations. Everybody is drunk. The Sovereign People is in a beastly state.' (See the article 'Temperance Movements' in the *Catholic Encyclopedia*, xiv. 487.)

Newman had little faith in movements like temperance societies and free public libraries as a corrective for the ills of man in society. He once shocked his brother Francis, after the latter had written in praise of a speech of Manning on temperance, by replying: 'As to what you tell me of Archbishop Manning, I have heard that some also of our Irish bishops think that too many drink-shops are licensed. As for me, I do not know whether we have too many or too few.' (*Contributions*, p. 110.)

49. 29 **I had subscribed . . . Record.**   This sentence does not appear in the Oratory MS. The previous sentence was originally followed in the MS. by the following cancelled paragraph:

'However, such was not the mode of action which would lead to any real success, nor was it the one natural to me. I instinctively fell into the "personal". The early Tracts are written in the first person; so are "the Church of the Fathers" and "Home Thoughts Abroad" which were at this time written for the British Magazine; and it was from a local centre and *from* among those, who knew me or had known me familiarly, that the movement was really to begin.'

50. 15 **not to the sixteenth century, but to the seventeenth**   That is, not to the Lutheran and Calvinist tendencies of Reformers like Cranmer and Ridley, but to the emphasis on Catholic tradition and doctrine associated with the names of Andrewes, Laud, and other famous seventeenth-century divines.

For a convenient and useful synthesis, made on Anglo-Catholic principles, of their work, see *Anglicanism*, ed. Paul Elmer More and F. L. Cross.

51. 3 **both of fierceness and of sport** 'Newman now is becoming perfectly ferocious in the cause, and proportionately sanguine of success. "We'll do them", he says, at least twenty times a day—meaning, by "them", the present race of aristocrats, and the Liberal oppressors of the Church in general.' *Letters of the Rev. J. B. Mozley, D.D.* (London, 1885), p. 36 and n.

51. 20 **I thought the mistake too pleasant to be corrected** If the mistake was the correspondent's, it was surely a natural one, for Article XXXI of the Thirty-nine Articles denied that the celebration of the Eucharist, or the Mass, involved a sacrifice. In Tract 90 Newman tried to show that only the Roman doctrine of the sacrifice was condemned—not all idea of sacrifice. (See *V.M.* ii. 324–5.) He later came to the conclusion that Anglican theology, including the Non-jurors and Pusey, was fundamentally opposed to Catholic doctrine on the sacrificial character of the Mass (Pusey had made clear in Tract 81 his denial that Christ Himself is offered up in the Mass); and accordingly that his interpretation of Article XXXI in Tract 90 could not be defended, though the Tract as a whole might be. (Ibid., pp. 351–6.)

51. 26 **the Wise man** Solomon. Prov. xxvi. 5.

51. 29 **I used irony in conversation** See *Letters*, i. 194.

51. 35 **Tract 15** *On the Apostolical Succession in the English Church.* The friend who furnished the matter was Palmer of Worcester. See his *Narrative*, p. 121, n. 4.

52. 1 **what it says about the Council of Trent** This was the General Council held at Trent in the Tyrol from 1548 to 1563, reaffirming Catholic doctrine including purgatory, indulgences, etc., against the Reformers. It was commonly regarded as shutting the door on a Protestant-Catholic reconciliation. Rome, says the Tract, 'was not heretical in the primitive ages. If she has apostatized, it was at the time of the Council of Trent. Then, if at any time, surely not before, did the Roman Communion bind herself in covenant to the cause of Antichrist.' (Tract 15, p. 10, in *Tracts for the Times*, i, London, 1834.) The cautious tone of the Tract and the praise of Luther and other Reformers with which it concluded were no doubt especially irritating to Froude. See *Letters*, ii. 185.

52. 5 **It is principally through Mr. Froude's Remains that this word has got into our language.** Through Newman's own *Arians*, according to the *N.E.D.* But there is no doubt that the *Remains* attracted far more attention than the *Arians*. For Newman's discussion of the word, see *Apo.*, pp. 241–2 and Note F, pp. 299–301; and *Select Treatises of St. Athanasius*, ii. 91–95. In the words of Brilioth, 'the doctrine of a *disciplina arcani*, and an *economy*, that is to say an adaptation in the imparting of the truth of faith with respect to the environment', which Newman derived from Alexandrian theology, 'were to come to play a fatal part during the Oxford Movement, more by the suspicions they roused than by their actual application'. (*The Anglican Revival*, p. 115.)

52. 22 This absolute confidence In manuscript this sentence first read: 'That absolute confidence in my cause which I have spoken of, showed itself in what I must call the fierceness as well as in the imprudence or extravagance of what I did.'

52. 25 In the Lyra Apostolica, I have said In LXXXI, 'Zeal Before Love' (November 20, 1832):

> And wouldst thou reach, rash scholar mine,
> Love's high unruffled state?
> Awake! thy easy dreams resign:
> First learn thee how to hate.

The next stanza began, 'Hatred of sin, and Zeal, and Fear, | Lead up the Holy Hill'. (Derby, 1836, p. 96. Reprinted with slight alteration as 'Zeal and Love' in *V.V.O.*, p. 64.)

52. 28 In one of my first Sermons I said See 'The Religion of the Day', *P.S.* i. 320–1. The sermon is dated August 26, 1832.

53. 1 a Northern dignitary See *Essays*, i. 279–80, referring to a Mr. T. The passage in the *Arians* occurs on pp. 234–5.

53. 14 one of my friends Newman's account here is not quite accurate. The friend was the Revd. Charles Girdlestone, one-time Fellow of Balliol and a leading Evangelical who had recommended Newman in 1824 for his first curacy at St. Clement's, Oxford. (See *Letters*, i. 74.) On November 1, 1833, Newman sent him a copy of the circular called 'Suggestions for an Association of Friends of the Church', together with a letter asking his support in the new movement and prophesying that 'the Church will shortly be delivered from its captivity under wicked men who are worse than Chushanrishathaim . . .'. Presently he added: '. . . we shall be truly glad of your co-operation . . . but if you will not, we will march past you'. A facsimile of Newman's letter, together with Girdlestone's impressive reply, appears in W. Tuckwell, *Reminiscences of Oxford*, 2nd ed. (London, 1907, New York, 1908), pp. 321–5. See also F. W. Newman, *Contributions*, p. 77.

The Biblical reference is to Judges iii. When, after the death of Joshua, the Israelites were unfaithful to the Lord and did not persevere in destroying the Canaanites, they were delivered for eight years into the hands of Chushan-rishathaim, King of Mesopotamia. The Lord finally sent them Othniel as a deliverer.

53. 19 St. Paul bids us avoid Rom. xvi. 17.

53. 20 you cause divisions Presumably a reference to Francis Newman's missionary activity with the fundamentalist Plymouth Brethren. For a revealing passage on the proper treatment of 'deliberate heretics and apostates', see *Arians*, pp. 85–86. This firmness of principle, which Newman never lost but later tempered with a warmer charity, explains his cold behaviour not only to Francis, but for a time to Whately, to the Catholic apostle of union, Fr. Spencer (*Apo.*, p. 117), and others.

53. 25 **He speaks bitterly and unfairly** In manuscript Newman originally quoted the following passage: 'Newman, who has raised himself into a Protestant Pope, and who, as sure as he lives, would persecute to the death if he had the direction of the civil power for a dozen years,—Newman expresses the utmost tenderness for those who, holding any opinions whatever, will only whisper them tremblingly into his ear.' (*The Life of the Rev. Joseph Blanco White*, ii. 213; see also ii. 222–3.)

53. 36 **Dr. Hampden** Renn Dickson Hampden (1793–1868) played an important role in the controversies aroused by the Oxford Movement. Fellow of Oriel and intimate friend of Arnold and Whately, he became tutor at Oriel by appointment of Hawkins after Newman and his friends refused to see that office in Hawkins's light. His Bampton Lectures of 1832, *The Scholastic Philosophy considered in its relations to Christian Theology*, and his pamphlet of 1834, *Observations on Religious Dissent*, distinguished Scripture and church doctrine in such a way as to threaten the certainty of the basic Christian dogmas, though he himself accepted them (see *Apo.*, p. 61). Both Evangelicals and Tractarians became alarmed; and when Lord Melbourne appointed Hampden Regius Professor of Divinity in 1836, a storm of protest broke out. Over forty-five books and pamphlets appeared; and though Melbourne stood firm in the appointment, the University voted overwhelmingly in May 1836 to exclude Hampden from his place on the board which appointed Select Preachers.

The agitation served to rally the Liberals against the Tractarians. To this day the fight against Hampden is cited as evidence of Tractarian bigotry (see Geoffrey Faber, *Oxford Apostles*, pp. 355 ff., *passim*), but there was clearly a question of principle involved, Faber himself admitting that Hampden's views 'certainly were' (p. 373) dangerous to dogmatic religion. See also Church, *The Oxford Movement*, pp. 139–54; and Maisie Ward, *Young Mr. Newman*, pp. 287–97. For the view that Newman 'did grievously misrepresent' Hampden's teaching, see E. A. Knox, *The Tractarian Movement*, pp. 166–74. Misrepresentation is also charged by Edwin A. Abbott, but on the ground of mental excitement rather than moral deficiency. See *The Anglican Career of Cardinal Newman* (2 vols., London, 1892), ii. 37–63.

54. 17 **the principle of dogma** For a discussion of dogma, see Newman's sermon 'The Theory of Developments in Religious Doctrine': 'Theological dogmas are propositions expressive of the judgments which the mind forms, or the impression which it receives, of Revealed Truth. Revelation sets before it certain supernatural facts and actions, beings and principles; these make a certain impression or image upon it; and this impression spontaneously, or even necessarily, becomes the subject of reflection on the part of the mind itself; which proceeds to investigate it and to draw it forth in successive and distinct sentences. Thus the Catholic doctrine of Original Sin, or of Sin after Baptism, or of the Eucharist, or of Justification, is but the expression of the inward belief of Catholics on these several points, formed upon an analysis of that belief.' (*U.S.*, pp. 319–20.)

He later adds: ' All that we know, strictly speaking, is the existence of the impressions our senses make on us; and yet we scruple not to speak as if they conveyed to us the knowledge of material substances. Let, then, the Catholic dogmas, as such, be freely admitted to contain no true idea of Almighty God, but only an earthly one, gained from earthly figures, provided it be allowed on the other hand, that the senses do not convey to us any true idea of matter, but only an idea commensurate with sensible impressions.' (p. 340.)

See also *Dev.*, pp. 122 ff.; and for the 'absurdities of the latitudinarian' or anti-dogmatic principle, *Loss and Gain*, p. 34. Much of this satirical novel is designed to illustrate these 'absurdities'.

55. 3 Such was the fundamental principle of the Movement of 1833. This is an important sentence by which to measure the later development of the Oxford Movement in the Church of England, which after Newman's conversion grew increasingly ritualistic but less dogmatic. For a brief sketch, see Humphrey J. T. Johnson, *Anglicanism in Transition* (London, 1938). See also Dawson, *The Spirit of the Oxford Movement*, pp. 135 ff. A distinguished Anglican religious philosopher, Clement C. J. Webb, explained later developments in part by saying that the principles of the Tractarian school 'prevented it from effectively resisting the tendency' to a changed view of the authority of the Bible, of the question of eternal punishment, and so on. See his *Religious Thought in the Oxford Movement* (London, 1933), pp. 148 ff.

55. 7 there was a visible Church The Evangelicals and Dissenters followed the Protestant tradition of minimizing the authority of the visible church and considering Christ's Church as primarily the invisible union of His followers.

55. 13 Laud William Laud (1573–1645), Charles I's Archbishop of Canterbury, enforced strict adherence to church discipline and ritual and attempted to steer a middle course between Rome and Puritan Calvinism. He was impeached by the Long Parliament, imprisoned in the Tower in 1641, tried in 1644, and executed January 10, 1645. A seven-volume edition of Laud's works (Oxford, 1847–60) is part of the Library of Anglo-Catholic Theology. See E. C. E. Bourne, *The Anglicanism of William Laud* (London, 1947).

55. 13 Bramhall John Bramhall (1594–1663), Bishop of Derry, loyal supporter of Charles and Laudian Anglicanism, refugee, and, after the Restoration, Archbishop of Armagh. Much of his writing is against Rome and Dissent, his works filling five volumes (Oxford, 1842–5) in the Library of Anglo-Catholic Theology. For some of his views on fundamental questions, see *V.M.* ii. 210–14. See also T. S. Eliot's essay 'John Bramhall', a review of W. J. Sparrow Simpson's *Archbishop Bramhall* (London, 1927), in *For Lancelot Andrewes* (London, 1928), pp. 33–48.

55. 14 Stillingfleet Edward Stillingfleet (1635–99), Bishop of Worcester, was a man of moderate views, a noted controversialist, antiquary, and preacher. His best-known work is *Origines Britannicae* (1685), an elaborate investigation of the sources of British church history. There is a six-volume edition of his works (1709–10), with a Life by his chaplain, Richard Bentley.

On November 3, 1833, Newman wrote to T. Mozley: 'As to Stillingfleet's Irenicon, I have been looking into it, since you mentioned it; perhaps I have not looked deep enough, but, as far as I have seen, he does not at all intrench upon the Tract headed "The Episcopal Church Apostolical". I am firing away in the Record, with what success I know not.' (MS. Letters, 'Movement Towards Rome'.) Stillingfleet's *Irenicum* (1659), advocating a union between Episcopalians and Presbyterians, opposed Nonconformity but treated the forms of church government as inessential. (*O.D.C.C.*)

55. 19 **St. Ignatius's Epistles** See 'The Theology of the Seven Epistles of St. Ignatius', *Essays*, i. 222–62.

55. 25 **Visitation Service** In which the sick are prepared for death. See *Apo.*, p. 87.

55. 29 **Commination Service** A service for Ash Wednesday that first appeared in the Book of Common Prayer in 1549, replacing the former distribution of ashes and the ejection from the church of those who had to do public penance. It anathematizes those who do not observe the law of God (hence the name, from L. *comminatio*: a threatening) and urges them to penance.

55. 36 **One passage** From the Epistle to the Magnesians, iii. See *Essays*, i. 255.

56. 26 **Vicariate** Until the restoration of the hierarchy in 1850, Roman Catholic England was governed as missionary territory by representatives of Rome called Vicars Apostolic. In 1840 Gregory XVI raised their number from four to eight, nominating Wiseman coadjutor to Bishop Walsh of the Central District.

56. 36 **Dr. Bagot** Richard Bagot (1782–1854), as Bishop of Oxford from 1829 to 1845, had the difficult task of mediating between the Tractarians and their various opponents. He recognized the service the Tractarians had done the Church and was friendly to Newman and other leaders. He was not especially interested in theology, however; and as time went on, he began to deplore the lack of judgement in their disciples' advocacy of Catholic principles. Newman's *Justification* and Palmer's *Narrative* are dedicated to him. In 1845, at his own request, he was translated to the diocese of Bath and Wells; but the excitement had been too much for him. He broke down in mind and body, and for some time his affairs had to be administered by the Bishop of Gloucester and Bristol. Eventually, however, he recovered. See Tristram, *Newman and His Friends*, pp. 72–74.

The manuscript of the *Apologia* describes Bagot as 'a man to whom (with one or two exceptions) no other Bishop on the Bench was fit to hold a candle'. In a letter of May 1, 1864 (MS. *Apo.* Letters), Copeland expressed his fear that such an expression might be thought inappropriate for this context and 'set up backs'. In letters to Copeland of May 8 and June 17, 1864, Newman indicates that he 'put the "Candle" out' on the 'bidding' of Keble and Copeland. (Copies in Oratory Personal Collection.)

Editor's Notes

57. 20 **the stanza in the Christian Year** The last stanza of the poem for November 5, 'Gunpowder Treason':

> Speak gently of our sister's fall:
> Who knows but gentle love
> May win her at our patient call
> The surer way to prove ?

57. 29 **St. Gregory I** (*c.* 540–604), usually called Gregory the Great, was Pope from 590. He was famous for his moral earnestness and missionary zeal; and in 597 he sent St. Augustine to convert England. But in Protestant eyes his strong affirmation of papal authority and of doctrines like purgatory and the intercession of saints marked him as a prototype of 'medieval' Christianity. See *Diff*. ii. 212–14, and *H.S.* iii. 130–41.

58. 14 **Carnival** The festival season immediately preceding Lent, widely observed in Catholic countries and elsewhere described by Newman as 'the special festival of the world, the flesh, and the devil'. (*O.S.*, p. 216.)

58. 15 **'the people sat down to eat . . .'** Exod. xxxii. 6.

58. 19 **St. Philip** That is, Philip Neri, 'my own special Father and Patron', as Newman calls him in a beautiful sketch in the *Idea of a University*, pp. 234–8. St. Philip devoted much effort to reclaiming the worldly and the irreligious. For a moving account of his aims and those of the Oratory, see 'The Mission of St. Philip Neri', *O.S.*, pp. 199–242.

59. 16 *Records*, **No. 24** The *Records* were extracts from the Fathers. See Liddon, *Life of Pusey*, i. 414–15. For the passage cited, see XXIV, 'St. Vincent of Lerins on the Test of Heresy', p. 7, in *Tracts for the Times*, vol. ii.

59. 27 **Bernard Gilpin** (1517–83) was an English clergyman known as the 'Apostle of the North' for his charities throughout the northern counties. Strongly influenced by Erasmus, he was highly critical of clerical abuses but reluctant to accept changes in doctrine, believing that Rome had kept the faith intact until the Council of Trent. In Tract 15, p. 10, Newman quotes the present passage at great length from *Wordsworth's Ecclesiastical Biography*, iv. 94.

60. 31 **If there was any thing** This sentence first read in manuscript: 'There was much in the Fathers which was different from the Anglicanism of the day, or as that system had ever been realized. What really had the *consensus* of the Fathers ought to be absorbed and assimilated into the belief of our people: what had not, might perplex or scandalize for a time, but could [?] die out from our [?] thoughts.'

60. 36 **Library of the Fathers** This was the *Library of Fathers of the Holy Catholic Church, anterior to the division of the East and West* (50 vols., Oxford, 1838–85). The huge project, undertaken by Pusey in 1836 with the help of Newman and Keble, proved highly influential in the revival of the Catholic spirit in the Church of England. The first volume was St. Augustine's *Confessions*, in Pusey's revision of an earlier translation by W. Watts and with a long preface by Pusey on patristic study. The second volume was *The*

Catechetical Lectures of S. Cyril, Archbishop of Jerusalem (1838), translated principally by R. W. Church and edited by Newman, who wrote a preface from which, p. xi, the passage he quotes here is taken. See Denys Gorce, *Newman et les Pères* (2nd ed., Bruges, 1947), pp. 55–59.

61. 8 'τῷ τελει . . .' Putting his faith in the finish or, as Newman has it, the event. (Sophocles, *Electra*, l. 735.) Orestes attempted to win a chariot race at the Delphian games by holding back until the other racers had entangled themselves.

61. 15 **the attack upon the University** Undergraduates at both Oxford and Cambridge had to subscribe to the Thirty-nine Articles before admission to a degree, and Oxford required subscription on matriculation as well. All non-Anglicans were thus excluded from the taking of degrees and even from attendance at Oxford. In 1834 Liberals and Dissenters joined forces to introduce a Bill in Parliament for removing these tests, which are referred to in the title of Hampden's pamphlet. It was defeated. In 1835 Oxford was agitated by a proposal to drop the requirement of subscription at matriculation, but it was also defeated. See Culler, *The Imperial Intellect*, pp. 98–114.

62. 10 **Phaeton has got into the chariot of the sun** A reference to the liberal triumphs at Oxford and in the Anglican Church beginning in the 1850s with reforms of a secularizing nature. (See Pattison's *Memoirs*.) Benjamin Jowett's critical study of St. Paul appeared in his edition of the Epistles to the Thessalonians, Galatians, and Romans (1855) and created a stir. *Essays and Reviews*, the first famous product of liberal Anglican theology, had appeared four years before the *Apologia* and was still a centre of controversy as Newman wrote. In a letter of October 12, 1881, Newman replied to an unnamed correspondent who had asked whom he was referring to in this passage: '. . . I made no personal allusion, when I spoke of Phaeton and the Sun. By Phaeton I meant liberalism in Religion—by the sun the Secular Power, the National Government viewed in its action.' (Orat. Miscellaneous Letters, 1881.)

63. 9 **a friend** Benjamin Harrison (1808–87), Domestic Chaplain to Archbishop Howley of Canterbury, later Canon of Canterbury and Archdeacon of Maidstone. He was an early supporter of the Movement, wrote Tracts 16, 17, 24, and 49, and drew Newman into the correspondence with the Abbé Jager which became part of his *Prophetical Office*. See Ward, *Life*, i. 374, and ii. 353–4; Williams's *Autobiography*, pp. 140–1; and Henry Tristram, 'In the Lists with the Abbé Jager', *Newman Centenary Essays*, pp. 203 ff.

63. 11 **my own verse about St. Gregory** St. Gregory Nazianzen (*c.* 329–90), Bishop of Constantinople, theologian, and famous preacher, had been ordained a priest against his will on the request of the people. His own inclination was for a life of ascetic retirement, and his life was marked by difficulties in performing his practical duties. The reference in the poem cited (*V.V.O.*, pp. 151–2) is to a retirement from his patriarchal throne:

> Thou couldst a people raise, but couldst not rule:
> So, gentle one,

Heaven set thee free,—for, ere thy years were full,
Thy work was done:
According thee the lot thou lovedst best,
To muse upon the past,—to serve, yet be at rest.

63. 34 **a gentleman was editor** James S. Boone (1799–1859), lecturer and writer on miscellaneous subjects. See Pattison's *Memoirs*, 200–1, and T. Mozley's *Reminiscences*, ii. 200–4. Mozley succeeded Newman as editor.

64. 3 **the writer who so handled it** Charles Webb le Bas, Fellow of Trinity College, Cambridge, and author of a life of T. F. Middleton, Bishop of Calcutta and Greek scholar. (H. T.) The article was 'Newman and Faber on Justification', xxiv (July 1838), pp. 82–119. See *Letters*, ii. 263.

64. 4 **an article against the Jesuits** Edward Churton's 'Revival of Jesuitism. Political View', xxv (January 1839), pp. 143–86. Newman in 1875 added this comment to Churton's letter of December 20, 1838: '. . . it shows my own disagreement with the tone of Churton's article on the Jesuits, and my disinclination (Dec. 1838) to oppose the devotions of the Immaculate Conception and the Sacred Heart'. (MS. Letters, 'Movement Towards Rome'.)

64. 7 **a friend** Charles P. Golightly (1807–85), Newman's curate at Littlemore in 1835–6, whose break with the Tractarians came over divergent views on baptismal regeneration but more especially over Golightly's intense fear and suspicion of Romeward tendencies in the Movement. He soon became the most indefatigable opponent of the Tractarians, of Newman himself in the affair of Tract 90, and later of the ritualistic movement: 'I have the sole charge of the Alarm-bell', as he once put it. In 1855 he was a leader of the opposition to the appointment of the liberal Benjamin Jowett as Regius Professor of Greek at Oxford. See *Letters*, ii. 91–94, 295, and 397–8; Maisie Ward, *Young Mr. Newman*, p. 328; E. A. Knox, *The Tractarian Movement*, pp. 252–3; and esp. R. W. Greaves, 'Golightly and Newman, 1824–1845', *Journal of Ecclesiastical History*, ix (1958), 209–28.

64. 11 **Fleury's Church History** Claude Fleury (1640–1725) was a learned French clergyman who, though tutor to royalty in a brilliant court, lived a modest, retiring life and wrote much, including a twenty-volume *Histoire Ecclésiastique* (Paris, 1691–1720) from the Ascension to the year 1414. (This was later continued to 1778 by J. C. Fabre and others.) Like his patron, Bossuet, Fleury was very conscious of the local rights of the Church, and his work reflects a restrained Gallicanism. This fact, together with his cordial relations with the Anglican Bishop Wilson of Sodor and Man, may help to account for Fleury's popularity with Rose and the Tractarians. See *Apo.*, p. 75.

A letter of August 9, 1835, from Newman to his sister Jemima, ascribes Rose's desire for a translation of Fleury to the feeling that 'we are perishing for want of a history—that the Clergy & c. are beginning to feel alive to the subject of the Church—and that there is nothing to recommend to them but Mosheim & Milner, and Milner and Mosheim—which is very true'. (Photostat in Oratory Archives.) Newman's assistants in translating portions of the history beginning with the Council of Constantinople in 381 (see *Letters*, ii. 255) included A. J. Christie of Oriel (vol. 1), George Buckle of Oriel (vol. 2), and Wm. Kay of Lincoln (vol. 3). Christie became a Roman Catholic priest, Buckle an evolutionary scientist, and Kay an Anglican bishop and conservative Biblical scholar.

64. 24 **Dr. Pusey** Edward Bouverie Pusey (1800–82) was elected Fellow of Oriel in 1823, where he became friendly with Keble and Newman. On the advice of Dr. Charles Lloyd, Regius Professor of Divinity, he studied at Göttingen, Berlin, and Bonn under such leaders of the 'higher criticism' as Eichhorn and Schleiermacher. Lloyd feared the results of the new approach, which Pusey soon realized that English theology was utterly unprepared to meet. He himself worked so hard at the study of Oriental languages that his health was impaired. He returned to England in 1827 and published *An Historical Enquiry into the Probable Causes of the Rationalist Character lately predominant in the Theology of Germany* (1828; part ii, 1830). This was an answer to Hugh James Rose, who in lectures at Cambridge had argued that this rationalism was due to the absence of the control supplied in the Church of England by her formularies of devotion and episcopal government. Pusey held rather that it came in reaction to a dead orthodoxy, a formal rather than vital belief such as he feared the Anglican Church itself was then threatened by.

In November 1828 Pusey was appointed Regius Professor of Hebrew, a position to which was attached a canonry at Christ Church, and so he was ordained. He proved an excellent teacher of Hebrew, and he devoted six years to completing the catalogue of Arabic manuscripts in the Bodleian Library. But his main work became the defence of orthodoxy as he thought the Fathers and the greatest English theologians had interpreted it, and which he felt could alone enable the English church to withstand the liberal attack. After Newman's retirement, Pusey became the leader of the Movement. There is something both noble and pathetic in the tremendous energy he devoted to apparently lost causes—he was to see the liberals triumph in both University and church, and his hopes for reunion with Rome were smashed by the first Vatican Council. His personal life was saddened by the untimely deaths of his wife and of three of his four children; but his great faith carried him through trials that might well have broken the majority of men.

H. P. Liddon's four-volume *Life* (1893–4) remains the standard biography and a very important source for the history of the Oxford Movement. However, for the view that Liddon 'succeeded in concealing Pusey's stature behind a pile of paper', and that Pusey's significance was moral and devotional rather than intellectual, see Owen Chadwick, *The Mind of the Oxford Movement*, pp. 46–52.

64. 26 ὁ μέγας the great one.

64. 30 **Tract on Fasting** No. 18, *Thoughts on the Benefits of the System of Fasting, Enjoined by our Church*, supplemented in no. 66. See Liddon's *Life*, i. 279.

65. 1 his family connexions Pusey's paternal grandfather was Jacob Bouverie, first Viscount Folkestone. His father was Philip Pusey, who adopted his surname on succeeding in 1789 to the estates of the old Pusey family of the small village of Pusey in Berkshire. Pusey's older brother Philip was an influential member of Parliament, a close friend of Robert Peel and Gladstone. He married Lady Emily Herbert, who was the sister of his intimate friend Lord Porchester, afterwards the third Earl of Carnarvon.

65. 15 Sir Robert Inglis (1786–1855) was a Tory of no special distinction who could always be counted on to oppose Roman Catholic claims. After defeating Peel in the by-election at Oxford in 1829 (see note 26. 10), he continued to represent Oxford till his retirement from Parliament in 1854.

66. 8 he put his initials to it Hence the Tractarians were often called *Puseyites*. This was ironic as Pusey was at first rather wary of the Movement; and according to a letter of Newman to Anne Mozley (April 18, 1878), 'when Pusey wrote Tract 18, he bargained with me he that might put his initials at the end of it, that he might separate from the Movement party'. (Copy of Mozley Family Letters in Oratory Archives.)

66. 9 his elaborate Treatise on Baptism Tracts 67–69.

66. 11 The Catenas of Anglican divines Tracts 74 and 76.

66. 36 a memorable appointment Melbourne's of Dr. Hampden as Regius Professor of Divinity.

67. 8 Lectures in London There were two series of lectures, one in the Sardinian Chapel in Lincoln's Inn Fields in the Advent of 1835, and the other in the Church of St. Mary's, Moorfields, in Lent of 1836. They were published as *Lectures on the Principal Doctrines and Practices of the Catholic Church*, and were reviewed by Newman in the *British Critic* for December 1836. One indication of their effect was the conversion to Roman Catholicism, after the second series, of Augustus Welby Pugin (1812–52), architect and leading figure in the Gothic revival. See *Letters*, ii. 195, and Ward's *Life of Wiseman*, i. 230–45.

67. 12 'The Prophetical office. . . .' According to Dawson, Newman in this work 'laid the foundation of a new theology for the Church of England, which has had an incalculable influence on the development of modern Anglicanism, and which perhaps still remains the best justification for the essential Anglican position'. (*The Spirit of the Oxford Movement*, p. 102.) F. L. Cross terms it 'perhaps the most enduring work that Newman produced . . . a magnificent apology for what may be termed the Anglican ethos.' (*John Henry Newman*, p. 70.)

67. 18 first written in the shape of controversial correspondence It seems rather to have grown out of lectures delivered in Adam de Brome's Chapel at St. Mary's, Oxford, between May 16 and July 11, 1836, into which portions of the correspondence with the 'learned French priest' were incorporated. This, at least, is the account in the 'Advertisement' to the *Prophetical Office* and 'on the whole represents the facts more accurately', according to

Fr. Tristram, whose account of the controversy has already been mentioned (note 63. 9). The priest was Jean-Nicolas Jager (1790–1868), Greek scholar and theologian, who collected the periodical correspondence in one volume published in 1836 under the title *Le Protestantisme aux prises avec la doctrine catholique.*

67. 29 **Tract 71** *Against Romanism.* This, together with several other important documents of these years, including Tract 90, is reprinted in *V.M.* ii. The first volume of *V.M.* contains *The Prophetical Office of the Church* along with Newman's criticisms of it written as a Roman Catholic.

68. 7 **It was published, I think, under the title** The title was *A Treatise on the Church of Christ* (London, 1838). For Newman's extended review in the *British Critic*, see *Essays*, i. 179–221.

68. 12 **Father Perrone in his Treatise** Giovanni Perrone (1794–1876), a Jesuit theologian who was Professor of Dogmatics at the Roman College, of which he eventually became head. His chief work is *Praelectiones Theologicae* (9 vols., 1835–42), which went through almost fifty editions by the end of the century. In 1846 at Rome Newman won Perrone's agreement on the compatibility with the Catholic faith of his ideas on doctrinal development. See Ward, *Life*, i. 184–7.

The reference to Palmer occurs in the *Praelect. Theol., Tract. de Loc. Theol.* § 189 n.: 'Inter eos Palmer doctrina ac moderatione ceteris praestare nobis visus est.' Fr. Tristram points out that the account in Ward's *Life*, i. 18—'Optime Palmer, Newman miscet et confundit omnia'—is not quite correct, as Perrone had not contrasted the two men but written at another point (§ 339 n.), 'Ita Newman op. cit. lect. VIII . . . ubi omnia permiscet atque confundit.' (Ward is quoting Fr. Ryder.)

69. 5 **a Whig appointment** Melbourne's, of Dr. Hampden.

70. 19 **a name which had already been applied** The conception of the Church of England as a middle way was not uncommon in the seventeenth century. Thus George Herbert, in his poem 'The British Church', asserted that 'The mean thy praise and glory is'; and Simon Patrick's *Account of the New Sect of Latitude-Men* (London, 1662, p. 7) described the liturgical 'virtuous mediocrity which our Church observes between the meretricious gaudiness of the Church of Rome and the squalid sluttery of fanatic conventicles'. (Both cited in *Anglicanism*, ed. More and Cross, pp. 11–12.)

Newman's more precise concept of the *via media*, however, was perhaps first adumbrated in a letter of Alexander Knox to John Jebb, written in 1813; and it appears to have been Newman himself who 'coined the term and gave it wide currency'. See Brilioth, *The Anglican Revival*, pp. 47–48. The first references to the term in the *N.E.D.* date from 1845, but Newman is not connected with any of them.

71. 3 **Andrewes** Lancelot Andrewes (1555–1626), Bishop of Winchester, first of the great Anglo-Catholic divines, and the one principally responsible for the English Bible. Patristic scholar, controversialist, and noted preacher, he combined great influence with a saintly life. His *Preces Privatae*, a manual

of devotions in Greek and Latin, has been widely used. Newman translated it (Tract 88) and kept the Greek text close by him to the end of his life. According to T. S. Eliot, the prose of Andrewes is 'not inferior to that of any sermons in the language, unless it be to some of Newman's'. See *For Lancelot Andrewes*, p. 32. The works of Andrewes are in the Library of Anglo-Catholic Theology (11 vols., Oxford, 1841–54). See Maurice F. Reidy, S.J., *Bishop Lancelot Andrewes* (Chicago, 1955), and Bouyer, *Newman*, pp. 167–9.

71. 3 **Hammond** Henry Hammond (1605–60), Fellow of Magdalen, was one of Charles I's most devoted chaplains. Barred from preferment for his loyalty, he wrote voluminously and is best known for his *Practical Catechism* (1644), the work which probably drew Charles's attention to him, and for his *Paraphrase and Annotations upon all the Books of the New Testament* (1653). His works appear in the Library of Anglo-Catholic Theology as *The Miscellaneous Theological Works of Henry Hammond*, 3 vols. in 4, 1847–50.

71. 3 **Wilson** Thomas Wilson (1663–1755), Bishop of Sodor and Man, was known for his reform and vigorous administration of church affairs in the Isle of Man. He was thoroughly anti-Erastian and engaged in many a struggle against interference by governors of the island with the discipline of the church. From his famous devotional writings many manuals have been extracted. Newman edited his *Sacra Privata* in 1838. Keble edited his works for the Library of Anglo-Catholic Theology (7 vols. in 8, 1847–63) and wrote a biography to introduce them. To the general reader, Wilson is probably best known from the many admiring citations of his maxims in the works of Matthew Arnold.

72. 28 **Dr. Howley** William Howley (1766–1848) became Archbishop of Canterbury in 1828. He was no friend of the Tractarians, but his opposition to the Reform Bill and the Church Temporalities Act of 1833 may have prompted Newman to think of him as sitting 'in the seat of St. Thomas the Martyr', i.e. Becket, archbishop from 1162 to 1170.

73. 17 **a paragraph inconsistent with it** See Liddon, *Life of Pusey*, i. 416. Pusey stressed the power of the Fathers to show 'modern Romanists' a way out of the 'secret infidelity' they were in great danger of lapsing into from the 'palpable errors of their own Church'.

74. 12 **a paradox in Luther's mouth** Luther, in reaction against abuses, denied any merit to man's works in winning him justification and held that we are accounted righteous through Christ's merits in the Atonement, which are imputed to us through faith alone. Newman evidently found it paradoxical that we should be accounted righteous if not in some way made righteous ourselves. In a note written as a Catholic for the third edition of his *Lectures on Justification*, he says of his appendix on the formal cause of justification:

'The purpose of this Appendix is to show that the cardinal question to be considered by Catholics and Protestants in their controversy about Justification is, What is its *formal cause*? When this is properly examined, it will be found that there is little or no difference of view between the disputants, except when the Protestant party adheres to the paradox of Luther:—"Sola

fides, non fides formata charitate, justificat: fides justificat sine et ante charitatem", and refuses to assign a formal cause.' (p. 343.) See also pp. 3–15
and 58–61.

74. 13 **a truism in Melanchthon's** Of Philip Melanchthon (1497–1560),
a humanist and pioneer Evangelical theologian, who wished to defend his
master Luther against the charge of doing away with good works, Newman
writes:

'Melanchthon, the most judicious defender of the chief doctrine of Protestantism, justification by the apprehensive power of faith, whom our Church
follows, makes that doctrine intelligible and true by admitting that it is not
to be taken literally, but as a mode of symbolizing a protest against the doctrine of human merit.' (*Justification*, p. 181 n.) And this passage Newman
later explains as follows:

'I say, then, that when Melanchthon and his school speak of faith only
justifying, they neither say with Luther that it is the *primary instrument*
(which it is not), nor with our Homilies, that it is an *instrument after* Baptism
(which it is), but with parts of our first book of Homilies, that it is an *emblem*
or *image* of the free grace of our redemption. To say we are justified by faith
only was in that Reformer's mouth a lively mode of speech (he calls it figurative), for saying that we are justified neither by faith nor by works, but by
God only. I do not deny that such a figure has something refined about it,
but it served effectually to exculpate the doctrine, which he had received from
Luther, from the charge of superseding good works, as showing that really
and practically it had nothing to do either with faith or works, but with grace.
And since when thus explained it was most true, and was a protest against
errors, which then were said to be widely spread in the Church, it was adopted
by our Reformers, without abandoning the modified *instrumental sense* of it
as above commented on.' (pp. 244–5.)

74. 33 **a Pamphlet** *A Letter Addressed to the Rev. the Margaret Professor
of Divinity, on Mr. R. Hurrell Froude's Statements Concerning the Holy
Eucharist, and other Matters Theological and Ecclesiastical.* In *V.M.* ii.
195–257. See especially pp. 235–7.

74. 38 **one of the earliest productions** *The Church of the Fathers* appeared from 1833 to 1836 under the heading 'Correspondence' to relieve the
editor of any responsibility. One of Newman's most charming works, it is a
series of sketches of the labours and trials of his fourth-century heroes like
Basil and Gregory Nazianzen, effected largely by an idiomatic translation of
their letters; and it is important for an understanding of Newman as well as
of the Movement. Published as a volume in 1840, it was later reprinted with
some omissions in *H.S.* i.

75. 5 **Church History** *Ecclesiastical History, from the Second Ecumenical
Council to . . .* A.D. 456 (3 vols., 1842–4). See note 64. 11.

75. 21 **Life of Pope Gregory VII** Gregory VII or Hildebrand, outstanding
reformer of clerical discipline and upholder of the rights of the church against
state encroachment, was Pope from 1073 to 1085. To him, Henry IV of

Germany made the famous submission at Canossa. Newman discusses Bowden's *Life and Pontificate of Gregory VII* (1840) in *Essays*, ii. 249–335. For his sketch of Bowden's life, see pp. 318–19.

75. 36 **the Tract on the Roman Breviary** No. 75, June 24, 1836. The Breviary is a collection of psalms, antiphons, responses, lessons, and other prayers forming the Divine Office of praise assigned to the canonical hours of the day: prime, terce, and so on. The term breviary (L. *breviarium*) comes from an abridgement made in the eleventh century when for convenience these prayers were collected in one place from their many sources. In the Middle Ages lives of the saints replaced many of the Scripture readings. The Council of Trent had the more apocryphal legends removed, and the *Breviarium Romanum* was issued in Rome in 1568. Various later reforms culminated in that carried out by Pius X, who in 1911 issued the present Breviary.

76. 2 **younger men began to translate** Samuel Wood, Robert Williams, and Frederick Oakeley. See Liddon's *Life of Pusey*, ii. 146–8 and 388–97.

76. 11 **an intimate friend** Frederic Rogers, the future Lord Blachford, according to his letter to Newman of June 15, 1864. (MS. *Apo.* Letters.) See *Apo.*, p. 150.

77. 1 **the words of Bramhall** 'No man can justly blame me for honouring my spiritual Mother, the Church of England, in whose womb I was conceived, at whose breasts I was nourished, and in whose bosom I hope to die. Bees, by the instinct of nature, do love their hives, and birds their nests. But, God is my witness, that, according to my uttermost talent and poor understanding, I have endeavoured to set down the naked truth impartially, without favour or prejudice. . . . My desire hath been to have Truth for my chiefest friend, and no enemy but error.'

Quoted in *V.M.* I. xii–xiii, from *The Works of . . . John Bramhall, D.D.* (1-vol. ed., Dublin, 1677), p. 141. See 'To the Christian Reader', a foreword to Bramhall's Discourse III.

77. 7 **I have spoken** *Diff.* i. 96–98. Omissions not indicated.

77. 35 **some light animadversions** See Liddon's *Life of Pusey*, ii. 52–64.

78. 1 **a Pamphlet** *A Letter to the Right Reverend Father in God, Richard, Lord Bishop of Oxford, on Occasion of No. 90, in the Series called the Tracts for the Times.* Reprinted in *V.M.* ii. For the passage quoted, see p. 398 and also Newman's letter to Pusey (Liddon, ii. 53), which indicates that the bishop was surprised at the deference shown his view: 'He did not fully consider the power of a Bishop's word, nor fancy we are so bound by professions . . . to obey it'; nor did he understand 'he has a *jurisdiction* over me'. Pusey was also surprised, and Liddon adds: 'There is no reason to suppose that Pusey ever held this theory. . . .'

78. 26 **the Articles** The Thirty-nine Articles, an attempt to define the dogmatic position of the Church of England in relation to sixteenth-century controversies, are a revision of Cranmer's forty-two articles of 1552. The Latin version was approved by Convocation in 1562 and the English in 1571.

The latter was published under the supervision of Bishop Jewel, one of the Tractarians' favourite targets among the Reformers. The Articles reveal Lutheran, Calvinistic, and Zwinglian influences and are not always easy to reconcile with the more Catholic-oriented Prayer Book. 'Since 1865 the clergy have been required only to affirm that the doctrine of the C of E as set forth in the BCP and the Articles is agreeable to the Word of God, and to undertake not to teach in contradiction of them, instead of giving a more particular subscription as before.' (*O.D.C.C.*) University student subscription to the Articles was abolished in 1871.

78. 32 **The actual cause of my doing so** According to Archbishop Tait, 'Ward worried him into writing Tract 90'. Wilfrid Ward, *William George Ward and the Oxford Movement* (London, 1889), p. 152.

79. 7 **Creed of Pope Pius IV** Pius IV was Pope from 1559 to 1565. In 1564, after the Council of Trent, he promulgated a profession of faith since required of all who hold ecclesiastical office in the Roman Church. It demanded faith in the creed as recited at Mass; in the Church's teaching on the seven sacraments; in the propitiatory and sacrificial character of the Mass; in the Church's teaching on original sin as formulated at Trent; in the Catholic doctrine of the Eucharist, including Transubstantiation; in purgatory, prayers for the dead, and the veneration of saints and their relics; and in the Catholicity and Apostolicity of the Roman Church. The creed ends with a promise of obedience to the Pope as Vicar of Christ and of acceptance of all that the Church teaches. In 1877 the form was slightly modified to include subscription to the decrees of the first Vatican Council. (See *The Catholic Encyclopedia Dictionary*.)

80. 3 **the seventeenth** On predestination and election.

82. 16 **Homilies** The Homilies are two books of sermons originally intended 'for the use of disaffected and illiterate clergy'. (*O.D.C.C.*) The first book, containing twelve homilies, mostly the work of Cranmer, appeared in 1547 and dealt with such topics as the reading of Scripture, true faith, good works, Christian charity, and the necessity for obedience; the second book, containing twenty-one, mostly by Jewel, was published in final form in 1571.

86. 12 **no need . . . to maintain every particular interpretation** See *V.M.* ii. 351–6, for Newman's later criticism of his earlier interpretation of Article XXXI as condemning 'not the authoritative teaching of Rome, but only the common belief and practice of Catholics, as regards Purgatory and private Masses'.

86. 24 **the hard names** They have never wholly disappeared, though no longer as blunt as the comment of the bishop who declared that he would not care to trust the author of Tract 90 with his purse. F. L. Cross (*John Henry Newman*, p. 127) quotes Gladstone: 'Tract 90 opened a joint in Newman's armour; it showed that in his wonderful genius there was a distinct flaw— a strong sophistical element'; and the remark of Yngve Brilioth, the Swedish Lutheran historian of the Oxford Movement (*The Anglican Revival*, p. 155): 'Tract 90 is and remains a very melancholy document. It shows how a really

great man can become little in a false and ambiguous position.' Cross then defends Newman, repeating Newman's own challenge, *Apo.*, p. 87.

For the charges of the bishops, see Meriol Trevor, *Newman: The Pillar of the Cloud*, pp. 257–61; and for a criticism of Tract 90 from the Evangelical viewpoint, see E. A. Knox, *The Tractarian Movement*, pp. 237–64.

86. 30 **no text in St. Paul** But see Rom. iv. 1–7, Gal. iii. 1–14, and similar texts often cited by Evangelicals; and *Justification*, pp. 58–65.

86. 31 **St. James expressly denies it** See ii. 14–26. The Epistle of St. James 'was disliked by M. Luther ("a right strawy epistle") and has generally been little valued by orthodox Protestants'. (*O.D.C.C.*)

86. 33 **'the Pillar and Ground of Truth'** I Tim. iii. 15.

86. 34 **'Let no man judge you . . .'** Col. ii. 16.

87. 6 **'He that is without sin . . .'** John viii. 7.

88. 17 **Dr. Hook** Walter Farquhar Hook (1798–1875) was then vicar of Leeds, where he brought new life to the church, and later Dean of Chichester. Though not formally a Tractarian, he had anticipated and sympathized with much of the spirit of the Movement; and in 1838, as a royal chaplain, he preached before the queen one of the most famous sermons of the century, 'Hear the Church', on the Catholic conception of the role of the church. In 1845 he voted against the condemnation of W. G. Ward and his *Ideal of a Christian Church*, though disapproving the book. It was his view that Rome had left the national church, and he was later much embarrassed by the Romeward tendencies and conversions at his old church of St. Saviour's in Leeds. His defence of Newman is contained in *A Letter to the Bishop of Ripon on the State of Parties in the Church of England* (1841).

89. 18 **an 'understanding'** The *Saturday Review* questioned this, saying that Newman 'rather accuses the Bishops of violating some compact into which they entered with him about Tract 90, but which compact we believe never existed'. (xvii [June 25, 1864], p. 786.) And even the *Dublin Review* called this reference to the conduct of the bishops the 'most obscure part' of the *Apologia*, attributing the obscurity to Newman's wish to spare the persons involved. (N.S. iii [July 1864], p. 167.)

However, in a letter of July 1, 1868, to W. J. Copeland, Newman wrote: 'I had been condemned by ecclesiastical authorities without a word said in my favour, though Jelf came to me, on the beginning of the row about it, from Archb. Howley to say that, if my friends would consent not to move, nothing should be done on the other side.' (Copy in Oratory Personal Collection.)

89. 18 **A clever man** The Revd. Edward Smedley (1788–1836), editor of the *Encyclopaedia Metropolitana*. See 'Additional Notes', *Apo.*, p. 332.

89 n. **the present Lord Houghton** Richard Monckton Milnes (1809–85), Cambridge 'Apostle', poet, critic, bibliophile, advocate of electoral reform. A man of great charm and broad sympathies, he was later to speak in the House of Lords against the condemnation by Convocation of *Essays and Reviews*.

90. 27 **'infandum dolorem'** For a discussion of this passage recalling the lines of Aeneas on the fall of Troy (ii. 3: 'Infandum, regina, iubes renovare dolorem'), see Walter E. Houghton, *The Art of Newman's Apologia* (New Haven, 1945), pp. 54–55.

91. 25 **declared on occasion of Tract 90** See 'A Letter Addressed to the Rev. R. W. Jelf, D.D. . . . in Explanation of the Ninetieth Tract in the Series Called *The Tracts for the Times*', in *V.M.* ii. 378–9.

91. 27 **with Bramhall a comprecation** '*A comprecation* both the *Grecians* and we do allow, an ultimate Invocation both the Grecians and we detest. . . .' 'Schism Guarded and beaten back upon the Right Owners', in *The Works of . . . John Bramhall* (Dublin, 1677), p. 418. A comprecation is a praying *with* rather than a direct invocation of the saints.

91. 28 **all but Transubstantiation** Transubstantiation is the Roman Catholic doctrine of the conversion at the consecration of the Mass of the whole substance of the bread and wine into the whole substance of the Body and Blood of Christ, only the accidents or appearances of bread and wine remaining.

In a note appended to Tract 90 in 1883, speaking of Pusey's view as outlined in Tract 81, Newman remarks: 'In the Introduction to the Tract, he says, p. 13, "The *false doctrine* was that ordinary persuasion, that in the Mass the Priest did offer Christ for the quick and dead." And this "false doctrine" was founded, he says, on the doctrine of Transubstantiation, so much so that, when there was no Transubstantiation, there was no real and literal offering of Christ; for he says, p. 7, "By *combining* the doctrine of Transubstantiation with that of the Sacrifice of the Eucharist, the laity were persuaded that not only a commemorative Sacrifice but that Christ was offered." Accordingly at p. 47 he puts into capital letters these words, "The doctrine of the Sacrifice cannot be the same where Transubstantiation is held and where it is not." This, I suppose, was my own view also; and it explains a passage in my *Apologia* in which I say, "I claimed" as an Anglican "in behalf of who would, the right of holding the Mass *all but* Transubstantiation with Andrewes. . . ."' (*V.M.* ii. 352–3.)

In the words of Andrewes: 'Do you take away from the Mass your Transubstantiation; and there will not long be any strife with us about the Sacrifice. Willingly we allow that a memory of the Sacrifice is made there. That your Christ made of bread is sacrificed there we will never allow.' Quoted from the *Responsio ad Apologiam Cardinalis Bellarmini*, in *Anglicanism*, ed. More and Cross, p. 465.

91. 29 **Hooker** Richard Hooker (1553–1600) was the foremost apologist of the Elizabethan settlement of 1559, author of the *Treatise on the Laws of Ecclesiastical Polity*, and a pioneer in the reaction against the earlier English reformers, whose direction was strongly Lutheran and Calvinist. He believed in the Real Presence of the Body and Blood of Christ in the communion elements but opposed attempts to define the precise manner of it. The question is discussed in bk. v, ch. lxvii of the *Laws*: 'Take therefore that wherein all agree, and then consider by itself what cause why the rest in question should

not rather be left as superfluous than urged as necessary.' (*Works*, ed. John Keble [3 vols., Oxford, 1836], ii. 452.) His views appear to favour a reception-ist theory—that the communicant receives with the bread and wine, them-selves unchanged, the true Body and Blood of Christ. (*O.D.C.C.*) See *Works*, ii. 450.

91. 31 **with Hammond** '. . . though I make it no matter of faith, because delivered neither by Scripture nor apostolic tradition, yet I shall number it among the *pie credibilia*, that no general council, truly such, 1. duly as-sembled, 2. freely celebrated, and 3. universally received, either hath erred or ever shall err in matters of faith.' See 'A Paraenesis', *The Miscellaneous Theological Works of Henry Hammond, D.D.* (3 vols. in 4, ii [3rd ed., Oxford, 1849], p. 350.)

91. 32 **or with Bull** See 'The State of Man before the Fall', *The Works of George Bull, D.D.* (7 vols. in 8, Oxford, 1846), ii. 52–53.

91. 34 **Thorndike** Herbert Thorndike (1598–1672), Fellow of Trinity Col-lege, Cambridge, and Canon of Westminster. A learned and systematic expounder of Anglo-Catholic principles who was more or less rediscovered by the Tractarians, he set forth his major views in *An Epilogue to the Tragedy of the Church of England* (1659). For his views on penance for post-baptismal sin, see 'Of the Laws of the Church', *Works* (6 vols. bound in 9, Oxford, 1844–54), iv, esp. pp. 203–6.

91. 35 **Pearson** John Pearson (1613–86), Bishop of Chester and noted patristic scholar and theologian. A popular exposition of his system is con-tained in *An Exposition of the Creed* (1659). '*There is no other name under heaven given among men whereby we must be saved, but* the name of *Jesus*; and that name is no otherwise given under heaven than in the church.' See Art. IX, 'The Holy Catholic Church', in *An Exposition* (London, 1887), p. 530.

92. 12 **an Article in the** *British Critic* April 1839. Reprinted in a slightly revised version as 'Prospects of the Anglican Church' in *Essays*, i. 263–308, where Newman identifies several of the authors alluded to in the following paragraph.

92. 18 **It is not altogether mine** See *Essays*, i. 308, where he modifies this statement by adding that 'it is from first to last my writing' and that what he borrowed from the friend is the topic worked out pp. 283–92: 'a theory, not mine, of a certain *metamorphosis* and recasting of doctrine into new shapes'. The friend may have been Palmer of Worcester—see *Essays*, i. 192.

92. 28 **One writer said** Baden Powell in *Tradition Unveiled* (1839), p. 4. Powell (1796–1860), Savilian Professor of Geometry at Oxford from 1827 till his death, was a liberal in theology and contributed to *Essays and Reviews*. He strongly opposed Tractarianism.

92. 33 **Another—'with the most rapid growth'** Edward Bickersteth in *Remarks on the Dangers of the Church of Christ* (London, 1839), p. 15. Bickersteth (1786–1850) was an ultra-Protestant Evangelical minister who

edited *Testimony of the Reformers* in 1836 to counteract Tractarianism. His Introduction on the 'Progress of Popery', afterwards published separately, created a stir.

92. 35 **Another: 'The Via Media . . .'** Identified only as the 'scoffing author of the Via Media'. (*Essays*, i. 264.)

92. 37 **Another: 'Were I to give you . . .'** C. S. Bird, *The Oxford Tract System considered with reference to the principle of Reserve in Preaching* (London, 1838), pp. 5–6. The quotation is slightly inaccurate and does not indicate omissions. See *Essays*, i. 304–5.

93. 8 **Another: 'The spread of these doctrines . . .'** Newman identifies him as the author of *The Natural History of Enthusiasm*: i.e. Isaac Taylor (1787–1865), in his lifetime a well-known lay theologian and man of letters, whose crusade against credulity and superstition led him to attack the church of the fourth century for those defects. See his *Ancient Christianity and the Doctrines of the Oxford Tracts* (2 vols., 1839–40), from which, i, p. xi, Newman's quotation is taken.

93. 14 **Another: 'The time has gone by . . .'** In *Essays*, i. 266, Newman attributes the words to a 'well-known Scotch Magazine'. Possibly the *Edinburgh Review*, which was consistently hostile to the Tractarians, but I have not traced the quotation.

93. 17 **Another: 'These doctrines . . .'** Newman originally identified the passage as from 'a new manufacture called' *Travels in Town*, by the 'silly, gossiping' author of *Random Recollections of the Lords and Commons*. This was James Grant (1802–79), journalist and devout Calvinist. Two volumes of *Travels* appeared in 1839. Newman's quotation, abridged, is from ii. 127.

93. 18 **One of the largest churches in Brighton . . . the church at Leeds** That is, throughout England, from south to north. Probably St. Paul's, Brighton, and W. F. Hook's church of St. Saviour's, Leeds, both centres of High Church activity in the nineteenth century.

93. 25 **a bishop in a charge** Sumner of Chester (*Apo.*, note 21. 28) in *A Charge Delivered to the Clergy of the Diocese of Chester at the Triennial Visitation in 1838* (London, 1838), p. 2.

94. 10 **Coleridge** Samuel Taylor Coleridge (1772–1834), whose essay *On the Constitution of the Church and State* held up the universal Christian Church as a divine institution independent of man's will. See Church, *The Oxford Movement*, p. 129; and the discussion by Yngve Brilioth of Coleridge and the other romantics here cited, *The Anglican Revival*, pp. 56–76. See also *Letters*, ii. 83 and 139. On the latter page, Newman calls Sir James Stephen 'too much of a philosopher, looking (in Coleridge's way) at the Church, Sacraments, doctrines, &c. rather as symbols of a philosophy than as *truths*—as the mere accidental types of principles'. Through his *Aids to Reflection* and *Confessions of an Inquiring Spirit*, Coleridge also had great influence on the rising liberal or Broad Church school in English theology. See James D. Boulger, *Coleridge*

as Religious Thinker (New Haven, 1961) and C. R. Sanders, *Coleridge and the Broad Church Movement* (Durham, N.C., 1942).

94. 20 **Southey and Wordsworth** 'Poetry. . . is our mysticism; and so far as any two characters of mind tend to penetrate below the surface of things, and to draw men away from the material to the invisible world, so far they may certainly be said to answer the same end; and that too a religious one.' (*Essays*, i. 291.) Not surprisingly, then, Newman was especially fond of Wordsworth's 'Ode: Intimations of Immortality'. In general, however, as Fr. Ignatius Ryder has said, 'I do not think he ever took cordially to Wordsworth. That poet's didactic tone, his almost sacerdotal pretensions, offended him, and he was wearied by his excessive deliberateness.' (Ward, *Life*, ii. 354.)

94. 27 **Knox** Alexander Knox (1757–1831), who spent a good part of his later life as a recluse in Ireland, upheld the view that the Church of England was Catholic, not Protestant; and he anticipated many Tractarian ideas. His opinions are contained in his *Remains* (4 vols., 1834–7). Newman is here quoting from i. 51 ff.

For the view that Knox, with his friend and correspondent Bishop Jebb of Limerick, was probably the chief pioneer in an Anglican renaissance distinguished from the Oxford Movement proper, see Brilioth, *The Anglican Revival*, pp. 45–55 and 331–3. Some idea of the special importance that Newman attached to the work of Knox may be inferred from the fact that before going on to speak of him as in a peculiar way the anticipator of renewed Catholic tendencies, he says of the writers named in the preceding paragraph: 'These writers, however, are to be noticed far more as indications of what was secretly going on in the minds of men than as causes of it.' (*Essays*, i. 269. See also *Letters*, ii. 82–83 and 119.)

94. 35 **a much venerated clergyman** Thomas Sikes, rector of Guilsborough, who died in 1834 and is described by Dean Church (*Oxford Movement*, p. 127) as 'an earnest High Churchman of the Joshua Watson type'. His remarks were made in conversation with Newman's friend W. J. Copeland and are given in full in Pusey's *Letter to His Grace the Archbishop of Canterbury* (1842), pp. 32–34. See also *Letters*, ii. 433–4, and Liddon's *Life of Pusey*, i. 257–8.

95. 19 **Mr. Churton** Edward Churton (1800–74) was the son of Ralph Churton, Archdeacon of St. David's. He was rector of Crayke in Suffolk, a theologian, and student of Spanish literature. He had left Oxford before the Tractarian Movement began, but he was in sympathy with it. See *Letters*, ii. 6, and *Corr.*, p. 101.

95. 23 **Mr. Dodsworth** William Dodsworth (1798–1861), Cambridge graduate and popular preacher, was drawn by Tractarianism from his Evangelical position. Perpetual Curate of Christ Church, St. Pancras, London, he became a Roman Catholic in 1851 after the Gorham judgement. See *Corr.*, p. 40. Newman's reference to the study of prophecy is presumably to Dodsworth's series of periodical articles published as *The Second Advent of Our Lord Jesus Christ, with an appendix on Jesus Christ as the Destroyer*

of Antichrist (London, 1835), unsigned, an attempt to show that the prophecies relating to the Lord's second coming have a practical and not merely speculative bearing on the Christian life. (Copy in British Museum.)

95. 23 **Mr. Oakeley** Frederick Oakeley (1802–80), Fellow of Balliol and former Evangelical, who, as minister of Margaret Chapel in London from 1839 to 1845, became famous for services marked by the increasing use of Catholic ritual. He was a leader with W. G. Ward of the pro-Roman wing of the Oxford Movement (*Apo.*, p. 151); and in July 1845 he was suspended from clerical duty for affirming that he, like Ward, held (without, however, teaching) all Roman doctrine. On October 29 of that year he entered the Roman Church and thereafter wrote much in her support. See his *Personal Reminiscences of the Oxford Movement with Illustrations from Dr. Newman's 'Loss and Gain'* (1855) and *Historical Notes on the Tractarian Movement* (1865). I have not traced the quotation Newman attributes to him here.

96. 23 **two or three of the writers** Isaac Williams conceived the idea, according to his *Autobiography* (pp. 96–99); and he and W. J. Copeland were joint editors of the *Plain Sermons*, which were intended 'to maintain a more practical turn in the movement', Williams himself being 'actuated with fears for the result of Newman's restless intellectual theories'. The sermons were simple and uncontroversial, with those of Thomas Keble considered as something of a model. Newman's contribution to the series is in *P.S.* vii and viii.

97. 9 **the two Mr. Kebles** John and his younger brother Thomas (1793–1875), from 1827 till his death vicar of the country parish of Bisley in Gloucestershire. A pioneer in the revival of daily service in the Church of England, he was a devoted pastor whose judgement and spiritual counsel were greatly esteemed. He contributed nos. 12, 22, 43, and 84 to the *Tracts*; and according to the account of Canon Overton in *D.N.B.* he probably first suggested the publication of *Plain Sermons*.

97. 9 **Isaac Williams** (1802–65), Fellow of Trinity College, Oxford, poet, and one-time curate of Newman at St. Mary's, owed much of his spiritual direction to John and Thomas Keble. Of a gentle and retiring nature and the highest moral ideals, he unwittingly became a storm centre twice in the Oxford Movement: once by his authorship of Tract 80 (followed up in 87), *On Reserve in Communicating Religious Knowledge*, which stressed the need for 'economy' in religious teaching and was denounced as insidious; and for the second time when he stood for the Professorship of Poetry in succession to Keble in 1842, but withdrew in the face of overwhelming defeat. He had won a measure of fame by his poem *The Cathedral* (1838), but his chances were spoiled when Pusey circulated a complaint that Williams was being opposed for his Tractarian principles. He withdrew from Oxford and lived a secluded life, but wrote much, especially poetry, sermons, and works on Scripture. His *Autobiography* remains an important source for the history of the Movement. See Henry Tristram, *Newman and His Friends*, pp. 79–82; and for many selections from his poems, Owen Chadwick, *The Mind of the Oxford Movement*, *passim*. Chadwick regards Williams as probably 'more than any of the others . . . a disciple and lover of George Herbert' (p. 64).

97. 35 **Fortes fortuna adjuvat** The proverb 'fortune favours the brave', was probably known to Newman especially from Terence's *Phormio*, 203, a work he knew very well, having played the role of Hegio at Ealing, September 22–24, 1813. Many years later he adapted the play for the students at the Oratory school.

98. 13 **any serious inroads** In a note to the revised edition of his works, Newman comments on these lines of the article as follows: 'It must be confessed, however, these formularies have not excluded it from the Anglican Church; still it has no stay in Anglicanism, or in any other religious communion, for it is a transition state, and is running its sure course, and in a great number of minds has already resolved itself into that avowed scepticism or infidelity which is its issue.' (*Essays*, i. 294.)

99. 17 **Tityrus's stags** See Virgil, *Eclogues*, i. 59–63. The reference is to a shepherd, Tityrus (presumably Virgil), who has recently visited Rome and seen the young 'god' Octavian, unforgettably: 'Sooner, then, shall the nimble stag graze in air . . . than that look of his shall fade from my heart.' (Transl. H. Rushton Fairclough, *Virgil* [2 vols., London, 1920], i. 7.)

99. 25 **Hildebrand and Loyola are alive** Gregory VII (1021–85), Pope from 1073, and St. Ignatius Loyola (1491 or 1495–1556), founder of the Society of Jesus, one of the chief instruments of the Counter Reformation: in other words, medieval and modern Catholicism.

100. 23 **Bellarmine** Robert Bellarmine (1542–1621), now a saint and Doctor of the Church, was an Italian Jesuit theologian and, in Newman's phrase, 'the foremost and pattern Catholic controversialist of the Reformation era'. (*V.M.* i. 74, n. 6.) His major work, containing what was widely recognized as a candid exposition of Protestant views and arguments, is *Disputationes de controversiis christianae fidei adversus hujus temporis haereticos* (1581–93).

100. 30 **This difficulty, however, had no tendency whatever to harass or perplex me: it was a matter which bore not on convictions, but on proofs** Newman maintained against Locke that as individuals we justifiably hold many beliefs with a certainty greater than strictly warranted by our adducible logical proofs. This argument is fundamental to his *Grammar of Assent*. The paragraph in the *Apologia* beginning p. 214, l. 13 may also throw light on this perhaps surprising remark, though it should be stressed that there Newman is speaking of 'difficulties intrinsic to the doctrines themselves' rather than of 'difficulties in the evidence'. See also Ward, *Life*, ii. 250.

101. 3 **Bishop Lloyd** Charles Lloyd (1784–1829), from 1822 Regius Professor of Divinity at Oxford, and from March 1827 till his death Bishop of Oxford. The article was his 'View of the Roman Catholic Doctrines' in the *British Critic* for October 1825. The distinction here made is prophetic of Tract 90, and Newman acknowledged the influence. Lloyd's private lectures on the Prayer Book, begun in 1823 and showing its relation to medieval and primitive Catholic works, were attended by several future Tractarians; and they had an important role in preparing for the Oxford Movement. See *Letters*, i. 96–99 (*A.W.*, pp. 69–72), and Oakeley's *Historical Notes*, pp. 12–15.

102. 23 **only a collection of crystals** For Newman's later extended comment on this argument, see *Essays*, ii. 89 ff.

103. 5 **Treatise of Vincentius** Vincent (d. *c.* 434) of Lerins, a small island off the south coast of France, was a monk of whose life little is known. His famous test for distinguishing heresy from true doctrine is found in his *Commonitorium*, ii. 3: in Newman's words, 'that is to be received as Apostolic which has been taught "always, everywhere, and by all". Catholicity, Antiquity, and consent of Fathers, is the proper evidence of the fidelity or Apostolicity of a professed Tradition.' (*V.M.* i. 51.) The *O.D.C.C.* points out that the text is 'quod ubique, quod semper, quod ab omnibus creditum est', this being 'very frequently misquoted with "antiquity" (*quod semper*) first by English writers in the 19th cent.' Newman, however, was aware of the correct order. See *H.S.* i. 383–4.

103. 19 **That paper** Reprinted in *D.A.* as 'How to Accomplish It'.

104. 11 **in July, 1841** See note 107. 7.

105. 11 **St. Cyprian** Bishop of Carthage from 248 till his martyrdom in 258. Newman's allusion is to his *De catholicae ecclesiae unitate*, iv. See *The Treatises of S. Caecilius Cyprian*, transl. Charles Thornton with a preface by Newman, in the Library of the Fathers (Oxford, 1839), pp. 134–5.

105. 12 **passage from St. Augustine** Augustine (354–430), Bishop of Hippo in Africa and greatest of the Latin Fathers, was a leader in the successful fight against the schism of Donatus of Casa Nigra, which began at Carthage in 311 and split the church in Africa for a hundred years. The Donatists objected to the appointment as Bishop of Carthage of Caecilian, on the ground that his consecration by an unworthy bishop was invalid and that sinners could not be members of the church. Augustine insisted on the objective character of the sacraments, their true minister being Christ. The passage Newman refers to occurs in Epistle 49 and is quoted in *D.A.*, p. 7.

105. 16 **St. Cyril's argument** Cyril (*c.* 315–*c.* 386), Bishop of Jerusalem and Doctor of the Church, to whose *Catecheses*, xviii. 12, Newman is alluding. See *The Catechetical Lectures of S. Cyril of Jerusalem* (Oxford, 1838), p. 252.

105. 32 **refuses us the Cup** Since about the twelfth century, communion has been given to the laity of the Roman Church in the species of bread only, the doctrine being that Christ is present under either form alone. Anglo-Catholics, like the Reformers in general, objected on the ground that this was not the primitive custom. For Newman's later defence of the practice, see *V.M.* ii. 106 n. One of the reforms promulgated by Pope Paul VI at the close of the second session of Vatican Council II (1963), permits the laity to receive communion under both species on special occasions.

106. 22 **In 1838 I illustrated it** In the *British Critic* for October, in a review of William Palmer's *Treatise on the Church of Christ*, reprinted in *Essays*, i. See pp. 209–10.

106. 31 *British Critic* **of January, 1840** 'The Catholicity of the Anglican Church', reprinted in *Essays*, ii. See p. 6 for this passage slightly revised.

107. 7 **July, 1841** In 'Private Judgment', reprinted in *Essays*, ii. See p. 367.

108. 2 **Commemoration** The annual celebration at Oxford in the latter part of June closing the academic year. Benefactors are commemorated and prizes announced.

108. 13 **Monophysites** As the fourth century was concerned in its theological controversies with the nature of Christ in determining that He was both God and man, so the fifth century was concerned with the mode of union of these two natures. The Nestorians had held that the two natures are one in the sense that husband and wife are one, though actually remaining two separate natures and persons. In their view, only the human nature or Jesus (as distinct from the Word or God) suffered and died on the cross. The consequences of this position for the doctrine of the Atonement were very significant, raising the question of whether the suffering of one mere man could be considered sufficient atonement for original sin and the sins of all men.

In reaction to the Nestorian view, the Monophysites (Gr. μόνος φύσις, one nature) held that after the Incarnation Christ had but one nature, the divine absorbing the human. This amounted to a denial that Christ was really human, sharing our nature, and again the theological consequences or implications of such a doctrine were startling.

The Catholic doctrine, formulated by Pope Leo the Great (d. 461) and accepted at the Council of Chalcedon (451), is that Christ is truly God and truly man, One Person 'in two natures, without confusion, without change, without division, without separation'. (Quoted in *Documents of the Christian Church*, ed. Henry Bettenson [New York and London, 1947], p. 73.) By the sixth century Monophysitism had become firmly established in the churches of the Copts and Abyssinians, the Syrian Jacobites, and the Armenians.

108. 16 **on the 30th of July mentioning** According to Fr. Tristram, the friend was probably Sir William Heathcote, with whom Newman dined after the dedication of Keble's church at Otterbourne. Newman's diary shows that he arrived in Otterbourne on the 30th and dined with Sir William on the 31st. The earlier references to Heathcote in the *Letters*, however, are not of such a nature as to suggest that Newman would have discussed this matter with him; nor would the words 'accidentally met' seem to apply here.

108. 20 **I have described in a former work** In *Diff.* i, Lecture XII, the whole of which should be read, as the ecclesiastical history to which Newman is referring is highly complex and no adequate picture can be drawn here. The reader who wishes to understand Newman's view of the crucial parallel case which did so much to destroy his faith in the *via media* as an untried but workable theory, should also read *Dev.* 297–316, and the comments of the editors, *Corr.*, ch. i. The pertinent historical documents may be found in *Documents of the Christian Church*, pp. 63–73.

108. 24 **I was a Monophysite** It is not the doctrines themselves which are significant for Newman's point here, but rather the mode in which a solution for the problem was reached: 'I thought I saw in the controversy . . . and in the Ecumenical Council connected with it, a clear interpretation of the present state of Christendom, and a key to the different parties and personages who

have figured on the Catholic or the Protestant side at and since the era of the Reformation.' (*Diff*. i. 373.)

Eutyches, abbot of a monastery near Constantinople, was condemned in 448 by a council at Constantinople, under the presidency of the Patriarch Flavian, for holding Monophysite views, though he claimed the support of the Fathers, the earlier Councils, and especially of Scripture for his doctrine and, says Newman (*Dev.*, p. 302), might have made a plausible defence of it. Eutyches appealed to Pope Leo, a General Council was called at Ephesus, with Dioscorus, Bishop of Alexandria and friend of Eutyches, appointed president by the Emperor Theodosius, also friendly to Eutyches. This Council, known in history as the *Latrocinium* or Robber Synod, was attended by 135 bishops. It reversed the condemnation of Eutyches and broke up in a riot, the Pope's legates having fled unheard and Flavian being fatally injured. Whatever the weakness or misbelief which led by an almost unanimous decision to the great offence of restoring Eutyches, says Newman, it 'was no local phenomenon, but the unanimous sin of Bishops in every patriarchate and of every school of the East'. (*Dev.*, p. 305.) 'If the East could determine a matter of faith independently of the West, certainly the Monophysite heresy was established as Apostolic truth in all its provinces from Macedonia to Egypt.' (p. 306.)

This decision was reversed in 451 by the Council of Chalcedon, attended by the largest number of bishops (about 600) ever to participate in a General Council, and almost all from the East. The Pope's legates took a prominent part; demanded and were granted that Dioscorus be barred for having held a council without the authority of the Apostolic See; read the Tome of St. Leo enunciating the Catholic doctrine, which was acclaimed in the words, 'Peter has thus spoken through Leo; the Apostles taught this' (*Dev.*, p. 309); and boldly succeeded in getting accepted into the definition of faith the Pope's phrase that Christ was not only *of* but *in* two natures. They threatened to leave the Council if this were not done, and were supported by the Emperor. The point was won, the Council adjourned and sent a note to Leo in which he is referred to as 'the very one commissioned with the guardianship of the Vine by the Saviour'. (*Dev.*, p. 311.)

The Churches of Egypt then disowned the authority of the Council as tyrannical. They gave up Eutyches, too, as an extremist and considered themselves Monophysites with teaching based on that of Athanasius and Cyril, who had pronounced 'One nature Incarnate'. Whether or not their difference was largely a matter of words, the significant point was that they refused to obey the voice of the Church and frequently found themselves associated with the Eutychians, though they had strongly disowned them. The Monophysite heresy, then, seemed to Newman to be an early *via media*, and the Eutychians early Protestants: 'Such a division of an heretical party into the maintainers of an extreme and a moderate view, perspicuous and plausible on paper, yet in fact unreal, impracticable, and hopeless, was no new phenomenon in the history of the Church.' (*Dev.*, p. 315.)

108. 29 **Petavius** See n. 25. 27. For his discussion of Eutyches, see *De Incarnatione*, lib. i, xiii–xviii, of his *Opus de Theologicis Dogmatibus* (Paris,

1644–50). I have not found Newman's precise phrase for Eutyches in Petavius, but for something similar, see I. XIV. v. in vols. 3 and 4 of the edition by F. A. Zacharia (6 vols. in 3, Venice, 1757): 'Praeclare omnino de hoc Eutychis inepto, ac secum pugnante delirio, Gelasius . . . observat. . . .' In his Tome, Pope Leo referred to Eutyches as 'an old man' and 'a rash and ignorant one', and Newman may be conflating the two sources. See *The Tome of Pope Leo the Great*, Latin text with transl., intro., and notes by E. H. Blakeney (London, 1923), chs. i and vi.

108. 35 **a passage from the account** See *Diff*. i. 387–8.

109. 24 **Sooner may my right hand** Ps.cxxxvii. 5 (A.V. Vulg. cxxxvi. 5).

109. 26 **as his who once stretched it out** The hand of Jereboam withered as he stretched it forth to order the seizure of a prophet foretelling the destruction of the king's altar of idolatry. (3 Kings [1 Kings] xiii. 1–4.)

109. 27 **Cranmers, Ridleys, Latimers, and Jewels** Note that the anathema is reserved for the first group of names: sixteenth-century Reformers under continental Protestant influence. Statues of the first three were erected at Oxford in 1839 as a Martyrs' Memorial in an attempt to force an issue with and embarrass the Tractarians, many of whom had slight regard for their doctrines or even their character.

Thomas Cranmer (1489–1556), first Protestant Archbishop of Canterbury. In the reign of Edward VI he did much to Protestantize the Church of England and is largely responsible for the First and Second Prayer Books and for the Thirty-nine Articles. A supporter of Lady Jane Grey, he was condemned to death for treason after the accession of Mary and later excommunicated. Shortly before his execution he made a complete recantation of Protestant doctrine. Seeing that his death was inevitable, however, he publicly repudiated the recantation and died bravely by fire in 1556 at Oxford, shortly after Ridley and Latimer had met the same fate.

Nicholas Ridley (*c*. 1500–55), for a time Cranmer's domestic chaplain, became Bishop of London in 1550, succeeding Bonner, whom he helped to depose. An active spokesman for the new views, he publicly renounced Transubstantiation, decried 'image worship', and was charged with the task of placing Protestantism on a firm basis at his University, Cambridge. Under Mary he was deposed, declared a heretic in a trial at Oxford and, after the passing of the statute *De haeretico comburendo* in 1555, condemned to the stake with Latimer on refusing to recant.

Hugh Latimer (*c*. 1490–1555) helped to establish the Reformation firmly in England by his widely popular sermons. On Cranmer's recommendation he became chaplain to Anne Boleyn and in 1535 was made Bishop of Worcester. In 1539 he resigned, having refused to accept the Catholic-minded Six Articles. He was confined to the Bishop of Chichester's palace for a time and later committed to the Tower of London. The accession of Edward VI gave him freedom. As Cranmer's confidant, he helped to prepare the Homilies. In general, his theology was Lutheran. In 1548 he resumed his preaching and, after Mary ascended the throne, again found himself accused of heresy. He died heroically for his principles.

John Jewel (1522–71) became Bishop of Salisbury in 1560, after a continental exile during Mary's reign. His scholarly *Apologia pro ecclesia Anglicana* (1562), maintaining that the English Church stood on the basis of the first six centuries, made him famous as a champion of the Elizabethan settlement. In 1571 he supervised the publication of the revised Thirty-nine Articles.

109. 28 **Bramhall, Ussher, Taylor, Stillingfleet, and Barrow** Seventeenth-century divines of, on the whole, a more Catholic tendency. Some have been mentioned already.

James Ussher (1581–1656), Archbishop of Armagh, whose theology was Calvinist, was a student of the Fathers who held that England had kept the primitive faith. He remained loyal to Charles I.

Jeremy Taylor (1613–67), one-time chaplain to Laud and later a bishop in Ireland, is especially famous for his devotional works, *Rule and Exercises of Holy Living* (1650) and *Rule and Exercises of Holy Dying* (1651).

Isaac Barrow (1630–77), Professor of Mathematics at Cambridge, was tutor of Isaac Newton. He later became chaplain to Charles II and in 1675 Vice-Chancellor of the University. He is perhaps best known for his *Treatise on the Pope's Supremacy* (1680).

109. 35 **by friends** The friend responsible was Robert Williams, according to *Letters*, ii. 256. See also Liddon, *Pusey*, ii. 152–4.

109. 36 **an article** 'The Anglican Claim of Apostolical Succession', vii. (August 1839), 139–80.

110. 11 **the palmary words** They are thus introduced in the *Review* by Wiseman: 'But it may perhaps be said, that the case between us and Protestants is by no means so simple as that of the Donatists and the Catholics of their times, but that the decision as to a case of schism must depend upon the examination of the points of difference. Now to this we reply, that by the Fathers, who combated the Donatists, the question was essentially considered one of fact rather than of right; that is to say, the very circumstance of one particular Church being out of the aggregation of other Churches, constituted these judges over the other, and left no room for questioning the justice of the condemnation. St. Augustine has a golden sentence on this subject, which should be an axiom in theology: "Quapropter SECURUS iudicat orbis terrarum, bonos non esse qui se dividunt ab orbe terrarum, in quacumque parte orbis terrarum."' (*Contra Epistolam Parmeniani*, bk. iii, ch. 3.)

This Wiseman translates: 'Wherefore, the entire world judges *with security*, that they are not good, who separate themselves from the entire world, in whatever part of the entire world.' (pp. 153–4.) Newman's version is: 'The universal Church is in its judgments secure of truth.' (*Essays*, ii. 101. See pp. 43 and 108–9 for his further comments on the implications.) The Monophysite history was 'a sort of alterative', with Augustine's phrase a 'dose at the end of it'. (*Letters*, ii. 256.)

'This saying of St. Augustine's', he later wrote to Maria Giberne, 'is in the teeth of the Anglican maxim: "Nothing is true but what is to [be] found in the Antenicene church.'" (October 15, 1870. MS. Birmingham Oratory Personal Collection.)

110. 34 **Turn again Whittington** Richard Whittington (d. 1423) was three times Mayor of London. Ill treated as a youth by a cook under whom he served as scullion, he ran away. Resting at Holloway, he heard Bow Bells ringing, as he fancied, the words

> Turn again, Whittington,
> Lord Mayor of London.

He returned to his master's house and a dramatic change of fortune. (See *Oxford Companion to English Literature*.)

110. 36 **'Tolle, lege . . .'** See *Confessions*, bk. viii, ch. 12. Augustine's conversion was wrought when, as he was weeping for his sins and asking for divine help, he heard a child's voice repeating, 'Take and read, take and read.' This he interpreted as a command to open the Bible, and the passage he turned to (Rom. xiii. 13) proved decisive.

111. 5 **to two most intimate friends** Frederic Rogers and Henry Wilberforce (H. T.)

111. 19 **It ends thus:** *P.S.* viii. 32.

112. 10 **'When I look back'** Originally called 'Discipline'. In *V.V.O.*, p. 187, as 'Semita Justorum':

> When I look back upon my former race,
>   Seasons I see at which the Inward Ray
>   More brightly burn'd, or guided some new way,
> Truth, in its wealthier scene and nobler space
> Given for my eye to range and feet to trace.
>   And next I mark, 'twas trial did convey,
>   Or grief or pain, or strange eventful day,
> To my tormented soul such larger grace.
> So now, when 'er, in journeying on, I feel
> The shadow of the Providential Hand,
> Deep breathless stirrings shoot across my breast,
> Searching to know what He will now reveal,
> What sink uncloak, what stricter rule command,
> And girding me to work His full behest.

(The work *sink* is an error for *sin*, the original reading.)

112. 11 **a memorandum** See *A.W.*, p. 5.

113. 22 **my Gradus** *Gradus ad Parnassum, sive novus synonymorum epithetorum, versuum ac phrasium poeticarum thesaurus.* This was a widely used thesaurus, especially by student-writers of Latin poetry. It was originally prepared from an earlier work ascribed to a Père Chastillon, by Paul Alers (1656–1727), a Jesuit who did much scholarly work at Cologne.

113. 26 **what I have already called it** *Apo.*, p. 20.

114. 3 **the fourth monster of Daniel** Dan. vii. 7.

115. 28 **to a friend in 1840** Presumably Keble. See *Apo.*, p. 124.

116. 20 **Preservative against Popery** *A Preservative against Popery in several Select Discourses upon the Principal Heads of Controversy between Protestants and Papists: Being Written and Published by the most eminent Divines of the Church of England chiefly in the Reign of King James II.* Collected by The Right Revd. Edward Gibson, D.D. (3 vols., 1738). Gibson (1669–1748) was Bishop of London, a High Church Whig, whose great work was the *Codex Juris Ecclesiasticae Anglicanae* (1713), still the most complete collection of English ecclesiastical statutes.

116. 25 **Letter about Tract 90** 'A Letter Addressed to the Rev. R. W. Jelf, D.D. . . . In Explanation of the Ninetieth Tract . . .', *V.M.* ii. See p. 369, and for Newman's later comment on the passage, pp. 392–3.

116. 33 **Hurrell Froude's words** See *Letters*, ii. 126.

117. 6 **the policy and acts of Mr. O'Connell** After achieving Catholic Emancipation, Daniel O'Connell attempted to win further reforms, including repeal of the Act of Union, which had deprived Ireland of any real self-government; and the abolition of the tithes by which Irish Catholics were forced to pay the expenses of the Protestant Establishment. In March 1835 members of the Whig and Radical parties met with O'Connell to arrange a campaign against the Tory government of Peel. O'Connell agreed to suspend his agitation against the Act of Union and to support the Whigs in Parliament; and they in turn, on coming to power, would commute the tithe, applying the surplus revenues of the Irish Church to secular purposes, and would press for certain other reforms in Ireland.

'The estimate of O'Connell which prevailed generally among his political opponents was that he was an uncouth and vulgar, foul-mouthed, and unscrupulous apostle of sedition and social disorder, consumed with hatred of the Established Church and the British Constitution, and ready to overthrow both in a convulsion of society should the opportunity offer. To these opinions the *Times* gave free and vigorous expression.' Michael Macdonough, *The Life of Daniel O'Connell* (London, 1903), p. 254. See the whole of ch. xiv, 'In Alliance with the Whigs, 1835–1839', pp. 241–70; and *Letters*, ii. 293.

117. 10 **taken up by the English Catholics** See Ward's *Life of Wiseman*, i. 289–308.

117. 17 **Mr. Spencer** George Spencer (1799–1864), younger son of Earl Spencer and brother of Lord Althorp, was converted to Roman Catholicism in 1829 and ordained shortly thereafter. He later helped to organize a crusade of prayer among Catholics on the Continent for union with the Church of England and wished Anglicans to join it. Newman's diary shows that on January 8, 1840, 'Mr. Spencer called on me with Palmer of Magdalen'. See *Letters*, ii. 264 and 267; *Corr.*, pp. 51–52; and Ward's *Wiseman*, i. 99–103.

119. 13 **some savage and ungrateful words** In 'The Catholicity of the Anglican Church', reprinted in *Essays*, ii, with slight revision. See pp. 71–73.

119. 25 **Ximenes, Borromeo, and Pascal** Francisco Ximénez de Cisneros (1436–1517) was a Spanish Franciscan cardinal famous as a patron of learning and founder in 1504 of the University of Alcalá; as the leader of Ferdinand's expedition against the Moors in Africa, where he took Oran by assault; and, on becoming Regent at Ferdinand's death, as a social reformer.

St. Charles Borromeo (1538–84) was a lawyer who became Archbishop of Milan, where he carried out great reforms and, by his piety and generosity, won the love and deep veneration of his people. He was also one of the organizers of the Council of Trent and writers of its Catechism.

Blaise Pascal (1623–62), mathematician and physicist, whose *Pensées sur la religion* has proved one of the most influential works in the literature of Christian apologetics. Resemblances between Newman's ideas and Pascal's have often been noted. They are vividly implied in T. S. Eliot's comment: '. . . I can think of no Christian writer, not Newman even, more to be commended than Pascal to those who doubt, but who have the mind to conceive, and the sensibility to feel, the disorder, the futility, the meaninglessness, the mystery of life and suffering, and who can only find peace through a satisfaction of the whole being.' (*Selected Essays* [3rd ed., London, 1951], p. 416.)

119. 31 **not to 'have dominion over our faith'** See 2 Cor. i. 24.

120. 24 **occurrences of an awkward character** The allusion is partly to sermons preached at St. Mary's by John B. Morris of Exeter College, a Tractarian of more zeal than common sense. Newman says that he gave a sermon on fasting, ' his one subject, for which he has a monomania', expressing the view 'that it was a good thing, whereas angels feasted on festivals, to make the brute creation fast on fast days; so I am told. May he (*salvis ossibus suis*) have a fasting horse the next time he goes steeple-chasing.' The following sermon gave his fretting hearers '*totidem verbis*, the Roman doctrine of the Mass; and . . . added, in energetic terms, that every one was an unbeliever, carnal, and so forth, who did not hold it. To this he added other speculations of his own still more objectionable.'

The Vice-Chancellor summoned Morris, reproved him, and called him to the attention of the bishop. Newman felt obliged to give an unfavourable judgement on Morris when questioned by the bishop. 'The worst part is that the Vice-Chancellor has not said a single word to me, good or bad, and has taken away his family from St. Mary's.' (*Letters*, ii. 260–1.)

Another awkward occurrence was that Newman's curate at Littlemore, J. R. Bloxam, had been incorrectly reported as having assisted at Mass and bowed his head at the elevation of the Host in the chapel of the Roman Catholic Lord Shrewsbury at Alton Towers. This story had disturbed the Bishop of Oxford. See *Corr.*, pp. 40–47; and R. D. Middleton, *Newman and Bloxam* (London, 1947), pp. 55–58 and 75–76.

120. 28 **the Article analyzed above** Pp. 92 ff.

121. 26 **Bellarmine had reckoned Temporal Prosperity among the Notes of the Church** Not precisely. The fifteenth and last of Bellarmine's Notes is '*Felicitas temporalis, divinitus iis collata, qui Ecclesiam defenderunt*': e.g. from Constantine to Charles V. See *De Notis Ecclesiae* in

Roberti Cardinalis Bellarmini Opera Omnia (8 vols., Naples, 1856–72), ii. 139.

121. 34 **an Article . . . 1840** *Essays*, ii. 1–111.

121. 37 **wrote then to Mr. Bowden** *Corr.*, p. 54. Omissions not indicated in text of *Apo*.

122. 21 **when I was speaking** pp. 78 ff.

123. 18 **Dr. Jelf** Richard Jelf (1798–1871), Fellow of Oriel and Canon of Christ Church, though an old friend of Pusey, took no real part in the Tractarian Movement and had a reputation for impartiality. Following the custom of writing a kind of white paper to such an observer in matters of controversy, Pusey and Newman both wrote him letters in defence of Tract 90. For the passage cited, see *V.M.* ii. 385.

124. 3 **a letter . . . in October 1840, to Keble** This letter, which does not appear in *Corr.*, is dated October 26, 1840. The date of October 29, tentatively suggested in the list of Supplemental Matter, *Apo.*, p. 312, is incorrect. In brackets above the manuscript letter in the Birmingham Oratory Personal Collection is written: '(This was to prepare him. JHN. Sept. 17, 1850.)' Cf. the letter to Rogers, November 25, 1840, *Letters*, ii. 284–6. Newman omits a few minor passages of his letter to Keble, among them this at the end: 'I have not mentioned the subject to Pusey. He is so apt from affection to adopt ideas put before him, that I know not how to proceed with him.'

125. 1 **the late Vice-Chancellor** Ashurst Turner Gilbert (1786–1870), Principal of Brasenose College from 1822, Vice-Chancellor from 1836 to 1840, and Bishop of Chichester from 1842. He was strongly opposed to anything he thought Roman in doctrine or ceremonial. He was the father of eleven children, one of whom, Elizabeth, blind from childhood and later famous for her philanthropic work among the blind, took special pleasure in Newman's services. See *Corr.*, p. 37; Williams's *Autobiography*, p. 146; and Middleton, *Newman and Bloxam*, p. 12.

125. 2 **the present** Philip Wynter (1794–1871) of St. John's, Vice-Chancellor during the critical years 1840–4. He is described by Dean Church as 'a kind-hearted man, but quite unfit to moderate among the strong wills and fierce tempers round him'. (*The Oxford Movement*, p. 284.)

125. 35 **Exeter Hall** The London site of the annual meetings of the Bible Society and other Evangelical groups, the Dissenters among which were usually hostile to the privileges of the Established Church and thus had something in common with O'Connell.

126. 16 **Rogers** See note 150. 6.

127. 12 **'hoisting of the engineer . . .'** *Hamlet*, III. iv. 206.

127. 33 **Milman's book** Henry Hart Milman (1791–1860), the future Dean of St. Paul's, was a student of Gibbon who had created a great stir in 1829 with his anti-miraculous *History of the Jews*. Newman here alludes to his

History of Christianity to the Abolition of Paganism in the Roman Empire (1840), a work in a similar vein which he had reviewed for the *British Critic* in January 1841. See 'Milman's View of Christianity', *Essays*, ii. 186–248.

130. 20 **I have said something on the subject** In *Diff.* i. 378–87, where he argues that both modern times and antiquity show Rome, Protestantism, the *via media*, and the State in the same relative positions.

Newman's point here is that the Anglican Church was like the followers of Eusebius of Nicomedia (d. *c.* 342), friend of the peace-seeking Emperor Constantine. They refused to carry Arianism (i.e. Protestantism) to its logical limits but employed 'cautious phraseology', finding it more consistent 'with their duties towards themselves' to fall back 'upon less assailable principles, to evade inquiry, to explain away texts, and to profess a submission to the voice of their forefathers and of the Catholic world; and they developed their formidable party in that form of heresy which is commonly called Semi-Arianism or Eusebianism' (p. 380): that is, holding the doctrine that the Son is of a like rather than the same substance with that of the Father. The Arians denied that he was of the same substance and held that the Son was a creature.

Semi-Arianism was embraced by Constantius, son of Constantine, and was in the ascendant for about thirty years, 'with quarrels and defections among themselves, restless attempts at stability in faith, violent efforts after a definite creed, fruitless projects of comprehension' (p. 385), when a new party (i.e. the Anglo-Catholic) arose:

'. . . towards the end of their domination, a phenomenon showed itself, which claims our particular attention, as not without parallel in ecclesiastical history, and as reminding us of what is going on, in a humbler way and on a narrower stage, before our eyes. In various districts, especially of Asia Minor, a considerable party had gradually been forming, and had exercised a considerable influence in the ecclesiastical transactions of the period, who, though called Semi-Arians and professing their symbols, had no sympathies with the Eusebians, and indeed were ultimately disowned by them. There seems to have been about a hundred bishops who belonged to this party, and their leaders were men of religious habits and unblemished repute, and approximated so nearly to orthodoxy in their language, that Saints appear among the number of their friends, or have issued from their school. Things could not stand as they were: every year brought its event: Constantius died; parties were broken up,—and this among the rest. It divided into two; as many as fifty-nine of its bishops subscribed the orthodox formula [before Athanasius at a council in Alexandria in 362], and submitted themselves to the Holy See. A body of thirty-four persisted in their separation from it, and afterwards formed a new heresy of their own.' (pp. 385–6.)

130. 24 **The Bishops . . . began to charge** See *Corr.*, pp. 211–27, *passim*; Liddon's *Pusey*, ii. 230–42; and Trevor, *Newman: The Pillar of the Cloud*, pp. 257–61.

130. 36 **On October 17th, I wrote thus to a friend** To Miss Giberne (MS. Birmingham Oratory Personal Collection). See note 207. 12.

131. 30 **the Jerusalem Bishopric** The project, which had social and economic as well as religious implications, appears to have been conceived by Frederick William IV of Prussia and the Chevalier Bunsen (note 42. 28) to give the Protestants a centre in the Holy Land and to inaugurate a great Protestant world movement. It was strongly supported in England by the future Lord Shaftesbury and the Evangelicals, who saw it as countering the Roman tendencies of the Oxford Movement. It also received the support of Palmerston; of Archbishop Howley of Canterbury and Bishop Blomfield of London; and of liberals like Thomas Arnold, who hailed the plan as an endorsement of his own ideas for church reform.

England and Prussia were to nominate in turn for the bishopric, and the bishop was to ordain German ministers on their subscribing the Protestant Confession of Augsburg. The bishop was to have jurisdiction over Protestant congregations which desired such an arrangement, and was even empowered to exercise jurisdiction over congregations in Syria, Chaldea, Egypt, and Abyssinia, where ancient schisms and heresies such as Monophysitism and Nestorianism were still prevalent.

All this was in obvious contradiction to Anglo-Catholic principles of the nature of the Church, but protests availed nothing. The Act became law October 5, 1841. It never worked well. For one thing, there were few Protestants in the Holy Land; and for another and in consequence, the project had aroused the political and religious distrust of Moslems and Orthodox. After the death of the third bishop in 1881, the King of Prussia made no attempt to fill the see, and the treaty of 1841 was dissolved in 1886.

See the account by Canon Ollard in the *Dictionary of English Church History*; Liddon, *Pusey*, ii. 248–60; R. W. Greaves, 'The Jerusalem Bishopric, 1841', *The English Historical Review*, lxiv (July 1949), 328–52; and the explanation in *The Greville Diary*, ed. Philip Whitwell Wilson (2 vols., London, 1927), ii. 302: 'Dec. 20, 1842: . . . We were talking at the Grove about the Bishopric of Jerusalem, when Clarendon told me that the history of our consenting to that ridiculous appointment was, that it was given to Ashley [Lord Shaftesbury] as the price of his negotiating with the *Times*, their support of, or cessation of opposition to, the Syrian War.' The editor adds that Ashley 'was nearly related to Lord Palmerston and Palmerston wanted the support of the *Times*. Hence, a bishop in Jerusalem.'

132. 19 **an article in the** *British Critic* 'Private Judgment', *Essays*, ii. 336–74. For the passage cited, see pp. 365–6.

133. 24 **the gravest suspicion** See *Letters*, ii. 316 and 333.

133. 26 **it had never been a Church** For further explanation, see the article on Newman in the *Dictionnaire de Théologie Catholique*, xi, col. 332.

133. 33 **I think he was a converted Jew** Yes—Michael Solomon Alexander (1799–1845), an ex-rabbi converted in 1825 and from 1832 Professor of Hebrew at King's College, London.

133. 34 **against the Epistle to the Galatians pretty nearly** After their conversion, the Galatians were taught by former Jews that all, including

Gentiles, should observe circumcision and other rites of the Mosaic law. St. Paul's epistle assails the view that man is justified 'by the works of the law'. Alexander's display of his Jewish descent evoked Newman's barb. Evangelicals in England who looked forward to a Hebrew national church, with its own language and customs, 'were in the habit of speaking of the new bishop, and of his bishopric, as "of the circumcision". Some churchmen, mindful how St. Paul had to withstand St. Peter, were troubled how literally this phrase was to be taken.' (Greaves, 'The Jerusalem Bishopric, 1841', *E.H.R.* lxiv. 343.)

133. 38 **Confession of Augsburg** An Evangelical profession of faith drawn up by Melanchthon, after consultation with Luther and others, for presentation before Charles V at the Diet of Augsburg in 1530. In this form it has been the chief creed of Lutheranism. The revised text issued by Melanchthon in 1540 is also accepted by Reformed or Calvinist churches in parts of Germany.

136. 3 **I observed** In a note to the published version of his sermon 'Outward and Inward notes of the Church', *S.S.D.*, pp. 340–1.

138. 10 **Torres Vedras** Three lines constructed by Wellington in 1810 during the Peninsular War, near the town of Torres Vedras, about twenty-five miles north of Lisbon, to be used as a retreat that would help render Lisbon itself impregnable. On October 10 Wellington was forced to enter these lines, where the advancing French General Massena could do nothing against him and in a month, during which his provisions ran low, had to retire. Wellington advanced again, to ultimate victory.

In 1858 Newman advised Acton and his *Rambler* magazine group regarding their conservative ecclesiastical critics: '. . . adopt the policy of Wellington in the lines of Torres Vedras, who kept within shelter, while the enemy scoured the plain, but kept a sharp eye on him and took him at disadvantage whenever it was possible.' (Ward's *Life*, i. 485.)

139. 23 **the promises** i.e. of indefectibility, through Christ's guidance. See Matt. xvi. 18 and xxviii. 20.

140. 8 **my article . . . in January, 1840** 'The Catholicity of the Anglican Church', reprinted in *Essays*, ii. For the passages quoted, see p. 59 and pp. 69–70.

140. 18 **resist Meletius** As a kind of unknown quantity theologically, St. Meletius (d. 381), noted for his simplicity and affability, was made Bishop of Antioch in 360, in the turbulent days of Arian troubles, when Catholics were zealous to maintain the views of the Nicene Council and feared any suspicion of heresy. He had once been a semi-Arian but had avowed orthodox doctrine. After making it clear that he was no Arian— but not clear enough to some—Meletius found himself caught in the midst of a schism between his followers and the Eustathians, named after an exiled bishop who had been a great defender of Nicene orthodoxy. During a period of exile for Meletius, decreed by the Emperor Constans under Arian influence, another bishop was consecrated, the Eustathian Paulinus. When

Meletius returned, the situation was worse than ever. Nevertheless, in spite of once losing the support of Athanasius and even of Jerome and Pope Damasus in the West, with the help of St. Basil he was restored in 378 and succeeded in effecting a large measure of unity in the Eastern Church. He was appointed to preside at the second Ecumenical Council of Constantinople but died during its sessions. The schism was not finally healed until 413.

Newman's point is that Meletius's 'meekness, gentleness, sweetness of temper, and generosity of feeling, seem to have been notes of his churchmanship, which outweighed his separation from Rome and Alexandria, and prove that Saints may be matured in a state which Romanists of this day would fain call schism'. (See *Essays*, ii. 62–65.)

140. 27 **another place** *Apo.*, p. 119.

141. 5 **I say in its Introduction** *V.M.* ii. 269–70.

141. 14. **In my Letter to the Bishop I said** *V.M.* ii. 421. Newman does not always indicate omissions from quotations. They are not significant, however.

142. 1 **Samaria** The reference is to the revolt of the ten tribes of Israel, *c.* 900 B.C., from the house of David (3 Kings [1 Kings] xv). Samaria became the capital of Israel, thenceforward distinct from Judah and the holy city of Jerusalem, seat of the great temple.

142. 4 **the purpose of Four Sermons** *S.S.D.* xxi–xxiv. They were preached on November 28, December 5, 12, and 19.

143. 25 **the multitudes on Mount Carmel** In Samaria, where before all Israel God rejected the sacrifice of the priests of Baal but sent a flame to consume the holocaust of Elias, who had prayed Him to witness that He was God of Israel. (3 Kings xviii.)

143. 26 **the Shunammite** A prominent woman of the town of Shunam who gave food and shelter to the prophet Elisha. (4 Kings iv.)

144. 17 **Christian Observer** The organ of the Evangelical party, founded in 1802 by the Clapham sect, it was of course strongly anti-Tractarian and anti-Catholic. In 1839 Newman thus summed up its view of him: 'One step alone is wanted—to say that I am the Pope *ipsissimus* in disguise.' (*Letters*, ii. 247.) See E. A. Knox, *The Tractarian Movement*, pp. 64–65.

146. 6 **Mr. Church** Richard William Church (1815–90), Newman's special confidant from 1841 to 1845, was elected Fellow of Oriel in 1838. He regarded Newman's famous sermon 'The Ventures of Faith' (*P.S.* iv. 295–306) as the turning point of his life. As junior proctor in 1845, he influenced his colleague Guillemard to veto the proposal to censure the principles of Tract 90 in Convocation. He later became well known as a man of letters, a leading High Churchman, and Dean of St. Paul's. His book *The Oxford Movement, 1833–1845* (1891), which he was completing at the time of his death, is still widely considered the best general account. The friendship of Newman and Church lapsed for about fifteen years after Newman's

conversion but was renewed with the happiest of results. See Newman's dedication to Church of the revised edition of his *University Sermons*; Tristram, *Newman and His Friends*, pp. 182–94; and B. A. Smith, *Dean Church, The Anglican Response to Newman* (London, 1958).

146. 12 **Moberly** George Moberly (1803–85) was Fellow and Tutor of Balliol from 1826 to 1834, where Manning and Tait, the future Archbishop of Canterbury, were among his pupils. He was later Headmaster of Winchester and in 1869, on Gladstone's appointment, became Bishop of Salisbury. He sympathized with the Tractarians and opposed the degradation of W. G. Ward. Married to the daughter of the widower who became the second husband of R. W. Church's mother, he was of great help in introducing Church to Oxford.

146. 18 **Marriott** Charles Marriott (1811–58), a pupil of Moberly at Balliol, was a Fellow and tutor of Oriel and a devoted disciple of Newman. After Newman's conversion he became Dr. Pusey's invaluable aide and was chiefly responsible for the Library of the Fathers. He was known for his gravity, his piety, and his influence over the young. See Church, *The Oxford Movement*, pp. 70–81.

147. 10 **Barter** William Brudenell Barter (1788–1858), one-time Fellow of Oriel and later rector of Burghclere, Hants. He broke off relations with Newman after the conversion but described him in a pamphlet at the time as 'save for this fatal deed the first of living characters'. See *Letters and Diaries*, xi (1961), 309.

Barter published a defence of Tract 90 entitled *Lord Morpeth's Remarks on Tracts for the Times Considered* (London, 1841), in which he explained that he was against the spirit in which the Tracts were opposed but did not agree 'with all the opinions advanced in those writings, especially on the subjects of sin after baptism, and reserve in communicating religious knowledge'. (p. 15.)

147. 16 **The Bishop of London has rejected a man** According to a letter of Pusey to Keble, December 30, 1841, 'The Bp. of London [Blomfield] rejected two candidates (I think two) for asserting the doctrine of the Real Presence and the Real Sacrifice; but on the second day they came fortified with quotations from our divines, and were admitted.' The editor adds that this 'circumstance seems to be referred to in Newman's "Apologia". . .'. (Liddon, *Pusey*, ii. 232, n. 1.)

148. 3 **holding the Holy Eucharist in a Socinian sense** That is, not as a sacrament or even a commemoration, but rather as a thanksgiving for the example shown us by Christ, a perfect man of miraculous birth but not divine. Socinianism strongly resembles Arianism. It derives its name from two sixteenth-century anti-Trinitarians, Lelio (1525–62) and his nephew Fausto Sozzini (1539–1604), who claimed to stand on the Bible as interpreted by reason alone.

148. 5 **our case is diverging from that of Ken's** Thomas Ken (1637–1711), Bishop of Bath and Wells, was famous for his eloquent preaching, his

books of devotion, and his saintly life. One of the original Non-jurors, he refused to preach before William and Mary and remained loyal to James despite the fact that he had been one of the seven bishops tried for refusing to publish in church the King's declaration of liberty of conscience in 1687.

Newman later described the Non-juring secession as 'based on no theological truth at all; it arose simply because . . . certain Bishops and clergy could not take the oaths to a new King. There is something very venerable and winning in Bishop Ken; but this arises in part from the very fact that he was so little disposed to defend any position, or oppose things as they were . . . his difficulty was of a personal nature, and he was unwilling that the Non-juring succession should be continued.' (*Diff.* i. 221.)

148. 27 **Worcester Palmer can whitewash the Ecclesiastical Commission and the Jerusalem Bishopric** In 1836 an Act of Parliament had been passed establishing a permanent body of Ecclesiastical Commissioners, a corporation with power to buy and hold land and propose the alteration and redistribution of ecclesiastical revenues. See Liddon, *Pusey*, ii. 149. For William Palmer's 'whitewash' of the Jerusalem Bishopric, see his letter to *The Times*, October 29, 1841, p. 3.

149. 19 **a very high churchman** Dr. Walter F. Hook. See *Corr.*, p. 100.

149. 24 **the heresy of their diocesan** John Bird Sumner (1780–1862), later Archbishop of Canterbury, on whose appointment to the see of Chester Newman had written in 1828: 'I have just heard of the appointment of John Sumner to Chester, which has given me sincere pleasure.' (*Letters*, i. 165.) Liddon describes him as 'wildly denunciatory' of the Tractarians as 'instruments of Satan to hinder the true principles of the Gospel'. (*Life of Pusey*, ii. 279.)

150. 5 **his brother Henry** Henry William Wilberforce (1807–73), youngest son of William Wilberforce, was a pupil of Newman during the latter's tutorship. In 1845 Newman described him as, since the death of Bowden, his oldest friend after Pusey. *Callista* is dedicated to him. During the troubled years of the Movement he lived away from Oxford in several vicarages. Ambrose St. John was his curate at Walmer, Newman once writing: '. . . that is the reason I love St. John so much because he comes from you and your teaching'. In 1850 he and his wife became Roman Catholics. See Tristram, *Newman and His Friends*, pp. 98–104.

150. 6 **Mr. Frederic Rogers** Frederic Rogers (1811–89) was elected Fellow of Oriel in 1833. He, too, had been tutored by Newman and became one of his closest friends. As Newman drew nearer to Roman Catholicism, however, Rogers felt obliged to separate himself from the man he had been accustomed to regard as the great hope of the English Church. The touching letter in which he did so is reproduced in *Newman and His Friends*, pp. 124–5. Rogers, a lawyer, went on to win fame as a colonial administrator, and in 1871 he became Baron Blachford. Like his good friend Dean Church, he renewed his friendship with Newman a short time before Kingsley's attack and was one of Newman's principal advisers in the writing of the *Apologia*. To him Newman dedicated the revised edition of his *Essays on Miracles*.

151. 1 **The most prominent . . . Mr. Oakeley** This remark, which Abbé Bremond thought an example of cruelty on Newman's part (*The Mystery of Newman* [London, 1907], p. 28), has been explained by Wilfrid Ward, the son of the man commonly regarded as the leader of the aggressive younger Tractarians: William George Ward (1812–82). Fellow of Balliol, logician, and stormy petrel of the Oxford Movement, Ward in 1844 published *The Ideal of a Christian Church*—i.e. Rome—for which Convocation deprived him of his degrees in 1845. He later became a Roman Catholic; and though devoted to Newman and a believer in his theory of knowledge in matters of religion, he proved so ultramontane in temper, exaggerating the limits of papal authority, that Newman had serious differences with him and another old friend and convert, Archbishop Manning.

Ward told his son Wilfrid, then a boy reading the still fairly new *Apologia*: '". . . the following pages are mainly a description of me. When I read them I realized for the first time how much I had irritated Newman at Oxford. He does not mention my name, and that is partly because of his present displeasure with me. But also it has a more friendly reason, for he did not wish to pass criticisms on me by name. He mentions Oakeley, who was identified with my views at Oxford, and then excepts him personally from his criticisms." The passage he specially pointed to as evidencing Newman's irritation in Oxford days, was that in which he intimates that the representatives of the avowedly Roman section of the Movement worried him by incessant argument and publicly claimed his assent—which they had forcibly extorted—to their own conclusions.' (*Apo.*, ed. Wilfrid Ward [London, 1913], p. xvii.)

Liddon, however, says that the 'two prominent men' of the younger group were Oakeley and Ward (*Pusey*, ii. 217); and there is some reason for believing that Oakeley, though influenced by Ward, was indeed somewhat better known than Ward at the time of which Newman is writing. For Newman's 'present displeasure' with Ward and good relations with Oakeley, see Edward Kelly, S.J., 'Newman's *Apologia* and the Ultramontanes', *passim*, esp. p. 34 in *Newman's Apologia: A Classic Reconsidered*, ed. V. F. Blehl, S.J. and F. X. Connolly.

152. 19 **in one of my earliest printed Sermons** 'The Reverence due to the Virgin Mary', a sermon for the Feast of the Annunciation. *P.S.* ii. 127–38.

154. 1 **in one of the Letters** To Dr. Jelf, *V.M.* ii. 386–7.

155. 4 **St. Leo had overset . . . Anglicanism** Because his authority had been acclaimed by antiquity at the Council of Chalcedon, as maintained in the preceding chapter.

155. 30 **'Non in dialectica. . .'** 'It has not pleased God to work the salvation of His people through dialectic.' (St. Ambrose, *De Fide*, i. 42.) This is the epigraph of the *Grammar of Assent*.

158. 18 **'Di me terrent . . .'** Turnus at bay retorts to the goading of Aeneas: 'It is not your hot words that frighten me, fierce man, but the gods and the enmity of Jupiter.' (*Aeneid* xii. 894–5.)

158. 28 **Ubi lapsus? quid feci?** 'Where was the fault? What have I done?' These words are said to have been adopted by the Powderham branch of the Courtenay family to express astonishment at a sudden and undeserved blow—the loss of the Earldom of Devon. See C. N. Elvin, *A Hand-Book of Mottoes* (London, 1860), p. 205.

158. 30 **Heads of Houses** An incident heightened in memory, it would seem. On August 28, 1850, Newman had written to J. M. Capes: 'I took the place at Littlemore in July 1841, put it to rights in the autumn—it made a talk all through the October term. I went up there the following Lent. I had already been two Lents (1840–41) there. I think I heard of Little Jenks [Jenkyns, Master of Balliol] & Big Ben [Symons, Warden of Wadham] going to see the progress of the building.' (Oratory Copied Letters, 1850.) Mark Pattison was apparently in error in saying that Newman had shut the door in the face of Symons, who had asked to see the monastery. 'We have no monastery here', Newman is supposed to have replied. (*Memoirs*, p. 190.)

159. 6 **a newspaper . . . of April 9** Identified in the draft of this letter (Orat. Miscellaneous Letters, 1842) as the John Bull Newspaper.

161. 26 **no 'monastery' is in process** This reply of a harried Newman is, strictly speaking, quite accurate. Littlemore was a kind of retreat house where all clergymen were welcome rather than a formal society governed by monastic vows. Yet Newman once had hopes for a monastery (*Apo.*, p. 123) there, those who lived there liked to call it a monastery, and certainly the life there was a very austere one—more so, indeed, than that of most monasteries. For a detailed description, see Middleton, *Newman and Bloxam*, pp. 69 ff. Fr. Dominic Barberi, who received Newman into the Roman Church, said Littlemore 'reminded him of Catholic monasteries of the strictest observance'. See Frederick Oakeley, *Personal Reminiscences of the Oxford Movement* (London, 1855), pp. 16–17.

162. 12 **young men in Oxford, whose testimonials for Orders had been refused** On December 7, 1841, Peter Young, M.A., though John Keble's curate, was refused admittance to his examination for priest's orders by the Bishop of Winchester 'on the ground of his declining positively to deny all mysterious Presence of our Blessed Lord's Body and Blood in the Holy Eucharist, excepting to the faithful receiver, he, the said Peter Young, desiring to leave the same an open question—that is, neither to affirm nor deny such Presence'. (From Keble's Protest in *Letters*, ii. 441. See also ibid., p. 313, and Liddon, *Pusey*, ii. 230–4.)

162. 28 **the unexpected conversion of one of them** William Lockhart (1820–92), of Exeter College, who received his B.A. in 1842 and, already wavering, joined Newman at Littlemore. Newman made him promise to wait three years before taking any action, but he entered the Roman Church in August 1843, the first of the Tractarians to do so. Newman regarded the affair as 'a very great scandal'—'I do not know how I can hold up my head again while I have St. Mary's.' (*Letters*, ii. 373–4; 378–9; and *Correspondence*, pp. 250–1.) Lockhart later became a priest of the Order of Charity

and in 1891 published *Cardinal Newman. Reminiscences of 50 Years Since, by One of His Oldest Living Disciples.*

163. 30 **June 20, 1843** This and the following letter, reproduced in full in *Corr.*, pp. 236–7 and 242, are early letters to Henry Wilberforce's curate, Ambrose St. John, to whom the *Apologia* is especially dedicated. See p. 252.

163. 35 **The Authorities find . . . military power** In May 1843 both Pusey and the Revd. T. E. Morris, a tutor of Christ Church, were rebuked by the University authorities 'under the provisions of the Statute Tit. xvi. § 11'—Pusey for his views on the Real Presence, Morris for his distinction between the intercession and invocation of saints (*Corr.*, pp. 229–30). Pusey, in a trial in which his accuser acted as one of the judges, was suspended from preaching for two years. See Liddon, *Pusey*, ii. 306–63.

164. 23 **A. B.** Lockhart.

166. 2 **a young clergyman** Bernard Smith (1815–1903), Fellow of Magdalen from 1836 to 1839 and then rector of Leadenham in the diocese of Bishop Kaye of Lincoln, the bishop here referred to, who had objected to Pugin's decoration and the ritualism of Smith's church. Smith became a Roman Catholic on December 15, 1842, a move that created a furore and prompted a strange correspondence in the *Morning Herald*, including a bogus letter by Smith denying his conversion. For a fuller account, including this correspondence and the correspondence Newman refers to, see R. D. Middleton, *Magdalen Studies* (London, 1936), pp. 231–67; and Ward's *Wiseman*, i. 409–13.

166. 7 **a Paper** *The English Churchman.*

166. 10 **Whoever is the author of it** The bishop's informant was the Revd. Henry Schneider, Smith's brother-in-law, who got the idea from a partially misunderstood remark of Smith's mother.

168. 34 **My last Sermon** 'The Parting of Friends', *S.S.D.* See *Letters*, ii. 378–9.

169. 6 **Mr. Stanley Faber** George Stanley Faber (1773–1854), Fellow of Lincoln College and from 1832 until his death Master of Sherburn Hospital, Durham, was a prolific Evangelical controversialist who had earlier engaged Newman in a fairly lengthy private debate on the subject of justification (MS. Orat. Personal Collection). According to a manuscript letter (undated) of his nephew, Faber made this particular charge in his *Letters on Tractarian Secessions to Popery* (1846). After a three-way exchange of letters, he withdrew it, only to renew it in 1851 in *Papal Infallibility, a Letter to a Dignitary of the Church of Rome*. See *Letters and Diaries*, xiii (1963), 302–3, 327–8, and 513; and xiv (1964), 332, 336, and 353.

169. 9 **His nephew** Francis A. Faber (1804–76), elder brother of Frederick Faber and Rector of Saunderton, Bucks. See *Apo.*, p. 332.

170. 27 **Catholic acquaintances** Most of the following letters are to the Revd. Dr. Charles W. Russell (1812–80) of Ireland, ecclesiastical historian

and student of Leibnitz, co-editor with Wiseman of the *Dublin Review*, and future president of Maynooth College, the chief Irish seminary. See *Apo.*, p. 176, where he is said to have 'had, perhaps, more to do with my conversion than any one else'. (But cf. pp. 332–3.) He began his correspondence with Newman on a sudden impulse on Holy Thursday, 1841, having been pained by Newman's remarks in Tract 90 on Transubstantiation. For his letters and more of Newman's, see *Corr.*, pp. 117 ff.; see also Tristram, *Newman and His Friends*, pp. 161–7. *Loss and Gain*, the story of a convert, is dedicated to Dr. Russell in the revised edition of Newman's works.

170. 28 **April 8** For the complete text of this letter to de Lisle, see E. S. Purcell, *Life and Letters of Ambrose Phillips de Lisle* (2 vols., London, 1900), i. 223–4.

172. 34 **I will not set my teeth on edge** See Ezechiel xviii. 1–3, where it is said that children should not be held responsible for sins of the parents.

173. 5 **a zealous Catholic layman** Ambrose Lisle Phillips or Phillips de Lisle (1809–78), as he was later known, a layman converted in youth and very eager for church reunion. He was instrumental in the founding at Paris in 1837 of the Society of Prayers for the Conversion of England. Through his correspondence in 1841 with J. R. Bloxam, one-time curate at Littlemore, Newman and other Tractarians were drawn into the discussion. See ch. v, 'Letters on Reunion', in Middleton's *Newman and Bloxam*.

174. 12 **the ἄνομος** The lawless one. The word is used in 1 John, but not as referring specifically to Antichrist, who is mentioned several times.

175. 16 **'approving themselves'** See 2 Cor. vi. 4.

176. 12 **He called again another summer** Newman's Diary for August 1, 1843: 'Walked into Oxford to lionize Mr. Russell of Maynooth.' (MS. Birmingham Oratory.)

176. 17 **Veron's Rule of Faith** *Règle de la foi catholique* (1649), a widely translated work by the chief French Catholic controversialist of his day, François Veron (*c.* 1575–1625), who had great success in winning converts. He was careful to separate authentic points of doctrine from opinions of the schools, popular legends, etc.; and he was noted for his considerateness to Protestants.

176. 17 **some Treatises of the Wallenburghs** Adrian (d. 1669) and Pierre (d. 1675) de Wallenburch, Dutch Catholic apologists, were brothers known for their theological learning and controversial skill. At Cologne, where Pierre in 1669 succeeded Adrian as auxiliary bishop, their works were collected in two folio volumes, *Tractatus generales de controversiis fidei* and *Tractatus speciales*.

176. 18 **St. Alfonso Liguori's Sermons** St. Alphonsus Liguori (1696–1787), Doctor of the Church and specialist in moral theology, founded the Congregation of the Most Holy Redeemer in 1732. He was also a poet and composer. He had a special devotion to the Blessed Virgin, and Pusey was

later to use his *Glories of Mary* (1750) as an example of Roman Catholic excesses. Newman, like so many of the old English Catholics but unlike such younger converts as Frederick Faber and his London Oratorians, was wary of the more unrestrained forms of continental devotion, both temperamentally and because he feared theological exaggeration. See *Apo.*, pp. 244 ff.; Ward's *Life*, i. 204 ff.; and *Diff.* ii. 89–118.

177. 23 **the Exercises of St. Ignatius** The famous manual of Ignatius Loyola for the amendment and sanctification of life. For a good outline of the work and its effect on a writer whose entry into the Society of Jesus Newman encouraged, see John Pick, *Gerard Manley Hopkins, Priest and Poet* (London, 1942), pp. 24–39. For Newman's account of the *Exercises* and of the books mentioned below, see *Dev.*, pp. 429–36.

178. 21 **to the principle of development** By reason of the scope of his famous *Essay*, the theory of development of doctrine is especially associated with the name of Newman, but in one form or another it may be traced back to the Fathers. See F. Marin-Sola, *L'Évolution homogène du dogme catholique* (2nd ed., Paris, 1924); Jean Guitton, *La Philosophie de Newman: essai sur l'idée de developpement* (Paris, 1933); Owen Chadwick, *From Bossuet to Newman, The Idea of Doctrinal Development* (Cambridge, 1957); and J. H. Walgrave, *Newman the Theologian*, transl. A. V. Littledale (London, 1960).

178. 23 **I had made mention of it** *Essays*, i. 284 ff.

178. 25 **had introduced it into my . . . Arians** Ch. ii, sect. iv.

178. 32 **a letter to a friend . . . July 14, 1844** Mrs. Wm. Froude.

179. 20 **The analogy of the Old Testament, and also of the New** See *Dev.*, pp. 64–74.

180. 1 **And I hold this still** The following two pages offer perhaps the best summary of the Newmanian theory of belief as outlined in the *Grammar of Assent.*

181. 29 **I made a formal Retractation** In the *Oxford Conservative Journal* and the *Oxford University Herald*. See *Letters*, ii. 363–5. The article is reprinted as the Conclusion of *V.M.* ii, the passage quoted below appearing on pp. 432–3.

185. 35 **Valeat quantum** *Valeat quantum valere potest*: Let it pass for what it is worth.

186. 2 **the following letter** The passages are taken from two letters addressed to Mrs. William Froude on April 3 and 4. See Gordon Huntington Harper, *Cardinal Newman and William Froude, F.R.S., a Correspondence* (Baltimore and London, 1933), pp. 38–42.

186. 3 **William's chief distress** William Froude (1810–79), brother of Hurrell and James Anthony, was a distinguished engineer and naval architect, to whose scientific achievements his biography in *D.N.B.* is entirely devoted. He was also deeply concerned with the problem of religious certi-

tude and never able to resolve his doubts. Though his wife and son became Roman Catholics, he remained unsettled, keeping up a correspondence with his close friend Newman, especially on the question of probable evidence. Ward prints two important letters in *Life*, ii. 465–6 and 587. The last one never reached Froude. From South Africa, where he had gone for distraction after his wife's death in 1878, he sent a letter to Newman outlining his religious position; but before Newman had finished correcting the rough draft of his reply, Froude was dead. See Tristram, *Newman and His Friends*, pp. 178–82.

186. 15 **Laud on Tradition** See 'A Relation of the Conference between William Laud . . . and Mr. Fisher the Jesuit', *Works*, ii (Oxford, 1849), esp. sect. xvi, pp. 70–131:

'The key that lets men into the Scriptures, even to this knowledge of them, that they are the word of God, is the tradition of the Church: but when they are in, they hear Christ Himself immediately speaking in Scripture to the faithful; and "His sheep" do not only "hear", but know, "His voice" . . . upon the matter we have a double divine testimony, altogether infallible, to confirm unto us, that Scripture is the word of God. The first is the tradition of the Church of the Apostles themselves, who delivered immediately to the world the word of Christ: the other, the Scripture itself; but after it hath received this testimony. And into these we do, and may safely, resolve our faith. As for the tradition of after ages . . . we believe them . . . because they do not preach other things than those former (the Apostles) left in *Scriptis certissimis*, "in most certain Scripture".' (pp. 115–16.)

188. 31 **the same friend** For the two following letters to Keble in full, see *Corr.*, pp. 219–20 and 225–9.

190. 4 **Lives of the English Saints** For the genesis of the idea, see *Letters*, ii. 308–9; on the difficulties involved, *Corr.*, pp. 280–8; and for the lives themselves, including biographical sketches of the authors, see *The Lives of the English Saints*, ed. A. W. Hutton (6 vols., London, 1900–1). Thirty-three lives out of a projected 300 were completed by some fourteen authors. Newman wrote the lives of Sts. Edelwald and Gundleus, the prose parts of St. Bettelin, and the advertisement for the vol. on the family of St. Richard. After the first two numbers, James Toovey (*c.* 1814–93), a London bookseller, succeeded him as editor. See also *Apo.*, Note D, p. 280. Mark Pattison and J. A. Froude emerged from the project well on the road to scepticism in reaction against working seriously on material in large part legendary. But see J. Derek Holmes, 'Newman's Reputation and *The Lives of the English Saints*', *The Catholic Historical Review*, li (Jan. 1966), 528–38.

190. 5 **a publisher** Francis Rivington (1805–85), son of the founder of the house which published the Tracts. He retired in 1859 and became a writer on religious and sociological problems. Among his works is *A Protest against Extreme Ritualism* (1867).

190. 25 **About thirty names follow** 'Bowden, Johnson (Observatory), Church, Haddan, Oakeley, Tickell (Univ.), Lewis, J. Mozley, Stanley

(perhaps), Lake, Macmullen, Faber (Univ.), Brewer, Coffin, Dalgairns, Ashworth, T. Ryder, Pattison, A. Christie, Pritchard (Balliol), Ormsby (Lincoln), Bridges (Oriel), Lockhart (Exeter), Harris (Magdalen), Barrow (Queens), Meyrick (C.C.C.), Chretien (Oriel), Murray (Ch. Ch.), Collings (Ch. Ch.), etc.' *Corr.*, p. 228.

191. 5 **Life of St. Stephen Harding** Stephen Harding (d. 1134) was Abbot of Citeaux and founder of the strict Cistercian Order. The life was written by John Dobree Dalgairns (1818–76), the principal contributor to the series. Dalgairns joined Newman at Littlemore, preceded him into the Roman Church, and later became a priest of the Oratory, succeeding Faber as Superior of the London Oratory in 1863. He was a member of the Metaphysical Society and well known for writings on philosophical, historical, and religious topics.

192. 4 **the author** Frederick Oakeley.

192. 9 **the authors have been considered 'hot-headed fanatic young men'** By Kingsley in *What, Then, Does Dr. Newman Mean?*

192. 13 **Mr. Johnson** See note 213. 5. Neither Bowden's nor Johnson's life was actually written.

192. 22 **Mr. A. B.** William Lockhart.

193. 10 **a Volume of Sermons** *S.S.D.* The four against moving are XXI–XXIV.

193. 13 **The late Mr. Goldsmid** Nathaniel Goldsmid (1807–60), of Exeter College, a lawyer friend of the Tractarians. In 1850 he and his wife became Roman Catholics.

193. 16 **a Scriptural image from Walter Scott** See Exod. xxiii. 19 and xxxiv. 26, and *Kenilworth*, ch. xli. The reference is to Foster's denunciation of the conspirator Varney for causing the death of Amy Robsart as she rushed forth in response to what she supposed was her husband's signal: 'Thou hast destroyed her by means of her best affections—It is a seething of the kid in the mother's milk.'

193. 19 **Victrix causa** The victorious side had the blessing of the gods but the vanquished had Cato's. The reference (Lucan, *Pharsalia*, i. 128) is to the breach between Caesar and Pompey in the First Triumvirate, with Caesar victorious. For Lucan, Pompey, and Cato were heroes, but Caesar was a villain. Cato symbolized truth and honour.

194. 16 **more than three persons** Rogers and Henry and William Wilberforce. See *Letters*, ii. 379.

194. 22 **the friend** Keble.

197. 10 **Je mourrai seul** The exact words, as Nédoncelle has pointed out, are *on mourra seul*. *Pensées de Blaise Pascal*, ed. Leon Brunschvicg (3 vols., Paris, 1904), ii, fr. 211, p. 129.

197. 30 **a gifted and deeply earnest lady** Maria Spencer Ruscombe Poole (1815–81), later Sister Mary Imelda, daughter of a solicitor at Bridgwater, was greatly influenced by Newman's sermons and Pusey's spiritual counsel. After moving to Bath in 1845, she and two of her sisters became Roman Catholics. She recounted her religious history in 'The Modern Pilgrim's Progress, or the History of Puseyism in a Dream', published in *The Rambler*, xi (Feb. 1853), 122–35. See *Letters and Diaries*, xi. 352–3.

198. 24 **The following three letters** These, with Manning's, are reprinted in *Corr.*, pp. 271–80. Both Manning and Gladstone felt that Newman was making too much of the strictures on Tract 90 and that the Anglican Church was becoming progressively more receptive to Catholic principles. Manning forwarded Newman's letter of October 14, 1843, to Gladstone. Manning replied to Newman October 23, and Gladstone to Manning on October 24. For Gladstone's letter see *Correspondence on Church and Religion of W. E. Gladstone*, ed. D. C. Lathbury (2 vols., London, 1910), i. 281–3.

198. 25 **Archdeacon Manning** Henry Edward Manning (1808–92), then Archdeacon of Chichester and from 1865 Archbishop of Westminster. Much has been written about the cool relations of the two men. They were never really intimate friends, and only during the period of these letters were they in close touch with one another. Fr. Tristram suggested that the ultimate source of Newman's distrust of Manning was Manning's behaviour at this time:

'Newman's self-revelation had a dramatic climax. Manning in a panic, feeling himself under the "painful, saddening, sickening necessity" of expressing his views on the Roman question, did so with no little vehemence in the Fifth of November Sermon [a strongly anti-papal sermon for Guy Fawkes' Day] at St. Mary's. On the following day Newman made this grim and laconic entry in his diary, "Manning called", but he did not add, what seems to have been the fact, that he refused to see him. It was J. A. Froude who revealed this. He happened to be at Littlemore that afternoon with Mark Pattison; and Newman sent him to the door to inform Manning that he was "not at home". So great was Froude's embarrassment that he escorted Manning back to Oxford without his hat, which in those days appears to have been a serious breach of the laws of decorum. There is no doubt that, whatever pleas Manning had to put forward in justification of his action, Newman never felt much confidence in him again.' (*Newman and His Friends*, pp. 151–2.) See E. S. Purcell, *Life of Cardinal Manning* (2 vols., London, 1896), i. 244–9.

Manning entered the Roman Catholic Church in 1851, and the two men were on good terms until Manning came to believe that Newman had joined Acton and Simpson in attacking his views on the Roman Question. Manning felt that the success of the *Apologia* made Newman a very dangerous spokesman for a worldly, minimizing type of Catholicism. See Trevor, *Newman: Light in Winter*, pp. 446–9.

199. 7 **Even my own Bishop has said** In a charge of May 23, 1842. The objectionable expression had been suggested to Bagot by a chaplain,

the Revd. F. E. Paget, who later wrote: 'I was guilty of doing much mischief by an honest but unguarded, and ill-considered opinion.' (Liddon, *Pusey*, ii. 286–7.)

199. 30 **Oct. 25, 1843** Manning sent this also to Gladstone, who replied October 28 and October 30. See Purcell, *Manning*, i. 242–3; and *Corr.*, p. 278.

201. 22 **one near friend** James Bowling Mozley (1813–78). See *Letters*, ii. 378–9 and 381. Mozley was a member of a family prominent in the Oxford Movement. His elder brother, Thomas, a Fellow of Oriel, wrote helpful though not always accurate *Reminiscences* and married Newman's sister Harriett; his sister Anne became the first editor of Newman's letters; and his brother John married Newman's sister Jemima. For ten years J. B. Mozley was editor of the *Christian Remembrancer*, which in 1844 succeeded the *British Critic* as the organ of the Tractarians. He wrote many works on theological subjects, including the *Theory of Development* (1878), a criticism of Newman's *Essay*. In 1871 he became Regius Professor of Divinity at Oxford.

202. 21 **A common friend of ours** Probably W. G. Ward but perhaps T. E. Morris. See *Letters*, ii. 314, and Liddon, *Pusey*, ii. 228–9.

203. 2 **another friend** Perhaps Manning—see conclusion of letter of October 25, 1843, *Corr.*, p. 278. But the word 'another' makes this doubtful.

203. 4 **Mr. James Hope, now Mr. Hope Scott** James R. Hope (1812–73), one-time Fellow of Merton, became perhaps the most noted parliamentary lawyer of his time. He published a protest against the Jerusalem Bishopric and after the Gorham judgement entered the Roman Church. He married the granddaughter of Sir Walter Scott and, on coming into possession of Abbotsford in 1853, assumed the name of Hope-Scott. See *Newman and His Friends*, pp. 104–8, and the deeply moving sermon Newman preached at Hope-Scott's funeral: 'In the World, but Not of the World', *O.S.*, pp. 263–80.

203. 13 **a dear and old friend** John William Bowden, Newman's oldest friend, who died September 15, 1844. *Letters*, ii. 380, *passim*.

205. 2 **to another friend** Ambrose St. John. *Corr.*, pp. 333–4.

205. 10 **Zoar** Vulg. Segor, little one. The little town where Lot took shelter and which the Lord spared on his prayer. Gen. xix. 18–22.

205. 12 **Moab and Ammon** The sons of Lot by his daughters. The Israelites were forbidden to dwell in their land. (Deut. ii. 9 and 19.) They here presumably stand for the Evangelicals and the Liberals.

206. 4 **Nov. 16, 1844** To Manning (Oratory Copied Letters).

207. 12 **a lady** Maria Rosina Giberne (1802–85), sister-in-law of the Revd. Walter Mayers, the classics teacher at Ealing who was so instrumental in Newman's early conversion. An old friend of the Newman family, she

corresponded with Newman for many years, became a Roman Catholic in 1845, and died as a nun of the Order of Visitation. See *Letters*, i. 155; T. Mozley's *Reminiscences*, ii. 42–47; and *Letters and Diaries*, xi. 341. The best account of Miss Giberne at present is to be found in Meriol Trevor's *Newman: The Pillar of the Cloud* and *Newman: Light in Winter*. The manuscript autobiography of Miss Giberne is in the Birmingham Oratory

208. 30 **the words of the Psalmist** Ps. lxxxvi (Vulg. lxxxv). 17.

209. 15 **Various measures** See Additional Notes, *Apo.*, p. 333, and *Corr.*, pp. 293 and 348–9. Gladstone suggested to Manning that by a discreet use of his knowledge he might influence some of the bishops to soften their charges; and that 'cords of silk' must be used to bind Newman to the Anglican Church.

209. 17 **an exceedingly kind article** J. B. Mozley's 'Recent Proceedings at Oxford', in the *Christian Remembrancer* for April 1845.

210. 16 **Badeley** Edward Lowth Badeley (1803–68), a lawyer specializing in ecclesiastical cases, was a close friend of Hope-Scott. He served as one of the counsel for the Bishop of Exeter in the Gorham case and entered the Roman Catholic Church after fruitless protest against the Gorham judgement. He was one of Newman's counsel during the Achilli trial; and to him, indirectly, we owe the *Apologia*, as it was he who advised Newman that Kingsley's proposed reparation for his insult was altogether inadequate. To him Newman dedicated *V.V.O.* See Tristram, *Newman and His Friends*, pp. 172–8.

210. 28 **you ought to measure** The doctrine of the 'economy' in a nutshell.

211. 12 **One of my friends at Littlemore** J. D. Dalgairns. See Ward, *Life*, i. 94–95, n. 1.

211. 14 **Father Dominic** Domenico Barberi (1792–1849) was a missionary priest of Italian peasant stock whose great ambition was the conversion of England to Roman Catholicism. In 1842 at Aston Hall, Staffordshire, after twenty-eight years of effort, he established the Passionist Order in England. He wrote several works of moral theology, devotion, and controversy. In 1911 he was declared 'Venerable' by Rome as the first step towards canonization; and in 1963 he was beatified or declared Blessed, as the second. See Dennis Gwynn, *Father Dominic Barberi* (London, 1948).

211. 21 **a number of friends** Thirty in all, according to Newman's entry in his journal for October 9: 'wrote to J. [his sister Jemima Mozley], Mrs. Wood, H. B[owden], Woodgate, Badeley, E. Coleridge, I. Williams, Wilson, Dr. Russell, Faber, Belaney, F. [probably Francis W. Newman], M. R. G. [Miss Giberne], Allies, Mrs. W. F[roude], Rogers, Rivington, Pusey, Anderdon, Manning, Barter, H. W[ilberforce], Miss Parker, Dodsworth, Mrs. Bowden, Watts Russell, R. Williams, Church, Capes, Dear.' (*Corr.*, pp. 388–9.)
The letter quoted is to R. W. Church. For it and some twenty of the others, see *Letters and Diaries*, xi. 3–15.

211. 28 **on St. John Baptist's day last year** Newman's Diary, June 24, 1844: 'Father Domenico called.'

212. 5 **Cardinal Acton** Charles Januarius Acton (1803–47), great-uncle of the historian Lord Acton, was the son of a Shropshire baronet who became Prime Minister of the Kingdom of Naples. Charles was educated in England and Rome, had a successful career in the papal diplomatic service, and was made cardinal in 1842. He was protector of the English College at Rome, and all important affairs of the church relating to England were referred to him.

212. 32 **Oscott** One-time Roman Catholic mission in Staffordshire and since 1793 a college, with Wiseman as president from 1840 to 1847. In the old building—Old Oscott or Maryvale, as they named it—Newman and five companions lived from February 23, 1846, till September 7, before going on to the English College at Rome.

212. 35 **'Obliviscere . . .'** 'Forget thy people and thy father's house.' (Ps. xliv [A.V. xlv]. 10.) On this concluding passage, see Houghton, *The Art of Newman's Apologia*, pp. 65–67; and Charles Reding's farewell to Oxford in *Loss and Gain*, pp. 374–5.

213. 5 **Mr. Johnson's** Manuel Johnson (1805–59) was a noted astronomer who, since 1839, had been in charge of Oxford's Radcliffe Observatory, a gathering place for the Tractarians, with whom Johnson sympathized. See Newman's letter to him, announcing the conversion of Mrs. Bowden, in *Letters and Diaries*, xi. 197–8.

213. 6 **Mr. Copeland** William John Copeland (1804–85) was a Fellow of Trinity who became Newman's curate at Littlemore in 1840 and remained in charge there after Newman's resignation. In 1862 an accidental meeting with Copeland in London began a renewal of relations with old friends which greatly heartened Newman and led to a new period of happiness and activity. As he confided to a notebook, 'Copeland, having met me accidentally in London, came to see us here, and he spread such a kind report of me, that Keble wrote to me, Rogers visited me . . . and Church proposed to do so. Williams too wished to come and see me—but *he* had never lost sight of me. The kind feeling was growing, when (Copeland accidentally being here) I began the Kingsley controversy, the effect of which I need not enlarge on. . . . And thus I am in a totally different position now [February 22, 1865] to what I was in January 1863. . . .' (*A.W.*, p. 261.) It was Copeland who, by re-editing Newman's *P.P.S.* (8 vols., 1868), gave him courage to reprint his Anglican works and go on with a collected edition. To him Newman dedicated *S.S.D.*

213. 7 **Mr. Buckle** George Buckle (1820–1900), B.A. Corpus Christi, 1842, and from 1848 to 1852 Fellow and Tutor of Oriel. He had translated one volume of Fleury. See Ward, *Life*, ii. 342–3, and *Letters and Diaries*, xi. 335.

213. 7 **Mr. Pattison** Mark Pattison (1813–84), Fellow and eventually Rector of Lincoln College, was an active Tractarian. He contributed lives

of Stephen Langton and St. Edmund to the series on English saints. He later became one of Oxford's leading liberal reformers.

213. 7 **Mr. Lewis** David Lewis (1814–95), Fellow and in 1845 Vice-Principal of Jesus College, was Newman's curate during his last years at St. Mary's. In May 1846 he entered the Roman Church and later helped to edit the *Tablet*, a Catholic newspaper. He also translated the works of St. Theresa of Avila and St. John of the Cross. See *Letters and Diaries*, xi. 344.

213. 8 **Dr. Ogle** James Adey Ogle (1792–1857), a mathematician, was Newman's private tutor at Trinity. In 1824 he became Aldrich Professor of Medicine and in 1851 Regius Professor. He remained a good friend of Newman but was not associated with the Oxford Movement. He was a prominent advocate of University reforms aimed at making science more important in the curriculum.

214. 26 **Ten thousand difficulties** See Ward, *Life*, ii. 250.

215. 15 **Sir Thomas More** (1477–1535), Henry VIII's Lord Chancellor, was canonized in 1935, the fourth centenary of his execution for refusing to acknowledge the ecclesiastical supremacy of the King. Macaulay's remarks are from his essay on von Ranke's *History of the Popes*, *Works* (London, 1879), vi. 458. See also *Idea*, pp. 435–8.

215. 25 **a rising school of philosophy now** Probably a reference to the empiricism of J. S. Mill, whose *System of Logic* engaged Newman's attention for a number of years after 1857, as manuscript philosophical papers at the Oratory indicate.

215. 33 **the doctrine of the Trinity** See *G.A.*, pp. 122–41.

216. 36 **Were it not for this voice** The approach to God through conscience, to Christianity through the sense of sin, the difficulty in many formal proofs, the importance of the whole man in reasoning (a subjectivity which is not mere relativism), a strong ethical bent—these are some of the ways in which Newman resembled his then almost unknown contemporary, Søren Kierkegaard (1813–55), the Danish theologian. Thus in a passage recalling Newman's 'two and two only absolute and luminously self-evident beings', Kierkegaard writes:

'The most objective truth which is necessarily and universally true for every one and for the whole of creation, the truth that God exists, is given to you—to *you* in the most emphatic sense of the word—most safely hidden by the most subjective truth which in all the immensity of creation is *only* valid for you, which you can communicate to no one except to God alone, and which remains for all eternity a secret between you and God and which you can only communicate to God because it was he who first communicated it to you in your conscience. Truth lies in subjectivity.' Quoted by Theodore Haecker, *Søren Kierkegaard* (London, 1937), pp. 23–24. See also pp. 57–58. For a valuable discussion of the role of conscience in Newman's thought, see Walgrave, *Newman the Theologian*, pp. 201–40 and 342–63.

217. 7 **the prophet's scroll** Ezek. ii. 9–10 (A.V.)

217. 24 **the Apostle's words** Eph. ii. 12 (A.V.).

218. 14 **Miracles as evidence** From Hume to Paley to T. H. Huxley the question of miracles was controverted in England. Not long before the *Apologia*, in his contribution to *Essays and Reviews* (1860), Baden Powell had attacked the idea of miracles, anticipating Huxley's view.

218. 25 **even the unaided reason** Newman is here affirming the teaching of the Roman Church. His own 'scepticism', of which much has been written, would thus seem to have had an historical rather than an epistemological basis. (However, see *U.S.*, pp. 347–9 and note, p. 349.) Thirty-four years earlier he had written about the possibilities of the unaided reason:

'When, then, religion of some sort is said to be *natural*, it is not here meant that any religious system has been actually traced out by unaided Reason. We know of no such system, because we know of no time or country in which human Reason *was* unaided. Scripture informs us that revelations were granted to the first fathers of our race, concerning the nature of God and man's duty to Him; and scarcely a people can be named, among whom there are not traditions, not only of the existence of powers exterior to this visible world, but also of their actual interference with the course of nature, followed up by religious communications to mankind from them. The Creator has never left Himself without such witness as might anticipate the conclusions of Reason, and support a wavering conscience and perplexed faith. No people (to speak in general terms) has been denied a revelation from God, though but a portion of the world has enjoyed an authenticated revelation.' (*U.S.*, pp. 17–18.)

219. 1 **atheism in one shape or other** *Agnosticism* became the common term, but it was not yet in use when Newman wrote. According to the *N.E.D.*, Thomas Huxley appears to have coined it in 1869.

219. 21 **Thirty years ago, education was relied upon** For Newman's views at the time, in a difference with Sir Robert Peel, see 'The Tamworth Reading Room', reprinted in *D.A.* Professor Harrold pointed out that even Carlyle shared the prevalent optimism about education, as witness the last chapters of *Sartor Resartus*, which appeared in *Fraser's* exactly thirty years before Newman was writing. See *English Prose of the Victorian Era*, ed. Harrold and Templeman (New York, 1938), p. 640.

219. 22 **ten years ago there was a hope that wars would cease** A reference to the spirit of the era symbolized by the Crystal Palace Exhibition of 1851.

219. 35 **in this day** An allusion to the 'Higher Criticism', then beginning to make itself more widely felt in England. *Essays and Reviews*, with its underlying principle that the truth of Scripture must be measured in the light of modern intellectual developments, had been, almost from its appearance in 1860, a centre of controversy which was reaching its climax as Newman wrote. Anglo-Catholics and Evangelicals alike opposed the book. Also under fire at the time was Bishop Colenso's *Pentateuch and Book of Joshua Critically Examined* (1862–3).

220. 28 **a defence of myself** This famous passage, beginning on p. 216, which according to Geoffrey Faber 'has a dark splendour, unmatched by anything in Gibbon' (*Oxford Apostles*, p. 3), is discussed at length by James Anthony Froude in 'The Oxford Counter-Reformation', *Short Studies* (4 vols., London, 1886), iv. 339 ff. To Froude, Newman remained 'one of the two most remarkable men whom I have ever met with' (p. 311—the other was Carlyle). But this passage, though 'so beautiful that the reader who has never seen it before will wish that it was longer', was 'a siren's song . . . the shore from which it came had been strewn for centuries with the bones of the lost mariners who were betrayed by such enchanting music.' (pp. 339–40.) Froude attempts an answer to the passage based on evolution and the idea of progress.

221. 15 **a statement of mine** *Diff*. i. 240, slightly altered. The objections to this passage and that quoted on p. 223 of the *Apologia*, were made by Kingsley in his pamphlet.

222. 28 **'Ye must be born again'** John iii. 7.

223. 3 **my own statement** *Diff*. i. 249–50.

223. 10 **'The publicans and harlots . . .'** Matt. xxi. 31. On the remark Newman is here defending, see Samuel Wilberforce, *Essays Contributed to the 'Quarterly Review'* (2 vols., London, 1874), i. 338–9.

223. 30 **I am not here determining any thing about the essential seat of that power** i.e. whether in the Pope alone or with a General Council. At the Vatican Council of 1870 it was defined that the *ex cathedra* teachings of the Roman Pontiff, speaking to the whole Church on doctrines of faith or morals, 'are of themselves, and not in consequence of the Church's consent, irreformable'. (See the article 'Infallibility' in the *Catholic Encyclopedia*.)

In a paper of February 15, 1868, Newman wrote: 'As to the Apologia, it must be recollected that it was not a didactic work—nor did it contain a statement of my own personal views about infallibility, but was addressed to Protestants *in order to show* them, what it was that a Catholic fairly undertook in the way of theological professions, when he became a Catholic. I myself, for instance, have ever held as a matter of theological opinion the Infallibility of the Pope; but I carefully abstain from asserting it in the general view which I give of Catholic doctrine. I felt I should be as obviously wrong in setting down theological opinions, when I was declaring the Church's doctrine as such, as I have thought Archbp. Manning obviously wrong in introducing into his Pastorals the Pope's Infallibility. . . .' See C. S. Dessain, 'An Unpublished Paper by Cardinal Newman on the Development of Doctrine', *The Journal of Theological Studies*, N.S. ix, pt. 2 (October 1958), 329–30.

225. 17 **St. Thomas** Thomas Aquinas (1225–74), Doctor of the Church, whose greatest work, the *Summa Theologica*, was a synthesis of philosophy and theology. For most of Newman's life Thomism was by no means intensively studied, even in the Roman schools. It was Leo XIII, the Pope

who made Newman a cardinal in 1879, who in the same year inaugurated the Thomistic revival with his encyclical *Aeterni Patris.*

226. 34 **Eutychianism** See notes 108. 13 and 108. 24.

226. 34 **Pelagianism** Named after Pelagius, fifth-century British heresiarch, who denied original sin and held that man of his own free will, without special aid or grace from God, can avoid sin and attain salvation. His teaching was condemned at the Councils of Carthage in 418 and Orange in 529.

226. 34 **Manichaeism** Named after the third-century Persian Mani or Manes, it became a problem in the fourth and fifth centuries, especially in Proconsular Africa. It held a dual creation between constantly struggling powers of good and evil, God and Satan. The spirit of man was from God; the flesh, from Satan. The Incarnation was denied, Christ having come in spirit only. Marriage was condemned. Manichaeism claimed to be able to explain all the mysteries of the Christian religion. For nine years St. Augustine was under its influence, afterwards writing some forty works opposing it.

226. 34 **Jansenism** Named after Cornelius Jansenius (1585–1638), Bishop of Ypres, it was an austere doctrine resembling Calvinism which divided Catholic France for a considerable time. It taught the radical corruption of human nature, the powerlessness of man to resist either grace or temptation, the death of Christ only for those predestined to salvation, the necessity of long and severe preparation for the reception of the sacraments, and the approach to God with fear and trembling.

227. 8 **it must ever appeal to them.** After this sentence, in the 1864 edition of the *Apologia*, appeared these words: 'Thus, in illustration, it does not extend to statements, however sound and evident, which are mere logical conclusions from the Articles of the Apostolic *Depositum*; again, it can pronounce nothing about the persons of heretics, whose works fall within its legitimate province.'

In his paper of 1868 on development (note 223. 30), after stating his agreement with the view that in a popular work 'theological opinions ought to be kept under', Newman adds: 'It was for this reason that I introduced into my statement two or three sentences from Chrismann, which professed less about the province of Infallibility than I held myself. . . . In the second edition I withdrew the two sentences from Chrissman because they seemed too strong an *assertion*, & to be taking a side,—whereas I wished it to be vague.'

Chrissman was an eighteenth-century German Franciscan, and Newman refers to his *Regula Fidei Catholicae et Collectio Dogmatum Credendorum* (Würzburg, 1854). Chrissman was a 'minimizer', and this edition of his work was put on the Roman Index in 1869. See Dessain in *Journal of Theological Studies*, ix, pt. 2 (October 1958), 329–30.

227. 29 **the Immaculate Conception** The doctrine that the soul of the Blessed Virgin, from the moment it was created and infused into her body, was free from the stain of original sin and filled with sanctifying grace. It

is often confused with the doctrine of the Virgin Birth. Pius IX officially defined the doctrine of the Immaculate Conception on December 8, 1854.

229. 3 **St. Bernard and St. Thomas, who scrupled at it in their day** Bernard of Clairvaux (1090–1153), Doctor of the Church, was a Cistercian monk and one of the most influential and appealing figures in medieval Catholicism. Though especially devoted to the Blessed Virgin, he attacked the feast of the Immaculate Conception as lacking a rational basis; but he held that the Virgin received sanctifying grace in the womb of her mother, so that her nativity rather than her conception was holy. See E. Vacandard, *Vie de Saint Bernard* (2 vols., Paris, 1895), ii. 84–87.

St. Thomas held that if the Blessed Virgin had not been stained by original sin, this would lessen the dignity of Christ as universal saviour. She was second only to Christ in purity, however, and was cleansed from the stain before her birth from the womb. (*Summa Theol.* iii, q. 27, art. 2, ad 2um.)

229. 28 **a remark contained in that University Sermon** See 'The Theory of Developments in Religious Doctrine', *U.S.*, p. 334.

230. 26 *pomoeria* Limits or bounds; originally a void space on either side of the walls of a city.

In the 1868 paper on development, after stressing the wisdom of playing down theological opinion in expositions of doctrine, Newman goes on to add: 'It was for this reason that I spoke so vaguely about the *Pomoeria*. I myself hold that the doctrines which may be considered as belonging to it are in some cases of obligation & in others not; but which are such & which not, is decided by theological opinion, & it varies. Such, for instance, would be the infallibility of canonization—to him who thinks it infallible, it is such. And there are two motives, short of fides divina, which occasion silence & acquiescence on such points, or at least very cautious & restrained avowals in opposition to them: the pietas fidei (which I think I did not refer to) and the duty of obedience. It was for the same reason that, in speaking of condemned propositions, I did not expressly say whether the condemnation was infallible or not, because a distinct assertion could not be made without turning a statement of 20 pages into a volume. All I did, was to say that such condemnations, from their general character, constituted no great burden for our faith to bear.' (Dessain, *J.T.S.* ix. 2 [Oct. 1958], 330.)

231. 7 **'O, it is excellent'** *Measure for Measure*, II. ii. 107–9.

231. 11 **the words of the Apostle** 2 Cor. iv. 7.

232. 3 **Origen** As indicated earlier (notes 36. 7 ff.), this is a complex subject, and modern authorities are divided on whether Origen and Origenism were ever officially condemned. But in the various Origenist crises such as that described below involving Theophilus, Origen's large-scale allegorizing of Scripture, his views on the subordination of the Divine Persons, on the creation, and on the universality of redemption were those which caused trouble. Personal and local motives of a nature scarcely edifying were closely bound up in the controversies.

232. 8 **Theophilus** Patriarch of Alexandria from 385 till his death in 412, Theophilus was a man of considerable zeal and some learning, but he was also unscrupulous and cruel in his methods and very elastic in his theology. He consecrated St. John Chrysostom (*c.* 347–407), the great preacher and reformer, Bishop of Constantinople in 398. He was forced to pass over his own favourite candidate, Isidore, an Origenist monk whom he had made Archpresbyter and *oeconomus* of his own patriarchate. Later a quarrel with Isidore over money matters helped turn him against Origenism, which he condemned at the Synod of Alexandria in 401, and against the monks of Nitria, who had given shelter to Isidore. He marched against the monks, drove them into exile, destroyed their homes, and mistreated those he captured.

Summoned to Constantinople to answer before the Emperor charges brought against him by some of the monks, to whom Chrysostom had given shelter, he used the opportunity to become head of the faction of ecclesiastics and courtiers whom Chrysostom's austerity and justice had offended —and these included the Empress Eudoxia. He failed in his first attempt, after the Empress lost courage, to exile Chrysostom; and he fled Constantinople. The second time, however, through influence exerted from a safe distance, he succeeded. In 404 St. John was led into a permanent and, his influence continuing, a progressively harsher exile which led to his death. Newman had a special devotion to St. John Chrysostom, whom he calls 'the most natural and human of the creations of supernatural grace'. (*H.S.* ii. 283.)

232. 9 **Vigilius** Pope from 537 to 555, he rose to that office through promises of leniency towards the Monophysites of Constantinople, through an offer of bribery, and through an election which involved the unjust deposition and harsh exile of his predecessor Silverius. He then refused, however, to support the Monophysites; and he assented to the condemnation of Origenism at a local council Justinian order convoked in Constantinople in 543.

As an Anglican, Newman had used the scandals of the Council of Ephesus and of the career of Vigilius as 'an effectual hindrance to any over-delicate and fastidious criticisms by Roman writers of our Reformation'. (*V.M.* i. 347–8.) The theological wavering of Vigilius was also cited at the first Vatican Council by opponents of the doctrine of papal infallibility.

233. 2 **a violent ultra party** A reference to the ultramontanist school of W. G. Ward, Archbishop Manning, Msgr. Talbot, Louis Veuillot, etc. In this discussion Newman is defending himself against Catholic suspicion of a lack of real loyalty to the papacy by attacking indirectly its over-ardent champions. Much of the chapter thus has a double-edged quality. See Ward, *Life*, ii. 36–41.

The chapter may also owe a good deal to Lord Acton, to whose plea for a frank discussion of the repressive policy in the Church 'which is adopted in order to avoid scandal', Newman replied, '. . . you may be sure I shall go as far as ever I can'. See Hugh A. MacDougall, *The Acton-Newman Relations: The Dilemma of Christian Liberalism* (New York, 1962), pp. 90–93.

234. 1 **a periodical, set up by Lord Byron and others** *The Liberal*, which lasted for only four numbers in 1822. The others were Shelley and

especially Leigh Hunt. In *Cain*, Byron had strongly attacked orthodox Christian theology. Newman's favourite, Southey, assailed Byron as leader of the 'Satanic school'. *The Liberal* contained Byron's stinging reply in *The Vision of Judgment*. For Newman, Byron was 'a great genius throwing off the fear of God, seeking for happiness in the creature, roaming unsatisfied from one object to another, breaking his soul upon itself, and bitterly confessing and imparting his wretchedness to all around him'. (*H.S.* ii. 144.)

234. 3 **a theological school, of a dry and repulsive character** The rationalism of Whately and the Noetics.

234. 38 **St. Augustine's beautiful words** 'Illi in vos saeviant qui nesciunt cum quo labore verum inveniatur, et quam difficile caveantur errores.' Newman's translation follows. *Contra Epistolam Manichaei Quam vocant Fundamenti*, I. ii. (Migne, *P.L.* xlii, col. 174.)

235. 26 **'beware', as the poet says** This is the moral of William Cowper's 'The Needless Alarm', ll. 132–3:

> Beware of desperate steps. The darkest day,
> Live till tomorrow, will have passed away.

It was a favourite quotation of Newman, who uses it in the same slightly inaccurate form, along with Augustine's *securus iudicat*, in a letter of 1870 to a French priest who, troubled by the proceedings of the Vatican Council, had left the Church. See Ward, *Life*, ii. 375–6.

235. 35 **recent acts of that authority** In December 1863 Pius IX addressed a Brief to the Archbishop of Munich asserting the authority of scholastic theology and the Roman congregations, which the noted theologian Döllinger had seemed to relegate to the past in a presidential address to a congress of Catholic scholars held at Munich in September of that year. Sir John Acton's learned and provocative *Home and Foreign Review*, already in trouble with Ward's ultramontane *Dublin Review* and others, had hailed the 'rare significance' of Döllinger's address and now suspended publication. Newman wrote to Acton regretting the end of the magazine but hoping that good might come out of a reaction: 'I don't think that active and honest minds can remain content under a dull tyranny. It seems impossible to conceive that they can remain quiet under the supremacy of Manning and Ward.' (*Life*, i. 566.)

Newman did not say that the papal brief required Acton's step, but in a careful analysis of the document he says: 'If I understand this brief, it is simply a providential intimation to every religious man, that, at this moment, we are simply to be silent, while scientific investigation proceeds—and say not a word on questions of interpretation of Scripture &c. &c., when perplexed persons ask us—and I am not sure that it will not prove to be the best way.' (Ibid., p. 567. The full text of Newman's analysis is given in an appendix, i. 641–2.)

236. 4 **'Fear ye not . . .'** Exod. xiv. 13–14.

236. 27 **the constantly cited case of Galileo** Galileo Galilei (1564–1642), the great physicist and astronomer, aroused fear and hostility among churchmen and even many scientists of his day by vigorous advocacy of the Copernican heliocentric instead of the Ptolemaic geocentric system commonly accepted and apparently demanded by Scripture. In 1616 the Congregation of the Holy Office at Rome condemned the Copernican system as anti-Scriptural and therefore heretical. Galileo promised not to spread his teachings but continued to do so indirectly, and for a dialogue published in 1632 he was called to trial for breach of contract and threatened with torture. He had to abjure his doctrine, which was again condemned, and was made a technical prisoner of the Holy Office though allowed to live at his own country home near Florence.

Though Newman defended the Church in the Galileo affair on the ground that the formal reception of so startling an hypothesis might have to be delayed until religious people were gradually prepared for it (*V.M.* i. liii–lviii), it seems clear that he is here citing the case of Galileo on the principle of once bitten, twice shy—not so much to defend the Church as to warn the ultramontanes of his own day that their repressive policy might work to the detriment of both science and religion. See his comment on the Munich Brief, *Life*, i. 642, and Ward's summary of Newman's view, ii. 421–5.

237. 17 **one point of doctrine** The pronouncement in 449 that Jesus Christ is one person in whom are two natures, divine and human, unconfused and unmixed.

237. 27 **Hilary** (*c.* 315–67), a convert from neo-Platonism, was Bishop of Poitiers and a militant foe of Arianism. *De Trinitate* is his best-known work. In his commentaries on the Psalms and St. Matthew, he is said to have closely followed Origen. According to the *O.D.C.C.*, he held an almost Monophysite Christology.

237. 28 **Ambrose** (*c.* 339–97), saint and Bishop of Milan, was partially responsible for the conversion of St. Augustine. For his debt to Origen, see F. Homes Dudden, D.D., *The Life and Times of St. Ambrose* (2 vols., Oxford, 1935), i. 113, no. 3, and *passim*.

237. 28 **Jerome** St. Jerome (*c.* 340–420), Doctor of the Church, produced the Latin version of Scripture or Vulgate, which became the basic text of the Roman Church, in a monastery near Bethlehem, where he lived an ascetic life. He also wrote commentaries on parts of the Bible and controverted Origenism and Pelagianism. Well versed in the classics, he was to Newman the 'literary Father . . . par excellence'. (*H.S.* ii. 450.)

237. 30 **the scarcely orthodox Eusebius** Bishop of Caesarea in Palestine, Eusebius (*c.* 260–*c.* 340) wrote an ecclesiastical history in ten books which has earned him the title of Father of Church History. It was well known to Jerome. Eusebius was connected with the Arian party and opposed to Athanasius. According to Newman, Eusebius was guilty of 'corrupting the simplicity of the Gospel with an Eclectic spirit'. (*Diff.* i. 381.) For a detailed account of what Newman meant by 'scarcely orthodox', see *Select Treatises of St. Athanasius*, ii. 97–106.

238. 5 **Malchion** A priest of Antioch, where he was head of the school of Greek literature. He took the leading part in the last of several councils against the worldly Bishop Paul of Samosata in 267–8. He procured the condemnation for heresy and the deposition of Paul, who seems to have held that the Son pre-existed only as an attribute of the Father, like reason, rather than as a person; and that Christ was essentially a man inspired from above. See *Arians*, pp. 3–6 and 27–28; and *Ath.* ii. 237–9.

238. 11 **St. Anselm at Bari** One of the most important of medieval theologians, St. Anselm (1033–1109) was the author of a famous ontological argument for the existence of God and of *Cur Deus Homo*, an influential treatise on the Atonement. In 1093 he became Archbishop of Canterbury and proved a champion of papal authority. In 1098 Pope Urban II convoked a council at Bari to deal with the long-standing difficulty of the position of the Greek churches on the procession of the Holy Ghost, and he invited Anselm to take a leading role. Anselm maintained the Roman doctrine of the procession from the Father and the Son against the Greek doctrine of procession from the Father only.

238. 13 **St. Bonaventura** (1221–74), Doctor of the Church, was a Franciscan who combined sanctity and learning to an unusual degree. His *Commentary on the Sentences, Breviloquium, Itenerarium Mentis in Deum*, and *De Reductione Artium ad Theologiam* provide the elements of a complete system of philosophy and are a compendium of dogma. They carried great weight at subsequent councils. See Louis de Castroplanio, *Seraphicus doctor Bonaventura in oecumenicis catholicae ecclesiae conciliis cum patribus dogmata definiens* (Rome, 1874).

238. 14 **Salmeron** Alphonsus Salmeron (1515–85) was a Jesuit Biblical scholar, one of Loyola's first companions, who wrote sixteen volumes of Scripture commentary. He served as theologian to Popes Paul III, Julius III, and Pius IV at various sessions of the Council of Trent, where he exerted great influence in discussions of justification, the Eucharist and the Mass, matrimony, the origin of the rights and duties of bishops, indulgences, and other subjects.

239. 37 **Zosimus** Pope from 417 to 418, Zosimus received the Pelagian Coelestius, who had been condemned by the preceding Pope, Innocent I, expelled from Constantinople, and condemned at Carthage; and he was won over to declare it uncertain that Coelestius really held the heretical views rejected by Innocent. Pelagius himself wrote a confession of faith and a new treatise on free will in which the heresy was carefully concealed; and Zosimus defended him, too, against the African bishops. A new synod of African bishops showed the Pope that he had been deceived; and after the steps taken by the Emperor Honorius against the Pelagians, he issued his *Tractoria*, in which Pelagianism and its authors were condemned.

240. 1 **Berengarius** Berengarius of Tours (*c.* 999–1088), director of the school of St. Martin, denied in *De Sacra Coena* 'that the "body of Christ is brought down from heaven and carnally present on the altar"', on the ground that Christ cannot be brought down from heaven before the Last Judgment'.

(*O.D.C.C.*) His views on the Nature of the Real Presence were changeable and not very clear, however, sometimes implying a merely figurative and at others a real presence of some kind. See *Dictionnaire de Théologie Catholique*, ii, cols. 735–6.

The view of Berengarius led to a more precise formulation of the doctrine by the Council of Rome in 1079. In spite of previous condemnations and his frequently contemptuous attitude, Berengarius was treated with kindness by Gregory VII, who, after a retractation, reconciled him to his bishops and forbade that he be penalized or called a heretic.

240. 35 **by giving us a Church of our own** A reference to the restoration in 1850 of the Roman Catholic hierarchy to England, previously governed ecclesiastically as missionary territory by Propaganda in Rome through bishops known as Vicars Apostolic.

241. 9 **a note upon one of my Sermons** 'Wisdom and Innocence', *S.S.D.*, pp. 297–8.

241. 10 **an admirable writer** Isaac Williams in Tracts 80 and 87.

241. 14 **Cast not your pearls** Matt. vii. 6.

241. 29 **'Disciplina Arcani'** From L. *arcanum*, a mystery or secret. The 'self-restraint and abstinence, practiced at least partially, by the Primitive Church in the publication of the most sacred doctrines of our religion' (*Arians*, pp. 49–50)—e.g. the Real Presence. See also *Dev.*, pp. 27–29. The term itself dates from the late seventeenth century.

241. 30 **Clement** That is, Clement of Alexandria, in *Stromateis*, vii. 8 and 9: 'Whatever is in his [the true gnostic or Christian philosopher's] mind, is also on his tongue; towards those who are fit recipients, both in speaking and living, he harmonizes his profession with his thoughts. He both thinks and speaks the truth; except when careful treatment is necessary, and then, as a physician for the good of his patients, he will lie, or rather utter a lie, as the Sophists say. For instance, the noble Apostle circumcised Timothy, while he cried out and wrote down, "Circumcision availeth not". . . . Nothing, however, but his neighbour's good will lead him to do this. . . .' (Newman's translation, *Arians*, pp. 73–74.)

242. 24 **Old Hall Green** A school and seminary in Ware, Hertfordshire, established in 1769 and reconstituted in 1793 as St. Edmund's College, to continue in southern England the work of the Catholic University at Douai, which had been suppressed during the French Revolution. Newman visited St. Edmund's and Ushaw soon after his conversion and was favourably impressed. See Ward, *Life*, i. 109–13.

242. 24 **Ushaw** A combined college and seminary near Durham founded in 1794 to continue in the northern district the work of Douai, which during the long period of Catholic civil and religious disabilities in England had supplied the Church with most of her priests.

242. 30 **a straightforward Englishman** William Bernard Ullathorne (1806–89), Bishop of Birmingham, who almost invariably stood by Newman in his later difficulties. See his letter, *Apo.*, pp. 316–18. One of the 'old Catholics' and a descendant of St. Thomas More, he was an important figure in the ecclesiastical history of his age. See Dom Cuthbert Butler, *The Life and Times of Bishop Ullathorne* (2 vols., London, 1926).

243. 11 **The Irish fever** Carried in by Irish emigrants during the famine years after 1845.

243. 14 **a bishop cut off** William Riddell (1807–47), Vicar Apostolic of the Northern district, who died of cholera November 2, 1847. See *Letters and Diaries*, xi. 354.

243. 18 **the cholera** There had been an epidemic in 1832. Newman himself was a volunteer when it broke out at Bilston in September 1849. See *Life*, i. 227.

243. 21 **'If in this life only. . .'** 1 Cor. xv. 19.

244. 4 **'It hath never been heard of . . .'** Baruch iii. 22–23.

244. 16 **by our accusers** In his pamphlet, Kingsley had charged Newman with becoming 'a convert to the *economic* views of St. Alfonso da Liguori and his compeers', adding: 'I am henceforth in doubt and fear, as much as any honest man can be concerning every word Dr. Newman may write. How can I tell that I shall not be the dupe of some cunning equivocation, of one of the three kinds laid down as permissible by the blessed Alfonso da Liguori and his pupils, even when confirmed by an oath, because then we do not deceive our neighbour, but allow him to deceive himself?'

In a decree of July 22, 1831, the Roman Catholic Church allowed her confessors to follow the opinions of Alphonsus, whose moderate ethical system called equiprobabilism, had long been a subject of contention in the Church, without weighing the reasons for them. (But see *Apo.*, p. 309.) In 1839 Alphonsus was canonized and in 1871 proclaimed a Doctor of the Church.

244. 18 **St. Alfonso . . . lays down that an equivocation** '*Amphibologia* triplici modo esse potest: I., quando verbum habet duplicem sensum, prout *volo* significat velle, et volare. II, Quando sermo duplicem sensum principalem habet, v. gr. *Hic liber est Petri*, significare potest, quod Petrus sit libri dominus aut sit libri auctor. III, Quando verba habent duplicem sensum, unum magis communem, alium minus, vel unum litteralem, alium spiritualem, ut verba illa quae dixit Christus de Baptista: *Ipse est Elias*. Et Baptista dixit: *Ego non sum Elias*. . . .

'His positis, certum est et commune apud omnes, quod ex justa causa licitum sit uti aequivocatione modis expositis, et cum juramento firmare. . . . Ratio, quia tunc non decipimus proximum, sed ex justa causa permittimus, up ipse decipiatur, et ex alia parte non tenemur ad mentem aliorum loqui si justa causa subsit. Justa autem causa esse potest quicunque finis honestus ad servanda bona spiritui, vel corpori utilia.' Lib. 4, Tract. 2, *Theologia Moralis S. Alphonsi de Ligorio* (9 vols., Mechliniae, 1845), ii. 316–17.

244. 34 **Taylor says** In *The Rule of Conscience*, bk. iii, ch. ii, rule v, par. 10. *The Whole Works*, ed. Reginald Heber (15 vols., London, 1839), xiii. 355. For a fuller discussion of Taylor's position, see the appendix to the 1864 edition, *Apo.*, pp. 459–61.

245. 6 **Milton says** Newman is quoting from *De Doctrina Christiana*, bk. ii, ch. xiii, *The Works of John Milton*, Columbia Edition, ed. F. A. Patterson et al. (18 vols. in 21, New York and London, 1931–8), xvii. 298–9. See also the appendix to the 1864 edition, *Apo.*, pp. 461 and 469–72.

245. 12 **Paley says** William Paley (1743–1805), Archdeacon of Carlisle and author of the famous *Evidences of Christianity* (1794). The reference here is to bk. iii, ch. v of his *Moral and Political Philosophy*, *Works* (6 vols., London, 1830), iii. 123. See also the 1864 appendix, pp. 461–2, where the quotation is incorrectly attributed to vol. iv.

245. 14 **Johnson** See *Boswell's Life of Johnson*, iv. 305.

245. 27 **Scavini** Pietro Scavini, Provost of the Cathedral and Vicar General of the Diocese of Novara in northern Italy. He was the author of *Theologia Moralis Universa*, a popular adaptation of St. Alfonso's ideas for the use of the clergy. The edition in the Birmingham Oratory Library is in three volumes; Brussels, 1847.

245. 34 **Hey** John Hey (1734–1815) was a clergyman and Cambridge lecturer on moral and theological subjects who, though defending subscription to the Articles, yet considered the differences between Anglicans and Unitarians as little more than verbal. See his *Lectures in Divinity* (3rd ed. rev., 2 vols., Cambridge, 1841), i. 475 ff. and ii. The lectures are divided into four books, the fourth and longest comprising an elaborate discussion of the Articles.

245. 34 **Burnett** Gilbert Burnet (1643–1715), Bishop of Salisbury and author of the famous *History of My Own Times*, published in 1699 an *Exposition of the Thirty-nine Articles* which was censured in 1701 by the lower house of Convocation as being latitudinarian, distorted in many passages, and dangerous to the Church of England. (It was Burnet's descendants who put the second *t* in the name.)

247. 8 **a late writer** See John Hill Burton, *Life and Correspondence of David Hume* (2 vols., Edinburgh, 1846), ii. 437 ff.

247. 21 **his Life** *The Life of St. Alphonsus Maria de Liguori*. Compiled from the Published Memoirs of the Saint by One of the Redemptorist Fathers (Baltimore, 1855), pp. 29–30. Newman's quotation varies slightly. The last sentence of the paragraph is not in the original and appears to be Newman's own comment.

249. 10 **Cardinal Gerdil** Hyacinthe Gerdil (1718–1802), theologian and philosopher, critic of Locke and Rousseau, who wrote widely in French, Latin, and Italian on dogmatic and moral theology and many other subjects.

In the appendix to the 1864 edition of the *Apologia*, p. 450, he is quoted as saying in part: 'Whoso swears binds himself in virtue of the words, not according to the sense he retains in his own mind, but in *the sense according to which he perceives that they are understood by him to whom the oath is made . . . whoso uses mental reservation or equivocation in the oath*, in order to deceive the party to whom he offers it, *sins most grievously* and is always bound to observe the oath *in the sense in which he knew that his words were* taken by the other party, according to the decision of St. Augustine. . . .' The quotation is from *Opuscoli Teologici Inediti* (Roma, 1851), pp. 28–29, Newman's copy of this work bearing the date 1864. The italics are his. The reference to St. Augustine is to Ep. 224.

249. 11 **Natalis Alexander** or Noël Alexandre (1639–1724), was a French Dominican theologian and ecclesiastical historian. The passage Newman quotes is from his *Theologia Dogmatica et Moralis*, lib. iv, c. iv, art. 3, reg. 11 (Cologne, 1698, p. 478). For the original, see the 1864 appendix, p. 465.

250. 2 **There we find** Pt. iii, ch. ix, 'The Eighth Commandment'. See *The Catechism by Decree of the Holy Council of Trent*. Translated into English and published with the original Latin text by J. Donovan, D.D. (2 vols., Rome, 1839), ii. 189–207, *passim*. Newman's translation is probably his own.

250. 7 **as the Apostle admonished** Eph. iv. 15.

250. 12 **the Apostle admonishes** Eph. iv. 25.

250. 21 **that maxim of St. Augustine's** The reference cited in the Catechism is to Augustine's Ep. ad Casulan. ap. Grat., but Newman apparently did not notice an editorial note to the effect that the quotation has not been found in Augustine. In any event, it is not in the letter to Casulanus (Ep. 36), to which it is attributed in Gratian's *Decretum*, pars ii, causa xi, qu. 3, cap. 80, in Migne, *P.L.*, vol. 187, col. 868. Because of Gratian's reference, perhaps, the passage is often attributed to Augustine in medieval writings.

251. 5 **as St. James says** Jas. iii. 11.

251. 32 **the Roman Oratorian** See Fr. Bacci, *The Life of St. Philip Neri, Apostle of Rome*, transl. F. W. Faber (2 vols., London, 1847), i. 293.

252. 15 **St. Philip's sons** The names commemorated are those of the original group of Oratorians—all that remained after the society enlarged and divided into two sections. Newman's 'external influence undoubtedly was great and widespread; but however far it extended, it should not be forgotten that the centre from which it radiated was the Oratory at Birmingham, and that to him the centre meant more than the circumference. It was the house of his sojourning; and after his connexion with Ireland came to an end in 1858, he seldom left it again, never for any appreciable time. . . . In 1864, when the *Apologia* came to be written, only the faithful remnant persevered,—just six and no more, all converts with one exception [Ryder]; and the one exception was the son of a convert.' (Tristram, *Newman and His Friends*, pp. 215–16.)

Cf. Pattison's *Memoirs*, pp. 209–10; Ward's *Life*, i. 112–13; and *The Letters of George Eliot*, ed. Gordon Haight, iv. 158–60.

252. 16 **Ambrose St. John** (1815–75), of Christ Church, became curate of Newman's close friend Henry Wilberforce at Walmer in Kent in 1841. Religious difficulties caused him to apply to Newman in 1843 for permission to spend some time—perhaps three months—at Littlemore. In the event, the visit lasted thirty-two years. The two men were rarely separated for any length of time thereafter and are buried, according to Newman's request, in the same grave in the little Oratorian cemetery at Rednal, near Birmingham. St. John was perhaps responsible for Newman's becoming an Oratorian by reminding him of a forgotten suggestion of Wiseman. Though he preferred the pastoral side of his vocation, he was an accomplished linguist and a student of German Biblical criticism and of Semitic subjects. His devotion to Newman never wearied: his last illness, in fact, was brought on by overwork in completing a translation of Fessler's *Die wahre und die falsche Unfehlbarkeit der Päpste*, which Newman wanted as a balance for Gladstone's *Vatican Decrees in their Bearing on Civil Allegiance*. Newman broke down repeatedly in giving the absolutions at St. John's Requiem Mass.

252. 16 **Henry Austin Mills** (1823–1903), the son of a Fellow of Trinity College, Cambridge, did not complete his course there. He was received into the Roman Catholic Church in January 1846; first joined the community of F. W. Faber, which in 1848 became affiliated with the Oratory; and from 1849 till his death lived a kindly, self-effacing life at Birmingham.

252. 17 **Henry Bittleston** (1818–86), of St. John's College, Oxford, took his B.A. degree in 1842, was ordained, and became curate at Leamington Priors in Warwickshire. Differing with his bishop on the subject of auricular confession, he left the diocese of Worcester in 1848, entered the Roman Church in 1849, and the Oratory in 1850. After thirty years he left the Oratory in July 1879, 'apparently because he had offended in some way, probably financial'. His last years were spent as the Catholic priest first at Barnet and then St. Albans. See *Letters and Diaries*, xiii. 510.

252. 17 **Edward Caswall** (1814–78) was educated at Brasenose College, Oxford, and as a young man won considerable success with two humorous works, *A New Art teaching how to be plucked, being a treatise after the fashion of Aristotle*, and *Sketches of Young Ladies by Quiz*, illustrated by Phiz. In 1839 he was ordained and became Perpetual Curate of Stratford-sub-Castle, near Salisbury. In 1847, influenced by Newman's *Development of Christian Doctrine*, he and his wife were received into the Catholic Church by Cardinal Acton at Rome, in Newman's presence. On her death of cholera at Torquay in 1849, he joined the Oratory and became known for his translations of hymns, which, according to the *Dictionary of Hymnology* 'have a wider circulation in modern hymnals than those of any other translator, Dr. Neale alone excepted'. See *Letters and Diaries*, xii. 429.

252. 18 **William Paine Neville** (1824–1905), a native of Ulster educated at Trinity College, Oxford, was a student at the time of Newman's conversion.

In 1849 he became a lay assistant in charge of financial and other secular affairs at St. Saviour's, Leeds, the centre of Tractarianism in the north in which Pusey had a special interest; and when that congregation broke up in 1851 after the Gorham judgement and many conversions to Rome, Newman, who had gone to Leeds, received him into the Roman Church and into the Oratory. He later became almost a second Ambrose St. John to Newman, serving as his secretary and finally as his literary executor, collecting, copying, and arranging Newman's papers and letters, wherever they could be found.

252. 18 **Henry Ignatius Dudley Ryder** (1837–1907) was a grandson of Henry Dudley Ryder, the first Evangelical to be named a bishop. His mother was one of four daughters of John Sargent famous for their beauty—the others married Samuel and Henry Wilberforce and Henry Edward Manning. His father, George Dudley Ryder, was received into the Catholic Church at Rome, together with his wife and children, in 1846. Henry received much of his education under Newman's direction and also studied at the Catholic University in Dublin and the English College at Rome. In 1863 he became a priest of the Oratory and, on Newman's death in 1890, Superior. Except for his pamphlets, *Idealism in Theology*, controverting W. G. Ward's views on papal infallibility, and several articles on a wide range of topics for English and American periodicals, he wrote little. He was a brilliant conversationalist, and in Ward's opinion the best theologian in England. He did not always see eye to eye with Newman. See Meriol Trevor, *Newman: Light in Winter* (London, 1962), pp. 541–4.

254. 4 **Count Montalembert and Father Lacordaire** Charles Forbes René, Comte de Montalembert (1810–70), lawyer, journalist, and historian, and Jean-Baptiste Lacordaire (1802–61), a Dominican priest and France's greatest preacher in the nineteenth century, were ardent Catholics who believed that religion was the mother of liberty and could best accomplish its purpose free of the state protection and influence which characterized the *ancien régime*. Free speech, freedom of education, and a free press were to be employed to defend the rights of the Church and enable it to come to terms with and christianize the aims of the modern democratic state. The bitter anti-clericalism of many French statesmen, inheritors of eighteenth-century scepticism and revolutionary zeal, made their position difficult and, in the eyes of Catholics like the influential editor of *L'Univers*, Louis Veuillot, highly dangerous.

Lacordaire, fearing identification of the Church with the empire of Napoleon III, attacked the new government in a speech in Paris in 1853, which in effect got him exiled to a military school chaplaincy. He died with the words: 'J'espère mourir en religieux penitent et en liberal impenitent.' Montalembert, shortly before his death, fearing that certain ultramontanes would exert undue influence at the Vatican Council, attacked the 'lay theologians of absolutism'. His position was analogous to Newman's in his troubles with Manning, Ward, and Talbot.

Newman's quotation is from the *Memoir of the Abbé Lacordaire*, by the Count de Montalembert (London, 1863), p. 19.

255. 2 **the University of Oxford woke up** For the University reforms, see *Idea*, pp. 1–3 and 154–8; Pattison's *Memoirs, passim*; and A. I. Tillyard, *A History of University Reform from 1800 A.D. to the Present Time* (Cambridge, 1913). The 'three or four colleges' alluded to below were Oriel, under John Eveleigh and Edward Copleston; Christ Church, with Cyril Jackson; Balliol, with John Parsons; and Magdalen, with Dr. Routh. Newman is speaking of the rise of the Noetic school.

256. 34 **Convocation** A general assembly or senate of the Masters of Arts of the University with power to approve or reject measures initiated by the council of Heads of Houses or Colleges known as the Hebdomadal Board. (Not to be confused with the ecclesiastical Convocations of Canterbury and York, which when Newman was writing had recently been revived after a century and a half of inactivity.)

256. 43 **Mr. John Miller** See note 30. 34.

257. 7 **He had the purity and simplicity of a child. He had few sympathies with the intellectual party** '[C]hildhood is a type of the perfect Christian state; our Saviour so made it when He said that we must become as little children to enter His kingdom. Yet it too is a thing past and over. We are not, we cannot be children; grown men have faculties, passions, aims, principles, views, duties, which children have not; still, however, we must become *as* little children; in them we are bound to see Christian perfection, and to labour for it with them in our eye. Indeed there is a very much closer connexion between the state of Adam in Paradise and our state in childhood, than may at first be thought; so that in surveying Eden, we are in a way looking back on our own childhood; and in aiming to be children again we are aiming to be as Adam on his creation . . . simple, inartificial, inexperienced in evil, unreasoning, uncalculating, ignorant of the future, or (as men now speak) unintellectual.' (*P.S.* v. 102–3.)

258. 6 **Dr. Johnson's saying** BOSWELL. 'Eld said, a Tory was a creature generated between a non-juring parson and one's grandmother.' JOHNSON. 'And I have always said, the first Whig was the Devil.' BOSWELL. 'He certainly was, Sir. The Devil was impatient of subordination; he was the first who resisted power: "Better to reign in Hell than serve in Heaven."' *Boswell's Life of Johnson*, iii. 326.

259. 16 **Hebdomadal Board** Before 1854 this supervisory board of Heads of Houses initiated legislation and in effect was the real governor of the University. In 'The Rise and Progress of Universities' (*H.S.* iii. 238) Newman describes it as an 'oligarchy indeed of twenty-four men, perpetual, sovereign, absolutely sheltered from public opinion, and purely irresponsible in their proceedings . . . a prodigy in the England of the nineteenth century'.

Early in February 1845 the Board voted to include in its measures against W. G. Ward for publishing his *Ideal of a Christian Church* a censure of the principles of Tract 90. Liberals like Stanley, Donkin, Jowett, and Greenhill joined the Tractarians in opposing the hasty and foreboding measure. The historic Convocation of February 13, in the Sheldonian Theatre, broke up in cheers when the Senior Proctor, Henry P. Guillemard of Trinity, arose and in the words 'Nobis procuratoribus non placet' suspended the voting on the measure. His younger colleague was R. W. Church. See *The Oxford Movement*, pp. 324–32.

259. 25 **the New Test** The original third proposal for Convocation, withdrawn after a storm of protest, was to add to the subscription of the Articles which the Vice-Chancellor might at any time call on a student to make in order to prove his orthodoxy, a declaration that the subscriber took them in the sense in which 'they were both first published and were now imposed by the University', with expulsion as the penalty for anyone who thrice refused such a declaration. See Church, *Oxford Movement*, pp. 326–8.

259. 26 **I took no interest at all** '. . . the pending matters do not disturb me in the least. I had not curiosity enough to open at once the note which brought the news of the Hebdomadal decision, and I now should, I think, be well content if Thursday, Friday, Saturday passed, without my knowing what had been the result of Thursday's proceedings.' (Newman to his sister Jemima, February 11, 1845, in the copy of the Mozley Family Letters at the Birmingham Oratory.)

This important and revealing letter goes on to say: 'The truth is that all the moderate men see that the Hebdomadal Board is playing into our hands —and that if I wished people to be unsettled and inclined towards Rome, I could not have better fortune than a condemnation of No. 90. I *do* wish people to agree with me in turning Romeward; but, as I do not wish them so to feel because *I* am so feeling, so do I deprecate their so feeling from mere disgust with what is happening among ourselves. Disgust makes no good converts; change of opinion is, commonly speaking, the work of a long time. People who are disgusted one way, may be disgusted the other.'

259. 33 **Mr. Hussey** Robert Hussey (1801–56), Regius Professor of Ecclesiastical History at Oxford, was not a Tractarian, but he objected to the censure in a pamphlet called *Reasons for Voting upon the Third Question to be proposed in Convocation on the 13th inst.*

259. 34 **the passage in Horace** See *Epist.* i, no. xvi. 71–79:

> The truly good and wise misused captive will dare to say,
> Like Bacchus to King Pentheus in the play:
> 'Ruler of Thebes, what undeserved woe
> Will you compel me now to undergo'?
>   'I'll strip you of your goods!' 'You mean, my plate,
> My couches, cattle, money, and estate?
> Take them, and welcome!' 'In a dungeon cell
> I'll keep you bound with gyve and manacle!'
>   'A god will set me free, when'er I please!'
> Meaning, methinks, Death as the god who frees,—
> Death, that shuts up the sum of all man's miseries.

(Transl. Sir Theodore Martin, *The Works of Horace* [Edinburgh and London, 1888], ii. 319.)

259. 36 **the Vice-Chancellor** Benjamin P. Symons (1785–1878), Warden of Wadham, one of Pusey's judges in the suspension of 1843, was an avowed enemy of the Tractarians who had been further inflamed against them by their concerted opposition to his nomination in 1844. See note 158. 30.

261. 21 'Whoso sheddeth man's blood. . .' Gen. ix. 6.

263. 9 **St. Gregory in Pontus** Gregory Thaumaturgus or Wonder-worker (*c.* 213–*c.* 270), Bishop of Neocaesarea in Pontus, Asia Minor. A convert of Origen, he is said to have found only seventeen Christians in his district when he became bishop and to have left only seventeen pagans on his death; and he is credited with a great number of miracles. For some of the more startling ones, based on an account by St. Gregory of Nyssa, see *Mir.*, pp. 117–21; and for a defence of the narrative, ibid., pp. 261–70.

263. 10. **St. Martin in Gaul** St. Martin of Tours (d. 397), Apostle of Gaul, monastic organizer and foe of Arianism, to whose intercession a great many miracles, both during and after his life, have been ascribed. For Newman's sketch of his life, based on a life by Martin's friend and disciple Sulpicius Severus, see *H.S.* ii. 185–206; and for some of the miracles, see *Mir.*, pp. 127–9.

263. 34 **I had said** See the 'Advertisement' to vol. 2 of *The Lives of the English Saints* (ed. Hutton), pp. 3–4. The 1864 version of this section is longer and very severe on Kingsley, charging him with confounding opinion and proof and with suppressing the fact 'that the miracles of St. Walburga are treated by the author of her Life as mythical', with the one exception of the medicinal oil.

264. 23 **as to St. Walburga** See Additional Notes, *Apo.*, pp. 334–7. Born in Devonshire, Walburga (*c.* 710–77) was the daughter of St. Richard, a West Saxon underking, and the niece of St. Boniface, Apostle of Germany, the first missionary to call women to his aid. In 748 she was sent to Germany, where she eventually became Abbess of Heidenheim, ruling over the monk's quarters as well as her own. She was celebrated for her virtue and the many wonders she is said to have worked. From the coincidence of her feast day with an old pagan feast designed to avert witchcraft, May 1 came to be called Walpurgis (Walburga's) night, familiar from Goethe's *Faust*.

When in 893 her casket was opened at Eichstadt in Bavaria, where her remains had been translated in 870, it was discovered that her body was immersed in an oil or liquid. Since the fifth century, at least, there are records of the use of oil or liquid flowing from the burial place of certain saints or poured over saints' relics, in the belief that it would cure physical or spiritual ills through the intercession of the particular saint. According to Michael Ott's article 'Oil of Saints' in the *Catholic Encyclopedia* (xi. 229), the oil of St. Walburga 'flows from the stone slab and the surrounding metal plate on which rest the relics. . . . The fluid is caught in a silver cup, placed beneath the slab for that purpose, and is distributed among the faithful in small phials by the Sisters of St. Benedict, to whom the church belongs. A chemical analysis has shown that the fluid contains nothing but the ingredients of water. Though the origin of the fluid is probably due to natural causes, the fact that it came in contact with the relics of the saint justifies the practice of using it as a remedy against diseases of the body and the soul.'

264. 25 **the Author of her Life** Thomas Meyrick (1817–1903), a Scholar of Corpus Christi, who entered the Roman Church in 1845 and became a priest. He twice joined and left the Society of Jesus, abandoned the Church for a time, but returned and spent his last years in a convent at Rome. See *Letters and Diaries*, xi. 346–7.

264. 32 **Scripture cannot be extravagant** This, of course, is precisely what the new Biblical criticism denied. Thus, T. H. Huxley was compelled to admit Newman's logic in such passages as the following and that on pp. 267–8, but he drew an opposite, ironical conclusion: '. . . I may express my satisfaction at finding myself in substantial accordance with a theologian above all suspicion of heterodoxy. With all my heart, I can declare my belief that there is just as good reason for believing in the miraculous slaying of the man who fell short of the Athanasian power of affirming contradictories [Arius], with respect to the nature of the Godhead, as there is for believing in the stories of the serpent and the ark told in Genesis, the speaking of Balaam's ass in Numbers, or the floating of the axe, at Elisha's order, in the second book of Kings.' (*Science and Christian Tradition* [London, 1894], p. 338.)

265. 19 **Basnage** Jacques Basnage (1653–1723) was a learned French Protestant clergyman, diplomat, and historian. For Newman's quotation naming the six writers see the Advertisement cited above to the second volume of *The Lives of the Saints*, p. 4. The passage in Basnage occurs in *Thesaurus Monumentorum Ecclesiasticorum et Historicum, sive Henrici Canisii Lectiones Antiquae . . . quibus prefationes historicas, animadversiones criticas, et notas in singulos auctores, adjecit Jacobus Basnage* (4 vols., Antwerp, 1725), tom. ii, pars. iii, p. 265.

265. 28 **Mabillon** Jean Mabillon (1632–1707), a famous French Benedictine historian and paleographer. See his *Annales Ordinis S. Benedicti* (6 vols., Paris, 1703–39), iii. 152–3.

What Newman more precisely said was: 'It may be right to add, that Mabillon, in his edition of Wolfhard's work, professes to omit, without assigning reason, some of the miracles it contains: which J. Basnage attributes to disbelief of them.' (Advertisement, p. 6.)

267. 25 **the alleged miracle of the Thundering Legion** See *Mir.*, pp. 241–54, for the story, a learned discussion, and the following passage slightly revised—Newman's quotations are from the original edition. According to the account of Eusebius (*Hist.* v. 5) and Tertullian (*Apol.* c. 5), supported as to the fact if not the reason by various pagan evidences, a Roman legion in Marcus Aurelius's war with Germanic tribes *c.* 175 was surrounded and perishing of thirst. Christian soldiers are said to have knelt on the ground before the startled enemy, a thunderstorm followed at once, the enemy was routed and the legion supplied with water. Claudius Apollinaris,

Bishop of Hierapolis, who wrote for Marcus a lost *Apology for Christianity* cited by Eusebius, incorrectly believed that this storm gave the legion the name 'Thundering' (*Fulminata*), but it was already in use. Pagans ascribed the aid to Jupiter Pluvius in a memorial sculptured on the Antonine column at Rome. Cf. the account and bibliography in *O.D.C.C.*

268. 5 **the death of Arius** See *Mir.*, pp. 327–33. In 336 Arius died suddenly in Constantinople on a Saturday evening before the day on which Constantine had ordered that he be received back into full communion by Alexander, the bishop. The latter, failing to dissuade the Emperor, prayed for the destruction of Arius lest his doctrine spread. That evening 'Arius was in the great square of Constantine when he was suddenly seized with indisposition. On returning, he was overtaken by what is commonly considered to be the fate of Judas, as described in the Book of Acts.' (*Mir.*, p. 328.) See Acts i. 16–18 and the account in Smith and Wace's *Dictionary of Christian Biography*. At the time of this event Arius was past 80, and Alexander was 96.

268. 24 **the apparent miracle** In the late fifth century, when the Arian Vandals ruled the Roman provinces on the African coast, an aide of Hunneric, whose father Genseric had begun a savage persecution of Catholics to force them into Arianism, collected the remaining Catholics of Tiposa— perhaps sixty—and cut off their tongues and right hands. That they continued to speak without their tongues was widely attested. For a detailed account, including identification of writers and sources mentioned, see *Mir.*, pp. 369–87.

269. 11 **an Article appeared** By 'E. T.', giving the sources for Milman's naturalistic interpretation of the event in his *History of Latin Christianity*. The article identifies the men named below. See also a reply by 'F. C. H.' in the number for June 12, 1858, p. 483.

270. 1 **for his stubborn incredulity** Gibbon thus ends his account: 'This supernatural gift of the African confessors, who spoke without tongues, will command the assent of those, and of those only who already believe that their language was pure and orthodox. But the stubborn mind of an infidel is guarded by secret incurable suspicion, and the Arian, or Socinian, who has seriously rejected the doctrine of the Trinity, will not be shaken by the most plausible evidence of an Athanasian miracle.' *History of the Decline and Fall of the Roman Empire*, ed. J. B. Bury (7 vols., London, 1898), iv. 91–92.

275. 14 **'muscular Christianity'** The term is believed to have beeen first applied to Kingsley's religion by the *Saturday Review* and was usually spoken in jest at an active and hearty but oversimplified and rather unintellectual version of Christianity. Kingsley's own illuminating discussion of the term, which he disliked, may be found in his *Life and Works*, iii. 219–20. See also the discussion in the *Edinburgh Review*, cvii (January 1858), 190–3, in the course of a review of *Tom Brown's Schooldays*, the once famous novel by Kingsley's close friend Thomas Hughes.

277. 19 **Mawworm** A once well-known character resembling Tartuffe in Isaac Bickerstaffe's play *The Hypocrite* (1769), adapted in part from Molière's work.

277. 29 **If he had undertaken to write a history, and not a romance** A sharp thrust, since Kingsley, whose romances such as *Hypatia* and *Westward Ho!* had been admired for their vividness but widely criticized for distortion, had become Professor of Modern History at Cambridge in 1860. His lectures were accorded a somewhat similar reception.

277. 35 **that in those very weeks from Christmas till over Easter ... I was but five times in the pulpit there** It is also true, however, as Douglas E. Pett has pointed out, that Newman preached every week from October 16 through December 18, 1842, as his diary shows; and that during the period from October till the end of February 1843, one half of the sermons in *S.S.D.* were preached. On the implications of this fact and on Newman's attitude toward Kingsley in this section, see 'The Newman-Kingsley Dispute Continues', *TLS*, February 17, 1961, p. xvi; and an exchange of letters in the issues of February 24, p. 121; March 3, p. 137; March 10, p. 153; and March 16, p. 169.

280. 8 **Bollandists** Jesuits responsible for the great collection of saints' lives known as the *Acta Sanctorum*. They were named after the Belgian John van Bolland, who in 1843 began the work, which still continues.

297. 14 **'the Bride of the Lamb'** Apoc. xxi. 9.

297. 16 **'I went by ...'** See Ps. xxxvi. 36 (Vulg.).

297. 19 **if the Holy See ever so decide** In September 1896 in the Bull *Apostolicae Curae*, Leo XIII, having received the report of a commission appointed to investigate the historical problems involved—a study which aroused great interest and hope for reunion, especially in English and French ecclesiastical circles—pronounced the decision that Anglican Orders were invalid. (But see the article 'Anglican Ordinations' in the *O.D.C.C.*) Newman discusses the question and explains what he means below by 'the urgency of visible facts' in a note on Essay X, 'The Catholicity of the Anglican Church', in *Essays*. ii. 74–111. It is an important document for the question of Newman's 'scepticism'.

297. 35 **had I been born in Dissent ...** On this passage, a manuscript by an unknown writer inserted in a copy of the 1883 issue of the *Apologia* in the Birmingham Oratory has the following comment: 'All kinds of Dissenters baptize their children, except Quakers and Baptists. The latter baptize those who make a personal profession of their faith.

'A few Congregations in England, formerly Presbyterian, lapsed into Socinianism, and by act of Parliament a few years ago had their chapels secured to them, where they had been a certain length of time in possession. After this the name Presbyterian was discarded, and they took the name of, and were called, Unitarians. The English Presbyterian Church, as now existing, is as anti-Socinian as the Anglican or any other Church.'

299. 25 **'winked at the times of ignorance'** Acts xvii. 30.

299. 26 **'because of the hardness of their hearts'** See Matt. xix. 8.

299. 29 **our Lord spoke harshly** Mark vii. 25–30.

299. 32 **Joseph 'made himself strange . . .'** Gen. xlii. 7 (A.V.).

299. 33 **Elisha kept silence** 2 Kings [4 Kings] v. 18–19.

299. 35 **'Circumcision availeth not'** See Acts xvi. 1–3; and Gal. v. 6 and vi. 15.

300. 8 **'mollia tempora fandi'** Suitable times for speaking, and for suitable words too. See *Aeneid*, iv. 293–4.

300. 14 **St. Paul expressly distinguishes** 1 Cor. iii. 2 and Heb. v. 13–14.

300. 24 **to which Bingham bears witness** Joseph Bingham (1668–1723), author of the influential *Origines Ecclesiasticae or the Antiquities of the Christian Church* (10 vols., London, 1708–23). Newman alludes here to bk. x, ch. v. See *Origines* (9 vols., London, 1843), iii. 379–98.

300. 25 **Basil** St. Basil the Great (329–79), Bishop of Caesarea and close friend of St. Gregory Nazianzen, is known as the Father of oriental monasticism. He was a reformer and a defender of the Church against the Arians. See *H.S.* ii. 3–74. For the references in Cyril, Theodoret, Chrysostom, and Basil, see *Arians*, pp. 42–79, *passim*.

300. 26 **Theodoret** (*c.* 393–*c.* 457), Bishop of Cyrus in Palestine, was long a defender of Nestorius in the struggle with the Monophysites. Deposed at the 'Robber Synod' of Ephesus by the efforts of Dioscorus, he was defended by Pope Leo, who held the deposition invalid; and he was allowed full membership in the Council of Chalcedon after agreeing to the anathema against Nestorius. He wrote many types of work, including an *Historia Ecclesiastica* from Arius to 429. See Newman's 'Trials of Theodoret', *H.S.* ii. 304–62.

301. 37 **'tell truth, and shame the devil'** *1 Henry IV*, III. i. 62.

303. 26 **He mentions defence of life and of honour** See *De Mendacio*, c. v–vii (*P.L.*, vol. 40, cols. 491–6).

303. 33 **St. Alfonso . . . 'Quicunque finis honestus . . .'** See note 244. 18.

303. 37 **Clement of Alexandria** *Stromateis*, lib. vii, c. ix.

303. 39 **the writer in the Mélanges Théologiques** The reference is to an unsigned article in a Belgian review of moral theology and canon law. See '*Examen de l'opinion de Bolgeni sur la licéité du mensonge en certains cas*', VIᵉ série (1852–3), 410–62.

303. 40 **Lessius** Leonard Lessius (1554–1623), a Jesuit Professor of Theology at Louvain known for his *De Justitia et Jure Actionum Humanarum Libri Quatuor*. The reference cited in the article is lib. ii. c. 42, n. 48.

304. 4 **Voit** Edmund Voit was an eighteenth-century Jesuit, rector of the noviciate at Mayence, and author of a *Theologia Moralis*. The reference cited in the article is tom. i, n. 538 (ed. Bassani et Venet., 1776).

304. 10 **St. Alfonso . . . quotes St. Thomas** *Theol. Moral.*, lib. iv, tr. 4, n. 483.

304. 17 **Kenrick** Francis P. Kenrick (1797–1863), an American theologian and Scripture scholar, Bishop of Philadelphia and later Archbishop of Baltimore. The reference is to his *Theologiae Moralis* (3 vols.; Philadelphia, 1841), i, tr. iii, c. xii, p. 147.

305. 9–306. 37 **When a question on the subject** The following passage is based on, and much of the documentation will be found in, an article called '*Examen de Quelques Thèses de Louvain*', *Mélanges Théologiques*, *III*ᵉ *Série* (1849–50), pp. 395–9. M. Vandenbroeck, a priest of Malines, had sustained certain theses at Louvain, the first on the reply of the Sacred Penitentiary at Rome to the question of the Archbishop of Besançon.

306. 8 **Viva** Domenico Viva (1648–1726), Jesuit theologian, Professor at the College of Naples. See his *Damnatae Theses ab Alex. VII, etc.* (Valentiae, 1728), p. 1.

306. 40 **Contenson** Vincent Contenson (1641–74), a Dominican theologian whose chief work is *Theologia Mentis et Cordis*. See Newman's 1864 appendix, pp. 465–6.

306. 40 **Concina** Daniello Concina (1687–1756), prolific Dominican theologian who severely attacked what he considered the lax opinions of the probabilists—followers of probable opinion in matters of conscience—of whom the Jesuits were champions. See 1864 appendix, pp. 466–7.

308. 11 **An instance is supplied** For the source of this anecdote, see Theodoret, *A History of the Church from A.D. 322 to the Death of Theodore of Mopsuestia, A.D. 427*, ed. and transl. E. Walford (London, 1854), bk. iii, ch. ix.

308. 14 **the satellites of Julian** That is, Julian the Apostate (331–63), who attempted to drive Athanasius from Alexandria.

308. 30 **St. Alban** A pagan of Verulamium (later St. Albans, Hertfordshire), who became Britain's first Christian martyr, *c.* 304, according to the legend. Moved by the good example of a cleric whom he sheltered during a persecution, he became a Christian and, disguised in his guest's cloak, gave himself up to the governor's emissaries. He was brought before a judge who recognized him and pleaded with him to deny his faith, but in vain. He was then scourged and beheaded.

310. 5 **Luther said, 'Pecca fortiter'** 'Esto peccator et pecca fortiter, sed fortius fide et gaude in Christo.' (Be a sinner and sin strongly, but more strongly have faith and rejoice in Christ.) Quoted in the *Oxford Dictionary of Quotations* (1941), p. 530, from *Letter to Melanchthon. Epistolae M. Lutheri* (Ienae [1556], i. 345).

310. 21 **If an early Father defends the patriarch Jacob** See Gen. xxvii for the story of Jacob's affirming himself Esau, with the aid of a slight disguise. His act is defended by St. Augustine in *Contra Mendacium*, c. 10.

319. 19 **something special and peculiar to myself** This is clearly the implication of Samuel Wilberforce's influential review of the first edition of the *Apologia* in the *Quarterly Review*, cxiv (October 1864), 528–73, which contains such remarks as 'Dr. Newman learned among us too much Catholicism to be ever a thorough Papist' (p. 563); and, on Newman's remarks on St. Alfonso as one authority among many, 'the consensus of living authority' is against Newman (p. 533). The review is reprinted in *Essays Contributed to the 'Quarterly Review'* (2 vols., London, 1874), ii. 334–93.

INDEX

(Page numbers in heavy type refer to editor's notes on persons, places, or subjects mentioned or alluded to in the *Apologia*.)

PRINTED IN GREAT BRITAIN
AT THE UNIVERSITY PRESS, OXFORD
BY VIVIAN RIDLER
PRINTER TO THE UNIVERSITY